S0-BAC-428

Teaching Content Reading and Writing

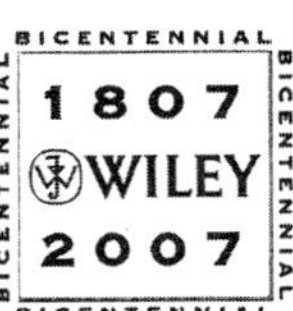

THE WILEY BICENTENNIAL–KNOWLEDGE FOR GENERATIONS

Each generation has its unique needs and aspirations. When Charles Wiley first opened his small printing shop in lower Manhattan in 1807, it was a generation of boundless potential searching for an identity. And we were there, helping to define a new American literary tradition. Over half a century later, in the midst of the Second Industrial Revolution, it was a generation focused on building the future. Once again, we were there, supplying the critical scientific, technical, and engineering knowledge that helped frame the world. Throughout the 20th Century, and into the new millennium, nations began to reach out beyond their own borders and a new international community was born. Wiley was there, expanding its operations around the world to enable a global exchange of ideas, opinions, and know-how.

For 200 years, Wiley has been an integral part of each generation's journey, enabling the flow of information and understanding necessary to meet their needs and fulfill their aspirations. Today, bold new technologies are changing the way we live and learn. Wiley will be there, providing you the must-have knowledge you need to imagine new worlds, new possibilities, and new opportunities.

Generations come and go, but you can always count on Wiley to provide you the knowledge you need, when and where you need it!

William J. Pesce
PRESIDENT AND CHIEF EXECUTIVE OFFICER

Peter Booth Wiley
CHAIRMAN OF THE BOARD

TEACHING CONTENT READING AND WRITING

FIFTH EDITION

Martha Rapp Ruddell

Sonoma State University

JOHN WILEY & SONS, INC.

To all my students, wherever they are
To all my family and friends
And to Perry, whom I love beyond all loving

VICE PRESIDENT AND PUBLISHER	Jay O' Callaghan
ACQUISITIONS EDITOR	Robert Johnston
EDITORIAL ASSISTANT	Eileen McKeever
MARKETING MANAGER	Emily Streutker
PRODUCTION EDITOR	Lea Radick
SENIOR DESIGNER	Kevin Murphy
SENIOR PHOTO EDITOR	Lisa Gee
PRODUCTION MANAGEMENT	Pine Tree Composition Inc.
BICENNTENIAL LOGO DESIGN	Richard J. Pacifico
COVER PHOTO	Photo Alto/Media Bakery

This book was set in Janson by Laserwords Private Limited, and printed and bound by R. R. Donnelley. The cover was printed by Phoenix Color.

ISBN 978-0-470-08404-5

Printed in the United States of America

10 9 8 7 6 5 4 3 2 1

PREFACE

When I mentioned to my granddaughter that I was finishing the last edition of this book, her immediate money-conscious-college-student response was, "Why do you authors always have to write new editions of your books? It just means we can't sell them back at the end of the semester!" (along with a few other disparaging remarks about the extent to which students read the books anyway). Good question. Why, indeed write new editions? Well, mainly because the world isn't the same today as it was when the last edition was published, and that means that the worlds of classrooms and schools are likewise different, as are the lives of the students and teachers in those classrooms and schools. Without a doubt, the middle level and high school classrooms that you'll teach in are dramatically different from those of my teaching experience, different from your own experience in middle school/high school, and even somewhat different from the experiences of this year's high school graduates. I've continued to spend time in secondary classrooms observing and interacting with students and teachers and learning about the lives of today's preadolescents and adolescents. I've contexutualized this edition within those changing worlds to help you make decisions about the most effective ways for you to teach *today's* learners. Second, we know more about preadolescent and adolescent literacy today than we did five years ago, and we also know how significantly the literacies that adolescents experience have changed in the last 5 years. My granddaughter has graduated from college now, but the answer I gave then is just as good today: new editors reflect new knowledge.

This fifth edition of *Teaching Content Reading and Writing* is grounded in the enduring wisdom that has accrued over the nearly half-century history of the field of adolescent literacy, and is informed most recently by knowledge generated through practice and research about adolescents and literacies in new times. Central to this notion is that the many literacies of preadolescent and adolescent lives (any number of which are highly technological and are changing as we speak) significantly affect their approaches and response to school, and thus are important for you to understand. I've explored this aspect of adolescence and literacy in greater depth in this edition. I've also increased the emphasis on technological approaches and resources for learning, secure in the knowledge that the technology will undoubtedly outpace me and make some of what I say obsolete before it is published (certainly, the possibilities I offer will be considerably widened before this sees print!). Because of the changing demographics and the heavy emphasis on "meeting the standards" in today's schools, I've added new information and instructional ideas for teaching second language learners, marginalized learners, and students with special needs in the hope that more teachers will be able to adjust instruction to facilitate all students' continued learning and growth. Also because the standards movement carries with it a correspondingly heavy emphasis on testing,

I've increased coverage of issues facing teachers and schools today with respect to assessment and instruction. Important in schools today also is the standard for **evidence based instructional practice**—instruction that is grounded in research showing it to be effective. Throughout the text and at the end of each chapter you will find citations for the research base that supports the instructional strategies and the assessments that are in this book. Following are features of the text that are intended to guide your reading, understanding, and application of ideas in the text.

FEATURES NEW TO THIS EDITION

Centerpiece Lesson Plans appear early in each of the chapters focused on instruction (Chapters 4, 5, 6, 7, 8, 10, 11). These and other lesson plans demonstrate how instructional strategies may be applied and adapted for specific content area lessons. All lesson plans include lesson objectives and their corresponding curriculum standards, procedures for guiding the lesson before, during, and after reading (into, through, and beyond), and assessments tied to the objectives. In early chapters, lesson plans are for mathematics, science, social studies, and English classes at both the middle school and high school levels; in Chapters 8, 10, and 11 they include physical education, music, and foreign language (Spanish) classes. The Centerpiece Lesson Plans are situated early in those chapters so you can see their application even before reading about them; other lesson plans follow discussion of a specific instructional strategy.

Creating Strategic Readers, Writers, and Learners. Throughout these same instructional chapters I stop occasionally to make suggestions for how you as a teacher can stimulate your students' abilities to become independent, strategic learners.

Sometimes the focus is on reading, sometimes on reading and writing, sometimes just on writing, and sometimes on reading, writing, and learning. I change the title of the feature to reflect that focus. The goal here is to give you ideas for helping your students take charge of their own learning, get good at doing the kind of reading and writing that are necessary for understanding your subject area, and begin to feel themselves to be competent, confident learners.

Video Vignettes. We have created 10 video vignettes of real teachers using instructional strategies from this text with real students at both the middle school and senior high levels. These are available online for you to view either in class or on your own. In each you will find a short introduction, the vignette, and then the teacher's reflection of how the lesson progressed. The goal of these vignettes is to let you see how these instructional strategies "live", how they play out in real life, and how they may be adapted in a variety of ways to meet specific instructional moments and needs.

ONGOING FEATURES

Double Entry Journal (DEJ) activities occur at the beginning and end of each chapter. At the beginning of the chapter, the DEJ activity is intended to stimulate your memory, thinking, and ideas about the main topic of the chapter you're about to read; essentially, the before-reading DEJ is a way of introducing topics, bringing your own prior knowledge and experiences to bear on the upcoming discussion, and giving you an experience-based foundation for the reading. The after-reading DEJ then builds on what you did before reading, and combines that thinking with ideas from the chapter to extend your understanding of the text. The best way to do the DEJ activities is to keep a journal specifically for them and to compare your DEJ thinking with a partner or small group; an alternative is to engage in online conversation with class colleagues, either informally in a listserve or in a Web CT/Blackboard forum.

Classroom Scenarios immediately following the opening DEJ give additional context for the material in the chapter and provide yet another avenue for connecting the chapter contents to kids and teachers and classrooms and schools. As you read the scenarios, think about how they reflect your experience or provide a new perspective to some aspect of school. In chapter discussions I refer back to the opening scenarios as is appropriate.

The **How To Do** feature occurs at irregular intervals in chapters focusing on instructional approaches (Chapters 4, 5, 6, 7, 8, 10, 11). The purpose of How To Do is to give you a step-by-step list of the things you need to plan, prepare, and/or consider in order to make a specific instructional strategy work in your subject area and classroom. How To Do generally follows explanations and discussions that are necessarily long and involved; my students like the succinct, listed format of How To Do and use it to guide their lesson and unit planning.

What Goes In My Portfolio? is a feature included because so many who read this text are also responsible for creating a portfolio of some type—either for the class or for a program; others reading this text may be in the process of developing a professional portfolio. The purpose of this feature is to give you some ideas of how you can represent your understandings from any given chapter in whatever kind of portfolio you are developing; my suggestions are prompts only, intended primarily for your personal adaptation.

The **Building Tables** that occur at the end of instructional chapters are intended to summarize in yet another way critical information about how to apply and combine the instructional approaches from this text in your teaching. Additionally, the purpose of the Building Tables is to allow you to see instructional connections across chapters that you may not see on your own (chapters have a way of creating rigid, and perhaps unnecessary, barriers), aid your planning efficiency, and give suggestions for increasing the power of the instructional strategies themselves.

In What This Chapter Means to You I use three or four statements to capture the essence of each chapter's point. The first statement links the opening scenario and chapter content to your teaching. The two or three others are intended to give you a final suggestion to think about in connecting the big ideas of the chapter and your teaching plans.

I hope you will find this book challenging, interesting, and useful in your teaching career.

ACKNOWLEDGMENTS

This fifth edition has evolved—as did the others—not only to meet the ever-changing realities of classroom life in middle and secondary schools and to include new information generated about preadolescent and adolescent literacy, but also from the responses of its users as well. What has become very clear to me is the influence of my own students and my professional friends (and their students) on the development of this text. My students are always especially adroit in their criticisms and comments and are both outspoken and reassuringly affirming in their views. Two of my most honest and loving critics are my good friends—Brenda Shearer at the University of Wisconsin, Oshkosh and MaryEllen Vogt from Long Beach State University—who use the book in their classes, give me their, and their students', ongoing feedback, and make suggestions that are unerringly apt.

It is most felicitous, I think, when students' work becomes part of what a teacher does, and it gives me extraordinary pleasure to acknowledge what students have contributed to my thinking and to this book. Hearty "thank yous" to Janet Rasmussen and Heidi Hayman-Ahders for their study maps in Chapter 7; to Jenny Fleischer and Jonathan Reveal for their insightful maps in Chapter 2 of the thinking-reading-writing processes; to Peter Santucci—for the CSSR visual in Chapter 5; and to David Hathorne whose experience leading group learning illuminates Chapter 11. Thanks also to Amy Holcombe, Eric Bohn, Eric Wycoff, Andrea Chambers and Leslie McKinley for letting me use their lesson plans to illustrate how ideas from this text may be applied to classroom practice. Thanks also to my good friend, Dianne Metzger, for her Spanish class lesson plan in Chapter 11, and to my colleagues and friends Karen Grady, for the *idea* for the Centerpiece Lesson Plans, and Rick Marks who taught me how to shelter an algebra lesson.

To my reviewers—Mary L. Agnew, University of Maryland Eastern Shore; Carol Bunch, Hannibal LaGrange College; Marilee Cosgrove, Rio Hondo College; Jacquelyn Culpepper, Mercer University; Katharine G. Fralick, Plymouth State College; Nancy L. Hadaway, University of Texas at Arlington; Susan Hall, University of the Incarnate Word; Laveria Hutchison, University of Houston; Barbara E. Karp, University of Bridgeport; Judy Lombardi, California State University – Northridge; Nancy L. Michelson, Salisbury University; Sheila A. Nicholson, Southwest Texas State University; Deborah L. Norland, Luther College; Barbara C. Palmer, Florida State University; Robert Perkins, College of Charleston; Mary J. Pickard, University of Idaho; Olivia Saracho, University of Maryland; Mary Spor, Alabama A&M University; and Patricia Wachholz, Florida Gulf Coast University—thank you for your thoughtfully detailed and honest reviews; your insights were highly useful guideposts for revision, and I returned to the reviews many times to keep myself on the right path. To my editors at John Wiley, Robert Johnston, and editorial assistant Eileen McKeever, thanks for your continuing support, thoughtful response to my many questions, and clear emphasis on quality. To Patty Donovan and the production staff at Pine Tree Composition, Inc. and my copy editor, Diane Burke, I am grateful for their professionlism and work on the project.

As I finished this edition, I lost a dear and wonderful friend, Dr. Patricia Monighan Nourot, a colleague of mine at Sonoma State University for eighteen years. Pat was an expert in early childhood education and was known internationally for her work in the area of children's play. Pat and I loved sharing stories about our experiences with kids—she with preschoolders and kindergarteners and I with seventh-graders and sophomores—and often remarked on the similarities, and the both similar and contrasting beauties, of the kids we described. She was an enduring and wonderful friend who left way too early but who, in the time she was here, influenced for the better the lives of many, many children. And my life too. Shortly after losing Pat, I also lost my 92-year-old mother Velma, who lived a long and eventful life. Mother taught me many things: She taught me early on that it's okay to be female and smart; she taught me how to look brave even when I'm scared; she taught me about leadership and initiative; and she taught me about unconditional love. She was very proud of all of her children's accomplishments, and kept track. As recently as last March when I went home to see her, she checked to see that I was still "writing" and wanted to know what article I had published lately. She was proud, beautiful, stubborn, smart, opinionated, and generous. She read voraciously, loved baseball, produced gorgeous embroidery and crochet, called all my friends "honey," and was the first person in the boat when a lake or river ride was about to happen. I shall miss her forever. This edition is dedicated to Mother and Pat.

As always, I'm thankful for my children—John, Amy and Paul, and Rob and Diane—and their children, the two "elders" Sarah and Ken and the three little ones Grace, Rebecca, and Madeline, and for all my wonderful family and friends. I am deeply, and forever, thankful for my husband Perry whose love and support are constants in my life and who is both a willing and perceptive listener and my most ardent fan.

INSTRUCTIONAL STRATEGY LOCATER

Startegies Referred to by Acronyms

(Continues)

Other Strategies

ABOUT THE AUTHOR

Photo by Scott Van Cleemput
vancleemputphotography.com

Martha Rapp Ruddell is Professor and Dean Emerita of the School of Education at Sonoma State University in Rohnert Park, California. She taught in the secondary teaching credential program and the graduate Reading and Language advanced credential and degree programs. Dr. Ruddell taught for 10 years in both rural and city schools in Missouri and Kansas. In addition to this text, Dr. Ruddell is author of numerous articles and book chapters and continues actively as a researcher, author, and presenter at professional conferences. She is Past President of the National Reading Conference, an international educational organization devoted to research in language and literacy. She is a member of the California Reading Association Reading Hall of Fame, and in 2003 she was honored with the Al Kingston Service Award of the National Reading Conference. Most recently she was named Distinguished Alumna by the University of Missouri, Kansas City, where she received the Ph.D. degree.

CONTENTS

CHAPTER 1

Literacy in Middle and Secondary Schools

Double Entry Journal

List everything you remember about reading in school using the following headings: Reading in Elementary School, Reading in Junior High School, and Reading in High School. List as many memories for each heading as you can. More memories may occur to you as you read the chapter. Add those as you wish.

PhotoDisc Red/PhotoDisc, Inc./Getty Images

Two people approach Washington High School with apprehension on this late-August morning. Jaime Lopez is on his way to school to start the first day of his freshman year. As a long distance runner, he'd already made some new friends because he'd started cross country practice last week, so he knew the coach, some other runners, and some friends from junior high. That helped, but Washington High was much bigger than the junior high, and everyone said it would be a lot harder. He wondered: What will my classes be like? What about all the teachers and kids I don't know? Will they like me? Will I like them? He'd gotten really into IM over the summer to stay in touch with his friends,and all of his group spent every minute they could playing video games. He had his iPod, his notebooks, and his backpack. Ready. Set. Go.

Ellie Burke is equally apprehensive. She is returning for her fifth year teaching American history, world history, and government and sponsoring the student senate. She had awakened this morning from the usual restlessness and light sleep of the night before the first day of school, and was feeling the same anxieties she'd felt every year she'd taught. (What will my students be like? Will they like me? Will I like them? Am I ready for this year?). She could also feel the familiar first-day butterflies in her stomach. She'd taken an instructional technology workshop over the summer and was really pleased with the website she'd created, and had lots of new electronic resources and strategies she planned to incorporate into her classes this year. She really wanted it to be a good year. Deep breath. Here we go.

• • •

Teaching in middle and secondary schools is a job for people with stamina, enthusiasm, knowledge, endurance, discipline, and a seemingly inexhaustible supply of energy. Nowhere else in schools are faculty expected to do so many things: teach five, six, or seven classes a day; sponsor clubs; coach sports; do hall duty; supervise dances; publish newspapers and yearbooks; direct plays; and sell refreshments at school events, to name a few. Life is hectic and, more often than not, regulated by forces outside teachers' control. I once taught in a consolidated school district in which one high school, one junior high, and six elementary schools served a rural community of about 13,000 people. Nearly all of the junior and senior high students were bused to school, so starting times were staggered to allow a limited number of buses to run multiple routes. The senior high began at 7:40 A.M., the junior high at 8:05 A.M., and the elementary schools at 8:45 A.M. At the beginning of one school year, about half of our junior high students were arriving 5 minutes late every day because the buses were unable to make their second run within the allotted time. In a school of 600 seventh-and eighth-graders, this created a situation bordering on chaos, and something clearly had to be done. Possible solutions seemed obvious: Start the senior high 5 minutes earlier and change the early bus schedule, or start the junior high and elementary schools 5 minutes later and adjust those bus schedules. Instead, the administration *set the junior high clocks back 5 minutes* and left everything else exactly as it was! So now, when the tardy bell rang at 8:05, it was really 8:10, but the students were in their seats, and the problem had been "solved," for everyone except us, of course. During the entire academic year, we lived and taught in a warp between "real time" and "junior high time" in which any discussion of out-of-school activity schedules was generally lost among confusion, laughter, and conjecture about the prevailing logic behind this decision.

School and classroom conditions, especially at the junior high and senior high levels, frequently make teachers' personal teaching goals and ideals exceedingly

ZITS © ZITS PARTNERSHIP, KING FEATURES SYNDICATE.

difficult to achieve. Class loads of 50 to 180 students a day, pressure to "get through the book" or "get students ready" for the next grade level or impending achievement and/or exit tests, insufficient or inappropriate instructional materials, absenteeism, and constant schedule interruptions are standard components of the secondary teacher's working milieu. And schools are becoming ever more complex: Changing school schedules, new instructional expectations, and high-stakes testing have increased considerably teachers' responsibilities and time demands for planning and preparation for teaching. Add to that the recurring and widely broadcast media focus on schools and persistent belief in the media and the general public that schools are failing, then top all that off with the continued tendency for teacher salaries to be well below levels in business and other professions, and you wonder why anyone remains a teacher at all. To their credit, middle school, junior high school, and senior high school teachers generally accept these conditions with a certain amount of grace and continue on.

(For clarity and consistency within this text, I refer to junior high and senior high schools and students as "secondary" because of distinctions between elementary and secondary teacher credentialing and school organizational patterns that are common to many states. Middle schools and students are called "middle" to distinguish them from elementary and junior high students and schools, which may or may not have overlapping grade levels. Although this usage of secondary and middle may not match standard usage in all states or geographic areas, no one set of labels is likely to do so. Nonetheless, at least we now have operational definitions useful for discussion throughout this text.)

Students' reading and writing abilities, and other issues surrounding literacy, are among the many important issues facing middle, junior high, and senior high teachers and schools today. Concern and discussion about these issues are not new. In fact, literacy and literacy achievement have been topics of widespread public and professional interest, discussion, and debate over the past 80 years. Where previously much of the focus of literacy issues, at least in the popular press, centered on elementary reading instruction (the relative effectiveness of certain instructional approaches, for example), today's discussion is aimed directly at, and is becoming decidedly louder about, issues of student literacy in secondary school.

Adolescent Literacy

Middle and secondary school students' reading and writing abilities are currently, and have been, the subject of much concern, and the debate over who is responsible for what continues. One reason for such intense and prolonged scrutiny is the critical role of literacy in students' overall academic success. (Until about the early- to mid-1980s, discussion focused almost solely on reading; since then, we have engaged in serious national discussion of the similarly important contribution of writing.) The issue essentially is that beginning at the upper elementary grades, and continuing on into middle school (or junior high) and senior high school, a steadily increasing amount of information is transmitted through the medium of written text; consequently, increasingly refined reading and writing skills at each level are necessary for continued learning in nearly all academic areas. These skills do not develop at the same rate for all students: In a class of 30 sophomores, we can expect, and do find, reading achievement test levels ranging from second grade through sixteenth grade (college senior), with concomitantly wide ranges in writing ability. Even in smaller, special classes—remedial reading or advanced placement chemistry, for example—a range of five to seven grade levels is not uncommon.

Complicating things further is the fact that adolescent literacy is complex and increasingly multifaceted. To measure or characterize it as a general, unitary thing (e.g., to say that someone is reading "on a ninth grade level" or that someone is a "good writer") is misleading and unrevealing of what it takes to be fully literate in middle and secondary school. Elizabeth Moje and her colleagues (2000) comment that many adolescents who have adequately mastered the literacy processes stressed in elementary school have not yet acquired the *practices* associated with the complex literacy forms that are expected in middle and secondary school, particularly those unique to specific disciplines.

DISCOURSES

James Gee (2002) describes the practices associated with literacy as different Discourses (ways of thinking, acting, speaking, believing, valuing, interacting) one encounters and must manage to understand or assume social roles. That is, one learns the Discourses appropriate to specific social situations and roles and, to be successful in each situation/role, shapes one's language, viewpoints, and behavior accordingly. Like chameleons, we are all highly capable of participating in a variety of Discourses. For middle and secondary students, learning the Discourses associated with a specific subject area—for example, the analytical thought, values, and language of the physical scientist designing, conducting, and reporting an experiment as opposed to the analytical thought, values, and language of the artist conceiving and executing a painting—is a critical aspect of success in school. Elizabeth Moje, Deborah Dillon, and David O'Brien elaborate:

> Learning in the secondary disciplines—or content areas—is shaped by reading and writing that learners do in those disciplines. Moreover, reading and writing in the disciplines is shaped by the unique conceptual, textual, and semantic demands of each area; for example, reading and writing historical narrative is different from reading and writing scientific exposition. (2000, p. 165)

Gee emphasizes that interactions and dialogue with more advanced peers and adults is crucial to acquiring the Discourses of different social and academic roles. Further, he and others emphasize that within the context of the Discourses they engage, adolescents construct specific, individual identities with regard to all aspects of their lives—that is, who and what they are as students (math student, English student, music student, etc.), children, athletes, siblings, musicians, friends, and so on. Thus, the different experience, familiarity, and facility that each individual has with the many Discourses of school (e.g., subject area Discourses, gender Discourses, in-crowd/out-crowd Discourses, teacher–student Discourses, textbook reading Discourses, etc.) must account in part for the wide disparity of students' literacy abilities in school. Bronwyn Williams (2006) describes the students who are skilled at academic Discourse:

> In . . . classrooms we recognize which students have mastered the discourse of academic culture. They are the ones who step back from the texts they are reading and connect them to others. They discuss ideas and themes without referencing their emotions or basing their opinions on likes or dislikes and don't display emotional involvement with a text or an argument. They frame their statements in a dispassionate, third-person rhetoric and support their ideas with evidence such as direct quotations or recognized scholarly works, which they know will resonate as relevant with their teachers. (p. 343)

TRACKING AND DETRACKING

No one can deny the wide range of students' literacy abilities. Experienced teachers watch daily as students struggle or idle their way through identical texts, but generally feel powerless to do anything about it. Experienced teachers know that regardless of the current reform or teaching trend, wide differences in students' literacy abilities tend to persist in secondary classrooms. And further, they know that tracking systems, honor programs, and "basic" classes, no matter how they are conceived and implemented, do not successfully deal with the differences among students' reading and writing abilities. Such approaches can only reduce the ability and achievement ranges to supposedly more manageable limits, but even then, substantial within-class achievement differences still occur. More importantly, perhaps, these tracking plans create as many problems as they solve and are themselves the source of serious concern and debate with respect to education equity and equality, the effect of teacher expectations on student achievement, and the quality of the educational experience in various school tracks.

THE KIDS *CAN* READ

Whatever the characteristics of a given school or district student population, it is not enough for middle and secondary teachers to accept the popular belief that "the kids can't read" or to blame elementary teachers for not doing their jobs; nor is it helpful to deny, ignore, or attempt to escape the diversity of student abilities and needs in our classrooms. First of all, the kids *can* read, although their reading and writing talents vary considerably and may or may not be the talents that are rewarded in school. With few exceptions, middle and secondary students *can read something:* Watch them go through *MAD* magazine, comic books, driver's training manuals, graphic novels, or whatever the current literary fad happens to be. Their skill in using new technologies is nothing short of astonishing. Second, elementary teachers *are* doing their jobs. They are teaching youngsters how to read and learn from elementary texts and to write in response to that reading—the Discourse of elementary school. To expect them to "preteach" all the literacy skills necessary for success in middle and secondary school is unrealistic, if not unreasonable. Beginning in middle school and continuing through high school, texts and writing task demands grow increasingly more difficult and different from those at the elementary level; literacy skills needed for success in reading and writing are similarly more complex and can be learned most efficiently as they are needed.

ADOLESCENTS AND LITERACIES IN NEW TIMES

A growing chorus of voices describe the many literacies that comprise adolescents' (and our) worlds and argue that these "multiliteracies" must be considered not only important, but also critical, to students' literacy and learning in school. In this chapter's opening scenario, consider how prevalent new technologies are in Jaime Lopez's and Ellie Burke's thoughts about beginning a new school year. In 2000 Don Leu stated:

> Fifteen years ago, students did not need to know word processing technologies. Ten years ago, students did not need to know how to negotiate through the rich information environments possible in multimedia, CD-ROM technologies. Five years ago, students did not need to know how to search for information on the Internet, set a bookmark, use a web browser, create an HTML document, participate in a mailing list, engage in a collaborative Internet project with another classroom, or communicate via e-mail. Today, however, each of these technologies and each of these environments is appearing within classrooms forcing teachers, students, and researchers to continually adapt to new definitions of literacy. (p. 759)

To get a sense of the complexity and sophistication of the literacy skills involved in just one form of new literacy, consider Cynthia Lewis's and Bettina Fabos's description of the literacy practices they found in their study of adolescent instant messaging (IMing); Lewis and Fabos found that the adolescents they studied routinely participated in at least four IM conversations at once—some of them many more—and were extremely adept at changing voice, style, and manner for each one:

> The literacy practices most evident in our findings are the performative and multivoiced nature of the IM experience. In order to be a proficient IM user, one must perform a version of one's self, shifting voices moment to moment for many audiences at once. Writers in digital environments frequently address and are addressed by multiple audiences simultaneously. To do this, users have to draw on the intertextual chains (The New London Group, 1996) that exist through the history of each exchange and the larger textual network. . . . Although face-to-face interaction is also performative, the need to fluidly shift performances from audience to audience is unique to the dyaic yet nearly simultaneous nature of IM. (2005, pp. 493–494)

Thus, we can no longer limit our view of literacy to just reading or writing or just academic reading and writing. We must include such activities as e-mailing, accessing and/or creating Web sites and blogs, burning CDs, faxing, video game playing and "bleading"–blog reading, and such sources as hypermedia, ATMs, electronic texts, cartoon and zine texts, PDAs, DVDs, and on and on. Further, we must understand the many ways in which adolescents use and respond to these multiliteracies. Tom Bean and his teenage daughters elaborate on the "multiple literacies of adolescents' lives"—the texts created by engagement with electronic texts and resources, magazine reading, video texts and games, and written and oral correspondence with friends. Bean and his daughters note that these multiple literacies have a profound influence on adolescents' lives. They state, "Content teachers must move away from a dependence on didactic, text-bound modes of teaching that place adolescents in passive roles. Recent research that includes adolescents' voices and views shows the sharp divide that exists between their lives outside school and inside school" (Bean, Bean, & Bean, 1999, p. 447).

THE MILLENNIALS

And who are these preadolescent and adolescent students populating today's middle and secondary schools? They are the "millennials," children born between the years of 1982 and 1998—during the presidencies of Ronald Reagan, George Bush Sr., and Bill Clinton—and who would be expected to graduate from high school between the years of 2000 and 2016. Millennials were born into and grew up in a technological age and accept multitechnologies and multiliteracies with unstudied ease. By the time the eldest of the millennials reached middle school, digitally enhanced movie and TV commercial action, the Internet, self-serve-pay-at-the-pump gas stations, and ATMs were common aspects of everyday life. Many have never known a world without them. Millennials are confused by certain old technologies, C. W. Nevius (2002) writes:

> The other day we needed some fives and ones instead of a $20 bill, so I took my son into the bank lobby to see an actual "teller." He was agog. These people are here all the time? Why don't these people in line use the machine? (p. E1)

Lori Norton-Meier (2005) cites the work of Prensky in her discussion of "digital natives" who have never known a world without the digital technologies of today, and an older generation of "digital immigrants" who must adapt and learn to function in a rapidly changing world. Prensky (2001) describes digital natives:

> They have spent their entire lives surrounded by and using computers, videogames, digital music players, video cameras, cell phones, and all the other toys and tools of the digital age. Today's average college grads have spent less than 5,000 hours of their lives reading, but over 10,000 hours playing video games (not to mention 20,000 hours watching TV). Computer games, email, the Internet, cell phones, and instant messaging are integral parts of their lives. (p. 1)

Of the millennials, Margaret Hagood, Lisa Stevens, and David Reinking (2002) say:

> For adolescents, literacy is multimodal, and rather than receive information from static texts, they actively create meaning dynamically across diverse media . . . such as [combining] computer technology with pencil art, programming codes with photo layout and web design, and music lyrics with dance movement. (p. 75)

Charles Elster refers to what he calls a "pragmatic" definition of literacy: "Literacy is the use of written language to get things done in the worlds in which one lives" (2003, p. 665). By that definition, the ability of children and youth to navigate new technologies, understand and use those technologies for their own purposes, and travel among and between old and new technologies are all signs of complex, competent literacy functioning. Some linguists believe that the language of IM is revolutionary and marks a permanent change to English. Others note that not only the language but also the traditions of instant messaging are changing the culture. David Silver, a University of Washington professor of communications, says that kids are "altering the language to suit the technology" (Dunnewind, p. D1) and notes that the strategic use of POS—parent over shoulder—is nothing short of "brilliant." He states,

> Say a teen is supposed to be doing homework but of course is on IM. A parent comes up and the kid quickly types "POS" and sends it out. Suddenly everyone is talking about *math* homework. (Dunnewind, 2003, p. D4)

Many teachers worry that the alternative language of IM will seep into the classroom and formal writing assignments although kids say that IM language is a "kid to kid" thing, thus indicating their understanding of code switching.

LINGUISTIC DIVERSITY

When we compound the complexities of differential talents, expanding technologies, and multiliteracies in adolescents' lives with the additional diversity brought about by rapidly changing school populations and the recent entrance of large groups of non- or new-English-speaking students into secondary schools, we begin to realize the extraordinarily complex responsibility teachers have for adjusting instruction to meet the literacy and learning needs of all their students. The fact is that our schools are populated by students who have come through our own K–12 system with widely disparate literacy achievement and abilities. Many, many students are progressing academically at a rate we consider highly satisfactory, others lag behind, and yet others are academically gifted or talented in special ways.

Immigrant students are often immersed quite suddenly in a cultural and language environment that is considerably different from their home culture and language and that may or may not honor their home culture and language. These and other bilingual students come to school with widely varying oral fluency in their first language and proficiency in first-language literacy and so have diverse linguistic abilities to support their progress in achieving English-language fluency and literacy. It is not unusual today for immigrant and native-born bilingual/bicultural students to choose to maintain strong ties with their cultural heritage and retain their first languages. For these students, and others, we need programs and classes that provide support for developing English-language fluency and literacy in content areas while at the same time maintaining students' primary language and culture.

Adding further to this mix in middle and secondary schools are students of all races and ethnicities who live below the poverty level, some of whom may come from homeless families. All these students, whether they are mainstream, immigrant, bilingual/bicultural, or representative of other types of diversity, are generally taught in schools and systems primarily focused on content knowledge rather than on teaching a diverse population of students how to read and write in the content areas.

Responding to Students' Learning and Literacy Needs

Thus, the increasingly diverse cultural, ethnic, and socioeconomic composition of school populations, in addition to the increasingly expanding range of literacies that impinge on adolescents' lives, requires us to take stock of just how complex the task of teaching in secondary schools is today. Mike Rose, in his stunning book *Lives on the Boundary* (1989), reminds us that in 1890, only 6.7% of 14–17-year-olds in the United States attended high school; by 1978, that figure had grown to 94.1%. However, our move from exclusive secondary schools that educated primarily the high achieving and affluent to inclusive schools that seek to educate *all* creates new challenges. According to *Reading Next—A Vision for Action and Research in Middle School and High School Literacy* (Biancarosa & Snow, 2004), over 8 million students in grades 4–12 are struggling readers and writers, 3,000 students drop out of school every day, only 70% of U.S. students graduate from high school on time, and over half of the high school graduates enrolled in postsecondary education have to take remedial literacy courses. The most recent report on high school graduation rates by the National Center for Educational Statistics (NCES) is that graduation rates varied between 72% and 74% in the 2002–2004 graduation years (Laird, DeBell, & Chapman, 2006). What we must understand is that ever-increasing diversity and just-as-ever-increasing literacies are the reality, the true fabric of U.S. middle and secondary schools. If we are to meet the needs of all (or any) students, middle and secondary school teaching—what goes on every day in every content classroom—must undergo a fundamental change (Alvermann et al., 1998; Goodlad, 1984; Newmann, 1992). Middle and secondary students—all of them—need additional literacy instruction to extend and refine the reading and writing abilities they already have. For this instruction to be most useful, classroom teachers, not reading or writing specialists, must provide it for them. It is, after all, classroom teachers, subject area specialists, who *know, understand, and expertly use the Discourses of each discipline*. Thus, the underlying assumption of this text is that *classroom teachers are able to develop students' literacy abilities without sacrificing attention to content subject matter*—and, in fact, that subject matter instruction is considerably improved by attention to reading and writing.

This assumption is not the product of wishful thinking or unrealistic ideals. Rather, it comes from knowledge acquired by researchers and educators over the past 80 years about secondary students and their literacy needs (Moore, Readence, & Rickelman, 1992); from a new focus on the special literacy needs of adolescent students; from the knowledge we have about how individuals develop fluency and literacy in a second language; and from the accumulated experience of middle and secondary teachers themselves. A quick outline of the history of the advent and growth of attention to middle and secondary reading and writing instruction in public schools in the next section of this chapter gives a sense of how this assumption came to be and how it has been operationalized in the past. The remainder of this book then focuses on middle school and secondary reading and writing instruction as it applies to content learning and presents effective ways for content reading and writing instruction to be implemented today and in the future.

The history outline that follows next focuses exclusively on reading instruction (as opposed to writing) up until the 1970s and 1980s because issues, instruction, research, and professional and public attention to reading have predominated heavily over writing in modern American education. Not until the late 1980s did writing begin to receive the same kind of emphasis and attention.

MIDDLE AND SECONDARY LITERACY INSTRUCTION IN PERSPECTIVE*

Literacy issues in middle and secondary schools are relative newcomers in the history of education in the United States. The reason is, in part, because U.S. reading instruction began in the mid-1600s as burgeoning communities organized to provide education for young children. Reading instruction was the nucleus of that education and was developmental in nature. That is, the major purpose for instruction was to develop children's reading from nonreading or prereading stages into beginning reading; from there, individuals advanced more or less independently toward mature reading.

Attention and emphasis on reading instruction beyond early grades, on the other hand, extends back only to about the late 1920s and early 1930s. At that time, educators and education movements began to acknowledge differences between literary and technical reading and to promote the practice of providing organized reading instruction for middle-grade and secondary students. Concurrent with this movement were revelations that many adolescents and adults were unable to perform well on newly developed reading tests, along with concerns regarding the literacy demands for soldiers during the First and Second World Wars. The major focus of secondary reading instruction in its earliest years was therefore *remedial*, rather than developmental, in nature. This difference accounts for the content and format of contemporary middle school and secondary reading instruction, and it assists us in understanding how this instruction evolved.

---

*Much of the information for the first 3½ decades of this discussion is taken from Nila Banton Smith's classic study, *American Reading Instruction* (1965).

THE 1930s

- This was the incubation period for secondary reading instruction.
- Research efforts were begun to determine the nature and extent of adolescent and adult reading problems.
- Few, if any, instructional programs were established.
- Interest and study during this period provided the foundation for much of the subsequent research and program development.

THE 1940s

- Rediscovery that many soldiers could not read well enough to carry out military work served as a final catalyst for the implementation of remedial reading programs in junior and senior high schools.
- The first attempt was made to provide systematic reading instruction to even one segment of the secondary school population.
- Leaders in the field of reading were recommending—not for the first time but with growing strength—that systematic reading instruction for all students continue into the middle grades and secondary school and called for the establishment of developmental reading programs for this purpose.

THE 1950s

- Secondary remedial programs expanded considerably.
- Reading instruction in general, and reading disability specifically, received intense professional and public scrutiny after publication of Rudolph Flesch's *Why Johnny Can't Read* (1955).
- With the launching of the Soviet satellite *Sputnik* in 1957, serious questions were raised concerning the quality of American education, with specific attention directed toward reading and reading instruction.
- Increased interest was shown in developmental secondary reading programs and content area reading instruction.
- In 1958, the National Defense Education Act (NDEA) provided massive federal funds for research, teacher education, school programs, and curriculum projects, much of which was allocated for both elementary and secondary reading.

THE 1960s

- Secondary remedial reading programs continued to grow.
- Most programs were funded wholly or in part by the Title I section of the Elementary and Secondary Education Act (ESEA) of 1965.
- Many programs, especially in junior high schools, were taught by relocated elementary reading teachers.
- Newly organized "developmental" reading classes appeared in greater numbers, usually designated as "basic English" or "remedial English" classes taught by willing and courageous, but untrained, English teachers who went on to become the secondary reading specialists of the 1970s and 1980s.

- Content area reading instruction received increasingly widespread recognition and support.
- A clear distinction was made between instructional approaches that addressed literacy development in the service of subject matter learning and traditional developmental reading instruction that focused specifically on learning how to read. However, his distinction was not always fully understood or practiced.

THE 1970s

- Remedial reading programs expanded widely.
- Programs in learning disabilities, English as a Second Language (ESL), and other special education fields emerged.
- Learning resource centers served an ever-expanding, and increasingly diverse, population.
- Developmental programs grew, especially in junior high schools, and were still generally intended for students identified as "reading below grade level."
- "Developmental reading" was almost universally interpreted as something that goes on outside the regular classroom.
- Right to Read campaign was launched, aimed at achieving universal national literacy by 1980 with "Every Teacher a Teacher of Reading" slogan adopted as its rallying cry.
- Minimum competency movement gained impetus, with much of the emphasis placed on testing to determine who would pass or graduate from junior high and senior high school and on a highly publicized "back-to-basics" approach to teaching the so-called basic skills of literacy.
- By the end of the decade, most schools were doing some type of minimum competency testing, either voluntarily or in compliance with state legislative mandate, and providing compensatory programs for students who did not meet the test standards.
- The combined impact of Right to Read and the minimum competency movement focused attention on the reading needs of secondary students.
- Expansion of secondary school reading programs continued, more universities and states required secondary teachers to take one or more reading education classes, and acceptance grew for instruction advocated by content area reading proponents.
- In 1973, the Bay Area Writing Project (affectionately called BAWP) was introduced at the University of California, Berkeley, with James Gray at its helm (Gray, personal communication, 1989).

THE 1980s

- Reading programs of one type or another were well established in most secondary schools.
- Although emphasis was still on remedial, developmental programs, accelerated programs, and attention to content reading instruction were growing.

- The middle school movement gained increasing attention and momentum.
- The nation experienced a major wave of education reform triggered by the report *A Nation at Risk: The Imperative for Educational Reform* (1983), followed in rapid succession by (among others) *High School: A Report on Secondary Education in America* (Boyer, 1983); *Horace's Compromise: The Dilemma of the American High School Today* (Sizer, 1984); *A Place Called School* (Goodlad, 1984); and *Becoming a Nation of Readers: The Report of the Commission on Reading* (Anderson, Heibert, Scott, & Wilkinson, 1985).
- In each report, literacy was a focal point, and in each, teachers, schools, textbook publishers, teacher education programs, and any other group even remotely responsible for schooling were severely taken to task for the failure of some students to become literate and of other students to move beyond the most basic, minimal literacy levels.
- The major reform emphasis was movement away from "basics" and toward a "critical thinking" and "critical reading" focus.
- "Writing Across the Curriculum" joined "Reading Across the Curriculum" as a major goal of secondary schools.
- The National Writing Project (previously BAWP) was well established.

THE 1990s

- As educators called for and schools restructured toward the end of more integrated, inquiry-based learning in middle and secondary schools and a more student-centered, caring curriculum, legislators and others outside the education community advocated, once again, "back to basics" in an effort to separate literacy instruction from content learning.
- National standards for performance (and graduation) were established in virtually all subject areas, with state and local standards in at least English and mathematics either in effect or in progress.
- High-stakes performance tests were mandated by states and school districts for the multiple purposes of evaluating individual students, teachers, and schools.
- School reform continued to dominate the attention of educators, legislators, and the public at large, with the ultimate effect of making education issues daily fodder for media reports and editorials.
- The end of the decade saw renewed attention to secondary literacy instruction, including issues of second-language learning and literacy and how to "take care of the problem" of the widely diverse reading and writing abilities of secondary school students.
- A national survey of high school programs for struggling readers and writers found that 67% of the 737 schools responding reported maintaining a program for students with reading difficulties (Barry, 1997).
- A few programs were based on collaboration between reading specialists and content teachers and/or focused solely on developing content teachers' abilities to provide instructional support for students.
- The growing trend in secondary schools for all students was to stipulate out-of-school reading requirements.

2000 AND BEYOND

As the first decade of the new millennium progresses, adolescent literacy and achievement in middle level and secondary schools, continue to be at the forefront of media and public awareness.

- Various forms of academic tracking, especially the expansion of Advanced Placement (AP) programs, are now well entrenched in high schools.
- More states are adopting exit examinations in at least English and mathematics for students to receive a high school diploma.
- The role of digital technologies in adolescent lives and in secondary schools is of high interest.
- Two new studies are influencing discussions of modern secondary education: *The Silent Epidemic: Perspectives of High School Dropouts* (Bridgeland, Dilulio, & Morison, 2006), and *Reading Next—A Vision for Action and Research in Middle School and High School Literacy* (Biancarosa & Snow, 2004).
- Issues of the effects of race, socioeconomic status, and gender on academic achievement are under increased scrutiny. In colleges and universities across the country, females outnumber males by about a 60%–40% ratio (Kovner, 2006); of the 3 million "less educated" young people in the country, African American males are disproportionately represented (Dionne, 2006); by 2004, 21% of black men who did not attend college were incarcerated (Eckholm, 2006).
- New calls are heard for increased support of students' literacy skills in every class using evidence-based instruction and promoting students' abilities to be strategic readers, writers, and learners.

THE ROLE OF MIDDLE/SECONDARY SCHOOLS AND TEACHERS IN ADOLESCENT LITERACY

Whatever the outcome of the interplay between adolescents' social and academic lives and the rapidly expanding role of electronic media in all our lives, it is clear that schools and teachers must pay attention to adolescents' literacy development. The International Reading Association's Commission on Adolescent Literacy issued a position statement that says, in part:

> Adolescents entering the adult world in the 21st century will read and write more than at any other time in human history. They will need advanced levels of literacy to perform their jobs, run their households, act as citizens, and conduct their personal lives. They will need literacy to cope with the flood of information they will find everywhere they turn. They will need literacy to feed their imaginations so they can create a world of the future. In a complex and sometimes even dangerous world, their ability to read will be crucial. Continued instruction beyond the early grades is needed. (Moore, Bean, Birdyshaw, & Rycik, 1999, p. 99)

Thus, the International Reading Association and many informed educators advocate for continued, systematic, and thoughtful attention to adolescent literacy for all of the following reasons:

1. *Attention to adolescent literacy acknowledges that literacy growth is continuous and does not stop at the end of fourth or sixth grade.* Neither should instruction. All students can, and should, have the opportunity to experience continued growth as readers and writers, and in order for them to do so, various types of instruction must be available.

2. *Attention to adolescent literacy provides for diversity of student literacy abilities and needs.* Middle school and secondary classrooms are filled with students who vary widely in literacy achievement and English-language fluency. This diversity in no way suggests that there is anything "wrong" with any students or casts aspersions on students' previous classroom learning or life experience; nor does it mean that only the bilingual/bicultural students require assistance with English-language fluency and literacy. Rather, it recognizes the reality of life in middle and secondary schools. Middle school and secondary reading and writing instruction provides for all students: those who are achieving satisfactorily, those who simply need more time to arrive at expected achievement levels, those who are in the process of becoming fluent and literate in a second language, and those whose achievement goes well beyond the norm.

3. *Attention to adolescent literacy allows students to learn new, more difficult reading/writing/study skills as* ***they are needed*** *to complete school tasks.* Many students find that the skills that served them well in elementary school simply are not adequate for success with the more difficult texts, heavier assignment load, and generally less personalized atmosphere of middle and secondary school. (In other words, the Discourse of elementary school is different from the Discourse of high school.) Reading and writing instruction in content area classrooms assist students in extending and adapting their skills to meet these new conditions.

4. *Attention to adolescent literacy places remedial reading and writing programs into a perspective that more accurately reflects reality.* When the only literacy instruction in middle and secondary schools was remedial, all discussion of reading, writing, and literacy was negative, and all attention and concern were focused on the relatively small percentage of the school population with literacy problems. Certainly, that population did and does exist; it would be foolish and irresponsible to suggest otherwise. The net effect, however, was that students, teachers, administrators, and parents alike saw reading and writing instruction as appropriate only for students who were experiencing serious difficulty. Little effort was made to acknowledge and provide for the many, many students who were progressing well. Negative attitudes linger, but expanded efforts to address reading and writing in all classes have done much to reduce this disparity.

A natural outgrowth of all this attention to literacy instruction in middle and secondary schools is that the responsibility for much of that instruction rests squarely on the shoulders of classroom teachers. Programs for students with reading problems and special needs continue to be needed. But for most students, the primary focus of literacy instruction should be in their subject area classrooms. The reasoning goes like this:

1. To think deeply in *any* subject area, students must learn the language (Discourse) of that subject area and be able to read and write fluently in that language. Therefore, it is the subject area specialist (the classroom teacher)—not the reading teacher down the hall—who is responsible for teaching them how to do so.

2. Literacy skills that serve students well in middle and secondary school are *different from* the skills that serve elementary students well. Therefore, it is the secondary classroom teacher—not elementary teachers—who are responsible for teaching those skills.

3. Students who are learning subject area content in a language that is not their home language need special guidance in learning the language, the skills, and the content of subject areas. Therefore, it is the subject area specialist (the classroom teacher)—not the ESL teacher—who is responsible for that instruction.

As we achieve the goal of understanding and addressing adolescent multiliteracies, contemporary middle and secondary reading and writing instruction thus appears to be moving toward the ideals first voiced by reading educators in the 1920s: continued, systematic literacy instruction for all students throughout their school years. As such instruction increasingly characterizes middle, junior high, and senior high schools, we will be able to turn our attention from literacy *problems* to address more adequately the literacy processes and practices of the students we teach.

PLAN OF THIS BOOK

Throughout the remainder of the book, we explore various aspects of middle and secondary school literacy instruction in subject area classrooms. This text presents a number of issues, instructional strategies, and classroom ideas for guiding students' literacy and language development in your particular subject area. Specifically, this book addresses the following:

Chapter 2 describes thinking, reading, and writing processes, as well as second-language development processes, and lays the foundation for the rest of the book. It presents a theoretical point of view and philosophical stance that are well recognized in the field of reading/language education. The instructional recommendations I make in the text follow logically from that point of view and philosophical stance.

Chapter 3 concerns context area texts—including traditional textbooks, fiction and nonfiction trade books, and electronic media—and presents various ways, including online resources, for evaluating the readability and overall appropriateness of texts.

Chapters 4 and 5 address the two processes of reading commonly considered to be preeminent aspects of most people's definitions and conceptualizations of reading: comprehension and vocabulary. These chapters demonstrate how both processes are central to learning in subject areas and how instruction may account for content (subject knowledge) and processes (comprehension and vocabulary) simultaneously. Evidence-based instructional strategies are provided in these and all other methodology chapters (6, 7, 8, 10, 11). Chapter 4 introduces two features that also continue in other methodology chapters: (1) Centerpiece Lesson Plans highlight and combine two or three of the instructional strategies in each chapter; they and other lesson plans show explicitly how to connect lesson objectives with curriculum standards, how to do the lesson step-by-step, and how to assess student performance during and after instruction. (2) Creating Strategic Readers, Writers, and Learners is a feature designed to synthesize and give specific ways for teachers to help students become increasingly independent learners. Lesson plans and demonstrations in Chapters 4 and 5 are in the subject areas of mathematics, social studies, science, and English.

Chapter 6 further extends the discussion begun in Chapter 2 by focusing on effective instructional activities for teaching subject matter content to bilingual/bicultural students in multilingual/multicultural classrooms. The central focus of Chapter 6 is how to shelter instruction for ELL students in subject area classrooms and how to analyze that instruction using the Sheltered Instruction Observation Protocol (SIOP). The Centerpiece Lesson Plan demonstrates sheltered instruction in science and how to shelter Chapter 4 and 5 lesson plans in English, mathematics, and social studies.

Chapters 7 and 8 extend the discussion begun in Chapters 4 and 5 by focusing explicitly on reading and writing across the curriculum. Comprehension and vocabulary development are certainly present in these chapters but are addressed as natural, and therefore assumed, parts of learning subject content. Chapter 7 introduces the idea of "flow," a learning experience where time flies and learners are totally engaged, and emphasizes alternative ways for students to seek and demonstrate knowledge, including online resources and media. Chapter 8 highlights the multiple and increasingly electronic mode of writing in which adolescents engage. The Centerpiece Lesson plan and other lesson plans in Chapters 7 and 8 are in the subject areas of social studies, science, and mathematics.

Chapter 9 explores issues of assessment and evaluation of literacy abilities in content areas and examines issues of high-stakes testing, standards, and authentic assessment, including development of rubrics and informal assessment. Although the emphasis here is on reading and writing, the recommended assessment information and practices can be generalized beyond literacy learning in many cases.

Chapter 10 extends discussions from earlier chapters about student diversity, multiculturalism, and teaching in pluralistic schools. Chapter 10 introduces the Difference Model for understanding and addressing diversity in the classroom. The focus is on marginalized learners, students with special needs, giftedness, gender, and creating learning classrooms for all students. The Centerpiece Lesson Plan and other lesson plan are in the subject areas of physical education and social studies.

Chapter 11 is another chapter focusing on instruction. It presents discussion, ideas, and specific directions for using collaborative, project-based learning activities in subject area classes. The emphasis remains on literacy learning in subject areas, and suggestions are made for connecting these strategies with those learned in previous chapters and for use of Internet inquiry in collaborative projects. The Centerpiece lesson plan and other lesson plan are in the subject areas of vocal music and foreign language.

Chapter 12 encourages you as teachers to promote your students' (and your own) lifelong reading and writing behaviors and to use literature to teach every content. It's a chapter devoted to pleasurable, interesting reading and writing—both in school and out—and based on the premise that, reading and writing can and should be captivating as well as informative. The premise of this chapter is that if we are to be truly successful teachers, we must not only teach students how to read and write in content areas but also promote attitudes and behaviors that lead students to choose to do both independently.

WHAT THIS CHAPTER MEANS TO YOU

1. The anxieties Ellie Burke and Jaime Lopez are experiencing are normal, reasonable, and common feelings. You will likely feel them at the beginning of every school year; keep in mind that your students are feeling them too. Middle and secondary schools are complex, multifaceted social organizations.

2. Adolescent literacy is comprised of multiple social, technological, and academic Discourses, and is made all the more complex by the individual identities students construct to define themselves. In order to reach preadolescent and adolescent learners, you will need to understand, acknowledge, and engage the multiliteracies of adolescents' lives.

3. Attention to adolescent literacy has evolved historically from instruction to help struggling readers and writers to an understanding of and focus on the various Discourses, literacies, and media that impinge on the lives of all adolescents and on subject area learning and teaching. As a classroom teacher you are a primary agent in guiding students' acquisition of the content, Discourses, and literacies of the subject you teach.

DOUBLE ENTRY JOURNAL

Write your own literacy history—an account of how you became literate and how you experienced literacy in elementary, middle level, and secondary school. Use your notes from your prereading Double Entry Journal (DEJ) to help you. Consider the many Discourses that you use in daily living and in the study of your subject area specialty, and the identities you constructed to define yourself as a student. Consider also the effect of various technologies on your learning from elementary school to today. Share your experience with your partner or group.

FEATURE *What Goes in My Portfolio?*

Create a portfolio artifact that shows your literacy history in relationship to the history of middle and secondary literacy instruction during the years you were in school. Use visuals and graphs, timelines, and/or samples of your adolescent reading and writing to create your artifact. Be sure to connect your literacy history to the history of literacy instruction, and the general history, of the time period.

RECOMMENDED SOURCES

*Alvermann, D. E., Hinchman, K. A., Moore, D. W., Phelps, S. F., & Waff, D. R. (Eds.) (1998). *Reconceptualizing the literacies in adolescents' lives* (pp. 3–26). Mahwah, NJ: Lawrence Erlbaum.

*Anderson, R. C., Heibert, E. H., Scott, J. A., & Wilkinson, I. A. G. (1985). *Becoming a nation of readers: The report of the Commission on Reading*. Washington, DC: National Institute of Education.

*Barry, A. L. (1997). High school reading programs revisited. *Journal of Adolescent & Adult Literacy, 40,* 524–531.

*Bean, T. W., Bean, S. K., & Bean, K. F. (1999). Intergenerational conversations and two adolescents' multiple literacies: Implications for redefining content area literacy. *Journal of Adolescent & Adult Literacy, 42,* 438–448.

*Biancarosa, G., & Snow, C. (2004). *Reading Next—A vision for action and research in middle school and high school literacy: A report to Carnegie Corporation of New York*. Washington, DC: Alliance for Excellent Education.

Bond, G. L., & Bond, E. (1941). *Developmental reading in high school*. New York: Macmillan.

*Boyer, E. L. (1983). *High school: A report on secondary education in America*. New York: Harper & Row.

*Bridgeland, J. M., Dilulio Jr., J. J., & Morison, K. B. (2006, March). *The silent epidemic: Perspectives of high school dropouts*. A report by Civic Enterprises in association with Peter D. Hart Research Associates for the Bill and Melinda Gates Foundation.

Chaskin, R. J., & Rauner, D. M. (Eds.) (1995). Special feature edition on youth and caring. *Phi Delta Kappan, 76*(9), 665–719.

Clifford, G. J. (1987). *A Sisyphean task: Historical perspectives on the relationship between writing and reading instruction* (Technical Report No. 7). Berkeley, CA: Center for the Study of Writing.

*Dionne, E.J. (February 21, 2006). Young, disadvantaged, and male. *San Francisco Chronicle* (originally *Washington Post* Writers Group), B7.

*Dunnewind, S. (2003, June 17). IM—Instant messaging by teens becoming a hybrid language. *The Press Democrat*, D1, D4.

Early, M. J. (1957). What does research reveal about successful reading programs? In M. A. Gunn et al. (Eds.), *What we know about high school reading*. Champaign, IL: National Council of Teachers of English.

Echevarria, J., Vogt, M. E., & Short, D. (1999). *Making content comprehensible for English language learners: The SIOP Model*. Needham Heights, MA: Allyn & Bacon.

*Eckholm, E. (March 20, 2006). Studies warn of deepening plight for black men. *The Press Democrat* (originally, *New York Times*), A5.

*Elster, C.A. (2003). Authority, performance, and interpretation in religious reading: Critical issues of intercultural communication and multiple literacies. *Journal of Literacy Research, 35*(1), 663–692.

*Flesch, R. (1955). *Why Johnny can't read*. New York: Harper & Row.

Freeman, D. E., & Freeman, Y. S. (2001). *Between worlds* (2nd ed.). Portsmouth, NH: Heinemann.

Gee, J. P. (1996). *Social linguistics and literacies* (2nd ed.). New York: Routledge-Falmer.

Gee, J. P. (2000). Teenagers in new times: A literacy studies perspective. *Journal of Adolescent and Adult Literacy, 43*(5), 412–420.

Gee, J. P. (2001). Reading as situated language: A sociocognitive perspective. *Journal of Adolescent and Adult Literacy, 44*(8), 714–725.

*Gee, J. P. (2002). Millennials and Bobos, *Blue's Clues* and *Sesame Street:* A story for our times. In D. E. Alvermann (Ed.), *Adolescents and literacies in a digital world* (pp. 51–67). New York: Peter Lang.

*Goodlad, J. I. (1984). *A place called school*. New York: McGraw-Hill.

Gray, W. S. (1948). Reading in the high school and college, *Forty-Seventh Yearbook, Part II, of the National Society for the Study of Education*.

Greenlaw, J., & Moore, D. (1982, December). *Reading programs in secondary schools*. Paper presented at the annual meeting of the National Reading Conference, St. Petersburg, FL.

*Hagood, M. C., Stevens, L. P., & Reinking, D. (2002). What do *They* have to teach *Us?* Talkin' 'cross generations. In D. E. Alvermann (Ed.), *Adolescents and literacies in a digital world* (pp. 68–83). New York: Peter Lang.

Harste, J. C. (1994). Literacy as curricular conversations about knowledge, inquiry, and morality. In R. B. Ruddell, M. R. Ruddell, & H. Singer (Eds.), *Theoretical*

*Cited in text.

models and processes of reading (4th ed., pp. 1220–1242). Newark, DE: International Reading Association.

Herber, H. L. (1978). *Teaching reading in content areas* (2nd ed.). Englewood Cliffs, NJ: Prentice-Hall.

Irwin, J. L. (1990). *Reading and the middle school student: Strategies to enhance literacy*. Newark, DE: International Reading Association.

Jiménez, R. T., Moll, L. C., Rodriguez-Brown, F. V., & Barrera, R. B. (1999). Latina and Latino researchers interact on issues related to literacy learning. *Reading Research Quarterly, 34*, 217–230.

*Kovner, G. (February 13, 2006). Collegiate gender gap just keeps growing. *The Press Democrat*, A1, A9.

*Laird, D., DeBell, M., & Chapman, C. (2006). *Dropout rates in the United States: 2004*. U.S. Department of Education.

Lenhart, A., Simon, M., & Graziano, M. (2001, September 1). *The Internet and education: Findings of the Per Internet & American Life Project*. Available: http://www.pewinternet.org

*Leu, D. J. (2000). Literacy and technology: Deitic consequences for literacy education in an information age. In M. L. Kamil, P. B. Mosenthal, P. D. Pearson, & R. Barr (Eds.), *Handbook of reading research volume III* (pp. 743–770). Mahwah, NJ: Lawrence Erlbaum.

*Lewis, C., & Fabos, B. (2005). Instant messaging, literacies, and social identities. *Reading Research Quarterly, 40*(4), 470–501.

Lucas, G. (1995, July 6). Legislators push basics in schools. *San Francisco Chronicle*, pp. A1, A9.

Luke, A., & Elkins, J. (2000). Special themed issue: Re-mediating adolescent literacies. *Journal of Adolescent and Adult Literacy, 45*(5), 396–398.

*Moje, E. B., Young, J. P, Readence, J. E., & Moore, D. W. (2000). Reinventing adolescent literacy for new times: Perennial and millennial issues. *Journal of Adolescent and Adult Literacy, 43*(5), 400–410.

*Moje, E. B. Dillon, D. R., & O'Brien, D. (2000, January/February). Reexamining roles of learner, text, and context in secondary literacy. *The Journal of Educational Research, 93*(3), 165–180.

*Moore, D. W., Bean, T. W., Birdyshaw, D., & Rycik, J. A. (1999). Adolescent literacy: A position statement. *Journal of Adolescent and Adult Literacy, 43*(2), 97–112.

*Moore, D. W., Readence, J. E., & Rickelman, R. J. (1992). An historical exploration of content reading instruction. In E. K. Dishner, T. W. Bean, J. E. Readence, & D. W. Moore (Eds.), *Reading in the content areas* (3rd ed., pp. 5–29). Dubuque, IA: Kendall/Hunt.

Moore, D. W., & Stefanich, G. P. (1990). Middle school reading: A historical perspective. In G. G. Duffy (Ed.), *Reading in the middle school* (2nd ed., pp. 3–15). Newark, DE: International Reading Association.

*National Commission on Excellence in Education. (1983). *A nation at risk: The imperative for educational reform*. Washington, DC: U.S. Government Printing Office.

*Nevius, C. W. (2002, August 18). Technology can keep us young if we let it. *The San Francisco Chronicle*, E1, E3.

*The New London Group (1996). A pedagogy of multiliteracies: Designing social futures. *Harvard Educational Review, 66*(1), 60–92.

*Newmann, F. M. (Ed.) (1992). *Student engagement and achievement in American secondary schools*. New York: Teachers College Press.

Nieto, S. (1999, December). *Language, literacy, and culture: Intersections and implications*. Paper delivered at the 49th annual meeting of the National Reading Conference, Orlando, FL.

Noddings, N. (1992). *The challenge to care in schools*. New York: Teachers College Press.

*Norton-Meier, L. (2005). Joining the video-game literacy club: A reluctant mother tries to join the "flow." *Journal of Adolescent and Adult Literacy, 48*(5), 428–432.

*Prensky, M. (2001). Digital natives, digital immigrants. *On the Horizon, 9*(5), 1–6.

*Rose, M. (1989). *Lives on the boundary*. New York: Penguin.

Shearer, B. A., Ruddell, M. R., & Vogt, M. E. (2001). Successful middle school reading intervention: Negotiated strategies and individual choice. In J. V. Hoffman, D. L. Schallert, C. M. Fairbanks, J. Worthy, & B. Maloch (Eds.), *50th yearbook of the National Reading Conference* (pp. 558–571).

*Sizer, T. R. (1984). *Horace's compromise: The dilemma of the American high school today*. Boston: Houghton Mifflin.

Smith, N. B. (1965). *American reading instruction*. Newark, DE: International Reading Association.

Stevenson, C., & Carr, J. F. (1993). *Integrated studies in the middle grades: "Dancing through walls."* New York: Teachers College Press.

Welner, K. G., & Oakes, J. (1996). (Li)ability grouping: The new susceptibility of school tracking systems to legal challenges. *Harvard Educational Review, 66*, 451–470.

*Williams, B. T. (2006). Home and away: The tensions of community, literacy, and identity. *Journal of Adolescent Literacy, 49*(4), 342–347.

CHAPTER 2

Literacy and Language Processes: Thinking, Reading, and Writing in First and Second Languages

DOUBLE ENTRY JOURNAL

Jot down ideas you have about the processes of thinking, reading, and writing. What is your definition of each? How do you think these processes are connected? Now overlay your ideas with what you know about second-language literacy development. After you've done that, organize your jottings and show any connections you can make among these literacy and language processes.

Creatas/Jupiter Images

The kids in biology lab 203 are a study in contrasts. One knot of five students in the far corner appears to be engaged in mighty verbal combat about how the group should proceed on its study of ocean ecologies. At lab tables around the room groups of two to five students work in a variety of ways. Two students converse avidly as they decide how they're going to represent their findings with the conceptual map they're creating on chart paper. At a computer, a group of four students is creating three-dimensional color charts and models; singleton students at tables and computers dot the room, reading, drawing, "mousing," word processing, and searching websites. Three students have taken over the lab cart on which they're creating an ocean ecology representation in the currently unused classroom aquarium. And at the board Jake Elrod, the teacher, is helping a group think through some major concepts and discover their knowledge gaps as they examine the issue of sustainable environments in the world's oceans.

• • •

How we think—how the human intellectual apparatus works—is an endlessly fascinating subject and has been an area of enduring interest to educators, psychologists, and other scientists for many, many years. Modern inquiry into human thinking can be dated to about the beginning of the twentieth century, and since that time cognition and cognitive processes have been the focus of much study, research, definition, speculation, and redefinition. Along the way, study of the relationship between thinking and learning as well as of the intricacies of various learning processes has led to additional interest in specific learning areas.

Reading emerged very early as a major focus of psychological theory and research, and, as the title of Thorndike's seminal study "Reading as Reasoning: A Study of Mistakes in Paragraph Reading" (1917) suggests, a clear linkage was made between cognition and literacy from early on. Today, information, theory, and research all support that linkage and further suggest that the relationship between reading and writing is direct and parallel—that is, they are different sides of the same coin. In this chapter, we will look first at current theory of cognition and cognitive processes; then we will connect those to reading and writing process theory. Following that, we will explore issues of second-language development and literacy.

THEORY AND PRACTICE

Before we go any further, however, let us talk for just a moment about theory. Much is made among students in education courses (and other courses as well) about the separation of "theory" and "practice." Long-standing education lore has it that to be "theoretical" is to be high-flown, impractical, and out of touch with the real world of the classroom. Nothing could be further from the truth. Although it is *possible* for a theorist to be all of those things, it is certainly not necessary—nor is it even typical, especially of good theorists.

Theory is nothing more (nor less) than an informed hunch about how things work. Theories are marked by *cohesion* (things within things "fit together"; things "fit" with other things), *organizing principles* (limited numbers of generalizations or rules explain numerous events), *hypothesis-testing capability* (theories and theory parts may be examined and judged), and *flexibility* (theories change as they are tested and reevaluated on the basis of incremental evidence).

The truly theoretical teacher, then, is one who *fits together* what he or she is doing with what the rest of the school is doing, who understands that how you treat students one day has direct consequences for how they behave the next, and who perceives the relationship of various curricula within the school. A theoretical teacher is also one whose behavior is *rule governed* rather than random; one who acts with foresight and thoughtfulness; one who reacts to classroom events predictably and reasonably; one who constantly seeks greater understanding of the classroom and school ecology by *analyzing events and testing hypotheses*; and one who *changes* classroom events, procedures, and interactions as conditions warrant. In short, to be theoretical is to make the classroom *make sense*—to yourself, to your students, and to anyone walking into the room. So, then, to be theoretical in the classroom is not to be high-flown, impractical, or out of touch with reality, all of which may be inconsiderate, thoughtless, foolish, sometimes silly, and maybe even dangerous—but certainly not theoretical. To be theoretical is to be down to earth, *utterly* practical, and fully in touch with reality. Thus, good theory is informed by practice and good practice is informed by theory. Without theory, then, what we do in the classroom—practice—is uninformed, random, inconsiderate, thoughtless, sometimes silly, and maybe even dangerous. Let us now look at important theory for guiding literacy learning.

COGNITIVE THEORY

I once sat in a teachers' lounge and listened to the vocational education teacher talk about how frustrated he was about a student we had in common. He finished by saying, with equal parts exasperation and affection, "That kid's just like a chicken—he wakes up to a new world every day!" I laughed along with the other teachers and rather admired the down-home flavor and humor of the comparison. Over the years, however, I've come to view that statement as a profound comment on human intelligence. What separates us from chickens is that we *don't* "wake up to a new world every day," and it is our ability to accumulate knowledge—to categorize, differentiate, generalize, make predictions, and acquire the many Discourses of our lives—that characterizes our intellectual power. *How* we accumulate knowledge, the cognitive processes that human thinking comprises, is a topic that has fascinated so many so long.

COGNITION

Current understanding of cognition is centered in *schema theory*, derived from the work of Sir Frederick Bartlett (1932) and Swiss epistemologist Jean Piaget (1950, 2001), and, somewhat in contrast to Piagetian theory, the work of Lev Vygotsky (1978, 1986). Other psychologists and educators expanded and refined early theory and research. Piaget defined *schemata* (plural for *schema*) as cognitive structures by which individuals intellectually adapt to and organize the environment. Schemata receive, sort, classify, and hold information about environmental events and objects; these events and objects comprise our world knowledge and are connected to one another by the logical operations we are capable of performing. Piaget's classification of developmental stages of cognitive growth identifies specific types of operations in each stage, from infant sensorimotor functioning to adult abstract reasoning.

Schemata are acquired, extended, and refined as a result of both direct and vicarious experience, and they carry with them *scripts*, or cognitive maps (Shank & Abelson, 1977), which tell us what to expect and how to behave in specific situations.

Rumelhart (1981) even refers to schemata as "little plays." James Gee extends the notion of scripts with his conception of Discourses that accompany schemata, and differentiates the capital-D "Discourse" he is talking about from the "stretches of language that make sense" definition commonly associated with the notion of little-d discourse (1996, p. 127). Gee defines Discourse as

> ways of being in the world, or forms of life which integrate words, acts, values, beliefs, attitudes, and social identities, as well as gestures, glances, body positions, and clothes. A Discourse is a sort of identity kit which comes complete with the appropriate costume and instructions on how to act, talk, and often write, so as to take on a particular social role that others will recognize. (1996, p. 127)

Knowledge accumulated in schemata, scripts, and Discourses helps us see relationships and interrelationships and to function successfully in various contexts.

Consider, for example, the development of your "library" schema and Discourse. Remember back to the first time you went to a library. The library was probably rather small; it might have been located in or near a local school. Someone probably showed you where books appropriate to your age were and gave you some information about how to act in a library—for example, speak quietly, take your books to the desk to be "checked out," sit on the floor or in a chair or at a table to read until it is time to leave, and so on (notice the values, attitudes, and beliefs embedded here). Knowledge residing in this new schema and its attendant Discourses subsequently made it possible for you to return to the library by yourself and function adequately (here is where you're you and a chicken is a chicken—no more "new world" for you, librarywise). You thus were able to classify information in your library schema/Discourse to allow you to know what to expect and how to act, just as you did in your "home" schema, your "dog" schema, your "family" schema, and on and on and on.

Along with classification, we are able to *generalize* schema knowledge and Discourse from one specific situation to another. We know that all libraries, even those we have never been inside, use classification systems to store books, periodicals, and electronic resources; furthermore, we can handle the vagaries of the Library of Congress classification system on the basis of what we already know about the Dewey decimal system, and we can use an online electronic index on the basis of our knowledge both of the Dewey decimal system and how computer file systems work.

Our ability to *differentiate* occurs when we distinguish between specific items or events both within and across schemata and Discourses. Although we understand that all libraries use a classification system for storing books, periodicals, and electronic resources, we also know that finding materials in a neighborhood library differs vastly from finding materials in a major research library. Further, classification systems are equally useful (and used) in department stores, fast-food restaurants, and fish markets; they're all different, and we must apply new classification system rules to each to use them. Our ability to differentiate across schemata and Discourses allows us to make those distinctions and to function appropriately.

And finally, we use schema and Discourse knowledge to *predict* specifics so that we enter both known and new situations with a set of assumptions and expectations that guide our behavior. On entering the library on your campus, you expect to find the main desk and major book sections exactly where they were when you were last there, and you expect to follow established procedures for using and borrowing materials; when entering a different library for the first time, you look for the same elements in similar or corresponding areas and learn the procedural variations necessary for library use.

COGNITIVE PROCESSING, CONCEPT FORMATION, AND LEARNING

We continually extend and refine schemata through the processes of *assimilation* (adding new information to old schemata) and *accommodation* (creating new schemata or changing old ones with new information). The sum of our schemata and Discourse knowledge can be thought of as our knowledge of the world. The more experience we have with various Discourses and the more accurately and precisely we classify, generalize, differentiate, and predict, the more likely it is that we are able to function successfully in many different contexts. Confusion, or non-sense, occurs when experience has not provided the appropriate schema or when there is a mismatch between the schema and Discourse we are using and the actual situation.

If we have no experience with libraries, it is unlikely we would know quite how to use one (luckily, we do have an adaptive schema that says, "When in doubt, observe or ask," so we look for the information desk or a friendly face). Mismatched schemata are typical of those odd, off-center conversations everyone has experienced when two people are talking, but not about the same thing. Comments don't "fit," and nothing makes sense until someone says, "Oh—*you're* talking about. . .; *I'm* talking about. . .;" Use of an inappropriate or mismatched Discourse is equally confusing. Gee (1996) uses the example of the disconnect that would occur if one used cocktail lounge language, protocol, and behavior in a biker bar. Critical to the process of unraveling confusion and non-sense is the monitoring aspect of well-established and refined schemata and Discourses. Such monitoring signals a problem and lets us know when our behavior, the behavior of others around us, or any variety of interactions are not "right." This monitoring function is crucial to our ability to operate successfully within a complex environment.

Vygotsky (1986) emphasizes the role of language in concept formation and learning. He states:

> It is the functional use of the word, or any other sign, as means of focusing one's attention, selecting distinctive features and analyzing and synthesizing them, that plays a central role in concept formation. (p. 106)

According to Vygotsky, we learn as we move cognitively from murky, undifferentiated object "heaps" to fully differentiated concepts through the medium of inner speech. Social interaction with family, teachers, and peers further serves to guide and direct learning as the learner observes, experiences, and practices the Discourse of the learning event. Vygotsky calls the distance between what we are able to do (or know) independently and what we are able to do (or know) with assistance the *Zone of Proximal Development* (ZPD) (1986, p. 187). The ZPD is the ideal space for learning to occur and thus serves as the centerpiece of Vygotsky's argument that with peer interaction or teacher guidance, individuals can do more than they are able to do alone (p. 187) and, further, that what one can do with assistance today can be done alone tomorrow (p. 188).

INTERTEXTUALITY

Doug Hartman makes the case that the notion of "text" need not be confined to printed language. Rather,

> A text can include both linguistic and nonlinguistic *signs*. As a result, a text can be an utterance, a gesture, a structure, or a piece of art, music, or drama. In this more inclusive sense, a text is any sign that communicates meaning. (1995, p. 523)

Thus, our lives themselves are texts filled with the many texts of our daily encounters and transactions and the "inner texts" (Pearson & Tierney, 1984) we create to interpret and represent that world. Intertextuality refers to the myriad ways in which we link these texts one to another in ongoing and ever-changing transactions with experience and events. These intertextual links create the Discourses we acquire through experience. Hartman suggests that any number of circumstances influence these linkages—our social history and/or our immediate social context, for example—and emphasizes the reconstructive nature of thinking as well. That is, not only do we construct meaning (or multiple meanings) for an immediate event, but also that meaning is shaded and colored by additional linkages we make in rethinking the event.

THE RELATIONSHIP BETWEEN THINKING AND READING

Reading is the act of constructing meaning while transacting with text. Just as we use information stored in schemata to understand and interact with the world around us, so do we use this knowledge to make sense of print. Notice that I have not said anything about the reader's "getting" meaning—from the author, the page, or anywhere else. I believe, as do others, that readers literally *make* meaning from the interaction between prior knowledge and previous experience (what they already know); from the information available in text; from the "stance" (Rosenblatt, 1994) or position they elect to take in relationship to the text; and from immediate, remembered, or shared social interaction and communication. Of this notion of "transaction," Louise Rosenblatt states:

> Every reading act is an event, or a transaction, involving a particular reader and a particular pattern of signs, a text, and occurring at a particular time in a particular context. Instead of two fixed entities acting on one another, the reader and the text are two aspects of a total dynamic situation. The "meaning" does not reside ready-made "in" the text or "in" the reader but happens or comes into being during the transaction between reader and text. (1994, p. 1063)

To this, Gee would add, "language . . . always comes fully attached to other stuff; to social relations, cultural models, power and politics, perspectives on experience, values, and attitudes, as well as things and places in the world" (1996, p. vii). And it is this "stuff" that comprises the Discourse of the reading event.

Consider how active this theoretical view of reading is—in other words, how different it is to "make meaning" from text than it is to "get meaning" from text. Consider also how it focuses on the *reader*, rather than on the text or the author, as the central element of the process and how it emphasizes individual constructions of meaning while accounting for socially negotiated meaning construction and the constantly evolving Discourses of the reading content and event. In essence, the reader brings to the reading event all the information residing in schemata and then constructs meaning as he or she links and relinks text information to that prior knowledge, all of which is influenced by the reader's interrelationships, Discourse context, and communication with others. Nancy Farnan shares a beautiful illustration of this point:

> Nowhere is the essence of this theory captured so elegantly as in [Gary] Paulsen's introduction to *The Winter Room* (1989), his wildly funny yet poignant story of two adolescent boys growing up in the northern Minnesota woods. The introductory chapter is a rich milieu of images, and he ends it this way: "If books could have more, give more, be more, show more, they would still need readers, who bring to them sound and smell and light and all the rest that can't be in books. The book needs you." (Farnan, 1996, p. 439; Paulsen, p. 3)

This view of reading is *constructivist* in nature, with its emphasis on the individual as *creator*, rather than *receiver*, of meaning. Just as importantly, this view of the reading process has clear instructional implications; that is, from this theoretical vantage point, one sees many opportunities for teachers to teach in ways that will increase students' reading abilities.

This definition is by no means the only definition of the reading process; others abound—many of them very different and many of them as fully supported by research and theory as this one. It is, however, the theoretical view of reading that guides and directs my thinking and thus serves as the foundation for this book. To reiterate:

> *Reading is the act of constructing meaning while transacting with text.* The reader makes meaning through the combination of prior knowledge and previous experience; information available in text; the stance he or she takes in relationship to the text; and immediate, remembered, or anticipated social interaction and communication.

Let us now look at the reading process.

THE READING PROCESS

PRIOR KNOWLEDGE AND PREVIOUS EXPERIENCE

At least two types of prior knowledge, residing in schemata, are critical to the reading process. The first is *world knowledge*, which is the total amount of information a person has accumulated through day-to-day living experience. The second is *text knowledge*, which is information accumulated from a reader's experiences with print.

World Knowledge World knowledge includes information within individual schemata, information involving networks of relationships between and across schemata, and information about embedded characteristics of schemata (Rumelhart, 1981). For example, the "library" schema has within it a large number of schemata we could enumerate: "desk," "chair," "classification system," and "book," to name a few. These schemata are related to, and in fact embedded in, various other schemata. Think about a library desk, a school desk, an office desk, a computer desk, a rolltop desk, and so forth, and you begin to get the idea. Each of these world-knowledge schemata carries with it the Discourses we discussed earlier, as well as procedural knowledge that makes it possible for the reader to organize information, allocate attention, draw inferences, carry out orderly memory searches, edit and summarize information, and remember information (Anderson, 1994).

During reading, world knowledge serves as both the foundation for and the building blocks for constructing meaning. That is, the amount, type, and kind of prior knowledge a reader has about a given topic and the manner in which the reader links known and new knowledge affects the meaning he or she constructs for the immediate text. Hartman describes this process as "moblization of potential knowledge fragments" in which the reader engages in "transposing texts into other texts, absorbing one text into another, and building a mosaic of intersecting texts" that lead to a reader's construction of meaning (1995, p. 526). World knowledge is thus constantly changing as the result of our ongoing transactions in the world around us and perceptions of incoming information; as a result, no two readings of the same text are ever the same. Generally, the greater the reader's world knowledge, the greater the likelihood that he or she will construct meaning congruent with the author's intended meaning. This is not always true, however. Rumelhart (1981, p. 22) suggests three explanations to account for lack of concurrence between reader text and author text. Gee's notion of Discourse adds to that explanation:

1. *The reader may not have the appropriate schemata (or Discourse).* In this case, the issue is the amount of world/Discourse knowledge; lacking either, the reader simply has no basis for constructing meaning. Have you ever read a book as an adult that you'd read as a child and found yourself astonished as you encountered ideas that you hadn't even known were there? The child could not make meaning of ideas for which he or she had no world knowledge. We've all experienced technical or other highly specialized text—legal documents, tax forms, bicycle assembly instructions—that left us baffled and defeated. That's "lack of appropriate schemata" in action.

2. *The reader may have the appropriate schemata (or Discourse), but the information available in text may not suggest them.* Here, the reader constructs incomplete or inappropriate meaning but could possibly construct appropriate meaning given addition textual (or other) information to direct attention to the intended schemata/Discourse. When mismatches do occur, the situation is not dissimilar to the odd, off-center conversations and miscommunications discussed earlier or to reading Far Side or Bizarro cartoons.

3. *The reader may construct a consistent interpretation of text but not the one intended.* In this instance, the reader "understands text" but misunderstands the author. This situation can occur when prior knowledge is inaccurate (Anders & Lloyd, 1989); when stylistic devices signaling author intent, such as irony or exaggeration, are not perceived; when reader linkages are significantly different from author linkages; or when the Discourse assumed by the reader is different from the Discourse assumed by the author (cocktail lounge behavior in a biker bar).

Hartman (1995) makes the important point that prior knowledge is not some static "thing" that readers bring to reading events and "unload" before they read. Rather, prior knowledge is constantly changing—and creating change—throughout reading, so that it influences and is influenced by all of the elements of the reading event.

Text Knowledge In addition to using world knowledge, readers also employ prior knowledge about text while reading. This highly specialized information, which is actually a subset of world knowledge rather than separate from it, contains all that the individual knows about how text is organized, how one processes text, how the language of text functions, what expectations are reasonable when approaching print, what procedures are useful in interacting with text, and countless other conventions of text and print.

Knowledge about text ranges in sophistication and complexity from the child's emerging awareness of "Once upon a time" as a stylistic marker for the beginning of a story to the mature reader's ability to distinguish not only between different types of text (narrative, expository) but between classifications within a given type (technical manual, school textbook, trade book, professional journal, popular magazine). It also includes information about such seemingly minor areas as how pronouns work, how connectives (such as *and*, *because*, *in addition to*) are used, and how print conventions (boldface headings, italicized words and terms, footnotes) are used to aid reader understanding of text. New text forms—such as e-mail, IM, and blogs and other Web sites—create new text conventions for us to learn, and we are all in the process of extending our text knowledge schemata and Discourses as these appear.

Knowledge about text information becomes increasingly sophisticated and complex as we have correspondingly wider experience with written text forms. This information creates a set of assumptions and expectations about text—in other words, a Discourse—that operates each time we begin to read and continues throughout the reader–text transaction. Consider, for example, the different assumptions and expectations you have for what the following texts will bring: advanced physics book, the current "steamy" bestseller, MySpace.com, nursery rhymes, graffiti, a grocery store aisle, Google.com, a bus schedule, and instructions for programming your remote control. Notice how your assumptions and expectations include both your knowledge about text and world knowledge. A student of mine recently said, "I wonder what's going to happen to the English language as I observe my 13-year-old daughter's e-mail communications with friends—no capital letters, disregard for spelling, new spellings that combine numbers and code with letters." We now identify this as IM text and understand that this text form, and its accompanying Discourses, continues to grow and change.

Even though we have discussed them separately, world knowledge and text knowledge are really rather difficult to sort out at times. Combined, they form the reader's base of prior knowledge and previous experience and thus assist the reader in constructing meaning. The reader's ability to construct meaning congruent with the author's intended meaning depends on the content of his or her prior knowledge and previous experience, on her or his ability to access that prior knowledge base and its attendant Discourse, and on the type and content of the linkages he or she makes between available texts.

INFORMATION AVAILABLE IN TEXT

The reader's ability to construct meaning also depends on her or his ability to use information available in text. Information in text may be new information or already known. Much of what we discussed in the previous section (on text knowledge) comprises information available in text—textual features that carry meaning. Some features are highly explicit (paragraphing and punctuation, for example); others are slightly less so, such as stylistic differences between comparison–contrast, cause–effect, and effect–cause writing. World-knowledge features are similarly available in text and are content laden; in subject area text, world-knowledge features include information that surrounds the topics of the text—for example, government structures, decimal points, and musical notation.

Text and world-knowledge features are available in text, whether or not the reader's prior knowledge base makes their meaning accessible. When the information in text is already known, that information is considered to be *redundant* because it requires less mental energy and cognitive processing time for meaning construction. For example, once a reader's text knowledge base includes the information that quotation marks are used to signal conversation and/or specialized use of language, that information is immediately accessed. Thus, the things in text that the reader knows before entering that text are redundant and, because of their redundancy, are readily processed.

World-knowledge information in text may be redundant as well. Consider the differences between your "history book" and "suspense novel" schemata. In each schema resides information that such texts focus on relationships between nations, often involve political conflict, and are concerned with some or all of the following: intrigue, economics, international disasters, famous people, war. Nevertheless, your prior knowledge about how history texts and suspense novels work—that is, the Discourse traditions of each—would lead to quite different expectations for both the form and substance, even when the subject matter of each is identical (World War II, for example). The degree to which individuals have experienced reading history books and suspense novels is the degree to which the information is redundant for each person. We create "slots" (Anderson, 1994) in our history book and suspense novel schemata for redundant elements that allow us to encounter them in text and process them with very little mental effort; thus, the amount of redundancy present in text determines, to some degree, the amount of mental energy we have available to concentrate on new information.

When readers use information both from their own prior knowledge base and from information available in text, they are able to enter text with expectations or predictions that assist in constructing the intended meaning. For example, I can predict with some confidence that a history book will proceed chronologically, will likely use a cause–effect or effect–cause format, will highlight important people and events of historical periods, and, if reasonably new, may use examples of historical "realia" and primary sources to illustrate or expand ideas. Just as confidently, I can predict that suspense writer John Le Carré will keep me in murk and fog for at least the first two chapters; Tom Clancy will give so much detail as to seem to be revealing national security secrets; and Helen Maclnnes will create exquisite tension. Such predictions assist readers in processing redundant information rapidly—in filling the "slots"— and allow them to concentrate energy on the nonredundant aspects of new information.

New, or nonredundant, information available in text is understood to the degree that the reader is able to create linkages between the new information and his or her prior knowledge base. New information is the information for which we literally have no slots; therefore, when text is highly abstract or obscure, creating cognitive links between the new and the known is difficult (Sadoski & Paivio, 1994). As readers working independently, we frequently give up or seek help constructing meaning for text with large amounts of new information. In school, teacher-led instruction, social interactions, and/or engaging in specific Discourses (e.g., thinking like a "scientist") often assist readers in creating links that allow understanding of new information.

READER STANCE IN RELATIONSHIP TO TEXT

Louise Rosenblatt, in her transactional theory of reading and writing (1978, 1994), states that in any reading act, the reader adopts, consciously or unconsciously, a stance that guides his or her progress through text. Reader stance involves selective attention, causing certain aspects of text to come to the forefront and others to recede, and literally creates the reading process for each reading event. What the reader attends to and his or her purpose for reading, in turn, determine to some degree the meaning constructed.

Consider for a moment what you know about 16-year-olds. Now consider differences in stance that the following reading materials might evoke among that group: a driver training manual, a current popular novel, instructions for operating a DVD player, *Julius Caesar*, a movie theater guide, a physical education class handout entitled "Rules of Baseball," a biographical article on a popular movie star, and 15 pages in a biology textbook. You get the picture. The point is that we cannot really talk about the reading process without discussing the reader, and the reader's intent—his or her reason for reading—is an important influence on the meaning he or she makes in the reading event. Rosenblatt believes that we have generally neglected this aspect of the reading process in our attempts to understand it. She states:

> The reading process that produces the meaning, say, of a scientific report differs from the reading process that evokes a literary work of art. Neither contemporary reading theory nor literary theory has done justice to this important distinction. The tendency in the past generally has been to assume that such a distinction depends entirely on the texts involved. The character of the "work" has been held to inhere entirely in the text. Such classification of texts as literary or nonliterary ignore the contribution of the reader. We cannot look at the text and predict the nature of the resulting work in any

> particular reading. Before we can assume, for instance, that a poem or novel, rather than a statement of facts will be evoked for the texts, say, of Frost's *Mending Wall* or Dickens's *Great Expectations*, we must postulate a particular kind of relationship between the reader and the text. (1989, p. 158)

Right now, we have a relatively imprecise understanding of how reader stance operates in individuals. Human knowledge, attitudes, beliefs, and motives are hidden from others' view, sometimes even from the individuals themselves, and are therefore difficult to study. We do, however, have some fairly reasonable hunches for explaining variations in reader stance. Certainly, the "ways of being" represented by Discourses, the values, attitudes, beliefs, and social identities that define individuals would appear to affect directly the stance readers select as they transact with text.

Other explanations of stance have to do with culture and language, social influences, and reader interest and investment. It's not unreasonable to believe that all of these factors—and others—influence reader stance both before and during reading. Thus, stance is flexible, changing as one reads to reflect the waxing and waning of interest, intent, and other variables.

SOCIAL INTERACTION AND COMMUNICATION

From the seminal work of Lev Vygotsky in the 1920s and 1930s (Vygotsky, 1986) and the current interest in collaborative thinking in classrooms, we have recently begun to reemphasize the influence of social interactions on readers' constructions of meaning. The Santa Barbara Classroom Discourse Group, a research consortium of teachers, graduate students, and university faculty, asserts that

> literacy [is not] a state of being that one arrives at like a state of grace. Rather, it is a dynamic process in which what literate action means is continually being constructed and reconstructed by individuals as they become members of new social groups. (1992, p. 120)

This influence extends to readers' meaning constructions. As readers, we negotiate meaning through discussions, exchanges of information, and remembered and anticipated conversations, even if these conversations are only in our own heads. The result is that the meanings we construct are shaped and changed by others' interpretations of text as well as our own.

And so, we come full circle in our discussion of the components in the reading process. We began with the reader—his or her prior knowledge and previous experience—and end with the influence of social interactions on the reader's constructions of meaning. Let us go back one more time to the original statement of the reading process; hopefully, newly gained redundancy will give it greater meaning than it had before:

> *Reading is the act of constructing meaning while transacting with text.* The reader makes meaning through the combination of prior knowledge and previous experience; information available in text; the stance he or she takes in relationship to the text; and immediate, remembered, or anticipated social interaction and communication.

MONITORING THE READING PROCESS

Recall for a moment the monitoring aspect of schema theory presented earlier—the part that tells you when things do or do not make sense. We call this *metacognition*, which means transcending or going beyond knowing. Metacognition monitors knowing; it is the ability to reflect on one's own cognitive processes. Metacognition tells us when we know and when we don't know; it tells us what we know and lets us glimpse what we don't know. Metacognitive behavior asks the all-important question "What's wrong with this picture?" that alerts us and causes us to short-circuit action in situations that do not make sense.

This same thing happens during reading. In effect, metacognitive behavior tells the reader, "Whoa! Stop. Go back and look at that again. The meaning you're making here is non-sense." Baker and Brown (1984) call this "dealing with failures to understand." Interestingly, it seems that very good readers have the most refined metacognitive sense while reading. (Just as interestingly, many not-so-good readers with not-so-good metacognition while reading have excellent metacognitive abilities in other contexts.) It appears that knowing when you don't know is every bit as important as knowing itself. At any rate, metacognitive functioning is a critical part of the reading process. It, too, contributes to the meaning the reader constructs by monitoring the quality of that meaning.

THE RELATIONSHIPS AMONG THINKING, READING, AND WRITING

As you have read and analyzed this theoretical view of reading as the act of constructing meaning while transacting with text, you may have already begun to see the relationship between reading and writing and the interrelationship of thinking to both. We could simply substitute *writing* for *reading* in our definition of the reading process—writing is the act of constructing meaning while transacting with text—and have a perfectly valid statement of the writing process.

THE WRITING PROCESS

PRIOR KNOWLEDGE AND PREVIOUS EXPERIENCE

It is a cliché in the lore of writing that one writes what one knows—that the most powerful writing comes from the authenticity of experience. Here, as in many cases, the cliché is true. What one knows *is* prior knowledge and previous experience, and it is from this pool of information that we produce written text. Consider the writing you do: all the many and varied tasks in any given day, ranging from jotting down telephone numbers to writing grocery lists to IMing to taking notes in class to writing letters or e-mail notes to family and friends. Prior knowledge and previous experience, both world knowledge and knowledge about text, affect all of these activities.

For example, if we compared an entire class's lecture notes for just one class period, I'm sure we would find large differences among individual note takers; we can explain these differences, at least in part, by individual differences in prior knowledge. Note takers use prior knowledge to process incoming information, concentrating their energy on the nonredundant parts, and then record that which they believe to be important on the basis of what they already know. Some note takers scribble bits and pieces of ideas, whereas others re-create almost verbatim what the lecturer says. Some use various print and textual conventions, such as outlining or indenting, whereas others write unbroken text or produce "maps," or schematic drawings.

These same individual differences carry over to other kinds of writing. Newly published authors are well known for producing work that is perceptibly, or even boldly, autobiographical. Other forms of writing—grocery lists, for example—are just as distinctive. My grocery lists are organized according to the store's organization, and because I shop at two stores, I organize my lists differently depending on which store I'm shopping. I frequently have such entries as "7 oz. chopped olives" and "13 oz. whole canned tomatoes." That's because I like to try new recipes, and from long (and hard) experience, I know that if I write only "chopped olives" and "whole canned tomatoes" for new recipes, it's awfully easy to get to the store and find myself wondering, "Now, was I supposed to have 7 ounces of chopped olives and 13 ounces of canned tomatoes, or was it 13 ounces of chopped olives and 7 ounces of canned tomatoes?" The difference makes a difference.

Prior knowledge and previous experience influence writing even when we write in a relatively new area. Let's go back to the very first "report" we each copied out of the *World Book* or the *Encyclopedia Americana*. (I believe *Wikipedia* is now the likely first choice.) First of all, we copied those reports because each of us knew so little about the topic that we literally had no words to discuss it. (Isn't it interesting that teachers feel compelled to send students off to do research on topics that the kids know nothing at all about? Wouldn't it be more interesting to find out what students would produce if we sent them off to do research on topics they know a lot about?) Anyway, the choices we made in our copying/writing ("I'll use it all; skip this paragraph; change that word," etc.) were grounded in prior knowledge, even though they often produced strikingly similar texts.

Then, as we became more sophisticated researchers and report writers, our wider base of world knowledge and knowledge about text produced increasingly individualistic text, so that now when we study and write on the same topics as others, we produce widely divergent text. Much of this difference can be explained by what we knew before we began writing, the Discourse within which we situate our writing, and the specific linkages we make between the texts we're writing about. Prior knowledge and previous experience inform us and direct our writing just as surely as they influence how we act in a library and how we read the morning paper or a music appreciation text.

INFORMATION EMERGING FROM TEXT

It is significant, I think, that one of the most important attributes of writing is that not only is it a way to demonstrate what we know—in a report, or a poem, or a set of class notes—but also it is a *way of knowing*, a way of working through confusion and fuzzy ideas, and a way of moving toward clarification and articulation of knowledge. This attribute of writing is often overlooked and undervalued. It should not be. Especially at those times when we are struggling to understand a new idea, to "fit" that information into our current knowledge base, and to arrive at coherent meaning, writing becomes a way of working through the process and moving toward insight. Thus, information emerges from text; *new ideas come as we write and from what we write*. All of us have faced the blank page. All of us have worked to put just the right words on paper, even when we didn't really know what it was we wanted to say. And all of us have had the light dawn, experienced insight, felt the "Aha!" Large or small, this insight grew from our writing, from the very process we went through to fill that empty page. This is the information emerging from text.

You may have noticed that I've changed this part of the reading-writing theory statement. With reading, I talked about information available in text; here, I'm referring to information emerging from text. I see them as mirror images of one another, indicative of the real differences that exist between reading and writing. The important connection between the two types of information is the constructed meaning resulting from or created by each.

WRITER STANCE IN RELATIONSHIP TO TEXT

With the writer's stance in relationship to text, as with prior knowledge and previous experience, we have a component of the writing process that is directly parallel to the reading process. The writer's intent, his or her purpose for writing, profoundly influences the resulting text. This intent is actually a little more obvious in the case of writer stance than it is for reader stance. As you reflected a moment earlier on the writing you do, in all probability each instance you identified had a purpose attached to it: grocery list (because I have to go to the grocery store and don't want to forget items), report for class (because it was assigned), e-mail to Mother (because I miss her), or note to roommate (because I want him to clean up his side of the room). Whatever they are, these reasons comprise the writer's stance, which, in turn, directs and situates the construction of text.

SOCIAL INTERACTION AND COMMUNICATION

As with reading, writing is influenced by social interaction with other thinkers and writers. Nearly always, we write with an audience in mind—even if it is only ourselves. Often we have the opportunity to share our writing with others with the purpose of getting their reaction or response. Such interaction creates and shapes the writing process itself, thus regulating mood, tone, style, and content and establishing our writing "voice." And it is in our writer's stance, or voice, that we enact explicitly (as we do with speech) the many Discourses of our lives, with all of their accompanying values, attitudes, beliefs, and styles. So, we write e-mails to friends in the Discourse of friendships; lab reports, essays, research papers, and analytic treatises in the various Discourses of academia; and love letters, sweet notes, and valentines in the Discourse of love.

Here, as with reading, we have come full circle. We began with the writer's background knowledge and ended with his or her voice. Let us look at our definition one more time in the context of writing:

> *Writing is the act of constructing meaning while transacting with text.* The writer makes meaning through the combination of prior knowledge and previous experience; information emerging from text; the stance he or she takes in relationship to the text; and immediate, remembered, or anticipated social interaction and communication.

MONITORING THE WRITING PROCESS

Metacognitive thought accompanies writing just as surely as it does reading; in fact, it is, if anything, more explicit in the writing process than in reading. Consider for a moment the revisions you do when creating text, whether the text itself is informal—a letter to a friend, for example—or polished, carefully honed text such as a term paper. Good writers have a sense of when their writing goes awry and have strategies for revising. That is metacognitive thought in action. Much of what goes on in classroom writing instruction today focuses on collaborative draft writing of text to increase students' awareness of various ways to monitor their writing and to engage them in metacognitive thought.

It seems clear that reading and writing are close, parallel processes. Although the specifics of the two processes are not identical, their similarity is striking. Tierney and Pearson (1986) make a strong case in their comparison of the reading and writing processes by identifying the "composing" aspect of each: planning, drafting, aligning, revising, and monitoring.

Figure 2.1 is a map constructed by Jenny Fleisher, one of my students, showing her understanding of the relationships among thinking, reading, and writing. I like Jenny's representation and think it effectively captures the view articulated in this chapter. Further, the map suggests the complexity of the relationships among these processes. When you add to the already complex relationships we've been discussing the additional complexity of thinking, reading, and writing in a second language (which we are about to discuss), you begin to grasp the enormity of it all. It truly is just a bit mind boggling.

FIGURE 2.1 *Map of Cognitive Processes*

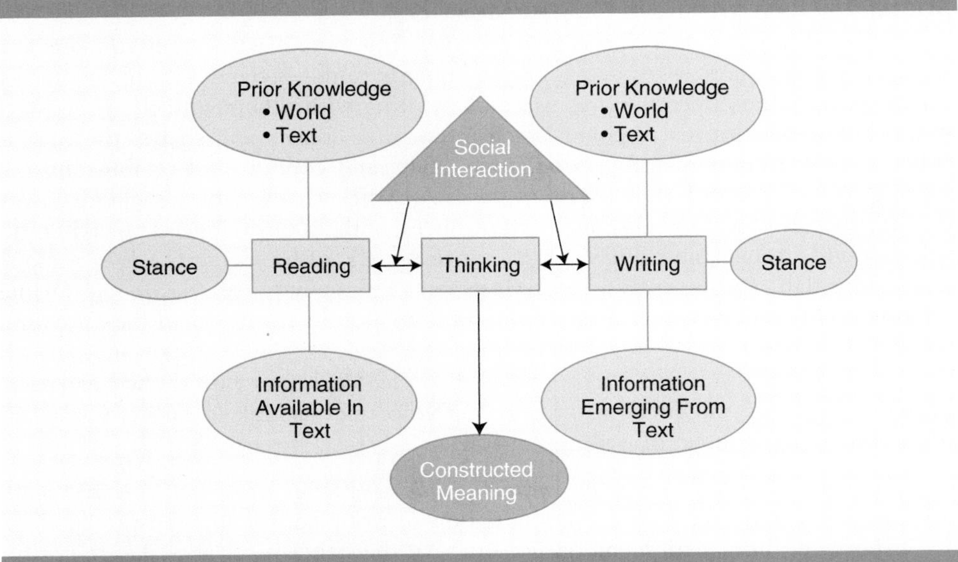

SECOND-LANGUAGE ACQUISITION AND LITERACY

How we acquire a second language and become literate in that language has also been the topic of much research and theory building over the years. Numerous theories exist to explain this process, each addressing second-language acquisition from a specific perspective. I'll not attempt to summarize all of them here; rather, I'll present two of the predominant theories. Understand, however, that although language-acquisition theories differ, they are not necessarily conflicting. Nearly all of them acknowledge the central role of first-language fluency and literacy in the acquisition of second-language fluency and literacy. Further, all but the nativist theories (those attributing language acquisition to innate abilities) account for, and in fact highlight, the importance of social interactions and transactions in second-language development. Finally, all theories focus on the learner and his or her home culture as central to the process; that is, that second-language acquisition is a process in which individual learning is assisted and shaped by social convention.

KRASHEN'S SECOND-LANGUAGE ACQUISITION THEORY

Stephen Krashen (1981, 1995) posits a model of second-language acquisition based on five hypotheses.

THE ACQUISITION–LEARNING HYPOTHESIS

The first hypothesis is the Acquisition–Learning Hypothesis, in which *acquisition* of a language occurs as a subconscious process as we encounter and use a second language for some communicative purpose. Conscious *learning* of a language, on the other hand, occurs as we study formally the grammar, structure, and lexicon of a language. Krashen considers acquisition, rather than learning, to be the primary means for second-language development. Gee (1996) articulates the same hypothesis for *all* language learning and the learning of the various Discourses in which we all engage.

THE NATURAL ORDER HYPOTHESIS

The Natural Order Hypothesis refers to the general order in which elements of a second language are acquired. Simply put, it means that we acquire the grammatical structures of a second language in a predictable order, even though linguists do not have complete understanding of what that order is for every structure in every language.

THE MONITOR HYPOTHESIS

The Monitor Hypothesis explains the relationship between acquisition and learning. Although acquisition—encountering and using language for specific communicative purposes—is responsible for fluency in a second language, conscious learning—what we know and can articulate about that language—serves as a monitor or editor in language use. Recall our discussion of cognitive monitoring, that facility of the mind that lets us know when things are going well and also when things are not (e.g., when it signals "Whoa. Go back. This is not making sense"). The second-language monitor serves the same purpose; it alerts the second-language speaker/reader/writer that the language construction she or he just used is not appropriate and allows for self-correction. Krashen emphasizes that for the monitor to be effective, the second-language user must *have time* to consult or reflect on language rules (such time is rarely available in normal conversation), *focus on form* or be thinking about correctness, and *know the rule*—a difficult task given the number and complexity of the rules and the time it takes to learn them.

THE INPUT HYPOTHESIS

The Input Hypothesis is, I think, the heart of Krashen's model. The Input Hypothesis states that we learn a second language by understanding language containing linguistic structures that are just beyond the structures we already know. Krashen calls this *comprehensible input* and symbolizes it as *i* (input) + 1. The notion of *i* + 1 is not at all unlike Vygotsky's ZPD; it is that place just a little bit beyond our current level of competence within which we are able to construct new meaning. We construct this new meaning (in this instance, understand the content of the communication and acquire more of the second language) using what we already know about the language, world knowledge, contextual information, and extralingual information. Krashen emphasizes that we acquire new structures in a second language (new words, new grammar rules, etc.) not by focusing on the structures themselves but by understanding the meaning of a communication containing those new structures.

Two interesting phenomena are explained by the Input Hypothesis. One is the *silent period*, the time during which the second-language acquirer does not speak. This is a time for collecting information, for getting a "feel" for the language, and for learning words and language structures by listening (although not all of the input is comprehensible). The silent period is an important stage in second-language acquisition, one in which the individual is particularly vulnerable, possibly even fearful, if he or she is required to produce language too early. I know, for example, that I am in a silent stage in acquiring Spanish: Given plenty of supporting context, I can read and construct reasonable meaning for sentences and even paragraphs in Spanish and can get the gist of some conversations—not all I hear—about common, ordinary topics and/or events in the immediate environment (but not technical or abstract topics). I do not participate in these conversations, however, beyond the word level (*bueno, gracias*), even when I know that the other participants would willingly tolerate errors. Because occasions to receive comprehensible input are relatively rare for me, my silent period continues; with additional input and time to acquire more language, I could progress.

The second phenomenon associated with the input hypothesis is the *Din in the Head* experience first described by Barber (1980). A linguist on a trip to Russia and struggling to bring her Russian to fluency, Barber noticed by the third day "a rising Din of Russian in my head; words, sounds, intonations, phrases, all swimming about in the voices of the people I talked with." This Din has been studied by other linguists and is often noted to be melodic. Bedford (1985) describes it as a "noticeable din or jumble of words, phrases, or even characteristic melody patterns" (p. 286). McQuillan and Rodrigo (1995) note the role of the Din in the Head with respect to reading, as well as speaking, in a second language. The Din is thought to be an involuntary mental rehearsal of bits and pieces of the new language that happens as we have $i + 1$ input; messages in the Din contain linguistic information not yet learned and allow the learner to practice the language mentally before having to produce and/or comprehend it. Once fluency is achieved or input is removed, the Din goes away.

The Affective Filter Hypothesis

Krashen identifies three affective variables that serve as "filters" or mental blocks that influence second-language acquisition. *Anxiety*, *motivation*, and *self-confidence* are the influencing filters: In situations in which we feel comfortable, in which motivation is high for acquiring the language, and in which we see ourselves as capable learners, acquisition of the second language is enhanced; the opposite effect occurs when anxiety is high and motivation and self-confidence are low. In the case of my Spanish-language acquisition, the affective filter is working full tilt. Even when I'm with friends and friendly acquaintances who will slow their speech and wait for me and ignore my mistakes, my concern about correctness (self-imposed high anxiety), my ability to get along very nicely in the English-language world I'm in at that moment, and my insecurity about my current level of fluency in Spanish all serve to slow my progress. Immersed in a Spanish-language environment, my need to get and give information (motivation) would at some point override the anxiety and insecurity. (A friend once told me that when visiting a country where the language is not one you know, the first words you learn are *Where's the bathroom?*) To the extent that the environment is friendly, inviting, and tolerant of my imprecise language attempts, my progress toward fluency will be heightened.

Krashen summarizes his theory this way: "People acquire second languages when they obtain comprehensible input and when their affective filters are low enough to allow the input in" (1995, p. 101). He suggests further that second-language acquisition will occur in classes taught in the second language if the student can understand what is going on in the class, that is, when input is comprehensible.

CUMMINS'S COGNITIVE AND LANGUAGE CONTEXT THEORY

Jim Cummins (1984) introduced the terms *basic interpersonal communication skills* (BICS) and *cognitive academic language proficiency* (CALP) to distinguish between students' second-language fluency and proficiency in social settings and their fluency and proficiency in classrooms. Essentially, this distinction is between the informal, ordinary language of daily life and the more structured, technical, and abstract language of academic discourse. Cummins estimates that ESL students acquire age-appropriate conversational proficiency (BICS) in about two years, whereas academic proficiency (CALP) requires five to seven years. He cautions us, therefore, to refrain from assuming that second-language students' proficiency in conversational English is a true measure of their proficiency in science, or social studies, or mathematics. This is particularly true in the situation in which we are using English-language tests to measure intelligence or academic skills. Cummins rightfully asserts that schools have all too often given ESL students "one-way tickets to special education classes" (1994, p. 39) through inappropriate testing practices based on faulty assumptions about students' English-language proficiency.

Cummins explains the discrepancy between the acquisition of social and academic language proficiency by examining communicative interactions associated with social and academic discourse. Figure 2.2 identifies two intersecting continua of cognitive and linguistic elements of language transactions. (Please note that this explanation is applicable to *all* language transactions, not just to those encountered by second-language learners.) The horizontal continuum describes the linguistic elements of context-embedded versus context-reduced language events. Context-embedded events are those in which "participants can actively negotiate meaning (by indicating when a message has not been understood, for example) and the language use is supported by a range of meaningful interpersonal and situational cues" (1994, p. 40). Social conversations, banter among friends, rereading well-known books or reading books by an author whose works you've read frequently are all examples of context-embedded language transactions. Context-reduced language events, on the other hand, are those in which participants must rely heavily on their knowledge of the language, rather than on interpersonal or situational cues, to construct meaning. Many classroom events are context reduced: reading from informational texts, writing reports and essays, and learning new vocabulary, to name a few. The vertical continuum describes extremes of the cognitive demand placed on participants in communicative events. Cognitively undemanding situations are those in which we already have lots of

FIGURE 2.2 *Range of Contextual Support and Degree of Cognitive Involvement in Communicative Activities*

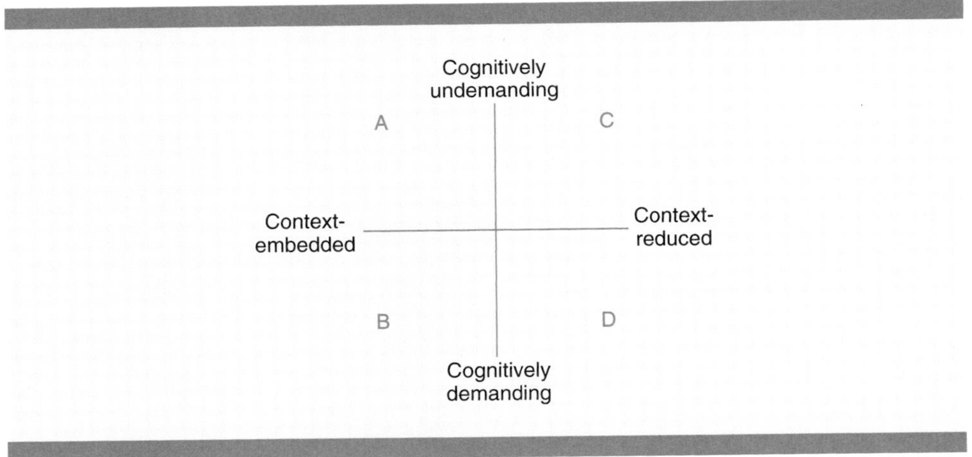

background and/or other information (i.e., redundancy) to support our participation in the language event and are thus easily able to enter into the event. Cognitively demanding activities are those in which we are learning new concepts and content or are articulating what we know about relatively new and/or abstract information—tasks that are commonplace in classrooms.

As you view the quadrants (A, B, C, D) created by these intersecting continua, you can see that social language proficiency (BICS) clusters in quadrant A, which is context embedded and cognitively undemanding; academic language proficiency (CALP), however, is primarily within quadrant D and is context reduced and cognitively demanding. Thus, we can see the reason for the three- to five-year lag between students' acquisition of social language proficiency and the acquisition of academic language proficiency. Cummins makes the further point that even as ESL students are acquiring skill in academic discourse, so, too, are native English speakers. Thus, ESL learners must "catch up with a moving target" (1994, p. 43) if they are to match the proficiency of native English speakers.

Figure 2.3 (p. 46) is a map created by another one of my students, Jonathan Reveal, showing his understanding of the thinking, reading, and writing processes in relationship to both the Krashen and Cummins theories of second language acquisition. This is yet another way to represent and grasp these highly abstract concepts.

IMPLICATIONS FOR LEARNING AND TEACHING

In this discussion, we have viewed reading and writing as parallel literacy processes that are inextricably linked with cognition, and we have explored issues of second-language development and literacy. Of immediate importance to us is that the views of literacy and language processes articulated in this chapter have clear instructional implications—that is, from the theoretical vantage points I have just described, one sees many opportunities for teachers to teach in such a way as to increase students' literacy and language abilities in content areas. What is critical to understand is that teaching in such a way as to increase students' literacy and language abilities does not dilute content instruction; in fact, *it increases students' learning of content*. That is what the rest of this book is about: issues and instructional strategies concerned with how students think and read and write within the context of subject area learning, whether they are native English speakers or English-language learners. All of the strategies are compatible with the theoretical viewpoints we have developed here, all of them are evidence-based—that is, tested by research and application—and all of them may be used by teachers for developing students' literacy and language skills simultaneously with teaching content. Because these instructional strategies take into account the diversity of secondary school students in today's schools and focus on literacy and language development in the service of content learning, they represent at least part of the fundamental change in secondary school teaching we discussed in Chapter 1. As you continue through the text, consider how such instruction may be applied in your subject area.

FIGURE 2.3

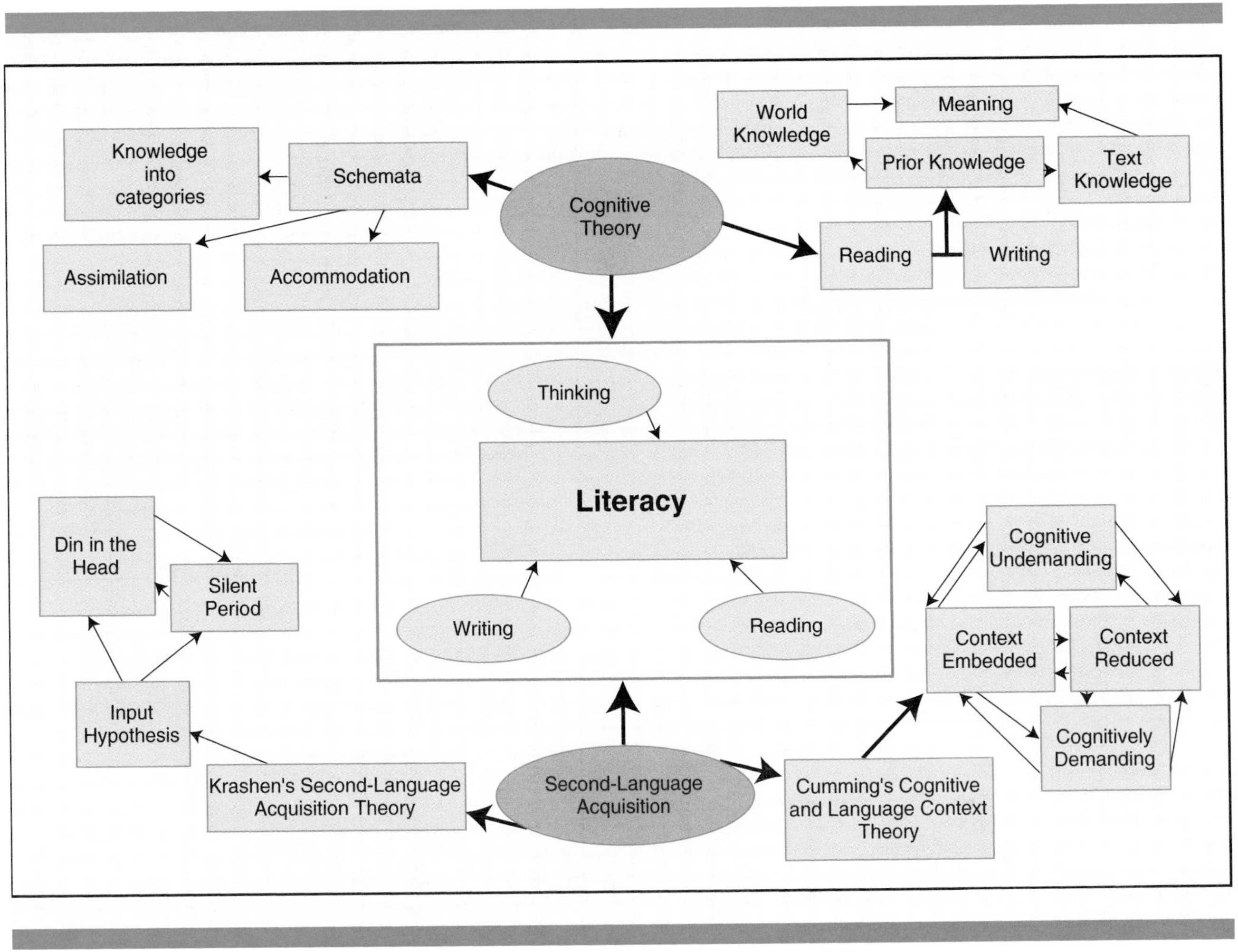

Knowledge into categories
Schemata
Assimilation
Accommodation
Cognitive Theory
World Knowledge
Meaning
Prior Knowledge
Text Knowledge
Reading
Writing
Thinking
Literacy
Writing
Reading
Din in the Head
Silent Period
Input Hypothesis
Krashen's Second-Language Acquisition Theory
Second-Language Acquisition
Cumming's Cognitive and Language Context Theory
Cognitive Undemanding
Context Embedded
Context Reduced
Cognitively Demanding

WHAT THIS CHAPTER MEANS TO YOU

1. The kids in biology lab 203 are engaging in various linguistic, cognitive, and social acts to create, extend, and adapt the understandings they already have about sustainable environments in the world's oceans. Guided by their teacher, they are participating in the Discourse of science learning and sustainable environments. Your job as a teacher is to create many opportunities for kids to do this in your classroom.

2. Knowing and learning grow from knowledge embedded in schemata and accompanying Discourses, social and linguistic interactions and transactions, and intertextual links between experience and events. In your classroom you can stimulate student learning most effectively by teaching so that students' prior knowledge serves as the basis for new learning, students actively participate in the Discourse of your subject area, social learning practices predominate, and implicit and explicit linkages are frequently made.

3. Reading and writing are acts of constructing meaning while transacting with text as readers/writers engage

- prior knowledge and previous experience;
- information available or emerging from text;
- stance in relationship to the text;
- and immediate, remembered, or anticipated social interaction and communication.

Your understanding and awareness of these complex processes will guide your selection of instructional strategies and activities to teach your subject area.

4. Students learning English as a second language become fluent and literate in English to the extent that the English-language environment supports their second-language learning with comprehensible input, and social and school English-language events encourage English-language learning. You will be an important agent in providing both English-language learning and content learning for ESL students in your classroom.

DOUBLE ENTRY JOURNAL

Now rewrite or create a map representing your definition of thinking, reading, and writing in first and second languages. Use the information you jotted down before reading, as well as information from this chapter. Make as many connections between these literacy and language processes and their attendant Discourses as you can. How are your definitions like or unlike those in this text? Compare your definitions with someone else's. If you're connected with classmates electronically, put your definitions out there and invite a dialogue.

FEATURE *What Goes in My Portfolio?*

Spend some time thinking deeply about thinking, learning, and literacy in first and second languages and the many Discourses of our social and academic lives. Create a portfolio artifact that represents your thinking on these topics. You may wish to use a graphic representation as Jenny and Jonathan did and accompany that with a written explanation, or you may prefer to extend and polish your postreading DEJ. Draw together and link information from other classes and sources for this artifact (e.g., Gardner's notion of "multiple intelligences" or other information you have about preadolescent and adolescent development).

RECOMMENDED SOURCES

*Anders, P. L., & Lloyd, C. V. (1989). The significance of prior knowledge in the learning of new content-specific instruction. In D. Lapp, J. Flood, & N. Farnan (Eds.), *Content area reading and learning: Instructional strategies* (pp. 258–269). Englewood Cliffs, NJ: Prentice-Hall.

*Cited in text.

Anderson, R. C. (1977). The notion of schema and the educational enterprise. In R. C. Anderson, R. J. Spiro, & W. E. Montague (Eds.), *Schooling and the acquisition of knowledge* (pp. 415–431). Hillsdale, NJ: Erlbaum.

*Anderson, R. C. (1994). Role of the reader's schema in comprehension, learning and memory. In R. B. Ruddell, M. R. Ruddell, & H. Singer (Eds.), *Theoretical models and processes of reading* (4th ed., pp. 469–482). Newark, DE: International Reading Association.

*Baker, L., & Brown, A. L. (1984). Cognitive monitoring in reading. In J. Flood (Ed.), *Understanding reading comprehension* (pp. 14–21). Newark, DE: International Reading Association.

*Barber, E. (1980). Language acquisition and applied linguistics. *ADFL Bulletin, 12*, 26–32.

*Bartlett, F. (1932). *Remembering*. Cambridge, England: Cambridge University Press.

*Bedford, D. (1985). Spontaneous playback of the second language: A descriptive study. *Foreign Language Annals, 18*, 279–287.

Bloome, D., & Egan-Robertson, A. (1993). The social construction of intertextuality. *Reading Research Quarterly, 28*(4), 305–333.

Bransford, J. N., & Johnson, M. K. (1972). Contextual prerequisites for understanding: Some investigations of comprehension and recall. *Journal of Verbal Learning and Verbal Behavior, 11*, 717–726.

Cambourne, B. (2002). Holistic, integrated approaches to reading and language arts instruction: The constructivist framework for an instructional theory. In A. E. Farstrup & S. J. Samuels (Eds.), *What research has to say about reading instruction* (pp. 25–47). Newark, DE: International Reading Association.

*Cummins, J. (1984). *Bilingualism and special education: Issues in assessment and pedagogy*. Clevedon, UK: Multilingual Matters.

*Cummins, J. (1994). The acquisition of English as a second language. In K. Spangenber-Urbschat & R. Pritchard (Eds.), *Kids come in all languages: Reading instruction for ESL students* (pp. 36–62). Newark, DE: International Reading Association.

*Farnan, N. (1996). Connecting adolescents and reading: Goals at the middle level. *Journal of Adolescent & Adult Literacy, 39*(6), 436–446.

Freeman, D. E., & Freeman, Y. (2001). *Between worlds: Access to second language acquisition* (2nd ed). Portsmouth, NH: Heinemann.

Gardner, H. (1983). *Frames of mind. The theory of multiple intelligences*. New York: HarperCollins.

*Gee, J. P. (1996). *Social linguistics and literacies* (2nd ed.). New York: Routledge-Falmer.

Gee, J. P. (2000). Discourse and sociocultural studies in reading. In M. L. Kamil, P. B. Mosenthal, P. D. Pearson, & R. Barr (Eds.), *Handbook of reading research volume III* (pp. 195–207). Mahwah, NJ: Lawrence Erlbaum.

Gee, J. P. (2001). Reading as situation language: A sociocultural perspective. *Journal of Adolescent and Adult Literacy, 44*(8), 714–725.

Goodman, K. S. (1994). Reading, writing, and written texts: A transactional sociopsycholinguistic view. In R. B. Ruddell, M. R. Ruddell, & H. Singer (Eds.), *Theoretical models and processes of reading* (4th ed., pp. 1093–1130). Newark, DE: International Reading Association.

Goodman, Y. M., & Goodman, K. S. (1990). Vygotsky in a whole language perspective. In L. Moll (Ed.), *Vygotsky and education: Instructional implications and applications of sociohistorical psychology*. Cambridge, England: Cambridge University Press.

Guthrie, J. T., & Wigfield, A. (2000). Engagement and motivation in reading. In M. L. Kamil, P. B. Mosenthal, P. D. Pearson, & R. Barr (Eds.), *Handbook of reading research volume III* (pp. 403–422). Mahwah, NJ: Lawrence Erlbaum.

*Hartman, D. K. (1995). Eight readers reading: The intertextual links of proficient readers reading multiple passages. *Reading Research Quarterly, 30*(3), 530–561.

*Krashen, S. (1981). *Second language acquisition and second language learning*. London: Pergamon Press.

Krashen, S. (1983). The din in the head, input, and the second language acquisition device. *Foreign Language Annals, 16*, 41–44.

*Krashen, S. D. (1995). Bilingual education and second language acquisition theory. In D. B. Durkin (Ed.), *Language issues: Readings for teachers* (pp. 90–115). White Plains, NY: Longman.

McQuillan, J. (1995, May). *Reading, acquisition, and the "din in the head": A new way to examine literacy*. Paper presented at the annual meeting of the International Reading Association, Anaheim, CA.

*McQuillan, J., & Rodrigo, V. (1995). A reading "din in the head": Evidence of involuntary mental rehearsal in second language readers. *Foreign Language Annals, 28*(2), 1–7.

*Paulsen, G. (1989). *The winter room*. New York: Dell.

*Pearson, P. D., & Tierney, R. J. (1984). On becoming a thoughtful reader: Learning to read like a writer. In A. C. Purves & O. S. Niles (Eds.), *Becoming readers in a complex society* (pp. 144–173). Chicago: National Society for the Study of Education.

*Piaget, J. (1950, 2001). *The psychology of intelligence* (M. Piercy & D. E. Berlyne, Trans.). New York: Routledge.

*Rosenblatt, L. M. (1978). *The reader, the text, the poem: The transactional theory of the literary work*. Carbondale, IL: Southern Illinois University Press.

Rosenblatt, L. M. (1989). Writing and reading: The transactional theory. In J. M. Mason (Ed.), *Reading and writing connections* (pp. 153–176). Boston: Allyn & Bacon.

*Rosenblatt, L. M. (1994). The transactional theory of reading and writing. In R. B. Ruddell, M. R. Ruddell, & H. Singer (Eds.), *Theoretical models and processes of reading* (4th ed., pp. 1057–1092). Newark, DE: International Reading Association.

*Rumelhart, D. E. (1981). Schemata: The building blocks of cognition. In J. T. Guthrie (Ed.), *Comprehension and teaching: Research reviews* (pp. 3–26). Newark, DE: International Reading Association.

Rumelhart, D. E. (1984). Understanding understanding. In J. Flood (Ed.), *Understanding reading comprehension* (pp. 1–20). Newark, DE: International Reading Association.

*Sadoski, M., & Paivio, A. (1994). A dual coding view of imagery and verbal processes in reading comprehension. In R. B. Ruddell, M. R. Ruddell, & H. Singer (Eds.), *Theoretical models and processes of reading* (4th ed., pp. 582–601). Newark, DE: International Reading Association.

*Santa Barbara Classroom Discourse Group. (1992). Constructing literacy in classrooms: Literate action as social accomplishment. In H. Marshall (Ed.), *Redefining learning: Roots of educational reform* (pp. 119–150). Norwood, NJ: Ablex.

Shank, R. C., & Abelson, R. P. (1977). *Scripts, plans, goals, and understanding*. Hillsdale, NJ: Erlbaum.

*Thorndike, E. L. (1917). Reading as reasoning: A study of mistakes in paragraph reading. *The Journal of Educational Psychology*, *8*, 323–332.

*Tierney, R. J., & Pearson, P. D. (1986). Toward a composing model of reading. In E. K. Dishner, T. W. Bean, J. E. Readence, & D. W. Moore (Eds.), *Reading in the content areas. Improving classroom instruction* (2nd ed., pp. 64–75). Dubuque, IA: Kendall/Hunt.

Tierney, R. J., & Pearson, P. D. (1992). Learning to learn from text: A framework for improving classroom practice, in E. K. Dishner, T. W. Bean, J. E. Readence, & D. W. Moore (Eds.), *Reading in the content areas: improving classroom instruction* (3rd ed., pp. 87–103). Dubuque, IA: Kendall/Hunt.

Van Den Broek, P., & Kremer, K. (2000). The mind in action: What it means to comprehend during reading. In B. M. Taylor, M. F. Graves, & P. Van Den Broek (Eds.), *Reading for meaning: Fostering comprehension in middle grades* (pp. 1–31). Newark, DE: International Reading Association.

Vygotsky, L. (1978). *Mind in society: The development of higher psychological processes*. Cambridge, MA: MIT Press.

*Vygotsky, L. V. (1986). *Thought and language* (Trans. & Ed., A. Kozulin). Cambridge, MA: MIT Press.

Weaver, C. (1994). Parallels between new paradigms in science and in reading and literacy theories: An essay review. In R. B. Ruddell, M. R. Ruddell, & H. Singer (Eds.), *Theoretical models and processes of reading* (4th ed., pp. 1185–1202). Newark, DE: International Reading Association.

CHAPTER 3

Evaluating Instructional Materials

Double Entry Journal

In your journal, list the qualities you would look for in selecting print, electronic, and visual texts and instructional materials for teaching your subject area. You may want to identify a specific grade, course, or level (e.g., sophomores, calculus, middle school) to help you focus your thinking. How do the qualities you list assist student learning?

Network Productions/© Index Stock Imagery

Jameela Moore, seventh-grade language arts teacher, feels like she's in a giant candy store. It's the second day of the International Reading Association annual convention, and she's in the Book Exhibition Hall on the bottom floor of the convention center. The exhibition hall is enormous—filled with over 400 booths of textbooks, books, software, hardware, graphic books, visuals, games, lesson planning guides, and other language arts materials. Since she's on her department committee for selecting new language arts textbooks for grades 7 and 8, one of her goals for attending the convention is to look at what the textbook publishers are offering in the very newest literature, English, and spelling series, and to see what is available in the way of writing resources. She's already gone to three author sessions—Kathrine Paterson, Gary Soto, and Chris Crutcher—and she can see new fiction and nonfiction books everywhere in the Exhibition Hall.

Her other objective is to find some really good software and Internet resources for teaching language arts. Five new computers will be delivered to her classroom this summer, compliments of a grant the district got, and an additional $500 is hers for purchasing software and other supplementary material. Nothing this big has happened to her in all her years of teaching, and she wants to get everything just right—books the kids will read, materials that are exciting and interesting and challenging, and wonderful ideas for making learning come alive that she can add to her already considerable teaching repertoire. Jameela looks around and realizes that a big part of the selection process will be examining all the possibilities and then narrowing her choices down to the very best.

• • •

Evaluating instructional materials is the right and responsibility of every classroom teacher. As the people charged with teaching curriculum concepts; with meeting state, school, and district curriculum standards; and with guiding students in the acquisition of content knowledge, teachers must be thoroughly knowledgeable about instructional materials and involved actively in selecting materials. Because the bulk of materials selection focuses on textbooks and other texts, much of what we discuss here in relationship to selection of instructional materials is likewise focused; however, teachers and departments are increasingly responsible for selecting software and on-line resources. We will therefore explore issues of selection and use of technological educational materials as well.

Most schools and/or school districts that you're likely to be a part of already have in place standard policies and procedures for textbook selection. And many states have clearly defined procedures and standards for textbook selection. Whatever the case, the process of materials evaluation and selection is intricate, and although the prospect of getting state-of-the-art textbooks and software is exciting, the process itself can be volatile and difficult.

The reasons for this begin with the fact that textbooks represent an enormous district investment. (Computer software is considerably less so for several reasons, not the least of which is that textbooks continue to dominate the education landscape.) Consider the cost of changing texts in *just one subject area* for an entire district, K–12; then think about the cost of keeping textbooks current in all subject areas. Districts can and do expect selection committee members and all teachers who will be using the new texts to spend time and energy in the decision-making process. For teachers, administrators, students, and parents serving on adoption committees and for all teachers affected by the process, time commitment for textbook selection is substantial. Added to the expense and time involved is the coordination that must occur for the adoption plan to be used, regardless of whether the plan is for new mathematics texts in grades K–12, new literature books for grades 7 and 8, or new health texts for grade 9 only.

Further, the process of textbook evaluation and selection is an exercise in compromise and accommodation. From the start, participants know that it will be impossible to find the one text that will please everyone, meet every teacher's needs, and be suitable for every student in the school/district. Yet, that's basically what the process attempts to do. The very makeup of the selection committee itself may be controversial, involving decisions of whether students, parents, school board, or other community groups should participate and such issues as community values, beliefs, and rights. The inevitable upshot is, of course, that after the textbook evaluation and selection process is over, some teachers are unhappy and displeased, and others feel their agenda and needs haven't been addressed. In addition, there will likely be some students for whom the books *are* inappropriate as well as some parents or community groups disgruntled by the final choice.

The list of problems goes on. My point, however, is not to discourage you from participating in textbook evaluation and adoption processes. Far from it. You need to be very actively involved; the only alternative is simply to avoid the process and use whatever textbooks other people pick. Early in your teaching career, you will, in all likelihood, use textbooks that others have chosen. (Opportunity for serving on a textbook selection committee generally comes after you've been in a school or district for a while.) As soon as you can, you will want to have a voice in textbook selection for your subject area. In the meantime, you will still need to evaluate the texts that others have chosen and that you are expected to use; and like Jameela Moore, you'll have any number of opportunities to choose or buy textbooks and other materials that do not require approval through the textbook selection process. Finally, you'll need to be able to explain to a department chair or principal in clear, crisp language why a given text should or should not be used with your students.

The purpose of this chapter is to give you information about traditional instruments for evaluation of instructional materials, demonstrate alternative approaches for looking at text difficulty and appropriateness, and suggest ways to increase the probability that the selection process—whether it involves you alone choosing some books or software for your classes or a full-blown, district-directed textbook adoption—will result in well-chosen materials suited to curriculum goals and teacher and student needs.

TEXT AND TEXTBOOK ISSUES

> If textbooks are not always boring, reading them is at least hard work. They tend to be impersonal, nonemotional presentations of facts; and, almost by definition, textbooks are difficult. Tremendous amounts of information and associated terminology are compressed into relatively few pages. . . . Add the fact that most secondary students choose neither the textbooks nor the courses in which they are used, and it is not hard to see why so many students consider so many textbooks to be so much drudgery. (Baldwin, 1986, p. 323)

Scott Baldwin's description and analysis of how textbooks are viewed by students is, I think, eloquent and accurate. Most textbooks are boring and/or difficult, even now that textbook publishers are giving concerted attention to increasing the quality of their products. To test this theory, the next time you're in a college or university bookstore, go to a subject area that you know very little about or have very little interest in. Choose a course textbook from that subject area at random and begin reading it. My guess is that you'll find it neither easy to do nor very much fun. If you want to extend this experiment a bit further, next go over to the trade book (popular press) side of the store and try to find some fiction or nonfiction book in the same general subject area. Try reading it. Chances are this book will at least be a little less difficult; chances are also that the experience will be a little more fun.

My point here is to support Baldwin's claim and to argue further (as he did) that we stand very little chance of turning students into lifelong readers and writers if the only thing they read and the only model of writing they see in classrooms is textbook text. This, however, appears to be pretty much the state of things in middle school and secondary classrooms, where a single required textbook is frequently the only source for reading and writing activities. Baldwin recommends supplementing required textbooks with selections from the many trade books available in all content areas; others recommend strongly that when and wherever possible, trade books be used to replace textbooks completely.

COMPARING TRADE TEXT AND TEXTBOOK TEXT

To illustrate the contrast between textbooks and trade books, I reproduce the following excerpt from William Manchester's book, *Winston Spencer Churchill: Alone. 1932–1940:*

> Often he was at his most dangerous when he seemed bored. Hunched over his seat below the gangway, within spitting distance of the Treasury Bench, he would appear to be inattentive to the business before the House. His eyes would close; he would breathe heavily. It was an ambush, of course, and twice MPs on the opposite side of the House lurched into it. The first asked loudly: "Must you fall asleep when I am speaking?" Winston replied: "No, it is purely voluntary." The second, more cautious, merely inquired whether he was asleep. Winston immediately answered: "I wish to God I were!" And he could stifle an effective jab with a sharper retort. As he finished a scathing attack on the cabinet, a backbencher called: "The Right Hon[orable] Gentleman, like a bad bridge player, blames his cards." Churchill snapped: "I blame the crooked deal." (1988, p. 108)

To see how this writing compared with textbook representations of Winston Churchill, I searched a secondary world history textbook, sophomore/junior level (Leinwand, 1994), to find all references to Churchill in the book. I found four. Of these, two were one-sentence statements in which Churchill's role in World War II was mentioned; for example: "Nevertheless, meetings involving the Big Three Allied leaders—Winston Churchill, Franklin D. Roosevelt, and Joseph Stalin—had taken place at several points during the course of the war" (p. 626). The two other references to Churchill were full paragraphs, one describing his "Iron Curtain" speech and the other telling of his fall from power as prime minister. The full text of the description of the Iron Curtain speech is as follows:

> In March 1946, in a speech made at Westminster College in Fulton, Missouri, British Prime Minister Winston Churchill stated: "From Stettin in the Baltic to

> Trieste in the Adriatic, an *iron curtain* has descended across the Continent." Churchill went on to say that on one side of that curtain, now known as Eastern Europe, was the Soviet Union and the Communist-dominated countries. On the other side, now known as Western Europe, were the democratic nations allied to the United States. Churchill urged that Great Britain and America work together against Soviet **expansionism,** or the drive to increase territory. (p. 635)

In my mind, there's little to compare between the Manchester and textbook text; I'll take Manchester any day.

Because of their very nature—the fact that trade books have the time and room to treat subjects in depth and the need for trade books to have broad-based and intrinsic appeal—trade books generally win hands down over textbooks when it comes to liveliness of text, depth of topic treatment, and interest. Textbooks are written for different purposes than trade books are and are held to standards of topic choice and coverage, pedagogical correctness, and information accuracy that do not affect trade-book publication. Furthermore, the people who select textbooks are not the audience for whom the books are intended. Alvermann and Moore state frankly, "A problem with textbook materials is that their contents are dictated by concerns other than appeal and comprehensibility to students" (1991, p. 973).

RESOLVING THE ISSUES

I am not recommending here that we should do away with all textbooks; textbooks serve very useful purposes as outlines of subject area curricula, compendia of information and ideas, and resources for students and teachers alike. I do believe, however, that if we want to capture students' imaginations and encourage them to become lifelong learners, we must give them large doses of the kind of writing exemplified by Manchester's masterful two-volume biography of Winston Churchill and much smaller doses of the less vibrant, sanitized, and space-constricted standard textbook text. Well-written and well-produced informational trade books must be much more than simple adjuncts to classroom life; they must become central to the reading and writing that students do and must be perceived by students and teachers alike as essential materials for learning.

Traditional Instruments for Evaluation of Classroom Texts

Whenever we talk about evaluating texts, we quickly realize that no single factor describes text quality. That is, we can't fully evaluate a book by saying, "The illustrations and graphics are well done and useful for interpreting text"; neither can we use, "This textbook covers all facets of our curriculum"; nor is the statement "This text is at an appropriate difficulty level for our students" by itself useful. Clearly, each of the foregoing aspects of text evaluation is necessary and pertinent to any such discussion; nevertheless, none is sufficient in and of itself to give us reasoned assessment of a specific text. The point here is that all of these factors, and many others, must be considered in relationship to one another for valid and useful evaluation to occur. Wendy Saul and Donna Dieckman note that content, writing, and design of texts are important factors in evaluating quality: "These aspects cannot, in the end, be separated from one another. The quality of a book has to do with how these elements work together" (2005, p. 505). The following discussion looks at a number of traditional instruments for evaluating instructional texts.

READABILITY OF TEXT

Readability is probably the most well-known aspect of text evaluation. Readability refers to (1) the difficulty level of text materials, an area of continuing concern for teachers, students, textbook authors, and publishers; and (2) the degree to which texts are considered to be "readable" by a target population. Readability is expressed in terms of grade level, so when a text is identified as having a readability level of seventh grade, the assumption is that to be able to read and construct meaning for that text, one would need to be reading at or above a seventh-grade level.

Readability is also a major focus of discussion, both in the public media and in professional journals, regarding the quality of school texts. Cited in allegations first made by former Secretary of Education Terrel Bell as the "dumbing down" of classroom texts (Farr & Tulley, 1985), the discussion centers on the efforts of publishers to produce textbooks written at levels that enable all students, even those who are less proficient readers, to read the text. Publishers and textbook authors are thought to be "writing to the [readability] formula" rather than producing well-constructed prose, thereby making textbooks "readable" but not very good (recall our earlier discussion). Concern exists over the appropriateness of this practice and the resulting quality, or lack of quality, of the textbooks produced.

READABILITY AND READABILITY FORMULAS

The notion of readability grew from reading research during the 1920s measuring the difficulty of content area textbooks and parallel research in vocabulary study. Essential to the notion of readability was the belief that if we could establish the level of competence required to read a particular text, we could then more accurately match texts with readers. This belief was the basis for early efforts to develop readability formulas to measure text difficulty and continues to be so in more recent ones.

Most readability formulas measure two dimensions of text difficulty: *semantic* (vocabulary) and *syntactic* (sentence) complexity. For each of these dimensions, the assumption of readability formulas is that longer = harder. Semantic complexity is therefore assumed to be associated with word length and multiple syllables; syntactic complexity is assumed to be associated with long sentences made so by modifiers and embedded phrases and clauses.

Clearly, these two dimensions do not account for all possible factors affecting text difficulty: The reader's prior knowledge and stance, text cohesion, and concept density, for example, influence textbook difficulty, along with such aspects as interestingness, understandability, and clarity (Irwin & Davis, 1980; Singer, 1992). Nor does the assumption behind the semantic and syntactic measures of complexity (longer = harder) always hold. "To be, or not to be; that is the question" is a relatively short compound sentence with only one two-syllable word; in all likelihood, it would register at first- or second-grade difficulty using a standard readability formula, yet any reasonable person would judge the concept level to be considerably above the second-grade readability level. Conversely, we know that unusual, multisyllabic words, words that would increase the level of difficulty as measured by a readability formula—*neighborhood*, for example—are readily learned by very young readers.

USEFULNESS OF READABILITY FORMULAS

Certainly, readability formulas have serious flaws that overlook important aspects of meaning construction; further, they may be (and, by the way, have been) improperly or inappropriately applied and interpreted. Nevertheless, readability formulas are one of the most researched and validated assessment tools in education; as long ago as 1989 Ed Fry noted that over 1,000 articles and reports on readability exist in the literature (p. 294). Furthermore, although various exceptions do exist ("To be or not to be"; *neighborhood*), Fry makes a strong case that *on the average*, the longer = harder assumption does indeed hold. He and others argue additionally that large numbers of studies suggest readability formulas to be valid tools for estimating the difficulty level of text.

In contrast, Weaver and Kintsch argue against the use of traditional readability formulas in light of recent knowledge regarding text structure, reader–text interactions, cognition, and knowledge construction. They conclude that "these [readability] formulas provide a scandalous oversimplification, more frequently a serious distortion [of text difficulty]. Nevertheless . . . they continue to be used" (1991, p. 242). Weaver and Kintsch recommend that we refine old formulas or develop new ways to assess readability that reflect more completely our current understanding of knowledge construction, reading, and learning.

My own position is somewhere between fully advocating readability formulas and wanting to abolish their use altogether. Although I do understand and acknowledge all the limitations and problems associated with readability formulas as they are today, I must agree with Fry that not using readability formulas is equally as limiting as the problems inherent in the formulas themselves. I am particularly wary of "throwing the baby out with the bathwater" here because I well remember when secondary subject area texts were written and published virtually without any regard for difficulty level. At that time (up until the mid- to late-1970s, in fact), secondary teachers were not very able judges of how difficult a text was. This was not out of malice or neglect but was related to the fact that until the 1970s, few secondary teachers took courses in content area reading. Therefore, they were not attuned to issues and concerns associated with adolescent literacy and difficulty level of text.

Just as importantly, secondary teachers were, and remain, subject area experts; they have spent years vitally interested and immersed in the literature of their discipline and have forgotten what it's like to be a novice: to know nothing of quarks, Wagner, sines and cosines, Chaucer's English, world political movements, and Impressionism, for example. Texts easy for the expert are not so for the novice, thereby leaving substantial room for error in their selection.

RECOMMENDATIONS FOR USING READABILITY FORMULAS

I recommend that we continue to use the readability formulas available to us today if for no other reason than to alert us to the *possibility* that a given text is not appropriate for our students. We must, however, be diligent to see that *we use the formulas appropriately and responsibly*. To do that, we must do the following:

1. Remember that readability formulas yield *estimates* (and imperfect estimates at that) of reading difficulty. Therefore, results should be interpreted cautiously and viewed in terms of grade-level *ranges* rather than specific, immutable grade levels.

2. Also remember that readability formula estimates of difficulty level cannot be interpreted as evaluations of other text or reader elements: for example, concept difficulty, suitability, interestingness, reader prior knowledge, and so on.

3. Use as many samples as time allows when applying a formula to a given text to account for varying levels of difficulty within that text.

4. Use readability formula estimates *in conjunction with* a variety of other means for evaluating text materials. (We will explore various ways for doing this.)

TWO READABILITY FORMULAS

Let's look at two highly popular readability formulas that teachers use to evaluate middle school and junior/senior high texts. There are other, much more complex formulas available on software for computer application; many schools and districts have these. There are also numerous online resources for measuring readability, including readability of Web sites. The formulas I'm presenting here are very easily applied and computed manually. After I've presented the two formulas, I'll suggest ways to help you understand and use them most effectively. Later in the chapter, we will explore text evaluation means that may be used as alternatives, or supplements, to readability formulas (see item 4 in the previous list).

FRY READABILITY GRAPH

The Fry Readability Graph (Fry, 1968, 1977) enjoys widespread use, especially for middle school, junior high, and senior high content texts. The graph and directions for its use are shown in Figure 3.1.

THE SMOG FORMULA

I've always liked the SMOG formula (McLaughlin, 1969), as much for its whimsical name—Simple Measure of Gobbledygook—as for its straightforward, easy procedures. The SMOG formula is applied using the following four steps:

1. Count 10 consecutive sentences near the beginning of the selection to be assessed, 10 in the middle, and 10 near the end. Count as a sentence any string of words ending with a period, question mark, or exclamation point.

2. In the 30 selected sentences, count every word of three or more syllables. Any string of letters or numerals beginning and ending with a space or punctuation mark should be counted if you can distinguish at least three syllables when you read it aloud in context. If a polysyllabic word is repeated, count each repetition.

3. Estimate the square root of the number of polysyllabic words counted. This is done by calculating the square root of the nearest perfect square. For example, if the count is 95, the nearest perfect square is 100, which yields a square root of 10. If the count lies roughly between two perfect squares, choose the lower number. For instance, if the count is 110, take the square root of 100 rather than that of 121.

4. Add 3 to the approximate square root. This gives the SMOG grade, which is the minimal reading level needed to understand the selection assessed.

FIGURE 3.1 *Graph for Estimating Readability—Extended*
By Edward Fry, Rutgers University Reading Center, New Brunswick, NJ 08904

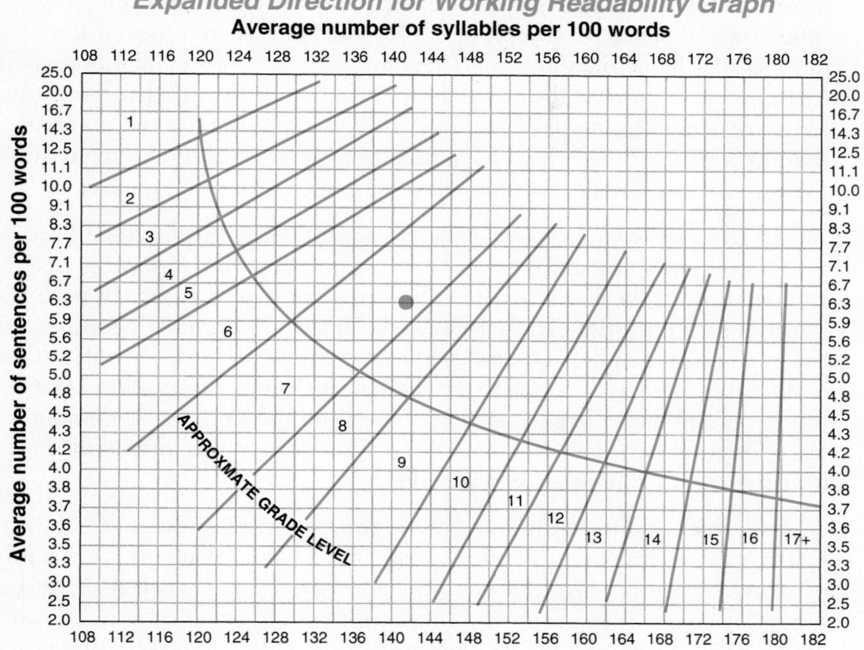

1. Randomly select three (3) sample passages and count out exactly 100 words each, beginning with the beginning of a sentence. Do count proper nouns, initialization, and numerals.

2. Count the number of sentences in the hundred words, estimating length of the fraction of the last sentence to the nearest one-tenth.

3. Count the total number of syllables in the 100-word passage. If you don't have a hand counter available, an easy way is to simply put a mark above every syllable over one in each word; then when you get to the end of the passage, count the number of marks and add 100. Small calculators can also be used as counters by pushing numeral 1, then push the plus sign for each word or syllable when counting.

4. Enter graph with average sentence length and average number of syllables; plot dot where the two lines intersect. Area where dot is plotted will give you the approximate grade level.

5. If a great deal of variability is found in syllable count or sentence count, putting more samples into the average is desirable.

6. A word is defined as a group of symbols with a space on either side; thus *Joe*, *IRA*, *1945*, and & are each one word.

7. A syllable is defined as a phonetic syllable. Generally, there are as many syllables as vowel sounds. For example, *stopped* is one syllable and *wanted* is two syllables. When counting syllables for numerals and initializations, count one syllable for each symbol. For example, *1945* is four syllables, *IRA* is three syllables, and & is one syllable.

UNDERSTANDING AND USING READABILITY FORMULAS

Notice that with the Fry formula, you are locating three 100-word passages and counting number of sentences and number of syllables; in the SMOG formula, you are locating three 10-sentence passages and counting number of words with three or more syllables. Do you see how these are simply two different ways of getting at semantic and syntactic complexity? One involves the number of long sentences and number of syllables in 300 words (the more long sentences and more syllables in a limited number of words, the more difficult the text); the other involves the number of long words in 30 sentences (the more long words in a limited number of sentences, the more difficult the text). I have used both of these formulas many times, and from that experience, I make the following suggestions for accurate use:

1. In the Fry formula, you are told to "randomly select" your three passages; the SMOG requires that sentence passages occur one at the beginning, one in the middle, and one toward the end of whatever material you are assessing. In both cases, random selection is appropriate so that you don't bias your choices; choosing passages from the beginning, middle, and end is equally useful with both formulas. The easiest way to do this is to open the book somewhere near the beginning, close your eyes, put your finger on one of the pages, open your eyes, find the nearest beginning sentence, and start counting (words or sentences). Do the same in the middle of the textbook and near the end for the other two passages.

2. You *must* duplicate the passages so you can write on them. Contrary to what Ed Fry says in his directions, you really can't use a hand calculator for this job, regardless of which formula you're using, and you really can't work directly from the text (unless it's okay to mark on it). You have to stop periodically to consider and make decisions, and you will forget whether you had already counted one syllable for the word you're considering or two, or whether you've counted anything at all; you'll need to mark your progress when you stop and have a record of what you've counted. Take my advice here: Make copies.

3. After counting your 100-word or 10-sentence passages, mark the beginning and end of each passage with brackets or a block line so you will know precisely where to begin and end counting. To count the sentences for the Fry formula, circle each period or other sentence-ending punctuation. Write the number in a margin or on a worksheet. To count syllables for the Fry formula, put a tick mark above each syllable in each word (or put a mark above each syllable over the basic one syllable that every word has), as Fry suggested. If you use the SMOG formula, put one tick mark above each polysyllabic word.

4. *You will need to read these passages aloud* (or, at the very least, whisper); otherwise, you'll find yourself counting words such as *stopped* and *learned* as two syllables, or accepting *prepared* as polysyllabic. In addition, you'll need to make some decisions that reading aloud will help you make. For example, if you're using the Fry formula, you'll have to decide how many syllables to assign to words such as *interesting* (in-ter-es′-ting = 4; in′-tra-sting = 3) and *vague*. You will find more words than you expect that cause you to make decisions, whichever formula you use. Regional and other dialects (your own and those in the area in which you teach) will enter into your deliberations here.

The best rule of thumb is to say each word as naturally as possible and count whatever you hear.

5. Before you enter the Fry graph, make sure you have converted your sentence and syllable counts to *averages.* You plot only once using the average sentence and syllable counts. First, take the total number of sentences for each passage and divide by the number of passages you used; do the same for the syllable count. Using the SMOG formula, add your counts of polysyllabic words from your three samples before finding the nearest perfect square. *If you choose to use more than three passages for the SMOG formula, you must use six or nine and make appropriate averaging adjustments.* The formula is based on the number of polysyllabic words in 30 sentences; if you use 40 or 50 sentences, you will distort the results. If you do use 60 or 90 sentences, you must total the polysyllabic words and then divide by 2 or 3, respectively, to arrive at the "average number of polysyllabic words in 30 sentences." Then find the nearest square root. Alternatively, calculate the entire formula two or three times if you use six or nine passages, and then compare results. Don't forget to add the 3 after finding the square root.

6. Hand-write or use your computer to create simple worksheets for your calculations. The two in Figure 3.2 are samples.

FIGURE 3.2 *Fry and SMOG Readability Graph Worksheets*

Worksheet: Fry Readability Graph

	Number of Sentences	Number of Syllables
Passage 1 (p. ______)	______	______
Passage 2 (p. ______)	______	______
Passage 3 (p. ______)	______	______
Total	______	______
Avg. (÷3)	______	______
	Grade Level (Range)	______

Worksheet: SMOG Readability Formula

	Number of Polysyllabic Words	
Passage 1 (p. ______)	________	
Passage 2 (p. ______)	________	
Passage 3 (p. ______)	________	
Total	________	
Nearest Square Root	________	
+3	________	Grade Level (Range) ________

READER-TEXT INTERACTIONS

One of the most frequent disadvantages cited for readability formulas is that they evaluate text in isolation from the reader. The concern is that the estimates produced by readability formulas for given texts tell us nothing about what will happen when readers interact with that text and bring to it their own prior knowledge base, attitudes and interests, and knowledge about how text works. Neither do formulas inform us regarding the effect of social interactions and classroom instruction on knowledge construction. These are particularly important concerns with content textbooks because of the influence of subject area prior knowledge on reading and learning and because social interaction and class instruction change the interaction between reader and text. Concerns about the reader–text interaction gain even greater importance as grade levels and text difficulty increase.

Earl Rankin (personal communication, 1974) made the point that regardless of what the readability formula says, and regardless of how much we know about the student's reading ability, "If the kid can't read the book, the kid can't read the book." Rankin's point, and the point of other critics of readability testing, is that we need information about the interaction that occurs when reader and text meet in order to have a clear understanding of the usefulness of a given text.

CLOZE TESTING

One of the first attempts to include the reader in text evaluation was the Cloze test introduced by Wilson Taylor in 1953. Cloze testing is based on the gestalt notion of "closure," which is the mind's ability to complete incomplete words, visual images, or thoughts. Closure depends, to a greater or lesser degree, on context. For example, if I wrote "Happy——," you might fill in the blank with *Halloween*, *Thanksgiving*, *Hanukkah*, *New Year*, *Valentine's Day*, *birthday*, *anniversary*, or *trails to you*, depending on the time of year, your immediate context, or any of a myriad of other personal proclivities. We all engage in closure events daily: for example, when we finish someone else's sentence, overlook typographical errors while proofreading, and deal with incomplete or disordered visual information.

Procedure for the Cloze Test The Cloze test Wilson Taylor proposed (1953) capitalizes on the mind's ability to create closure. In the test, the reader replaces systematically deleted words of a text passage; the percentage of correct replacements gives us information about how effectively a given reader handles a given text. Because the Cloze test is a sample of its larger environment (i.e., the textbook itself), we then make some assumptions about how the reader will be able to read and construct meaning from that textbook as a whole.

Cloze testing and the percentage standards used for establishing levels of effectiveness with text have been subjects of considerable research, particularly during the 1960s and 1970s, when the technique was relatively new. From that body of research, we have developed fairly standard administration and scoring procedures for cloze testing and percentage levels for evaluating reader effectiveness. Cloze testing differs in significant ways from Cloze teaching strategies (see Chapter 5), and the two should not be confused. Cloze tests are carried out using much more rigid rules for word deletion and for determination of correctness of word replacement. To arrive at interpretable results of a Cloze test, the following procedures should be used for constructing, administering, scoring, and interpreting the test:

Construction

1. Select a passage by finding a section of relatively unbroken text from a portion of the text to be evaluated that students have not yet read; you will need a passage of 275 to 300 words. It is not necessary that this passage be randomly chosen; in fact, it is best if you deliberately select a passage that typifies the text.

2. Word process the passage double-spaced. Leave the first sentence intact. Then, starting at a random spot in the second sentence, delete every fifth word using a standard 10- or 15-space underline to show the deletions. Take care not to split deletion lines from one line of text to another. Number the deletions consecutively. When you have deleted 50 words, type the remainder of that sentence intact. Add one more intact sentence. It helps to mark all of this on a copy of the text, including space numbers, before beginning the word processing.

3. Prepare an answer sheet by creating two columns of numbered blanks (1 to 50) spaced to allow plenty of room for students to write one-word responses. Be sure to include a place for students' names and any other information you want on the answer sheet.

4. Prepare a scoring template with exact replacements written in the same formation as the answer sheet.

5. Duplicate sufficient copies of the test and answer sheets for your students. *Be sure that both the test and the answer sheet are cleanly duplicated so that smearing, smudges, and dark copies do not interfere with your results.*

Administration

1. Explain to students the purpose of the Cloze test and reassure them that it will have no effect on their grades in your class.

2. Demonstrate several examples of deletion replacement on the board or an overhead projector so students will know what they are expected to do. Be sure to demonstrate how to use the answer sheet.

3. Give students as much time as they need to complete the test.

Scoring

1. Count as correct exact replacements only. You will undoubtedly find synonym replacements that appear to be absolutely correct and others that are "sort of" correct; do not count these as correct. For purposes of evaluating text difficulty, synonym replacement increases the complexity of the scoring (e.g., where do you draw the line between "absolutely correct" and "sort of correct"?) but does not increase appreciably the precision or accuracy of the results. Percentage levels for interpretation are based on exact replacement scores.

2. Determine each student's total correct replacements; multiply by two. This product represents the student's percentage score.

Interpretation

1. Scores ranging between 61% and 100% represent the *Independent Reading Level.* Students who achieve these scores should be able to read this text with ease. If a number of students score in the upper ranges of this level, the text is probably not challenging enough for this class.

2. Scores ranging between 40% and 60% represent the *Instructional Reading Level.* Students achieving these scores should be able to read the text with instruction—that is, with guidance and assistance from the teacher. The most appropriate text for any group of students should have a relatively large majority of students scoring in or slightly above this level.

3. Scores ranging between 0% and 39% represent the *Frustration Reading Level.* Students achieving these scores will probably experience considerable difficulty reading the text. If a significant number of students score within this level, the text is likely to be too difficult for this group.

Advantages and Disadvantages of Cloze Tests Remember, the purpose of Cloze testing is not to determine if students know the meaning of the words in the passage per se; rather, it is to tell whether they can read and construct meaning from text when these words are missing. Cloze tests, therefore, give us more information than do readability formulas: Instead of yielding an estimate of the reading grade-level ability needed for students to read a given text, the Cloze test estimates how well each student functions when engaged with that text. To this extent, Cloze tests have an advantage over readability formulas. In addition, Cloze tests are easily constructed, administered, scored, and interpreted.

Unfortunately, Cloze tests have one very significant disadvantage: They are difficult, and students generally do not like to do them. Cloze tests present students with a large number of unknowns in a small space, causing some students to become totally discouraged and unwilling to attempt completion, and even the best students to experience some level of irritation and discomfort. Brenda Shearer (personal communication, 2000) recommends that Cloze testing be done by sampling your class—ask for volunteers and pay attention to ascertain that they represent ability ranges in the class; show students how to do the Cloze test, and then use their results to estimate how the general population of students will function with that text.

When Cloze Testing Cannot Be Used There are at least two circumstances in which Cloze testing is neither useful nor appropriate. The first is with texts in which there is not enough running text to allow for a 275- to 300-word sample. In such texts, clearly, construction of meaning does not depend on interpretation of large amounts of connected prose. Mathematics and foreign language texts are often written in such a way. These, and other similar texts, must be evaluated using methods other than Cloze testing.

The second circumstance in which Cloze testing is not useful is in anthology texts and books of readings or articles in which several or many authors with varied writing styles, genres, and levels of difficulty are presented. Certainly, no one sample of such a text could represent the entire text. Literature texts and article collections are examples; however, even texts with a single author may vary in difficulty from chapter to chapter. These, too, must be evaluated alternatively.

THE GROUP READING INVENTORY (GRI)

The Group Reading Inventory (GRI) is yet another way, and far superior to Cloze testing, I believe, to determine how students interact with text. GRIs go beyond Cloze testing by focusing on students' abilities to understand and use book parts and study aids (such as tables of contents, indexes, chapter titles, marginal notes, charts, maps, illustrations, and tables) as well as to comprehend text content and vocabulary. Numerous forms and formats for GRIs have been recommended over the years, ranging from representative passages from the text accompanied by questions constructed to evaluate comprehension to elaborate questionnaires that direct students to locate information in the text, use text graphics and aids, and answer multiple-choice comprehension and vocabulary questions for one or more passages.

Usefulness of GRIs GRIs require a considerable amount of time to construct, administer, and score, but they are worth it. They are most useful for learning to what degree students perceive and can use the basic structure of the textbook, the written and visual aids, and the book parts. In addition, they are usable with both kinds of texts that cannot be evaluated by readability formulas or Cloze testing—texts with mathematical or other symbols, texts of article or literature collections, or foreign language texts. Information from GRIs is useful in determining how much assistance students will need to be successful in reading and learning from the text. I prefer short, open-ended inventories to the more elaborate ones generally recommended, and I like to evaluate students' comprehension with broad, open-ended questions rather than with multiple-choice questions. Brevity has the advantage of time efficiency, and open-endedness allows a richer view of students' abilities than do responses on multiple-choice items.

Representative GRIs The following are representative samples of what I think are useful GRIs:

Mathematics

1. In the lessons in our book, how can you tell the *examples* from the *explanations?*
2. What does the green highlighting signal in the text?
3. Where can you find the *generalizations* or *rules* in each lesson?
4. If you were doing your homework and forgot how to do the exercises, where would you look to get help?
5. List, in order, what steps you would take to figure out how to do the exercises.

Health

1. What are the Check Your Understanding sections for? How could you use them to guide your study?

2. What might you do with the information in the Chapter Summary and Do You Remember sections?

3. Where in this book would you look if you needed to know the meaning of a word?

4. How would you interpret Figure 23.9, Edith, on page 364?

5. Read Section 4, "Intoxication and Society" (pp. 250–252). In your own words, tell what you think that section is about.

Literature

1. Where would you look in the text to get information on the effect of the Enlightenment on the English language?

2. What is the organizational scheme for the sequence of literature in this book?

3. How can you use the line notes and footnotes in this text?

4. Where in this book would you look to find definitions of literary terms?

5. Read the first chapter of Charles Dickens's *Great Expectations* (pages 595 through 597). In your own words, tell what you think this chapter was about. What do you think it will lead to? (You may wish to read about Charles Dickens in the introduction to the Victorian period on the preceding two pages.)

Science

1. What is the significance of the white numerals in blue circles scattered through the chapters?

2. Look at the investigation into solar heating on page 239. In your own words, list the steps you must take to carry out this investigation.

3. What is the relationship of the dark black headings to the gold capitalized headings in each chapter? How can you use these headings to help you study?

4. Where would you look in this text if you wanted to locate a particular topic? What is the name of that section? What pages does it cover?

5. List everything you know about tornadoes; draw a line after your last item. Then read the section on tornadoes (pages 198 through 199). Go back to your list and add new information under the line you drew. Put an asterisk (*) beside anything you already knew that you found in the book.

I strongly encourage you to develop a short GRI for evaluating your students' abilities to use classroom texts, including electronic texts. I think you can see how they combine aspects of content writing and students' understanding of text design. Administering a GRI will give you a great deal of information about your students' reading abilities and will help you decide how you can most effectively guide their continued reading growth in your subject area.

ALTERNATIVE APPROACHES FOR EVALUATING CLASSROOM TEXTS

Much of our most recent efforts to find alternative means for evaluating text grew from widespread discontent with the limited focus of readability formulas. Although Cloze testing and GRIs do enlarge the scope of text evaluation to include the reader, even these measures do not account for some important aspects of the interaction between reader and text. In the 1990s, we increased considerably our understanding of the reading process and how knowledge is constructed from text. This new understanding ultimately led to parallel expansion of our definitions of what constitutes well-written text. We now know that what makes a text readable concerns not only the reader's prior knowledge but issues of Discourse—attitudes, interests, beliefs, and predispositions—as well. Further, we are now examining text in new ways to determine text elements that contribute, or do not contribute, to readers' constructions of meaning. Therefore, variables other than semantic and syntactic complexity of text and readers' abilities to understand and use the text must be considered in our evaluations.

Alternative approaches for evaluating instructional text seek to account for the interactions that occur when readers bring their prior knowledge, interests, and attitudes to those texts. The results of these efforts have yielded several instruments, each with its own signature focus on text, that can be used singly or in tandem with other measures to deepen our knowledge of textbooks under review. Irwin and Davis (1980) focused on the variables "understandability" and "learnability," and Singer (1986) adopted the computer-world notion of "user friendly" to discuss "friendly" text.

THE READABILITY CHECKLIST

Irwin and Davis (1980) developed the Readability Checklist (see Figure 3.3, pp. 70–72) with the express purpose of providing teachers with both the information about how readable a text is and the knowledge of what teacher aids may be supplied to make it more readable. The checklist has two main areas for analysis:

1. *Understandability.* Understandability refers to the degree to which the text accounts for reader prior knowledge and background experience, the ways in which concepts are developed in the text, various aspects of syntactic difficulty (sentence construction, main idea and detail arrangement, and explication of ideas), and resources for providing aids to comprehension.

2. *Learnability.* Learnability includes the clarity and usefulness of how the book, chapters, and special features (e.g., the index) are organized; included in the learnability analysis are reinforcement (the type and amount of practice provided) and motivation (the presence of features that interest readers).

At the end of the checklist are questions designed to assist the evaluator in summarizing the text's strengths and weaknesses. The checklist includes provision for readability testing (Understandability). The Readability Checklist and directions for using it are shown in Figure 3.3.

FIGURE 3.3 *Readability Checklist*
From Irwin and Davis, 1980 (pp. 129–130).

This checklist is designed to help you evaluate the readability of your classroom texts. It can best be used if you rate your text while you are thinking of a specific class. Be sure to compare the textbook to a fictional ideal rather than to another text. Your goal is to find out what aspects of the text are or are not less than ideal. Finally, consider supplementary workbooks as part of the textbook and rate them together. Have fun!

Rate the questions below using the following rating system:

5 – Excellent
4 – Good
3 – Adequate
2 – Poor
1 – Unacceptable
NA – Not applicable

Further comments may be written in the space provided.
Textbook Title: ______________________________
Publisher: ______________________________
Copyright date: ______________________________

Understandability

A. _____ Are the assumptions about students' vocabulary knowledge appropriate?
B. _____ Are the assumptions about students' prior knowledge of this content area appropriate?
C. _____ Are the assumptions about students' general experiential backgrounds appropriate?
D. _____ Does the teacher's manual provide the teacher with ways to develop and review the students' conceptual and experiential backgrounds?
E. _____ Are new concepts explicitly linked to the students' prior knowledge or to their experiential backgrounds?
F. _____ Does the text introduce abstract concepts by accompanying them with many concrete examples?
G. _____ Does the text introduce new concepts one at a time with a sufficient number of examples for each one?
H. _____ Are definitions understandable and at a lower level of abstraction than the concept being defined?
I. _____ Is the level of sentence complexity appropriate for the students?
J. _____ Are the main ideas of paragraphs, chapters, and subsections clearly stated?
K. _____ Does the text avoid irrelevant details?
L. _____ Does the text explicitly state important complex relationships (e.g., causality, conditionality, etc.) rather than always expecting the reader to infer them from the context?
M. _____ Does the teacher's manual provide lists of accessible resources containing alternative readings for very poor or very advanced readers?

FIGURE 3.3 *continued*

Learnability

Organization

A. _____ Is an introduction provided for in each chapter?
B. _____ Is there a clear and simple organizational pattern relating the chapters to each other?
C. _____ Does each chapter have a clear, explicit, and simple organizational structure?
D. _____ Does the text include resources such as an index, glossary, and table of contents?
E. _____ Do questions and activities draw attention to the organizational pattern of the material (e.g., chronological, cause and effect, spatial, topical, etc.)?
F. _____ Do consumable materials interrelate well with the textbook?

Reinforcement

A. _____ Does the text provide opportunities for students to practice using new concepts?
B. _____ Are there summaries at appropriate intervals in the text?
C. _____ Does the text provide adequate iconic aids such as maps, graphs, illustrations, etc., to reinforce concepts?
D. _____ Are there adequate suggestions for usable supplementary activities?
E. _____ Do these activities provide for a broad range of ability levels?
F. _____ Are there literal recall questions provided for the students' self-review?
G. _____ Do some of the questions encourage the students to draw inferences?
H. _____ Are there discussion questions which encourage creative thinking?
I. _____ Are questions clearly worded?

Motivation

A. _____ Does the teacher's manual provide introductory activities that will capture students' interest?
B. _____ Are chapter titles and subheadings concrete, meaningful, or interesting?
C. _____ Is the writing style of the text appealing to the students?
D. _____ Are the activities motivating? Will they make the student want to pursue the topic further?
E. _____ Does the book clearly show how the knowledge being learned might be used by the learner in the future?
F. _____ Are the cover, format, print size, and pictures appealing to the students?
G. _____ Does the text provide positive and motivating models for both sexes as well as for other racial, ethnic, and socioeconomic groups?

Readability analysis

Weaknesses

1) On which items was the book rated the lowest?
2) Did these items tend to fall in certain categories?

(continued)

FIGURE 3.3 *continued*

3) Summarize the weaknesses of this text.
4) What can you do in class to compensate for the weaknesses of this text?

Assets

1) On which items was the book rated the highest?
2) Did these items fall in certain categories?
3) Summarize the assets of this text.
4) What can you do in class to take advantage of the assets of this text?

THE FRIENDLY TEXT EVALUATION SCALE

Harry Singer (1992) developed the Friendly Text Evaluation Scale (Figure 3.4) to be used along with readability formula evaluation so that the evaluator can discern and specify what makes one text friendlier than another (p. 161). Singer's scale organizes and categorizes items somewhat differently from Irwin and Davis's checklist, itemizes more in some areas (e.g., Instructional Devices), and offers examples and explanations right on the checklist itself; essentially, however, the two checklists are comparable. Singer emphasizes the importance of going beyond determining readability levels and friendliness of text:

> If a prediction is to be made on how well students in a classroom situation are likely to comprehend a text, then a third step is to determine how a particular teacher is likely to enhance the friendliness of a text, the readers' resources, and the interactions between the text and the reader. (p. 161)

Singer concedes that no scale is available to predict teachers' responses to friendly and unfriendly text. The Friendly Text Evaluation Scale and directions for using it are shown in Figure 3.4.

THE CARTER G. WOODSON BOOK AWARD CHECKLIST

Increasingly in the United States, we have become attuned to and acknowledge the contributions of the many groups of people who comprise the nation's population, whether these groups are identified by race, ethnicity, culture, gender, physical ability, social and economic status, or life experience. This awareness is reflected in modern textbooks, fiction and nonfiction texts, and other instructional materials and will continue to be so. As classrooms become more diverse, and as textbooks begin to speak from the voices of many people to this diversity, evaluation of instructional material also needs to address issues related to pluralism.

Sharon Pugh and Jesus Garcia (1990) emphasize the notion of cultural pluralism and its importance in school texts. Such efforts are particularly timely in light of calls for a return to primary sources and unexcerpted text and a general upgrading of the quality of classroom texts. Pugh and Garcia recommend that texts and materials used in the classroom be evaluated with the checklist used for reviewing nonfiction texts

FIGURE 3.4 *Friendly Text Evaluation Scale*
From Singer, 1992 (pp. 162–163).

Directions: Read each criterion and judge the degree of agreement or disagreement between it and the text. Then circle the number to the right of the criterion that indicates your judgment.

1. SA = Strongly Agree
2. A = Agree
3. U = Uncertain
4. D = Disagree
5. SD = Strongly Disagree

	SA	*A*	*U*	*D*	*SD*
I. ORGANIZATION					
1. The introductions to the book and each chapter explain their purposes.	1	2	3	4	5
2. The introduction provides information on the sequence of the text's contents.	1	2	3	4	5
3. The introduction communicates how the reader should learn from the text.	1	2	3	4	5
4. The ideas presented in the text follow a unidirectional sequence. One idea leads to the next.	1	2	3	4	5
5. The type of paragraph structure organizes information to facilitate memory. For example, objects and their properties are grouped together so as to emphasize relationships.	1	2	3	4	5
6. Ideas are hierarchically structured either verbally or graphically.	1	2	3	4	5
7. The author provides cues to the way information will be presented. For example, the author states: "There are five points to consider."	1	2	3	4	5
8. Signal words (conjunctions, adverbs) and rhetorical devices (problem–solution, question–answer,cause–effect,comparison and contrast, argument–proof) interrelate sentences, paragraphs, and larger units of discourse.	1	2	3	4	5
Discourse consistency					
9. The style of writing is consistent and coherent. For example, the paragraphs, sections, and chapters build to a conclusion. Or they begin with a general statement and then present supporting ideas. Or the text has a combination of these patterns. Any one of these patterns would fit this consistency criterion.	1	2	3	4	5
Cohesiveness					
10. The text is cohesive. That is, the author ties ideas together from sentence to sentence, paragraph to paragraph, chapter to chapter.	1	2	3	4	5
II. EXPLICATION					
11. Some texts may be read at more than one level, e.g., descriptive vs. theoretical. The text orients students to a level that is appropriate for the students.	1	2	3	4	5

(continued)

FIGURE 3.4 *continued*

	SA	*A*	*U*	*D*	*SD*
12. The text provides reasons for functions or events. For example, the text, if it is a biology text, not only lists the differences between arteries and veins but also explains why they are different.	1	2	3	4	5
13. The text highlights or italicizes and defines new terms as they are introduced at a level that is familiar to the student.	1	2	3	4	5
14. The text provides necessary background knowledge. For example, the text introduces new ideas by reviewing or reminding readers of previously acquired knowledge or concepts.	1	2	3	4	5
15. The author uses examples, analogies, metaphors, similes, personifications, or allusions that clarify new ideas and make them vivid.	1	2	3	4	5
16. The author explains ideas in relatively short active sentences.	1	2	3	4	5
17. The explanations or theories that underlie the text are made explicit. E.g., Keynesian theory in Samuelson's economic text, Skinner's theory in Bijou and Baer's *Child Development*, behavioristic or gestalt theories in psychology texts.	1	2	3	4	5
III. CONCEPTUAL DENSITY					
18. Ideas are introduced, defined, or clarified, integrated with semantically related ideas previously presented in the text and examples given before additional ideas are presented.	1	2	3	4	5
19. The vocabulary load is appropriate. For example, usually only one new vocabulary item per paragraph occurs throughout the text.	1	2	3	4	5
20. Content is accurate, up-to-date, and not biased.	1	2	3	4	5
IV. METADISCOURSE					
21. The author talks directly to the reader to explain how to learn from the text. For example, the author states that some information in the text is more important than other information.	1	2	3	4	5
22. The author establishes a purpose or goal for the text.	1	2	3	4	5
23. The text supplies collateral information for putting events into context.	1	2	3	4	5
24. The text points out relationships to ideas previously presented in the text or to the reader's prior knowledge.	1	2	3	4	5
V. INSTRUCTIONAL DEVICES					
25. The text contains a logically organized table of contents.	1	2	3	4	5
26. The text has a glossary that defines technical terms in understandable language.	1	2	3	4	5
27. The index integrates concepts dispersed throughout the text.	1	2	3	4	5

FIGURE 3.4 *continued*

	SA	*A*	*U*	*D*	*SD*
28. There are overviews, proposed questions, or graphic devices, such as diagrams, tables, and graphs, throughout the text that emphasize what is to be learned in the chapters or sections.	1	2	3	4	5
29. The text includes marginal annotations or footnotes that instruct the reader.	1	2	3	4	5
30. The text contains chapter summaries that reflect its main points.	1	2	3	4	5
31. The text has problems or questions at the literal, interpretive, applied, and evaluative levels at the end of each chapter that help the reader understand knowledge presented in the text.	1	2	3	4	5
32. The text contains headings and subheadings that divide the text into categories that enable readers to perceive the major ideas.	1	2	3	4	5
33. The author provides information in the text or at the end of the chapters or the text that enables the reader to apply the knowledge in the text to new situations.	1	2	3	4	5
34. The author uses personal pronouns that makes the text more interesting to the reader.	1	2	3	4	5

Score Total ____________

Add the numbers circled.

Score range: 34 to 170 points

Interpretation of scores:

A score closer to 34 implies the text is friendly; scores closer to 170 suggest the text is unfriendly.

nominated for the Carter G. Woodson Book Award, which "recognizes authors who treat issues of race relations and minority and ethnic groups accurately and sensitively" (p. 21). This checklist not only is useful for looking at treatment of race and ethnicity but also is appropriate for evaluating books treating other aspects of diversity, including gender, ability, sexual orientation, life experience, and others. The checklist and directions for using it are presented in Figure 3.5 (p. 76).

SUMMARY OF ALTERNATIVE APPROACHES FOR EVALUATING TEXT

The three alternative approaches just discussed for evaluating instructional text represent real progress in how we select materials for classroom use. They build on and acknowledge traditional approaches, and at the same time they turn our attention to areas that traditional approaches do not address. In addition they are highly compatible with and adaptable to criteria developed by professional educational organizations for evaluating the quality of books and other texts in specific fields. Generally, these criteria focus on the combination of elements that Saul and Dieckman identified—content,

FIGURE 3.5 *Checklist—Carter G. Woodson Nomination*

Title of book ____________________ Identification of evaluator ____________
Author ____________________ Date ____________________
Publisher ____________________ *Place summary comments on reverse side

General guidelines	Superior	Acceptable	Unsatisfactory	Not applicable
1. Reflects respect for personal and cultural differences and the worth and importance of individual(s)/group(s) presented.				
2. Offers a factual, realistic, and balanced treatment of the past and present.				
3. Focuses on problems/issues that provide insight into the experience of racial and ethnic groups.				
4. Focuses on the interactions among racial/minority groups and the dominant culture.				
5. Avoids portraying the group(s) as "problem oriented"; stresses positives and negatives.				
6. Develops concepts related to cultural pluralism at a level appropriate for the intended audience.				
Guidelines—Illustrations				
7. Shows cultural diversity in illustrative materials.				
8. Avoids distortions and stereotyping.				
9. Presents the group(s)/individuals(s) in a variety of settings.				
Guidelines—Narrative				
10. Possesses a narrative theme that is believable, realistic, and unpatronizing of the targeted group(s).				
11. Describes narrative characters with feelings, emotions, and values equal to those of other individuals.				
Sum points				
Total points				

2 = S = Superior
1 = A = Acceptable
–1 = U = Unsatisfactory
0 = NA = Not Applicable

*The checklist should be used to evaluate the overall strengths and weaknesses of a book. Place a single value (2, 1, -1, 0) where appropriate and note page reference. You need not place a value in each category.

writing, and design—and are easily accessible at professional organization Web sites. Aspects of the Readability Checklist, the Friendly Text Evaluation Scale, and the Carter B. Woodson Book Award checklist are readily adaptable for use with criteria developed by professional organizations to create a comprehensive, useful evaluation instrument for choosing new texts for your classroom. Thus, unlike readability formulas, these alternative approaches may be used flexibly and in combination with other criteria to evaluate texts. Jameela Moore will be wise to use and adapt these and other evaluation instruments as she selects new books for her classroom.

MAKING THE TEXT EVALUATION AND SELECTION PROCESS SUCCESSFUL

It should be apparent by now that text evaluation is multifaceted and complicated, as it should be. After all, our subject disciplines, the knowledge we want our students to acquire, and our students themselves are similarly complex. To the extent that criticisms of textbooks persist (Sewall, 1988), as schools in the United States become increasingly diverse and pluralistic, and if textbooks continue to predominate as the focus of instruction in classrooms, textbook evaluation and selection processes will likely become even more complex and critical in the future than they are today.

Farr and Tulley outline many of the problems and complications of textbook adoption processes and even suggest the possibility that future efforts in textbook adoption could have lasting influence on the quality of textbooks themselves. It becomes important, therefore, that whether teachers are working individually to select texts for their classes or participating in school- or district-mandated adoption committees, the process be as orderly and thoughtfully planned as possible. Farr and Tulley offer the following suggestions (1985, p. 471):

1. *Do not confuse the textbook with the curriculum.* Finding one single textbook to cover all aspects of a curriculum is impossible and often leads to a choice of coverage over quality. Farr and Tulley state, "A single textbook series should be part of the curriculum, not the total curriculum" (p. 471).

2. *Limit the scope of the review to a few important features rather than attempting to cover every possible factor.* Long lists of features to review overwhelm and clutter the process; Farr and Tulley found criteria lists ranging from 42 items to 180 items. They recommend a list of no more than 12 items.

3. *Try out procedures and instruments and identify exemplars of excellence before launching the evaluation process itself.* These safeguards increase the validity and reliability of the procedures and the process and reduce confusion and/or mistakes.

To their suggestions I add the following:

4. *Involve students in the textbook-selection process.* If at all possible, involve them from the very beginning; if not, get information from them at some point. At the very least, ask them what they like and don't like about the current text. Then listen to them. Students will give you insightful and important information about school texts.

5. *Remember, you are engaged in a process that has the goal of meeting many teachers' and students' needs.* At some point in all adoption processes involving more than one person, comparative ranking occurs. The tendency is to focus attention on the top rankings, but don't forget the bottom rankings—the texts identified by teachers as the ones they least want to adopt. When making final decisions, it is sometimes best to choose a text from the top three that may not have gotten the most "first" rankings but that did get the fewest "last" rankings. You have to live and work with the other teachers when this process is over.

6. *Carefully select several evaluative instruments to be used in conjunction with one another to show different facets of textbooks under review.* I recommend one (and only one) readability formula, parts or all of one of the checklists discussed (Readability, Friendly Text, Carter G. Woodson) in conjunction with professional organization criteria, and some spot-checking with either a Cloze test or a short GRI.

7. *Develop a summary sheet for final review of all texts under consideration.* I offer the one shown in Figure 3.6 as a prototype.

FIGURE 3.6 *Text Evaluation Summary*

Text: ______________________________
Authors: ______________________________
Publisher: ______________________________ Date of Publication __________
____

Reviewer: ______________________________ Date: __________

Readability Level: Formula ______________________ Grade Level/Range: ________

Results from other sources (Select one or more):

Readability Checklist:

Friendly Text Evaluation Scale:

Cloze Test (circle one): Independent, Instructional, Frustration Level

Group Reading Inventory (GRI):

Carter G. Woodson Award Checklist:

Professional Organization Criteria:

Overall Evaluation (High, Medium, Low): ________ Rank: __________

Total: First ranks _____ Second ranks _____ Third ranks _____ Last ranks _____

Final Decision: ______________________________
____

EVALUATION OF ELECTRONIC AND SOFTWARE TEXTS

Electronic text, multimedia hardware and software, and Internet resources are in classrooms to stay, and give every indication of becoming increasingly more important in every aspect of learning and teaching in school. And I don't believe it's stretching the truth to say that many, many preadolescents and adolescents come to school skilled in the use of on-line navigation and aware of electronic resources and software products in ways that adults, both parents and teachers, cannot even conceive. Here is a recent description of one adolescent's daily interaction with electronic texts:

> One winter Friday just as the sun was going down, Nathan Yan settled at the computer table in his . . . living room and began what he calls "my rounds." That includes checking his e-mail, friends' blogs, his Wikipedia watch list, and scanning for news about *Lost*. If he has time, he might post a blog, peruse his spreadsheet of baseball statistics, or cyber window shop, watching the price of camera equipment he can't afford drop almost daily. He also listens to music, using headphones so he won't bother his parents or younger brother, who often sits at an adjacent computer, also wearing headphones, ensconced in a game. . . .
>
> [Nathan] estimates he spends five to six hours a day on the computer, including doing his homework—often concurrently with other activities. But even when he's working on "noncomputing activities," he's usually in front of his computer. Tonight he'll probably be on until about midnight. (Seligman, 2006, p. 5)

It is the role and responsibility of teachers to evaluate the quality and educational appropriateness of electronic texts just as surely as it is for textbooks and other classroom materials. The big difference here, of course, is the immediate accessibility of Internet resources (students don't have to wait for a committee review process to begin using them), the sheer volume of the material on the Internet itself, adolescents' tendencies to use the Internet much like Nathan Yan, and the elusive nature of some Internet sources (here today and gone tomorrow). Various forms of educational software also abound, much of which gives students (and you) the capability of creating extended, elaborated, illustrated, and in some cases streamed video texts. What electronic and software resources add to our canon of traditionally published textbooks, trade books, and other written resources are the many ways our interactions with electronic text can *change the text itself*, so that our resource environment changes from static, cast-in-print textbooks, trade books, and journals to dynamic, fluid, created–recreated–re-re-recreated representations on computer screens.

Evaluation of electronic text presents new challenges, not the least of which is the fluidity of text and the capability for alternative visual representations. Phil Moore (1999) notes the multiple authorship common to software and websites: "It is impossible to know how many hands have been at work when a word-processed file is read" (p. 53), and the nonlinearity of electronic texts, as opposed to the traditional linear text of published books.

> With a book, it is clear where to start and where to finish, and it is easy to understand that page 15 comes before page 73. Reading an Internet text, on the

ZITS © ZITS PARTNERSHIP, KING FEATURES SYNDICATE.

> other hand, is like a frog jumping around a three-dimensional pond: It can be difficult to stand back from the text to see where you are as a whole. (p. 54)

The same holds true for software texts, so the evaluation task must include consideration of issues of the *dynamics* of text and the text's own ability to guide the learner through.

EVALUATING INTERNET TEXTS

Martha Rekrut (1999) emphasizes the need for teachers to "separate substance from smoke" on Web sites (p. 553) by visiting the sites to evaluate both their content and presentation and by seeking evaluative information. She and Caruso (1997) recommend the following:

1. Determine the expertise and capability of the site author.
2. Consider the reliability and scope of the content.
3. Determine if the site is free.
4. Check to see when the site was created and updated.
5. Assess the site quality and intent.

Numerous Web site evaluative resources are available. The Infopeople site (www.infopeople.org/resources/bkmk/select.html) provides a checklist for evaluating Internet resources that asks pointed questions related to the following:

- Authority of the originator
- Affiliation of the author/site
- Currency of the information
- Purpose for the information
- Intended audience for the information
- Comparison of site to other work, including non-Internet sources
- Conclusion/decision to bookmark

Many other sites offer similar criteria and procedures for evaluating Internet resources—for example, www.yahooligans.com. Figure 3.7 lists some of the online resources available for evaluating Internet sites and educational software. A number of these contain within them links to other evaluative resources.

FIGURE 3.7 *Resources for Evaluating Software and Internet Sites*

www.rtec.org/—The Regional Technology in Education Consortia. Provides many, many resources including links to other evaluation criteria and procedures.
www.iste.org/—International Society for Technology in Education. Technology standards and annotations of resources.
www.pcuser.com.au/—Reviews hot sites, vendors.
www.superkids.com/—SuperKids Educational Software Reviews: Reviews of children's software by parents, teachers, and kids.
www.worldvillage.com/—Software Reviews and Evaluations: Software reviews and evaluations by the Summit County Instructional Software Preview Center.
www.pt3.org—Preparing Tomorrow's Teachers for Technology site. Links to current project site, each of which links or lists evaluation resources.
www.Yahooligans.com—Teacher Resources provide information regarding acceptable use policy and evaluating websites.
www.clearinghouse.k12.ca.us/—The California Instructional Technology Clearinghouse. Provides evaluation of software and websites. Tied to California curriculum standards but is accessible to educators across the country.
www.infopeople.org/resources/bkmk/select.html—Provides an evaluation protocol for websites.
www.scout.cs.wisc.edu/scout/report—Provides a juried Internet surfing resource.

EVALUATING SOFTWARE

You will undoubtedly have occasion to select software for your students' use, either with the computer(s) in your classroom or in a school lab. Any number of issues must be addressed here, ranging from the capabilities of the hardware to use recently developed software, to the examination of how specific software contributes to and enhances students' learning in your subject area, to the *intent* of the software and your purposes for using it (e.g., Is the purpose to provide practice in a specific skill? Is it to guide students in thinking critically about issues or ideas? Is it to challenge students in problem solving of some kind?). You may or may not have much experience or knowledge about computer technology and possibilities for your teaching; if you don't, I recommend that you find someone who does or participate in workshops that may be available in your district or county, at a local university, or at professional conferences.

One approach is rating software using a checklist such as the one shown in Figure 3.8 on pp. 82–83 (adapted from Shade, Davis, & Perron, 1999). Shade et al. recommend a total score of at least 77 (out of a possible 110) for the software to be considered appropriate. You may not wish to hold to that standard always, but even when you don't, evaluation helps clarify the strengths and weaknesses of the program itself.

And finally, any number of online resources offer criteria and processes for evaluation of software. Here are a few I found:

- http://www.glencoe.come/sec/teachingtoday/educationupclose/phtml/30
- http://www.teachervision.fen.com/tv/resources/technology/evalsoft_index.html

FIGURE 3.8 *A Better Comprehensive Developmental Evaluation (ABCDE) Scale*
Adapted from Shade, Davis, and Perron (1999)

Student Usage and Content Features

Accommodates divergent thinking ______
Active learning emphasized ______
Age-appropriate concepts ______
Student can use independently ______
Student controlled interaction, pace ______
Student is agent of change ______
Student can start over at any time ______
Concrete representations function accurately ______
Discovery learning ______
Experimentation is possible ______
High performance ceiling ______
Instrinsically motivating ______

Lacks violence ______
Low entry ______

Makes use of unique computer media ______

Models a consistent and familiar world ______
Not skill drilling ______

Keyboard mastery not required ______
Process supersedes product ______

Simple and precise directions ______

Technical Features

Student can save and print work ______

Fast installation, set-up ______
Realistic sound effects, music ______

Realistic high-res graphics ______

Teacher Features

Animation other than reward ______
Can be customized ______
Student proof ______
Consistency of required responses ______
Constructive instructional feedback ______
Curriculum integration possible ______
Extended usability ______
No excessive intro or reward animation ______
Mixed gender and equity ______
No socially unacceptable behavior ______
Relevant educational content ______
Does not only portray stereotypic family styles ______

Does not exclusively portray traditional ability levels ______
Does not promote the desirability of one particular age group over another ______

Does not promote a single ethnic or racial group exclusively ______

Requires no particular cultural background ______

Supplemental to curriculum ______
Technical support information offered ______
User friendly manual ______
Multiple languages ______

Special Needs Bonus

Can adapt reinforcement individually ______
Built in scanning ______
Can be used with adaptable access software utilities ______

FIGURE 3.8 *continued*

Speech is clear, distinct	_____	Single-switch interface	_____
Screen layout is clear, clean	_____	Special keyboard, touch screen touch pad	_____
Fast processing speeds, minimal waiting	_____		
No distracting music, sounds; turn off, on	_____	2 points for each ✔ Minimum = 77 points	
Hot spot—icons are available	_____		
Intuitive interface	_____		

- http://www.owlet.rice.edu/~ling417/guide.html
- http://www.seamonkey.ed.asu.edu/emc300/software/evalform.html

Many, if not most, professional journals now have more articles and/or recurring columns focused on evaluation of electronic texts in classrooms.

SOME FINAL WORDS ABOUT EVALUATION OF INSTRUCTIONAL TEXTS

Information about instructional texts—how difficult, interesting, useful, and appropriate they are—will be vital to you throughout your teaching career. You will use this information often in selecting texts and other materials and in deciding how they should be used in your classroom. Use one or more of the instruments in this chapter to find out about the textbooks, software, and on-line sites already chosen for the classes you teach. Consider how the results of the readability formula, checklist, or Cloze test correspond to your initial impressions. Don't forget to ask students what they like and don't like about the texts. Undoubtedly, you will discover some discrepancies between your prior impressions and the results of your review; that's fine. It only demonstrates that those of us who are experts in any given field are sometimes not very good at choosing textbooks and other materials for novices in that same field. Armed with that knowledge, you are sensitized to many of the important issues involved in evaluating instructional materials and much more likely to consider those issues when you become responsible for that selection yourself.

WHAT THIS CHAPTER MEANS TO YOU

1. Just like Jameela Moore, you will have many opportunities to serve on textbook adoption committees and purchase and use books, software, Internet resources, and other materials for your classroom. You will be successful at this to the extent you are able to choose vibrant, rich, readable, and inviting traditional and electronic texts.

2. Various evaluative instruments and approaches provide important information in the text selection processes. You will find it helpful to use several ways to evaluate text, including asking students their opinion, when you adopt textbooks and supplementary materials for your classroom.

3. Evaluation of electronic texts represents an ongoing challenge as on-line and software texts and technology change. You can find many resources to assist in this process, on-line and through professional reading and development.

DOUBLE ENTRY JOURNAL

Summarize your current understanding of the issues surrounding evaluation of instructional materials. Which one of them do you expect to be most important in your teaching? How will you address this issue?

FEATURE *What Goes in My Portfolio?*

Use at least three of the instruments/approaches featured in this chapter—at least one of which involves students—to evaluate either a hard copy text or an Internet/software text. Summarize what you found in your evaluation and make recommendations as to how and/or whether this text should be used.

RECOMMENDED SOURCES

*Alvermann, D. E., & Moore, D. W. (1991). Secondary school reading. In R. Barr, M. L. Kamil, P. Mosenthal, & P. D. Pearson (Eds.), *Handbook of reading research* (vol. II, pp. 951–953). New York: Longman.

Applebee, A. N., Langer, J. A., & Mullis, I. V. S. (1987). *Literature and U.S. history: The instructional experience and factual knowledge of high school juniors.* Princeton, NJ: Educational Testing Service.

*Baldwin, R. S. (1986). When was the last time you bought a textbook just for kicks? In E. K. Dishner, T. W. Bean, J. E. Readence, & D. W. Moore (Eds.), *Reading in the content areas* (2nd ed., pp. 323–328). Dubuque, IA: Kendall/Hunt.

Bernstein, H. T. (1985). The new politics of textbook adoption. *Phi Delta Kappan, 66*, 463–466.

Bruce, B., Rubin, A., & Starr, K. (1981). *Why readability formulas fail.* Champaign, IL: Center for the Study of Reading.

*Caruso, C. (1997). Before you cite a site. *Educational Leadership, 55*(3), 24–25.

*Cited in text.

Chall, J. S. (1988). The beginning years. In B. L. Zakaluk & S. J. Samuels (Eds.), *Readability: Its past, present, and future* (pp. 2–13). Newark, DE: International Reading Association.

Dale, E., & Chall, J. S. (1948). A formula for predicting readability. *Educational Research Bulletin, 27*, 11–20, 37–54.

Dolch, W. W. (1928). Vocabulary burden. *Journal of Educational Research, 17*, 170–188.

Duffy, T. M. (1985). Readability formulas: What's the use? In T. M. Duffy & R. Waller (Eds.), *Designing usable texts*. New York: Academic Press.

*Farr, R., & Tulley, M. A. (1985). Do adoption committees perpetuate mediocre textbooks? *Phi Delta Kappan, 66*, 467–471.

Flesch, R. F. (1948). A new readability yardstick. *Journal of Applied Psychology, 32*, 221–233.

*Fry, E. B. (1968). A readability formula that saves time. *Journal of Reading, 11*, 513–516.

*Fry, E. B. (1977). Fry's readability graph: Clarifications, validity, and extension to level 17. *Journal of Reading, 21*, 242–252.

*Fry, E. B. (1989). Readability formulas—maligned but valid. *Journal of Reading, 32*, 292–296.

Garner, R., Gillingham, M. G., & White, C. S. (1989). Effects of "seductive details" on macroprocessing and microprocessing in adults and children. *Cognition and Instruction, 6*, 41–57.

Goetz, E. T., & Sadoski, M. (1995). The perils of seduction: Distracting details or incomprehensible abstractions? *Reading Research Quarterly, 30*(5), 500–511.

Goodlad, J. I. (1984). *A place called school*. New York: McGraw-Hill.

Gray, W. S., & Leary, B. E. (1935). *What makes a book readable, with special reference to adults of limited reading ability, an initial study*. Chicago: University of Chicago Press.

*Irwin, J. W., & Davis, C. A. (1980). Assessing readability: The checklist approach. *Journal of Reading, 24*, 124–130.

Klare, G. R. (1976). A second look at the validity of readability formulas. *Journal of Reading Behavior, 8*, 129–152.

Klare, G. R. (1989). Understanding the readability of content area texts. In D. Lapp, J. Flood, & N. Farnan (Eds.), *Content area reading and learning: Instructional strategies* (pp. 34–42). Englewood Cliffs, NJ: Prentice-Hall.

*Leinwand, G. (1994). *The pageant of world history*. Needham, MA: Prentice-Hall.

Lively, B. A., & Pressey, S. L. (1923). A method for measuring the "vocabulary burden" of textbooks. *Educational Administration and Supervision, 9*, 389–398.

Lorge, I. (1939). Predicting reading difficulty of selections for children. *Elementary English Review, 16*, 229–233.

Manchester, W. (1983). *Winston Churchill: The last lion*. Boston: Little, Brown.

*Manchester, W. (1988). *Winston Spencer Churchill: Alone, 1932–1940*. Boston: Little, Brown.

*McLaughlin, G. H. (1969). SMOG grading—a new readability formula. *Journal of Reading, 12*, 639–646.

*Moore, P. (1999). Reading and writing the Internet. In J. Handcock (Ed.), *Teaching literacy using information technology: A collection of articles from the Australian literacy educators' association*. Newark, DE: International Reading Association.

*Pugh, S. L., & Garcia, J. (1990). Portraits in Black: Establishing African American identity through nonfiction books. *Journal of Reading, 34*, 20–25.

Rankin, E. F., & Culhane, J. W. (1969). Comparable cloze and multiple-choice comprehension test scores. *Journal of Reading, 13*, 193–198.

*Rekrut, M. D. (1999). Using the Internet in classroom instruction. *Journal of Reading, 42*(7), 546–557.

Sadoski, M., & Paivio, A. (1994). A dual coding view of imagery and verbal processes in reading comprehension. In R. B. Ruddell, M. R. Ruddell, & H. Singer (Eds.), *Theoretical models and processes of reading* (4th ed., pp. 582–601). Newark, DE: International Reading Association.

*Saul, E. W., & Dieckman, D. (2005). Choosing and using information trade books. *Reading Research Quarterly 40*(4), 502–513.

Seligman, K. (2006, May 14). Young and wired. *San Francisco Chronicle Magazine*, 5–9, 15.

Sewall, G. T. (1988). American history textbooks: Where do we go from here? *Phi Delta Kappan, 69*, 552–558.

*Shade, D. D., Davis, B. C., & Perron, K. (1999). *A Better Comprehensive Developmental Evaluation (ABCDE) Scale*. Newark, DE: University of Delaware.

Shepherd, D. (1982). *Comprehensive high school reading methods*. Columbus, OH: Merrill.

*Singer, H. (1992). Friendly texts: Description and criteria. In E. K. Dishner, T. W. Bean, J. E. Readence, & D. W. Moore (Eds.), *Reading in the content areas* (3rd ed., pp. 155–168). Dubuque, IA: Kendall/Hunt.

*Taylor, W. L. (1953). Cloze procedures: A new tool for measuring readability. *Journalism Quarterly*, *30*, 360–368

*Weaver, C. A., III, & Kintsch, W. (1991). Expository text. In R. Barr, M. L. Kamil, P. B. Mosenthal, & P. D. Pearson (Eds.), *Handbook of reading research* (vol. II, pp. 230–245). New York: Longman.

Zakaluk, B. L., & Samuels, S. J. (1988). Toward a new approach to predicting text comprehensibility. In B. L. Zakuluk & S. J. Samuels (Eds.), *Readability: Its past, present & future* (pp. 121–144). Newark, DE: International Reading Association.

C H A P T E R 4

Comprehension Instruction in Content Areas

D O U B L E E N T R Y J O U R N A L

You've heard the term reading comprehension many times. List ideas or concepts you associate with reading comprehension and ways you think we learn to comprehend. Now think of your most difficult subject area. How might teachers have made it easier for you to understand this material? How do you suppose teachers teach comprehension?

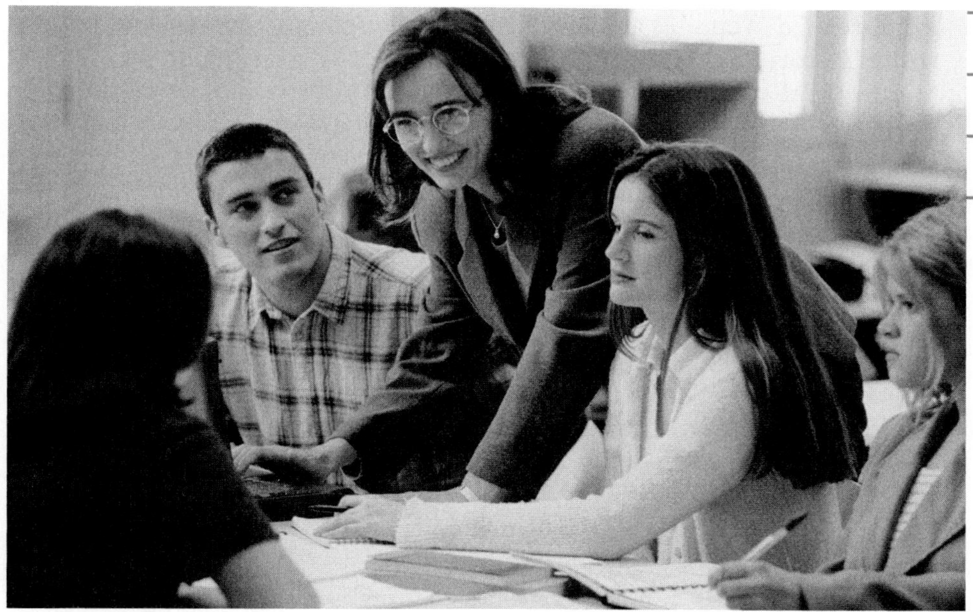

PIXTAL/Age Fotostock America, Inc.

Dave Lowery stares out the open classroom window. Sixth period. He's bored. And to make everything worse, it's a beautiful autumn day. He'd rather be sitting under that tree outside the window, or doing anything outside, than making it through another world history class. The drone of class discussion hums on the periphery of his attention, but he couldn't care less. Ms. Dahlmann is right in the middle of her lecture and about ready to review last night's homework. He didn't read the chapter and he didn't answer any of the questions, so he couldn't join in the discussion if he wanted to. What he did do was spend last night playing video games, even digging out *Warcraft III—Reign of Chaos* for old time's sake. The new games are incredible—so complex that it takes him hours, days, weeks to figure out strategies and codes. He's nearly obsessed with finding game-related Web sites and playing games at night and on weekends. He wishes history class could be so interesting.

It's not that he can't read; he can, and he always gets decent scores on the yearly reading tests. It's just that he's not interested in history, and all the names and places and events are hard to keep track of. Plus, the world history book is boring and the chapters are long, and all they do in class is talk, talk, talk. Even when he tries to read his homework, he often gets to the end of a page or a chapter and can't remember one thing he read. Answering the questions is just another boring assignment.

• • •

PART I: *The Comprehension Process and Comprehension Instruction*

The most common academic goal of reading is text comprehension—the construction of meaning that in some way corresponds to the author's intended meaning. (The fact of individual differences in both prior knowledge and stance in relationship to text suggests that this correspondence is never exact or identical from reader to reader.) In school, however, reading has three additional goals:

1. **Subject Matter Learning.** Students read not only to understand text but to extend their knowledge in subject areas as well.
2. **Increasing Reading Skills.** At each grade level, students are expected to become better readers and to read increasingly difficult text.
3. **Knowledge Application.** Throughout the middle and secondary grades, students are expected to apply knowledge constructed from their reading of subject text.

Think about this for a moment: It is no small thing we ask students to do. We expect them, from their very earliest reading experiences, to understand the author's intended meaning; at the same time, we expect them to learn more in each and every subject area taught (whether they like it or not), to become progressively sophisticated readers and writers (arriving at some mythical level of "maturity" around the eleventh or twelfth grade), and, finally, to apply newly constructed content knowledge in novel situations. We expect these accomplishments of all students and are often quite vocal in our complaints when we believe that expectations are not being met. Unfortunately, we just as often overlook the fact that what we expect of students—comprehending, learning, developing reading proficiency, and applying knowledge—are interrelated academic abilities. To focus on one ability and exclude the others is to hinder progress in all. The obvious counterpoint is that to develop students' abilities in one area, instruction must address all.

In the past, much of the comprehension "instruction" in secondary schools was little more than teachers *telling* students to read and understand ("Read Chapter 3 and be prepared to discuss it." "Read pages 54 through 67 and answer the questions on page 68."). Long a tradition in secondary schooling, this approach today seems more than a little shortsighted, especially when viewed in light of the heavy expectations we hold for student learning and development of literacy skills and abilities. Simply *telling* students to read and understand assumes students will be able to do all that we expect them to do without our help. Further, it equates *telling* someone to do something with *teaching* her or him how to do it, and such an equation is simply not valid.

If middle school and secondary school students are to meet the expectations held by teachers, parents, the school, and society as a whole, they need *real* instruction—instruction that guides their progress through text, promotes learning, teaches them how to become better readers and writers, and provides adequate support for application of new learning. That is what this chapter is about: first, to examine comprehension as it relates to our agreed-on view of the reading process (or, if you will, the view presented by this book), and second, to present instructional strategies compatible with both that theoretical stance and the criteria for real instruction—instruction that guides students through text, promotes subject matter learning, develops reading proficiency, and fosters knowledge application.

CENTERPIECE LESSON PLAN

Before we get into a larger discussion of comprehension and instructional strategies, I want to direct your attention to the **Centerpiece Lesson Plan** for this chapter. This lesson plan is an application of two important instructional strategies in the chapter, the Directed Reading-Thinking Activity (DR-TA) and the Group Mapping Activity (GMA). You will see Centerpiece Lesson Plans in other chapters as well.

I'm putting this lesson plan here in the chapter so that before you read about literacy processes and instructional practice you can see how specific instructional strategies may be applied in real classrooms. In this particular chapter, I want you to see how guided comprehension before, during, and after reading looks in advance of our discussion about the comprehension process and recommended instruction. Later, as you read about DR-TA and GMA, I encourage you to come back to this lesson plan to see again how the strategies were adapted and applied.

Please note the following elements in this Centerpiece Lesson Plan (and other lesson plans in the book):

- Identification of what **lesson** is being taught, the **course and grade level** the plan is for, and the **materials** needed for the lesson.
- Identification of LESSON OBJECTIVES that state clearly what students are expected to **know** and **be able to do** when the lesson is over.
- Identification of CONTENT STANDARDS associated with each lesson objective. I use standards from my state and, upon occasion, from national professional organization; you have state and/or district standards that are parallel.
- Statement of LESSON PROCEDURES written in such a way that a knowledgeable substitute could pick up the lesson and teach it essentially the way the teacher intended.

- Identification of LESSON ASSESSMENTS that directly reflect the lesson objectives Lesson assessments include teacher observation during class, as well as grades given for homework and other assignments to demonstrate student mastery of the objectives. Notice how the observational assessment evaluates both content learning and literacy development (in this lesson, comprehension of text).
- Provisions for guiding students before, during, and after the learning event. In this chapter, we focus on guiding students' comprehension of text; we'll have different emphases in other chapters, but lesson plans in all chapters will have the before, during, and after procedural elements. Many people identify this sequence as **Into, Through**, and **Beyond** (in fact, many district require new teachers to develop lesson plans using the Into, Through, and Beyond structure).

Let's turn now to the Centerpiece Lesson Plan for comprehension.

DR-TA, GMA CENTERPIECE LESSON PLAN, *Mathematics*

Lesson: Solving Multi-Step Equations
Course/Grade: Algebra I, 9th Grade
Materials: Algebra I book, paper, pencils

LESSON OBJECTIVES (WITH CONTENT STANDARDS)

Upon completion of this lesson, students will be able to

- Combine like terms (Standard 4.0—students simplify expressions before solving linear equations in one variable, such as $3(2x - 5) + 4(x - 2) = 12$).
- Use properties, such as distribution, additive, inverse, etc. (Standard 1.0—students identify and use the arithmetic properties).
- Solve multi-step equations (Standard 5.0—students solve multi-step problems, including word problems, involving linear equations in one variable and provide justification for each step).

LESSON PROCEDURES

Before Reading: Into—DR-TA

1. Have students silently read the chapter title ("Solving Multi-Step Equations") and objectives for the section. *Ask*: What do you think this lesson will be about? Why do you say that? *As discussion unfolds, follow up by asking* What do you think it means to "combine like terms"? What do you think "multi-step" means in this context? What do you think will be expected of you when we finish this lesson? Why?
2. *Say*: Before we get into solving multi-step equations, let's review.

3. Write x + 5 = 7 on board. *Ask*: What do we do to solve for x? Why do we subtract 5? Why do we do it to both sides? *Check for understanding. Give examples where addition, multiplication, and division are needed to solve. Mention* additive inverse *and other inverse relationships as appropriate.*

During Reading: Through

4. *Say*: Now read the first example problem and its explanation. What do you think we need to do? Why?
5. Write 4x + 1 = 17 on board. *Ask*: What do you think we do first? Why? Work with the person next to you to figure out how to solve for x. *Have teams come to the board and show/explain the steps of their solution. As needed, probe*: Why did we subtract 1 first? Why couldn't we divide by 4 first?
6. *Say*: Now look at the second example and its explanation. Write 4(x + 1) = 17 on board. *Ask*: What is different about this equation? (*Make sure first equation with solutions steps is still on the board.*) What do we need to do first? Why? *Go through the solution process getting student input on steps or thinking out loud as you work. Ask:* Why didn't we get the same answer for this equation?
7. *Say*: Now look at the next problem. Write on board 3(x – 2) + 6 = 12. *Say*: What is new here? Work with your partner to solve this problem. *Have some teams show and explain their work. Highlight both ways to solve problem.*
8. *Say*: Okay, last example. Write on board 5x – 9 = 3x + 1. *Ask*: How is this problem different? What do we need to do first? Why? Then what? *Work through the problem with students giving the steps.*

After Reading: Beyond—GMA

9. *Say*: With your partner create a map or visual representation that will help you understand and remember how to do multi-step equations. You may create your map any way you wish—there is no right or wrong way. Be prepared to tell us about your map. You have about five minutes to do your map.
10. *Say*: Hold your maps us so we can all see them. Who'd like to share their map? *As students share, draw out their responses. Probe:* What made you decide to put that information there? How does the map help you remember how to do multi-step equations? What are the really important ideas on your map?
11. *Say*: Now it's time for more practice. Write these five problems on the board: 4n + 3n + 5 = 12; 5y – 3 + 2y = 39; 6(2x – 4) = 36; 2(4z – 4) – 3 = 21; 4x + 6 + 3x = 2x + 31. *Say*: You may work with your partner or alone. Be sure to use your map or the textbook to help you solve. Make sure that both partners have a copy of your map.
12. *Say*: Homework for tomorrow: These five problems plus the even-numbered problems in your book. Select one problem and write in sentence form the steps you took to solve it. Write your explanation for someone who has never seen a multi-step equation before. Be sure to use your map and the book to help you do the homework. We will grade the problems in class, and I will collect your maps and your written explanations.

LESSON ASSESSMENTS

13. Observational Assessment—During discussion, spot check the class, partners, and individuals; are they getting it? When partners/individuals work, move through room to see what students are writing; offer assistance/explanations as needed. Pay close attention to student explanations and their maps.
14. Homework Assessment—Grade homework and record grades. Collect written explanations and maps. Review these to check for understandings and misunderstandings. Give written feedback on each; record completion of each.

THE COMPREHENSION PROCESS

In Chapter 2, we described reading as the act of constructing meaning while transacting with text. The meaning one makes (or what one comprehends) from text during this transaction is a result of the linkages one makes between prior knowledge and previous experience and the information available in text; one's stance in relationship to the text; and immediate, remembered, or anticipated social interaction and communication. Let's now elaborate on that description of the reading process. Essentially, what happens is this: The reader approaches text with prior information about a topic, assumptions about both the text itself and the appropriate Discourse to engage, and a reason for reading. What the reader already knows can range from nothing (in which case, little, if anything, will be comprehended) to total knowledge of a given topic (and there are those who would argue that this reader will comprehend nothing *new*). Most often, however, readers begin knowing something well within these two extremes. Reasons for reading are similarly variable, with an unspecified number of possible affective, cognitive, social, and practical overlays. For example, whether the reader's purpose for reading is intrinsic or extrinsic—internally or externally imposed—is one; the reader's prior success in reading such text is another; others are the degree to which the reader views the material as useful, interesting, important, and so on.

With this background information and reason(s) for reading, the reader enters text with certain predictions, or expectations, about the text: whether it will be known information or relatively new, easy to read or difficult, interesting or dull, useful or not, and so forth. The reader then progresses by sampling text, making intertextual linkages and new predictions based on this sample, resampling, and confirming or adjusting linkages and predictions in light of new information. The amount of redundancy present in text—elements and information already known to the reader—controls to some extent the rate of progress and focus of reader energy and attention.

So, for example, the more one knows about the topic under discussion, and the more skilled one is in the Discourse appropriate for this text, the greater the likelihood that reading will be evenly paced, uninterrupted, and relatively rapid. On the other hand, when the reader knows little about the topic, chances are that reading will be slower, somewhat erratic, and interrupted by "thinking" pauses that provide the reader time to process new language and information and/or consider metacognitively how much sense he or she is constructing.

As reading continues, all of the elements of comprehension—prior knowledge and previous experience, information available in text, reader stance, and social interactions—become impossibly intertwined. New information merges with old; reasons for reading change, waxing and waning with value attached to what is in the text; prior knowledge shades or influences the meaning one makes of certain portions of text; previous discussion and/or anticipated social interchange shade interpretations; and on and on. The point is, comprehension is both cyclical and cumulative; it is driven by a predict—read (sample text)—repredict—resample cycle that seems to gather speed and strength and force as it continues successfully forward. (The opposite is also true—the cycle very rapidly loses speed and strength and force when progress is hindered.) As I mentioned in Chapter 2, its complexity is mind-boggling.

Given this complexity and the dynamic aspect of reader–text transactions, it becomes important to get a sense of how successful readers approach and process text if we are to assist students in understanding subject texts. Pearson, Roehler, Dole, and Duffy (1990) summarized a body of comprehension research about what strategies good readers use to construct full, rich meaning from text. From the many studies reviewed has emerged a profile of proficient readers—Pearson and his associates call them "expert" or "thoughtful" readers—that increases our understanding of what happens during successful reader–text transactions. According to Pearson and colleagues, thoughtful readers:

- Constantly search for connections between what they know and what they encounter as new information in the text.
- Constantly monitor the adequacy of the models of text meaning they build.
- Take steps to repair faulty comprehension once they realize that they have failed to understand something.
- Learn very early to distinguish important from less important ideas in the text they read.
- Are especially adept at synthesizing information within and across texts and reading experiences.
- Make inferences during and after reading to achieve a full, integrated understanding of what they read.
- Sometimes consciously (almost always unconsciously) ask questions of themselves, the authors they encounter, and the texts they read.

In 1995 Michael Pressley and Peter Afflerback summarized the results of over 40 studies in which readers read text and told researchers what they were doing and thinking as they read. They found a pattern of behaviors that "mature readers" use that is quite similar to those identified for thoughtful readers. According to Pressley and Afflerback, mature readers use the following processes flexibly and selectively as they read (cited in Pressley, 2000, pp. 550–551):

- Being aware of their purposes for reading
- Overviewing text before reading
- Reading selectively
- Making associations between new ideas and prior knowledge
- Evaluating and revising predictions as reading progresses
- Revising prior knowledge that is inconsistent with ideas in text
- Figuring out meanings of new words

- Underlining, rereading, making notes
- Interpreting text through imaginary conversations with the author
- Evaluating the quality of the text
- Reviewing after reading
- Thinking about how to use/apply the information in the text

To these profiles Scott Paris, Marjorie Lipson, and Karen Wixon (1994) add their notion of "strategic reading"—that is, reading in which the reader not only knows what to do but also knows how to do it and when to do what. They label these kinds of knowledge "Declarative" (knowing what to do), "Procedural" (knowing how to do it), and "Conditional" (knowing when to do what). They emphasize that skilled readers know the purpose of the task at hand and the options for completing it successfully; less skilled readers are often unaware of both (p. 796). I would add that the profiles above of thoughtful readers and mature readers, suggest strategic readers: readers who have a wide repertoire of available actions that they use flexibly and effectively to comprehend written text—in other words, readers who know what to do to be effective, how to do it, and when to do what.

GUIDED COMPREHENSION

Clearly, an important goal for all students is that they become thoughtful, mature, strategic readers of content texts. And one of the most powerful ways to help them to get there is to teach in such a way that they develop the characteristics of thoughtful, mature, strategic readers. Instruction that guides students' comprehension of text while teaching content knowledge does just that. Thus, the goals of the instructional strategies in this chapter are focused on guiding comprehension; just as important, however, these instructional practices assist students in learning and applying content knowledge as well.

THE DIRECTED READING-THINKING ACTIVITY (DR-TA)

The DR-TA was introduced by Russell Stauffer in 1969 to develop higher level thinking while reading, and over the years has received considerable attention as a recommended instructional strategy. I'm placing it first in the chapter because it is such a sturdy instructional approach, one that is adaptable for endless varieties of content areas and texts. You've already seen in the Centerpiece Lesson Plan how the DR-TA can be used in mathematics class (you may want to review that now); before we are through you will see a lesson example, a lesson demonstration, and lesson materials for using DR-TA in science, English, and the social studies.

The key element of DR-TA is prediction. The teacher structures a DR-TA lesson in such a way that students (1) make predictions about what they're going to read, (2) read to see if the predictions were accurate/useful, (3) reconcile their predictions with what they read, (4) revise or add predictions, and (5) read again.

Frank Smith makes a strong argument for DR-TA and DR-TA-like instruction that focuses on students' predictions and subsequent reading of text:

> Now at last prediction and comprehension can be tied together. Prediction means asking questions, and comprehension means being able to get some of

> the questions answered. Comprehension, basically, is the absence of confusion. As we read, as we listen to someone talking, as we go through life, we are constantly asking questions, then we comprehend. The person who does not comprehend how to repair a bicycle is the one who cannot ask and find answers to such questions as "Which of these nuts and bolts goes where?" at appropriate times. And the person who does not comprehend a book or newspaper article is the one who cannot find relevant questions and answers concerning the next part of the text. There is a *flow* to comprehension, with new questions constantly being generated from the answers that are sought. (1994, p. 19)

You have already seen a lesson plan for using DR-TA in an Algebra I class. Reproduced below is a section of the first page of a chapter of a physics text, *Physics: Its Methods and Meanings* (Taffel, 1992). Following that is an example of how DR-TA can be used in a science lesson with this text.

TEXTBOOK EXCERPT *Physics*

4 Vectors, Force, and Motion

AIMS

1. To note that energy is often associated with matter in motion and that motion is controlled by forces.
2. To learn how to represent forces and motion by vectors.
3. To learn how to obtain the combined effect of two or more vectors acting upon the same point of a body.
4. To understand how a vector can act in directions other than its own.

VECTORS AND SCALARS

4-1 CHANGE, MOTION, AND FORCE

Practically all of the changes we see in the world about us are the result of motion. Day and night are caused by the rotation of the earth on its axis. The winds and their effects are caused by the motion of air. The conversion of raw materials into the products we need in everyday living is brought about by various motions. These include transporting the materials to factories, combining them, shaping them into finished products, and transporting the products to market. Change and motion go hand in hand.

When a car stalls, it must be pushed to get it going. When the engine is running, it is the engine which pushes the car forward. In either case, a force is being used to change the state of the car from rest to motion. In order to make the car slow down or to stop altogether, the brakes are applied. Again, a force is being applied to change the motion of the car. These examples illustrate that motion is controlled or changed by means of force.

4-2 DISPLACEMENT IS A VECTOR

Motion generally involves a change of position of the object being moved. A change of position is called a displacement. Suppose a body is moved from a point A to a second point B 10 meters to the northeast of A. How shall we describe this displacement? It is not enough to say that the body has moved 10 meters from A. Its final position could then be any point on the circumference of a circle centered on A and having a 10-meter radius. To state exactly how the position of the body changed, we must also state in what direction it was moved. Thus, the displacement from A to B is described as one of 10 meters northeast.

DR-TA LESSON EXAMPLE *Physics*

To initiate DR-TA instruction, the teacher asks students to cover everything on the page except the chapter title:

> **4 Vectors, Force, and Motion**

The teacher then asks, "Based on this title, what do you think the chapter will be about?" Following each student response, the teacher probes for support (if it has not spontaneously been stated): "What makes you say that" or "Why?" Then the teacher asks students to look at the aims statements below the chapter title:

> AIMS
> 1. To note that energy is often associated with matter in motion and that motion is controlled by forces.
> 2. To learn how to represent forces and motion by vectors.
> 3. To learn how to obtain the combined effect of two or more vectors acting upon the same point of a body.
> 4. To understand how a vector can act in directions other than its own.

At this point, the teacher encourages more predictions ("What do you think we're going to learn?") and evaluations of logic and thinking ("Why?"; "What makes you say that?") Students are then asked to read the first three paragraphs of the chapter:

> VECTORS AND SCALARS
>
> 4-1 CHANGE, MOTION, AND FORCE
>
> Practically all of the changes we see in the world about us are the result of motion. Day and night are caused by the rotation of the earth on its axis. The winds and their effects are caused by the motion of air. The conversion of raw materials into the products we need in everyday living is brought about by various motions. These include transporting the materials to factories, combining them, shaping them into finished products, and transporting the products to market. Change and motion go hand in hand.
>
> When a car stalls, it must be pushed to get it going. When the engine is running, it is the engine which pushes the car forward. In either case, a force is being used to change the state of the car from rest to motion. In order to make the car slow down or to stop altogether, the brakes are applied. Again, a force is being applied to change the motion of the car. These examples illustrate that motion is controlled or changed by means of force.
>
> 4-2 DISPLACEMENT IS A VECTOR
>
> Motion generally involves a change of position of the object being moved. A change of position is called a displacement. Suppose a body is moved from a point A to a second point B 10 meters to the northeast of A. How shall we describe this displacement? It is not enough to say that the body has moved 10 meters from A. Its final position could then be any point on the circumference of a circle centered on A and having a 10-meter radius. To state exactly how the position of the body changed, we must also state in what direction it was moved. Thus, the displacement from A to B is described as one of 10 meters northeast.

Discussion continues, with increasingly specific discussion of content: "What other ideas do you think we'll find in this chapter?" "Why?" "What do you think we'll know when we're through?" "Why?" "Anything else?"

Next, the teacher directs students to read larger sections of text, stop at appropriate points to evaluate previous predictions, draw conclusions, examine and possibly revise logic, and make new predictions. The lesson then continues with the activities and exercises that support content learning.

The DR-TA is relatively simple to do, but it almost needs to be seen to be understood. So I'm going to demonstrate a DR-TA for an English class lesson using a short story called "The Splendid Outcast" (Markham, 1987). I have chosen to use a sample demonstration of the DR-TA for several reasons. First, in my mind, the DR-TA is a very important instructional strategy: it clearly replicates the predict-sample text-repredict-resample process we discussed earlier as a critical component of comprehension; it encourages the behaviors of thoughtful, mature, and strategic readers; and, with its emphasis on prediction and discussion, it stimulates full, rich understanding of text.

Second, I believe the DR-TA is worth knowing a lot about because it is adaptable to many different text styles as well as to other media. Two of the best DR-TA lessons I've ever seen were one done in a music appreciation class as students listened to a piece of music for the first time, and one in a homemaking class to teach students how to use a dressmaking pattern.

Third, the DR-TA is particularly useful for accommodating the wide cultural, language, and literacy differences students bring to secondary classrooms and for supporting all students in constructing new knowledge. Further, it encourages students to construct meaning collaboratively, and it stimulates a great deal of student talk and verbal interchange, thus bringing into the classroom the real-life transactions and mutual sharing of knowledge and ability that are characteristic of everyday learning. Most importantly, the wide-ranging, rich classroom discussion of a DR-TA exposes speakers with limited English to the very language they are trying to learn. (Of course, language-rich classrooms are just as beneficial for the most accomplished language users as well.)

And finally, the presentation of an extended lesson here allows me to illustrate the use of four different instructional strategies—two in this chapter, one in Chapter 5 (Vocabulary Learning in Content Areas), and one in Chapter 8 (Writing Across the Curriculum). After the demonstration, I discuss the DR-TA further and show other ways it may be applied to various subject area texts.

DR-TA LESSON DEMONSTRATION *English*

Setting: Senior English Class *Topic:* Short Story

Teacher: I'm giving each of you a blank sheet of paper that I will call your "cover sheet." Open your books to page 34 and cover everything except the title and author of the story.

> THE SPLENDID OUTCAST
>
> by
>
> Beryl Markham

Teacher: With a title like that, what do you think this story will be about?

Student: About a person who's doing something that's not particularly acceptable, or maybe something outside the ordinary. But something that's exciting.

T: Why do you say that?

S1: Well, because I know who Beryl Markham is.

T: Who is Beryl Markham?

S1: If I recall, she's famous aviator from the turn of the [last] century and was a great flier and lover of the African outdoors . . . a horse trainer. She was also a horse trainer.

T: Yes, she was a horse trainer. And she's a bit later than turn of the century—more like in [the twentieth] century. Yes, what were you going to say?

S2: I was thinking it was somebody who was outside of the social clique but doing quite well on their own.

T: Why?

S2: Because of the word *splendid.*

T: *Splendid* in the title. Okay. That's an interesting idea. What else? Does anyone know this story? Any other ideas?

S3: I was thinking of an eccentric who was really having a good time at it.

T: An eccentric who was having a good time of it! That sounds like fun. Any other ideas?

S4: I think that *splendid* might mean that someone else admired this outcast. This outcast doesn't care whether he's an outcast or not.

T: All right. Move your cover sheet so you can read just the first paragraph.

> The stallion was named after a star, and when he fell from his particular heaven, it was easy enough for people to say that he had been named too well. People like to see stars fall, but in the case of Rigel, it was of greater importance to me. To me and to one other—to a little man with shabby cuffs and a wilted cap that rested over eyes made mild by something more than time.

T: (After students read.) Now what do you think?

S1: It's about the horse.

T: All right, it's about a horse. What else?

S1: Well, he used to be well known, but something's happened.

T: What do you think it might be?

S1: Injury?

T: It could be.

S1: Like a racehorse.

T: Certainly. Any other ideas?

S2: He had some kind of connection to this little guy. Maybe the guy was a jockey or somebody else that had been connected with him for a while and something that happened to the horse had an impact on this guy.

T: Why do you suggest that he might have been a jockey or might be a jockey?

S2: Because it said "little man" and I know jockeys are little.

T: All right. Okay. Any other ideas? Read the next four paragraphs.

> It was Newmarket, in England, where, since Charles I instituted the first cup race, a kind of court has been held for the royalty of the turf. Men of all classes come to Newmarket for the races and for the December sales. They come from everywhere—some to bet, some to buy or sell, and some merely to offer homage to the resplendent peers of the Stud Book, for the sport of kings may, after all, be the pleasure of every man.
>
> December can be bitterly cold in England, and this December was. There was frozen sleet on buildings and on trees, and I remember that the huge Newmarket track lay on the downs below the village like a noose of diamonds on a tarnished mat. There was a festive spirit everywhere, but it was somehow lost on me. I had come to buy new blood for my stable in Kenya, and since my stable was my living, I came as serious buyers do, with figures in my mind and caution in my heart. Horses are hard to judge at best, and the thought of putting your hoarded pounds behind that judgement makes it harder still.
>
> I sat close on the edge of the auction ring and held my breath from time to time as the bidding soared. I held it because the casual mention of ten thousand guineas in payment for a horse or for anything else seemed to me wildly beyond the realm of probable things. For myself, I had five hundred pounds to spend and, as I waited for Rigel to be shown, I remember that I felt uncommonly maternal about each pound. I waited for Rigel because I had come six thousand miles to buy him, nor was I apprehensive lest anyone should take him from me; he was an outcast.
>
> Rigel had a pedigree that looked backward and beyond the pedigrees of many Englishmen—and Rigel had a brilliant record. By all odds, he should have brought ten thousand guineas at the sale, but I knew he wouldn't, for he had killed a man.

T: (After students read.) Now what do you think?

S1: The writer is wanting to buy this horse who is an outcast. That's real clear from it. I wish I knew the difference between guineas and pounds. That would be helpful.

T: Yes. I don't really know the difference. I know what pounds are. I don't think guineas are used in the British monetary system anymore, but I don't know. I can't answer it. Anybody know? All right. We'll hang on to that and look it up. What else? What do you think?

S2: This horse is really special. She's come six thousand miles to buy him. Breed him, I guess.

T: Okay. What else?

S3: I get the impression that his price is going to be lower. I'm not sure of the exact cost.

T: The horse?

S3: Rigel. Because she (or he) is not worried about anybody getting him.

S4: Either not worried or has enough money that he doesn't have to.

T: Right. (Beryl Markham is a woman, by the way.)

S4: Right. But I thought in the story it might be a character.

T: I would imagine because she was a horse trainer. . .

S4: That it's autobiographical.

T: Yes. That she's speaking of herself. Okay. Anything else? The comment that you made about Rigel being cheaper. Why would that be?

S3: He probably was once a good runner. And he probably had some kind of accident or injury or something happened that made him not a good runner. My guess is that there might be a genetic weakness.

S4: No one dares to buy him unless they have somebody they think is heaven-sent who is going to take care of this horse.

T: Why?

S1: Because of the killings, and he's just impossible to take care of. In the back of my mind, though, she's watching this little man who she thought was probably a jockey, so I'm thinking that he figures very closely in the story as somebody in her future with this horse.

T: Okay.

The class continues reading as the story unfolds to reveal that the storyteller and the little man do, indeed, become rival bidders for Rigel. Both, however, are clearly short on funds. In the meantime, Rigel becomes wildly uncontrollable as he is being shown for auction by the stable hands working at the sale. The stable hands are frozen into inaction by Rigel's raging presence; the little man enters the ring and approaches the flailing horse.

T: Now what do you think?

S1: Maybe she'll let him have Rigel because of her admiration for him or because he really won him. He's the only one with courage to approach him.

T: All right.

S2: I think she knows the horse is nothing without him—absolutely nothing—that their lives depend on each other.

T: Anything else?

S3: I think the auctioneer is going to say, "Sold."

T: And give Rigel to her?

S3: No. Give it to the other guy.

T: To him.

S3: He's a tight spender.

T: Oh, that's right, that's right. He's got the four hundred eighty.

S4: She won't get the five hundred out of her mouth, I don't think.

T: All right.

S5: I think she'll have the chance if she wants to.

T: Okay. So, we've got our three suggested alternatives here [suggested earlier]: She's going to get the horse and hire the man; she's going to let him buy the horse; she's simply going to get the horse and he'll be out of it.

S5: She's going to give the horse to him. She knows it. Even if she could outbid him, the horse would still be his.

T: All right. Finish the story.

Thus ends the Directed Reading–Thinking Activity. (It does not end class discussion of the story, however, but I'll get back to that later.) Let's examine the steps in the DR-TA; then I will give directions for classroom use and demonstrate other applications.

STEPS IN THE DR-TA

Step 1 Identifying Purposes for Reading

The DR-TA begins with students setting individual and group purposes for reading as they create intertextual links by combining prior knowledge with information in text to predict what the text is going to be about. Purpose setting continues throughout the reading each time students repredict, raising new questions ("What connection does the little man have with the horse?"; "Will Markham 'let' him buy the horse or will she outbid him?"; "What is the bond between the two characters?"), and then sample increasing amounts of text. In discussion, new links occur, and students therefore return to text repeatedly with a purpose for reading; to get answers to questions arising from their predictions or to see whether new information will cause these predictions to be revised.

In our lesson-demonstration discussion, notice how broad and speculative early predictions were in contrast to the last ones just before students were directed to finish reading ("About a person who's doing something that's not particularly acceptable, or maybe something outside the ordinary" versus "She's going to give the horse to him. She knows it. Even if she could outbid him, the horse would still be his."). This same progression from general to highly specific predictions is just as typical when reading expository text—physics and algebra texts for example—as it is with narrative.

Notice also how this contrast illustrates what we said earlier about comprehension. In the first prediction, the reader had very little information to go on; the last prediction, however, was focused and informed by prior knowledge, increased amounts of information in the text, the readers' own intertextual linkages, and input from other readers. By this point, the readers had gotten a great deal of information, both from the text and from the discussion accompanying reading, and each had clearly made a decision about the final outcome.

DR-TA with Narrative and Extended Expository Text The teacher's role during discussion is to accept student predictions, making no judgment about how "correct" the predictions are, and to concentrate on follow-up probe questions after reading that assist students in making linkages between what they predicted and what they found and in articulating the reasons, logic, and evidence for the predictions that were made. Teachers interject information only when student comments indicate misinformation or misunderstanding (recall the clarification from the teacher about Beryl Markham). Critical to this point is that the teacher's role involves much more listening than talking.

Look back at the discussion in the lesson demonstration and you'll see that the teacher really said very little. The major responsibility for discussion was on the students: They were the ones bringing up new ideas, they were holding the floor most of the time, and they occasionally left the teacher out altogether to discuss the story among themselves. That is precisely as it should be. Good DR-TA teachers quite often find themselves standing in front of a class calling on students, nodding, and saying, "Why?", "What makes you say that?", "Um-hmm", "Really?", and "Any other ideas?" The teacher encourages students to support predictions and opinions through metacognitive talk—that is, to examine aloud how they know something or reveal their line of reasoning and to clarify the logic of their thinking. As reading progresses, students reexamine their logic to achieve a "fit" between their prior knowledge base and new ideas. The purpose of DR-TA is not anything-goes, wild conjecture but, rather, *disciplined inquiry* in which students use prior knowledge and evidence from the text to arrive at new linkages, insights, and understandings, whether these new ideas come from within the immediate text or across multiple texts. Because students bring different experiences, language and cultural backgrounds, and logic systems to the learning task, individual predictions will differ. These differences are to be expected and even celebrated. One of the greatest values of a DR-TA is the sharing of diverse individual experiences and perceptions. This, however, does not mean that DR-TA lessons compromise the integrity or precision of what is to be learned; they do not. Rather, the lesson acknowledges that students may take very different paths toward that understanding. Understanding of subject matter information is the final outcome of a DR-TA lesson.

DR-TA with Other Texts Go back to the Centerpiece Lesson Plan on pps. 92–94 for a moment, and you can see that in this mathematics text, discussion will progress slightly differently than it did in the English class lesson demonstration. First, because the text itself is different: mathematics texts generally have much less extended exposition and often combine exposition with other sign systems, as do foreign language texts, grammar texts in all languages, some science texts, and other specialized texts such as recipes, music—both with and without libretti—repair manuals, and game or sport How to Play texts. Second, information is usually very densely packed in these texts, so it requires more discussion in fewer pages; in the algebra DR-TA discussion steps 4–8 covered only one-and-a-half pages of the algebra text, whereas the full text of "Splendid Outcast" is 15 pages.

That said, however, the progression of thinking in both discussions is quite similar. In each, student acquisition of new information informs and strengthens their predictions as they progress through text. So, by the time algebra students get to $5x - 9 = 3x + 1$, the practice they've had solving earlier problems allows them to predict with some certainty that a likely place to start is to get all x's on one side of the equals sign. Because of the precision required to do algebra (or conduct science experiments or read music), teachers' DR-TA questions in such texts may be a bit more frequent and pointed; nevertheless, note how the questioning at each step in the algebra lesson plan begins with prediction ("What do you think we do first?" "What is new here?" "What do we need to do?") and requires students to use a combination of prior knowledge and information in the text to answer.

The Teacher's Role It is important that you really listen to what students say during DR-TA discussion. As students speculate and support their predictions and conclusions, you can learn a great deal about their prior knowledge base and how they are creating textual links between what they know and what they are learning. So, too, can you gain insight into different constructions of meaning that stem from diverse cultural, social, and critical viewpoints and guide students toward understanding of the information to be learned.

The *value* here, then, is the sharing of personal background and reasoning, different as these may be, to increase everyone's fund of knowledge, hone thinking skills, and provide immediate purposes for reading. The net effect is that students engage much more willingly, effectively, and deeply with content text: Discussion is a real exchange of information by active learners (rather than rapid-fire responses to factual questions) and is comprised of the real "stuff" of learning—information and experiences that shape students' meaning constructions. Purposes for continuing to read grow naturally from questions that arise in the course of that discussion, and the whole of the information exchange is directed specifically toward the ultimate goal of learning subject matter content.

Step 2 Adjusting Rate to Purposes and Material

Rate adjustment occurs along two dimensions in a DR-TA: (1) rate and flow of information (teacher determined) and (2) reading rate (student determined). The teacher determines the amount of text to be revealed between stop-points and the length of discussion time at each. In the physics lesson, text units varied from one line (the chapter title), to the stated aims of the text and the section title, to the first three paragraphs; the next reasonable unit of text would have been to the rest of the section; from there, the next entire section could be read. The English lesson was similar: Stop-point intervals went from the title, to one paragraph, to a page and a half, to several pages. In the algebra text, after the lesson title, text units were about equal. It is equally workable to use a DR-TA to *introduce* an article, chapter, or story by reading the first several paragraphs in class DR-TA-style and then assigning the remainder to be read at home for discussion in the following class.

Rate and Flow of Information The first stop-point should occur immediately following a title or opening line. Here, students are invited to speculate about all the possible contexts into which the title (or line) might fit. Predictions will vary from literal to highly abstract and from reasonable to silly. (By the way, silly predictions generally go away after one or two DR-TA lessons—the teacher helps them go away by not giving them much attention. Good, hearty, *funny* predictions happen forever.) As they share predictions in class, students examine a variety of experiences—their own and others'—that not only present a range of possibilities but also raise the question "Which of these will it be?"

The second stop-point may be after one or two paragraphs in some texts where introductory information provides clues as to the central ideas of the text, or it may be with other texts after the stated goals/aims/objectives of a chapter in which such information also resides. The point here is to launch readers into the cycle of predicting–sampling text–repredicting–resampling that is so important to comprehension. In effect, it gives students practice doing what good readers do (monitoring, adjusting predictions, connecting across texts, and so on); so, while focusing student attention on comprehension of immediate text, these stop-point predictions help them become better readers as well.

From this point forward, the nature of the text determines the amount of text between stop-points. Generally, with narrative and extended expository text the goal is for students to read increasingly longer amounts of text between stop-points; with other texts (as with the algebra lesson plan), the length of text units remains relatively consistent. A good rule of thumb is to have no more than four or five stops in one lesson.

Critical to the guidance provided is the amount of discussion time at each stop-point. The amount of time allowed determines how long students will have to think and draw conclusions or make decisions about what they are reading. It depends, in part, on the amount of information available and the degree of student participation. Of prime importance is the teacher's sensitivity to student needs and willingness to wait for ideas to occur. There are points when the text does not offer much to be discussed or when students want to get on with the reading. At such times, the best course of action is to let them read. At other times, response is slow because students need time—time to ponder, to consider possibilities, and to synthesize information from a variety of sources. Wait time, when the room is absolutely quiet and no one (not even the teacher) is talking, is necessary for this kind of thinking to take place. It can be uncomfortable for students and teachers who are used to rapid-fire questions and answers; frequently, however, the liveliest discussions and most interesting predictions result from these moments.

Rate Adjustment The second dimension of rate adjustment occurs spontaneously as students alter their reading rates to meet both their own needs and the needs of the discussion. Some students, being given the direction "Read to the end of . . ." will first skim quickly through the section to get a general idea of the content (actually, to see if their predictions come true) and then go back and read carefully to fill in details because they know they will be asked to support any conclusions drawn or predictions made. Others will read carefully from the start and go back later to scan the text for ideas that reinforce or support their opinions. Students with known learning disabilities and who struggle with reading text will need to be given a bit extra reading time and reassurance that this is not the only reading of the text and that they will have time to return to the text later. The degree and amount of rate adjustment vary considerably from individual to individual.

Important here is that, for all students, situational demand requires the application of a reading skill that increases their efficiency and effectiveness as readers. Each time a student scans text to find a word or phrase to support a prediction or conclusion, each time a student races through the reading to see how well he or she predicted and then goes back to get the details, and each time an entire class returns to text to search for overlooked ideas, this skill is reinforced.

Step 3 Observing the Reading

In many classrooms, especially in middle and secondary schools, reading of text that goes beyond word, sentence, and paragraph boundaries usually takes place in one of two ways: Either students are assigned such passages for independent seat work or homework or they take turns reading the entire assignment aloud, paragraph by paragraph, droning up one row and down another, around the room in the dreaded Round Robin Oral Reading. In the first instance, teachers somehow feel that time spent reading silently in class is wasted, that there are more important things to do, and that students should be able to "get it on their own." In the second, teachers frustrated by students' seeming inability to get it on their own resort to Round Robin Oral Reading because it is the only way they know to make sure that everyone is at least exposed to the content of the text.

Unfortunately, neither of these practices is terribly useful. The one simply leaves students on their own to sink or swim; the other promotes dependency by removing all responsibility for reading from them. Just as importantly, perhaps, Round Robin Oral Reading is unfair to everyone: It's deadly dull for everybody in the room when not-so-good readers read, and a source of immediate, abject terror for those students whose oral reading skills are not good. Jim Cope reports from a survey of 300 high school seniors about reading that "the most intensely personal negative experience for students was being forced to read aloud in class" (1997, p. 21). Round Robin Oral Reading really does not belong in the classroom, even when teachers don't make the less able readers participate. I know it is common practice in schools; I know also that teachers often use Round Robin Oral Reading because some students clamor for it and because they believe it helps the less able readers and ESL students to "read along" silently as someone reads fluently aloud. There are far better ways for teachers to engage students in oral reading, and the fact is that less able readers aren't "reading along" with the uninterrupted flow of fluent reading. Rather, their visual focus is disrupted by trying to follow along and so lags behind the text being read or strays to the window (Singer, 1970).

For instruction to be effective, a certain amount of guided silent reading needs to be done in school; it is not wasted time. Teacher observation during that reading yields much valuable information about students' silent reading abilities and allows the teacher to assist those students who do need help. Whether in small groups or with an entire class, the teacher can quickly learn which students are faster readers and which are slower, which students are actually reading and which are not, which students exhibit signs of serious reading problems (inattention, extreme slowness, stress symptoms, and so on), what strategies students use to get meaning from text or figure out an unknown word, and many other details. Of critical importance here is that unless teachers provide opportunity for students to read silently in class, teachers can have no idea of how students read independently; few, if any, students attempt to complete out-of-class reading assignments by reading text aloud. The most useful, informative way to learn about students' reading abilities is to observe silent reading.

Along with silent reading, purposeful oral reading can and should take place, either spontaneously when a student reads from text to support an opinion, or focused by teacher direction. Over time, teacher observation of both silent and oral reading yields information about individuals and the group that is useful not only for conducting the lesson at hand but also in (1) planning subsequent lessons, (2) selecting materials that are appropriate and useful with this class, (3) determining the amount and kind of guidance needed for future instruction, and (4) making recommendations for students to be screened for special programs. Observation and planning of this kind are the essence of reflective teaching.

Step 4 Developing Comprehension

By now, it should be clear that developing comprehension is an integral part of all phases of the DR-TA. It occurs as students combine prior knowledge and new information to make predictions, read to confirm or adjust their predictions, and then draw conclusions and speculate during class discussion. It also occurs during the periodic discussions as students compare their knowledge base with others', review and revise their own logic, and add others' ideas and viewpoints to their thinking. During this process, it is the teacher's responsibility to see that new concepts are developed and reinforced and that students can anchor them within the framework of their prior knowledge base.

Think back to our English class DR-TA lesson demonstration when the student raised the question of the difference between pounds and guineas. In this instance, the teacher *did not know the answer* to the question. (Surprise!) The teacher offered what little information she had and then asked if anybody knew anything more. Her final comment, "We'll hang on to that and look it up," was both an acknowledgment of the importance of the concept and a promise to students that she would help them fill in that information when the time was right. This same thing can happen during silent reading; it is not unusual in a DR-TA for a student to interrupt the reading by asking aloud, "What does———mean?" The teacher or another student responds and reading continues. Later, during discussion, if the word in question is important to the concept being developed, the teacher extends the immediate definition in an appropriate manner.

Also critical to developing comprehension in the DR-TA are the questioning strategies that teachers use to initiate and extend discussion. It is here, with the questions that teachers use to guide discussion, that the DR-TA differs most remarkably from traditional instruction. The standard DR-TA has essentially two types of questions:

1. *Questions that require speculation, prediction, and critical analysis:*
   "With a title like that, what do you think the chapter (or story or article) will be about?"
   "Now what do you think?"
   "What information do you think we'll find in this chapter?"
   "What do you think will happen next?"

   Followed by:

2. *Questions that require drawing conclusions and/or providing support:*
   "What makes you say that?"
   "Why?"
   "How do you know that?"

Here, I reproduce verbatim teacher questions asked during our example physics lesson and demonstration English lesson DR-TAs:

Physics

"Based on this title, what do you think the chapter will be about?"
"What makes you say that?"
"Now what do you think?"
"Why?"

"What other ideas do you think we'll find in this chapter?"
"Why?"
"What do you think we'll know when we're through?"
"Anything else?"

English

"With a title like that, what do you think this story will be about?"
"Why do you say that?"
"Who is Beryl Markham?"
"What were you going to say?"
"Why?"
"What else? Does anyone know this story? Any other ideas?"
"Any other ideas?"
"Now what do you think?"
"What else?"
"What do you think it might be?"
"Any other ideas?"
"Why do you suggest that he might have been a jockey or might be a jockey?"
"Now what do you think?"
"What else? What do you think?"
"What else?"

You get the idea. It is important to note that none of these questions asks students to state the literal meaning of text, a fact that probably leads to some teacher skepticism or discomfort with the DR-TA. Although DR-TA questions may not specifically ask about literal meaning, this is not to say that literal information is not discussed. It is. Students use literal information in the course of making predictions, drawing conclusions, and supporting their responses. It therefore becomes unnecessary to reiterate this information through specific questioning.

In the DR-TA, questions other than those that require making and supporting predictions and drawing conclusions are generally probes to assist students in articulating their thinking. Notice in the algebra lesson plan, the teacher wrote out probes that might be useful for doing this ("Why did we subtract 1 first?" "Why didn't we get the same answer for this equation?" "What did we need to do first? Why?"). Notice also how very high level these questions are, even though they are very specific. The open-ended questions of the DR-TA focus attention on the larger issues, and thus literal meaning remains in rightful perspective. *It is only when student response to the open-ended question indicates misunderstanding that literal questions are asked.* Literal questions are asked immediately to clarify and remove the misunderstanding; as soon as that is accomplished, teacher questions should return to the types described earlier.

Step 5 Developing Fundamental Skills and Assessment

When the reading is completed, the teacher directs the class in developing skills that are appropriate to student needs and instructional goals. Activities should not require students to write answers to literal questions about what they have just read and discussed. The quality of the discussion and the level of understanding students have achieved have gone well beyond literal comprehension already. Activities should extend student response to text in some important way and may include solving problems, writing experiment logs, vocabulary study, various activities to organize and combine information, or any of numerous writing activities. We look at several strategies for developing follow-up activities later in this chapter and in other chapters as well. Of prime importance here is that (1) follow-up activities are thoughtful, meaningful additions to the reading experience; and (2) assessments that accompany these activities reflect what students were taught and the lesson objectives and content standards identified for the lesson.

OTHER APPLICATIONS OF THE DR-TA

Recall I said earlier that the DR-TA is a sturdy instructional strategy. It is. You have seen ways in which the DR-TA may be adapted for guiding students' comprehension in English, physics, and mathematics classes with very different kinds of texts. I want to present yet another way the DR-TA may be adapted, this time using a social studies lesson/text. This application, however, is good for any extended narrative or expository text; the difference between it and the DR-TAs we've looked at so far is that it guides students as they read independently, rather than as part of a class activity. This application is thus good for use in guiding students' comprehension of homework reading. What follows are two DR-TA reading guidesheets that are alternative formats for the same social studies assignment. Do note that the guidesheets engage students in essentially the same process as the in-class, teacher-led DR-TA.

DR-TA SAMPLE GUIDESHEET *Social Studies*

I. **New State Governments**

The following is a list of the subheadings for Section I of our chapter:

Following Old Patterns
Ways of Constitution Making
Written Constitutions
The New State Constitutions
Equality in the States
First Moves Against Slavery

On the basis of these subheadings, what information do you think you'll find in the "New State Governments" section of our chapter? On the lines for Predictions, list the kinds of information and ideas you think you will find in the reading. After you've finished reading, use the Important Information lines to list important information you find. Put an asterisk (*) beside important information you found that you had predicted you would find. Be prepared to discuss your predictions and choices of important ideas.

Predictions: ______________________________

____

____

____

____

____

Important Information: ______

______

______

______

______

______

DR-TA SAMPLE GUIDESHEET *Social Studies*

The subheadings for Section I of our chapter, "New State Governments," are given in the following list. For each subheading, use the Predictions lines to write your predictions about the information and ideas you're likely to find in that subsection. Complete all your predictions before reading. Then, as you read, use the Important Ideas lines to jot down important ideas you find in each subsection. Put an asterisk (*) beside any ideas you found that you predicted you would find. Be prepared to discuss your choices of important ideas.

I. ***New State Governments***

Following Old Patterns. **Predictions:** ______

______

Important Ideas: ______

______

Ways of Constitution Making. **Predictions:** ______

______

Important Ideas: ______

______

Written Constitutions. **Predictions:** ______

______

Important Ideas: ______

______

The New State Constitutions. **Predictions:** ______

______

Important Ideas: ______

______

Equality in the States. **Predictions:** ______

______

Important Ideas: ______

______

First Moves Against Slavery. **Predictions:** ______

______

Important Ideas: ______

______

CLOSING THOUGHTS ABOUT THE DR-TA

Students and teachers frequently ask me whether I would use DR-TAs "all the time." The answer is, "No. I wouldn't recommend using anything 'all the time.'" But without getting too overblown about it, I must say that the DR-TA has a way of becoming a habit. It sort of gets in your blood. It does not take long before you find that regardless of the instructional strategy you're using, you hear yourself asking, "What do you think will be important in this chapter?" and "What made you say that?" and all the language from a DR-TA that causes students to make connections and to predict and to examine text critically. Well, fine. If that happens, it just means you've internalized a process that is useful and effective in the classroom. What is so powerful about the DR-TA is how it stimulates and engages students in reading and thinking about subject matter text, even the Dave Lowerys of the class who work so hard at staying disengaged.

Creating Strategic Readers

There is much talk in secondary schools today about the importance of students become strategic readers (we even discussed it earlier in the chapter). Carol Santa (2006) makes the very important point that for students to become truly strategic readers, writers and learners, they need more than a "bundle of procedures" to be applied as they read. I agree. Becoming a strategic reader is not *just* about learning "the strategies," it's about becoming introspective with respect to one's self as a learner. In essence, it requires metacognitive thought. The DR-TA is a good start-point for helping students think about their own literacy and learning, and increasing their reading/learning proficiency. After you've done a few DR-TAs with your students, say something like this:

> "Do you notice that I ask you to make predictions as you're reading? Why do you suppose I do that?" *Field answers.* "Making predictions helps you connect what you already know to new information, so it increases your understanding as you read. Before reading, look at titles and headings, instructional goals (if they're in the text) and any marginal notes. Make some predictions. What do you think you'll learn? Then read to see if your predictions were right, or how close you came to being right. Pay attention if you're way off the mark and go back to see what led you in a different direction from the text. Try to get better each time you predict."

Spend a little time each week helping your students think introspectively about their reading and learning.

You will undoubtedly at one time or another have students in your class who for one reason or another—either because they speak little English, or because they are very shy, or because of special needs, or because they have experienced many years of school failure—do not participate initially in the DR-TA. For a while, that's okay; let them become accustomed to the routine and comfortable with your willingness to accept a range of responses. If you have a number of these students in class, use the DR-TA often but with short units of text, and look for every opportunity to call on them and give them positive feedback for responses. Gradually their participation will increase.

How to do . . . .

A DR-TA

A DR-TA is relatively easy to prepare. The most difficult part of preparation is deciding where to place stop-points, and for novice DR-TA teachers, the tendency is to stop more often than necessary, as opposed to less. The only other hard part is learning to ask open-ended, DR-TA–type questions rather than lots of literal questions and becoming used to lesson episodes in which students do most of the talking. *When you first begin using a DR-TA, you may want to use it simply to introduce students to their homework reading assignment. To do so, just ask them to make predictions from the title and the first and second paragraphs, record the predictions, and use them for opening discussion the next day. Later, when you and your students are comfortable with this kind of questioning, move on to a full-text reading with DR-TA.* Here are the preparation steps:

1. Select the reading assignment (chapter, article, story, and so on).
2. Determine stop-points. Stop first after the title. Then use logical breaks, such as subheadings, mathematics problems, chapter parts, and so forth, to establish three or four additional stops.
3. Prepare questions to be asked at stop-points; for example, "Based on this title, what do you think the chapter will be about?"; "Why?"; "Now what do you think?"; "Why?"; "What do you think we'll learn or find out next?"; "Why?"
4. Obtain/prepare cover sheets for students to use to cover text following stop-points (if needed).
5. Determine and prepare assessments needed for the lesson.

CRITICAL LITERACY AND GUIDED COMPREHENSION

The notion of critical literacy has grown from many sources but can be understood as a natural outgrowth of critical theorists' claim that literacy is "reading the word and the world" (Freire & Macedo, 1989). That is, to be literate is to go beyond simple literal construction of meaning to engage in critical examination of the world with respect to issues of power, politics, economics, voice, and available Discourses, and one's position in relationship to all. It is, in fact, to question (i.e., critique) the text, to challenge the assumptions embedded in the text, and to reposition oneself in light of ideas, values, and attitudes suggested by the text. Bakhtin earlier called this "independent, discriminate thinking" (1981). Allen Luke recommends using the following questions to engage students in critical examination of texts they read:

- Which/whose version of events is foregrounded (i.e., most prominent)?
- Which other versions are excluded? Whose interests are served by this representation?
- How does the text construct reality (i.e., what kind of language or voice does it use?)?
- How does the text try to position you in relation to its messages? (2000, p. 457).

Luke notes that consideration of such questions makes readers "text participants" (p. 455) engaged in reading not only as a cognitive process, but also as a sociological and cultural process as they examine the Discourses and ideologies underpinning the text. Obviously, not all texts lend themselves to these considerations.

Tom Bean and Karen Moni (2003) use a slightly different approach to guide students in the same sort of critical analysis of text. They propose four types of critical discussion prompts (p. 645) (these were originally intended for reading novels; I have adapted them for the reading of other texts as well):

1. Structural Prompts
   - Where does the text come from?
   - What function does it serve?
2. Subject and Reader Positioning
   - How does the author construct the world?
   - Who is the ideal reader for this text?
3. Gaps and Silencing
   - Who gets to speak and have a voice in this text and who does not?
   - Who is left out of this text?
4. Classroom Transformations
   - How might we rewrite this text to deal with the gaps and silences?

Colin Harrison (e-mail communication, September 2001) suggests a media studies approach to critical literacy with respect to the media coverage of September 11 in which the following questions are asked of both written and visual text:

- What did we see (read)?
- Why were we shown (told) this?
- What were some of the effects of its being shown (told, written) this way?
- What might have been some of the effects of its being done differently?

Such critical examinations of text are easily incorporated into the DR-TA and other instructional strategies by asking such questions as the following:

"Whose voice(s) are we hearing here? Whose (or what) voices are not heard?"

"How is the author positioning him/herself? How is the author positioning the reader?"

"What are we being told? What is being left out?"

"How does what we're reading fit with your experience? How does it not?"

(Ruddell & Marker, 2006, p. 19)

As you can see from these sets of questions, critical reading of text is a political act, one that teachers may find "too hot to handle" (Luke, 2000) in a school setting. Nevertheless, it is our responsibility to give adolescents the opportunity and the wherewithal to engage in critical examination of texts they read.

THE GROUP MAPPING ACTIVITY (GMA)

The Group Mapping Activity (GMA) was introduced by Jane Davidson (1982) as a means of assisting students in organizing information after reading. Quite simply, maps are visual and written representations of readers' understanding of text. Maps have become relatively common in classrooms. Many teachers encourage students to use them both to represent meaning constructed from reading as well as to plan and prepare for intended writing. Davidson's approach to mapping begins with these instructions (or something like them) to students:

> On your cover sheet, and without looking back at the text, map your perceptions of what we have just read. A map is simply a diagram of what you think the reading (or chapter) was about. There are no right or wrong ways to map. A map may have shapes, lines, figures, words, anything you want it to have. (Adapted from Davidson, 1982)

After students have completed their maps, the teacher then invites them to display the maps. The display shows clearly how different the maps are, and students may, at first, be a bit disconcerted at having to show their maps. The teacher then invites students to share their maps by telling what the symbols and writing on the maps represent and waits for a student to volunteer to share his or her map. (Figure 4.1 on p. 116 shows one way our physics chapter could be mapped.) The wait for a volunteer can seem long, but it rarely exceeds 20 to 30 seconds. The student explains her or his map and tells why she or he chose to map the reading as she or he did. The teacher asks generative questions to expand the explanation; for example, "What made you decide to put directional arrows between *force*, *motion*, and *change?*" Several maps are shared in this manner, with the teacher leading and guiding the discussion.

A GMA is an ideal activity to follow a DR-TA lesson because it helps students organize and retain information from the text; this is one way teachers assist students in learning and applying subject area information. Additionally, it gives teachers on-the-spot assessment of students' understanding and learning. The discussion that occurs as the maps are displayed and explained allows students to elaborate and expand the knowledge they construct from text. Readers' constructions of meaning continue to be

FIGURE 4.1 *Physics Chapter Map Drawn in a Group Mapping Activity*

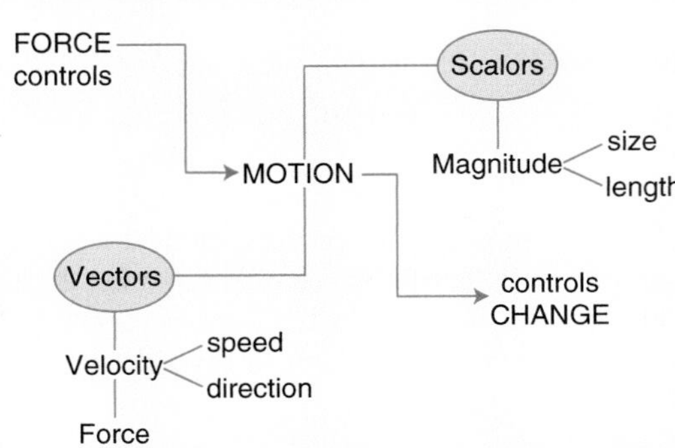

shared during this interchange. When the DR-TA is used to introduce a chapter or article and reading is completed at home, the opening activity in the next class period can be the creation of maps. Alternatively, after students are experienced mappers, they can create maps at home and share them during the next class.

I used group mapping immediately following our DR-TA demonstration English lesson. Here is one of the map explanations from the GMA for "The Splendid Outcast":

S: I did some highlighting to show that I had two things going at the same time. I had her train of thought—the horse auction, and that she was interested in the horse and that she remembers his dangerous past but also his breeding. A reference to her own horse business, and that it was getting toward the end of the auction, and then she notices the man (that comes back down here) but prior to that Rigel is brought out in chains—real defiant, real dangerous. And then the bidding takes place in here, and again he comes in (every time I highlight it with pink, he's coming in again).

T: The man?

S: Right. Then the stallion goes berserk, and she passes on the bidding, he gets the horse, and in the end he's revealed as a rebel. So, I just put down train of thought.

T: You show your train of thought there. The man, the jockey, seems to come in there at the beginning, and then come around like this. Did you have a specific reason for highlighting his interaction in there?

S: In the center? Yeah. He seemed to be central to all this peripheral stuff that was going on. It kept coming back to him. Down here, he seemed to be in most of the passages, most of the action. He seemed like a peripheral figure, and yet he seemed central at the same time.

Here is another map explanation. Notice how differently this student organizes and classifies information. Notice also the teacher's role.

S1: Well, mine's really simple. I saw a parallel between the actual buying ring and sort of like a Venn diagram. If I'd had more room, they'd have been the same size. Rigel, being the center of the story, is the center of the ring. Then the regular buying crowd is all around. Then Beryl and the jockey are each in their own sphere, and they're the only ones who have an interest in Rigel as far as buying him, so they're interacting with him, in a way. Then ending up with Rigel and the jockey, totally overlapped, totally intersected.

T: Oh. This is Rigel and the jockey here? Okay.

S1: Surrounded by the total interest of Beryl and just slightly overlapped by the regular buying audience.

T: So what you have is this great big circle here that looks real powerful and it becomes this one here. And this small ellipse here has become the big circle here. So, it's a transformation.

S1: Yeah. But I would have made them more the same size if I'd had more room.

GROUP MAPPING AND MEANING CONSTRUCTION

From these map explanations, it is clear that response to text is a highly individual, personal matter. It is clear, too, that provision for differences in student background and construction of knowledge does not in any way violate or distort the author's intended meaning of a text. These two students, both of whom participated in the same DR-TA lesson, took very different impressions from that reading, illustrating yet again that readers *make* meaning, rather than *get* meaning, from text. It serves also to highlight one of the two ways that the GMA differs from other mapping strategies.

First, the GMA uses free-form directions to students that *allow* them to respond to text from their own knowledge base and preferred means of representation. Other mapping strategies tell students, step-by-step, how to map. Although there is nothing *wrong* with that approach, my experience has been that it tends to lock students in to one "right" way to map; it leaves little room for experimentation and difference. It also tends to focus on literal meaning and thus reduces the possibility that students will move away from the literal into the critical and abstract. The GMA does neither of these. Of particular importance to English-language learners who need assistance with English, and other students as well, is that free-form maps allow students to use symbols other than words to represent meaning—or to combine symbols, words, and languages—thus broadening and expanding significantly the range and complexity of the ideas they can represent.

Transmediation The value of allowing students to invent their own means for representing text can be found in the notion of "transmediation"—translation of content from one sign system to another (Suhor, 1984). In this instance, the sign systems we're moving across are written English text and symbolic/pictorial text. Marjorie Siegel, in her work with students reading mathematics text, found that the act of sketching (or mapping) from text produced reflective and generative thinking that increased and deepened students' understanding of the text. She describes Tim and Eric's experience of reading and sketching "Mathematics and the Marketplace":

> As they explained to their classmates, they did not begin the sketching process with much understanding of the text, let alone any way to represent "all that mumble jumble [referring to the article] . . . going around in our head." Instead, they found that experimenting with the new expression plane itself helped them find an entry into the text. In other words, "messing about" with various images gave rise to the star image [the central image of their sketch] and, as they said, this image served as a "key" that allowed them to open the text and begin an exploration of the interrelationship of mathematics and the marketplace . . . .Their own reflections on the experience indicate that literally "picturing" their thinking gave them a way to engage in meaningful learning. (1995, p. 467)

Free-form mapping is not at all unlike the free-form sketching Siegel describes; it is, in fact, so open-ended that it presents the temporary problem of causing student concern about how to invent their maps: The very first time you tell students to "map your perceptions of what you think the reading was about," they'll get a little anxious. They get anxious because you're not telling them specifically what to do, and they're afraid they'll be "wrong." (They don't believe you when you say there is no right or wrong way to map.) I solve this problem by displaying "dummy" maps, such as those shown in Figures 4.2 and 4.3, which are maps I've made of texts different from the one students are currently reading. I show them very quickly, saying, "A map can look like this, or like this, or any way you want it to look." That gives students ideas for mapping without providing a pattern they feel compelled to copy. By the time they get to their second mapping experience, students know what you want: They've seen other maps, they have a number of new ideas about how to map, and they've seen that you really do accept their individuality and differences in interpretation and representation.

Map Sharing The second major difference between the GMA and other mapping strategies is sharing the maps and map explanations in class (that's the "group" part). Sharing is the most powerful aspect of the GMA and should not be omitted. It is here, after they have mapped, that students can say what they understand about text; explore ideas both in text and beyond; and arrive at conclusions, generalizations, and abstractions. And, as Siegel suggests, the maps serve as a medium for developing insight and generating new ideas; map sharing is yet another form of transmediation, and it is not unusual for students to arrive at deeper understanding in the very act of telling about their maps. This process not only provides for high-level comprehension but is the cornerstone of learning as well. It gives students practice using new ideas and practice articulating these into oral language. Just as importantly, as students listen to one another explain and explore map meanings, everyone's construction of knowledge is increased and expanded.

Once again, as with the DR-TA, the teacher's role is to facilitate, rather than dominate, the process. The teacher is responsible for asking questions that help students clarify their thinking, articulate new understanding, and arrive at deeper insights. Recall when the teacher asked if the student had a reason for placing the jockey in the center of her map. The student was then able to say what she hadn't said

FIGURE 4.2 *Sample "Dummy" Map for Health Lesson*

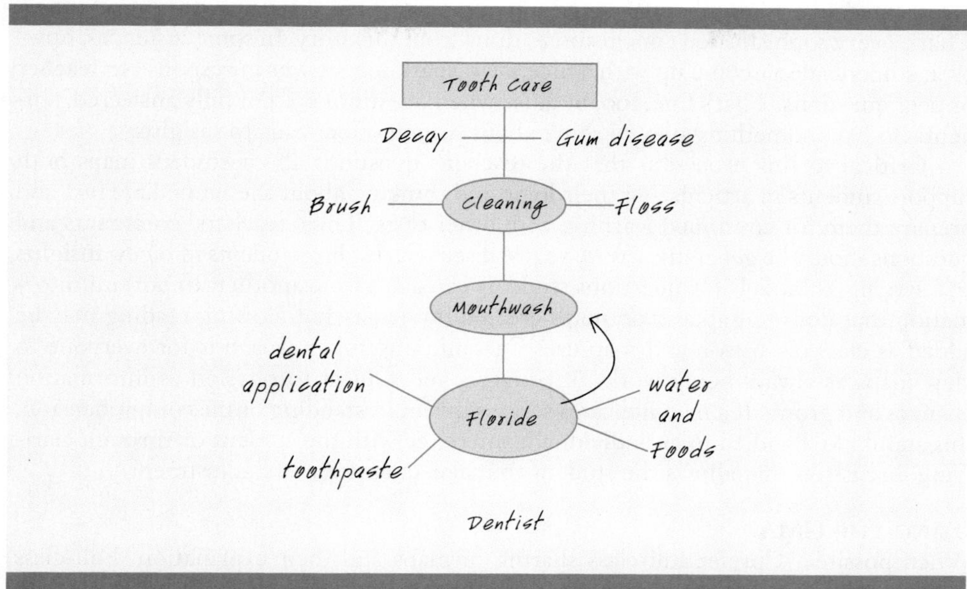

FIGURE 4.3 *Sample "Dummy" Map for English Lesson*

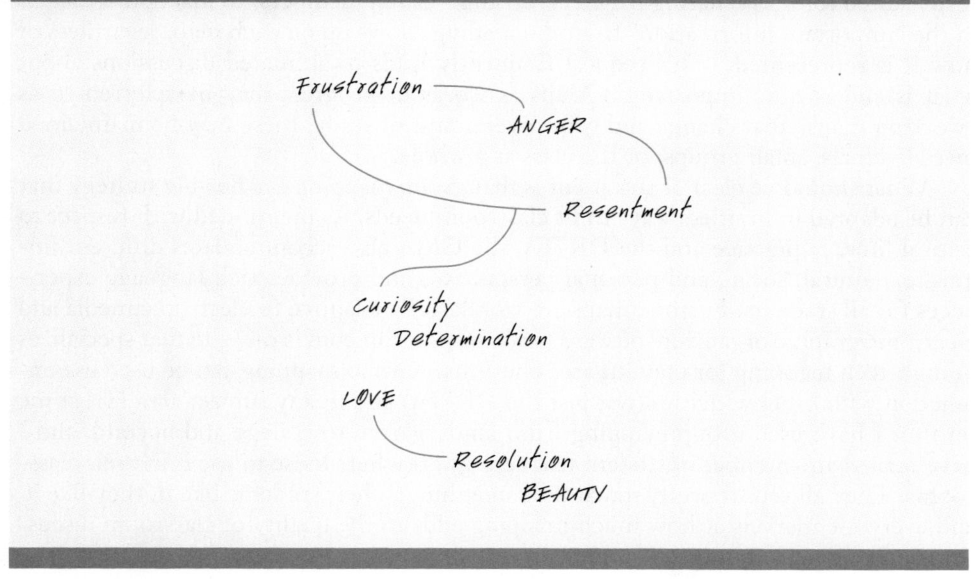

before: "Yeah. He seemed to be central to all this peripheral stuff that was going on . . . . He seemed like a peripheral figure, and yet he seemed central at the same time." That's a very sophisticated conclusion to draw from this story. In some instances, however, students don't come up with a nice, new, sparkling answer in response to teacher or peer questions. That's fine, too, because when questions are not fully answered, students do have something new to think about, which often leads to insights.

Critical to this process is that the teacher's questions about student maps both support students in articulating their logic and thinking about the immediate text and prepare them for continued learning with other texts. Thus, teachers' comments and questions should be generative, as we've just discussed, leading students into new insights and serving as models for questions students can ask of one another. Important information that does not appear on maps created immediately following reading may be added as class discussion and map uses warrant; a useful approach is for everyone to view maps as always being works in progress and subject to revision as information changes and grows. If a map indicates serious misunderstanding or miscomprehension, this should be handled in an individual conference with the student or through clarifying discussion that allows the student to make an appropriate adjustment.

USING THE GMA

When possible, I prefer full-class sharing of maps and their explanation. Full-class participation is especially important in the first few experiences with mapping. You may not always have time for full-class sharing, however, so other arrangements are possible. Frequently, I have students share with a partner or in small groups. After hearing the teacher's questions, students become quite good at generative questioning; they may need to be reminded to be tolerant of others' representational schemes or text interpretations. When the maps are intended as study aids, which they are perfectly suited for, I ask sharing partners (or small-group members) to make sure that all of the "important information" from the reading shows up on each map, regardless of how it is represented. (This request frequently leads to animated discussions about what is and is not "important.") Maps as works in progress may be referred to as "working maps" that change and grow over a unit of study; these may be maintained by individuals, small groups, or the class as a whole.

What should be clear at this point is that group mapping is a flexible strategy that can be adapted in limitless ways to fit classroom needs. As mentioned with respect to critical literacy practice and the DR-TA, the GMA also accommodates different linguistic, cultural, social, and personal perspectives and provides rich language experiences for all students. Further, maps are wonderfully adaptive to electronic media and electronic graphic organizer software (www.inspiration.com is one site that specializes in high-tech mapping for content area concepts). Group mapping can be used in conjunction with other activities (not just the DR-TA) and in any subject area. Trust me on this: I have used group mapping from kindergarten to college and beyond, and I have turned any number of student teachers and teachers loose to use it in their classrooms. They all report pretty much the same thing: Their students like it, they like it, and everyone marvels at how much mapping adds to the quality of classroom discussion and student learning.

Creating Strategic Readers and Writers

The GMA, like DR-TA, is a perfect strategy for encouraging introspection and metacognitive thought in students. The map sharing itself is an exercise in metacognition when the teacher or student colleague asks, "What made you decide to put———in the center of your map?" In addition, the act of mapping requires students to organize the information they just read into a cogent whole with important ideas and supporting details shown, one of the things successful learners do. And, finally, mapping is an excellent precursor to writing because ideas are now organized and ready for discussion.

After you've had students map a few times, begin expanding discussion by asking occasionally, "If you were going to map this information a different way, how would you do it? Why?" Encourage students to revise and update their maps. *Talk* to them about how useful maps are for remembering information (recall that in the Algebra GMA the teacher's instructions were to "create a map or visual representation that will help you understand and remember how to solve multi-step equations") and/or for preparing for tests and writing assignments. Ask them, "How does that map help you understand———?"

How to do . . . .

A GMA

In content learning, maps serve as useful learning tools. Not only do they help students organize information after reading but they are powerful study tools as well. Use these steps to direct group mapping in your classroom:

1. Prepare "dummy" maps.
2. After reading, instruct students to map their perceptions of the reading. Use the following means for clarification and additional guidance:
   a. "A map is a diagram of what you think the reading is about. There is no right or wrong way to map. You may use geometric shapes, words, or pictures on your map."
   b. Show "dummy" maps, saying, "A map may look like this . . . like this . . . like this . . . or any way you want it to look."
3. Have students display maps.

4. Allow students to tell about their maps—either to a partner or to the whole class. Focus on how the student chose to map and why rather than on a given standard of "rightness."
5. Encourage, and model, questions that allow students who are sharing their maps to clarify and extend their thinking.
6. Determine and plan assessment procedures.

PART II: *Comprehension Levels, Teacher Questions, and Comprehension Instruction*

Earlier in this chapter, we discussed the quality of meaning students construct, both during and after reading, and the teacher's role in guiding students toward insightful, rich comprehension of text. The point was made that what the teacher does, or does not do, has clear implications for all four goals associated with secondary school reading:

1. Comprehending
2. Learning subject area content
3. Increasing reading skills, and
4. Applying new knowledge

In this section, we continue that line of reasoning with some shift of emphasis: Where we earlier characterized the teacher as a thoughtful facilitator of the reading/learning process—one who designs the instructional progression and then steps back and allows students to lead—in this section we place the teacher in the more traditional, visible role of thoughtful, explicitly active participant in the instructional episode. Specifically, we will look at how skillful teacher questioning supports comprehension and learning.

LEVELS OF COMPREHENSION

Every reading methods text has a section on "levels of comprehension," and/or levels of questioning that guide students' comprehension. Generally, such taxonomies identify three or four levels of comprehension; a notable exception is the six levels of Bloom's taxonomy (1956), which a number of people have adopted to discuss reading comprehension. Mainly, however, authors focus on three comprehension levels. I am most comfortable with Herber's (1978) Literal, Interpretive, and Applied labels, and my description shares much with his work. For our discussion, let's use the following definitions of reading comprehension levels:

> *Literal comprehension* refers to meaning derived from "reading the lines," in which the reader constructs meaning that accurately reflects the author's intended message. Literal comprehension is text explicit; that is, answers to literal questions require reader understanding of ideas stated directly in text.

Interpretive comprehension refers to meaning derived by reading "between the lines," in which the reader perceives author intent or understands relationships between text elements that are not stated directly. Interpretive comprehension is text implicit; answers to interpretive questions require the reader to draw conclusions in response to unstated cause–effect relationships or comparisons, perception of nuance, and/or symbolic use of language and ideas.

Applied comprehension refers to meaning derived by reading "beyond the lines," in which the reader understands unstated relationships between information in text and information in his/her prior knowledge base. Applied comprehension is schema implicit (or experience based, if you prefer); answers to questions at this level require integration of new information into the reader's previous fund of knowledge, from which new relationships emerge.

Literal, interpretive, and applied levels of comprehension constitute a hierarchical arrangement of the quality of meaning a reader constructs during and after encounters with text. At the lowest level, the reader understands the author's intended meaning; at the second, the reader draws conclusions and sees implied relationships; and at the highest, the reader perceives new relationships. The goal of comprehension instruction is to teach students how to achieve all three levels.

Our discussion of the DR-TA, critical literacy, and the GMA clearly demonstrates their usefulness in developing all levels of comprehension. A more traditional approach than any of these strategies is class discussion led by direct teacher questioning, in a Socratic question-response-question-response sequence. In this type of approach (as with the less traditional approach), teacher questions become critical in determining the quality of student comprehension.

TEACHER QUESTIONS

Teacher questions and teacher-led discussion have been the subject of much study and concern since the mid-1960s. In 1967, Frank Guszak published research that reported the kinds of questions teachers ask in reading and subject area instruction. He found that 74% of teacher questions were at the literal level, 8% at the interpretive level, and 19% at the applied level. (The applied-level question percentage is somewhat inflated because 14% of those applied questions could be answered by a simple yes or no—for example, "Did you like the story?") Guszak found additionally that 90% of teachers' literal questions were answered correctly, which led him to conclude that students learn very early to give teachers what teachers want: correct answers to literal questions.

Guszak's results have been replicated in studies at various grade levels in many different settings and schools. The pattern of results from such studies continues to say what Guszak's results suggested in 1967: An overwhelming majority of instructional time is devoted to students' supplying literal answers to teachers' literal questions. The obvious conclusion must be that we systematically limit the intellectual boundaries of the classroom by focusing on bits and pieces of information rather than using those bits and pieces to explore the larger picture. John Goodlad describes this as part of the "frontal teaching" practices he found to predominate in junior and senior high schools. Frontal teaching occurs when the teacher stands in front of the class telling, explaining, and asking

> specific questions calling essentially for students to fill in the blanks: "What is the capital city of Canada?" "What are the principal exports of Japan?" Students rarely turn things around by asking the questions. Nor do teachers often give students a chance to romp with an open-ended question such as, "What are your views on the quality of television?" (1984, pp. 108–109)

Life in the classroom becomes a game of "Can you guess what I'm thinking?" in which teachers ask known-information questions—questions for which they already have the answers (Mehan, 1979)—and search the room until they get a response that matches the one in their head. Donna Alvermann and David Moore describe the common scene:

> The dominant pattern during whole-class presentations in secondary classrooms consists of the following moves: the teacher solicits a student to answer a question; the teacher listens to the student's response; and the teacher evaluates or modifies the student's response. Student-initiated comments or questions are rare. This pattern of communication persists during postreading checks as well as during any other time set aside for whole-class presentation. (1991, p. 969)

Such questioning often produces instructional discussions bordering on the bizarre: Helen Gillotte (1991) describes a classroom she observed in which the teacher spent *15 minutes* attempting to elicit the word *clever* from students who had been asked to describe a story character. This is in direct contrast to real questions that teachers ask to find out how students construct meaning from text (e.g., "What do you think will be important in this chapter? Why?").

I believe that teachers use literal, known-information questions because of their honest (and legitimate) desire to make sure students understand text—that students "get it"—when reading the assignment. Often, these discussions get bogged down in trivia, or time gets wasted in the search for the one correct answer (e.g., *clever*), so that teachers never get around to the higher-level questions they had planned to use; or teachers simply don't know how to get beyond literal questions into higher-order questions or activities that challenge and expand the use of the mind. You already know that the DR-TA, critical literacy practices, and the GMA are effective ways to move students toward higher-order thinking; there are others.

TEACHER QUESTIONS AND GUIDED COMPREHENSION

THE DIRECTED READING ACTIVITY (DRA)

The Directed Reading Activity (DRA) (Betts, 1946) was designed originally for the purpose of increasing students' comprehension of text by removing barriers to comprehension, encouraging guided silent reading of text, and embedding skill development into lessons focusing on conceptual understanding. Although often associated with the "Direct Reading Instruction" most commonly used in elementary reading instruction, the five steps of the DRA—(1) preparation for reading, (2) guided silent reading, (3) comprehension development, (4) skill development and application, and (5) extension and follow-up activities—are quite like, if not directly parallel to, the five-step lesson model presented (with varying labels and terminology) in most secondary curriculum methodology texts.

In fact, the DRA has, for some time, appeared in one form or another in secondary textbook teacher guides; it has been and can be successfully adapted for "Indirect Reading Instruction" (Herber, 1978) in which there is clear focus on subject area content, rather than reading skills per se, and reading skills are taught only as they are needed to learn content. The DRA, however, is subject to much variation in how teachers interpret and apply it in the classroom, and therein lies the key to its effectiveness. Let's examine the sequential steps of the DRA more closely. Following that, is a DRA social studies lesson plan.

STEPS IN THE DRA

Step 1 Preparation for Reading (Before Reading: Into)

The DRA begins with two types of reader preparation. First is vocabulary presentation, in which selected words from the chapter are pretaught for the purpose of reducing or removing barriers to comprehension. This is based on two very important assumptions: (1) that the identified words are *critical to comprehension of the passage* and (2) that the words, as they appear in the passage, are *unfamiliar to the students*. Generally, these words are content specific; that is, their use and meanings are directly related to the topic under discussion. They do not have to be, however; they simply may be noncontent-specific words in text that meet the two assumptions given above.

Whatever the case, it is important for teachers to select these words carefully, by prereading the text and/or choosing from a list suggested by the textbook author(s), and to tailor their choices specifically for the students being taught. Otherwise, teachers will find themselves standing in front of a class of students teaching words the students already know, only to find later that there were any number of other critical words the students *didn't* know. (Believe me. This will happen even with careful selection—I've done it.)

Presentation of the vocabulary words must be done in context so that students will have sufficient information to understand how each word is used in the text and to draw on their prior knowledge base for speculating about possible meanings. The teacher writes the words on the board in sentences or phrases taken directly from text (e.g., "Germany made an *alliance* with Austria and Italy"; "*Points* are ideas") or asks students to find the words in the passage to be read ("Find the word *alliance* on page 297, paragraph 2"). Students are invited to contribute ideas they have about each word's meaning in this context (prior knowledge and previous experience combined with information available in text), and discussion continues until a satisfactory definition is reached. The CSSD progression for analyzing unknown words (Gray, 1946) is useful for this process. (I elaborate on CSSD in Chapter 5.) Here it is in brief:

Context. First, try to construct the meaning of the word from the meaning of the surrounding text.

Structure. Second, look for known word parts (prefixes, roots, suffixes) to help you construct the meaning of the word.

Sound. If that doesn't work, pronounce the word to see if it sounds like any word you know.

Dictionary. When all else fails, look it up.

Because the purpose of vocabulary study during preparation for reading is to help students comprehend text by giving them information about new words and new concepts they will encounter in that text, it is usually short and to the point. It should be, so as not to delay unnecessarily topic discussion and the actual reading. At the most, prereading vocabulary presentation should take no longer than five to 10 minutes. If it does, then reading assignments should be shortened to reduce concept load. It is important, also, to understand that prereading presentation is not the only instruction and practice necessary for long-term vocabulary retention and acquisition. Additional attention to vocabulary can and should follow reading. This is discussed at length in Chapter 5.

The second part of preparation for reading focuses student attention on the subject matter of the text and engages student interest and participation. It begins with the teacher's focusing statements and questions: "Today we are going to begin our unit on woodworking. What do you already know about woods and the handling of them?" or "How many of you know what an empire is? What empires do you know about in the nineteenth and twentieth centuries, and what was their purpose?"

The discussion following such questions activates students' prior knowledge and previous experience by allowing them to recall both direct and vicarious experience related to a given topic. Further, it creates a pool of shared knowledge that becomes the basis for new learning—in essence, the collective class schema that sensitizes students to the information they will encounter in text. This discussion is valuable for all students and is particularly useful as a means of bringing into play diverse viewpoints, perceptions, and cultural experiences. Just as importantly, it stimulates interest in learning as students perceive points of commonality across various sets of knowledge and experience, points of difference, and unresolved questions.

Step 2 Guided Silent Reading (During Reading: Through)

Guided silent reading begins with a statement of purpose for reading given by the teacher; for example, "Read pages 191 through 198 to find out how winds affect weather" or "Read the article to find out how environment and culture influence people's needs and wants." This statement of purpose, along with the previous discussion, shapes the reader's stance in relationship to text. The purpose statement should be prepared in advance and should correspond directly to the teacher's instructional objectives.

Discussion leading to statement of purpose for reading may require, however, that the statement change. You may find out that students already know how wind affects weather or how environment and culture influence people's wants and needs. If that's the case, seriously reconsider whether the reading should be done at all. If it should, determine what *new* purpose students might have for doing it or develop a new purpose collaboratively with students.

More than likely, you will have a pretty good idea of what your students do and do not know about a subject, so you will not have to deal with major adjustment (although it's not unheard of). But *do* pay attention to discussion before reading so that you will know what kind of and how much adjustment of the purpose-setting statement is necessary. Then adjust as quickly and smoothly as you can and have students begin reading. (This is called informed decision making and/or reflective teaching. It means that you look at and listen to your students, analyze their response to what happens in the classroom, and change your plans as conditions warrant. It's scary to make such on-the-spot decisions, but learn to do it. If you persist in teaching something that students already know *as though they didn't know it*, you'll destroy your own credibility and any interest students have in the topic as well. So, *do something—anything;* it may not be perfect, but it'll beat the alternative.)

Frequently, guided silent reading assignments involve an entire chapter, article, essay, or short story that is too lengthy to finish in one class period. You can handle this by initiating silent reading in class, so that you have time to observe students as they read and give assistance to those who need it, and then assigning unfinished reading to be completed as homework.

Discussion of the reading occurs on the next day of class after a short (three- to five-minute) review period. When the text is particularly long or difficult, however, you may wish to provide more guidance by dividing the reading into sections, stopping at the end of each section for discussion, and then suggesting another purpose for continued reading. This allows you to monitor student progress a bit more carefully and see to it that concepts important to comprehension of subsequent information are developed. I find this "sectional" approach particularly useful with concept-dense texts and with books in which text is predominantly numeric and/or graphic (e.g., mathematics books) rather than lexical. Leading students through such a text with purpose-setting statements is useful in teaching them how to read it.

Step 3 Comprehension Development (After Reading: Beyond)

As with the DR-TA, comprehension development begins the moment we initiate the DRA lesson: in our discussion of the language of text (vocabulary presentation), schema activation and sharing of prior knowledge (focusing questions), and right on into statement of purpose for reading (guiding silent reading). Immediately following the reading (or at the beginning of the next class), the purpose-setting statement is asked as a question to initiate discussion; for example, "What are some of the effects of wind on weather?" or "How do people's environment and culture influence their wants and needs?"

It is imperative that you ask the purpose-setting question first and that discussion of it be substantive (involving students' prior knowledge as well as new information from text). If not, students learn that the purpose-setting statement is just something the teacher says, that it has no value and no implications for what is to follow, and that they can ignore it with impunity. Silent reading is then no longer guided.

The very best readers in the class can tolerate this—they'll set their own purpose for reading (even if it's only to get through the assignment) and slog on—but most of the others cannot. The good readers will give it a try—they'll at least come up with the gist of the assignment; average readers will run their eyes over print and take what they can get (about half); the not-so-good readers will flounder through paragraphs and pages of text and construct little, if any, meaning; and the really-not-so-good readers will give up—they're the ones sleeping, heads on desks, while the rest of the class works. Purpose-setting statements that are followed up as opening-discussion questions teach students how to enter text with focused intent and increase the possibility that all students will construct purposeful meaning from text.

Following response to the purpose-setting question, discussion then should be focused on exploration of many aspects of the reading and application of that information to students' lives (middle school, junior high, and senior high students always want to know "What's in this for me?"). At this point, the questions you use to guide discussion are critical; they can and should be complex, interesting, and directly related both to textual information and the lives of the students in the class. They should not be concerned solely with literal-level questions designed to "check" to see if students read the chapter. You will discover soon enough, in response to complex questions, whether students understand literal information (and, incidentally, whether they read the chapter). If student responses indicate noncomprehension, then it is time to back up, see where the problem lies, resolve it, and continue on at the interpretive and applied levels. If students already *do* understand the literal information (i.e., have constructed meaning that accurately reflects the author's intended meaning), then point-by-point reiteration of it in question–answer "discussion" is nothing more than a poorly disguised, boring (let's be honest) test. Unfortunately, these tests are all too common in secondary classrooms. Recall Goodlad's observation that "teachers [rarely] give students a chance to romp with an open-ended question" (1984), and our decades' worth of documentation that literal questions are teachers' questions of choice about 75% of the time.

So it is here, during discussion, that much of the quality of the DRA is established, and it is the *teacher* who determines the tone and content of that discussion. The following guidelines are intended to help you move toward the goal of becoming an accomplished question asker and discussion leader:

- *Take the time to articulate clearly your instructional objectives for units of study and lesson plans.* Determine what you want students to know or to be able to do when they are through with this lesson; these are your instructional objectives. Evaluate them: How useful/important are they? Do they reflect what you really want students to learn? Then choose the very best and write questions that relate directly to them.
- *Focus your time and energy on higher-level questions and initiate discussion with them.* Do not believe that in order to ask higher-level questions, you have to lead up to them with lower-level questions. It is simply not true. In fact, Martin Haberman (1991) calls the notion of basic-level thinking before higher-level thinking "the pedagogy of poverty," not only because it is so predominant in schools with large populations of low-income students but also because the practice of beginning always with literal information gets in the way of real learning. *Start* with the higher-level questions; trust that your students can think abstractly and deeply and want to think abstractly and deeply, that they really *like* latching on to a problem and having to use intellectual power to solve it. They do.

  Ask questions that allow students' minds to "click." As students grapple with larger questions, they will use and learn literal facts and information. If you find that you need to ask literal-level questions, they will come to you with little effort; you do not need to have these questions written out in advance. You do need to have higher-level questions thought out and written out, however; it is best to focus your energy on them.

- *Constantly seek to connect subject matter content to students' lives.* Build on what students *know* rather than trying to "catch" them unable to recite what they don't know. Design questions that link the known with the new and help students see that carbon-dating tables, Ping-Pong tables, multiplication tables, and water tables all have bearing on their lives. Our most recent study of high school dropouts (Bridgeland, Dilulio, & Morison, 2006) found that 47%—nearly half—of adults who dropped out of school did so because classes were uninteresting: "boring, nothing I was interested in" (p. 4). Connecting learning to students' lives helps make school interesting.
- *Write and ask questions that you find interesting, intriguing, and provocative.* Chances are, your students will feel the same way. Certainly, if you find writing the questions to be boring, class discussion will be correspondingly dull.
- *Don't be afraid to let students learn from one another.* Teacher-led discussions need not be limited to the one-person-response model. Put students in groups or let them work with partners. Ask big-picture questions and receive group consensus responses. Students will teach one another and learn from one another. They will cover main points and use details and facts to support their group response; they will also assist those students who need help. After all groups have contributed, give students time to reflect and comment on variations in the original responses. This has a way of chaining into wonderfully satisfying, rich discussion. When that happens, comprehension is correspondingly satisfying and rich.
- *After writing your questions, check to see what comprehension levels you've addressed.* Check to see how many of your questions require
  - *Reader understanding of ideas directly stated in text*—Literal-Level Comprehension.
  - *Reader conclusions drawn from text elements not directly stated* (unstated relationships or comparisons, nuance, symbolic language)—Interpretive-Level Comprehension.
  - *Reader integration of new information with world knowledge from which new relationships emerge*—Applied-Level Comprehension.

Step 4 Skill Development and Application (After Reading: Beyond)

Skill development and application should follow logically and reasonably from discussion that has taken place and from the lesson objectives. It may, in fact, occur as part of the discussion during and immediately following reading. The intent of this part of the DRA is to give students the opportunity to practice doing what they've just learned to do, whether it's observing and recording weather conditions, solving arithmetic equations, reading and interpreting Shakespeare, playing basketball, or understanding the historical forces that led to the Vietnam War. Obviously, some activities are "skillsier" than others. The questions are: How *important* are they? And how significantly do they contribute to your students' ability to function in your content area? Answers to these questions allow you to decide if your skill development and application activity should be some sort of drill, vocabulary study, expository/narrative writing, group mapping with discussion and analysis, individual or group projects, or some combination of these activities.

Step 5 Extension and Follow-up Activities (After Reading: Beyond)

Sometimes it is difficult to decide where skill development and application ends and lesson extension and follow-up activities begin. That's all right. In real life, step-by-step procedures have a way of getting blurred at the edges. What is important is that extension and follow-up activities allow both *closure*—bringing a lesson to a satisfying end—and *extension*—pursuing an exciting idea well beyond immediate lesson boundaries. So, these "5th-Step Activities" (Davidson, 1989) may be small or large, a big deal or a little deal, short and sweet, or long and involved. The larger ones tend to be easily identifiable: major course projects; skits, plays, and productions; science fairs; completed furniture, paintings, clothing, and meals; research papers; or any number of other more-or-less elaborate activities. It is frequently the case that these activities are a primary basis for assessment of how well students achieved lesson and unit goals.

One activity that I recommend for all subject areas is the Three-Minute Write (which some people refer to as a Quick Write). Very simply, the Three-Minute Write is 3 minutes of time, at the end of a lesson or class, in which students are asked to write about what they learned, what they didn't learn, what they understood, what they didn't understand, what they want more of, and what bothered them—in short, to write about their immediate analysis of their learning and of the class period. These may be signed or anonymous and are turned in to the teacher (also sometimes called Exit Slips—the students' passports for leaving class). The wise teacher reads these writings carefully, noting where confusion/noncomprehension occurred, looking to see what should be repeated and what should not, checking to see if damage-control efforts need to be launched, and facing honestly his/her own strengths and weaknesses as perceived by the students.

DRA LESSON PLAN—SOCIAL STUDIES

The following DRA lesson plan was written to guide reading and study of a newspaper article titled, "Architecture: Now you see it, now you don't" which raises issues in contemporary urban and community planning.

As you read the lesson plan, notice how different this lesson is from the daily routine that Dave Lowery describes in his social studies class. The DRA in this lesson is structured to engage students' minds, energy, and attention. It builds on what students already know and then extends that knowledge with new information. Along the way it guides their reading and supports both their learning and their development as readers and thinkers.

DRA LESSON PLAN, *Social Studies*

Lesson: Urban and Community Planning

Course/Grade: American History/11th Grade

Materials: Newspaper Article, "Architecture: Now you see it, now you don't," paper, pens/pencils

LESSON OBJECTIVES (WITH CONTENT STANDARDS)

Upon completion of this lesson students will:

- Be able to identify ways that planning and development affect urban and community life (Standard 11.2.2—students describe the changing landscape, including the growth of cities linked by industry and trade, and the development of cities according to race, ethnicity, and class).
- Be able to identify current issues related to city and community planning, both in the local community and across the nation (Standard 11.8.6—students discuss the diverse environmental regions of North America, their relationship to local economies, and the origins and resolution of environmental problems in those areas.
- Understand the impact of city and community planning on their own lives, both current and future (Standard 11.5.7—students discuss the rise of mass production techniques, the growth of cities, the impact of new technologies and the resulting prosperity and the effect on the American landscape.

LESSON PROCEDURES: DAY ONE

Before Reading: Into

Step One Preparation for Reading

1. Vocabulary Presentation: Write the following on the board:
   - Parks, sidewalks and building lobbies are the un-volumetric or formless living room where we are redefining public space versus private domain. (Context, structure.)
   - It is the Super Tool of our times that has jettisoned privacy from the confines of a phone booth. (Context.)
   - . . . the start of a fluid phantom world in which street furniture, belvederes, gazebos, balconies and footbridges were unrecognized attempts to reconnect with nature. (Context, sound.)
   - Tall, towering symbols of power—totems and obelisks that every ancient culture erected—are reimagined as lookout posts (what the Eiffel Tower is to Paris) or lifeguard stations. (Context.)
2. *Read sentences/fragments aloud, say*: What do you think———means? How did you figure that out? *Continue discussion until reasonable definitions are developed.*
3. Focusing Event: *Say something like*, Today we're going to read about how technology has altered the buildings of our landscape, the "look" of our cities and communities, and how we connect to the natural landscape. What are some of the local issues of this nature? *List on board as students respond.*
4. What do you think are the "hot topics" of this nature in our community today? *List on board.*

During Reading: Through

Step Two Guided Silent Reading

5. Purpose-Setting Statement: Read the article to find out ways in which we have redefined public and private space using technology and other means.

After Reading: Beyond

Step Three Comprehension Development

6. *Ask:* What are ways we have redefined public and private space? *Record responses on board. Probe for how technology and other means created the redefinitions.*
7. *Say:* Let's go back to our lists of issues and hot topics in our community. Now that we've read the article, what additions might we make? *Students justify responses. Add to lists on board.*
8. *Say:* What are the possible areas of controversy inherent in this kind of city and community development and redefinition? *List.*

Step Four Skill Development and Application

9. *Put students in groups of four to five. Say*: Working in your group, develop a list of what the group believe to be the **five most controversial architectural, development, or building projects for our community**. For each of your five items, develop a written rationale giving reasons for your choice. Identify the person or agency you think will carry primary responsibility for the project. You will need to

   Brainstorm with your group a wide variety of issues—you aren't limited by what we have on the board.

   Seek information from many sources, including newspapers, parents, and the Internet.

   Gather lots of opinions and positions regarding your choices; look for underlying information.

10. *Allow students time to work in groups. Say*: Tonight as homework, choose from the list your group generated your own top five issues in rough priority order. Come to class tomorrow prepared to work toward group consensus on your list.

LESSON PROCEDURES: DAY TWO

11. *Allow first half of the period for groups to arrive at their consensus lists Circulate and assist as needed.*
12. *Say*: One member from each group please come to the board and list your five issues in order of priority. *Have each group give a short explanation of their rationale and reasons for its list of issues and the priorities they established.*
13. *Say*: Now we're going to create a class list. We'll need to do this by consensus and possibly compromise. Let's begin with issues that were at or near the top of all lists. *Guide students in working through this*

process. Make sure that each group has at least one of its items on the final class list.

Step Five Extension and Follow-up

14. *Say*: As homework I want each of you to select one item from our class list and write a statement that justifies this issue as a priority issue for our community to discuss and decide upon. Be sure to use thoughtful, reasoned logic in your statement. This is a formal writing assignment that I will grade. Be sure you edit carefully for logic and well-developed rationale and for grammar and presentation.

LESSON ASSESSMENT(S)

15. Observational Assessment—During discussion check to see that students have a secure hold on the topic and issues. Circulate as groups work, and listen in to see if they're making progress. On Day Two check to see that all students have individual lists and are contributing to group discussion; note the quality of the final lists that groups develop.
16. Homework Assessment—Grade students' written statements for content and presentation.

How to do . . . .

A DRA

The DRA has been criticized in the past as being too focused on teacher talk and not focused enough on student thinking and as being too closely connected with direct reading instruction rather than emphasizing content learning. I think at least some of this criticism is misplaced. The biggest problem with the DRA is that teachers misuse it (such as when questions do not get beyond the literal level or when an entire class discussion is suspended while the teacher searches for the word *clever* or when discussion ignores the content and focuses solely on reading skills). The strategy is not at fault here. The fact is, the DRA is a solid, useful instructional strategy when it is used intelligently and appropriately. It is particularly useful for teachers who feel a need for a bit of structure to support them as they negotiate the complex classroom culture. Use the following guidelines to develop scintillating and subject matter-rich DRA lessons:

1. Select the reading assignment and estimate number of class periods needed to complete prereading, reading, skills development, and follow-up activities. Establish homework assignment(s), if any.

2. Choose vocabulary words to be presented prior to reading. Determine how they will be presented in context: on the board, in a duplicated

handout, or in the text. Note probable means for defining (i.e., context, structure, sound, and dictionary).

3. Write the purpose-setting statement and accompanying question for initiating discussion.
4. Write probable discussion questions.
5. Identify skills to be developed and practiced and the activities to be used for that purpose. Prepare any needed handouts, materials, equipment, and so forth.
6. Identify extension and follow-up activities. Prepare needed materials/ equipment, make any necessary special arrangements, and establish timelines and assignment dates, if appropriate.
7. Determine appropriate assessments.

REQUEST

ReQuest was designed by Anthony Manzo (1969a, 1969b) for the purpose of increasing students' comprehension through a process of reciprocal questioning between teacher and student. It is based on two important notions about constructing meaning from text: first, that asking the right question is as important as (and possibly more important than) knowing the right answer, especially when one's purpose for reading includes learning the information in text (recall Frank Smith's belief that comprehension is all about getting answers to questions one poses). Our most recent research supports this notion. Ana Toboada and John Guthrie (2006) found that questions students ask before reading support their comprehension with or without a strong prior knowledge base. Further, they found that the *level* of questions students asked corresponded to the level of comprehension they demonstrated; thus, literal level questions tended to yield literal level understanding and high-level conceptual questions tended to lead to fuller text representations. A second important idea is that teachers serve as powerful models for student behavior—if students are repeatedly exposed to teachers asking good questions about text, students will adopt similar strategies and begin doing the same thing.

The point of ReQuest is to use student-to-teacher/teacher-to-student questioning interactions to engage students in the same type of purposeful reading and rich comprehension processing as is found with DR-TA. In fact, Manzo considers ReQuest to be a DR-TA-like instructional strategy (Manzo, personal communication, 1974). Originally intended for one-to-one instructional settings, ReQuest is equally adaptable to small-group and large-group instruction. It is, in fact, one of my favorite ways of teaching, which I used extensively during my last two years in the public schools. I describe its use for group instruction here; later, in Chapter 10, I show you how it can be used when working with individuals. For ease of presentation, I have divided ReQuest into sequential steps.

STEPS FOR USING REQUEST

Step 1 The teacher and students silently read a segment of text (the amount of text is predetermined and announced by the teacher). After reading, the teacher closes her/his book, and students are invited to ask as many questions as they wish about the text. They are encouraged to ask "teacher-type" questions. The teacher answers all questions as fully as possible.

Step 2 After students have finished questioning, they close their books and the teacher asks questions, following up on items/ideas students raised, raising new issues, and/or calling students' attention to other important information. The teacher is responsible for asking good questions and for asking questions at all levels of comprehension; Manzo recommends seven categories of questions, which are identified and demonstrated immediately following this discussion.

Step 3 The next segment of text is read, and the reciprocal questioning between students and teacher continues. By the second segment, and continuing throughout the procedure, the teacher's questions should include those that explicitly integrate information from one reading segment into discussion of another: for example, "In the last paragraph, we found out that there is a direct relationship between wind and wave. What effect do you think prevailing winds have on ocean currents?" This step ensures that students will perceive the importance of this kind of integration and accumulation of knowledge.

Step 4 The procedure continues until students can reasonably predict what is going to happen, what further information they are going to get, and what they need to do to complete activities and/or exercises. At that point, the teacher asks, "On the basis of what we have read so far, what do you think the rest of the chapter will be about? What question can we ask that you think the chapter/story will answer?" (Alternatively, "What do you think you'll be asked to do in the exercises/activity following the reading? What will you need to know to do them/it? What question(s) can we ask that will help us complete the exercises/activity?")

Because of the clear focus on question asking in the ReQuest procedure, it is critical that teachers help students turn their prediction statements into questions (e.g., "What question can we ask that you think the chapter will answer?"). It is not important that the final purpose-setting question be "perfect" or match the question the teacher has in his/her head. Imperfect questions can be dealt with in follow-up discussion and are themselves vehicles for developing a sense of what constitutes a "good" question.

Step 5 Students write the purpose-setting question and complete the reading/activity assignment. To initiate discussion, the teacher begins by asking the purpose-setting question and allowing students to answer and evaluate it. (As with the DRA, it is important for this to be the first question addressed; afterward, discussion broadens to include many other topics and areas.) A purpose-setting question the class formulated that was not answered by the text (i.e., an "imperfect" question) is identified as such at the onset of discussion when the teacher asks it. That is, when the teacher asks,

"What is the relationship between color and light in oil painting?" if the text did not address this topic, students will likely answer, "We don't know. The article wasn't about that." The teacher then can say, "All right. If the article didn't answer our question, what question did it answer?" and allow students to ask a question that leads into the content discussion that needs to occur.

Later, the teacher should go back to the "imperfect" question and let students analyze how they came to ask it; for example, "What was it that led us toward this question? Was it something in the book? Something we already knew about the topic? A combination of both?" In this way, students can engage in metacognitive thought by examining and reexamining their own logic and line of reasoning in comparison with the logic of the text. Following discussion, the teacher assigns or guides follow-up activities as appropriate.

CATEGORIES OF QUESTIONS FOR REQUEST

As mentioned earlier, Manzo (1969a) suggests seven categories of questions teachers should ask during a ReQuest interaction. You will readily see that his category list includes all three levels of comprehension (literal, interpretive, and applied); however, these are implicit within his categories and are not addressed directly as such. I like his list because it adopts a slightly different perspective toward questioning than standard categories do and can be helpful in formulating questions, especially if you're new at the game of question asking. It's a rather nice alternative to the traditional, hierarchical comprehension-level model. The category explications below were taken very nearly verbatim from Manzo; sample questions for each category were written for a junior high mathematics text; the lesson was about *angles*.

The following types of questions should be asked during a ReQuest interaction:

1. Questions for which there is an immediate reference; questions that can be answered by looking at the text: "How do you read $m\angle ABC$?" "What does *vertex* mean?"

2. Questions that relate to common knowledge and for which answers can be reasonably expected: "If you hadn't seen the illustration here, how would you expect a right angle to look? Why?"

3. Questions for which the teacher does not expect a "correct" response but for which she or he can provide related information: "Have you ever seen a quilt made from angled pieces? Let me show you one my grandmother made . . ."

4. Questions for which neither the teacher nor the selection is likely to supply a "right" answer but that are nonetheless worth pondering or discussing: "I wonder how any of us could use comparison of angles in our daily lives?"

5. Questions of a personalized type that only the students can answer: "What do you find hardest about using a compass or protractor?"

6. Questions that are answerable but are not answered by the selection being read; further reference is needed: "I wonder how sophisticated computers and computer programs are in generating and measuring geometric figures these days?"

7. Questions requiring translation—for example, from one level of abstraction to another, from one symbolic form to another, from one verbal form to another: "In your own words, how do we tell an obtuse angle from a right angle? from an acute angle?"

Lead-in for developing the final purpose-setting question: "On the basis of what we've done so far, what do you think the practice exercises will require you to do? What information will you need to have in order to do them? What questions will you be answering in completing the exercises?"

I think you can see how the reading lead-in questions follow naturally from questions asked during the teacher–student question exchange. All seven categories of questions are not needed at each stop-point during the discussion; however, in the course of any complete ReQuest lesson, you should ask the full range of question types. It is the teacher's responsibility to see that this occurs. When I first started using ReQuest, I kept a small file card in my book with the category types jotted on it to remind myself of them; I found that I very quickly internalized the question categories and was easily able to keep mental track so that all types of questions were asked in each lesson.

USING REQUEST

During ReQuest, it is critical that the teacher listen carefully to the questions students ask, not only to monitor the kinds and quality of those questions, but also because often students "beat you to the punch" by asking all the questions you'd planned. That's all right (in fact, it's wonderful!) as long as you don't plow forward and ask the same questions anyway. As in so many other situations, you've got to be light on your feet and able to conjure up new questions (or have the presence of mind to say you don't have any questions, compliment the class on a job well done, and move right along).

ReQuest is a powerful strategy for increasing students' comprehension, teaching lesson content, and developing students' reading/learning skills. After using ReQuest for only half a semester, I was more than a little surprised to find my own words coming right back at me from my students. (I discovered I asked "What do you suppose . . ." questions a lot!) Not only that, students even modeled my manner of speech, body language, and strategies for gaining clarification. Once, after I had asked a really muddled question (I was trying to think and ask a question at the same time—not an easy task) the most unlikely student—a painfully shy, never-assertive young man who had been in special reading classes most of his 10 years in school—responded to my muddled question by asking me, "Would you *rephrase* that question, please?" with the most *teacherly* intonation. It was wonderful. I could have jumped for joy. Instead, I thanked him for giving me the opportunity to start over and asked him a crisp and articulate question. I wanted to make sure he felt rewarded for daring to use the strategy of asking me to rephrase my question and encourage him to continue using it and other information-getting strategies in the future. He did, on both counts. He answered the question quite nicely, and, in fact, proceeded to become rather bold in my classroom. I've seen many students nurtured toward intellectual curiosity and increased classroom proficiency with ReQuest. I know that it does indeed change the dynamic in traditional classrooms like Dave Lowery's and foster the kind of reading and learning we've been talking about through this entire chapter.

Following is a lesson plan using ReQuest

REQUEST LESSON PLAN, *Mathematics*

Lesson: Exponential Growth

Course/Grade: Algebra I, 9th–11th Grades

Materials: Textbook, pens for dry-erase board, pencils, notebooks

LESSON OBJECTIVES

Upon completion of this lesson students will be able to

- Interpret and evaluate exponential functions and will be able to model real-world situations with exponential functions (Standard 13—Students add, subtract, multiply, and divide rational expressions and functions. Students solve both computationally and conceptually challenging problems by using these techniques).
- Make predictions using exponential functions (Standard 15—Students apply algebraic techniques to solve rate problems, work problems, and percent mixture problems. Standard 16—Students understand the concepts of a relation and a function, determine whether a given relation defines a function, and give pertinent information about given relations and functions.)

LESSON PROCEDURES

Before Reading: Into

1. *Write* "Exponential Growth" *on the board.*
2. *Say*: Yesterday we learned about exponents and powers. On the basis of what we learned then and what you know about "growth," can you predict what this lesson on exponential growth will be about? *Probe:* Why do you say that? What else? Any other ideas?

During Reading: Through

3. *Say*: Read silently up to but not including Example 1.
4. *After reading, close book and* Say: Now you may ask me questions about what we read. Try to ask "teacher type" questions. *Respond to questions.*
5. *Say*: Now you close your books and I'll ask questions. *Ask (unless already asked)*:
   - How do you write a percent as a decimal?
   - What does the solution "84" represent?

- In your own words, what does "growth factor" mean?
- If you hadn't seen this solution, how else would you have solved this problem?
- Which step in this solution did you find to be the most difficult?

6. *Say*: Now read Example 1.
7. *After reading, Say: Now you ask questions. Respond.*
8. *Say*: Close your books and I'll ask:
   - Where did you see the growth factor, as it was used in the last paragraph, used in this example?
   - What was the exponent used to find the population after two years? After three years?
   - What do you expect the exponent will be to find the population after five years? After 10 years?

9. *Say*: Read the next page included Example 2.
10. *After reading, Say*: Your turn for questions. *Respond.*
11. *Say*: Now I'll ask.
    - When can you use the exponential growth model $y = a(1 + r)^x$
    - What does the a in the model represent?
    - What does the r in the model represent?
    - What is the growth factor in the model?
    - How do you read the equation $y = a(1 + r)^x$
    - What value should be substituted for the x, the exponent, in Example 2? Why?

12. *Say*: Read "Think and Communicate" questions 1–3.
13. *Say*: Ask questions.
14. *Ask*:
    - On the basis on what you learned in the last section we read, what value of x would you substitute in the equation $y = 84(1.12)^x$ to estimate the number of peregrines now?
    - How many peregrines would there be now, according to this equation?

15. *Say*: Read the next page up to "Think and Communicate."
16. *Say*: Ask questions.
17. *Ask:*
    - What do you think the graph will do if you continue drawing the graph to the right?
    - What happens to y as x grows larger?
    - Do x and y grow at the same rate?
    - I wonder how any of us could use exponential growth in our daily lives?
    - What do you find hardest to understand about exponential growth?

18. *Say*: Read "Think and Communicate" and do question 5.
19. *Say*: Who'll share their answer and explanation? *Respond and probe as needed.*

After Reading: Beyond

20. *Ask*:
    - On the basis of what we've done, how would you now define exponential growth? *Allow several students to respond.*
    - What do you think you will be asked to do in the exercises at the end of the lesson?
    - What will you need to know in order to do them?
    - What question or questions might we ask to help us complete the exercises?

21. Say: Take the next 10 minutes to do Checking Key Concepts 1–6 on your own. *After students have finished,* Say: Who'll share the first answer? *Continue.*
22. Homework: Section 9.2, numbers 1, 4, 5, 9, 17, and choose any three in numbers 10–15.

LESSON ASSESSMENT(S)

23. Observational Assessment—During discussion and as students work on practice problems, check to make sure they're understanding. Circulate during seatwork and see that all are on the right track.
24. Homework Assessment—Go over homework in class. Collect papers and grades.

How to do . . . .

ReQUEST

ReQuest is rather easily learned by teachers and students alike. It is particularly useful in short vignettes that stimulate activation of students' prior knowledge base. It serves as a marvelous mechanism for students to obtain information *without having to admit ignorance.* (They treat your answers as responses to known-information questions they've asked!) As such, it allows students to fill empty slots in their prior knowledge base, gain access to key language to express half-known or emerging concepts, and enter text with a richer sense of the content knowledge itself. The following steps are useful for preparing and teaching ReQuest:

1. Select the reading assignment and determine length and number of reading/questioning segments.
2. Preread material, making note of areas you consider to be important enough for questioning (correlate these with already-stated lesson objectives).
3. Determine lead-in question for eliciting student-generated purpose-setting question.

4. Identify follow-up activities and/or assignments.
5. Prepare assessments.

SOME CONCLUDING THOUGHTS ON COMPREHENSION

At the opening of this chapter, I stated that the ultimate goal of reading is comprehension: constructing meaning that is in some way congruent with the author's intended meaning. In addition, I suggested that moving students toward critical analysis of texts is important to their development as readers and learners. The instructional strategies presented here—DR-TA, GMA, DRA, ReQuest—share a clear focus on guiding student comprehension of text. They are, however, valuable resources for doing much more. Certainly, they address the three other goals associated with secondary school reading: learning subject matter content, increasing reading skill, and applying new knowledge. But more importantly, they accomplish all three of these goals in such a way as to differ significantly from the frontal teaching John Goodlad found to be the unrelenting staple of the secondary school day, the kind of teaching we glimped at the beginning of the chapter in Dave Lowery's class. They do, indeed, let students "romp with open-ended questions" and allow them to "turn things around by asking questions [themselves]." Further, they all focus squarely on higher-order thinking and critical examination of ideas and texts.

I made reference earlier in the discussion of the steps in the DRA to the recent landmark study, conducted in 2005, of adults who dropped out of high school. In that study over 465 adults, ages 16 to 25, told focus group leaders and interviewers that the number one reason for dropping out of school was boredom—lack of interesting classes and instructional activities and information that had any relevance to their lives. Once again, we are reminded of Dave Lowery's experience in social studies class. DR-TA, GMA, DRA, and ReQuest help change that experience. They are productive ways to develop students' comprehension, teach subject matter, increase students' reading skills, or guide application of new information, and they encourage critical literacy as well. Each of these instructional strategies provides for students with diverse cultural, linguistic, and academic backgrounds: They allow many voices to be heard in the classroom and opportunities for students to validate their own experience while learning content. These methods immerse students in extended, full discussion of content; at the very least, students who feel constrained to participate have access to important subject matter information. As students gain increasing mastery of the language of that content—which can come only from consistent, repeated opportunity to use it—they will increasingly participate in class discussion and learn the content itself. And finally, this kind of instruction creates opportunity for all students to become thoughtful, strategic readers of content text. As you review the characteristics of thoughtful, mature, and strategic readers earlier in this chapter, you will notice that the instructional strategies presented here guide students in developing such characteristics. All of this is important, both for you and for your students. I firmly believe that if you used nothing more than these instructional approaches in your classroom, you would be a good teacher. You need not, however, be limited to these. There are many other equally productive and useful tools, which will be discussed in the upcoming chapters.

WHAT THIS CHAPTER MEANS TO YOU

1. Dave Lowery is learning very little world history in Ms. Dahlmann's class, but he is developing a world-class negative attitude toward it. And the pattern Ms. Dahlmann has established of read-the-chapter-answer-the-questions-listen-to-the-teacher-lecture is doing nothing to change that situation or increase Dave's ability to read and learn world history. You don't want to create Dave Lowerys in your class.

2. Guiding students' reading of text is a primary means to increase both their comprehension of text and their ability to read increasingly difficult subject matter text. You now know four instructional strategies for guiding comprehension; the DR-TA, GMA, DRA, and ReQuest. All of these strategies are adaptable to many different texts.

3. Critical literacy practices allow students to analyze and critique texts for the purpose of making transparent the underlying attitudes, values, Discourses, and sociocultural stances that texts represent. Open-ended questions allow students to begin such analysis and critique.

FEATURE *What Goes in My Portfolio?*

Create a portfolio artifact from this chapter by applying one or more of the instructional strategies to your subject area. Write a lesson plan demonstrating your ability to guide students' comprehension of text using a DR-TA, GMA, DRA, or ReQuest (or combining GMA with one of the other three). The "How to do . . ." and Building Table features of the chapter (and the sample lesson plans for the DRA and ReQuest in the chapter) should assist you in developing your lesson plan. If possible, teach your lesson and include your reflections and samples of students' work with your lesson plan.

DOUBLE ENTRY JOURNAL

What new ideas do you now have to add to or revise your definition of reading comprehension? What role can you see for comprehension instructional strategies in your subject area and for your own teaching? How can you use or adapt instructional strategies from this chapter to avoid frontal teaching practices and to help students who find your subject area their most difficult? Share your ideas with someone who teaches a subject area different from yours. How do your conclusions compare?

RECOMMENDED SOURCES

*Alvermann, D. E., & Moore, D. W. (1991). Secondary school reading. In R. Barr, M. L. Kamil, P. B. Mosenthal, & P. D. Pearson (Eds.), *Handbook of reading research: Volume II* (pp. 951–983). New York: Longman.

Applebee, A. N. (1993). *Literature in the secondary school: Studies of curriculum instruction in the United States* (Research Report No. 25). Urbana, IL: National Council of Teachers of English.

*Bakhtin, M. M. (1981). *The dialogic imagination: Four essays by M. M. Bakhtin)*. (M. Holquist, Ed.; C. Emerson & M. Holquist, Trans.). Austin: University of Texas Press.

*Bean, T. W., & Moni, K. (2003). Developing students' critical literacy: Exploring identity construction in young adult fiction. *Journal of Adolescent and Adult Literacy, 46*(8), 638–648.

*Betts, E. A. (1946). *Foundations of reading instruction*. New York: American Book Company.

*Bloom, B. S. (1956). *Taxonomy of educational objectives: Handbook I, cognitive domain*. New York: Longman, Green.

*Bridgeland, J. M., Dilulio Jr., J. J., & Morison, K. B. (2006). *The silent epidemic: Perspectives of high school dropouts*. A report by Civic Enterprises in association with Peter D. Hart Research Associates for the Bill & Melinda Gates Foundation. http://www.gatesfoundation.org/nr/downloads/ed/TheSilentEpidemic3-06/FINAL.pdf.

*Cope, J. (1997). *Beyond Voices of Readers:* Students on school's effect on reading. *Journal of English, 86*(3), 18–23.

*Davidson, J. L. (1982). The group mapping activity for instruction in reading and thinking. *Journal of Reading, 26*, 52–56.

*Davidson, J. L. (1989). *The DR-TA reading series*. Monroe, NY: Trillium Press.

*Cited in Text.

Durkin, D. (1978–1979). What classroom observations reveal about reading comprehension instruction. *Reading Research Quarterly, 14*, 481–533.

*Freire, P., & Macedo, D. (1989). *Literacy*. Westport, CT: Greenwood Press.

*Gee, J. P. (1996). *Social linguistics and literacies* (2nd ed.). New York: Routledge-Falmer.

*Gillotte, H. (1991, April). *The examination of literature-based series: Potential problems for minority students.* Paper presented at the annual meeting of the American Educational Research Association, Chicago, IL.

*Goodlad, J. I. (1984). *A place called school.* New York: McGraw-Hill.

Gray, W. S. (1946). *On their own in reading.* Chicago: Scott Foresman.

*Guszak, F. J. (1967). Teacher questioning and reading. *Reading Teacher, 21*, 227–234.

*Haberman, M. (1991). The pedagogy of poverty versus good teaching. *Phi Delta Kappan, 73*, 290–294.

Haggard, M. R. (1988). Developing critical thinking with the directed reading-thinking activity. *Reading Teacher, 41*, 526–533.

Hartman, D. K. (1995). Eight readers reading: The intertextual links of proficient readers reading multiple passages. *Reading Research Quarterly, 30*(3), 520–561.

Heath, S. B. (1982). Questioning at home and at school: A comparative study. In G. Spindler (Ed.), *Doing the ethnography of schooling: Educational anthropology in action* (pp. 102–131). New York: Holt.

*Herber, H. L. (1978). *Teaching reading in the content areas* (2nd ed). Englewood Cliffs, NJ: Prentice–Hall.

*Luke, A. (2000). Critical literacy in Australia: A matter of context and standpoint. *Journal of Adolescent and Adult Literacy 43*(5), 448–461.

*Manzo, A. V. (1969a). The ReQuest procedure. *Journal of Reading, 13*, 123–126.

*Manzo, A. V. (1969b). *Improving reading comprehension through reciprocal questioning.* Doctoral dissertation, Syracuse University (University Microfilms No. 70–10, 364), Syracuse, NY.

*Markham, B. (1987). The splendid outcast. In M. S. Lovell (Ed.), *The splendid outcast: Beryl Markham's African stories* (pp. 33–47). San Francisco: North Point Press.

*Mehan, H. (1979). "What time is it, Denise?", Asking known information questions in classroom discourse. In *Theory into Practice*, (vol. 18, pp. 285–294). Columbus, OH: College of Education, Ohio State University.

Newmann, F. M. (1992). Higher-order thinking and prospects for classroom thoughtfulness. In F. M. Newmann (Ed.), *Student engagement and achievement in American secondary schools* (pp. 62–91). New York: Teachers College Press.

*Paris, S. G., Lipson, M. Y., & Wixon, K. K. (1994). Becoming a strategic reader. In R. B. Ruddell, M. R. Ruddell, & H. Singer (Eds.), *Theoretical models and processes of reading* (4th ed., pp. 788–810). Newark, DE: International Reading Association.

*Pearson, P. D., Roehler, L. R., Dole, J. A., & Duffy, G. G. (1990). *Developing expertise in reading comprehension: What should be taught? How should it be taught?* (Tech. Rep. No. 512). Champaign: University of Illinois at Urbana-Champaign, Center for the Study of Reading.

*Pressley, M. (2000). What should comprehension instruction be the instruction of? In M. L. Kamil, P. B. Mosenthal, P. D. Pearson, & R. Barr (Eds.), *Handbook of reading research*, volume III (pp. 545–561). Mahway, NJ: Lawrence Erlbaum.

*Ruddell, M. R., & Marker, P. M. (2006). Literacy and social justice: The place where the sidewalk ends. *California Reader, 39*(3), 13–21.

*Santa, C. M. (2006). A vision for adolescent literacy: Ours or theirs? *Journal of Adolescent and Adult Literacy, 49*(6), 466–476.

*Siegel, M. (1995). More than words: The generative power of transmediation in learning. *Canadian Journal of Education, 20*(4), 455–475.

*Singer, H. (1970). Research that should have made a difference. *Elementary English, 47*, 27–34.

*Smith, F. (1994). *Understanding reading* (5th ed.). Hillsdale, NJ: Lawrence Erlbaum.

*Stauffer, R. G. (1969). *Directing reading maturity as a cognitive process.* New York: Harper & Row.

*Stauffer, R. G. (1980). *The language-experience approach to teaching reading* (2nd ed.). New York: Harper & Row.

Suhor, C. (1984). Towards a semiotics-based curriculum. *Journal of Curriculum Studies, 16*, 247–257.

*Taffel, A. (1992). *Physics: Its methods and meanings* (6th ed.). Needham, MA: Prentice-Hall.

Tierney, R. J., & Pearson, P. D. (1992). Learning to learn from text: A framework for improving classroom practice. In E. K. Dishner, T. W. Bean, J. E. Readence, & D. W. Moore (Eds.), *Reading in the content areas: Improving classroom instruction* (3rd ed., pp. 87–103). Dubuque, IA: Kendall/ Hunt.

Tierney, R. J., Readence, J. E., & Dishner, E. K. (2000). *Reading strategies and practices: A compendium* (5th ed.). Boston: Allyn & Bacon.

*Toboada, A., & Guthrie, J. T. (2006). Contributions of student questioning and prior knowledge to construction of knowledge from reading information text. *Journal of Literacy Research, 38*(1), 1–35.

BUILDING TABLE

CHAPTER 4	DR-TA	GMA	DRA	REQUEST
FOCUS ON	Content reading and discussion	Content reading and organization	Content reading and discussion	Content reading and discussion
GUIDES STUDENTS	Before and during reading	After reading and before writing	Before, during, and after reading	Before and during reading
USE TO PLAN	Lessons	Lessons	Lessons	Lessons
MAY BE USED	Whole class, small groups	Whole class, cooperative groups, partnerships	Whole class, small groups	Whole class, small groups, individuals
MAY BE COMBINED WITH (known strategies)	GMA	DR-TA, DRA	GMA	GMA
MATERIALS PREPARATION	Light	None to light	Moderate to extensive	Light
OTHER PREPARATION	Moderate	Moderate	Moderate to extensive	Light
OUTSIDE RESOURCES	Not needed	Not needed	Useful	Useful
HOW TO DO	Page 113	Pages 121–122	Pages 133–134	Pages 140–141

CHAPTER 5

VOCABULARY LEARNING IN CONTENT AREAS

DOUBLE ENTRY JOURNAL

Can you remember an incident when you were elementary school age in which you learned a new word or incorporated a word into your speaking vocabulary? In your journal, write the word and describe the incident as fully as possible. Can you remember an incident when you were junior high or high school age in which you learned a new word or incorporated a word into your speaking vocabulary? Write the word and describe the incident as fully as possible.

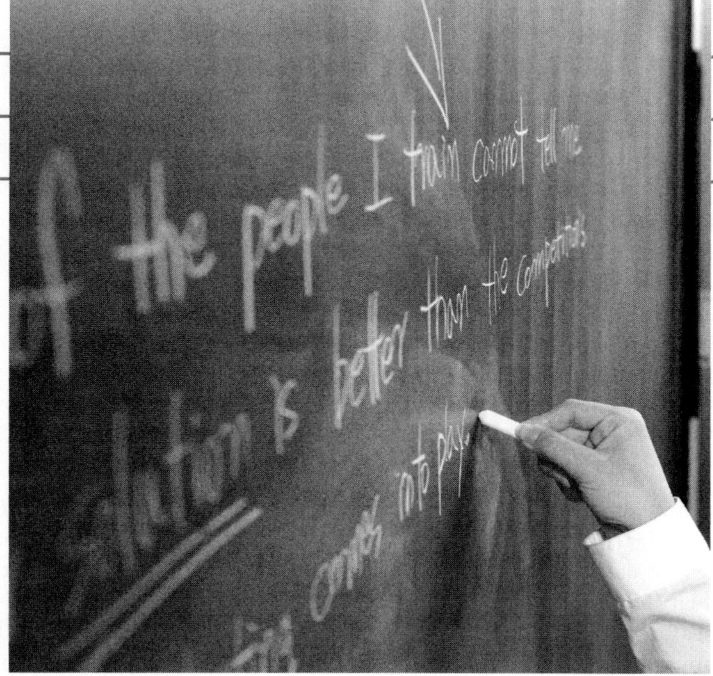

TongRo Image Stock/Jupiter Images

Zena Logan sits at her desk working on her vocabulary assignment—finding the words in the dictionary and writing definitions on the word sheet. The 20 words Mr. Whitaker assigned this week go from *lackey* to *mendicant.* She looks at the clock. Nineteen minutes left in third period. She can hear the tick-tick-tick as the second hand s-l-o-w-l-y makes its way around again. Her stomach growls softly. At least lunch comes next. Better get back to the list and her dictionary.

lackey—a male servant

laconic—expressed with few words

lambent—softly bright or radiant

latent—potential, hidden, concealed

God, this is boring. I wonder if I'll see Michael at lunch. Will he see me? Maybe talk to me? Better keep going. Eight minutes.

laudable—commendable

lenient—not harsh or severe in judgment

lethargy—drowsiness

That's it—*lethargy*, "drowsiness"—that's just how she feels. Gotta rest. Stretch. Yawn. Sigh. Two minutes. Time to finish and get out of here. Only 13 words to go.

• • •

Vocabulary knowledge has long been accepted as a critical component of text comprehension and learning in all subject areas. Virtually everyone agrees that learning the language of a subject area is an important aspect of learning the subject itself. The important relationship between vocabulary, comprehension, and learning is, however, more universally proclaimed than it is operationalized in the classroom. All too often, vocabulary instruction is isolated: contiguous in time, perhaps, but not connected to the true point of the classroom and almost never connected to the lives of the students themselves. We all have memories of such vocabulary lessons: Definitions dictated by the teacher at the beginning of each reading assignment; words on the chalkboard to be written down, looked up, and defined verbatim from the dictionary; and the Dreaded Word Lists. Such instruction is contrary to much of what we know about vocabulary learning. In an extensive review of research on vocabulary development, I arrived at the following generalizations about word learning.

- Words are known on a variety of levels and in gradients of understanding; similarly, words are learned not in one fell swoop but in a more or less gradual way over time. Word learning involves a constellation of learning resources and abilities.
- By adulthood, individuals have well-developed, personalized strategies for learning new words: instruction directed toward teaching students how to apply various word-learning strategies is, by and large, highly successful.
- We know that students acquire strategies for learning and remembering new words, but we have almost no understanding of how, or whether, students systematically and selectively apply these strategies while reading and learning.
- Much and varied information resides in text, and it is this information that makes up the context that readers use to construct meaning while reading.
- The general consensus is that context does indeed facilitate meaning construction.
- Substantial evidence suggests that readers spontaneously use context to construct meaning for new words.

- We have little knowledge of how readers transact with words in text and the stances they adopt for understanding new words, learning new words, remembering word meanings, and applying that knowledge in everyday reading, writing, and learning events.
- We are just beginning to explore the influence of social interactions on word learning. The limited evidence we have suggests that positive effects occur as the result of social interactions during word learning. (Ruddell, 1994, pp. 436–437)

Figure 5.1 on page 153 is a word list I picked up from the floor of an area high school at the end of school one day and is not at all unlike the list Zena Logan is grappling with. Notice how it marches, shall we say, inexorably, through the alphabet, contextless and forbidding; notice also that this student has decided that it takes only a synonym or two to define some pretty powerful words. This list, and other similar materials, actually encourage a definition-by-synonym approach to vocabulary instruction in which no context, or text of any kind, is present to aid in meaning construction, add depth, suggest nuance, or indicate any connections with one's prior knowledge base. Further, long and contextless word lists typify precisely Bill Nagy's charge (1988) that much vocabulary instruction is ineffective because

1. Most instruction fails to produce in-depth word knowledge.
2. Most instruction is targeted toward a set of words considered to be "difficult," when, in fact, the difficulty of a given word lies not in the word itself but rather in the word *in relationship to* the context within which it is used.

CENTERPIECE LESSON PLAN

Before we discuss effective vocabulary instruction and instructional strategies, let's look at this chapter's Centerpiece Lesson Plan. This lesson plan combines three instructional strategies; it embeds semantic mapping into a Directed Reading Activity (DRA) and combines that with the Vocabulary Self-Collection Strategy (VSS). Two things you should note about this lesson plan are (1) it illustrates appropriate vocabulary instruction both for removing barriers to comprehension and for long-term retention of word meanings, and (2) it shows how to do a DRA in which you alternate guided reading with discussion of short pieces of text.

SEMANTIC MAPPING, DRA, VSS CENTERPIECE LESSON PLAN *Science*

Lesson: Motion

Course/Grade: Physical Science/8th Grade

Materials: Textbooks, pens, pencils, paper

LESSON OBJECTIVES (WITH CONTENT STANDARDS)

Upon completion of this lesson, students will be able to

- Recognize the distinguishing factors among the concepts of *speed, velocity,* and *acceleration* (Standard 1d—Students know that velocity of an object must be described by specifying both the direction and the speed of the object. Standard 1e—Students know changes in velocity may be due to changes in speed, direction or both).
- Apply their understanding of rate, speed, velocity, and acceleration in practical situations (Standard 1b—Students know that average speed is the total distance divided by the total time elapsed and the speed of an object. Standard 1c—Students know how to solve problems involving distance, time, and average speed).

LESSON PROCEDURES: DAY ONE

Before Reading: Into—Semantic Mapping, DRA

1. Vocabulary Development: Place students in partner teams. Write the word *motion* on the board.
2. *Say*: Working with your partner, list as many features, ideas, or things you associate with the word motion as you can. Do this quickly. *Allow two to three minutes.*
3. *Say*: Let's share ideas. What are some things you thought of for *motion? As students share, write ideas in any order around the word motion, discussing ideas as you go.*
4. *Say*: Now let's create a semantic map of the ideas we generated for *motion.* How might we organize those ideas and group them around "motion"? *Guide students in categorizing and organizing words sensibly around the central topic creating a semantic map as you go. Accept new words/ideas as they occur. Continue until all or most of the words have been entered on the semantic map.*
5. *Say*: Everyone make a quick copy of our semantic map. As we go through the lesson and unit you may add to or revise your map.
6. Focusing Event: *Say*: This week we'll be exploring the concept of motion. We'll be reading in the textbook, doing some problems, creating problems of our own, and reading other things as well. Here's the first challenge to lead us into reading: You hear two friends arguing; one says that the fastest sprinter alive runs at 20 miles per hour, and the other insists he speeds along at 20 miles per second. Who is right? Can they both be? *Write challenge on board.*

During Reading: Through—DRA

7. Purpose-Setting Statement: *Say*: Read Section 2.1, "Motion is Relative" and write a brief answer to the challenge questions. Be sure you can justify your answers. When you're reading, share your answers with your partner and resolve any differences. List two other examples of *rate* and *relative motion.*

8. Comprehension Development: *After students have finished say*:
   - Does the fastest sprinter alive run 20 miles per hour or 20 miles per second? How do you know? *Receive responses. Probe, clarify.*
   - Can both the 20 miles per hour and 20 miles per second be right? Why or why not?
   - What additional examples of rate and motion did you list? Why did you choose them?
   - How can we now define *rate* and *relative motion*? Where might we locate those on our semantic map? *Guide class in doing this.*
9. New Purpose-Setting Statement: *Say*: In a race car last year, the top driver averaged 100 miles per hour over a 200-mile course. The course looked something like this: *Draw a racing oval on the board.* On the straightaway, he was clocked at 200 miles and hour. Read Section 2.2, "Speed" to see how to describe the race in terms of *instantaneous* and *average speed.*
10. Comprehension Development: *After students have finished say*:
    - How can you describe the race in terms of instantaneous and average speed?
    - How do we determine average speed? *Receive responses; clarify.*
    - What was the driver's average speed? How did you figure that out?
    - What are some other examples of how we might use instantaneous and average speeds?

After Reading: Beyond—VSS

11. Vocabulary Self-Collection Strategy (VSS): *Say*: Now I want you and your partner to choose one word or term from our reading and discussion today that you think should be on the vocabulary list for our study of motion. You'll nominate your word for our list. I get to nominate a word as well. Be prepared to
    - Tell where you found the word
    - Tell what you think the word means
    - And tell why you think it should be on our vocabulary list.

    Words you nominate may or may not already be on our semantic map.
12. *When students are ready say*: Okay, who has a word to nominate for our vocabulary list? *Receive words and have students tell where they found it, what they think it means, and why they're nominating it.* ***Be sure to add your own word and give the same accompanying information.***
13. *After all partner teams have shared say*: Let's pick the top five words from the nominations for our vocabulary list. We'll add more as we go through the chapter. Which words do you think we should keep on our list? *Lead discussion to arrive at consensus; make sure that* rate, speed, velocity, *and* acceleration *are either (1) on the list, or (2) already fully understood by all. Circle the final 5 words selected.*

14. *Say*: Let's refine and agree on our definitions. *Go through the list of five words and craft a definition for each from student input, your knowledge, and use of reference sources (glossaries, dictionaries, online references, etc.). Write each final definition on the board.* Everyone copy the words and their definitions in your vocabulary journal. Let's also put them on our semantic map and mark them with an asterisk. *Lead discussion.*
15. Homework: *Say*: By any method you choose, determine your average speed of walking. Be prepared to share your findings and method tomorrow. Prepare a written summary of how you calculated your average speed of walking and the results. Use your book and our VSS words to help develop your method and explanation. You will turn this paper in for a grade.

LESSON ASSESSMENT(S)

16. Observational Assessment—During semantic mapping, after-reading discussions, and VSS discussion check to see that students have accurate understandings and justifications for conclusions. Note the importance of words selected in VSS.
17. Homework Assessment—Grade students' papers for accuracy and creativity in development of the means for determining average speed of walking. Add points for correct use of VSS words/terms.

EFFECTIVE CONTENT VOCABULARY INSTRUCTION

Effective content vocabulary instruction must, if nothing else, *connect*. It must connect with reading/writing assignments, class topics, and the content to be learned; it must connect with students' prior knowledge and previous experience, with their interests and needs for learning content, and with their daily lives; and it must connect with all that goes on in the classroom, the "whole fabric" of classroom life. Graves (2001) suggests that to be effective, vocabulary instruction needs to be a four-part program involving wide reading, teaching individual words, teaching word-learning strategies, and fostering word-consciousness. Nagy (1988) states that effective vocabulary instruction must include the properties of *integration*, *repetition*, and *meaningful use*, which all imply connectedness. Graves and Prenn (1986) highlight yet another type of connecting: the teacher's awareness of and sensitivity to varying task needs and levels of word knowledge that influence how words should be taught. Graves and Prenn identify three vocabulary-learning tasks associated with reading, each with its own distinct instructional implications:

1. Learning to read words already in students' listening or speaking vocabularies but not in their reading or writing vocabularies.
2. Learning to read words that are not in students' listening, speaking, reading, or writing vocabularies but for which a concept is available.
3. Learning to read words for which students do not yet have a concept.

FIGURE 5.1 *The Dreaded Word List*

203. immutable
not changeable

204. impale
to torture

205. impasse
deadlock

206. impeccable
without error

207. impediment
an obstruction

208. impervious
not capable of being influenced

209. implacable
unforgiving

210. impunity

211. inadvertent
unintentional

212. inane
lacking sense, foolish

213. inarticulate
not clearly defined

214. incarcerate
to imprison, jail

215. incessant
ceaseless

216. incipient
beginning

217. inclement
rough, stormy, harsh

218. incognito
[something-adj?] hidden, disguised

219. incongruous
not in keeping, unsuitable

220. incorrigible
beyond control

221. incredible
difficult to believe

222. incubus
an evil spirit, nightmare

223. indigent
poor, impoverished

224. indomitable
undefeatable

225. inert
not moving, active [sic]

226. inexorable
relentless, unyielding, inflexible

227. inexplicable
cannot be accounted for, unexplainable

228. inference
educated guess based on info

229. ingenious
very clever

230. ingenuous
naive

PURPOSES FOR CONTENT VOCABULARY INSTRUCTION

Integration, repetition, meaningful use, connectedness—all of these are critical components of effective vocabulary instruction. An equally important but often overlooked instructional component is that teachers need to understand the different goals, or purposes, for vocabulary instruction and know when and how to use various instructional strategies and activities to achieve them. I find, for example, that very few people distinguish between two different purposes for teaching content vocabulary.

The first purpose is to *remove barriers to comprehension* of text. This is the instruction we do prior to reading, as we did in the DRA in Chapter 4 and this chapter's Centerpiece Lesson Plan, to preteach vocabulary. Preteaching vocabulary before reading is a traditionally recommended practice, and it is currently receiving renewed attention because of its usefulness in assisting ESL students' acquisition of both the language and the content knowledge in subject area classrooms. For the most part, this instruction focuses on key words and concepts central to the content of the immediate text; thus, both the words and their meanings are often specialized, technical, and lesson specific or context specific. In this instruction, multiple meanings, nuance, and meaning extensions generally are less important than is the goal of building meaning and developing concepts pertaining to a particular topic or text. *Immediate* use predominates as the goal of prereading vocabulary instruction, with periodic review of words and terms as they occur across topics and texts. The task needs Graves and Prenn (1986) describe (e.g., learning to read words already partially known, learning to read words for which a concept is available, and learning to read words for which no concept is available) are pertinent to and influence the form this instruction will take.

A second purpose for content vocabulary instruction is to *promote long-term acquisition and development of the language of an academic discipline.* The rationale for this instruction is based, in part, on the conviction we all hold that increased command of the language of a subject will deepen and enrich students' understanding of the subject itself, and also because we know (whether intuitively or through our own study and observation) that the mark of an educated person in any discipline is his or her ability to function easily in the language of that field. We want our students to acquire this proficiency and to have the depth of understanding that signifies real learning. Further, we want them to become independent word learners and active knowledge seekers as well. Instruction designed to achieve this goal focuses on extending, refining, adding to, and changing schemata; developing multiple meanings; making connections within and across academic disciplines; and adding nuance and subtlety to word meaning and constructions of knowledge. This instruction is directed primarily toward in-depth understanding and requires exploration of words in relationship to the context in which they are embedded—and I would extend Nagy's notion of written context to include the Discourse of the discipline as a whole.

To summarize, then, one goal of content vocabulary instruction is focused clearly on immediate, short-term learning needs, with emphasis on identifying what students know and preparing them for the reading and learning to follow. The other goal involves development and extension of students' mastery of a discipline through integration of new ideas into their existing knowledge base and assimilation of new words into working vocabularies. One occurs immediately prior to reading text, whereas the other is most reasonably accomplished after reading. One is short, sweet, and to the point; the other is extended, exploratory, and wide ranging.

CONFOUNDING THE PURPOSES FOR CONTENT VOCABULARY INSTRUCTION

Problems occur in teaching content vocabulary when we confuse instruction intended to remove barriers to comprehension with instruction aimed at long-term vocabulary acquisition and development and/or when we attempt to combine instruction to achieve both goals at once. Certainly, there is some overlap between the two; words taught prior to reading may eventually become words targeted for long-term development, and learning that occurs in the prereading period feeds into and strengthens instruction that follows. When instruction is designed for one purpose (preparing students to read, for example), however, and teachers expect outcomes associated with the other (long-term retention), *expectations are rarely realized* and everyone ends up thinking that time spent teaching content vocabulary actually impedes subject learning by taking time away from teaching the content itself.

Attempts to combine purposes are just as problematic: It is not until *after* reading that we really know what words need to be pursued for long-term acquisition. Students' prior knowledge and previous experience determine that, and more often than not, the "real" list is considerably shorter than the list of potential words that any book chapter or other text selection would yield. Consequently, if we attempt to preteach all the words that could interfere with comprehension of a passage *in combination with* all the words that we predict are important for long-term acquisition, the list becomes so long that vocabulary lessons in fact do delay or derail completely the content lesson itself.

So it is important for teachers to distinguish between these two related but different content vocabulary instructional goals. One is aimed at removing barriers to comprehension (instruction that should occur *before* reading); the other is intended to encourage long-term acquisition and development of the language of an academic discipline (instruction that should occur *after* reading). This chapter considers both prereading and postreading content vocabulary instruction and includes three of the four program parts for effective vocabulary instruction that Graves (2001) recommends: teaching individual words, teaching word-learning strategies (both addressed in prereading instruction), and fostering word-consciousness (postreading instruction). Wide reading is covered in Chapter 12.

Content Vocabulary Instruction: Removing Barriers to Comprehension

As content area teachers, we have two major responsibilities regarding vocabulary instruction and comprehension of text. First, we are responsible for ensuring that our students will experience some level of success in constructing meaning from text; this frequently is accomplished, in part, during prereading instruction by direct teaching of selected vocabulary words. We do this to remove barriers to comprehension and "boost" students' understanding of key concepts and ideas they will encounter as they read. This is the kind of vocabulary instruction that most frequently occurs in secondary classrooms and is commonly referred to as "direct vocabulary instruction." It usually combines some degree of lecture, questioning, explanation, and discussion as teachers determine students' prior knowledge levels.

A second responsibility teachers have in prereading vocabulary instruction is to provide students with the means for dealing *independently* with unknown words. That is, we must make sure students have a *functional system* for learning new words, an effective answer for the question "What do you do when you come to a word you do not know?" Further, we must ensure that students have instruction and practice using this system *in the classroom of every subject area in which they are expected to read, write, think, and learn.* This is much more far-reaching than direct vocabulary instruction, and it takes a little more time than direct vocabulary instruction, but we cannot ignore the responsibility for it by limiting instruction to teaching simply a selected set of words.

Consider for a moment the futility of attempting to teach every new word students need to learn in the course of a school year in your class. It simply cannot be done; part of your instructional time must therefore focus on teaching and reinforcing students' ability to handle unknown words on their own. (Sorry. The elementary teachers can't do this one for you. You can't teach a third-grader how to construct meaning for words in an advanced chemistry text, a woodworking manual, or one of Shakespeare's plays.) It is middle school and secondary teachers, then, who must assume the responsibility for both direct vocabulary instruction (teaching individual words) and instruction to assist students in developing a functional system for learning the language of middle school and secondary texts (teaching word-learning strategies).

PREREADING INSTRUCTION: DIRECT VOCABULARY TEACHING

Recall the vocabulary portion of our sample DRA lesson in Chapter 4 (reproduced below).

1. Vocabulary Presentation: *Write the following on the board*:
   - Parks, sidewalks, and building lobbies are the un-volumetric or formless living room where we are redefining public space versus private domain. (Context, structure.)
   - It is the Super Tool of our times that has jettisoned privacy from the confines of a phone booth. (Context.)
   - . . . the start of a fluid phantom world in which street furniture, belvederes, gazebos, balconies, and footbridges were unrecognized attempts to reconnect with nature. (Context, sound.)
   - Tall, towering symbols of power—totems and obelisks that every ancient culture erected—are reimagined as lookout posts (what the Eiffel Tower is to Paris) or lifeguard stations. (Context.)
2. *Read each sentence/fragment aloud*, Say: What do you think———means? How did you figure that out? *Continue discussion until reasonable definitions are developed.*

This is an example of direct prereading vocabulary instruction, and it is representative of a fair amount of the direct instruction that teachers do; however, any number of other activities may be used in addition to, or instead of, the "What do you think this word means?" discussion used in this lesson. Herber (1978) and Nelson-Herber (1986) suggest clustering vocabulary words around critical lesson concepts and teaching them with a Structured Overview model to introduce both the words and important lesson concepts prior to reading (see Figure 5.2). Nelson-Herber emphasizes the importance of extended class discussion of the structured overview and its usefulness for:

1. Teaching content words and concepts.
2. Refining and extending meanings of words previously learned.
3. Introducing the reading itself.

Many of the vocabulary activities presented in this section and later in the chapter are also good substitutes for the straightforward discussion we used with the DRA and may be adapted according to students' needs; that is, instruction may:

1. *Provide pronunciation* for a word that is in students' speaking/listening vocabularies.

FIGURE 5.2 *Structured Overview: Science*

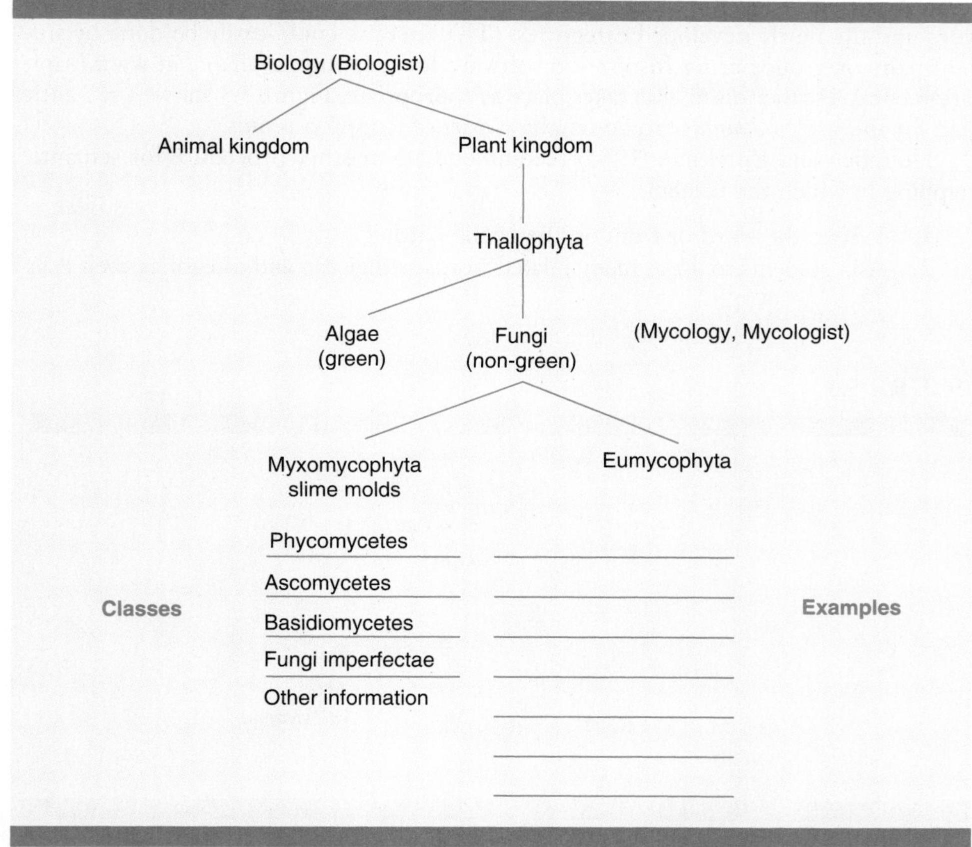

2. *Tell what a word means and link it* to known concepts.
3. *Provide extended definition and discussion* of words for which concepts are incomplete or not available (Graves & Prenn, 1986).

SEMANTIC MAPPING

Semantic mapping (Johnson, Toms-Bronowski, & Pittelman, 1981) is a whole-class, small-group, or individual activity that develops associations and encourages personal response to targeted vocabulary words. You have already seen semantic mapping in our Centerpiece Lesson Plan. Semantic mapping is particularly useful for prereading instruction because it assists in activating students' prior knowledge of key concepts to be encountered in text.

As a whole-class activity, semantic mapping may be done in a variety of ways. One way that is slightly different from what the teacher did in our Centerpiece Lesson Plan begins with the teacher writing one of the selected vocabulary words on the board: for example, *measurement.* Students free-associate words, terms, or phrases they associate with the word *(inches, precision, testing, numbers);* these are written on the board around the targeted word in random order as they are suggested. When students are finished suggesting ideas, they work in small groups or pairs or individually to categorize associations and label the categories. Students then produce their own maps for the word and the newly developed categories. (This exercise could easily be done by student pairs or groups using Inspiration software for mapping, available at www.Inspiration.com). Further discussion takes place as appropriate. Figure 5.3 shows a semantic map for the word *advantage* to be taught as part of a unit on tennis.

Heimlich and Pittelman (1986) recommend yet another procedure for semantic mapping in which the teacher:

1. Writes the word or term on the chalkboard.
2. Asks students to list as many related words as they can and categorize their lists.

FIGURE 5.3 *Semantic Map: Tennis*

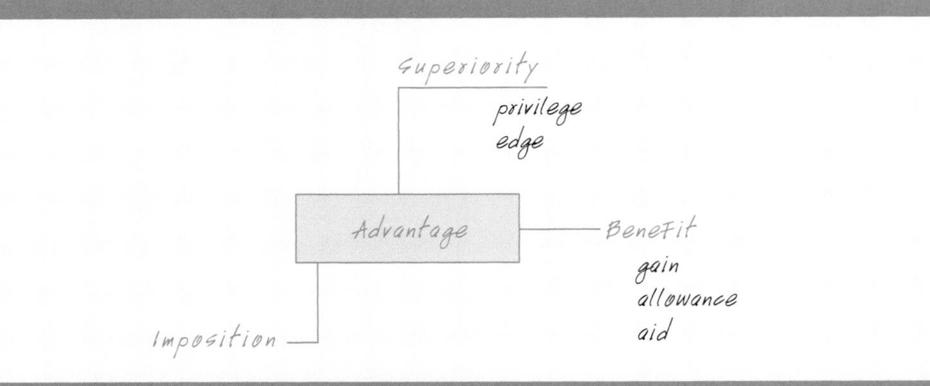

3. Conducts discussion in which students share the prepared lists orally and write these on the class map.
4. Asks students to label the categories.
5. Continues discussion as appropriate.

Heimlich and Pittelman emphasize the importance of discussion in semantic mapping to provide much opportunity for students to connect prior knowledge with content concepts and terminology, thus increasing students' comprehension of text. Dyer's research with seventh-grade students (1985) supports this view, as does her subsequent work with college students in basic skills classes (Dyer, personal communication, 1991). Stahl and Vancil (1986) got similar results with their research with sixth-graders; semantic mapping plus discussion was more effective in word learning than was semantic mapping alone. I support these findings. Semantic mapping is particularly well suited as a prereading activity precisely because it teaches content vocabulary and is an effective preview for text comprehension as well. Semantic mapping led easily into text reading in our Centerpiece Lesson Plan. Later, semantic maps were revisited as instruction warranted.

List-Group-Label

Moore, Readence, and Rickelman (1989) suggest List-Group-Label, a vocabulary-development strategy designed originally for social studies and science. List-Group-Label is similar to semantic mapping. It begins with students generating a *list* of all the words and terms they associated with a targeted vocabulary word; words are listed in random order. After no more associated words and terms are forthcoming, students then *group* the words into categories and *label* each. This part of List-Group-Label is best done in small student groups or pairs and should include a requirement that students provide a rationale for their category labels. List-Group-Label can be productively combined with semantic mapping.

Characteristics of Direct Vocabulary Teaching

One characteristic of effective direct vocabulary instruction is that it is *short*. It is, in other words, limited to a few critical words and concepts (time constraints alone prohibit in-depth instruction for all possible unknown words). Recall Nagy's charge that most vocabulary instruction fails to produce in-depth word knowledge; more often than not, this results from teachers' attempts to preteach 10 or 15 words before reading instead of 5 (remember those long lists of words on the board). A realistic solution here is to adopt the position that it is far better to teach a few words well rather than many words poorly. Careful preselection of targeted words is therefore vital.

A second characteristic of direct content vocabulary instruction is that it is *connected explicity to the actual text* students are to read, so that no one can miss the connection; it must begin and/or end with target words embedded in sentences and paragraphs directly from the text to be read. This connection is strengthened when direct content vocabulary instruction involves an opportunity for students to reconcile prior knowledge with new information acquired during discussion, allows students to predict meanings and generate informed guesses, and encourages students to support their predictions and guesses with personal experience and accounts.

PREREADING INSTRUCTION: DEVELOPING A FUNCTIONAL SYSTEM FOR LEARNING NEW WORDS (CSSR—CONTEXT, STRUCTURE, SOUND, REFERENCE)

When I was a junior in high school, one of my teachers said to our class, "Good readers read with the dictionary by their sides. When they come to a word they do not know, they look it up." This statement confused me and made me feel more than a little guilty. I knew I was a good reader, but I also knew that I rarely did what she said good readers do. "Looking it up" was bothersome and disruptive; it interrupted the flow of text and interfered with my reading. So, I just got the general meaning from context and went right on; sometimes, I'd stop and work on a word, if I felt like I needed to; on *very rare* occasions, I'd check a reference if it was handy; sometimes, I'd just skip the word and go on reading. What I didn't know then (but do today) is that I had a very effective, functional system for learning new words.

For mature readers, the most efficient approach for constructing the meaning of new words is the four-step interactive process Gray (1946) labeled CSSD (this was briefly discussed in Chapter 4):

Step 1, arriving at a gist of the meaning through *context;*

Step 2, examining the *structure* of the word (prefixes, suffixes, roots, etc.) and combining that information with context:

Step 3, pronouncing a word (identifying its *sound*); and

Step 4, checking an outside *reference* by looking the word up or asking someone. Gray limited this last step to dictionary. I have expanded the step to include any reference resource; I therefore refer to the process as *CSSR.*

Jane Harmon, in her vocabulary research (1998), found that "readers activated multiple strategies during single encounters with unfamiliar words . . . but not necessarily in any consistent order" (p. 593). However, the most proficient reader in her sample used a progression very like CSSR.

CSSR is functional and efficient because it uses steps in a sequence of descending probability of success. It begins with context, which has the highest probability of payoff, and it moves through structural analysis to phonic analysis, which has the lowest; it leaves the most disruptive, but generally surest, activity (looking it up) for last. It is, in fact, a system commonly used by good readers almost unconsciously and deserves mention in your classroom, if for no other reason than to encourage its continued use. I can't describe how good it felt when I discovered that what I had been doing was right instead of wrong; I've seen the faces of high-achieving students and teachers alike when I describe the system to them. Their eyes reflect the same pleasure and relief I felt.

For less able readers and writers, it is even more important that we teach a functional system to provide access to high-payoff strategies and to release them from the laborious, often futile, sound-it-out approach they typically use for every word they do not know (Harmon, 1998). Sounding it out is time consuming and difficult; further, in the world of middle school and secondary content reading, it is often impossible and/or nonproductive (try, for example, to determine meaning by sounding out *parabola*, *stare decisis*, *inveigle*, *per se*). Even when less able readers do use high-payoff sources of information (context, for example), they seem to do so nonsystematically and thus ineffectively; that is, they don't know what to do with the information they get from context or where to go if context does not assist them in constructing meaning. For English-language learners, discovering a functional system for learning new words gives them more information about how English works and gives them one more way to manipulate and use the language effectively. Teaching the system requires that we (1) reveal the system to students, (2) provide instruction and practice using the parts of the system, and (3) demonstrate how to put the system together.

REVEALING THE CSSR SYSTEM

The easiest, most direct way to reveal the CSSR approach is simply to tell students about it. You may wish to use a schematic to illustrate and remind students of CSSR, such as the one in Figure 5.4, developed by Peter Santucci in MaryEllen Vogt's content area reading class. Begin instruction by saying, "When you come to a word you do not know, here's what to do":

FIGURE 5.4 *CSSR: What to Do When You Come to a Word You Don't Know*

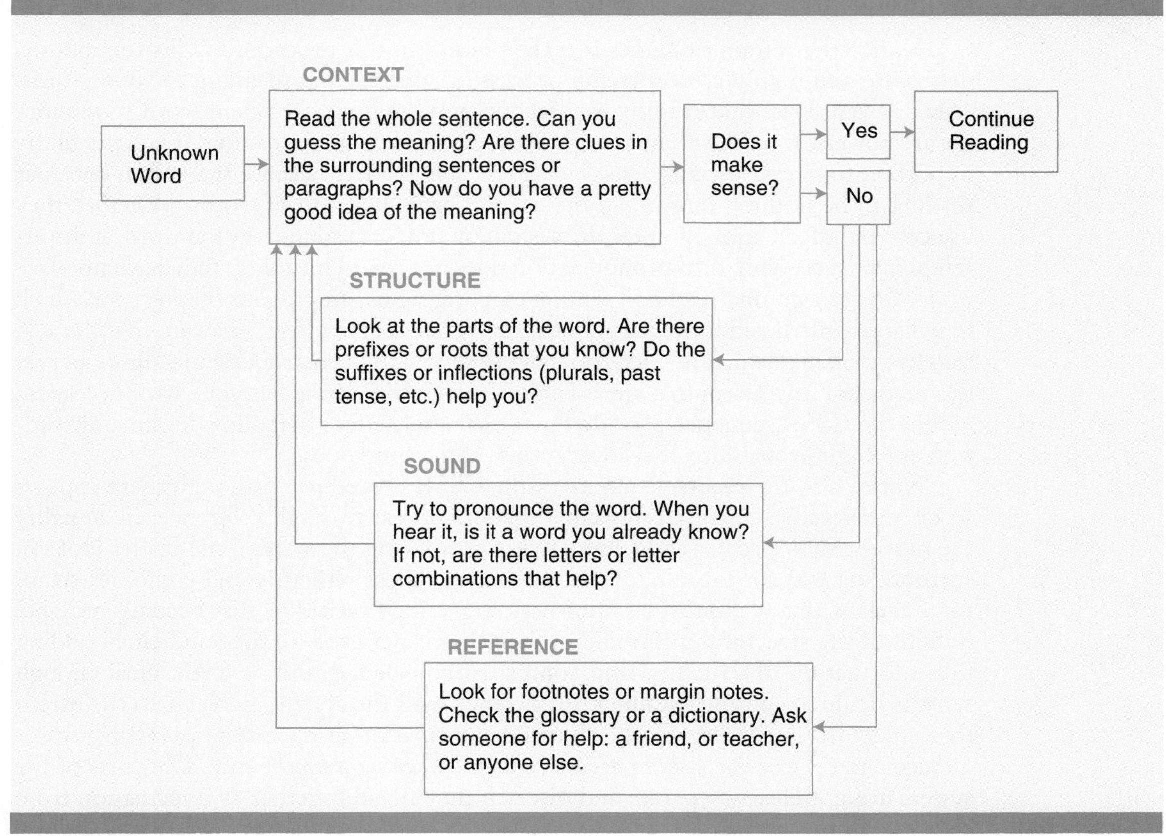

1. Read to the end of the sentence. Can you guess the meaning? Are there any clues in the surrounding sentences or paragraphs that help you? Now do you have a pretty good idea of the meaning? Does it make sense? If so, keep right on reading.

If not,

2. Look at the parts of the word. Are there prefixes or roots that you know? Do the suffixes or inflections (plurals, past tense, etc.) help you? Combine this information with context information to arrive at a meaning. Does it make sense? If so, go right on reading.

If not,

3. Try to pronounce the word. When you hear it, does it sound like a word you already know? If not, are there letters or letter combinations that help (e.g., the *ct* in *tract* as opposed to the *ck* in *track*)? Combine this information with information from context. Does it make sense? If so, go right on reading.

If not,

4. Look for footnotes or margin notes. Check the glossary or a dictionary. Ask someone for help: a friend, or me, or anyone else. Combine this information with information from context. Does it make sense?

Notice the refrain of "Does it make sense?" in this procedure. This reminder is deliberate and highly critical to the process of constructing meaning for new words. "Making sense" is what reading is all about, and the most proficient word pronouncers are powerless if they do not construct some modicum of meaning. It is particularly important to stress "making sense" with less able readers because they often consider reading to be nothing more than the correct pronunciation of words. Whether they use context information or enter the system by trying to sound out the word, if the attempt is unsuccessful, or if pronunciation does not reveal meaning, they have no place to go. So they go on "reading" sentences, paragraphs, and whole chapters for which they have constructed little, if any, meaning. They are, in effect, unaware that the system has broken down. The focus on making sense—on constructing meaning—serves as a metacognitive alarm that alerts students when something has gone wrong; choices within the CSSR sequence provide functional alternatives that allow minimal disruption and high probability of recovery when something does.

Notice also the recursive nature of the CSSR procedure. Although there appears to be a generally sequential movement from context through reference, in actuality the movement is circular and cumulative. On entering the system, the reader looks in surrounding text for meaning; then the reader checks structure and combines structural clues with any contextual information obtained earlier or that became available in light of the structural information; then the reader goes on to sound clues, adding this information to structural and contextual knowledge, and so forth, until enough sense is made to continue reading. Proficiency with the system increases to the extent that students (1) use previously obtained information at each new point in the sequence and (2) exit the system *as soon as useful meaning is constructed*. The parts of the system are not clearly separate and distinct; they blend together as information from one part influences how other types of information are used and as reader decisions for exiting the system are made.

For students to acquire proficiency using the parts of the CSSR system, they need instruction and practice *in content areas.* All of the recommendations given below assume this condition: that activities will be developed from texts used in the class so that students will be learning the language of the discipline as they are learning a functional system for learning new words in that discipline. Keep in mind also that the activities recommended here are not intended to be full-blown, class-long lessons; rather, they are lesson parts that occur during the class period in the course of teaching content. Note that when you're teaching CSSR and its parts, you're teaching word-learning strategies. It is strange but true that occasionally it takes longer for me to tell you about these instructional strategies and activities than it will take you to use them.

USING THE PARTS OF THE CSSR SYSTEM: CONTEXT

Context is an important source of information for learning new content words. By context, we mean the semantic and syntactic information contained in the words, sentences, and paragraphs of text. Jenkins et al. (1989) conclude from the results of a number of studies that instruction in how to use context increases students' ability to do so effectively. The purpose of such instruction is to make students aware of contextual information—the *context clues*—and to demonstrate how such information may be used to determine the meaning of an unknown word. Text conventions and types of context clues vary from subject area to subject area; therefore, a general "knowledge of context clues" does not transfer automatically from one text to another. Students need instruction and practice in using context that is specific to text in each subject area.

One versatile and effective way to do this is through the use of the Cloze teaching technique (Taylor, 1953), which is substantially different from the Cloze *testing* technique I described in Chapter 3. A Cloze teaching activity begins with a reproduced passage from text (the class textbook or other subject text) in which selected words (rather than every fifth word) are deleted and replaced with a blank line. The purpose of the task is for students to use information in the passage (context clues) to replace the deleted words.

Interactive Cloze Meeks and Morgan (1978) describe the Interactive Cloze activity, which is particularly good for subject area instruction. It begins with the preparation of a Cloze passage using a text students have not previously read. (This may be any reading material you're using, or it may be taken directly from the class text. I find that students generally do not read ahead in their regular textbooks.) The passage should be rather short, and the deletions should not exceed 10 to 15 words; a good portion of the first and last sentences of the passage should be left intact. When using Cloze as a teaching technique, there is no set rule for deciding which words to delete; a good rule of thumb is to delete words/terms that would appear to stimulate lots of discussion about possible replacements. Figure 5.5 on page 164 shows a science passage prepared for Interactive Cloze (Miller & Levine, 1995, p. 516).

Students are allowed to work singly or in pairs to replace the deleted words. They then meet in groups of four or five to compare their responses and to arrive at a group consensus on the best replacement for each deletion. Final choices can be selected from individual responses or from suggestions made during the course of small-group discussion. After all groups have finished, group answers are compared in whole-class discussion, along with the reasons for each choice, and class agreement for replacements is reached. An easy way to do this is to project the deleted passage using an overhead projector or LCD screen and record each group's replacement word for each deletion slot. Following this, the original intact passage is read to determine how close class replacement came to it; students are then given an opportunity to decide which they like best—their own replacements or the original. The entire procedure should take no longer than 8 to 10 minutes.

From this simple instructional strategy, an extraordinary amount of instruction and practice in using context occurs. Individual replacement choices are made on the basis of meaning each student constructs for the passage, including his or her prior knowledge and experience with the topic. Reasons for replacement choices are then shared, debated, and challenged in small-group discussion. It should be emphasized that much of the learning occurs during these small-group discussions, so it is unnecessary to go over every explanation with the whole group. In all probability, discussion there will center around three or four key words or issues, ranging from consideration of "best fit" to topic knowledge to synonym distinctions and beyond.

To understand the type and kind of information exchanged during such a lesson, use the passage in Figure 5.5 to do an Interactive Cloze with a group of friends or classmates. During the small-group stage, you may wish to ask one member to observe and take notes for your analysis of the process at its completion. (The intact passage is provided at the end of this chapter.)

Once students become experienced with this technique, any number of variations and adaptations may be used. Passages may be longer or the number of deletions may be increased. Interactive Cloze may be used for direct prereading instruction by deleting target words, rather than presenting and discussing them, and allowing students

FIGURE 5.5 *Interactive Cloze Passage: Science*

PLANT GROWTH AND DEVELOPMENT

You have probably heard the old saying "Mighty oaks from tiny acorns grow." But have you ever thought about the amazing _____ that take place during the long life of such a _____? A tiny embryo oak plant sits _____ an acorn for months, maybe even years. Then one spring, it sprouts. Its roots grow deep into the soil in search of water and _____. Its leaves reach toward the sun—toward the light _____ that powers the life of the plant. In autumn, growth _____. The oak's leaves turn color and fall to the ground. The entire plant undergoes the _____ _____ to survive the approaching cold winter weather.

Many years later the tree _____. Suddenly it produces hundreds, perhaps even thousands, of flowers. Some of the flowers produce _____ that mature into acorns. When the acorns ripen, they fall to the ground, where they may be buried or eaten by squirrels. With luck, the _____ of growth begins again.

to discover the words as they discuss the constructed meaning of the passage. Alternatively, the element of "deletion systems" may be introduced.

Yossarian's Game Yossarian's Game is for students who have become competent at Interactive Cloze (I named this activity after the main character in *Catch-22* [Heller, 1955] who worked as a censor during wartime and used a different one of his own "systems" for censoring mail each day; his ultimate system was born the day he deleted everything except articles—*a*, *an*, and *the*). The class is divided into groups, and each group is given a different intact passage. (*Remember*. These are passages from the classroom text or other content-focused material—students will be learning and discussing content as they consider and manipulate words.) Each group is to decide on its own system for deleting words and prepare the passage accordingly. I strongly advise some ground rules here. For example, you may require that the first and last sentences remain intact, or you may limit the number of deletions that may be made. The deleted passages are duplicated and distributed to the other groups. Groups then work together to complete the passages prepared by the other groups and to figure out the deletion criteria. Group decisions are shared with the whole class and compared to original-group criteria; general discussion follows.

Yossarian's Game is particularly well suited for use with computers and word-processing software. You should prepare the intact passages on a computer, if possible, for ease of preparation of deleted passages; it's even better if students have computer access and can prepare deleted passages themselves.

The value of Yossarian's Game is that in their efforts to make solving the passage difficult, students will first have to explore a variety of deletions systems to find one that will not be immediately apparent to others. To do this requires lots of brainstorming and exchange of ideas and information. Students may key on anything from initial letters (words beginning with *g*) to word counts (every eighth word) to content (words associated with water), to any combination of the above (every third word beginning with *t;* every second word referring to government services, etc.). The possibilities are endless. What is important is that students use substantial word, text, and content knowledge to develop their deletion criterion. In addition, once the system is selected, students analyze and evaluate undeleted parts of the passage to determine how difficult the solution will be for the rest of the class. In doing so, they will decide what information is given by the intact part to suggest replacement possibilities for the naïve reader, dredging every clue they can from the context provided—including much that comes from their knowledge of the content and topic itself. That summarizes the *point* of these activities: Students are involved in acquiring content reading skills as *they learn content*.

USING THE PARTS OF THE CSSR SYSTEM: STRUCTURE

Structural features of words that provide information for analysis are roots, affixes (prefixes and suffixes), inflections (plurals, past-tense endings, possessives, etc.), and compounds. Of these, roots, prefixes, and compounds generally yield the most information directly tied to meaning. Suffixes and inflections do carry meaning (e.g., *-ist*, meaning "one who"; *-s*, *-es*, denoting plural; *-ed*, denoting past tense), but it is general rather than specific. For example, in the word *geologists*, knowledge that *-ist*, means "one who" and *-s* indicates "more than one" is relatively useless unless we understand that *geo-* means "of or having to do with the earth," and that *-ology* is a combining form meaning "the science or study of." That is not to say that suffixes and inflections are unimportant to teach but only that much of the instruction in structural analysis should probably concentrate on roots, prefixes, and compound words.

Structural Analysis One approach for teaching structural analysis is to guide students in connecting structural elements across words. It begins with a structural element contained in a critical word of the reading assignment or chapter. For example, in a social studies chapter dealing with international trade, the element *-port* in the words *import* and *export* might be chosen. Begin instruction by writing a known word containing that element on the board—*portable* or *transportation*, for example—underlining the targeted element (port able.) Ask students to determine the meaning of the element port on the basis of what they know about the word *portable*. Once the meaning of "to carry" has been established, ask students to name other words with the port element and "to carry" meaning.

As words are generated, list them on the board, explore and discuss meanings, and give specific attention to the way in which each word is *similar to* and *different from* the original word *portable*. After a few words are discussed, allow students to work in pairs or groups to list as many words as they can with the element *port*. (Have dictionaries or on-line resources handy to settle disputes.) Group words are presented to the class with appropriate discussion. Then, if they have not already been mentioned, the vocabulary words from the reading, *import* and *export*, are introduced in context by having students locate them in the textbook. Discussion now centers on the specific meaning of these words and their relationship to the content of the lesson at hand. If other important words in the chapter contain *port*, these should likewise be located and discussed.

Several significant features are part of this instructional approach. First, as emphasized in Chapter 4, this approach uses a learning pattern that moves from what students already know to what is to be learned. We began with a known word and concept, allowed students to explore and verify that knowledge, and then applied that information to a new situation.

Second, and perhaps even more important, we gave students the *means for making the transfer*. We walked them through the process of expanding their knowledge base and articulated the process to them. With continued instruction and practice, the process itself will become internalized and available to students in any number of situations and thus a critical component of their ability to learn words independently.

Third, we increased student knowledge of words and word structure in an exponential, rather than additive, way. We could have effectively added to their knowledge by direct teaching of the words *import* and *export*. Instead, we taught the generic *port*, thus making many new associated words available to students. In addition, this approach has a way of spiraling out in other directions as well. In the course of discussing the word *portable*, the suffix *-able*, meaning "capable of being," is also defined. The same thing happens with the words *transportation*, *deportment*, *porter*, *important*, and, finally, *import* and *export*, so that what we really teach is a constellation of structural elements and forms with emphasis on a particular one.

Fourth, and finally, we used the students' own text and immediate assignment in a subject area as the medium for teaching a functional skill. Just as importantly, we demonstrated to students the value of this knowledge for learning the content of that subject area. Most disciplines contain at least some critical language that contains structural elements worth learning: *equals, equation, equivalent; judge, judicial, prejudice, adjudicate; isobars, isostasy, isotherms, isotopes; dermis, dermatology, epiderm; piano, pianissimo, forte, fortissimo*. It's worth some time to show students how to make connections between such words when they occur as part of the content being studied.

Verbal–Visual Word Association Gary Hopkins and Tom Bean (1998/99) recommend using an activity for teaching structural elements in which students create vocabulary boxes which each contain four squares. They write the structural element in the upper left square, its definition in the bottom left, the target word in the upper right, and a visual representation of the target word in the lower right. Figure 5.6 shows vocabulary boxes for the import/export target words associated with the social studies lesson we discussed previously. Hopkins and Bean found that this approach personalized vocabulary learning in such a way that students were able to "use their strengths as well as address their weaknesses" (p. 279) with respect to word learning and that it fostered independent problem-solving skills.

USING THE PARTS OF THE CSSR SYSTEM: SOUND

For all intents and purposes, teaching the sound part of the CSSR is outside the purview of middle school and secondary school classrooms for a number of important reasons. Most secondary teachers have little knowledge or training in "phonics" or pronunciation rules, and very few have any interest in gaining such. Rightly so: It is unreasonable to expect that middle school and secondary classroom teachers are equipped to—or *should*—teach pronunciation rules and the like in their classrooms. Contrary to media assertions (and many people's perceptions), all students have been taught "phonics rules"; in fact, we have evidence to suggest that the least-accomplished students have been taught the most phonics and other basic skills (Allington, 1978; Collins, 1986). What must be understood, however, is that pronunciation rules are most useful

FIGURE 5.6 *Vocabulary Boxes: Social Studies*

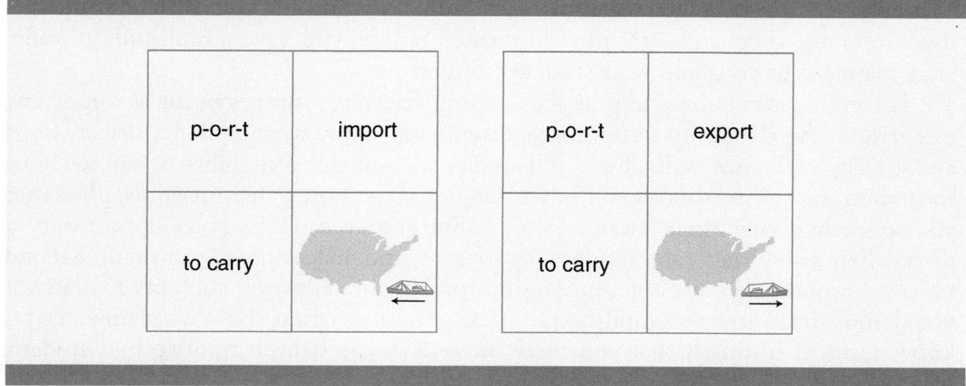

for recognizing new words in the primary, learning-to-read grades when the pool of new words encountered in text is relatively small and generally well within students' listening and speaking vocabularies. That is, in the early grades, most new words encountered in text are words that, once pronounced, are known to readers. Not so in later grades. Beginning at about fourth grade and rapidly increasing thereafter, students read a wide variety of texts, for both study and pleasure, that include an extraordinary range of new and difficult words. Many of these words do not conform to the pronunciation rules (remember *parabola, stare decisis* and *per se:* consider *schedule, placebo,* and *lagniappe*), and even when they do, they frequently are so far removed from student experience and knowledge that pronunciation alone does not bring meaning (define, for example, *egregious, chancre,* and *contact sheet conference*). The point here is that for middle school and secondary school students, phonic analysis has low utility, and it is therefore inefficient to continue spending large amounts of time teaching or reteaching phonics rules (Greenleaf, Jiménez, & Roller, 2002). Certainly, when application of pronunciation rules is useful, subject area teachers should point this out to students and encourage its use. The primary goal, however, should be to guide students as they apply and extend what they already know, and to place pronunciation rules appropriately within the functional system so that they are useful to students.

USING THE PARTS OF THE CSSR SYSTEM: REFERENCE

Learning to use reference sources—whether they are part of the class text, housed in a dictionary or the reference section of the library, on the Internet, or in the form of another person—is of great importance as students move toward independence in reading, writing, and learning. This is particularly true for middle school and secondary school students who encounter new, and often highly abstract, concepts in their daily reading. To be sure, there are so-called basic skills associated with using reference sources: knowledge and application of diacritical markings; use of indexes and tables of contents; first-, second-, third-, and fourth-letter alphabetizing; use of head words; effective web search strategies; and selection of contextually appropriate definitions, to name a few. Like phonics, many of these skills have been taught in elementary school; middle school and secondary school teachers are responsible for demonstrating how such skills are applied to text and other materials used in their classes.

Much can be done toward this end by filling your classroom with all sorts of reference materials, thus signifying that you consider these books, objects, software, and other electronic resources to be important and worthwhile for your own and students' use. Certainly, if your classroom is connected online, you have a multitude of reference materials at your and your students' fingertips.

Effective instruction and practice in using reference sources occur as opportunities arise in the classroom to reinforce, extend, and apply what students already know about using reference skills. First, tell students about the availability of reference information in their textbooks and other materials: footnotes, margin notes, glossaries, and so forth; review their knowledge of online resources. Take every opportunity to direct their attention to these reference sources, and encourage use of them. Second, become a model of good reference-using behavior by allowing students to watch as you demonstrate how accomplished learners get information about what they need to know. Critical to this is that you *think out loud* as you demonstrate so that students have access to the process. Consider the following scene:

The word *befouled* is encountered in an environmental studies lesson discussion of a newspaper editorial about a Pew Oceans Commission report on the condition of America's ocean waters. The teacher might say, "Hmm. It says here 'befouled waters.' I'm not sure I know exactly what *befouled* means. It sounds like something dirty or wrong. Does anyone know?" [A few tentative guesses] "Let's check." Opening the online dictionary, the teacher uses headwords to locate *befouled* continuing to think aloud. *bee hive,* [scrolling], *been, beetle, beet sugar, befall, befit, before,* . . . here it is, *befoul.* It's pronounced just like it looks: bēfoul' [writing the pronunciation on the board] and has two definitions: '1. to make fifthy: dirty; soil. 2. to cast aspersions on; slander.' Okay, the sentence we read was, 'The image of vanishing underwater life and befouled waters is striking enough.' So, it must be the first definition, and it does mean 'dirty,' but it includes the idea of agency; to *have been made filthy* suggests that it wasn't dirty or soiled or filthy before. Someone or something must have caused it. What would be some of the sources for dirtying of our ocean waters?"

The scene ends. Notice what happened. The students saw an active, inquisitive mind at work and watched as a whole set of skills was integrated in the search for understanding through the use of headwords, entry words, and diacritical markings and applying definition to context, and not so incidentally using an online dictionary. Notice also the *positive* approach to "not knowing," rather than its negative counterpart. The teacher acknowledged that she didn't know the precise meaning of the word and offered some possibilities ("dirty" or "wrong"), read the two dictionary definitions, and went back to sentence context to adjust meaning. The end result is a much more refined understanding of the word and the sentence, and nobody appeared dumb. In fact, somebody appeared very bright indeed.

Two postscripts are in order. First, consider the possibilities of the class discussion that might follow the teacher's heuristic question ("What would be some of the sources of the dirtying of our ocean waters?"). Second, in a sentence later in the editorial, the word *daunting* appears. It would seem entirely reasonable for a teacher now to direct students as they practice using the model (just presented) of how-to-get-the-meaning-of-a-word-when-all-other-attempts-fail. Here, as with the other parts of the CSSR system, instruction and practice in a functional skill are paired with meaningful discussion of content. Each reinforces the other, and not knowing becomes a springboard for learning rather than a source of embarrassment. This very same sequence of events could occur to model effective use of a textbook glossary, a thesaurus (hard copy or computer based), page footnotes or other written and graphic text aids, a search engine, and any or all informational software.

PUTTING THE CSSR PARTS TOGETHER

Earlier, I stated that the easiest, most direct way to let students know about the CSSR system was simply to tell them about it and demonstrate it. The same principle applies to teaching them how to put the parts together. Tell students how to use the system and give them practice doing it. When new words are introduced in context, ask students, "Can we tell from context what this word means? Does it make sense?" If not, ask, "Where do we look now?" and so on, until meaning is developed.

It is important to remember that the main purpose of the system is to be functionally efficient; that is, it has to work, and it has to work in the least possible time. Therefore, a major goal of instruction should be to teach students to exit the system *as soon as meaning is achieved.* This means you must not continue through predetermined lessons if students short-circuit your plans. You may have planned to use *daunting* as a means of teaching and practicing reference skills, but during discussion someone figured it out by combining previous experience and context. If this happens, stop the lesson, compliment the students on their skill, and go on to whatever is next. In this case, meeting the immediate goal of teaching reference skills goes counter to the overall goal of providing a functional system for learning new content vocabulary words—the students have done exactly what you wanted them to do. It's now up to you to be perceptive and flexible enough to reward their accomplishment.

Creating Strategic Readers

The ability to understand the meaning of new words in text is the absolute hallmark of proficient readers, and the downfall of those who do not read well. So it is particularly important for students to think about and be able to answer the question, "What do I do when I come to a word I do not know?" Teach them CSSR. Put a schematic or written reminders on the wall. Help them practice using context and structure. Find occasions to ask your students, "What do you do when you come to a word you do not know?" and help them develop a multi-step answer by asking, "What do you do then? What then?" and so forth. This is a reading skill worth teaching in your classroom.

How to do . . . .

PREREADING CONTENT VOCABULARY DEVELOPMENT (Semantic Mapping, List-Group-Label, Interactive Cloze, CSSR)

Let me reiterate: Prereading content vocabulary instruction should be short, sweet, and to the point. It should focus on a few key words that have been carefully preselected by the teacher and should use actual content text as the basis for instruction. Whenever possible, prereading vocabulary instruction should combine teaching words, teaching content, and teaching a functional system for learning unknown words. Use the following guidelines to develop prereading content vocabulary lessons:

1. Preview the material to be read and select five or six words to be taught.

2. Determine the type of instruction most appropriate for these words: (a) Direct instruction—telling, linking to known concepts, or conducting elaborated definition and discussion; (b) Instruction About or Within the CSSR System—using the system or using one or more parts of the system.
3. Prepare for instruction: for example, duplicate Cloze passage, write sentences with underlined targeted words on the board, determine stimulus word(s) for semantic mapping or structural analysis, establish groups.
4. Identify link from vocabulary discussion to the reading and content topic.

CONTENT VOCABULARY INSTRUCTION: LONG-TERM ACQUISITION AND DEVELOPMENT

Content vocabulary instruction directed toward long-term acquisition of words may be seen as an extension of prereading vocabulary study and as useful in and of itself. It extends prereading instruction because many of the words presented prior to reading are chosen for further discussion and study after reading; it may be used, however, whether or not prereading instruction was provided. (It also does not necessarily need to be linked with reading. It may follow any type of instruction: lecture, discussion, media presentations, writing, etc.)

POSTREADING INSTRUCTION: THE VOCABULARY SELF-COLLECTION STRATEGY (VSS)

The Vocabulary Self-Collection Strategy (VSS) (Haggard [now Ruddell], 1982), is an instructional strategy intended to foster long-term acquisition and development of the vocabulary of academic disciplines. You saw one way to do VSS in our Centerpiece Lesson Plan. VSS has as its primary goal incorporation of new content words into students' working vocabularies. Unlike the Dreaded Word List that Zena Logan's teacher uses, VSS focuses on content words that students need to know, words that are important to them and about which they have expressed interest and curiosity. Further, VSS gives students the skills necessary for continued, independent content vocabulary growth by simulating natural word-learning processes. I developed VSS some years ago and used it in my own classrooms with students ranging from seventh grade to high school sophomores and juniors to college freshmen to first-year pharmacy students in graduate school. I know firsthand how powerful it can be and how easy it is to do.

USING VSS

VSS begins following reading and discussion of text (or any learning event) and is initiated by the teacher asking students to nominate one word or term that they would like to learn or to know more about and that they think should appear on a class vocabulary list. The teacher also nominates one word. Students are encouraged to find words/terms that are important to the topic at hand and are required to tell:

1. *Where they found the word.* (Read the sentence if in text or recall the context if from discussion or other learning event.)
2. *What they think the word means in this context.*
3. *Why they think the class should learn it* (i.e., identify the word's importance to the content topic).

In most classrooms, this part of VSS is most efficiently done with students in nominating teams of two to five people, depending on the number of words the teacher wishes to have in the nominated pool (A good rule of thumb is eight to ten words, with a target of five to six words for the final class list.) Don't forget that the teacher nominates one of the original pool words as well. Generally, three to five minutes is sufficient time for groups to reexamine text and find words, prepare their definitions from text, and develop a rationale for learning each word; it is often useful to rush students a bit, keeping them on task and leaving little time for extraneous discussion and then extending the time if it is really needed. The teacher also is wise to predetermine his or her selection (and, in fact, have two or three on deck in the event of duplication with student choices) in order to be free to monitor group functioning and answer questions.

As soon as groups are ready, a spokesperson from each group presents a nominated word and tells where it was found, what the group believes it means, and why it was chosen. The teacher writes the words on the board and leads discussion to define each, first from context as nominators tell what they think their word means, and then, if needed, from any references available in the room. Discussion should include contributions from other class members as well, so that definitions are extended and personalized.

The focus is always on the meaning of the word in the specific context of the immediate content topic or text; however, conversation is likely to range across other meanings or contexts that are part of students' prior knowledge and experience. These other meanings serve as useful intertextual links to the topic-specific meaning under discussion. After all words/terms have been nominated, a final class list is established by eliminating duplicates, any words or terms the class feels it already knows, and any that do not appear to be appropriate. (At this time, the teacher spot-checks to see if any content words introduced prior to the reading appear, or should appear, on the final class list.)

During this process, words chosen for the class list are circled (or identified in some way), and eliminated words are simply left alone so that nothing is erased from the board. Words chosen for the vocabulary list are then redefined and written with definitions in vocabulary journals or any ongoing unit or lesson documents (e.g., entered in appropriate places on study maps). Words not chosen for class study may be recorded by students who wish to include them on their own personal vocabulary lists.

VSS LESSON EXAMPLE—ENGLISH

The partial transcript below will give you a sense of what happens in VSS lessons, although it's difficult to capture the energy and spontaneity of the discussion. This lesson followed the DR-TA and GMA for "The Splendid Outcast" presented in Chapter 4.

VSS LESSON EXAMPLE *English*

Students in groups of three to five

T: I want you to find two words or terms that you think should be on our vocabulary list for this story—two words or terms that you think we should know, or study, or know more about. Listen carefully: I want you, as a group, to locate the words and be prepared to tell where the words are in the story, what you as a group think those words mean, and why you as a group think we should learn them. Got it? You have about four minutes.

Overheard as groups discuss:

Here are two that I had questions about . . .

Go ahead, influence me.

Weren't there a couple words you wanted to know? (Laughter.)

Second paragraph . . . okay, that's one; there's another one here . . . (Silence as students search text.)

Yeah, that's a good one.

Something interesting . . .

I know that there's one in here.

Where did you find one?

That's a good word. I missed it; I wonder what it means.

There on page 39. . . .

Of course, we have to tell why we're choosing them—the importance to the story . . .

Okay, we know that *encomiums* is, uh . . . it says here, "He listened to the encomiums," so you can tell it's a noun.

Yeah, okay, do you suppose that's a particular speech pattern . . . [do you] suppose it's a term that auctioneers use?

It just has a gorgeous sound. It does. That's a good reason.

That doesn't really tell *why* we're going to use that word.

Where was *Lilliputian?* Do you remember?

T: Ready, got your words?

(Continued discussion.)

T: Table 1, have you got your words? What about you, Table 2? Table 3, got your words? Okay, quickly.

(Waits.)

T: Okay, ready? Table 4?

(In background, "Who used *Lilliputians?* Where was *Lilliputian* used?" Continued discussion in groups.)

T: Who'd like to nominate a word? Okay, we're ready. (Murmurs continue.)

S1: Encomiums.

T: (Writing word on board.) All right. Is that e-n?

S1: e-n-c-o-m-i-u-m-s

(Continued murmurs and discussion in groups.)

T: Where did you find *encomiums?* Okay, everybody, stay with us . . . . Read the sentence for us.

S1: "He stared down upon the arena as each horse was led into it, and he listened to the dignified encomiums of the auctioneer with the humble attention of a parishioner at mass."

T: What do you think *encomiums* means?

S1: Something as simple as "words" or "saying."

T: Okay, it could be that. Anything else?

S2: We thought it was peculiar to the auctioneer—language that an auctioneer uses.

S3: Flattery, praises, related to money.

T: Descriptions that he was giving of the horses . . . . Why did you choose this one, group?

S1: Because we didn't know what it meant.

(Much laughter.)

T: That's as good a reason as any to choose one. Okay, another one.

S1: Lilliputian.

T: *Lilliputian.* Did they have that capitalized?

S1: Yes. Page 46. "They watch with open mouths as the giant Rigel, the killer Rigel, with no harness save a head collar, follows his Lilliputian master, his new friend, across the ring."

T: (Writing on board.) L-i-l-l?

S1: Yes. i-p-u-t-i-a-n.

T: *Lilliputian*, which means . . . ?

S1: Very, very small. (In a very, very small voice.)

T: Very small. Why did you choose *Lilliputian?*

S1: Do we have to be honest? (Laughter.)

T: Yes! (Laughs.)

S1: Partially because you just like to hear yourself say it. It's such a colorful word.

T: *Perfect* reason to learn a word—that it sounds wonderful. *Lilliputian.*

T: Table 1. Did you guys have one?

S1: Those two. (Laughter.)

T: Are there any others that we haven't given?

S1: Oh yeah, we wanted to know what *guineas* were for sure.

T: All right, spell *guineas*.

S1: g-u-i-n-e-a-s.

T: (Writing word on board.) Read where you found it.

S1: Page 39. "'A hundred guineas!' I stand as I call my price, and the auctioneer is plainly shocked—not by the meagerness of the offer, but by the offer itself."

T: Okay, we know it's part of the monetary system, we don't know what part of the monetary system, but it was a part, okay? So your purpose here, your reason for choosing it is . . . you by gosh want to know what it is. Fine.

I have a word. It's *votary*. (Writing word on board.) Page 36: "They were the cultists, he the votary, and there were, in fact, about his grey eyes and his slender lips, the deep, tense lines so often etched in the faces of zealots and of lonely men." I think *votary* must be connected to, or synonymous with, zealotry. I'm not sure of the exact meaning, but I chose it because I don't think I've ever heard it before. Okay, who has got another one? Any others?

T: Everybody like these words?

("Um hmms" around.)

T: Go back to your map, and for right now—we'll do other things with them later—enter the words on your map in an appropriate place, and put an asterisk by them so that you remember they are our vocabulary words. You may already have them on your map. If you don't, find a place to enter the words on your map. (Waits.) If you can't find a place that feels good for each word, then simply list those words that you can't put on the map at the top, or bottom, or someplace on that piece of paper.

S1: (Interrupting work silence.) I wonder if guineas and pounds are interchangeable. She said she had five hundred pounds, but she started bidding in guineas.

T: (Trying to bring lesson to close.) Right.

S2: Yeah, it does later. I remember, uh, you know, reading later, it said five hundred pounds. So they are the same.

T: You think they're the same?

S2: I think so. (General conversation and agreement.)

T: I don't think so.

S1: Well, then why would she start bidding in guineas? I mean, she'd gotten . . .

T: Well, the English, the old British system. See, we're so used to a decimal system: ten pennies make a dime; ten dimes make a dollar. It was not based on a decimal system back then, and so a guinea could be any given part of a pound.

S1: It must be *close*, though, because she said she'd bid four hundred fifty, hoping he wouldn't know there was so little to follow. So she knew she didn't have much left of her five hundred pounds.

T: Right. Well, we'll find out. (Trying *again* to bring lesson to a close.)

S3: Maybe pounds is a more formal way of referring to money. And I could see the "cultists" using pounds and not reverting to guineas, whereas people who are more blue collar. . .

T: Ah. So it'd be equivalent to saying, uh, a quarter versus two bits.*

S3: Right.

T: All right, that may be it. Well, we'll find out. Has everybody got your words on your map?

*Author note: A guinea was 21 shillings and a pound was 20 shillings in the old British monetary system; the guinea was so named because the original guinea coins were made from gold imported from Guinea. Use of *guinea* and *pound* was indeed, a language marker for social class: the lower socioeconomic class people dealt in guineas and the upper socioeconomic class in pounds.

This lesson is typical of a VSS discussion. Notice the diversity of words chosen—*encomiums*, *Lilliputian*, *guineas*, and *votary*—and the equally diverse reasons for choosing them—new words, partially known words, old words, interesting-sounding words. But the most important aspect of this lesson—and what makes it typical of a VSS lesson—is the intensity with which students participated. They had to be *pulled* into whole-class discussion to share choices because they did not want to stop their in-progress small-group discussions about words. And these groups were on task! Then, they were not about to turn loose of the discussion of *guineas;* recall that this discussion began during the initial story reading (in Chapter 4). Each time the teacher attempted to close the VSS lesson, beginning with her directions for students to enter the words on their maps, students brought the subject up again and simply conducted their own discussion. The teacher was constrained to yield the floor and allow time for the discussion to take place. This is not typical of classroom vocabulary lessons; it is, however, not in the least unusual for VSS discussion.

POSTREADING INSTRUCTION: FOLLOW-UP ACTIVITIES THAT EXTEND VSS

Vocabulary instruction is never complete without follow-up activities to reinforce initial content word learning. When using VSS, after the selection process (and with any vocabulary instruction), it is necessary for the teacher to design activities for extended study and practice so that students will attend to, use, and manipulate words sufficiently to incorporate them into working vocabularies. It must be emphasized that without planned opportunity for students to use new content vocabulary, it is unlikely that many students will be very successful learning the words and, in fact, learning the content itself.

Activities intended to promote content vocabulary acquisition and development must be adapted to and integrated with content instruction, if for no other reason than efficient use of time, but more importantly, because of the vital role language plays in the construction of content knowledge. Keep in mind that only the teacher needs to know what part of a follow-up lesson is directed toward "vocabulary" and what part is focused on content.

PRINCIPLES FOR DESIGNING VOCABULARY LESSON ACTIVITIES

A wide variety of activities may be used to assist students in the process of integrating new content words into their working vocabularies. It is important, however, that these activities contain the properties we have already discussed—integration, repetition, meaningful use, and connectedness—because these properties are the intertextual links that promote in-depth understanding and integration of new content words and concepts into one's prior knowledge base. Further, the assumption here is that VSS activities, just as prereading vocabulary study, will extend and reinforce content learning itself. The following principles are important standards for designing and adapting activities for use in VSS and other vocabulary lessons:

1. *Activities should allow students to use content words in a meaningful way.* Meaningful use of words is a form of repetition and connectedness. It is important that whatever activities teachers assign following identification of new words, these assignments be a form of repetition that makes sense to students and genuinely involves them in the learning event. Repetition for repetition's sake (writing words or sentences over and over) or rote word practice (writing formulaic sentences or filling in blanks mindlessly) are of little value here. Further, implausible use is just as valueless (writing sentences using high-flown words inappropriately; for example, "I'd like to continue the redundance of my 'problem' and further segregate the crux of the issue."). Meaningful use of newly acquired content vocabulary requires that students write or speak reasonably, exploring new ideas and language, making connections, and reinforcing what they have just learned.

2. *Activities should allow students opportunities to associate new content words and concepts with their own experience.* As we have learned from adult drop-outs, making connections between what students already know and what they are to learn is one of the single most powerful learning tools available to teachers. Activities that reflect this principle are usually generative—students speaking or writing from their own experience—and often reveal students' logic and thinking as well as their prior knowledge. Because they are generative, they generally require time for students to interact with one another, to explore ideas in writing, and to refine and extend meaning.

3. *Activities should develop associations with other content words.* Related somewhat to the previous principle, this one reminds us to provide activities that connect explicitly new content words with other, related, words and terms. This is important for all students learning the language of a content discipline and is particularly necessary for students who are learning English, subject content, and the language of the content concurrently. Learning associated words thus boosts learning the language of any subject area—for example, musical notation (quarter note, half note, rest), literary elements (plot, theme, characterization, irony, satire), key components of the U.S. Constitution (legislative, judicial, executive branches of government; individual versus state and federal rights), art movements (Impressionism, Dadasm, Cubism, realism), the sport of baseball (ERA, ground-rule double, blooper, ribby, six-to-four-to-three). Important here also are associations and distinctions made for multiple-meaning words both within and across disciplines (oil-base paint, third base, base versus acid, base numbers, base word, the base of a triangle, etc.). These associations and distinctions are usually developed through activities that invite comparison and contrast and allow students to articulate their thinking and line of reasoning.

4. *Activities should encourage higher-order thinking.* Higher-order thinking requires "deep processing," in which students make more cognitive connections between new and known information or expend more mental effort to learn something than they would if information were processed more shallowly (Stahl, 1986). Higher-order thinking, by definition, goes beyond the surface, the quick response, the easily accomplished. Activities that promote higher-order thinking therefore are extended and often are, themselves, extensions and elaborations of work that has gone before.

5. *Activities should lead students to many different resources.* One of the most pervasive preadolescent and adolescent tendencies in response to assigned questions is to look no further than the first answer they get, especially if that answer is in the one resource they typically use for getting answers. (This tendency does not necessarily hold when the question is "May I use the car tonight?" and the first answer is "No.") In the area of vocabulary study, a text glossary or class dictionary is the usual single resource. Rarely do students use the many other resources for vocabulary information available to them, including text notes and marginalia, encyclopedias, journals and magazines, on-line and other electronic resources, newspapers, friends, parents, neighbors, experts, visual media, and so on. The first requirement for activities that encourage use of various resources is that some variety of resources be available in classrooms and schools; the second is that teachers actively seek opportunities to direct students to diverse, and often unusual, sources for information.

6. *Activities should acknowledge and capitalize on the social nature of learning.* We have discussed previously the argument that there is a strong interrelationship among language, thinking, learning, and the social world of the individual. Much of what students learn, they can and do learn from one another through discussion, shared experience, and exchange of ideas and information. Although we're just beginning to explore the effect of social interactions on vocabulary learning, preliminary research suggests a strong positive relationship between the two (Beck, McKeown, & Omanson, 1987; Stahl & Vancil, 1986). Cooperative and collaborative grouping in content classrooms encourages social interaction, and every vocabulary/content activity presented in this chapter is readily adaptable to any variety of small-group and partnership configurations. (We will explore various collaborative learning approaches in Chapter 11.) None is nearly as effective when assigned as individual student homework or seat work and left undiscussed. Much of the power of VSS comes from the discussion that occurs from the very beginning of the learning episode; that same power operates in the follow-up activities that reinforce initial learning.

The following activities are particularly well suited for developing understanding and knowledge of new content words. Note how each of them meets at least one of the principles listed above; most satisfy two or more. These activities also may be adapted for prereading vocabulary introduction.

SEMANTIC FEATURE ANALYSIS (SFA)

Semantic Feature Analysis (SFA) (Johnson Toms-Bronowski, & Pittelman, 1981) is useful both for developing word associations and for extending content knowledge. To do SFA, the teacher prepares a grid (Figure 5.7) in which words listed vertically and features listed horizontally are related to a given category; one or more of the words and features are taken from the VSS list. Working in pairs or small groups, students indicate which features are associated with each word by marking a plus (+) in intersecting squares for those that are and a minus (–) for those that are not. Group decisions are then shared in whole-class discussion, generally to the tune of lively debate and disagreement. Be aware that you may need to assist groups in resolving these disagreements. After the initial SFA, student groups are invited to add to the "words" and "features" lists and continue the exercise with these additions. Further exploration of ideas may be introduced by replacing the "yes/no" (+/–) coding with "always," "sometimes," or "never" criteria using additional coding symbols.

Numerous other extensions and elaborations of this activity are possible. For example, discussion about relationships between specific words and features may lead to reanalysis of text information or further research; or such discussion may stimulate extended writing and/or formal essays supporting a position or point of view, particularly when issues remain unresolved. Paragraph summaries or analyses of the topic category are useful follow-up study aids or supplements to class notes. At some point, student groups should be encouraged to create their own SFA grids using their choice of VSS words; these may be duplicated and distributed to other groups, and then they may serve as the basis for a discussion comparing responses.

FIGURE 5.7 *Semantic Feature Analysis, Social Studies*

	Protec-tionist	Expan-sionist	Inclusive	Exclusive	Globali zation*	Import*	Export*
High Tariffs							
Low Tariffs							
Out-sourcing*							
NAFTA*							
EU*							

*VSS Word

SEMANTIC MAPPING AND LIST-GROUP-LABEL ACTIVITIES

Semantic mapping is just as appropriate for use with VSS content words as it is for prereading instruction. The procedure is essentially the same; however, discussions may be more elaborated because students will have encountered the words in text and discussed them during the VSS nomination process.

List-Group-Label activities also work well. Semantic maps may be used independently of or in conjunction with text maps students have constructed (e.g., maps following reading). Semantic maps and List-Group-Label exercises also are useful beginning points for developing formal outlines or summary notes for topic study and as the basis for further writing.

EXTENDED WRITING

As already mentioned, open-ended or focused writing assignments, in which students are encouraged to use their VSS content words in written elaborations of lesson ideas, are extremely valuable for in-depth word learning. We know that writing itself is a powerful means for construction and clarification of knowledge and highly useful for combined content/vocabulary learning. In the very act of meaningful writing using new content vocabulary, students will arrive at new insights and understanding. It is important that we provide numerous opportunities for them to do so. A partial list of vocabulary writing activities follows. (We will discuss the full use of writing activities in Chapter 8.)

Journal writing is a means for students to elaborate their personal response to vocabulary words or the vocabulary lesson; journals may or may not be read by the teacher.

Response group summaries require that a working group of students decide on a group response to a given prompt about one or more vocabulary words and produce a written summary of that response.

Lab reports require students to analyze new words/concepts as they summarize steps of an experiment, report and analyze results, compare results with preexperimental expectations, draw conclusions, and evaluate the experience.

Quick Writes, *Three-Minute Writes*, *Exit Slips* (as adapted from Chapter 4), interspersed during or at the end of class, allow students to identify what they learned about new vocabulary, what is problematic, what they liked about the lesson, and what they didn't like.

Extended narrative and expository writing include all manner of stories, poetry, drama, essays, and reports using new vocabulary appropriately within the context of content lesson goals.

Any number of other written responses to text and/or a content lesson may be used to provide opportunity for students to practice using new words, as long as they *do not involve requirements for students to copy definitions from the dictionary* (recall Zena) or *write a series of unrelated, non-content-specific sentences for the express purpose of using and underlining targeted vocabulary words.*

WORD TREASURE HUNTS

Word treasure hunts (Haggard, 1989) direct students to "Find out everything anyone would want to know" about one of the chosen VSS content words or terms. Students are encouraged to ask people they know; look the word up in various dictionaries, encyclopedias, and other text or on-line reference sources; and add their own knowledge and ideas. Students record information and report back to class. Ideas are put on the board in much the same way that is done for semantic maps, discussed, and used for other categorizing, mapping, and writing activities. Word treasure hunts are well suited for out-of-class and homework assignments and/or Webquest activities in which students search various on-line sources and bring information back for class consideration and discussion.

CATEGORIZING/RECATEGORIZING

Categorizing occurs in a number of the activities already discussed (e.g., semantic mapping); however, it may be used effectively to demonstrate word relationships and the effect of differing categorical criteria. In categorizing, the teacher prepares a series of words taken from the reading, including as many VSS words as possible. Students, in pairs or groups, are asked to categorize the words in any way they choose (similar to List-Group-Label). Group solutions are then presented to other groups, either with explanation or with directions for other groups to determine the group criteria. Following this, students may be asked to recategorize the words using a new criterion.

Davidson (1984) suggests the activity Which One Doesn't Belong? (Figure 5.8), in which students are shown groups of words in rows and columns, where it's not clear whether the groups are the rows or the columns. Students are asked to identify one word in each group that does not belong (this requires them to decide whether the groups are the rows or the columns) and state the reason for their choices. Which One Doesn't Belong? works best in small groups in which students can spend some time debating their reasons for deciding on rows or columns and for deciding which words don't belong. A great deal of prior knowledge and text information is used in making these decisions. As a follow-up, teachers may then direct students to redo the exercise by arranging the words differently or by using a different criterion for eliminating words.

FIGURE 5.8 *Which One Doesn't Belong?: Science*

DIRECTIONS TO STUDENTS:

Look at each series of words and think about how the words are related to one another. For each series, find one word that doesn't belong with the others. Be prepared to explain why the word doesn't belong and what the others have in common.

Magnitude	Temblor	Fault	Seismic
Tectonic	Aftershocks	Tremor	Compressional wave
Love wave	Energy	Magnitude	Rayleigh wave

WORD SORTS

After students have accrued an extended list of vocabulary words over several weeks' time, a useful activity is to have them sort the words in their lists according to a given criterion: for example, words that *describe*, words that are *function words*, words that are associated with the *respiratory system*, words that relate to *rhythm*, words associated with *solving equations*. The value of word sorts is that students see how concepts and vocabulary connect across lesson and unit topics and that students make new associations between words.

The activities just presented are not the only effective ways to encourage long-term acquisition and development of content vocabulary. They are, however, remarkably generative: You can design many different lessons from one or more of these activities. Consider also ways to adapt prereading activities to VSS lessons; the structural analysis activity is well suited to that end, and Interactive Cloze, with some thought and planning, could be adapted as well.

BENEFITS OF USING VSS

Two of the most obvious benefits of VSS are its versatility and ease of use. VSS can be used in any subject area, with any size class, and following any type of lesson. It requires nothing in the way of new materials or equipment, and it makes no demand that text from which words are to be chosen be of any particular form or meet any standard. VSS words can be collected from a video, a lecture, or any other class activity just as readily as they can from a textbook, magazine, or primary source. In this chapter you've seen VSS used with a science textbook in the centerpiece lesson plan and with a short story in our on-going English class reading and follow-up to "The Splendid Outcast." It takes only a little planning, a willingness to spend a portion of class time on content vocabulary study, and some time and effort developing reinforcement activities to implement VSS very effectively.

A third benefit is that words and language become a vital part of classroom discussion and students' lives. That statement may sound hyperbolic, but it is not; my experience with VSS has been that everybody gets excited about words, and the biggest problem the teacher has is moving the lesson on to other important topics. It happened in "The Splendid Outcast" lesson, and it will happen in your class. The value here is that students become attuned to words in textbooks and the subject discipline itself, alert to new and increasingly difficult words, and eager to satisfy their curiosity. Brenda Shearer and I (Ruddell & Shearer, 2002) studied the effect of using VSS with seventh- and eighth-grade at-risk students in special reading classes. Students were asked to bring to class each week a word or term they wanted to learn or know more about. Here are a few of the words from a list collected over a six-week period: *potassium*, *insensate*, *magnetosphere*, *chaos*, *reign*, *epochs*, *conscientious*, *nebula*, *carbohydrate*, *spelunking*, *embezzle*, *aisle*, *recapitulate*, *quadrilateral*, *aerobic*, *nocturnal*. A number of things can be said about this list. First, these are all difficult words, by any standard (in fact, these words could easily be mistaken for words collected in a gifted class); and second, they reveal both personal interests and the curriculum of students' subject area classes. Thus, students integrated VSS instruction in their reading class into the other parts of their personal and academic lives. Students really *like* collecting vocabulary words. Alvermann and her colleagues asked students about this:

> Yet, when [the teacher] asked the students if they would prefer that she preteach the vocabulary that would likely present some trouble, they said

"no." Laura explained, "When you tell me, I don't want to know. If I come across it on my own, I have a reason to find it." Jason and Mark agreed, while Jonathon noted, "If you tell us, it might focus more attention on the word than it really deserves." (1995, p. 29)

VSS certainly meets Graves's requirement that effective vocabulary instruction include fostering word-consciousness. Years ago, I demonstrated VSS to a secondary reading methods class by having students bring words for our class to learn. One man brought the word *pottle* to class and defined it as a container that holds 1-1/2 quarts of liquid. I was intrigued. I'd never heard the word before, so I began questioning him. For further clarification, he compared *pottle* to *hottle*, the container used for one serving of coffee or tea by hotel room service. He said that a hottle is half a pottle. I was now enchanted; I'd been using hottles for years but had never known they had a name. A year or so later, I wanted to tell this story and give accurate definitions for *pottle* and *hottle*. To my surprise, I could find only *pottle* (container for holding 1/2 gallon liquid) in my dictionary. No *hottle*. I called the main library, and neither the reference librarian nor the science librarian could find anything. I recounted this to a group of teachers a year or so later, and a district curriculum supervisor told me that I could have gotten accurate definitions from a restaurant-supply house because they are "container" terms: *pottle* is a combined word meaning "pot-bottle," and *hottle* comes from and means "hot-bottle." Now, dictionary.com defines both.

Word-consciousness is clearly evident in the list of words collected by the seventh- and eighth-grade students Brenda Shearer and I studied; students found words in classes, at home, in church, and in myriad personal reading—comic books, newspapers, popular magazines, song lyrics, and others. Students not only became attuned to words in their environment, but also they became very thoughtful about the usefulness of words in their lives. Here are some of the reasons students gave for selecting words. *Dormant*, "I asked Mr. D. [science teacher] what it meant. We need to know about volcanoes." *Acquaintance*, "It's tricky with the 'ac' and 'qu.'" *Nebulous*, "I thought it was a cool word and I wanted to know what it meant." *Affluent*, "I'm interested in words in other classes." *Embezzle*, "It's a cool word with the two z's. I bet other kids don't know it." *Federation*, "It's important to history." *Frequent*, "Bigger word for 'often.'" Notice how metacognitive these reasons are, touching on needing to know, coolness, interestingness, importance, and utility. And it is here, at the intersection of word awareness and metacognitive discussions, that VSS appears to yield big payoff for students by helping them build what Louise Rosenblatt calls "linguistic-experiential capital" (1994, p. 1083), much like investors build financial capital with compound interest. The more linguistic-experiential capital one has, the greater one's wherewithal to get more. In other words, the more students explore and seek out new, interesting, important, and tricky words and consider the value of those words to their learning, the more aware they become of such words and the more they will continue to do such exploration. Thus, VSS, used over time, engages students in word learning that results in an exponential knowledge growth pattern.

With VSS, students really do get excited about learning and actively seek knowledge. *They* nominate the pool of words and determine the final list, and because they invest so much of themselves in the word- and list-selection processes, they develop abiding interest in the learning that follows. Their interest and involvement grow from one powerful source: These words touch them in some special way—a sound, an association, a need to know—and the impact of that internal motivating force is exceptionally strong.

In my research on the conditions that precipitate word learning (Haggard, 1980, 1986a), I found that adolescents enjoy playing with the sound of words and with the words themselves. Thus, an entire population of high school students adopted the catchword *behooves* after hearing an assistant principal tell them in an all-school assembly, "It behooves you not to show affection in public." *Four years later*, students (now seniors) were still saying to one another, "It *behooves* you not to hold hands in the hall." "It *behooves* you to study for the test!" Clearly, these students enjoyed playing with and using that word. VSS encourages this response and playfulness, and so such words as *gymnosperm*, *ignominy*, and *behoove* find their way onto word lists. These words are just as difficult as the ones on the Dreaded Word List like the one Zena Logan is working listlessly through, but VSS words belong to students in a way no word list can ever duplicate. My own earlier research and my and others' current research confirm not only the long-lasting learning benefits of VSS but also the close and vital connection with words that VSS engenders (Pariza, 2002; Ruddell & Shearer, 2002). In the VSS classroom, word list definition-by-synonym yields to elaborated discussion in which exploration of content word meanings, connections with students' prior knowledge, and increased depth of understanding and learning are common. VSS words are content words students *need to know*, words that lead to independent, active learning and that, in turn, develop and support content learning.

Strategic Readers

VSS is, in and of itself, a means for creating strategic readers because it involves ongoing introspection about learning new words. When you ask, "Why do you think we need to have this word/term on our word list?" you immediately engage metacognitive thought. Why, indeed, is this word important? becomes the underlying rationale for each new choice. In addition, the very act of looking for new words to learn or know more about heightens students' sensitivity to important words and concepts in an academic discipline. Students who are given lots of practice doing this get very good at it and become increasingly able and willing to do so independently.

How to do . . . .

VSS

Student teachers' and teachers' first concern about VSS is the feature that allows students to select the words to be learned. The question I most frequently hear about VSS is "Won't the students choose the simplest words?" The answer is a resounding no. You have seen that the VSS words seventh- and eighth-grade students identified as "at risk" collected for their reading class were not easy. The simplest words are not the most interesting or useful or important to learning content. Students quickly discern the value word study has *and* see that by choosing interesting and important words they (1) make classroom learning more fun and (2) serve their own goal of learning the subject matter (and getting good grades). Students love VSS; so do teachers who have tried it. The following guidelines will be helpful as you adapt VSS for your subject area:

1. After reading (or other learning event), ask student groups to find a word or term that they would like to study or learn more about. Students are to be prepared to:
   a. Identify the word/term in context.
   b. Tell where they found it in the text.
   c. Tell what they think the word/term means.
   d. Tell why they think the word/term is important to the topic and should be on the class vocabulary list.
2. Accept word/term nominations with discussion of possible meanings and reasons for learning (a through d above). Encourage extension and refinement of meanings through collaboration and pooling of information.
3. Nominate the word you wish to have on the list and supply all of the requisite information (a through d above).
4. Narrow class list to predetermined number (if needed).
5. Refine definitions as needed for each word/term.
6. Direct students to record final list words/terms and definitions (as developed in class discussion) in vocabulary journals, on maps, or wherever you wish.
7. Develop VSS lesson activities for reinforcement (e.g., SFA grid).
8. Provide time for students to complete lesson activities (e.g., semantic mapping) and/or make out-of-class assignments.
9. Incorporate vocabulary items into end-of-chapter/unit assessments, as appropriate.

WHAT THIS CHAPTER MEANS TO YOU

1. Zena Logan's experience working her way through the Dreaded Word List is not unlike many other students' experience (and quite possibly your own). This kind of vocabulary "instruction" runs counter to everything we know about teaching and learning, and not incidentally, adolescents' propensities to play with language. It is of questionable value and not likely to contribute positively to your students' learning. If you must have a long list of words, let students generate one using VSS.

2. It is important to distinguish between *prereading* vocabulary instruction intended to remove barriers to comprehension and *postreading* vocabulary instruction intended for long-term vocabulary acquisition and development. Prereading instruction is short, sweet, and to the point; postreading instruction is extended, exploratory, and wide ranging.
3. Effective vocabulary instruction needs to teach individual words, teach word-learning strategies, and foster word-consciousness through integration, repetition, and meaningful use. You now know that CSSR, VSS, and other activities—semantic mapping, SFA, List-Group-Label, word treasure hunts, and so on—all do just that.

DOUBLE ENTRY JOURNAL

In my vocabulary research, I found that I could categorize people's experiences with word learning. I called these categories precipitating conditions for word learning. Here's what I found in descending order of frequency:

Elementary Years:

The word was learned because of its sound or adultness.

The word was learned as the result of an incident involving strong emotions.

The word was learned as the result of immediate usefulness.

The word was learned as the result of peer group usage.

Secondary Years:

The word was learned as the result of peer group usage.

The word was learned as the result of immediate usefulness.

The word was learned as the result of an incident involving strong emotions.

The word was learned because of its sound or adultness.

Where in these categories do your words and incidents fit? What conclusions can you draw about how middle school and secondary school students respond to words? What are some ways you can encourage students to develop their vocabularies in your subject area? Share your thinking with others.

FEATURE *What Goes in My Portfolio?*

Create a portfolio artifact that demonstrates how you can develop students' vocabulary in your subject area. You may want to demonstrate both prereading and postreading vocabulary instruction; you may want to combine your comprehension and vocabulary artifacts by revising the lesson plans you wrote for Chapter 4; and you may want to show how your lesson plan links to the principles of good instruction outlined both in that chapter and in this one.

FIGURE 5.5 *Intact Passage (See page 164)*

PLANT GROWTH AND DEVELOPMENT

You have probably heard the old saying "Mighty oaks from tiny acorns grow." But have you ever thought about the amazing *changes* that take place during the long life of such a *tree*? A tiny embryo oak plant sits *within* an acorn for months, maybe even years. Then one spring, it sprouts. Its roots grow deep into the soil in search of water and *nutrients*. Its leaves reach toward the sun—toward the light *energy* that powers the life of the plant. In autumn, growth *slows*. The oak's leaves turn color and fall to the ground. The entire plant undergoes the *changes necessary* to survive the approaching cold winter weather.

Many years later the tree *matures*. Suddenly it produces hundreds, perhaps even thousands, of flowers. Some of the flowers produce *seeds* that mature into acorns. When the acorns ripen, they fall to the ground, where they may be buried or eaten by squirrels. With luck, the *process* of growth begins again.

RECOMMENDED SOURCES

*Allington, R. L. (1978). *Are good and poor readers taught differently? Is that why poor readers are poor readers?* Paper presented at the meeting of the American Educational Research Association, Toronto.

*Alvermann, D. E., Weaver, D., Hinchman, R. A., Moore, D., Phelps, S. F., Thrach, E. C., & Zalewski, P. (1995). *Middle-and high-school students' perceptions of how they experience text-based discussion: A multicase study.* (Reading Research Report No. 36). Athens, GA: National Reading Research Center.

Anders, P. L., & Bos, C. S. (1986). Semantic feature analysis: An interactive strategy for vocabulary development and text comprehension. *Journal of Reading, 29*(7), 610–616.

Beck, I. L., McKeown, M. G., & Omanson, R. C. (1987). The effects and uses of diverse vocabulary techniques. In M. G. McKeown & M. E. Curtis (Eds.), *The nature of vocabulary acquisition* (pp. 147–163). Hillsdale, NJ: Lawrence Erlbaum.

*Collins, J. (1986). Differential instruction in reading groups. In J. Cook-Gumperz (Ed.), *The social construction of literacy* (pp. 117–137). New York: Cambridge University Press.

*Davidson, J. L. (1984). *Inquiry approaches to content learning.* Paper presented at the annual meeting of the International Reading Association, Atlanta.

*Dyer, P. A. (1985). *A study of the effect of prereading mapping on comprehension and transfer of learning.* Doctoral dissertation, University of California, Berkeley.

Freedman, S. W. (1987). *Peer response groups in two ninth-grade classrooms* (Technical Report No. 12). Berkeley, CA: Center for the Study of Writing.

Gee, J. P. (1996). *Social linguistics and literacies* (2nd ed.). New York: Routledge-Falmer.

Gee, J. P. (2000). Teenagers in new times: A literacy studies perspective. *Journal of Adolescent and Adult Literacy, 43*(5), 412–420.

*Graves, M. F. (2001). A vocabulary program to complement and bolster a middle-grade comprehension program. In B. M. Taylor, M. F. Graves, & P. Van Den Broek (Eds.), *Reading for meaning* (pp. 116–135). Newark, DE: International Reading Association.

*Graves, M. F., & Prenn, M. C. (1986). Costs and benefits of various methods of teaching vocabulary. *Journal of Reading, 29*(7), 596–602.

*Gray, W. S. (1946). *On their own in reading.* Chicago: Scott-Foresman.

*Greenleaf, C. L., Jiménez, R. T., & Roller, C. (2002). Conversations: Reclaiming secondary reading interventions: From limited to rich conceptions, from narrow to broad conversations. *Reading Research Quarterly, 37*(4), 484–496.

*Haggard, M. R. (1980). Vocabulary acquisition during elementary and post-elementary years: A preliminary report. *Reading Horizons, 21*, 61–69.

*Haggard, M. R. (1982). The vocabulary self-collection strategy: An active approach to word learning. *Journal of Reading, 26*(4), 203–207.

*Haggard, M. R. (1985). An interactive strategies approach to content learning. *Journal of Reading, 29*(3), 204–210.

*Haggard, M. R. (1986a). The vocabulary self-collection strategy: Using student interest and world knowledge to enhance vocabulary growth. *Journal of Reading, 29*(7), 634–642.

*Haggard, M. R. (1986b). The vocabulary self-collection strategy: Implications from classroom practice and research. In M. P. Douglass (Ed.), *Reading: The quest for meaning, 50th yearbook of the Claremont Reading Conference* (pp. 340–351). Claremont, CA: Claremont Reading Conference.

*Haggard, M. R. (1989). Instructional strategies for developing student interest in content area subjects. In D. Lapp, J. Flood, & N. Farnan (Eds.), *Content area reading and learning: Instructional strategies* (pp. 70–80). Englewood Cliffs, NJ: Prentice-Hall.

*Harmon, J. M. (1998). Constructing word meanings: Strategies and perceptions of four middle school learners. *Journal of Literacy Research, 30*(4), 561–599.

*Heimlich, J. E., & Pittelman, S. D. (1986). *Semantic mapping: Classroom applications.* Newark, DE: International Reading Association.

*Heller, J. (1955). *Catch-22.* New York: Simon & Schuster.

*Herber, H. L. (1978). *Teaching reading in content areas* (2nd ed.). Englewood Cliffs, NJ: Prentice-Hall.

*Cited in text

*Hopkins, G., & Bean, T. W. (1998/99). Vocabulary learning with the verbal-visual word association strategy in a Native American community. *Journal of Adolescent and Adult Literacy, 42*(4), 274–281.

*Jenkins, J. R., Matlock, B., & Slocum, T. A. (1989). Two approaches to vocabulary instruction: The teaching of individual word meanings and practice in deriving word meaning from context. *Reading Research Quarterly, 24*, 215–235.

*Johnson, D. D., Toms-Bronowski, S., & Pittelman, S. D. (1981). *A review of trends in vocabulary research and the effects of prior knowledge in instructional strategies for vocabulary acquisition* (Theoretical Paper No. 95). Madison: Wisconsin Center for Education Research.

Jongsma, E. (1971). *The Cloze procedure as a teaching technique.* Newark, DE: International Reading Association.

*Meeks, J. W., & Morgan, R. F. (1978). Classroom and the Cloze procedure: Interaction in imagery. *Reading Horizons, 18*, 261–264.

*Miller, K. R., & Levine, J. (1995). *Biology*. Englewood Cliffs, NJ: Prentice-Hall.

*Moore, D. W., Readence, J. E., & Rickelman, R. J. (1989). *Prereading activities for content area reading and learning* (2nd ed.). Newark, DE: International Reading Association.

*Nagy, W. E. (1988). *Teaching vocabulary to improve reading comprehension.* Newark, DE: International Reading Association.

*Nelson-Herber, J. (1986). Expanding and refining vocabulary in content areas. *Journal of Reading, 29*(7), 626–633.

*Pariza, J. L. (2002). *A description of vocabulary learning in at-risk college freshmen cooperatively involved in generative study of self-collected words.* Doctoral dissertation, Northern Illinois University.

Pittelman, S. D., Heimlich, J. E., Bergland, R. L., & French, M. P. (1991). *Semantic feature analysis: Classroom applications.* Newark, DE: International Reading Association.

*Rosenblatt, L. M. (1994). The transactional theory of reading and writing. In R. B. Ruddell, M. R. Ruddell, & H. Singer (Eds.), *Theoretical models and processes of reading* (4th ed., pp. 1057–1092). Newark, DE: International Reading Association.

*Ruddell, M. R.-H. (1992). Integrated content and long-term vocabulary learning with the Vocabulary Self-collection Strategy (VSS). In E. K. Dishner, T. W. Bean, J. E. Readence, & D. W. Moore (Eds.), *Reading in the content areas: Improving classroom instruction* (3rd ed., pp. 190–196). Dubuque, IA: Kendall/Hunt.

*Ruddell, M. R. (1994). Vocabulary knowledge and comprehension: A comprehension-process view of complex literacy relationships. In R. B. Ruddell, M. R. Ruddell, & H. Singer (Eds.), *Theoretical models and processes of reading* (4th ed., pp. 414–447). Newark, DE: International Reading Association.

*Ruddell, M. R., & Shearer, B. A. (2002). "Extraordinary," "tremendous," "exhilarating," "magnificent": Middle school at-risk students become avid word learners with the Vocabulary Self-Collection Strategy (VSS). *Journal of Adolescent and Adult Literacy, 45*(5), 352–363.

*Shearer, B. A., Ruddell, M. R., & Vogt, M. E. (2001). Successful middle school reading intervention: Negotiated strategies and individual choice. In J. V. Hoffman, C. M. Fairbanks, D. L. Schllart, J. Worthy, & B. Maloch (Eds.), *National Reading Conference Yearbook 51* (pp. 558–571). Chicago: National Reading Conference.

Singer, H. (1964). Substrata-factor patterns accompanying development in power of reading, elementary through college levels. In E. Thurston & L. Hafner (Eds.), *The philosophical and sociological bases of education. Fourteenth yearbook of the National Reading Conference.* Marquette, WI: National Reading Conference.

Stahl, S. A. (1986). Three principles of effective vocabulary instruction. *Journal of Reading, 29*(7), 662–668.

*Stahl, S. A., & Vancil, S. J. (1986). Discussion is what makes semantic maps work in vocabulary instruction. *The Reading Teacher, 40*, 62–67.

Stanovich, K. E. (1991). Word recognition: Changing perspectives. In R. Barr, M. L. Kamil, P. Mosenthal, & P. D. Pearson (Eds.), *Handbook of reading research* (vol. II, pp. 418–452). New York: Longman.

Stewart, J. (1991). *Vocabulary learning of high school sophomores: A comparison of traditional list instruction with VSS.* Unpublished master's program paper, Sonoma State University, Rohnert Park, CA.

Stewart, J., & Ruddell, M. R. (1992). *Vocabulary learning using VSS with high school sophomores.* Unpublished manuscript.

*Taylor, W. L. (1953). Cloze procedures: A new tool for measuring readability. *Journalism Quarterly, 30*, 360–368.

BUILDING TABLE

CHAPTER 5	SEMANTIC MAPPING	LIST-GROUP-LABEL	INTERACTIVE CLOZE	VSS
FOCUS ON	Content vocabulary and concept learning	Content vocabulary and concept learning	Contextual analysis of content vocabulary	Content vocabulary and concept learning
GUIDES STUDENTS	Before and after reading	Before or after reading	Before reading	After reading
USE TO PLAN	Lessons	Lessons	Lessons	Lessons, units, semester
MAY BE USED	Whole class, collaborative groups, partnerships, individuals	Whole class, collaborative groups, partnerships, individuals	Collaborative groups	Whole class, collobrative groups
MAY BE COMBINED WITH (known strategies)	VSS, GMA, DR-TA, DRA	DR-TA, DRA, VSS, GMA	DRA	DR-TA, GMA, semantic mapping, DRA, ReQuest
MATERIALS PREPARATION	None	None	Moderate	Moderate
OTHER PREPARATION	Light	Light	None to light	Moderate
OUTSIDE RESOURCES	Useful	Useful	Not needed	Necessary
HOW TO DO	Pages 170–171	Pages 170–171	Pages 170–171	Pages 184–185

CHAPTER 6

Teaching Bilingual/Bicultural Students in Multilingual/Multicultural Settings

DOUBLE ENTRY JOURNAL

Picture yourself, a successfully literate adult and competent learner, newly arrived in a country whose language and culture is different from your own. Jot down some of the problems and feelings you might experience in such a situation. Now imagine yourself a

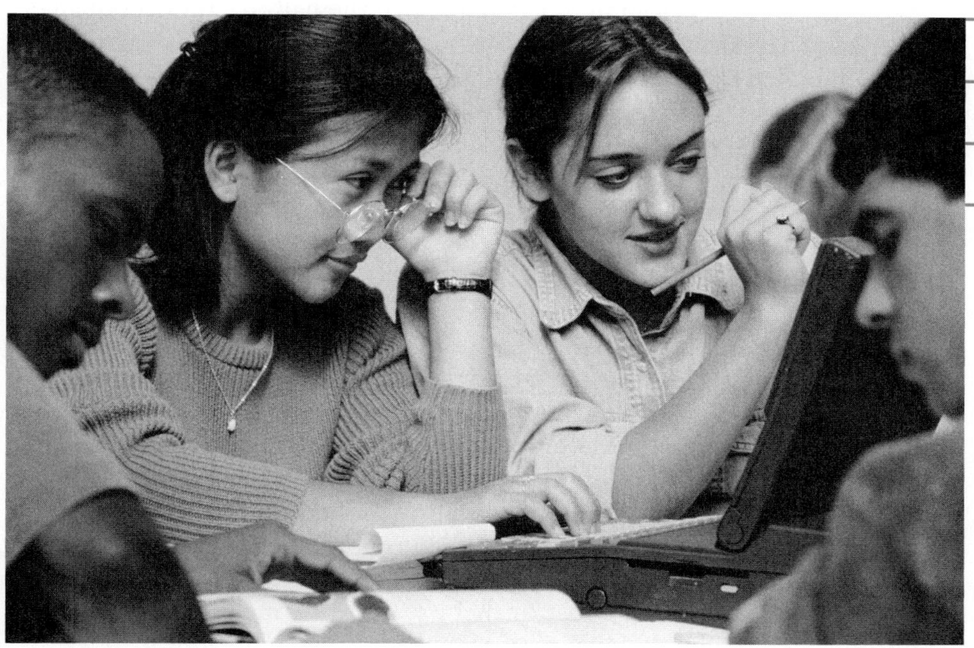

Arthur Tilley/Taxi/Getty Images

preadolescent or adolescent in school in this new country, language, and culture; spend a little time listing the likely problems and feelings you might have had as an adolescent. What strategies might you have used to function successfully in that environment and learn the content of school subjects? Share your perceptions with a friend.

Kim Marchand walks contemplatively down the hall. It's the end of another busy day for her at Center North Junior High. She sighs, trying to figure out what she can do to help all the newcomer students she's got in her classes this year. She's had three really good, hard-working years teaching eighth-grade social studies, and she had hoped that in this, her fourth year, she wouldn't have to do major revisions on her lesson and unit plans. But it looks like she will have to after all. During her first three years most of her bilingual students had been well established in the school, fluent English users, and quite good students. For the very few who were transitioning from the ESL class, she had had time to give them extra attention and assistance and to adjust instruction and assignments as needed. This year is different. With all the newly arrived immigrant families along with the migration of families out of the inner city to this changing neighborhood, she now has as many as five to eight bilingual kids in each of her classes—different languages, different fluency levels, and different levels of education in their home countries. She just can't ignore their needs; nor can she even hope to provide adequate individual attention for them if she doesn't change her teaching somehow. The kids are great. Most of them seem to be making friends and adjusting to the school. They're sweet and charming and appear to want to do well in class, but some of them clearly aren't able to handle the reading assignments or the class discussions. She's got to find a way to make the lessons understandable to them. She's got to get them interested and participating in class. If she doesn't do something soon, they'll shut down from sheer boredom if nothing else. Maybe she'd better go back to her books and class notes from her credential program. She remembers reading and talking about bilingual learners in her classes.

• • •

One in every five children in public schools today is either an immigrant child or a child of immigrant parents (Zenatella, 2005), with the dispersion of immigrants in this country no longer limited to border states. Thus, bilingualism in schools is "not only a California issue or a New York issue, but also a Kansas issue and a South Carolina issue" (Suárez-Orozco & Suárez-Orozco, 2001, in Qin-Hilliard, 2002, p. 398). Indeed, the 2005 U.S. Census American Community survey shows large increases in immigrant populations in the Upper Midwest, New England, and the Rocky Mountain States (Lyman, 2006). In today's schools, according to Echevarria, Vogt, and Short:

> Students who are learning English as an additional language are the fastest growing segment of the school-age population in the United States and almost

> all candidates in teacher education programs will have linguistically and culturally diverse students in their classes during their teaching careers. (2004, p. 18)

Classrooms in the United States are increasingly like Kim Marchand's—multilingual and multicultural, with various combinations of bilingual/bicultural students in them; the National Center for Education Statistics noted a 138% increase in the English language learner (ELL) population in U.S. schools from 1979 to 1999 compared with a 6% increase overall. In 2001, ELL students comprised 4 million students in public schools—about 10% of the total school population (Llana & Paulson, 2006). It should be noted that individuals' intent to develop bilingual fluency and literacy (or, in some cases, multilingual fluency and literacy), though relatively new to most monolingual U.S. Americans, is not considered unusual in many parts of the world (Portes & Rumbaut, 1990, pp. 182–183). Unfortunately, the issue of bilingualism is all too often viewed as a *problem* in the United States (you need only to read the popular press to perceive the magnitude of this belief), when in fact just the opposite should be true. In a world of increasing globalization, where access to other countries, cultures, and peoples is microseconds away via the Internet, and where hybridity—that is, cross-cultural identity—is increasingly apparent, especially among adolescents (Luke, 2002; Moje, 2002), one can only conclude that in such a world, crossing boundaries and borders—geographic, linguistic, cultural—can most easily be accomplished when one is fluent in two or more languages. Thus, bilingualism becomes a personal, professional, and educational *asset* rather than a problem, and those of us who remain monolingual are at a decided disadvantage.

BILINGUAL/BICULTURAL AND NON-ENGLISH-SPEAKING STUDENTS

Before we discuss issues associated with non-English-speaking students and bilingualism, you may wish to review the discussion in Chapter 2 regarding second-language acquisition and development. Keep in mind that for many students, English is not a second language but a third or fourth. Our discussion will focus on bilingualism and bilingual learning because that is the most common pattern; however, issues I raise and suggestions I make for bilingual students apply to multilingual students as well.

Keep in mind also the very close connections among language, culture, and community (Zentella, 2005). Regardless of whether students are learning English as a second, third, or even fourth language, much of what they bring to school from their primary language represents the beliefs, attitudes, behaviors, and values of their home, their primary culture, and community as well, the Discourses of their lives. Lee Gunderson (2000) cautions, "Language and culture are inextricably linked. Unlike the Gordian knot, nothing comes from separating them because they have little or no meaning apart from each other" (p. 694), and he reminds us of the reality of life in school for many immigrant adolescents:

> The youngest members of the newest most visible diasporas cling together in litter-strewn secondary school hallways amidst lockers filled with the delicious and dangerous tokens of the dominant culture. They learn to speak a "first"

> second language, not the six-o'clock news standard, but a patois steeped in MTV, rap, rebellion, and world domination. [These are] high school students who struggle with the impossible task of becoming adults, being submerged in a dominant second language and culture, learning English and learning in English and surviving as immigrants. (p. 694)

Gunderson's perception of the experience of adolescent Canadian immigrants is borne out by the experience of Leonard Peters who immigrated as a teen from Samoa to the state of Hawai'i.

> English is my second language. It was tough to learn. I don't think I really prepared for it. Any kid who come from (other) Pacific Islands, you're put in what they call a step class. They teach you English and stuff like that, break it down for you a little bit slower. It was pretty hard. I used to always think in Samoan first, then try to translate it in my head. It was even harder for me in Hawai'i. It wasn't only English (spoken) where I lived. It was pidgin. You're trying to learn English and pidgin at the same time. You're trying to learn two languages instead of one. (Tsai, 2006, p. C4)

Kiana Davenport (1994), in her novel *Shark Dialogues*, speaks about the experience of the native-born young adult who grew up in a Hawai'ian creole–language home, the close relationship between language and culture, and the pain associated with eradicating one's primary language:

> And entering university in Manoa Valley, frightened every day. What am I doing there, who do I think I am? . . . Silently swearing I will wear my fingers down, my eyes, I will die becoming something better. Smoothing out my English. Swallowing Pidgin, denying it, saving it for home, for "slang." This tongue I was born with, raised on, this part of my mouth demeaned, thrown out like garbage. Mama trying to keep up with me, ironing out her Pidgin, ironing other people's clothes. (p. 193)

To teach bilingual and multilingual students effectively, we need knowledge and understanding of their language, culture, and community; we need to honor and respect the knowledge represented by students' homes and communities (Kana'iaupuni, 2005; Moll & Ruiz, 2002); and we need to understand the relationships among these important influences on students' lives. We need also to recognize that many monolingual English-speaking students are at the same time bicultural. Some of the issues regarding bilingualism are just as appropriately applied to monolingual/bicultural students as they are to bilingual/bicultural students.

For the most part, non-English-speaking students in United States schools are immigrant rather than indigenous. Bilingual students, on the other hand, may have been born in the United States to immigrant parents or reared in a family where a language or dialect other than English predominates in the home; these students may or may not be literate in their first language. The Navaho, Eskimo-Aleut, and other Native Americans and the Louisiana French are examples of such indigenous populations as are native Hawai'ians, Sea Islanders from the Carolinas to northern Florida, and African Americans. All of these variations—from immigrant non-English-speaking students, to indigenous students with home language fluency preceding English language fluency, to students whose home language and/or dialect develop concurrently with English—are present in our schools. Newly apparent within this general population are the immigrant students Lee Gunderson referred to, and Leonard Peters identified himself as, who learn an English dialect, rather than mainstream English, first and who must then transition a second time into the English of the classroom. All of these variations of language learning in some way affect students' language and literacy development in English. The remainder of this chapter addresses issues related to second-language acquisition, bilingual students and programs, and appropriate subject matter instruction for bilingual/bicultural students in multilingual/multicultural settings.

BILINGUAL STUDENTS AND PROGRAMS

In the literature of bilingualism, you will find a number of generally standard terms and abbreviations used to describe or refer to non-English-speaking and bilingual students. It is helpful to learn these terms and, in so doing, begin to get a sense of the students themselves.

Bilingual describes students who speak two languages (*multilingual*, more than two languages). Many bilingual students have achieved full English language fluency and are biliterate in English and their other language. These students generally function as effortlessly in classroom English as do their monolingual English language peers, and do not require special assistance in learning English. Others have not reached that level of English language fluency and literacy.

LEP refers to Limited English Proficient students, those who demonstrate some level of oral-language fluency in English but who have not attained minimal levels of academic and oral-language English proficiency.

L1 stands for "first language"; *L2* is "second language." Various authors use the terms *primary language*, *native language*, *home language*, *heritage language*, or *mother tongue* to refer to L1.

ESL, or English as a Second Language, is used to designate classes that are immersion English classes. In these classes, students generally have various primary languages and varying levels of English literacy and oral fluency. As suggested earlier, students in the classes may be learning English as a third or fourth language. Often, ESL classes are taught by teachers who are monolingual English speakers; instruction is in English and focused on acquisition of English language skills. Most L1 interaction in ESL classes is between students with common home languages. ESL is also used to refer to students who speak English as a second language, whether or not those students are actually in ESL classes.

ELL refers to English Language Learners, a term gaining prominence as the preferred means for referring to immigrant students who are not fluent in English. Some authors shorten this to EL.

Bilingual Education programs provide instruction in students' primary language, focusing on content learning while providing instruction in English during part of the school day. Most bilingual classes are in elementary schools, and most of those are at the primary grade level. Some do exist at intermediate grades and in middle schools, and a few can be found in junior high or high schools. Bilingual classes require that everyone in the class have the same L1 and so generally are found in schools with large concentrations of immigrant students from the same country or who speak common languages; they also require teachers who are fluently bilingual and bilingually literate. Bilingual education programs in some states have been banned or severely restricted by legislation aimed at "English-only" instruction.

Dual Immersion programs provide instruction in English and another language by alternating languages by curriculum (subject areas) or time (morning, afternoon). Students in immersion programs enter with either English or the other language as their L1; the goal of immersion programs is for all students to exit the program fluently bilingual and biliterate. Teachers in immersion programs are both.

Transition programs are intended to bridge ESL and bilingual classes and regular classrooms. Students who have been in ESL and bilingual classes who need a bit more assistance before being completely immersed in regular classes are often put into transition classes. Many transition classes focus on sheltered instruction (SI) as the primary means for instruction; some are even called "sheltered" classes. We will discuss sheltered instruction at some length later in this chapter. Transition classes are often found in middle, junior high, and senior high schools.

Maintenance bilingual programs are available in some very few middle and secondary schools for the purpose of maintaining and developing students' language and literacy proficiency in their first language. Such programs are grounded in two key beliefs: (1) that unless ELL students have opportunity to continue instruction in their first (or heritage) language, they are at risk of becoming partial bilinguals and semiliterates in their first language and (2) that eradication of students' first language undermines cultural identity and causes loss of communication between parents who maintain the first language and their children who have lost that language (Fillmore, 1990; Hones, 1999). Lily Wong Fillmore (1990) describes this generational rift as "tragic." Fillmore states, "What is lost is the ability for parents and children to communicate about the deep and critical experiences of growing up. What the parent has to teach the child and what the child is able to share with the parent are irretrievably lost when their means of communication are lost to them" (p. 46). The end result can thus interfere with students' social, emotional, *and* academic development. Immigrant students who are fluent bilinguals (those fluent and literate in both their primary language and English) do better in school than those who are English monolingual (those who have lost their primary language) and those who are limited bilinguals (those with limited proficiency in both languages) (Portes & Rumbout, 2001). Tse (2001) points out that in most families the heritage language is completely lost by the third generation. Thus, not only do maintenance bilingual programs validate students' primary language and culture and continue developing their L1 language and literacy abilities (therefore encouraging fluent bilingualism), but in so doing, these programs positively affect these students' English-language literacy and overall academic achievement as well.

APPROPRIATE PLACEMENT IN PROGRAMS FOR BILINGUAL STUDENTS

Lee Gunderson (1991) emphasizes the importance of appropriate instruction for ELL students and appropriate placement of these students into available bilingual, ESL, reading, and regular classrooms. He uses a graduated scale to define degrees of English (L2) oral-language proficiency that is helpful in understanding second-language development, especially growth from "basic interpersonal communication" (BIC) to cognitive academic language proficiency (CALP) (Cummins, 1984). Please note that Gunderson's "O-Level English" and "Very Limited English" may, in fact, describe a student in the silent period. The levels he uses are described below (adapted from Gunderson, 1991, p. 26):

O-Level English
Cannot answer yes/no questions.
Unable to identify and name any objects.
Understands no English.
Often appears withdrawn and afraid.

Very Limited English
Responds to simple questions with mostly yes/no or one-word responses.
Speaks in one- to two-word phrases.
Attempts no extended conversation.
Seldom, if ever, initiates conversation.

Limited English
Responds easily to simple questions.
Produces simple sentences.
Has difficulty elaborating when asked.
Uses syntax/vocabulary adequate for personal, simple situations.
Occasionally initiates conversation.

Limited Fluency
Speaks with ease.
Initiates conversations.
May make phonological or grammatical errors.
Makes errors in more syntactically complex utterances.
Freely and easily switches codes.

Gunderson uses a "decision heuristic" that combines students' L1 literacy (the number of years they have experienced literacy instruction and/or literacy in their primary language) and L2 oral-language proficiency (English) to guide decision making about ESL student placement (p. 27). The Secondary Decision Heuristic—English Ability—is shown in Figure 6.1 on p. 200.

This heuristic may be used to decide what kind of instruction would be most beneficial for students: Students with O-Level or Very Limited L2 proficiency and no or

FIGURE 6.1 *The Secondary Decision Heuristic—English Ability*

	L-2 Oral Proficiency		
L1 Literacy	0-Level Very Limited	Limited	Limited Fluency
None			
2 to 6 Years			
7+ Years			

very few years of reading and writing instruction in their primary language (upper-left box in Figure 6.1) would be very unlikely to benefit from placement in regular subject area classrooms; students with limited oral fluency and 7 or more years of L1 literacy would probably function very effectively in regular classes. Between these extremes, students would probably function better or less well in regular classrooms, depending on where their abilities fall on the heuristic.

I present Gunderson's oral-language proficiency description and the decision heuristic here because my experience suggests, and reports from middle school and secondary teachers confirm, that bilingual and non-English-speaking students are often misplaced in schools, particularly at the senior high level. Misplacement of bilingual students occurs with greater frequency as resources dwindle, negative attitudes and legislation prevail, and teachers and staff with expertise and experience in bilingual and ESL programs are removed from schools. Misplacement of ELL students can have significant impact on their educational progress. A study of 5,000 immigrant high school students in Vancouver revealed that 40% of them dropped out of school, most often after leaving ESL class (Gunderson, 2006).

In the event that you find yourself in a school that has minimal staff and facilities for evaluating and placing bilingual students in programs and classrooms, you need to have some basis for making this evaluation yourself. (Recall Kim Marchand's experience. Recall also Echevarria and colleagues' assertion that most teachers will work with bilingual/bicultural students at some point in their careers.) Similarly, even with staff and facilities, you may find bilingual students in your class whom you believe to be misplaced. To check the placement and appropriate instruction for students in your classes, use the authentic assessment instruments discussed in Chapter 9, as appropriate, and check records to determine everything you can about students' prior schooling and L1 literacy; then apply that information to Gunderson's heuristic. You may or may not be able to change students' placement if this analysis suggests they are misplaced; however, at the very least, knowledge gained from the analysis should guide your decision making about classroom instruction and activities for these students.

ACADEMIC SUCCESS AND BILINGUAL/BICULTURAL STUDENTS

It is important to emphasize at this point that many bilingual/bicultural students succeed splendidly in school. Their success stories are well known, and the students (and their stories) are in front of our eyes daily. Jiménez, García, & Pearson (1996) summarized research on the characteristics of successful Latina/o readers. Successful Latina/o readers:

- Understand the unitary nature of reading, whether the process is in Spanish or English (e.g., "When I learned to read in English I just needed to know the pronunciation and spelling of the words"; "[E]verything's the same that you have to know [to read in English and Spanish]" [p. 99]).
- Use a variety of techniques to identify unknown vocabulary, including context, prior knowledge, inferencing, searching for cognates (English/Spanish words with similar pronunciation), and translating.
- Monitor their comprehension by checking to make sure their constructions of meaning make sense.
- Make large numbers of inferences during reading that serve as temporary meaning units to be confirmed or disconfirmed by further reading and/or additional information.
- Occasionally ask questions to assist in meaning construction.

This list is strikingly similar to the list of strategies used by successful readers in general (i.e., "thoughtful" or "mature" readers) described in Chapter 4. An important finding of this study was the heightened awareness among successful Latina/o readers of the parallel nature of the process of reading in two languages and their active search for cognates as bridges between their first and second languages.

Other ELL students do not succeed in school for many and varied reasons. John Ogbu (1988) distinguishes between immigrants—people who moved "more or less voluntarily" to the United States for economic, political, or personal reasons—and involuntary minorities—people who were brought into U.S. society through slavery, conquest, or colonization (p. 41). Involuntary minorities in the United States include African Americans, Native Americans, Native Hawai'ians, and Mexican Americans of the Southwest. Ogbu makes the point that differential success rates of various cultural groups in acquiring fluent English, independent literacy, and academic success may be explained, in part, by differences in how different cultures were originally brought into the mainstream culture. He suggests further that among involuntary minority youth, behaviors that reject mainstream culture, language, and academic values may reflect students' "disillusionment about their ability to succeed in adult life through the mainstream strategy of schooling" (p. 54), rather than reflecting differential abilities and intelligence for school learning across racial and ethnic groups. Shawn Kana'iaupuni (2005) notes the educational disconnect that occurs when school practice conflicts with cultural beliefs and standards of the students schools serve and/or when assumptions held by teachers, administrators, and the public in general include an assumption of "failure to succeed." And Gutiérrez et al. (2002) note that many immigrant students are part of the "new poor" and that the real issue is "not poverty but rather how being a poor child becomes a debilitating condition in schools. So the issue is how schools treat poor children" (p. 329).

We must acknowledge that we have in our schools students of many cultures and primary languages who represent a wide range of language, literacy, and learning abilities and achievement in English (and in their primary language). And, whatever their socioeconomic, cultural, or other characteristics, it is important that we teach our respective subject areas in ways that make content accessible to all students and increase their English-language and literacy development in subject areas. The rest of this chapter focuses on appropriate instruction for ELL students—students who have not achieved fluency and literacy in English commensurate with their level of schooling. When I refer to ELL students, I am not talking about those bilingual students who have achieved high levels of fluency and literacy and for whom sheltered instruction is not needed.

Candace Harper and Ester de Jong (2004) identify three understandings teachers must have in order to provide appropriate content instruction for ELL students. First, teachers need to know that while L1 and L2 learning are highly similar, they are not identical processes; thus, teachers need to do more than immerse students in an L2 environment by ensuring that ELL students have the language skills needed for a given task. Second, teachers need to understand the role of learner variables in L2 acquisition and development—the affective, cultural, and emotional differences among ELL students—that may cause them to progress at different rates. And, finally, teachers need to go beyond simply helping ELL students "get around" L2 academic language, by direct instruction of L2 vocabulary words. Specifically, Harper and de Jong recommend that in addition to good L1 instructional practice, teachers need to

- Identify the oral language and literacy demands of their content area.
- Set instructional objectives and select classroom tasks that promote academic and social language as well as content learning.
- Provide appropriate and sufficient feedback to scaffold students' mastery of the L2 functions, structures, and vocabulary of the subject area. (p. 159)

CENTERPIECE LESSON PLAN

Let us now look at this chapter's Centerpiece Lesson Plan, a two-day lesson for a science class with ELL students. This sheltered lesson combines the Directed Inquiry Activity (DIA) with two strategies you've seen in previous chapters—the Group Mapping Activity (GMA) and the Vocabulary Self-Collection Strategy (VSS). You will note at least two differences in this Centerpiece Lesson Plan from others: (1) it includes a section called "Language Skills" in which the teacher identifies how ELL students will engage in listening, speaking, reading, and writing in the lesson; and (2) the lesson plan is longer (even than the two-day DRA lesson plan in Chapter 4) and requires more materials for demonstration and illustration, and more time for preteaching vocabulary and concepts.

DIA, GMA, VSS CENTERPIECE SHELTERED LESSON PLAN, *Science*

Lesson: Forms of Energy (Two Days)
Course/Grade: Earth Science/6th Grade
Materials:

- Items for illustrating energy: hammer, nail and board; light socket and bulb; hotplate and teakettle, two magnets.
- Five sets of pictures for small groups, each set containing a picture of: a windmill, waves crashing on shore, a person ironing clothes, a dam with water rushing through, a hot air balloon, a house with solar panels, a sail-boat, a nuclear power plant, an X-ray of lungs.
- Handouts for all students with one inquiry question at the top of each sheet, additional paper, pencils/pens.

  Inquiry Questions

  a. What are the different forms of energy?
  b. How do we use energy, and what are the outcomes of that use?
  c. Why is it important to consider issues related to energy resources?
  d. How do we tell the difference between kinetic and potential energy resources?
  e. What are some important questions we need to explore?
- Text Set—Energy
- Web sources:
  http://www.eia.doe.gov/kids/energyfacts/science/formsofenergy.html
  http://www.ftexploring.com/energy/enrg-types.htm
  http://projectsol.aps.com/energy/energy_changes2.asp
- Large sheets of butcher paper and five sets of marking pens.

LESSON OBJECTIVES (WITH CONTENT STANDARDS)

Upon completion of this lesson students will be able to

- Give examples to show that energy exists in different and varied forms (Standard 6—Students know that sources of energy and materials differ in amounts, distribution, usefulness, and the time required for their formation).
- Classify sources of energy as renewable or nonrenewable (Standard 6.a—Students know different natural energy and material resources, including air, soil, rocks, minerals, petroleum, fresh water, wildlife, and forests, and know how to classify them as renewable or nonrenewable).
- Understand the practical and social, immediate and future consequences of energy use (Standard 6.b—Students know the utility of energy sources is determined by factors that are involved in converting these sources to useful forms and the consequences of the conversion process).

LANGUAGE SKILLS

Listening: Participating in Into discussions, group discussions, map presentations.
Speaking: Contributing to whole class and small group discussions.
Reading: Doing research to answer group inquiry question.
Writing: Contributing to creation of group map, creating final map.

LESSON PROCEDURES

Before Reading: Into—Day One, DIA

1. BRINGING THE LESSON TO LIFE. *Arrange all of the items for illustrating energy (hammer, nail, and board, etc.) on a table in front of the room. Say*: Today we're going to begin our study of energy *write "forms of energy" on the board. Pound nail into board, say*: This is energy changing form. What form of energy is this creating? (*mechanical/kinetic*) *Let students suggest possibilities and help them arrive at the answer, ask*: What other kinds of mechanical energy can you think of?

2. Continue through this process with the other items.

3. SETTING THE STAGE. *Divide students into five groups with the ELL students distributed across the groups. Give each group a set of pictures, say*: Working together in your group decide what kind of energy each picture represents. *Circulate as groups are working.*

4. PRETEACHING VOCABULARY. *Mount one set of pictures on the board, Say*: Okay. Let's look at some different forms of energy. Which group will tell us what form of energy is represented by this windmill? *Let groups answer; resolve any differences. When such answers as "wind," "mechanical," "electric" are given, write each label on the board under that picture. Make sure the word/picture pairings are easy for everyone to see. Point several times from the picture to the labels; refer back to items on the table and say/connect them with labels. Continue in this manner through the pictures.*

5. *Give each group the inquiry question handout, say*: Working with your group, read each inquiry question, think about our lesson topic *point to on the board*, "forms of energy" and the forms of energy we've talked about *gesture to vocabulary pictures on the board and the table display of energy forms*, and write some predictions about what answer we'll get to the inquiry questions. *Circulate.*

6. GUIDING INITIAL LEARNING. *Say*: What are some of your predictions about our inquiry questions? *Read the first inquiry question and field responses. Write predictions on board or butcher paper. After finishing, assign each group one of the inquiry questions and say*: Okay groups. You're going to work as a team to become our "resident experts" on your question. You are to use your textbook, the text set books on the cart, and the Web sites I have already opened on our computers to answer your question. For now, all you need to do is get information recorded on your handout sheet. Later I'll tell you what I want you to do with it. You may get to work right now.

During Reading: Through—End of Day One, Day Two

7. GUIDING PRACTICE. Circulate as groups work, making sure that ELL students are participating in gathering and discussing information related to the questions, and helping groups stay productive.

After Reading: Beyond—GMA, VSS

8. After groups have compiled sufficient information, give each group a sheet of butcher paper and a set of marking pens. *Say*: Now I want each group to create a map or other visual representation of what you've learned. Be sure to include enough information so that we will all have a good understanding of your information. *Circulate and assist groups. When all groups are finished, mount each map on the wall. Say*. Group 1. What were some of the predictions the class made about the different forms of energy? *Read or have students in Group 1 read them. Display (on an overhead, LCD, butcher paper) the original list of predictions. As group presents/explains map, probe, ask questions, refer back to predictions. Be sure to include metacognitive questions*, Ask: How closely did your research match our predictions? Why did your group organize your map that way? Why did you put ——— where you did? etc. *Continue similarly until all groups have presented.*

9. *Say*: Now I want each group to go back to your reading and information collection and choose two words or terms that you think should be on our vocabulary list. Be prepared to tell where you found it, what you think it means, and why you think it should be on our list. I'll nominate two words too. *Move this along. When groups are ready*, Ask: Who'll nominate a word? *Receive words and write each on board. Make sure group reads word in context, gives a definition, and tells why it should be on list. Continue until all words are nominated (about 12)*, Ask: Which of these words do we want on our list? *Arrive at final list.*

10. Develop final definitions of each vocabulary word. Write these definitions on the board and have students copy them in their vocabulary journals.

11. GUIDING INDEPENDENT PRACTICE. *Say*: Continue working in your groups to create maps that combine information from all of our group maps. You may each create a different map or all do the same one, but you must make sure that everyone in your group has the important information on their maps. Be sure to put our vocabulary words on your maps and mark them some way so you'll remember they are vocab words. We're going to be looking at forms of energy and some of the issues raised by our reading over the next few days, so it's really important that these maps are complete. You'll turn your maps in to me today and I'll return them to you tomorrow.

LESSON ASSESSMENT(S)

12. Observational Assessment—As students respond to Into activities, note their background knowledge and understandings. During the two days, check to see how well students are developing familiarity with concepts and issues and how their explanations gain specificity and fullness. Note completeness of group maps, importance of VSS words.

13. Language Assessment—Note how well all students are increasing their vocabularies. Pay particular attention to ELL students' development of concept vocabulary, fluency of expression, and ease with written text.

14. Other Assessment—Review individual or group maps checking for understanding, completeness. Provide feedback. Record maps as completed.

IMPLICATIONS FOR INSTRUCTION

The clear implication from what we know about second-language learning and second-language learners is that ELL students need to be in classrooms in which they receive sufficient comprehensible input to allow both the learning of content information and the further acquisition and development of English-language proficiency. Indeed, we have evidence from a recent study of U.S. and Canadian ELL students (Hakuta, Butler, & Witt, 2000) that not only supports Cummins's estimate that it takes ELL students five to seven years to arrive at English-language proficiency levels needed for fluency in the classroom (CALP), but suggests the possibility that five to seven years may be an *under*estimate. Further, instruction for ELL students must include support and scaffolding activities when instructional expectations fall in quadrant B of Cummins's intersecting continua; that is, when cognitive demand is high, instruction must be highly context embedded to give students many extralingual and situational cues for constructing meaning. This has the effect of reducing negative affective filters (e.g., high anxiety, low self-confidence, low motivation), boosting positive affect, and increasing students' willingness to participate in learning events.

INSTRUCTION FOR BILINGUAL/BICULTURAL STUDENTS

One of the most important issues in instruction for bilingual students in middle and secondary schools is who is responsible for that instruction. In their book *Overlooked and Underserved: Immigrant Students in U.S. Secondary Schools*, Ruiz-de-Velasco, Fix, and Clewell (2000) note that many content teachers believe that addressing the needs of ELL students is "not my job" (p. 60), and that ESL programs are "remedial." Gunderson (2000) also notes the status implications of academic placement for ELL students. In his 10-year study of over 35,000 immigrant students in Canadian schools, he found a clear discrepancy between students' experiences in ESL and regular classrooms:

> When I knew I was put in the ESL class, I was very disappointed. In the first week I was totally upset and was in a very low mood because I didn't have many friends, and all things around me were unfamiliar. Besides, I didn't want to be distinct from others. I wanted to be a regular student. However, after the first day of integration, the master of hell told me where heaven was. As I first stepped in the regular classroom, I could easily feel the coldness and bitterness in the air. Everyone was indifferent to me. I was standing in front of the classroom like a fool waiting for the teacher to come. I was so embarrassed

> that I wanted to cry out and run back to the ESL class. As time went by, I made more friends in the ESL class and we studied together like brothers and sisters. We cared for and helped each other. But I remain an unconcerned visitor in the regular class after six months. I talk to no one. So I am traveling now between heaven and hell, back and forth. (female—Cantonese—Hong Kong—15 years). (p. 699)

Warm though they may be, however, much of the instruction that goes on in ESL and/or the low-track classes in which ELL students are placed *is* remedial. Danling Fu (1995) describes such instruction:

> Through the specific examples and detailed description of Tran, Paw, and Cham, refugee children tracked at the low level in their school learning, my study typifies the situation of all students ranked at the bottom. These students are bombarded with endless worksheets, surrounded by meaningless mechanical skills and decontextualized spelling words, and suffocated with frequent tests and quizzes. Every day they numbly move disconnected words from books to worksheets and are trained to passively follow the rules. (p. 202)

No student should be condemned to life at school in the kind of low-track classes that Fu describes (we'll talk more about this in Chapter 10 as well), and *all* teachers must accept responsibility for meeting the language and learning needs of ELL students. All teachers must do what they can to make the curriculum accessible to all learners, including ELL students.

Another important concern in the education of ELL students is the degree and quality of communication between all parties involved in that education. All too often, there is too little, it is too late, or the lines of communication break down (Díaz, Moll, & Mehan, 1986). If you have ELL students in your classes, you need to initiate contact with whomever is responsible for counseling, making assignments, and watching over these students' progress, if that person does not contact you. Do whatever is needed to maintain close communication.

Once again, the point must be made that instruction for bilingual/bicultural students need not, and indeed *should not*, be "remedial" in nature. Rather, it should be the kind of *good instruction* emphasized throughout this text, involving:

- Rich language interaction
- A focus on students' prior knowledge base
- Careful lesson planning
- Integrated/collaborative learning
- Cultural breadth
- An emphasis on student strengths
- Authentic assessment
- Multiple sources of information
- Multiple response modes

In addition to

- Attention to language
- More time for everything

- Repetition of ideas and concepts
- Allowance for students to choose which language to use at any given moment
- Low-risk environment for second-language users
- Deemphasis of on-the-spot correction of language miscues

ELL students are best served by solid, well-designed instruction suitable for all students that focuses on content learning and that provides needed support for students who are in the process of developing English-language and literacy skills. Of prime importance is that this instruction provides for and increases student facility with the academic language of subject areas.

Further, such instruction should provide for cultural attributes other than language, including nonverbal communication, perspectives and worldviews, behavioral styles, values, methods of reasoning and validating knowledge, and cultural identification (Anderson, 1988). Hee-Won Kang, Phyllis Kuehn, and Adrienne Herrell (1994), in an ethnographic study of Hmong adult literacy classes, found numerous areas of cultural misunderstanding between the Hmong students and their native U.S. teachers. For example, much laughter was heard in the room as students worked, enough so that one observer concluded that the Hmong students were not serious about their study. Closer observation showed, however, that students laughed or giggled when they made a mistake, or were having problems, or were unsure about what they were doing or saying in English. Thus, instead of being a sign of lightheartedness or play, the laughter was a signal to the teacher that the student needed help.

MAKING THE CURRICULUM ACCESSIBLE FOR BILINGUAL LEARNERS

Two approaches for modifying instruction for ELL learners in subject matter classrooms are Specially Designed Academic Instruction in English (SDAIE) and Sheltered Instruction (SI). Although some authors make distinctions between these approaches, most use them interchangeably, as I will. Certain principles of instruction underlie these approaches. They are as follows:

- *Active participation:* Students learn both content and language through active engagement in academic tasks that are directly related to a specific content.
- *Social interaction:* Students learn both content and language by interacting with others as they carry out activities.
- *Integrated oral and written language:* Students become more able language learners when language processes are integrated in a variety of ways for a variety of purposes.
- *Real books and real tasks:* Students learn to read authentic texts and to write for useful purposes.
- *Background knowledge:* Students' prior knowledge of a topic may be activated through classroom activities drawn from a variety of language sources. (Díaz-Rico & Weed, 1995, p. 116)

As you can see, these principles are highly congruent with everything we've discussed previously in terms of what constitutes good instruction for all students. Miramontes, Nadeau, and Cummins (1997) make the point that instruction for ELL students must include provision for students to (1) fully understand and interact with the content,

(2) learn new content through the second language, (3) develop second-language academic proficiency, and (4) interact cross-culturally with their peers (pp. 156–157).

SHELTERED INSTRUCTION (SI)

Sheltered instruction is viewed today as the most effective and appropriate approach for students in ESL transition classes and in subject area classes that house students who are not fully fluent in English and have not achieved English literacy (Díaz-Rico & Weed, 1995; Echevarria et al., 2004). Kim Marchand's best hope for meeting the needs of her ELL students is to adjust instruction using SI techniques.

Watson and colleagues (1989) suggest that teachers use SI techniques to bridge the gap between students' English-language and literacy abilities, the teacher's language, and the content to be learned. Sheltering involves the following:

1. Adjusting language demands of a lesson by modifying speech and vocabulary, providing rich context, using models and visuals to illustrate concepts, and relating instructions to students' experiences.
2. Teaching both the content vocabulary and the words used to explain the lesson.
3. Repeatedly using the same general lesson format (not activity) initially so that students do not have to figure out how the teacher is presenting information from day to day.
4. Minimizing lecture time, making lectures short and direct, and emphasizing small-group collaborative learning activities.
5. Providing charts, schematics, pictures, organizers, and other visuals to illustrate and support information and concepts developed through oral or written language.
6. Using pictorial schematics to illustrate directions for completing tasks and activities.
7. Incorporating tasks into lessons, as appropriate, that do not depend heavily on language and literacy abilities.

Specifically, the elements of a sheltered lesson are as follows:

Bringing the lesson to life

Setting the stage

Preteaching vocabulary

Guiding initial learning

Guiding practice

Guiding independent practice

You saw there elements identified in our Centerpiece Lesson Plan. Echevarria et al. (2004) describe the effective SI classroom:

> Accomplished SI teachers modulate the level of English used with and among students and make the content comprehensible through techniques such as the use of visual aids, modeling, demonstrations, graphic organizers, vocabulary previews, predictions, adapted texts, cooperative learning, peer tutoring, multicultural content, and native language support. They also make specific connections between the content being taught and students' experiences and prior knowledge and focus on expanding students' vocabulary base.

> In effective SI lessons, there is a high level of student engagement and interaction with the teacher, with each other, and with text which leads to elaborated discourse and thinking. Students are explicitly taught functional language skills as well, such as how to negotiate meaning, confirm information, argue, persuade, and disagree. . . . Through instructional conversations and meaningful activities, students practice and apply their new language and content knowledge. (p. 14)

SHELTERED INSTRUCTION—DIRECTED INQUIRY ACTIVITY (DIA)

The Centerpiece Lesson Plan in this chapter begins with a sheltered version of Keith Thomas's Directed Inquiry Activity, DIA (Thomas, 1986). Thomas developed the DIA to apply the predicting elements of a DR-TA to meet the expressed needs of middle and secondary school students and teachers. The point of the DIA is to allow student involvement in learning while preserving the teacher's prerogative to determine what information is to be learned. Thomas sees this strategy as one that directs students through text with specific emphasis on inquiry directed to Who? What? When? Where? Why? and How? (1986, p. 279).

In its original format the DIA begins with the teacher presenting five or six inquiry questions about the chapter or material to be read. These may be listed on the board, leaving plenty of space for recording predictions, or they may be duplicated on a handout. Students are then asked to survey a portion of the material to be read: the title and some introductory paragraphs; the headings listed in the table of contents; the introduction and the summary; or even just the title alone for a very short selection. Students then predict responses to the inquiry questions using information from the survey and any background information they have. The teacher records predictions on the chalkboard or has students record them on their handouts.

In our sheltered DIA, we begin by introducing concepts associated with energy through demonstration (hitting the nail with a hammer, etc.). These concepts are then reinforced by vocabulary instruction using a task in which small groups of students (with ELL students distributed across groups) use pictorial representations of forms of energy to name and label those forms. Subsequently, in whole class discussion additional links are made between the pictures and written vocabulary words. Notice throughout this process that the teacher continually gestures to both the pictorial and written symbols to provide explicit linkage. The inquiry questions that are the foundation of the DIA are introduced only after students have considerable experience with lesson concepts and vocabulary; this experience serves as the preview of the lesson that forms the basis for making predictions about possible answers to the inquiry questions. In this lesson the teacher provides further assistance to ELL students by having students work again in their small groups to make predictions that are to be subsequently shared in whole class discussion and recorded on the board.

At this point, everyone in the room has the advantage of the visual display of the items used to illustrate energy, the pictures with types of energy labeled underneath, and the list of predictions for each inquiry question. The teacher now assigns each group just one of the inquiry questions to "become experts on" and guides groups as they read the textbook and/or work online or with the materials on the library cart to answer their question. Thus, the sheltered DIA in our Centerpiece Lesson Plan covers the before reading (**Into**) and during reading (**Through**) part of the lesson and the first five steps of sheltered instruction.

Creating Strategic Readers

Georgia García, in her review of research on instruction for ELL students (2000), notes that much of that research points to the effectiveness of teaching ELL students how to be strategic in their English language and literacy development and in content learning. So it is important that you (1) teach ELL students useful strategies for learning in your subject area, and (2) engage them in metacognitive thought about those strategies. The DIA emphasizes prediction, a strategy regularly—and possibly unconsciously—used by successful readers and learners. Include discussions of strategy with discussions of content.

> *Ask*, "How were you able to make predictions about our inquiry questions?" *Field answers. Extend any response that mentions prior knowledge.* "How can asking predictions help us read and do research?" *Field responses.* "What do we know now after reading that we didn't know before?" *Compare predictions with information from reading/research. Ask*, "So, what is one way you can become a better (science) reader?" *Make a list and summarize:* "Before you read, preview the text, think about what you already know, and make a prediction or two to guide your reading."

How to do . . . .

A SHELTERED INSTRUCTION DIRECTED INQUIRY ACTIVITY (DIA)

The sheltered DIA is relatively easy to use. Once again, the key is to establish well-articulated lesson objectives and to write clear, useful inquiry questions. Your inquiry questions should meet two criteria: First, they should stem directly from and explicitly reflect your lesson objectives; second, they should be generative, rich questions that stimulate the kind of classroom talk, writing, and participation found in classrooms where students engage actively in knowledge construction. Sheltering a DIA simply makes the learning experience richer for everyone in the room. A reasonable extension of the DIA is group mapping or VSS, or both. Use the following steps to do a sheltered instruction DIA:

Bring the lesson to life

1. Determine content and language objectives.
2. Write five or six inquiry questions.
3. Collect realia for demonstrations and visuals for teaching vocabulary.

4. Collect resource materials (textbooks, online sources, text set).

Set the stage

5. Establish small groups with ELL students distributed across groups.
6. Plan small group vocabulary task(s).

Guide initial learning

7. Plan small group prediction task.
8. Plan whole class discussion of predictions
9. Determine focus for answering inquiry questions (e.g., "experts").

Guide Practice

10. Plan working time and procedures.

Guide Independent Practice

11. Determine follow-up and assessments.

SHELTERED INSTRUCTION—DIRECTED READING-THINKING ACTIVITY (DR-TA)
In Chapter 4 you saw how to do a DR-TA using a physics text (Vectors, Force, and Motion) a mathematics text, a short story ("The Splendid Outcast"), and a social studies text. A DR-TA already has many of the characteristics of sheltered instruction noted earlier—active participation, social interactions, use of predictions and students' prior knowledge, high level of student engagement, elaborated discourse, and higher-order thinking. And, when followed by GMA, DR-TA includes provision for individualized response to reading, variety of visual representation, and encouragement for students to respond in one or more languages. DR-TA can be further sheltered for ELL students by adding early and ongoing visuals and by explicitly teaching vocabulary. Following are examples of how the four DR-TA lessons you've seen previously can become sheltered instruction.

Sheltering the DR-TA Algebra Lesson In the review of one-step equations (number 3 on the lesson plan), write $x + 5 = 7$ on the board. In advance prepare a very light, opaque bag with two marbles in it. Using a pan balance, place the bag on the left pan; announce that the bag = x (point to equation on the board). Then place five loose marbles on the left pan and seven loose marble on the right pan. Count everything out as you do it, and make sure that everyone understands that the contents on the pan balance represent the equation on the board. Remove a loose marble from one side; note the imbalance. Then remove one marble from the other side; now the pans are balanced. Now ask, "What do we need to do to keep balance?" "How can we find out how many marbles are in the x bag?" Remove five loose marbles from each pan (subtract 5 from each side of the equation on the board). Check the x bag to verify the presence of two marbles.

Prepare in advance the same materials needed for the next equations; have students predict what they need to do for the next problem and note how quickly they respond. If their response is slow or incorrect, demonstrate with marbles and pan balance.

Continue similarly. Make sure you prepare for $5x - 9 = 3x + 1$ because this is the first equation with a variable (unknown) on both sides of the equals sign.

Sheltering the DR-TA English Lesson Place students in groups, with ELL students distributed evenly throughout the groups. Give each group several pictures and/or magazines depicting aspects of horse racing—the races themselves, jockeys, horses, training routines, and so on. Ask the groups to create a group list of things they know about racehorses. Have groups share with the class a few of the items they've listed. Show a short video of a horse race, perhaps a clip from the movie *Seabiscuit*. Then initiate story discussion as with the original DR-TA. After reading the title, "The Splendid Outcast," ask, "With a title like that, what do you think this story will be about?" "Why?" Continue through the story, stopping periodically for discussion. Allow, and even encourage, groups to confer among themselves before contributing to the class discussion. Follow the DR-TA with paired mapping and VSS.

Sheltering the DR-TA Physics Lesson Before introducing the chapter title, show a PowerPoint presentation of pictures or place pictures around the room that illustrate *motion*, and specifically illustrate the motions described in the text—rotation of the earth on its axis, various pictures of the effects of wind, conversion of ore into steel, and many others. Ask, "What do these pictures have in common?" "What do we already know about (motion)?" Then show the chapter title and ask, "Based on this title, what do you think the chapter will be about?" "What makes you say that?"

Now ask the students to look at the AIMS section of the text. Show a PowerPoint slide of one of the pictures shown previously in which the word *motion* labels the action of wind or rotation (alternatively, attach a label of *motion* under one of the pictures displayed in the room and then *rotation* under another). Next, illustrate on one of the pictures the direction and velocity of the motion and label that *vector*. Then ask, "Now what do you think?" and "Why?"

Students then read the first three paragraphs, followed by the same questioning. Show illustrations of a car being pushed and the label *force* along with the new position of the car and the label *displacement*. Continue questioning more specifically about content. "What other ideas do you think we'll find in this chapter?" "What makes you say that?" Spot check to make sure that everyone knows the meaning of *motion*, *vector*, *force*, and *displacement*.

Sheltering the DR-TA Social Studies Lesson This lesson about the establishment of state constitutions follows the unit on the creation of a federal government and national constitution. Its title is "From Confederation to Nation." Begin the lesson by displaying around the room maps and other visuals the class created to define the principles and procedures that were the basis for creation of the U.S. Constitution. Put students in groups of two or three with ELL students distributed across the groups. Initiate discussion by reviewing the displayed materials with the class; create a summary listing on the board of some of the key aspects of how the federal government was created. Then have the groups work together to make predictions from the text headings about how state constitutions were created. Have groups share predictions; list these on the board in a "key word" fashion that will preview some of the important ideas students will find in the text. Allow students to work with their group as they read.

SHELTERED INSTRUCTION—GROUP MAPPING ACTIVITY (GMA)

By now you probably have a good sense of why GMA is a useful sheltered instructional strategy. First, GMA allows initial conceptual representation of text and meaning in ways not bound by words—all manner of symbols are useful and used on maps. Second, the actual mapping is followed by whole class or partner sharing in which lesson concepts *are* put into words, but the framing of those words is rehearsed in the construction of the maps themselves. And, finally, teachers can encourage ELL students to elect to use their first language in the construction of their maps if that language is helpful to them; this can then be a springboard for teaching the English equivalent of the L1 word or phrase.

In our Centerpiece Lesson Plan sheltered GMA, the GMA is adapted so that the initial mapping is a group activity in which small group discussion must occur in the planning and construction of the map. This gives ELL students much needed support in articulating lesson concepts in English. Note also that by giving each group a set of colored pens, students use colors to categorize and organize information on their maps; thus, ELL students, and all other students as well, have the additional support of color coding to assist in learning and remembering important concepts and vocabulary. Later, after the group maps of inquiry questions are shared and mounted on the wall, once again the entire class has access to visual representations that answer all five inquiry questions. Students then are asked to create their own individual maps (or a group map if preferred) with each group assuming responsibility of making sure everyone has all the important information on his/her map. Later, students will add VSS words to their maps, and, again, they may elect to color-code VSS words to identify them as such. This is, by now, the fifth or sixth time students have been through

Strategic Readers, Writers, and Learners

One of the most valuable strategies for retaining information after reading is organizing that information in a way that makes sense for individual learners. GMA is particularly useful for ELL students because it allows them to use a variety of representations: pictorial, visual, and written L1 or L2, as needed. When initiated as group work, much of the discussion about how the map should look is metacognitive, centered around how the organizational plan makes sense and how it reflects the content of what was learned. Talk to students about their maps:

> "What made you decide to organize your map that way?" "How did you determine your color scheme?" "Can you see another way you could have organized this information?" "How can you use your map to write a paragraph about ———?"

Remind them how to use maps to gather their thoughts and prepare for other activities. Show them how to go from mapping to outlining or formal field notes this information. Concepts and vocabulary should be sufficiently in place to proceed to the next phase of the lesson.

SHELTERED INSTRUCTION—VISUAL LITERACY ACTIVITY

Sinatra, Beaudry, Stahl-Gemake, & Guastello (1990) recommend a "visual literacy" activity for culturally and linguistically diverse students that has students working in pairs to construct photo and written essays. In the sixth- and seventh-grade classrooms Sinatra and his associates describe, the teacher used 20 cameras donated by a camera manufacturer as the basis for the collaborative project. (Disposable cameras are available if you don't have access to donated cameras, and disposable cameras are recyclable.)

Students are given the task of creating photo storyboards, using a semantic map framework, around a central theme. Themes at this level are general. For example, students in the project Sinatra and his colleagues describe were exploring various aspects of their own neighborhood community—hence, the theme "Wonderful Williamsburg" (New York). With this activity, each student pair is responsible for deciding what aspect or subtheme it wishes to photograph, planning specific shots, and taking the pictures. As soon as the pictures are developed, pairs determine the organization of their storyboards, prepare and mount the photos, and follow that with a written essay based on the photo essay. The beauty of visual literacy activities is their application to widely varied themes. Themes and storyboards and written essays may include scientific as well as social observations, analysis of physical movement as well as art or literature, and commentary on plant or animal as well as human attributes.

The value of this activity is the extended, independent collaborative planning and decision making it requires, along with the language-rich environment such planning and decision making create. The activity begins with a class-determined project. Then student pairs must discuss the topic theme and subthemes at some length to arrive at their own plan for developing an idea. Next they must sort, classify, and organize their photos to communicate whatever they wish to say. Sinatra and his associates found three patterns of storyboard organization developed by the students (Figure 6.2, p. 216). These organizational patterns provide support for students engaged in the final collaborative activity of constructing a written essay to accompany their photo essay.

For ELL students, the amount of language interaction during planning and preparation of the storyboards and the availability of photos to convey mutually agreed-on meanings increase considerably their access to meaning and to language. Sinatra and colleagues state:

> The images and ideas captured by the photos transcended the language differences of this diverse student population while providing a common base for communication. Indeed, the "deep" structure of a picture is processed by a viewer for meaning regardless of his or her facility with the "surface" structure of language. (1990, p. 613)

The collaborative strategy Sinatra and his associates propose, with its language interaction and photo support, thus encourages and increases the oral and written English-language development of bilingual student in subject areas.

FIGURE 6.2 *Three Patterns of Storyboard Organization for Photo Essay and Written Composition*

(A) Sequential organization

A Day with Our Principal

Photo 1 → Photo 2 → Photo 3 → Photo 4 → Photo 5 → Photo 6 → etc.

(B) Thematic organization

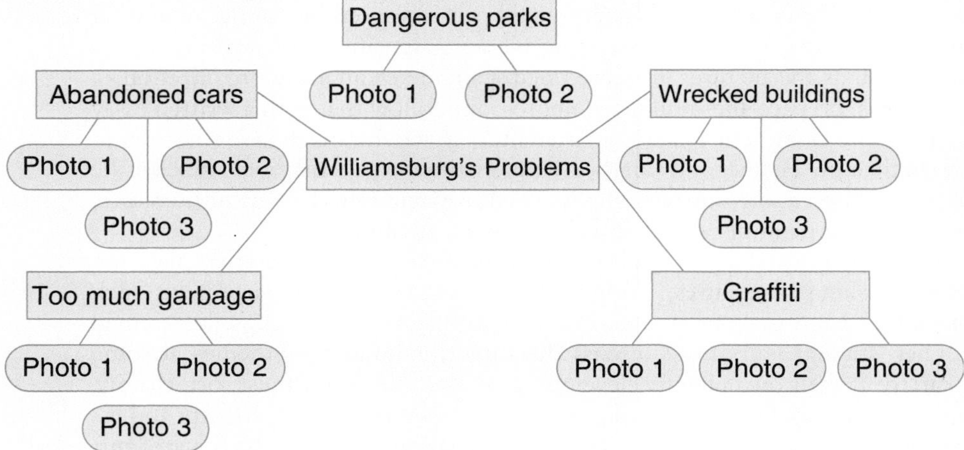

(C) Organization by classification

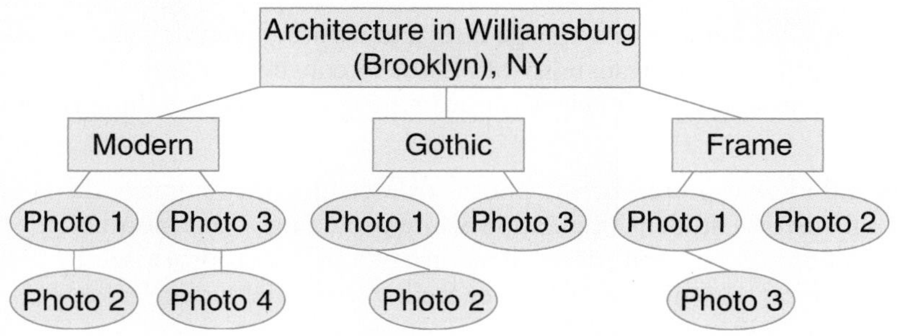

How to do . . . .

SI LESSONS (DR-TA, VISUAL LITERACY PROJECTS, ETC.)

The principles of SI are not at all unlike the kind of content and literacy instruction we've discussed throughout this text. The major difference is the linking of graphic, pictorial, and visual representations of concepts with the written word(s) both in presenting lessons and in student responses, to anchor content concepts for ELL students. The felicitous effect of using SI in classrooms with mixed L1 is that inclusion of graphic, pictorial, and visual representations is just as helpful to native-English-speaking students as it is for ELL students.

Step 1 ***Think of ways to bring lessons to life.***

- Develop objectives for content and language.
- Identify visuals and manipulatives.
- Identify concrete and pictorial materials to illustrate ideas, concepts, and task directions.

Step 2 ***Set the stage.***

- Present a broad overview of the unit/lesson content.
- Begin each lesson with a short review of what was learned yesterday and/or predictions of what will happen today.

Step 3 ***Preteach two vocabulary sets.***

- Teach words necessary for understanding content.
- Teach words that will be used to explain content.

Step 4 ***Guide initial learning.***

- Use consistent lesson formats, at least initially.
- Find ways to animate instruction with role playing, realia, experiments, and activities.

Step 5 ***Guide practice.***

- Provide examples and tryouts.
- Demonstrate explicitly how practice activities relate to initial learning.

Step 6 ***Guide independent practice.***

- Maximize student interactions (dyads, groups, collaborative learning).
- Evaluate students using student-developed products and tests.

SHELTERED INSTRUCTION—TEXT SETS

One of the most useful ways to shelter instruction is to use multilevel texts and resources for teaching lessons and units. *Text sets*—groups of books connected thematically but widely varying in difficulty and type—are perfectly suited for addressing the needs of ELL students in your class and are at the same time just as useful for addressing the needs of all students. The secret to creating good text sets is to find books and other resources that span a wide range of difficulty levels, interests, genres (short story, nonfiction, novel, poetry, picture book, etc.). Don't be afraid to include children's books, especially since so many of them are beautifully illustrated; in fact, get yourself to the children's section in a bookstore or library and discover all the wonderful resources there to teach whatever unit or lesson you're teaching. Include websites, videos, and other electronic resources for your text set. So, for example, if you're teaching *The Odyssey* in a sophomore English class you might gather the following texts to be used as primary sources for the unit:

D'Aulaires' Book of Greek Myths, elementary, illustrated

Usborne Illustrated Guide to Greek Myths and Legends, middle level, illustrated

Roman Myths and Legends retold by Anthony Masters, middle level, illustrated

Usborne Illustrated World History: The Romans, middle level, illustrated

Eyewitness Books Ancient Greece, all levels, illustrated

Edith Hamilton Mythology, high school/college, not illustrated

Myths of the Greeks and Romans by Michael Grant, high school/college, not illustrated

For a sports and fitness unit, you might use the following:

Skateboarding in Action, elementary/middle, illustrated

Gail Deavers a Runner's Dream, elementary/middle, illustrated

Step-by-Step Ballet Class: The Official Illustrated Guide, middle level, illustrated

Baseball's 25 Greatest Moments, high school, illustrated

Baseball's Best Shots, all levels, photography

Exercise Addiction: When Fitness Becomes an Obsession, middle level/high school, illustrated

Breakthroughs in Science, The Human Body, middle level/high school, illustrated

Using text sets, you can create highly effective SI lessons and units with many different instructional strategies. The DIA is a perfect match with text sets and note that we used a text set in our Centerpiece Lesson Plan because each group member is able to select the resource or resources he or she wants to use for answering the inquiry questions.

SHELTERED INSTRUCTION AND VOCABULARY KNOWLEDGE

Hee-Won Kang and Anne Golden (1994) make the critical point that direct instruction of vocabulary must be viewed as only the starting point for ELL learners—as it was in our lesson—and that a far more important instructional task is for teachers to help ELL students develop the skills and abilities needed to learn new vocabulary on their own. Kang and Golden emphasize the need for bilingual students to learn words that they see as important to their own situation and interests and to become skilled at constructing meaning for new words from contextual cues and information. (Recall our discussion in Chapter 2 of Krashen's hypothesis of comprehensible input in which what ELL students hear is just beyond the English they already know. This is how comprehensible input—*i* + 1—increases language fluency.) According to Kang and Golden, simply telling students the meaning of English words is of very limited usefulness in vocabulary development. "The least valuable information about a word is a word in another language" (p. 66). I could not agree more, and I encourage you to consider very seriously the implementation of the VSS as a way of helping ELL students become independent English word learners, increasing their sensitivity to the language of your subject area, developing their ability to gain meaning from context, and providing rich, active transactions with the English language.

Two aspects of vocabulary development occur in our sheltered Centerpiece Lesson Plan. First, as part of the DIA we preteach vocabulary words that are critical to the understanding of lesson content; in this lesson the words were labels for forms of energy. We link the written representations of the words with both objects and pictures to give ELL students as many ways as possible to acquire the word-concept knowledge that will be critical to their reading and research to answer inquiry questions. The teacher makes a concerted and conscious effort to reinforce word-concept linkages by pointing to the word-picture displays and by using the vocabulary words repeatedly.

The second aspect of vocabulary development occurs in the VSS that follows the DIA and GMA. Here, the goal is long-term retention of new content vocabulary. Students and the teacher nominate words/terms for the class vocabulary list, and it is in the act of choosing and nominating words that ELL students have the opportunity to determine what words are important to them—the words they *need to know*. Clearly, the unspoken end-point is that these are the words they need to know to learn the subject matter information. This same benefit accrues to all students; thus, they become individually and collectively invested in the vocabulary and in the lesson itself.

SHELTERED INSTRUCTION AND STUDENT WRITING

Danling Fu (1995), in her study of the experiences of four Laotian students (brothers and sisters) in middle school and high school in the United States, found that when they were placed in remedial (or low-track) English classes, they were expected to follow a highly structured, prescriptive formula for writing: teacher-assigned topics and organization of writing into topic sentences followed by details. The problem was that the topics teachers chose were usually abstract and removed from students' personal experience, and the organizational structure itself was highly abstract. (How does one teach the concept of *topic sentence* to someone who does not know the meaning of *topic* and who may have a tenuous understanding of the concept of *sentence* in English?) Thus, the writing these students produced in such assignments was tortured and conceptually fragmented—almost meaningless—and was vastly inferior to the English writing they produced when given the opportunity to write from their own experience in a form that was meaningful to them. The lesson here is that in our zeal to "help" ELL students by giving them lots of structure to guide their writing, we may actually be impeding their writing progress by having them write about things that are, essentially, outside their knowledge and experiential base and by having them write within

Creating Strategic Readers

VSS is of particular usefulness in helping ELL students become strategic because it specifically asks students to identify words and terms that they need to learn or know more about. A useful approach in helping ELL students become strategic vocabulary learners is to highlight and focus their attention on cognates—words that are similar in appearance and pronunciation in their L1 and English (e.g., *night*, English; *nuit*, French; *nacht*, German; *noch*, Russian. Spanish-English: *problema-problem; nación-nation; farmica-pharmacy*, etc.). Use of cognate knowledge is a strategic way for ELL students to increase English knowledge rapidly. During VSS collection discussions, highlight cognates, discuss them, and encourage students to look for them.

A second important strategy is for ELL students to learn how to use context to help them understand new words. When you ask in a VSS discussion (after "Where did you find that word?"), "What do you think it means?" elaborate on student responses and identify specific context clues that helped students construct meaning for the word. Spend some time discussing how one gets meaning from context to help understand a new word. Review CSSR (from Chapter 5).

the confines of an organizational structure that is nonsensical to them—a daunting task for anyone, even in one's native language. Is it any wonder that the writing they produce is well below their spoken English-language fluency, disjointed, and riddled with grammatical and usage errors?

Díaz, Moll, and Mehan (1986) emphasize the importance (as does Fu) of using the students' L1 language skills "in the service of academic goals in their second language" (p. 218) and recommend development of academic activities that connect the home and community with the school. They describe a student-developed project in which ELL students surveyed people in their community and wrote a report describing the benefits of being bilingual. Such activities are particularly effective when students' primary language and culture are incorporated into content learning. Díaz and associates also emphasize that writing activities for ELL students, as for all students, should focus on writing for communication and intellectual advancement.

The use of mixed-ability/mixed L1 collaborative learning groups—much like the groups established for the sheltered DIA, GMA, VSS lesson—that engage students in such writing activities provides much support for bilingual students at all levels of English proficiency and for other students as well. Recall our discussion in Chapter 1 of the "multimodal" nature of adolescents' literacy. Composing on-line or in electronic environments allows mixed use of written language, pictorial, auditory, hypertext, and other visual forms for student writing that significantly changes the skills that comprise expert functioning. GMA before writing helps students organize and prepare their

FIGURE 6.3 *Continued*

	Highly Evident		Somewhat Evident		Not Evident	NA
11. Explanation of academic tasks clear	☐	☐	☐	☐	☐	☐
12. Uses a variety of techniques to make content concepts clear (e.g., modeling, visuals, hands-on activities, demonstrations, gestures, body language)	☐	☐	☐	☐	☐	☐
Comments:						
3. Strategies	**4**	**3**	**2**	**1**	**0**	**NA**
13. Provides ample opportunities for student to use strategies	☐	☐	☐	☐	☐	☐
14. Consistent use of scaffolding techniques throughout lesson, assisting and supporting student understanding, such as think-alouds	☐	☐	☐	☐	☐	☐
15. Teacher uses a variety of question types throughout the lesson including those that promote higher-order thinking skills throughout the lesson (e.g., literal, analytical, and interpretive questions)	☐	☐	☐	☐	☐	☐
Comments:						
4. Interaction	**4**	**3**	**2**	**1**	**0**	**NA**
16. Frequent opportunities for interactions and discussion between teacher/student and among students, which encourage elaborated responses about lesson concepts	☐	☐	☐	☐	☐	☐
17. Grouping configurations support language and content objectives of the lesson	☐	☐	☐	☐	☐	☐
18. Consistently provides sufficient wait time for student response	☐	☐	☐	☐	☐	☐
19. Ample opportunities for students to clarify key concepts in L1	☐	☐	☐	☐	☐	☐
Comments:						
5. Practice/Application	**4**	**3**	**2**	**1**	**0**	**NA**
20. Provides hands-on materials and/or manipulatives for students to practice using new content knowledge	☐	☐	☐	☐	☐	☐
21. Provides activities for students to apply content and language knowledge in the classroom	☐	☐	☐	☐	☐	☐
22. Uses activities that integrate all language skills (i.e., reading, writing, listening, and speaking)	☐	☐	☐	☐	☐	☐
Comments:						

(continued)

FIGURE 6.3 *Continued*

	Highly Evident		Somewhat Evident		Not Evident	NA
6. Lesson Delivery	**4**	**3**	**2**	**1**	**0**	**NA**
23. Content objectives clearly supported by lesson delivery	☐	☐	☐	☐	☐	☐
24. Language objectives clearly supported by lesson delivery	☐	☐	☐	☐	☐	☐
25. Students engaged approximately 90% to 100% of the period	☐	☐	☐	☐	☐	☐
26. Pacing of the lesson appropriate to the students' ability level	☐	☐	☐	☐	☐	☐
Comments:						
III. Review/Assessment	**4**	**3**	**2**	**1**	**0**	**NA**
27. Comprehensive review of key vocabulary	☐	☐	☐	☐	☐	☐
28. Comprehensive review of key content concepts	☐	☐	☐	☐	☐	☐
29. Regularly provides feedback to students on their output (e.g., language, content, work)	☐	☐	☐	☐	☐	☐
30. Conducts assessment of student comprehension and learning of all lesson objectives (spot checking, group response) throughout the lesson.	☐	☐	☐	☐	☐	☐
Comments:						

progress. Involving the students themselves in assessment procedures through self-report, think-alouds (events in which students speak aloud what they are thinking as they construct meaning from text or other class activities), and response logs and journals (García, 1994) adds considerably to the teacher's understanding of the full measure of what students know and are able to do. For ELL students, high-stakes testing is particularly meaningful: The stakes are high indeed when their educational progress is based solely on standardized test results, pop quizzes, and end-of-unit multiple-choice and short-answer tests. We will address a variety of assessment issues, including high-stakes testing and authentic assessment practices, in Chapter 9.

Of immediate importance in classrooms is that ELL students are given multiple opportunities and means for demonstrating their understanding of content knowledge (and the degree to which they meet lesson objectives). This means that ways other than paper-pencil tests are needed for students to show what they've learned—oral reports, pictorial representations, PowerPoint presentations, multimedia shows, group projects—the list is long and varied. (By the way, all students, not just the English learners, benefit from this approach to assessment.) The key here for ELL students is that many times their understanding outpaces what they can demonstrate by reading and writing (paper-pencil tests); using alternative assessments allows the teacher to get a more accurate measure of students' knowledge. In addition, and just as important, informal assessment provides teachers with immediate information about the nature and degree of sheltered instruction appropriate for each student. Observation of students during instruction is also critical to teachers' understanding of ELL students' language and content needs. Our Centerpiece Lesson Plan provides both observational and alternative assessment.

OTHER ISSUES

Several other issues concerning ELL learners need to be addressed at this point. The first issue concerns student mistakes. Teachers are often unsure how they should respond to the language mistakes and reading miscues that English-language learners make. Hilda Hernández (2000) reminds us that making mistakes is a normal part of learning. She recommends that teachers focus on the content of what bilingual students are saying or doing rather than such features of language as pronunciation, syntax, and grammar. She suggests further that correction of these language features should be covert (that is, rephrasing or repeating with correct pronunciation or syntax) rather than explicit. I support her recommendations. For ELL students, such an approach gives them the freedom to concentrate on learning content without worrying about language differences. English-language learning will occur, as does L1 learning, rapidly and naturally with continued exposure to a language-rich environment and experimentation with English.

The second issue is one I've touched on earlier in this chapter and will revisit in Chapter 10 as well. It concerns our perceptions of second-language learners and the effect that our perceptions have on them. It is essential that ELL students' cultures and primary languages be respected and valued in classrooms, that classroom situations and activities be structured to include ELL students as *mainstream participants in the class*, and that all bilingual students be treated as capable, contributing class members. Thus, we must allow ELL students the latitude to respond variously in English, in their primary language, in other visual forms, and in assorted other ways because we know that each response system supports their English-language and academic development. We must create and construct classroom activities that invite ELL students to contribute information from their cultural and knowledge base that might not have been available without their presence in class, and we must develop enough understanding of the cultures represented in our classes to avoid misinterpreting students' behaviors and abilities (Kang et al., 1994). We must also understand the cultural *and* language differences that may be present among students with common languages; for example, Cuban, Puerto Rican, Mexican, and Salvadoran students (Zenatella, 2005). We must ensure that bilingual students have access to academic conventions and strategies that lead to success in school (Delpit, 1995). And finally, we must encourage students' first-language and literacy development through maintenance classes and programs, thereby assisting their English-language development and asserting the advantage of bilingualism in this society.

The final issue I want to address concerns families, communities, and bilingual/bicultural learners themselves. Luis Moll and his associates (Moll, 1994; Moll, 1997) have spent considerable time over the past years studying the households of language-minority communities. What they have found is a complex, rich system of "funds of knowledge" through which individuals, families, and other groups share information and skills for the betterment of all. Moll makes the point that not only are these community resources often unperceived by teachers and schools but, more importantly, that teachers, classrooms, and schools would benefit greatly by having access to them. This requires reaching out to the community rather than waiting for parents and community leaders to come to school. Such reaching out is particularly important when you consider the reality of bilingual/bicultural students' lives. Voon-Mooi Choo and Taffy Raphael characterize bicultural students as "walking in two worlds" and summarize the experience as follows:

> Learning to walk in different worlds is complex. The journey involves dealing with the unknown, and can be very lonely. Bicultural students exist in a confused, confusing, and deeply troubled hybrid world. (1995, p. 3)

Lee Gunderson elaborates:

> Members of the diasporas in this study were lost in the spaces between various identities: the teenager, the immigrant, the first-language speaker, the individual from the first culture, the individual socializing into a second language and culture, the individual with neither a first nor a second culture, but one not of either culture. (2000, p. 703)

It therefore seems powerfully important that teachers and schools not wait for parents and the community to come to them. The only reasonable way to provide support for students walking in two worlds—or lost in the spaces between worlds—is to develop programs and events that bridge those worlds.

Donald Hones (1999) describes the notion of "bilingual liaisons" as a means of building bridges between the community and schools. Bilingual liaisons are community members who serve as "border crossers" between the cultures of the community and school with the sole intent of creating greater mutual understanding and knowledge. In the Wisconsin community he describes, the culture was Hmong and the liaison was Shou Cha, who came to school each day and worked with children individually and in groups and who met with school faculty and staff and the community in his role as "peacemaker." Hones cites Henry Trueba's poignant plea:

> Could anyone really question the universal need for healing? The daily stories about hatred, cruelty, war, and conflict dividing nations, regions, states, cities, and neighborhoods reveal clearly the open wounds and hurts of many. We all carry profound emotional injuries that affect another deeper sense of self and the ability to recognize who we are individually and collectively. (1994, p. viii)

Many on-line resources are available for increasing your ability to provide appropriate instruction for ELL students. Both the National Association of Bilingual Education (NABE) and its state affiliates and the National Clearinghouse for English Language Acquisition (NCELA) provide rich resources and links to others. Their websites may be found at www.nabe.org and www.ncela.gwu.edu/ respectively.

SOME FINAL WORDS ABOUT TEACHING BILINGUAL/BICULTURAL LEARNERS IN MULTILINGUAL/MULTICULTURAL CLASSROOMS

Several years ago, I supervised a student teacher in a tenth-grade mainstream social studies class in which about half the students were native Spanish speakers of varying English-language fluency. The teacher, Nancy Case (a former student of mine), is fluently English–Spanish bilingual. When Nancy was in the room, I noticed that she chatted with

BUILDING TABLE

Chapter-6	Sheltered Instruction DIA	Sheltered Instruction Visual Literacy Projects, DR-TA
FOCUS ON	Content reading and discussion; information organization	Content reading and discussion; information organization and articulation
GUIDES STUDENTS	Before, during, and after reading	Before, during, and after reading and writing
USE TO PLAN	Lessons, units	Lessons, units
MAY BE USED	Whole class, collaborative groups, partnerships	Whole class, collaborative groups, partnerships
MAY BE COMBINED WITH (known strategies)	GMA, VSS, semantic mapping, word treasure hunts	GMA, VSS, SFA, semantic mapping, word treasure hunts
MATERIALS PREPARATION	Light	Moderate
OTHER PREPARATION	Moderate	Moderate to extensive
OUTSIDE RESOURCES	Useful	Necessary
HOW TO DO	Pages 211–212	Page 217

CHAPTER 7

READING ACROSS THE CURRICULUM

DOUBLE ENTRY JOURNAL

Remember a time in your life when you were learning something new—whether in school or out—in which you were totally engrossed: when time flew and you felt that zing of energy, pleasure, and accomplishment go through your entire body. Name that moment. What were you learning? What can you remember about the time, place, and learning environment? What did you feel and think? Jot down what you remember of that event. Keep it in mind as you read this chapter.

teachers could pretty confidently assume that students would have a knowledge base. (In classes with predominantly immigrant students, the discussion may have to begin with constitutions in general, then lead in to the U.S. Constitution.) Note that the "things we already know" are written on the board (or overhead projector or butcher paper) or projected on an LCD screen, reproduced, and given to students as a handout and then later referred to in the WebQuest discussion (#5 on the lesson plan). The purpose for this is threefold:

- To articulate and acknowledge what students already know. Several benefits accrue here: (1) What students already know is a good portion of their strength; it makes them feel capable when they're able to show that strength. (2) This gives teachers a real look at what students do know and thus an idea of what needs to be learned, where misconceptions may lie, and the distance between what students know and what you want them to learn.
- To guide students in the strategic process of making predictions, reading/learning to how well they predicted, making new predictions, and continuing to read. Having students note with asterisks information in their reading that they had predicted they would find reinforces that process and leads them toward more independent use of strategic literacy practices. Thus it both builds on their strength and increases their learning capabilities.
- To serve as the set-point for students and the teacher to use throughout the WebQuest and at the end of the unit to assess what students have learned. The great value here is that not only the teacher, but also the *students*, do this assessment so that students become attuned to their own learning and growth.

GMA and VSS provide further opportunity for students to organize information after reading. These, too, are part of Antowan Reid's lesson. Because we have already discussed the basic structure for both GMA and VSS in previous chapters, the discussion here will be short and will focus on specific ways to extend the content uses of GMA and VSS by converting maps into clearly designated study aids.

GROUP MAPPING ACTIVITY (GMA) AS A STUDY AID

In our Centerpiece Lesson Plan, we used mapping informally to organize information before reading. I like to use GMA, as a combined idea organizer and study aid, in a slightly more structured way than the very open-ended way described in Chapter 4. Instructions for the initial mapping activity, when you use it in this more structured way, should be something like the following:

> Without looking back at the book and without talking to anyone, map your perceptions of the reading you just did on the rules and regulations for playing field hockey (or about state governments or stringed instruments). You are going to use this map to record important information as we go through the field hockey unit; at the end of the unit, you'll find it a useful study aid in preparing for our field hockey test. Be sure to include on your map all of the information you consider to be important.

After completing the maps, students are directed to share their maps with their partner (orgroup) by telling the partner *what* they considered important, *how* they chose to organize the information, and *why* they made the choices they made. Partners are to respond by eliciting elaboration about important information (e.g., "What made you choose that point?") and by looking to see what relationships are shown on the map.

Emphasis is placed on the value of the maps as the basis for further study or as starting points for individual and group projects throughout the unit. Further, students are reminded that their and their partner's maps *do not have to look alike;* rather, whatever the information and organization scheme used, the map must be complete. After one map is discussed, partners then exchange roles. During this discussion, the original text is consulted repeatedly to verify information and add details and ideas missed in the original mapping. Full-group discussion may then be initiated, in much the same way as discussed in Chapter 4.

Study maps are marvelously expansive and can continue to grow as new ideas are encountered. They also may be used to teach students how to do more formal organization of information: summary writing, précis writing, single-idea development and elaboration, and (The Really Big One) outlining. One of the interesting components of Inspiration software (mentioned in Chapters 4 and 5) is that it will convert a map to an outline, thus demonstrating how that is done. One caution I would give about mapping: If you decide to use maps as study aids, which gives added weight and permanence to their content, you must be prepared to accept varying map structures and constructions of meaning. Harry Singer said it best:

> Different cultural backgrounds and perspectives are likely to result in a range of acceptable variations in interpreting texts and events. . . . [The teacher should be willing to] accept as accurate a whole band of interpretations. (1985, p. 13)

Your willingness to accept a "band of interpretations" need not in any way reduce your requirement for precision or understanding of specific information, including formulas, theories, core knowledge, and/or important facts in any subject area. Rather, use discussion to clarify and define these elements within the context of students' constructions of meaning; this will allow students to elaborate further on their own understanding. Following such discussion, either with a peer or in a whole class, students may decide to restructure their maps for added precision or the inclusion of other ideas. Figures 7.4 and 7.5 (pp. 247 and 248) show study maps developed from a TPRC lesson on the feeding habits of humpback whales. These maps are original conceptualizations that have been shared with a partner. The maps are now ready to be reconsidered and/or redrawn to reflect that discussion and in preparation for use throughout the whale unit.

VOCABULARY SELF-COLLECTION STRATEGY (VSS) AS A STUDY AID

As with mapping, VSS may be used essentially as described earlier (see Chapter 5). In this chapter's Centerpiece Lesson Plan, students first presented words in their small groups and then each group nominated two words for the class list. To be useful study aids, however, VSS words must be recorded in such a way as to give context to the

FIGURE 7.4 *Study Map Derived from TPRC Lesson: Biology*

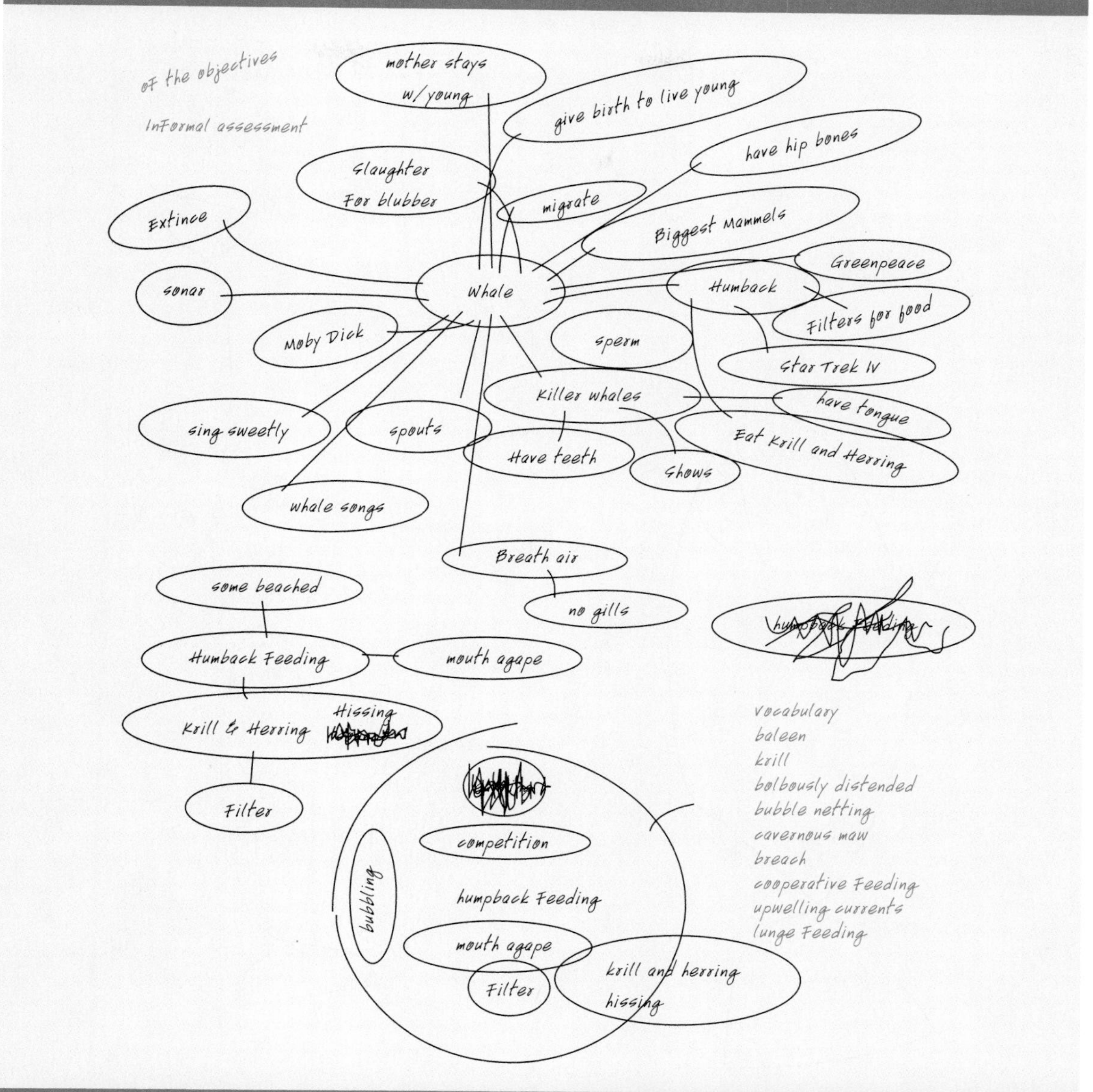

FIGURE 7.5 *Study Map Derived from TPRC Lesson: Biology*

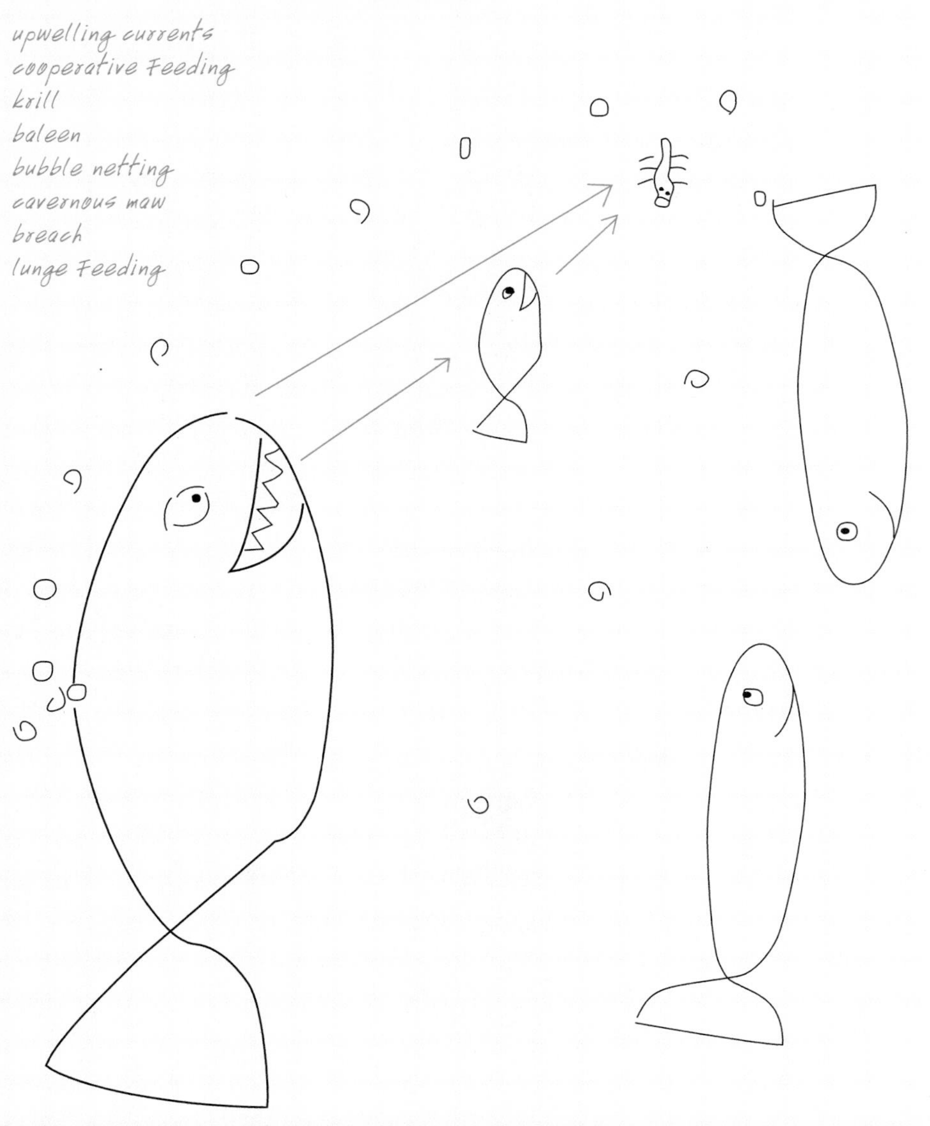

FIGURE 7.6 *Semantic Feature Analysis: VSS Words from the Whale Lesson: Biology*

Humpback Whales	Characteristic	Behavior	Learned	Unlearned				
*Baleen								
*Lunge feeding								
*Bubble netting								
*Breaching								
Cavernous maw								
Cooperative feeding								
Competitive feeding								
*VSS word/term								

words themselves. For example, the teacher may direct students to enter their VSS words on their study maps "where the words make sense." VSS words should be marked in some way on the map (with an asterisk or by underlining, highlighting, or circling) and should be given attention through follow-up activities just as general vocabulary words are, on VSS words may be entered in Vocabulary journals. Figure 7.6 shows a Semantic Feature Analysis (SFA) grid for the VSS words chosen as part of the lesson on whales.

How TPRC, GMA, and VSS Guide Students Before, During, and After Reading

Notice that this progression of events—TPRC, GMA, and VSS—provides ample opportunity for students to do all the things we said earlier they need to do: organize information before, during, and after reading; synthesize and articulate new learning; learn the content vocabulary; and create something new. Notice also that students are given a great deal of support in the three reading/study stages (before, during, and after reading), as well as practice in strategic reading. Of particular importance is that this progression—TPRC, GMA, VSS—provides a context for reading and learning that assists students in seeing the *significance* of the text with which they are engaged. If students do *not* perceive that significance, then ideas in text become an arbitrary list of things that make little sense and are easily forgotten (Bransford, 1985). TPRC, GMA, and VSS, then, develop important linkages between the known and the new, prepare students to extend learning, and develop students' strategic reading/learning abilities. Following is the lesson plan for teaching the Feeding Habits of the Humpback Whale.

TPRC, GMA, VSS LESSON PLAN, *Science*

Lesson: Feeding Habits of the Humpback Whale
Course/Grade: Life Science, 7th Grade
Materials: Copies of *National Geographic* article on humpback whales, TPRC worksheets, student notebooks, pens, pencils

LESSON OBJECTIVES (WITH CONTENT STANDARDS)

Upon completion of the lesson students will

- Be able to identify the feeding habits of the humpback whale (Standard 1c—Students know the nucleus is the repository for genetic information in plant and animal cells).
- Understand the controversy regarding cooperative versus competitive feeding (Standard 2.c—Students know an inherited trait can be determined by one or more genes; Standard 3.a—Students know both genetic variation and environmental factors are causes of evolution and diversity in organisms).

LESSON PROCEDURES

Before Reading: Into—TPRC

1. Classroom partnerships already established. *Say:* You and your partner will need this TPRC worksheet (*hand out worksheets*) and a pencil. Working together, think about everything you know about whales *(write "whales" on board)*. List your ideas under "Think" on your worksheet. Do that now. *Allow six to eight minutes for students to work. Have students share some of the items on their lists.*

2. Say: Today we're going to read about the feeding habits of the humpback whale (*write "feeding habits of the humpback whale" on the board*). Go back to your list and put a checkmark in the "Predict" column by an item on your list that you think will be in the reading. Add any new ideas that you have. *Allow about two minutes for this. Say:* Okay. What are some things you predict you'll find in your reading? *Collect ideas and write them on board.*

During Reading: Through

3. *Say*: I'm handing out the article. As you read, put an asterisk, or some other mark, by anything on your list that appears in the article.

4. *After reading. Say:* Let's look at some of your predictions *(on board)*. Did you find any of these in your reading? *Field responses. Add to list. Say:* What are some connections you can make between what you knew and what you learned in the article?

5. *Say:* What are some things you found in the article that you didn't already know? *Spend lots of time here on discussing and clarifying feeding issues, especially the competition vs. cooperation issue.*

After Reading: Beyond—GMA, VSS

6. *Say:* Now I want you to map what we just read. Please do your mapping without looking back at the article or talking to your partner. You'll have opportunity to do both later. Be sure to get all the important information on your map.

7. *After students have finished mapping, Say:* Share your map with your partner. Partners, your job is to make sure that your partner's map has all the important information from the article. It is NOT necessary that your maps look the same. Share with each other the reasoning you used to create your map.

8. *Give partners plenty of time to share maps. Circulate in room and join discussions so you can look at maps and hear what students are saying. After map sharing, Say:* Now go back to the article with your partner and find one word or term that you think we should have on our class vocabulary list. Be prepared to tell where you found it, what you think it means, and why you think it's important. I get to nominate a word, too.

9. *Rush students a bit in getting their words. Say:* Who has a word to nominate? *Lead discussion until all words are nominated, defined, and discussed. Have class narrow list; go back to designated words and establish final definitions and have students write these in their vocabulary journals. Say:* Everyone enter the vocabulary words on your map in an appropriate place. Find a way to identify them as our class vocabulary words.

10. *Say:* Turn your maps in to me; I will record them as complete and return them to you tomorrow.

LESSON ASSESSMENT(S)

11. Observational Assessment—Note students' prior knowledge about whales in TPRC and how they were able to identify genetic/environmental elements contributing to feeding habits in subsequent discussion. Pay close attention in partnership map sharing and in words groups selected to learn.

12. Other Assessment—Carefully examine maps for misconceptions, etc. Record completion grades. Develop end-of-unit test, including vocabulary items.

How to do . . . .

TPRC, GROUP MAPPING, AND VSS

One of the nicest things about TPRC is how easy it is to use with just about any text or other learning medium. It requires no special materials or equipment, no elaborate preparations, and no alteration of text or textbooks. What is critical is that you define *explicitly* the lesson topic and goals you wish to address so that you can establish clear focus for what the students respond to in the ***think*** and ***predict*** stages. The Think stage is always focused on the *general topic:* the prior knowledge and previous experience students have *related* to the specific subject of study. This general knowledge is the text from which students will create linkages to the new information. The Predict stage focuses attention on the *specific subject* of the lesson; predictions are made on the basis of students' general knowledge base. I recommend that you prepare the TPRC worksheet for students to use in thinking about and predicting before reading. The following steps will lead sequentially through TPRC, GMA, and VSS.

TPRC

1. Ask student teams to ***think*** about and jot down everything they know about a *general topic* (e.g., whales, baking, algebra, baseball)—6 to 8 minutes.
2. Announce *specific topic* (e.g., feeding habits of humpback whales, yeast bread baking, factoring, fielding).
3. Ask students to ***predict*** what information on their lists might appear in the reading [✓]; add any new predictions they have—2 to 3 minutes.
4. Ask students to ***read*** the assignment; note how well they predicted [*].
5. Lead a short discussion to ***connect*** the predictions with the reading (e.g., "How well did you predict?"; "How many of your ideas appeared in the reading?"; "What new ideas appeared?").

GMA STUDY AIDS

6. Ask students to map their perceptions of the reading without talking to anybody and without looking back at the reading. (Have "dummy" maps ready if mapping is a new activity.) Remind them that the maps will be used as study aids and should include all information they consider important.
7. Ask partners to share their maps with one another and to assist each other in elaborating on what they considered important, how they chose to organize it, and why they made the choices they made. Allow students to refer to the reading as they wish.
8. Lead whole-class display and discussion of selected study maps.

VSS STUDY AIDS

9. Have student teams choose a word or term that students believe to be important to the chapter. Teams should be prepared to tell where they found the word/term, what they think it means, and why they think it is important. (You also nominate a word/term.)

10. Lead discussion as words are nominated and defined; write all nominated words/terms on the board.
11. Lead discussion for students to choose the final class vocabulary list; review and refine definitions of words/terms on the list.
12. Have students enter vocabulary words on their study maps where the words fit the map. Mark vocabulary words with an asterisk.
13. Develop follow-up activities for using the vocabulary words meaningfully.
14. Provide opportunities for students to elaborate on what was learned.
15. Design observational and other assessments.

WEBQUESTS

With the rapidly increasing presence of technology in our homes and schools and lives, the benefits of incorporating technology, electronic resources, and electronically generated information into subject area classes becomes increasingly evident. WebQuests have become a popular way to use the resources offered by the web in an integrative way in content classes. Antowan Reid, for example, made WebQuests a centerpiece of his unit on ecosystems as our Centerpiece Unit Plan did.

WebQuests were created and popularized by Bernie Dodge and Tom March. Dodge (1997) defines WebQuest as "an inquiry-oriented activity in which some or all of the information that learners interact with comes from resources on the internet" (p. 1). In our Centerpiece Lesson Plan, you saw how a WebQuest may be used with other instructional strategies. WebQuests are located on-line and present students with a problem to solve, instructions for the final product they are to create, links for gathering information, and rubrics for evaluating the final product. Dodge differentiates between short-term WebQuests, which require learners to grapple with a significant amount of new information, and longer-term WebQuests in which the learner "analyzed a body of knowledge deeply, transformed it in some way, and demonstrated an understanding of the materials by creating something that others can respond to on-line or off-" (p. 1). The critical attributes of a WebQuest are as follows (Dodge, 1997):

1. An *introduction* that sets the stage and provides some background information.
2. A *task* that is doable and interesting.
3. A set of *information sources* needed to complete the task. Most of these are web based—for example, web documents, experts available via e-mail, databases—and are identified in advance so that "learners are not left to wander through webspace completely adrift" (p. 2).
4. A description of the *process* the learners should go through to accomplish the task.
5. Some *guidance* on how to organize the information required.
6. A *conclusion* that brings closure to the quest, reminds the learners of what they have learned, and encourages them to extend their learning.

The format of our Centerpiece Lesson Plan WebQuest is typical: A problem or issue is set before students (attending the Constitutional Convention as a delegate, reporter, or public relations firm) with a major task for students to complete (research the perspectives and points of view of delegates and the thinking that went into the creation of the U.S. Constitution). Typical also is that the bulk of the resources for completion of the task are found online; however, a teacher-created text set or open access to materials in the library add to the online resources. What is particularly attractive about this WebQuest are the various alternative formats for students to demonstrate knowledge. As delegates, they may prepare notes for a talk show host *or* create a videotape to be shown on the talk show; as reporters they create a newsletter and individually may report on the convention in written articles *or* graphics; and as a PR firm they may create a brochure *or* a video *or* a Web site. Thus, do we allow students to work from their capabilities and interests—that is, create flow—and thus do we *build* on those strengths in the service of content learning. Possibilities for WebQuest tasks are almost endless, and many, many WebQuests are available for teachers to use.

How To Do . . . .

WEBQUEST

WebQuests are amenable to various formats and uses. You may use any of the myriad available ones already online, or you may create your own and upload it for your students' use. The following general steps will assist you in using WebQuests.

1. Determine your lesson/unit objectives and link these with curriculum standards.
2. Find or create a WebQuest that meets your objectives and is appropriate for your students.
3. Determine how you can initiate student interest in the topic; e.g., the first part of a TPRC or some other means for linking to students' experiences.
4. Determine groups and working rules for group functioning and use of computers in and outside the classroom.
5. Find online and other resources such as a text set for students to use in their research.
6. Establish finished product(s) and rubrics for assessment.
7. Determine total assessment procedures and criteria for the lesson/unit.

Probably the very best way to get a sense of the many forms WebQuests may take is to visit sites where many are available. One of the best is at San Diego State University (where Bernie Dodge is) at http://webquest.sdsu.edu/. Hundreds of WebQuests for the content areas in middle school and high school are available there. For other sites, type "webquest" into the Google search engine (www.google.com). There are also many sources of assistance for creating your own WebQuests. The Bernie Dodge site listed earlier gives step-by-step information and instructions for creating them. Filamentality, at http://www.kn.pacbell.com/wired/fil/, provides both instructions and a template for creating your own WebQuest, as does www.webquest.org.

The value of WebQuests is that they engage students in active inquiry, allow students to respond to the task in a variety of ways, and require students to produce something new through the transformation of prior knowledge with new information. Equally important, WebQuests use technology and the Internet in an integrative, generative way to increase student learning. This is not drill-and-practice; rather, it is a rich application of technology in classrooms *and* it guides student before, during and after reading.

K-W-L PLUS

K-W-L Plus (Carr & Ogle, 1987) is a combination of Donna Ogle's original K-W-L (1986) with mapping. K, W, and L stand for *know*, *want to know*, and *learned*, respectively, and are used to guide students through text in much the same manner that the TPRC does. Students begin by brainstorming everything they know about a topic and then categorizing their knowledge and listing it on a K-W-L worksheet (Figure 7.7 on p. 256) under *K*. Following this, students generate a list of questions about what they want to know and anticipate learning from the text. Want to know questions are listed under *W*. Barbara Boyd (2003) recommends that, with respect to *W*, teachers ask students, "Where and what are the possible sources for finding out what we want to know? the net? books? journals? community or human resources?" As the reading progresses, students may generate additional questions they want to explore. After reading, students summarize what they have learned by listing that information under *L*. The worksheet then is used as the basis for mapping; students categorize the information under *L* on the worksheet and develop their own maps using those categories and content. Carr and Ogle recommend alternatively that written summaries may be used to extend K-W-L learning. Figure 7.8 (Carr & Ogle, 1987) shows a map developed from the ninth-grader's K-W-L worksheet shown in Figure 7.7 (p. 256).

K-W-L Plus is clearly designed to assist students throughout the learning event (before, during, and after reading). As with other, similar strategies, K-W-L Plus builds on what students already know, engages them in prediction and anticipation of the reading, and then leads them through organization, reorganization, and development of information after reading. K-W-L Plus seems perfectly suited to partnership and small-group work. Just as many other lessons are made more powerful through group interaction, so is K-W-L Plus.

FIGURE 7.7 *Ninth-Grade Student's K-W-L Worksheet for a Lesson on Killer Whales*

K (Know)	W (Want to Know)	L (Learned)
They live in oceans. They are vicious. They eat each other. They are mammals.	Why do they attack people? How fast can they swim? What kind of fish do they eat? What is their description? How long do they live? How do they breathe?	D—They are the biggest member of the dolphin family. D—They weigh 10,000 pounds and get 30 feet long. F—They eat squids, seals, and other dolphins. A—They have good vision under water. F—They are carnivorous (meat eaters). A—They are the second smartest animal on earth. D—They breathe through blowholes. A—They do not attack unless they are hungry. D—Warm blooded. A—They have echo-location (sonar). L—They are found in the oceans.
Description Food Location		

Final category designations developed for column L, information learned about killer whales:
A = abilities; D = description; F = food; L = location.

FIGURE 7.8 *Ninth-Grade Student's Map Generated from K-W-L Worksheet*
From Carr and Ogle, 1987

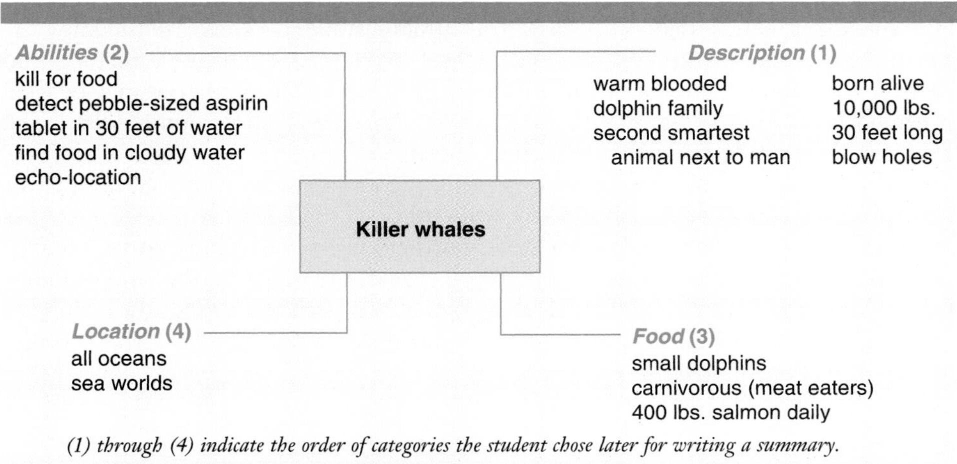

(1) through (4) indicate the order of categories the student chose later for writing a summary.

Creating Strategic Readers, Writers and Learners

Whether you choose to do an extended TPRC, WebQuest, VSS over a two-week period, or a single lesson using TPRC, GMA, VSS, from start to finish you are guiding students through a process that contributes to their ability to be increasingly capable learners. K-W-L Plus accomplishes the same. Talk to students about how starting with what they know helps them understand their reading or learning activity. Review the steps with them. The first question is, "What do I already know about this topic?" Then comes, "What do I think I'll learn?" followed by, "How well did I predict?" and, "What connections can I make between what I knew and what I learned?" All of this is metacognitive thought. Make it explicit by talking to students about it. Do the same with the GMA and VSS, always with the emphasis of how doing this helps them read, think, and learn.

How to do . . . .

K-W-L PLUS

You may want to prepare a K-W-L Plus worksheet, with the *K*, *W*, and *L* columns labeled and defined, which you then print and distribute to students. This gives the work at each stage of the reading an official air that adds to its appeal and importance. These worksheets would also be ideal for placement in students' portfolios or whatever you use to document student progress. The following steps are useful in developing K-W-L Plus lessons:

1. Ask students or student teams to brainstorm about what they *know* about the topic of the lesson.
2. Direct students to organize and categorize their knowledge and list it under *K* on their worksheets.
3. Ask students to anticipate what they will read as they list questions they *want to know* or have answered under *W*.
4. Ask students to read the assignment, adding questions to their list as needed.
5. Have students list the information they *learned* under *L* on their worksheets.

6. Ask students to generate categories for the information they learned and to develop individual maps.
7. Lead a discussion in which students display and explain their maps.
8. Assign further writing and idea development as desired.
9. Design assessments.

SAMPLE WORKSHEET *K-W-L*

K (Know)	W (Want to Know)	L (Learned)

PREDICT-LOCATE-ADD-NOTE (PLAN)

PLAN, or Predict-Locate-Add-Note (Caverly, Mandeville, & Nicholson, 1995), combines many of the prediction and mapping activities we've previously discussed. PLAN begins with students creating a map based on their predictions of what the reading on a topic will be about. Students place the topic title (e.g., "The Solar System" or "Poetry" or "Westward Migration" or "The Baroque Period") in the center of a piece of paper. They then *predict* by generating a probable map of the text content using the subtitles, highlighted words, and other text features they find while previewing the reading. After the map is constructed, students *locate* known and unknown information on their maps by putting check marks (✓) beside information they know and questions marks (?) by information unfamiliar to them. As they read, students then *add* words, phrases, or ideas at appropriate places on their maps that fill in information, explain unknown ideas, or add to concepts already known. Finally, students *note* what they have learned, by either revising or redoing their maps, creating new representations, writing in their journals, or participating in small-group or whole-class discussion.

Caverly and his associates comment on how important it is to teach the PLAN strategy over time and to provide instruction that gives students ample models for what they are to do. For example, they note that middle school students tend to copy whole sentences rather than key words when creating their prediction maps (p. 197); you can remedy this by having students use text messaging language to create their prediction maps. In addition, they found that spatial organization of a large amount of text onto one page is problematic at first for some students, especially middle-grade students. The key to using PLAN is to provide ample guidance, practice, and collaborative work opportunities so that students learn how to (1) preview reading and make predictions, (2) determine what information on their maps is new or known (before reading), (3) add information and ideas to extend map representations, and (4) reorganize the now-detailed information on their maps.

How to do . . . .

PLAN

PLAN is more elaborate than any of the other instructional strategies we've discussed so far. Thus, it will take more preparation and more guidance on your part to be taught effectively. I recommend that you attempt PLAN only with students who are experienced predictors, mappers, vocabulary collectors, and such—that is, those who are already used to such instructional strategies as DR-TA, TPRC, GMA, VSS, K-W-L Plus, and DIA. Further, you (and your students) will probably be well served if you initially teach the four steps separately, one each in four lessons, to give students time to learn how to do each step. Then provide follow-up and practice for the entire strategy over time. The following steps are useful in teaching PLAN:

1. Determine your lesson objectives.
2. Identify the reading(s) using, at the outset, "considerate" text that is easily parsed for important ideas and supporting detail.
3. Using an overhead projector and class copies of a text, model for students the full PLAN process: how one goes about creating a prediction map, locating known and unknown information, adding supporting detail, and taking note of new learning. Think aloud as you work on the overhead projector; allow students to see your missteps and rethinking and to ask questions after you've finished.
4. Have students work with a partner to create a prediction map of a different text. Share these with the class and discuss how the mapped information was obtained. Discuss also how students will locate known and unknown information.

5. Have students and their partners locate known and unknown information.
6. Direct students to read the text and, with their partners, add words/phrases to their maps to explain concepts.
7. Conduct a class discussion in which students share their maps and discuss how they will go about representing their new knowledge.
8. Design assessment plans.

THREE-LEVEL READING GUIDES

Three-level reading guides are part of the functional, indirect teaching of reading approach introduced by Harold Herber (1970) as the most useful means of teaching reading in the content areas. Herber's instructional strategies and approaches—which include graphic organizers, reaction guides, reasoning guides, structured overviews, and others, as well as the three-level guide (1970, 1978)—have been enormously popular since Herber first introduced them.

The three-level guide is a direct outgrowth of the three levels of comprehension—literal, interpretive, and applied—that we discussed in Chapter 4. Herber emphasizes that the intent of the guide is, first, to maintain a classroom focus on subject matter while teaching reading and study strategies indirectly, as they are needed for learning content; second, to "show students how to do what they are required to do" (1978, p. 6); and finally, to provide a structure that will assist students before, during, and after reading.

Three-level reading guides, used as Herber intended, provide the structure and stimulus for individual learning within the context of small-group discussion and exploration of ideas associated with written text. Each section of guide lessons allows students to read and respond to text, support their response choices through the combination of previous experience and information in the text, and compare their responses with those of the group. Specifically, three-level guide lessons progress as follows:

Part I (Literal Comprehension)

1. Students individually read the written directions and statements for Part I of the three-level guide.
2. Students read the assigned section of text.
3. Students reread statements in Part I, marking those that they believe to be supported by the text and deciding how the text supports their choices.
4. Small groups meet for students to identify, support, compare, debate, and discuss individual responses to Part I statements.

Part II (Interpretive Comprehension)

5. Students individually read and respond to Part II statements.
6. Small groups meet for students to identify, support, compare, debate, and discuss these responses.

Part III (Applied Comprehension)

7. Students individually read and respond to Part III statements.
8. Small groups meet for students to identify, support, compare, debate, and discuss these responses.
9. The teacher leads a short whole-class discussion for students to share the nature of the exchange in each group, to summarize discoveries/insights achieved from the reading, and/or to clarify or elaborate ideas from the reading and small-group discussions.
10. The teacher makes follow-up assignments for elaboration of information, continuation of the lesson, or reinforcement of lesson ideas or skills. Following is an example of a Three-Level Guide for mathematics.

THREE-LEVEL GUIDE EXAMPLE *Mathematics*

I. ***Directions:*** Read the statements below; then read the Simple Probability section of your text to see if it contains the information in each statement. Put a check beside each statement that you believe can be supported by the text. Provide evidence for why you mark each statement as you do.

_____Outcomes are the result of specific events.

_____When we talk about probability, all possible outcomes have an equal chance of occurring.

_____The number of ways an outcome can happen in relationship to the total possible outcomes determines the probability of an outcome's happening.

II. ***Directions:*** Read the following statements and consider how they relate to the information you just discussed. Put a check beside the statements below that you believe to be logical inferences based on your reading. Be prepared to support your choices. Discuss this section before going on to Section III.

_____Probability is a type of ratio.

_____Outcomes are lawfully related to probabilities.

_____Probability is associated with common events.

III. ***Directions:*** Read through the following statements and consider how they relate to information in your text, inferences you have drawn, and ideas from your discussion. Check the statements below that you believe are reasonable conclusions from your reading, discussion, and any other information you have. Be prepared to support your choices.

_____Knowledge about probability can be useful when playing card, dice, and spinner games.

_____You can make better "educated guesses" if you know something about probability.

_____Probability and possibility are terms that have a special relationship.

As you can see, the three-level guide encourages rich, active participation and student exchange of ideas. It does all the things we've talked about throughout this chapter: guides students before, during, and after reading; assists students in organizing information; demonstrates the significance of the text by linking it to students' prior knowledge and by showing relationships; engages students in "substantive discourse" about text; and promotes strategic reading of text. What is critical to understand about three-level guides, however, is that to use them *without* the small-group discussion, without stopping periodically to discuss student responses and reasoning, is to *misuse the guides.* You may well have had the experience of making your way through long lists of reading guide statements in high school classes: 25 to 50 statements for each reading assignment, to be done on your own and brought to class for discussion. That was three-level guides at their worst. Three-level guides at their best stimulate lively, animated discussion and debate. To achieve this, you will need to attend to several critical aspects while writing the guides and directing the lesson.

WRITING THREE-LEVEL READING GUIDES

When writing three-level reading guides, use the following principles to guide your work:

1. *Establish clear lesson objectives.* You simply cannot write statements for guiding students through the reading without knowing what the learning objectives are. Ask yourself, "What do I want my students to know or be able to do when they are through with this lesson?" Using whatever format works for you, write these objectives down and link them to content standards used by your district or state.

2. *Read the selection to:* (a) identify essential information and main ideas, (b) determine relationships between ideas, (c) determine generalizations or conclusions that can be drawn from the ideas and their relationships, and (d) decide how the text information does (and does not) meet your lesson objectives.

3. *Write declarative statements* (not questions) for each level of the guide. *Literal* statements should answer the questions "What is the essential information contained in this assignment? What are the important ideas here?" *Interpretive* statements reflect the questions, "What relationships can be seen from this information? What inferences might be drawn? What important point is the author trying to make here?" *Applied* statements should answer the questions "What conclusions can be drawn by combining what students already know with what information is here (or implied)? How does all of this relate to students' lives or to what they know of the world?"

Keep in mind that you do not need to write "foils" (statements that are misleading or deliberately incorrect); rather, write statements that are reasonable, defendable, and reflective of a variety of perspectives and interpretations.

4. *Monitor the number and quality of the statements.* For a number of reasons, it is far better to have too few rather than too many statements. Important among these reasons is that too many statements will overwhelm the very students you're trying to assist. A few well-chosen statements will serve to launch the interesting, animated small-group discussions you're attempting to stimulate and should reflect rather directly the lesson objectives you've established. If you have trouble winnowing your list of statements down to that well-chosen few, you may not have real clarity about the lesson objectives themselves. In that case, go back to the objectives, rewrite as necessary, and get that clarity; then look at your statements again.

5. *Double-check* to see that the applied statements (level III) show relevance of information to students' lives. These statements should clearly allow for students to apply new insights to their lives and to the world at large. They should *broaden* students' knowledge so that both the students and the lesson go beyond the text. This is one of the ways that teachers increase the power of text.

6. *Write directions to assist students in working through the guide.* These directions must be adjusted to students' grade level. This can easily be done by adjusting the instructional practices you use with the guides so that younger students, or those who are not experienced using guides, are given more teacher guidance and more hands-on experience while using the three-level guide (as you can see in the lesson plan that follows).

USING THREE-LEVEL GUIDES

When actually using the three-level reading guide, the following principles should guide you:

1. *Make sure instructions for each discussion include specific, explicit directions for students to support their choices.* It is not enough for students simply to compare statements to see who agreed with what. Monitor small-group discussions to make sure students are looking at rationale, individual reasoning, and logic. If you find they are not doing it, model with them the kind of probe questions that lead to such discussion.

2. *Have students do something with the information discussed.* Go back to your objectives and see what you want students to know or be able to do that goes beyond the text. Have students map (or add to their maps), write position statements, do practice problems, summarize group response to the text, write summary-response logs, identify vocabulary words, complete an experiment, or play a game of volleyball: in other words, *use the new information meaningfully.* Following is a lesson plan for using the Three-Level Reading Guide—Mathematics below.

THREE-LEVEL READING GUIDE LESSON PLAN *Mathematics*

Lesson: Probability

Course/Grade: Mathematics/6th Grade

Materials: Textbook, blank cubes, spinners, dice, pennies, paper, pencils

LESSON OBJECTIVES (WITH CONTENT STANDARDS)

Upon completion of the lesson students will

- Understand outcomes (Standard 3.1—Students will represent all possible outcomes for compound events in an organized way and express the theoretical probability of each outcome).

- Understand probability outcomes (Standard 3.2—Students will use data to estimate the probability of future events).
- Be able to complete probability problems accurately (Standard 3.3—Students will represent probabilities as ratios, proportions, decimals between 1 and 0, and percentages between 0 and 100 and verify that the probabilities computed are reasonable).

LESSON PROCEDURES

Before Reading: Into

1. *Put students in groups of four to five. Give students the Three-Level Guide. Read aloud and explain the directions for Section I of the guide. Say:* Remember that after you read and mark your guides, you are then to compare your choices and tell why each of you made the choices you made. Do that now.

During Reading: Through

2. After groups have compared their choices, give each group a blank cube and have them perform the cube experiment in the text. Then do the spinner, die, and/or penny experiments as time allows.
3. *Ask:* Does any of the information from the experiments change your previous choices? If so, how? If not, why?
4. *Direct students' attention to Section II of the guide. Read it and explain. Say:* Remember to use information from what you read, from your previous discussion, and from the experiments in making your decisions. Share your thinking in your group discussion.

After Reading: Beyond

5. *After groups have finished discussing, Say*: Share with the class some of the thinking in your group. How did you talk about the statement, "Probability is a type of ratio?" *Lead discussion. Continue similarly for the other two statements.*
6. *Say:* Now do Section III of your guide. Be prepared to share your thinking with the class. *Lead Discussion and spend significant time discussing how probability is used in everyday life.*
7. *Say*: For homework do the problems on page 93. You will turn homework in for a grade. Bring to class one example of how probability works in your life.

LESSON ASSESSMENT(S)

8. Observational Assessment—Monitor group discussions and in whole class discussion to make sure students understand outcomes and probability.
9. Homework Assessment—Grade homework and record grades.

Following is a Three-Level Guide that can be taught using a similar lesson plan.

THREE-LEVEL GUIDE *Biology (Homeostasis)*

I. Read the following statements; then read pp. 419–424 in your text. Put a check (✓) beside those statements you find in your reading. The statements may or may not be worded exactly as found in the book. Discuss the statements in your group, making sure everyone understands the reading, and provide evidence for your choices.

_____ The exchange of materials with the environment involves two general problems: (1) maintaining homeostasis, and (2) removing wastes.

_____ Osmosis, diffusion, and contractile vacuoles are mechanisms for materials exchange in protists.

_____ Dew is a form of waste removal.

_____ Grasshoppers excrete nitrogenous wastes in the form of uric acid.

_____ Ammonia is very toxic and requires dilution in large quantities of water.

II. Read the following statements. Put a check (✓) beside those statements you agree with on the basis of the reading assignment. In discussion, give reasons for your choices.

_____ Unproductive transfer occurs when organisms take in unneeded materials or excrete needed ones.

_____ Contractile vacuoles and flame cells serve related functions.

_____ Land animals and land plants have the common need to conserve body water.

_____ Land organisms and water organisms have evolved different ways to excrete nitrogenous wastes.

_____ The excretory system of the grasshopper is more complex than the excretory system of planariums.

III. Read the following statements. Put a check (✓) by those statements you agree with. Use information from this chapter and any other information you have to support your choices. Discuss your reasoning in your group.

_____ Failure or malfunctioning of the excretory system would cause an organism to die.

_____ An organism's excretory system is a product of both evolution and environment.

_____ In human organisms, the respiratory system serves an important role in the excretory process.

_____ Characteristics of the excretory system of an organism can be determined roughly through knowledge of the organism's environment.

_____ Human organisms have the most complex excretory system of all living things.

How to do . . . .

A THREE-LEVEL READING GUIDE LESSON

I think you can see that three-level guides require considerably more teacher preparation than do TPRCs, GMAs, VSSs, and K-W-Ls. They do take more time, but they're worth it, especially when the reading material is particularly difficult or the topic unwieldy. Three-level guides help *you* organize your thinking and lesson planning and so help students also. *One cautionary note:* Although it is important that you understand and can differentiate between literal, interpretive, and applied levels of comprehension and then write corresponding declarative statements, it is not important for your *students* to be able to do so. *You do not need to teach the three comprehension levels to students or refer to the statements by their comprehension-level names.* As with any other instructional strategy, three-level guides are not to be used with every lesson or assignment. I recommend that you build a "library" of guides over time, writing several new ones each year and adapting old ones to meet the needs of subsequent units, lessons, and students. The following steps will assist you in writing and directing a three-level guide lesson:

1. Identify lesson objectives.
2. Read the selection to identify important ideas, relationships, and conclusions that may be drawn from it.
3. Write declarative statements to correspond to the three levels of comprehension: literal, interpretive, applied.
4. Write directions for students to follow for reading the text and discussing statement responses at each level.
5. Direct students as they work individually and in small groups to read and discuss the lesson. Activities should alternate between individual response and small-group discussion of responses to each section of the guide.
6. Upon completion of individual/small group activities, lead a whole-class discussion to compare small-group experiences, summarize responses, and clarify information.
7. Assign follow-up activities for elaboration of information, continuation of the lesson, or reinforcement of lesson skills.
8. Design assessment(s).

ANTICIPATION GUIDES

Anticipation Guides are somewhat similar to Three-Level Reading Guides because they present a set of statements for readers to consider before reading text and thus help readers focus their attention on the salient ideas in the text. Anticipation Guides differ from Three-Level Guides because they *begin* with statements from real life that reflect possible conclusions one could draw from the text. Below is an Anticipation Guide developed by Rebecca Siegert (2003) to guide students' reading and discussion of *Hamlet.*

ANTICIPATION GUIDE *English*

Hamlet

ANTICIPATION GUIDE

Part One:

Read each statement and write YES in the blank if you believe the statement and could support it, or put NO in the blank if you do not believe the statement and could not support it. After we read the play, we'll revisit the statements and see if your answers change.

Before		**After**
_____	1. It's OK to take someone's life in order to further your own aspirations.	_____
_____	2. A person's actions cannot drive another person literally insane.	_____
_____	3. It's OK to marry your sister-in-law/brother-in-law after your brother/sister dies.	_____
_____	4. The quest for revenge can lead people to their demise.	_____
_____	5. It's OK to keep secrets from your spouse.	_____
_____	6. A person cannot be held accountable for his actions if he is in a deep depression.	_____
_____	7. Suicide is never an option, even in the darkest of times.	_____
_____	8. Loyalty to the government is less important than loyalty to family and/or friends.	_____

Part Two:

Pick one of the questions to explore further. Write a one-page response (on the back of this page or on another sheet of paper) suporting why you answered the question the way that you did.

As you can see, the point of the Anticipation Guide is first to engage students' consideration of real-life application of the themes and issues raised by the text. Their decisions about the statements before reading and then after reading allow them to reconsider these issues based on the text reading. And finally, they are asked to take and support a position on one of the statements. Thus, Part I guides students into and through the reading, and Part II guides them beyond the reading. Anticipation Guides are easily written for many subject areas.

GUIDING STUDENTS BEFORE AND DURING READING (INTO AND THROUGH)

The following instructional strategies are useful for initiating reading and guiding students through text. They may be combined with other follow-up instruction (see Building Table, pp. 284–285) after reading.

THE PREREADING PLAN (PREP)

Judith Langer's PReP strategy (1982), provides students with a means of organizing information before reading. It begins with the teacher's saying, "Tell me anything that comes to your mind when I say——['bowling' or 'sculpture' or 'human needs,' etc.]." The students' free associations are recorded on the board. The teacher then asks, "What made you think of——[each student's response to the first statement]?" while pointing to the response on the board. After responses have been discussed, the teacher says, "On the basis of our discussion, have you any new ideas about——['bowling,' 'sculpture,' 'human needs,' etc.]?" Students then read the assignment to see how their old and new ideas apply. PReP is a useful introductory activity that may be done on a whole-class basis or directed in small-group discussions. You may wish to have students make a prediction or two after new ideas are discussed to give them immediate reasons for doing the reading. Any number of discussion/elaboration activities or instructional strategies may be used to follow the reading.

QUESTIONING THE AUTHOR (QTA)

Questioning the Author, or QtA, was developed by Isabel Beck and her associates (Beck, McKeown, Hamilton, & Kucan, 1997) to promote student engagement with text to build understanding (p. 3). QtA is based on the assumption of author fallibility—that is, that authors are limited both in the extent of their knowledge and in their ability to communicate that knowledge to students. The intent here is to "depose the authority of the text" in such a way that students come to view texts as "less impersonal, authoritative, and incomprehensible" (p. 18). A second key feature of QtA is the notion of "queries" in place of teacher questions. Queries in the QtA dialogue are probes teachers use to initiate and sustain discussion; they are distinct from traditional dialogic teacher questions in the way they "prompt students to consider meaning and develop ideas rather than to retrieve information and state ideas" (p. 7). QtA uses the kind of segmented text that we've discussed previously with the DR-TA and ReQuest. The teacher determines appropriate stopping points in text by prereading and identifying text segments congruent with the major understandings that comprise lesson objectives. The teacher's role is to guide discussion using *initiating* and *follow-up* queries that focus student attention on construction of meaning. Beck and her associates state that an important aspect of teaching QtA is to convince students that readers have to "take on" a text, little by little and idea by idea; thus, it's worth stopping and talking about text while reading. Initiating queries are of three types:

- What is the author trying to say here?
- What is the author's message?

- What is the author talking about?

After initiating queries begin the discussion and exploration of the text, they are followed by such follow-up queries as

- Does this make sense with what we read before?
- How does this connect with what we read earlier?
- What does the author mean here?
- Why do you think the author tells us this now?

The role of the teacher in the discussion is to keep students engaged in the process of meaning construction (do note how very DR-TA-like the queries are and how they address critical analysis of text). Teachers do this using what Beck and her colleagues refer to as "discussion moves" (p. 81). The discussion moves include the following (pp. 82–92):

- *Marking*—responding to student comments by drawing attention to certain ideas: "Oh, so human-built levees may solve one problem and create another?"
- *Turning back*—both (1) turning responsibility back to students for thinking ideas through and (2) turning student attention back to text for clarification and extension of ideas: "How did you arrive at that conclusion?"
- *Revoicing*—rephrasing and interpreting student response so ideas can be discussed further: "What I think you're saying is that Gershwin uses minor key, glissando, and syncopation as distinctive features in his body of work."
- *Modeling*—thinking aloud to give students access to aspects of meaning construction: "When I first read this I thought it was confusing; then I realized that the word *functions* helped me begin to sort out the meaning."
- *Annotating*—providing information to fill in the gaps; "Beryl Markham was indeed an aviator and horse trainer; she lived more in the twentieth century than at the turn of the nineteenth century."
- *Recapping*—pulling together and summarizing main ideas so the discussion can move forward: "Okay, we've agreed that buildup of economic, military, and industrial strength was happening simultaneously in various countries. Now let's see what the outcome was."

How to do . . . .

QtA

QtA is an instructional strategy that may be used with any variety of texts. This strategy is particularly notable for its intent to reconstitute students' approach to academic text; I really like the assumption of author fallibility and the focus on deposing the authority of text. "Because the book said so" is truly not a useful basis for drawing conclusions and making decisions about subject matter information; rather, our focus needs to be on students exploring ideas, finding the intertextual linkages that promote construction of new knowledge, and developing growing awareness and confidence in their own powers as readers and learners. Following are the steps for developing QtA lessons:

1. Determine lesson objectives.
2. Select the reading and preread to segment the text according to major concepts identified in the learning objectives.
3. Determine alternative queries for initiating and developing the discussion.
4. Prepare a notecard with possible queries and discussion moves for initial lessons.
5. Lead the reading and discussion.
6. Plan assessment(s).

GUIDING STUDENTS DURING AND AFTER READING (THROUGH AND BEYOND)

The two activities detailed in this section are highly useful for developing rich responses from students during and after reading. They, too, may be combined with other instructional strategies quite successfully.

READING RESPONSE GROUPS

Reading response groups are, by now, rather well accepted in middle school and secondary classrooms. They are also referred to as conversational discussion groups (O'Flahavan, 1989), and reading–writing workbench (Tierney, Caplan, Ehri, Healy, & Hurdlow, 1989). Most activities involving reading response groups center around transforming classroom discussion of text from "gentle inquisitions" to "grand conversations" (Eeds & Wells, 1989). The point of the activity is to engage students in gently directed small-group discussions of text that have all the characteristics of the spontaneous discussions that occur when an idea captures, sparks, and excites a group. Fundamental to reading response group instruction are two major assumptions (Ruddell, 1990):

1. Meaning derived from text is highly individualized and is constructed from personal transaction between reader and text.
2. Reader understanding is deepened through social transactions between peers for the purpose of sharing personal constructions of meaning, asking questions, and building group meaning.

TEACHING CONTENT WITH READING RESPONSE GROUPS

Reading response groups generally are considered to be productive additions to the classroom. They are not without some difficulties, however, most of which are usually associated with what happens when students are turned loose to discuss on their own, specifically with regard to the quality of group discussion and participation by group members. Despite these potential drawbacks, reading response groups offer important opportunities for students to work together to construct content knowledge and generate new ideas. Although current designs for reading response groups are most frequently tied to literature study, I see no reason why the benefits associated with rich constructions of knowledge for a novel or short story would not apply equally as well to constructions of knowledge for subject matter texts, or any reason why novels and short stories, and many types of nonfiction, should not be used in conjunction with subject matter texts. Reading response groups are perfect settings for using text sets (as introduced in Chapter 6). When using reading response groups, the teacher should do the following:

1. Establish heterogeneous (nonability grouped) reading response groups, generally consisting of four to five students per group.
2. Develop and teach guidelines for groups to function effectively. (We will discuss these at some length in Chapter 11.)
3. Focus student attention on the specific kinds of responses they are to construct from the text.
4. Monitor student groups as they develop and discuss responses. (More about this in Chapter 11 as well.)
5. Design follow-up activities for students to apply responses and elaborate further on them.

PROMPTS FOR CONTENT READING RESPONSE GROUPS

Focusing response group discussion (the third item in the list above) is critical to the success of reading response group activity. The following sections present various ways to focus student response in a unit on fitness.

Prior Knowledge, Text Meaning, and Reaction Response Prompts O'Flahavan (1989) suggests that the teacher leave three questions with each group that address the following areas: (1) background knowledge—how student experiences relate to the text; (2) ideas derived from the text—how students construct text meaning; and (3) ideas that go beyond the text—how students interpret or react to the text. For a fitness unit and reading assignment, these questions might be as follows:

- What fitness needs do you see in your own life? What might you like to be able to do (or do better) that you can't do now?
- On the basis of what you read, how would you define *fitness?* Support your definition.
- If you were to design a fitness program for your own needs, what element or elements would be your first priority? Why?

These three types of questions loosely reflect the three comprehension levels (literal, interpretive, applied) we've discussed previously. The difference here is that the focus of the first question is more on students' prior knowledge base than on information available in text.

Perception, Reaction, and Feelings Response Prompts Bleich (1978) asks students to react *in writing* to slightly different focusing categories: (1) text perceptions—how students "see" (or construct meaning from) the text; (2) reactions to the text—how students respond to the text; and (3) associations with the text—feelings and thoughts students have in relationship to their perceptions of the text. So students are asked to write about, and then discuss, what they think the text theme is, how they respond to it, and how they feel about it:

- In your own words, what do you think the authors are saying about fitness?
- Do you accept the authors' definitions of fitness? Why or why not?
- What is your attitude toward fitness? Would [do] you work out? Why or why not?

Following discussion, students then may develop a fitness program for themselves, with teacher guidance, or pursue further an exploration and study of fitness and health.

Stages of Understanding Response Prompts The reading–writing workbench approach (Tierney et al., 1989) begins at a thematic level and progresses in three general stages. In the fitness unit, for example, groups might begin by exploring a large question, "What is fitness?" (stage 1). From this discussion, students read the central assignment, as well as other resources, to explore many aspects of the notion of fitness. During this exploration, they are encouraged to experiment with various reading and writing activities to get more information, express what they are learning, and share information with one another. Some type of culminating activity occurs: development of one's own fitness program with written rationale; group dramatization of "From Fragile to Fit"; compilation of various low-impact methods for achieving fitness (stage 2). Finally, students are asked to reflect on and assess what they have learned and what meaning this learning will have in their lives (stage 3). Thus, the prompts for this reading–writing workbench might be

- What is fitness?
- What will you produce to summarize this unit?
- What have you learned in this unit that applies to your own life?

How to do . . . .

READING RESPONSE GROUPS

As you can see, reading response groups may be used in daily, short-term classroom activities, or they may be the central organizational foundation for major units of study. However you wish to use them, teacher planning is critical to their success. First and foremost, you must define your unit and lesson objectives. Second, you must decide how extensively you wish to use response groups. Many teachers start on a small scale when first using reading response groups and gradually progress to major response group projects. Finally, you need to develop useful focusing activities and prompts that promote the response and interaction you are intending. The following steps are appropriate for using reading response groups:

1. Determine unit/lesson objectives.
2. Establish response groups (four to five students per group).

3. Decide how you want groups to function, develop guidelines for group behaviors, and teach students how to do what you want them to do in their groups (see Chapter 11).
4. Prepare focusing questions or statements and develop necessary directions for students' guided responses.
5. Observe groups as they work, troubleshoot when necessary, and provide access to resources students need.
6. Lead reflection and follow-up discussion for students to evaluate response group functioning.
7. Plan assessment(s).

READ, ENCODE, ANNOTATE, PONDER (REAP) AND iREAP

REAP—Read, Encode into your own words, Annotate, Ponder—is an instructional activity introduced by Marilyn Eanet and Tony Manzo (1976) that guides students after reading. In it, students respond to reading by writing different types of annotations, or notes, that reflect various perspectives on the text itself. REAP may be used with students working independently or with groups. Recently, Manzo, Manzo, and Albee (2002) renamed REAP as iREAP to "represent its currency and contribution to Internet community building" (p. 42). In addition, they have expanded the original seven types of annotations to four reconstructive annotations—understanding the essence of the author's meaning—and eight constructive annotations—going beyond the author's meaning to form personal schema connections (p. 43). Following are the author's definitions of reconstructive and constructive annotations. I have added illustrative annotations from a health class handout of a newspaper editorial on blood pressure:

RECONSTRUCTIVE ANNOTATIONS

Summary. Stating the main ideas of the text: for example, "The main idea of this article is that we don't know as much about high blood pressure as we thought. Elements and factors other than sodium—calcium, for example—may affect high blood pressure."

Telegram. Stating the main idea in the briefest way possible—a crisp, telegram-like message: for example, "Researchers question knowledge base about blood pressure. We don't know as much as we think."

Heuristic. Using the author's words to stimulate a reaction: for example, "The author of this article states that 'high sodium may not be the villain of high blood pressure; rather, low calcium may be more at fault.' I wonder what this will do to advertising and food companies who are currently making a bundle on low-sodium products."

Question. Asking a question related to major ideas in the selection: for example, "If low calcium rather than high sodium could be the real culprit in high blood pressure, what and how many other unexplored or unresearched variables might be involved?"

CONSTRUCTIVE ANNOTATIONS

Personal View. Answering the question, "How do your views and feelings compare with what the author says?": for example, "I agree; I think this is one more reason we should be wary of simple solutions to the complex health issues."

Humorous. Bringing a smile: for example, "We're all such lemmings—we all jump on the "in" health fad. Remember oat bran?"

Critical. Examining the author's point of view and the annotator's reaction: for example, "I don't see a heavy 'point of view' in this article except that by its presence it suggests alternative viewpoints to current beliefs about high blood pressure. I was glad to see someone presenting such a possibility. I've never understood how high sodium could be so harmful to some people and not to others."

Contrary. Stating a logical alternative position, even if it is not necessarily what the student believes: for example, "Medical wisdom and considerable research have for some time supported the link between high sodium intake and high blood pressure. Until we have significant evidence to the contrary, we should continue to treat high blood pressure by reducing sodium intake."

Intention. Speculating on the author's intent in writing the text; for example, "I think that the intent here is to inform the public so reasonable personal decisions may be made about one's health. Dire warnings over a number of years about the effects of high sodium may have been overstated and caused inappropriate actions. At the very least, the article appears to be intended to get people to look at this issue."

Motivation. Identifying or considering the author's motivations: for example, "This article was probably motivated by two things: (1) the occurrence of research results that run counter to accepted knowledge and previous research, a sort of 'shock' factor; and (2) the prominence of high blood pressure as a threat to health in a country where a substantial portion of the population is above middle age or at risk for developing high blood pressure."

Discovery. Stating one or more practical questions that need to be answered before the selection can be judged for accuracy or worth: for example, "What specific evidence have researchers found to call into question our current understanding of the relationship between sodium and blood pressure?"

Creative. Suggesting different and perhaps better solutions, views, and connections: for example, "With our knowledge of genetics today, it would seem reasonable to look for hereditary influences on high blood pressure."

The *ponder* step of REAP is usually best done in a group setting, perhaps a reading response group, so that students have the opportunity to interact with one another, comparing and elaborating on their original annotations. What is critical is that students move within and across the different types of annotations, thus internalizing what Manzo, Manzo, and Albee call "spectrum thinking" (p. 45)—that is, the ability to change one's own thinking and to think from "different perspectives so that it becomes a habit of mind: a familiar, comfortable, almost automatic mental strategy" (p. 45). Thus, students not only engage in viewing issues and problems from various perspectives, but also they have the opportunity to see their peers doing the same thing. Manzo, Manzo, and Albee recommend that teachers require students to follow initial annotation responses with another, different type, each of which is shared with others. The result of such discussion is student development of the kind of critical literacy stance described in Chapter 4.

The REAP/iREAP procedure may be adapted in many ways for use with various students and classes. Its focus is on guiding students after reading (rather than before or during), and it may be most easily used, at least initially, in an informal way—by having students work in pairs or groups to do their first few annotations, for example. Another possibility is to have students annotate after mapping and map sharing. This procedure allows students to respond to text in ways other than simply retelling or identifying main ideas. Further, the annotations themselves are useful as springboards to extended discussion or other major activities. In addition, iREAP annotations may become part of on-line threaded discussions in a Blackboard or Web CT environment that allow students to continue discussion beyond the classroom space.

ISSUES RELATED TO TECHNOLOGY USE IN CLASSROOMS

Many schools are developing, or have developed, rather elaborate policies and procedures for computer use, access to the Internet, and software installation on school and home computers. New developments in software, hardware, and electronic networks happen stunningly quickly, leaving us all breathless a good deal of the time—not the least of which is access to the Internet via cell phone.

At some point, every teacher makes a decision about the degree and type of technology he or she will use in the classroom. Martha Rekrut, in a 1999 journal article, summarizes the results of various teachers' decisions to have their students use the Internet in classes, from student experiences e-mailing other students, to teacher and student evaluation of science Web sites, to evaluation of information obtained from newsgroups. Rekrut offers useful advice for teachers who are novices at using Internet resources in their classrooms (p. 556):

- Determine your instructional goals, or objectives. Do enough research to know whether the Internet is the best, or at least a good, source for what you want the students to learn, and whether what you intend the students to discover is readily accessible.
- Set Internet lesson(s) in the context of ongoing instruction, as part of the regular curriculum. Students should regard the web as a research tool like any print, oral/aural, or visual source.
- Understand the literacy demands of the assignment, especially as students access websites. Be aware of the vocabulary they may see, and monitor their

comprehension. A quick lesson on unfamiliar terms they will encounter before they go on-line can reduce students' anxiety and confusion.

- Formulate specific objectives for each Internet session. These should be conceived in terms of intended student learning rather than be merely a list of activities. Be aware that the length of the class period may affect what students can accomplish in each Internet session.
- Include a written component in each lesson, a product the student (or group) hands to the teacher at the end of the period or that becomes a part of the final outcome. This may be a progress report of what the student found on the Web, a record of e-mail sent, a completed worksheet, or a downloaded document. This embeds the Internet in normal classroom practice and helps students see tangible results of their electronic efforts.
- If possible, help students publicize their findings. They may post their research results to a newsgroup, continue their e-mail correspondence, offer critiques of websites, or develop a class home page. Student activities can also be described on the school's website, on display posters, or in public discussions.
- Ask the students to evaluate their Internet experience in class discussion by answering survey questions or by responding to a writing prompt that requires them to describe what they learned and discovered about the Internet as a resource. Use their comments to improve your next foray on the World Wide Web.

STUDY SKILLS AND CONTENT AREA READING

Earlier in this chapter I made a point that the study skills perspective was not sufficient for developing strategic subject area readers and learners, so I think it is important to address the rightful place of study skills in content learning. Certainly, there are definable reading/study skills—for example:

1. Understanding and using book parts (tables of contents, indexes, marginalia, glossaries, etc.)
2. Alphabetizing, using headnotes and pronunciation guides, understanding abbreviations in reference sources (dictionaries, encyclopedias, atlases, etc.)
3. Using other references (telephone directories, newspapers, on-line indexes, etc.)
4. Using the library (databases, Dewey decimal system, etc.)
5. Adjusting reading to purpose (skimming, scanning, intensive reading)
6. Reading graphs, charts, maps, globes, and other pictorial information
7. Notetaking
8. Finding main ideas; separating main ideas from important details
9. Outlining
10. Summarizing

What is important to understand is that instruction and guidance in these skills is least effective when it is isolated from the normal work of the subject area classroom—that is, when commercial worksheets and generic drill exercises replace "real-life" learning and application of study skills. To be effective, study skill instruction must be embedded in, or the outgrowth of, activities critical to students' acquisition of subject matter knowledge. Thus, they may be taught and reinforced when and as students need them in the course of making and evaluating their predictions about text, revising and refining study maps, turning maps into formal outlines, or identifying important ideas in text. Viewed this way, teaching study skills becomes a natural and useful part of all learning events.

SQ3R and *notetaking/underlining* are two instructional practices that have traditionally been used to develop students' study skills. I present them here because of their wide popularity; however, for each I raise questions regarding the usefulness of teaching the strategy to students.

SURVEY, QUESTION, READ, RECITE, REVIEW (SQ3R)

SQ3R (Robinson, 1946), if not the oldest study strategy around, is certainly one of the oldest, as well as one of the most frequently cited. SQ3R is intended to guide students before, during, and after reading. It is also meant to be used independently by students after they become adept at its use. The steps in this activity are as follows:

1. *Survey the text* by skimming the assignment, looking at headings and subheadings, and examining illustrations, charts, and so on.
2. *Ask Questions* about what you are to read by converting subheads to questions.
3. *Read the text* to answer the questions.
4. *Recite* by stating answers to the questions.
5. *Review* by going back over the information, filling in details in your answers, and recalling answers over time.

SQ3R contains provisions for guiding students through all stages of reading and meaning construction; however, we have little evidence that it is particularly useful (Caverly & Orlando, 1991). More importantly, my experience suggests that, however solid a technique it is, students don't like doing SQ3R independently. It's more than a little bit cumbersome and requires substantial instruction for students to understand; unfortunately, it does not stick with students very long, no matter how carefully it is taught. My experience is supported by Caverly and Orlando's review of the SQ3R literature (1991), in which they suggest that students will need to be made aware of "the effort required in using this strategy" (p. 149). I suggest either teacher-directed or informal use of SQ3R—that is, getting students into the habit of looking through what they're going to read before reading it, developing questions or predictions about what they think they'll be reading, and looking back and making sense of what they've read when finished. That is the goal of every instructional strategy we've discussed, not only in this chapter but throughout this text: teacher-guided practice at effective study reading that yields rich, full meaning construction. That is the ultimate "study skill."

SURVEY, QUESTION, PREDICT, READ, RESPOND, SUMMARIZE (SQP2RS)

MaryEllen Vogt (2000, 2002) suggests that the problem with SQ3R may lie in our expectation that students will use it independently rather than in the strategy itself. She developed SQP2RS, loosely based on SQ3R, as an instructional framework for teachers to use to teach content rather than something we teach students how to do and then expect students to do it independently. SQP2RS incorporates aspects of DR-TA, ReQuest, TPRC, and other similar instructional strategies. It requires the teacher to guide students through each step.

Survey. The teacher leads students through whatever text is to be read, perhaps initially thinking aloud so students can see how one samples text to get the gist of what it is about.

Question. Students with teacher guidance suggest questions that they expect to be answered by the text. Instructions can be, "Write two or three questions that you can't answer now that you think you'll be able to answer after you read" (Vogt, 2000).

Predict. Building on the questions previously generated, have students predict two or three things they believe they'll learn reading this text.

Read. Students may read independently, in pairs, or in small groups. Or the teacher may read the text to students. Generally, long chapters or articles should be chunked into several SQP2RS events.

Respond. Direct students' attention to the questions and predictions generated earlier and look to see which have been answered or met. Guide students as they decide which questions/predictions were not addressed by the reading and have students speculate as to why.

Summarize. Students can work collaboratively to create summaries of their choice—perhaps maps or annotations or other types of representations that allow them to elaborate their learning and serve as a record of the information learned.

The first time you use SQR2RS, it is good to demonstrate each step using a think-aloud technique that allows students to see how to do it. In her study of this strategy with ninth-grade students (2002), Vogt found that SQR2RS appears to be effective in teaching students cognitive and metacognitve strategies for learning. After experience using this strategy, students come to view themselves as strategic readers and learners who have at their disposal a variety of strategies for comprehending expository text. She also notes that she always uses VSS after SQP2RS but that she didn't put it in the strategy name "because then it would be SQP2RSV2S and that is just over the top" (personal communication). I agree with her on both counts: VSS works wonderfully well with SQP2RS, and SQP2RSV2S is definitely over the top. Do combine these two instructional strategies.

UNDERLINING AND NOTETAKING

Underlining (or highlighting) and *taking notes* while reading are two independent study skills that nearly every student is expected to use at one time or another, especially in college and beyond. Caverly and Orlando (1991) identify underlining as having "grown in popularity to become one of the most ubiquitous strategies used in postsecondary schools" (p. 107).

The most striking statement we can make about underlining and notetaking from text is that those students who underline or take notes spontaneously (generally average readers and above) tend to do it well: Their underlining and notes capture ideas central to the major points of the text and eliminate the least-significant details. Students taught or induced to underline or take notes (generally low-average readers and below) do not do it well: Their underlining and notes are random, with little differentiation between important ideas and insignificant details (Brown, 1985; Caverly & Orlando, 1991). In their summary of 31 studies on underlining and 30 studies on notetaking from text Caverly and Orlando conclude that attempts to teach underlining and notetaking, especially to students who are having difficulty with the text, are not likely to be effective.

Barbara Boyd (2003) uses a technique for teaching students how to underline text effectively by duplicating copies of the text pages. She begins by modeling underlining of part of the text using an overhead projector. She then divides students into groups and has them read a specified number of paragraphs (she used nine paragraphs); she asks each group to choose *one sentence per paragraph* to underline or highlight as the most important sentence. Next she allows them to go back and choose five additional sentences across the nine paragraphs to underline that each group feels to be pertinent to the topic of the text. After all of this is done, the teacher reads the full passage aloud with the groups choral reading with her only those sentences their group chose. The teacher then points out the loudest sentences (in other words, the sentences chosen by most groups), debriefs the groups on their reasons for choosing the sentences, and leads a discussion for final selection of the most important sentences to underline.

Important also is to spend class time engaging students in the complex, elaborative activities recommended in this chapter, and throughout this text, and to use those as a springboard for teaching notetaking and underlining. Thus, students develop ways to organize information that will ultimately result in a variety of effective study practices. Using maps to represent important ideas in text, with provision for map sharing and reconstructing, provides a foundation for outlining, notetaking, and underlining skills. Adding VSS words to maps "where they make sense" teaches students how to link concept labels with supporting information. Maps produced from K-W-L and PLAN lessons, as well as REAP and iREAP annotations, illustrate alternative ways to identify main ideas and summarize supporting details. As students become sophisticated in using these strategies, they are more fully prepared to benefit from demonstrations of effective underlining and notetaking practices.

CONCLUDING THOUGHTS ABOUT READING ACROSS THE CURRICULUM

If I were to identify the single most voiced complaint about middle school and secondary students, it is undoubtedly, "The kids can't read and write." You'll hear it often. You may even be tempted to say it. I hope, instead, that you'll say what needs to be said: *"The kids can't read and write in my classroom if I do not support their literacy progress* [in English, math, physical education, etc.] *and provide for its growth."* That's a pretty weighty statement, but it is true—in each and every subject area. If teachers are to support students' literacy progress and provide for its growth, they need to use the kind of instructional approaches we've discussed in this and other chapters, to teach content. Just remember how much more you know about your subject than students do: You only have to *activate* your schemata; students are *constructing* theirs. You are *remembering* and *recalling* formulas, principles, ideas, and concepts; students are *learning* them. Now consider the extraordinary increase in difficulty we add if we attach "as they are learning English" to what students are required to do. Teachers therefore need to center their classrooms around *real* learning and literacy, building on students' strengths and creating flow conditions in classrooms that leads to engagement, in-depth learning, and integration of knowledge and information. Csikszentmihalyi's powerful notion of "flow" alludes to classroom interactions that are full, rich, and meaning-laden; it suggests exchanging ideas in an environment of diversity and open inquiry by involved, active learners. It sounds complex, exciting, demanding, and rewarding. I can't think of any better way to conduct school.

WHAT THIS CHAPTER MEANS TO YOU

1. Antowan Reid does indeed have a winner: lesson and unit plans that build on students' prior knowledge and previous experience, engage them in meaningful learning tasks, allow multiple and varied responses to these tasks, and require students to use new information meaningfully by creating something new.

2. In order for students to be able to read and think deeply about subject matter knowledge, they must become engaged with the subject matter and perceive themselves capable of completing classroom tasks successfully. Teachers can encourage both by creating conditions of flow in classrooms, using instructional approaches that build on students' strengths, and teaching students how to become increasingly able learners in their subject area.

3. Whether by traditional means or by using the Internet, the degree to which we engage students in rich learning events that guide their ability to (a) organize information before, while, and after reading, (b) articulate new learning, (c) learn new vocabulary that labels important concepts and relationships, and (d) create something new is the degree to which we teach students how to study and learn in each subject area—the true study skills.

DOUBLE ENTRY JOURNAL

Go back to your pre-reading DEJ notes about a time in your learning when you experienced flow. Now that you've read this chapter, what elements of that learning event can you capture in your own teaching? How can you craft lessons and units in your class so that you 1) teach your subject content, 2) guide students' reading of that content, and 3) create conditions of flow? Use these ideas to develop lesson and unit plans for your teaching.

FEATURE *What Goes in My Portfolio?*

Create an artifact for your portfolio that provides a plan of action you will use in your classroom that increases flow conditions, increases student learning in your subject area, and develops students' study skills in your subject area. You may wish to include lesson/unit plans in your action plan and consider the role of technology in your plan. Explain how your plan of action accomplishes these goals.

RECOMMENDED SOURCES

*Beck, I. L., McKeown, M. G., Hamilton, R. L., & Kucan, L. (1997). *Questioning the author: An approach for enhancing student engagement with text.* Newark, DE: International Reading Association.

*Bleich, D. (1978). *Subjective criticism.* Baltimore, MD: Johns Hopkins University Press.

*Boyd, B. (2003, April). *Issues in teaching content area literacy to high school teachers:Social sciences.* Presentation at the Issues in Secondary Reading Regional Reading Faculty Meeting, CSU Center for the Advancement of Reading, Sacramento, California.

*Bransford, J. D. (1985). Schema activation and schema acquisition: Comments on Richard C. Anderson's remarks. In H. Singer & R. B. Ruddell (Eds.), *Theoretical models and processes of reading* (3rd ed., pp. 385–397). Newark, DE: International Reading Association.

Brown, A. (1985). Metacognition: The development of selective attention strategies for learning from texts. In H. Singer & R. B. Ruddell (Eds.), *Theoretical models and processes of reading* (3rd ed., pp. 501–526). Newark, DE: International Reading Association.

*Burke, J. (2004). *School smarts: The 4 C's of academic success.* Portsmouth, NH: Heinemann.

*Carr, E., & Ogle, D. (1987). K-W-L Plus: A strategy for comprehension and summarization. *Journal of Reading, 30,* 626–631.

*Caverly, D. C., Mandeville, T. F., & Nicholson, S. A. (1995). PLAN: A study-reading strategy for informational text. *Journal of Reading, 39*(3), 190–199.

*Caverly, D. C., & Orlando, V. P. (1991). Textbook study strategies. In R. Flippo & D. C. Caverly (Eds.), *Teaching reading & study strategies at the college level* (pp. 86–165). Newark, DE: International Reading Association.

*Csikszentmihalyi, M. (1997). *Finding flow: The psychology of engagement with everyday life.* New York: Basic Books.

Davidson, J. L. (1982). The group mapping activity for instruction in reading and thinking. *Journal of Reading, 26,* 52–56.

Davis, C. (1995). The I-search paper goes global: Using the Internet as a research tool. *English Journal, 84*(6), 27–33.

Dewey, J. (1910). *How we think.* Boston: Heath.

*Dodge, B. (1997). *Some thoughts about WebQuests* [On-line]. Available:http://edweb.sdsu.edu/courses/edtec596/about_webquests.html

*Eanet, M. G., & Manzo, A. V. (1976). REAP—a strategy for improving reading/writing study skills. *Journal of Reading, 19,* 647–652.

*Eeds, M., & Wells, D. (1989). Grand conversations: An exploration of meaning construction in literature study groups. *Research in the Teaching of English, 23,* 4–29.

Golden, J. M. (1986). Reader–text interaction. *Theory into Practice, 25,* 92–96.

*Goodlad, J. I. (1984). *A place called school.* New York: McGraw-Hill.

*Guthrie, J. T., & Wigfield, A. (2000). Engagement and motivation in reading. In M. L. Kamil, P. B. Mosenthal, & R. Barr (Eds.), *Handbook of reading research,* volume III (pp. 406–424). Mahwah, NJ: Erlbaum.

*Haggard, M. R. (1985). An interactive strategies approach to content reading. *Journal of Reading, 29,* 204–210.

*Haggard, M. R. (1989). Instructional strategies for developing student interest in content area subjects. In D. Lapp, J. Flood, & N. Farnan (Eds.), *Content area reading/learning: Instructional strategies* (pp. 70–80). Englewood Cliffs, NJ: Prentice-Hall.

*Herber, H. L. (1970). *Teaching reading in content areas.* Englewood Cliffs, NJ: Prentice-Hall.

*Herber, H. L. (1978). *Teaching reading in content areas* (2nd ed.). Englewood Cliffs, NJ: Prentice-Hall.

*Langer, J. (1982). Facilitating text processing: The elaboration of prior knowledge. In J. A. Langer & M. T. Smith-Burke (Eds.), *Reader meets author/bridging the gap: A psycholinguistic and sociolinguistic perspective* (pp. 149–162). Newark, DE: International Reading Association.

*Manzo, A. V., Manzo, U., & Albee, J. J. (2002). iREAP: Improving reading, writing, and thinking in the wired classroom. *Journal of Adolescent and Adult Literacy, 46*(1), 42–47.

Newmann, F. M. (1991). Linking restructuring to authentic student achievement. *Phi Delta Kappan, 72,* 458–463.

*Cited in text.

*O'Flahavan, J. (1989). *An exploration of the effects of participant structure upon literacy development in reading group discussion.* Doctoral dissertation, University of Illinois-Champaign.

*Ogle, D. (1986). K-W-L: A teaching model that develops active reading of expository text. *The Reading Teacher, 39*, 564–570.

Probst, R. (1989). Teaching the reading of literature. In D. Lapp, J. Flood, & N. Farnan (Eds.), *Content area reading and learning: Instructional strategies* (pp. 179–186). Englewood Cliffs, NJ: Prentice-Hall.

*Rekrut, M. D. (1999). Using the Internet in classroom instruction: A primer for teachers. *Journal of Adolescent and Adult Literacy, 42*(7), 546–557.

*Robinson, F. P. (1946). *Effective study* (2nd ed.). New York: Harper & Row.

*Ruddell, M. R.-H. (1990, December). *The year of silence: An analysis of high achieving readers' non-participation in a reading response group.* Paper presented at the annual meeting of the National Reading Conference, Miami Beach, FL.

*Ruddell, M. R.-H. (1992). Integrated content and long-term vocabulary learning with the Vocabulary Self-Collection Strategy. In E. K. Dishner, T. W. Bean, J. E. Readence, & D. W. Moore (Eds.), *Reading in the content areas* (3rd ed., pp. 190–196). Dubuque, IA: Kendall/Hunt.

Shanahan, C., Shanahan T., & Misischia, C. (2006, November) *Frameworks for literacy in three disciplines.* Paper presented at the annual meeting of the National Reading Conference, Los Angeles, CA.

*Shearer, B. A., & Ruddell, M. R. (In press). Engaging students' interest and participation in learning. In D. Lapp, J. Flood, & N. Farnan (Eds.), *Content area reading and learning* (3rd ed.). Mahwah, NJ: Erlbaum.

*Siegert, R. (2003, April). *Issues in teaching content area literacy to high school students: English.* Presented at the Issues in Secondary Reading Regional Reading Faculty Meeting of the CSU Center for the Advancement of Reading, Sacramento, California.

Silva, P. U., Meagher, M. E., Valenzuela, M., & Crenshaw, S. W. (1996). E-mail: Real-life classroom experiences with foreign languages. *Learning and Leading with Technology, 23*(5), 10–12.

*Singer, H. (1985). A century of landmarks in reading research. In H. Singer & R. B. Ruddell (Eds.), *Theoretical models and processes of reading* (3rd ed., pp. 8–20). Newark, DE: International Reading Association.

*Smith, M., & Wilhelm, J. (2002). *Reading don't fix no Chevys: Literacy in the lives of young men.* Portsmouth, NH: Heinemann.

*Smith, M., & Wilhelm, J. (2005). Boys and reading: It's more complicated than you think. *California Reader, 38*(4), 5–11.

Stauffer, R. G. (1969). *Directing reading maturity as a cognitive process.* New York: Harper & Row.

*Tierney, R. J., Caplan, R., Ehri, L., Healy, M., & Hurdlow, M. (1989). Writing and reading working together. In A. H. Dyson (Ed.), *Collaboration through writing and reading: Exploring possibilities?* Urbana, IL: National Council of Teachers of English.

*Vogt, M. E. (2000). Content learning for students needing modifications: An issue of access. In M. McLaughlin and M. E. Vogt (Eds.), *Creativity and innovation in content area teaching* (pp. 329–351). Norwood, MA: Christopher-Gordon.

*Vogt, M. E. (2002, December). *Engaging students' metacognition during expository text reading with SQP2RS.* Paper presented at the annual meeting of the National Reading Conference, Miami, FL.

BUILDING TABLE

CHAPTER 7	TPRC, GMA, AND VSS	Web Quest	K-W-LPLUS	PLAN	THREE-LEVEL GUIDES
FOCUS ON	Content reading and discussion; information organization	Content reading and discussion; information organization	Content reading and discussion; information organization	Content reading and discussion; information organization	Content reading and discussion; information organization
GUIDES STUDENTS	Before, during, and after reading; before writing	Before, during, and after reading	Before, during, and after reading	Before, during, and after reading	Before, during, and after reading
USE TO PLAN	Lessons, units	Lessons, units	Lessons, units	Lessons, units	Lessons, units
MAY BE USED	Partnerships, collaborative groups	Collaborative Groups, Individuals	Whole class, collaborative groups, partnerships	Whole class, collaborative groups, partnerships	Collaborative groups
MAY BE COMBINED WITH (known strategies)	Reading Response Groups	TPRC, K-W-L, VSS, GMA	VSS, REAP, Reading Response Groups	Reading Response Groups	GMA, VSS, K-W-L Plus, REAP
MATERIALS PREPARATION	Light to moderate	Moderate to extensive	Moderate	Moderate	Extensive
OTHER PREPARATION	Moderate	Moderate to extensive	Light	Light	Moderate
OUTSIDE RESOURCES	Necessary	Online and Other, Necessary	Necessary	Necessary	Useful
HOW TO DO	Pages 251–253	Page 254	Page 258	Pages 259–260	Page 266

PReP	QtA	Reading Response Groups	REAP/iREAP
Content reading and concept learning	Content reading and discussion	Content reading and discussion	Content; information organization
Before reading	Before and during reading	Before, during, and after reading	After reading; during writing
Lessons	Lessons	Lessons, units	Lessons
Whole class, collaborative groups, partnerships	Whole class	Collaborative groups	Collaborative groups, partnerships
DRA, VSS, DIA	VSS, REAP	GMA, VSS, K-W-L Plus, REAP	DR-TA, DRA, GMA, DIA, TPRC
None	Light	Light to moderate	Light
Light	Light	Light	Light
Not needed	Not needed	Necessary	Useful
———	Pages 269–270	Pages 272–273	———

CHAPTER 8

WRITING ACROSS THE CURRICULUM

DOUBLE ENTRY JOURNAL

Consider your most recent observations of middle school, junior high, or senior high classes in your subject area. What amount and kind of writing were students doing? List what writing activities you observed. How do these recent observations compare with your own junior high/senior high school writing experiences in your subject area? How do they compare with your knowledge of how and what adolescents write outside of school today?

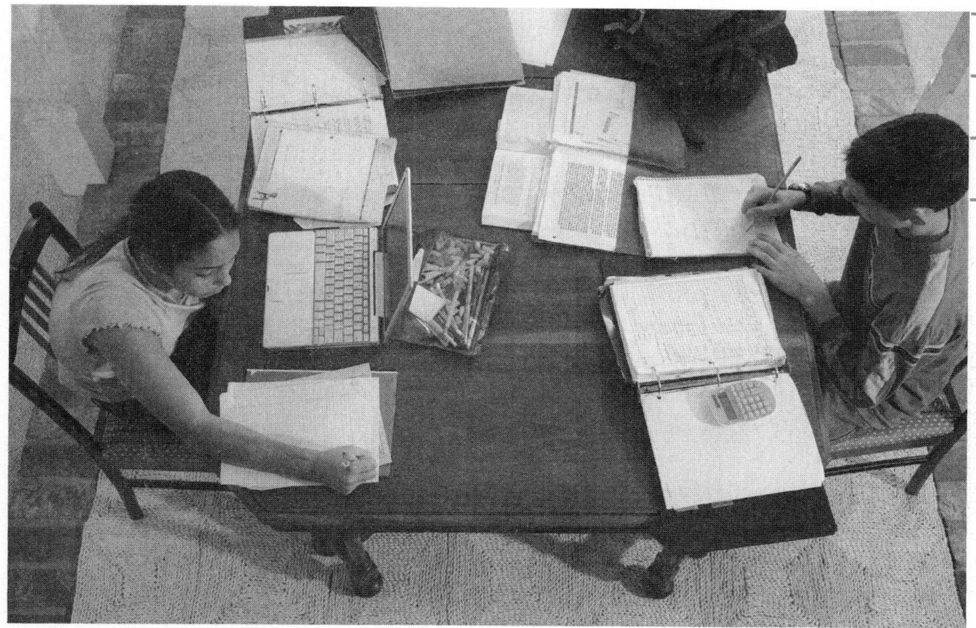

Hill Street Studios/Brand X Pictures/Jupiter Images

The Lafayette High School gymnasium is inordinately quiet during this part of fourth period. Scattered across the floor are students writing with real concentration in their journals. Nikki Tran, a sophomore, pauses a moment then writes rapidly, pauses again and writes. She's searching for just the right words to describe how she did in tennis skill practice and play today. She knows that it's important to capture each day's experience so that she'll have the information she'll need at the end of the tennis unit to write a formal analysis of her own developing tennis game and herself as a tennis player.

When Coach Williams announced that they would be keeping daily journals for each unit of the Lifetime Sports class *and* that at the end of each unit part of their grade would be based on the completeness of the journal along with the formal written analysis, Nikki had groaned along with the rest of the class. It sounded like such a drag, and it wasn't even P.E.! She'd never had to do this before. Surprisingly, though, she'd rather gotten to like it. It was nice to have some quiet time at the end of class, time to think about and reflect on what she'd done. Best of all she could feel herself becoming a pretty good tennis player—both singles and doubles—and she knew deep down inside that somehow the writing and reflection had contributed to her development. She wasn't sure how. What is really fun now, though, is to look back and reread her journal entries from early in the unit. Wow. What a difference! She has come a long way. Not only that, but she's learned the value of paying attention to her body and form during practice and play to see what feels right and what doesn't (oh there's nothing to compare with the feeling of a perfectly hit ball—the serve when the arc of her racket and the fall of the ball are timed just right, the return that she hits right on the racket's sweet spot). She makes mental notes during class so that she'll remember things she wants to write in her journal each day. She knows that the written analysis of herself as a tennis player will be much, much better than what she turned in for bowling. Her journal entries are longer and more detailed, she's paying more attention to her progress, and she knows that there's a connection of some sort between her analytical thinking during class, her journal writing, and her tennis game.

• • •

"Writing across the curriculum" is an often misunderstood catch-phrase in the world of literacy development and instruction. It is misunderstood because some people associate writing across the curriculum with five-paragraph essays, grammar and punctuation exercises, research papers, creative writing, and all the other aspects of writing instruction that have been or are now part of the English curriculum. Or they associate writing across the curriculum with the formal written reports we all trudged through in the middle level and high school years that were, in actuality, thinly veiled plagiaristic renderings of whatever resources we could find.

What, then, *is* writing across the curriculum? Very simply, it is the opportunity in *each and every class* for students to work through ideas in writing, to articulate their thinking by writing, and to polish and refine ideas in written form. Writing across the curriculum may indeed involve themes and essays, but just as likely it will be accomplished in jottings, quick writes, notes, and other ways of writing housed in learning logs, lab books, journals, laptops, notebooks, and all manner of other media that are vastly different from the written essays we all did in English classes.

Further, writing across the curriculum is concerned mainly with writing as a *process*—as a medium for learning—rather than with writing as a polished product. That is, the act of writing assumes greater importance here—when students jot down everything they know about a topic, list questions they have about an idea or an assigned reading, write about their reactions to an experiment or performance, or respond to a classmate's ideas in writing—than the actual writing that is produced. (In fact, the term *process writing* is frequently used to designate content and writing instruction with this focus.) Often, the product of that writing will be developed further into a polished piece; sometimes, it will not.

Our most recent national evaluation of writing (NCES, 2003) assessed 277,000 fourth-, eighth-, and twelfth-grade students and found that 84% of eighth-graders and 78% of twelfth-graders were at or above a basic writing level. For the eighth-grade sample, 58% scored at the basic level (partial mastery of proficient skills), 27% at the proficient level (solid academic performance), and 1% at an advanced level (superior performance). For twelfth grade, 57% scored at basic, 22% scored proficient, and 1% scored at advanced. Writers below basic level were 16% of the eighth-grade sample and 22% of the twelfth-grade sample. These results are slightly higher than the 1998 NAEP results for eighth grade, and about the same for twelfth grade. (However, serious questions are emerging about how writing assessment should be done in a world where word processing is commonplace and assessments are typically handwritten; more about this in Chapter 9). A significant finding of the 1998 study was that the highest-performing students reported that they were used to instruction that is typical of classrooms where process writing predominates—writing several drafts of their work, having teachers who talked to them about their writing, and using computers for part or all of their writing.

The value of process writing across the curriculum is thus twofold: (1) it stimulates the deep processing of information required by the act of writing itself and the very real phenomenon of people achieving insight and developing concepts as *writing progresses*, as opposed to merely writing down what they have already understood or perceived; and (2) it encourages writing growth and proficiency when students elect (or are assigned) to develop a piece of their writing beyond the first draft and possibly into a polished product.

CENTERPIECE LESSON PLAN

The Centerpiece Lesson Plan for writing is intended to be a culminating activity in which a formal piece of writing, collaboratively produced by small groups of students, will initiate the last half of a four-day lesson. The instructional strategy is titled Role/Audience/Format/Topic (RAFT) for its focus on guiding students' consideration of these four aspects of the writing process in their planning and development of a written analysis of a subject matter topic.

RAFT CENTERPIECE LESSON PLAN, *Biology*

Lesson: Structure of the Heart and How Blood Flows
Course/Grade: Biology, 10th-12th Grades
Materials:

- LCD Screen and Laptop
- PowerPoint slides of Figures 31.7 and 31.9 from textbook
- Students bring textbooks and maps created yesterday
- Large size chart paper for each group

LESSON OBJECTIVES (WITH CONTENT STANDARDS)

Upon completion of the lesson students will be able to

- Understand the circulatory system (Standard 9.a—students know how the complementary activity of major body systems provides cells with oxygen and nutrients, and removes toxic waste products such as carbon dioxide).
- Know the structure of the heart (Standard 9.a—above).
- Be able to trace blood through the pulmonary and coronary systems (Standard 9.a—above).
- Understand pulse, with introduction to blood pressure (Standard 9.a—above).

LESSON PROCEDURES

Students yesterday did a TPRC, GMA, VSS on pp. 718–721 of the text: Structure of the Heart and How Blood Flows.

Before Writing: Into

1. Using the LCD screen, laptop, and PP slide of Figure 31.7, ask students to describe the structure of the heart using the VSS words from yesterday: *atrium*, *ventricle*, *valves*, *pulmonary*.
2. Have students trace the routes of blood flow through the heart and body using slide of Figure 31.9.
3. With the help of the slide ask students where they can find/feel a pulse on their body. They should be able to identify a few places, including radial artery, femoral artery, carotid artery, dorsalis pedis, and anterior tibial. Have students attempt to find their own pulse in at least two places. Further define pulse and discuss relationship of pulse to pressures in the vascular system
4. Have students review their maps with partners to see that information from this discussion is reflected in each map. Assign students to groups.

5. Create a written statement having to do with these aspects of the circulatory system: the heart, blood flow, and pulse. *Say:* In your groups you will construct a group map that represents the information from our reading yesterday and our discussion today. You may use your individual maps to help create your group map. Do that now, please.

6. As groups work, circulate to assist. *Say:* Look carefully at the topics and subtopics on your map. Choose one that appeals to the group. Brainstorm in your group a number of questions that you have about that topic or subtopic.

7. As student work, write on board

   R—Role of the writer (Who are you?)
   A—Audience (To whom are you writing?)
   F—Format (What form will your writing take?)
   T—Topic (What are you writing about?)

8. *Say:* The writing you're going to do today should come from one or more of the questions you've asked. What are some of those questions? *Receive questions from groups. Say:* Good. Those questions will become your Topic. *Point to Topic on board and read, "What are you writing about?". Say:* Now you get to decide what Role you want to assume, *point*, what Audience you will write to, *point*, and what Format you will use. *Point, say:* Let's start with Role.

9. Write on the board

   <u>ROLE</u> <u>AUDIENCE</u> <u>FORMAT</u> <u>TOPIC</u>

10. Guide students through the process of selecting a role by having them brainstorm possible roles. List these on the board in the Role column. If students have trouble thinking of roles, provide some, e.g., a red blood cell making its way through the heart (or through the body), a ventricle receiving and passing blood through the heart, a heart valve opening and shutting, a pulse point as blood flows through, etc.

11. Have each group consider one or more roles they might assume. For each role have them answer the following questions:
    - What do we know about this role?
    - In order to assume this role, what will we need to know?
    - What are some sources of information we could explore to help us write from this perspective?

    After considering various roles, each group selects its Role.

12. Follow this general procedure for guiding groups in selecting their Audience and Format. Spend time with each group to make sure they are clear on their selections for each aspect of RAFT.

During Writing: Through

13. Allow groups time to do the exploratory work they need to do to clarify their perspectives and topics.

14. Provide time for groups to begin writing. *Say:* In your groups assign homework for each member so that your writing can be finished during class tomorrow. We will meet in the computer lab; bring any materials you'll need. You know how to e-mail homework texts to the lab computer for use in your finals drafts tomorrow. Turn in to me a sheet listing each person's homework assignment. *Circulate among groups to assist as assignments are made. Help groups clarify how homework assignments will move work forward.* Lesson to continue tomorrow.

LESSON ASSESSMENT(S)

15. Observational Assessment. During initial discussion, make sure students have stable concepts about the circulatory systems with emphasis on structure of the heart and blood circulation. During RAFT discussions, see that students have a clear understanding of the tasks and task processes.

16. Homework Assessment. Circulate among groups. Have each student display homework work; record completion for each student.

17. Other Assessment. Assign a group grade for each written statement and its presentation.

WRITING IN SUBJECT AREA CLASSROOMS

TRADITIONAL WRITING INSTRUCTION

Until very recently, almost everyone viewed writing in the secondary school as a sort of academic dance—a stylized task in which a teacher assigns "topics" that students "write about" and submit for the teacher to "grade." This notion of writing was focused almost exclusively on students' recording and documenting their learning rather than gaining insight or elaborating knowledge through the writing process itself. The point of writing from this traditional perspective was for students to "show what you know," even if they used others' words to do it.

Arthur Applebee captured such a view of secondary writing in his national *Study of Writing in the Secondary School* (1981), and what he found then remains true in many schools and classrooms today. As part of the study, Applebee, over a two-year period, periodically visited 15 students' classes unannounced to see what was going on when students were writing. He found the following:

1. A lot of writing went on outside English classes (about 60% of what he observed).

2. Almost half of all writing tasks required only that students write or respond to words or sentences; almost none (about 3%) required response to or development of full-bodied text beyond the word/sentence level.

3. On the average, only three minutes were devoted to thinking time for writing assignments (the time from the moment students realized writing was to happen to the moment they began to write).

4. Teachers typically abandoned students during the time when students were actually writing. The general practice was, as suggested earlier, that teachers assigned topics, students wrote (often outside the class), and teachers evaluated.

5. Most writing assignments asked students to demonstrate knowledge rather than encouraging them to speculate, question, or explore ideas.

6. Many writing assignments centered around what Applebee (1983) called "impossible topics": for example, "Describe the social, political, cultural, and religious changes Europe was going through at the Reformation."

7. Most assignments required students to give knowledge to someone who knew more about the topic than they *and who could therefore make sense out of nonsensical writing*. The entire exercise—the dance [my language]—consisted of students writing on topics they knew very little about in an attempt to demonstrate what it was they did know, followed by teachers using their greater experience and knowledge of the topic to construct meaning from students' less well constructed writing attempts.

NEW VIEWPOINTS ABOUT WRITING

Applebee's picture is a pretty discouraging one and, I think, a fairly accurate reflection of the writing experiences we all had in secondary school. Happily, the picture is changing, and this about-face in teachers' thinking is typified in Susan Mauney's teaching experience:

> I realized that reading science references and writing up reports was a very limited use of the written word in my classroom. I believed I had missed opportunities to use language—particularly writing—for years because I used writing primarily as an end-product exercise. We would do lab and write about it or conduct research and write about it. Writing was used at the end of an activity as a summative evaluation rather than as a tool for use during all stages of learning. I knew that writing things down helps me learn, but I had not given my students the most beneficial kinds of writing tasks. They had not had much opportunity to put their understandings about science into their own words. (Mauney, Lalik, & Glasson, 1995, p. 193)

What Mauney and others now recognize is that students need to write daily in all their classes and that writing includes all of the traditional types of notetaking and such, but also includes jotting down ideas, creating maps, doing quick writes, and a myriad of other writing forms and functions.

Jamie Myers and Richard Beach (2001) comment on the many changes wrought by the multimodal technologies available to authors today:

> Literacy instruction has recently been enabled and broadened enormously through the rapidly developing array of technological tools used to create hypermedia. Our representations of the world are viewed electronically as quickly as we move whole paragraphs to change the flow of words and position of graphics. Discussion groups and live chat rooms provide wide-open

> spaces for the negotiation of subjectivities and the construction of our possible identities. The image, the animation, video, and music spill in and out of our desktop computers contributing to the expanding intertext we create. (p. 539)

They and others note the impact of multimedia on adolescents' identities, the alternatives students have for representing ideas through combinations of media, and the ways in which available media have altered our ideas of what constitutes text and how it is created. Thus, today we talk of "authoring" hypertexts that are multimodal as acknowledgment that "writing" is too limited a description of how hypertexts are created. Myers and Beach recommend Storyspace™, found at www.eastgate.com, as a primary tool for constructing hypertexts. As teachers become more sophisticated users of all kinds of electronic media, classroom projects and daily authoring assignments using hypertext are becoming commonplace. In some schools it already has:

> One student teacher, as part of her social studies placement in a senior high school, required of her student groups that they create a business, develop a business plan, and create a technology production that advertises or tells about the business they created. She showed for us a PowerPoint presentation, created by a group of her students about their business—"PONG'S The Ultimate Gaming Experience!"—a nightclub for adolescents that was all about gaming; no alcohol allowed. The presentation was breathtaking—it held an audience of adults spellbound with its humor and movement and music and force. We all agreed that it had all of the pizzazz, professional appearance, and teen appeal for commercial use (given some necessary copyright permissions). Another teacher challenged her high school English students to create a PowerPoint presentation to teach each other the parts of speech; this they did with visuals, spinning letters, and lots of sound. (Ruddell, 2001, p. 8)

Clearly, the act of writing, composing, and authoring in classrooms is changing with breathtaking speed. Just as importantly, students' out-of-school literacy, and especially authoring, practices are changing with equally breathtaking speed. Consider the after-school life of an adolescent girl described by researcher Gloria Jacobs:

> A girl I'll call Lisa in on the telephone and is facing the computer, her back to the door, as I enter the room. The television is on; it's a game show of some sort. She turns slightly, smiles, and waves. . . . She then turns back to the computer, snugs the telephone receiver beneath her left ear, and begins typing. She appears to ignore me as I fumble about the room setting up my two cameras, although she does glance at me and giggle as I trip over a cord and nearly send a camera crashing to the floor. (Jacobs, 2004, p. 394).

The only things missing in this scene are the iPod with ibuds in ears and the cell phone standing ready for additional calls or IM and e-mail capability (and I suspect that the only reason they are not there is the pre-2004 date of this observation). Scenes of young people multitasking—e-mailing, IMing with multiple partners, watching TV, listening to music, and all the while cognizant of the immediate surroundings—are legion. Clearly, these adolescents are either in a state of flow or in a state of "continuous partial attention" in which their multitasking causes them to give only partial attention to everyone and everything (Friedman, 2006).

Whatever the case, the challenge for us in schools is to engage students in writing events, whether written, visual, aural, or a combination that results in deep consideration of subject matter concepts. The journaling that Nikki Tran is doing meets those criteria. William Zinsser, in his book *Writing to Learn* (1988), explains the "why" of writing across the curriculum; the point he makes about writing holds equally well for composing in new media:

> Writing is a tool that enables people in every discipline to wrestle with facts and ideas. It's a physical activity, unlike reading. Writing requires us to operate some kind of mechanism—pencil, pen, typewriter, word processor—for getting our thoughts on paper. It compels us by the repeated effort of language to go after those thoughts and to organize them and present them clearly. It forces us to keep asking, "Am I saying what I want to say?" Very often, the answer is "No." It's a useful piece of information. (p. 49)

WRITING PROCESS

A number of generally agreed upon descriptions of the writing process exist, most of which include the aspects of prewriting (rehearsal), drafting, revising, editing, publishing (sharing with others), and evaluating one's own writing. Virtually all current views of the writing process avoid descriptions of a series of "writing steps" that all writers proceed through to create written text. Rather, they recognize the fluid and interactive/transactive path of the writing process that writers traverse in creating new text. For ease of discussion, I've organized the following description of writing process into the categories of before writing, during writing, and after writing, even though the boundaries between the three categories are somewhat hazy.

BEFORE WRITING: PREWRITING

Prewriting is frequently the foundation for a variety of writing, reading, thinking, and learning events. It might best be described as mulling ideas over, whether immediately before beginning to draft a written piece or while simply thinking about what one knows about a given topic. Prewriting occurs in journals, logs, lists, diaries, e-mails, chat rooms, and maps, and in one's own head; it is comprised of jottings, speculations, predictions, forecasts, and other compilations of ideas. Consider how we began the TPRC in Chapter 7 by asking students to list "everything you know about the U.S. Constitution" and the topic brainstorming used in Carr and Ogle's "K-W-L Plus." That's prewriting; it is a listing of ideas at the beginning of a learning event that can ultimately lead to an elaborated writing experience later on. We extended the TPRC listing and transformed it into prediction by focusing attention on the topic for the WebQuest—viewpoints and perspectives of those who attended the Constitutional Convention—and asking students to mark anything on their list they believed would be in the reading. K-W-L Plus extends similarly by requiring students to list what they want to learn before reading. That's also prewriting. The predictive mapping and information-adding steps of PLAN are prewriting activities, as are the questions and predictions generated in SQP2RS. Every bit of this is prewriting with a purpose—the purpose being to activate prior knowledge and set the stage for learning and, in all likelihood, additional writing.

Prewriting activities are a major way for us to hear students' voices, to find out what students know and do not know about a given topic, and to learn about the different perspectives and content knowledge bases afforded by various cultural and experiential backgrounds. Clearly, this kind of activity need not be confined to preparation for reading and writing. It can, and should, be used to prepare students for discussion, film/video viewing, experimentation, action, and many other classroom events. What is important is that we keep firmly in mind that what we're doing here is using writing as a medium for learning (we are, indeed, engaging students in "writing across the curriculum activities") as *we teach content* and consider ways that we can extend this writing with activities that are authentically related to our discipline.

DURING WRITING: DRAFTING

Drafting extends prewriting as students create a new text from what they have read, seen, done, thought about, or examined. Nancy Spivey (1989) describes this process as one in which the reader constructs knowledge through interaction with the text or event; transforms that knowledge through organizing, selecting, and connecting ideas; and then constructs new meaning in a new written text. Sometimes this process is highly structured, as in formal laboratory reports or major research papers; other kinds of writing, such as biographies, reviews, and informal analyses are less structured.

There are many other authentic ways for students to engage in drafting substantive text in all academic disciplines. High on the list are student surveys and analyses of their own and others' ideas, actions, attitudes, knowledge, and beliefs in relationship to whatever topic is being studied. WebQuest activities are excellent drafting events as students create the variety of texts required for completion of the quest itself.

AFTER WRITING: REVISING, EDITING, PUBLISHING (SHARING), EVALUATING

Revising and Editing Revising and editing generally occur in ways idiosyncratic to each writer; many writers like to get as much as they can on paper as rapidly as possible without any revision, while others prefer to polish their writing sentence-by-sentence (sometimes word-by-word) as they go. Most process writing instruction encourages students to draft with as little revision as possible in order to get ideas on paper; however, writers who want to polish their writing as they go have a way of stubbornly refusing to write without revision. Even when they do revise as they write, some form of after-drafting revision and editing occurs. In addition, revision and editing involve many of the same cognitive and writing processes as drafting. The difference is that in the revision and editing process, students are truly transforming information and incorporating it into their own knowledge base. According to Spivey (1989), "They dismantle source texts and reconfigure content they generate from stored knowledge." *This is where students make knowledge their own*, and we increase substantially the probability they will do so when we give them many opportunities for their writing to be taken to the revision and editing level.

Recall again our TPRC lesson on the U.S. Constitution. We have already done some of the prewriting in the preparation for the WebQuest. Students did research constructed knowledge, and drafted some conclusions about their task. Student groups then used these constructions of individual knowledge to create the polished final product of the written statements, news reports, and PR brochures.

Such writing activity is appropriate for in-class writing, an overnight homework assignment, a full-blown research project, or some combination of the three. How it is used should be determined by student and curriculum needs. Most likely, you'll use the majority of assignments more in the course of daily work than you will as full-blown research projects. Keep in mind that your choice to extended students' writing through revision and editing does not mean that you will now have to grade 150 to 180 papers. Instead, the position statements may simply be recorded as completed and then used as the basis for a full-scale class debate. Grades may be assigned on the combined basis of completed papers, PowerPoint presentations, and contribution to the debate.

This brings us back to my original point: that writing-across-the-curriculum writing is not part of the traditional academic dance; it does not include teachers assigning topics, students writing essays to fit those topics, and teachers putting grades at the top and notes/corrections in the margins of the paper indicating how successful students were in achieving that fit. Writing across the curriculum becomes something students do for themselves and each other rather than simply for the teacher. Its focus, once again, is process—the opportunity for students literally to *write their way through* knowledge construction and articulation. This process benefits all students, particularly those learning and writing in a second language, and gives everyone advantages and assistance in learning content. More importantly, perhaps, is that writing evolves into a natural, integral part of learning and of the classroom environment itself.

Publishing (Sharing) and Evaluating In most classrooms, published writing takes the form of the final paper turned in to the teacher or a formal class presentation. In some cases, students share their writing/composing in small or large groups. The WebQuest proposal described above is a case in point. What is critical to the process is that students be given an opportunity to self-evaluate what they have written and the process they've experienced in arriving at the formal written document (or hypertext). This adds to their metacognitive awareness of themselves as both writers and learners of content.

Many instructional approaches guide students before, during, and after writing. We will begin by looking at instruction that does all three; then I present instruction that guides students before and during writing; and finally, I describe strategies that guide students before writing.

Instruction That Guides Students Before, During, and After Writing

Writing Workshop

The essential notion of the writing workshop is that in every classroom time is set aside, daily if possible, when everyone in the room is immersed in writing. This time is established and maintained consistently, so that students can depend on its daily (or alternating-day or three-times-a-week) occurrence. The purpose of the workshop is to give students frequent, regularly scheduled opportunities to write about the subject matter of that class and their relationship to it. Calkins states:

> The content of the writing workshop is the content of real life, for the workshop begins with what each student thinks, feels and experiences, and with *the human urge to articulate and understand experience* [emphasis mine]. The structure of the workshop is kept simple so that teachers and [students] are free from choreography and able to respond to the human surprises, to the small discoveries, to the moth as it pokes its antennae over the top of the desk. (1986, p. 8)

The point of the writing workshop is to write and to use writing as a means for making sense of the world; in subject area classrooms, the world we are talking about is the world of content disciplines: physics, government, art, physical education, trigonometry, family living, accounting, auto mechanics, and so forth. Thus, Nikki Tran writes every day in her physical education class for the purpose of analyzing her ongoing development as a tennis player (bowler, golfer, etc.); this is done to focus her thinking on how her mind and body function each day and how her progress goes. In the end, she creates a formal written analysis of her own physical development in that sport. Part of the point of the writing workshop is that we are not attempting to "motivate" students to write; we are *turning them into writers* in our subject area. There is a major difference between the two. The reason a regular schedule is so important, the reason everyone must be able to depend on the workshop regularity, stems from a wonderful tendency of the human mind. When students know that they will be writing at a certain time and place, their minds begin to collect ideas and rehearse, that is, prewrite (during class, out of school, in the middle of lectures and reading and experiments), gathering information, ideas, and ways of saying things to use during the writing time. This is an important event, for it means that students are thinking, analyzing, and *processing* content information—just as Nikki is; it also means that they are internalizing information and ideas that are part of the class. That, I believe, is precisely what we want them to do.

WRITING WORKSHOP APPLIED IN CONTENT CLASSROOMS

How, then, do we make writing workshop happen in a middle school or junior/senior high classroom and still have time to teach content? To begin with, *let us keep firmly in mind that we are teaching content in the writing workshop.* Perhaps a better way to say this is that students are learning content as they perform writing workshop activities. The writing activities that comprise writing workshop—prewriting, drafting, revising, editing, publishing, evaluating—are all directed toward enriching students' learning in the subject area.

I recommend setting aside 10 to 15 minutes at either the beginning of class or end of class daily for writing workshop. Both of those times are frequently used for routine tasks or are not particularly productive anyway—when the teacher is taking roll and doing other recordkeeping tasks at the beginning of the period, and when everyone is sitting books-in-arms ready to leave at the end of the period. Combine an already-lost five minutes with 10 more, and you have a solid 15-minute block of time for writing workshop. If you want to open class with writing workshop, the rule can be, "When the tardy bell rings, you are to be in your seat and writing." If you want to end class with writing workshop, the rule can be "Everyone writes until the dismissal bell rings."

THE STRUCTURE OF WRITING WORKSHOP

One way to structure writing workshop is to decide how you would like students to be thinking about your subject area—whether it is algebra, economics, drawing, French, choir, biology, or family living—and shape the writing workshop to encourage that thinking. Randy Bomer (1999) suggests "noticing" as a way to do this. Here is how I interpret Bomer:

- First, decide what you want students to *notice* in their daily lives—even at school—about your subject. Frankly, I cannot think of a more important question that teachers could ask themselves if they truly are interested in connecting their subject to students' lives: "What do I want my students to *notice* in their lives about algebra or economics or drawing or family living?" These questions guide students' observations and what they notice; students record their "noticings" during writing workshop and use them for further thinking and reflection. (Recall, Coach Williams wants students to *notice* what their bodies are doing as they progress in playing tennis.)
- Second, encourage students to begin asking questions about what they notice and record those questions and attendant responses in a journal or log. (As Nikki is doing.)
- And finally, have students then look for themes that connect their noticings and questions; these themes become the subject for drafting an exploration of the relationship of the subject area to students' lives. (Nikki's formal analysis of her tennis game and her progress as a tennis player.)

However you structure it, critical to the success of writing workshop is how the teacher interacts with students and perceives his or her role as students write. Remember, I said earlier that the writing we're talking about here is different from the traditional academic dance; the teacher doesn't simply assign, abandon, and grade. Instead, the teacher *guides.* He or she designs instruction that leads students toward independent thinking and writing, rather than assigns topics; consults with student writers and assists them in finding resources and thinking reflectively, rather than abandons; and gives feedback, response, and focusing direction, rather than merely affixes grades. All of this is done with the goal of enhancing students' understanding of class content and developing their ability to become independent, competent learners and writers in the subject area. When noticing, questioning, reflecting, and writing become the daily fare of subject area classes, students truly do become immersed in the subject and eager, confident learners.

TEACHING WRITING SKILLS IN WRITING WORKSHOP

On any number of occasions, you will want your students to develop their process writing into polished products (revising, editing, publishing). These pieces will be graded for their final content and form, and students will be expected to follow all the conventions of formal writing. It is important to understand, however, that you cannot expect formal writing instruction and learning processes and conventions that students learn in English classes to transfer automatically to your class. You are responsible for guiding that transfer by providing instruction and assistance in the kinds of writing appropriate to your subject area and your standards of quality (particularly for polished products).

To do this most effectively, you will need to teach, and the easiest way to do that is through writing workshop "mini-lessons" (Calkins, 1986, 1994). Mini-lessons are short, to-the-point instructional episodes in which one *something* is taught. For example, perhaps the major written product you want from your students is a formal essay comparing the work of any three Impressionist painters. You have noticed that students' learning logs reveal students' singular focus on differences in artists' work, with little if any attention to similarities. So, you conduct a mini-lesson on comparison versus contrast—nothing more. You deal with no other aspect of the assignment. The lesson is short (three to five minutes long). The examples you use come from language samples you've gathered from learning logs in this or other classes. You engage students in identifying themes that unite as well as separate artistic expression in the Impressionist movement.

Mini-lessons on library research procedures, report writing, grammar, editing strategies, and limitless other topics are useful in guiding students toward polished written products. An electronic method of giving students feedback (either from the teacher or a peer) as they revise and edit their writing is the **Comment** feature of Microsoft Word software, found in the **Insert** menu (in Windows, the **Comment** feature has a sticky-note icon next to it). The student sends the draft to the teacher (or peer editor) as an e-mail attachment; the teacher saves the attachment to a Word file, and while reading it on the monitor clicks on the **Comment** feature, which allows insertion of teacher comments and feedback in a comment pane at the bottom of the text. The point at which the insert was made will be highlighted. When finished reading, the teacher saves the document again (now with comments) and sends it back to the student as an e-mail attachment. The student saves the attachment and, when reading, moves the cursor to the highlighted areas, which will cause the teacher's comment to pop up in a bubble. The student responds to the comment and removes the highlighting by putting the cursor there and hitting **Delete.**

Creating Strategic Writers

A powerful way to get students thinking strategically about their writing is to have them think about their out-of-school digital literacies (IM, chat, gaming, etc.) and how these differ from school literacies (Lewis & Fabos, 2005). From a mini-lesson discussion about that you can engage them in metadiscussions about how strategies they use in out-of-school writing can be applied to school literacies. IM, for example, is generally an exchange in which adolescents rapidly change voice, style, and topic according to who is participating in the discussion; analysis of just this element of IM writing could lead students to consider audience and voice in their school writing.

In addition to written and electronic feedback, writing workshop teacher conferences with individuals or groups are frequently helpful. Calkins (1994, p. 222) lists a set of questions that are useful in developing students' writing. Even if you do not view yourself as a "writing teacher," you may find these questions valuable when you want to assist students in moving from their journals or learning logs into more formal writing in your class. These questions (or something like them) might even be written on poster board and displayed in the room so that students can see them daily.

QUESTIONS FOR GUIDING MY WRITING

1. What have I said so far? What am I trying to say?
2. How do I like it? What's good here that I can build on? What's not so good that I can fix?
3. How does it sound? How does it look?
4. What will my reader[s] think as they read this? What questions will they ask? What will they notice? Feel? Think?
5. What am I going to do next?

INSTRUCTION THAT GUIDES STUDENTS BEFORE AND DURING WRITING

ROLE/AUDIENCE/FORMAT/TOPIC (RAFT)

Carol Santa (1988) developed the Role/Audience/Format/Topic (RAFT) writing strategy to increase the quality of students' writing by personalizing the task and transforming students' perception of both the writing topic and writing event. From our Centerpiece Lesson Plan, you already know that the RAFT acronym stands for:

R—Role of the writer (Who are you?)

A—Audience for the writer (To whom are you writing?)

F—Format of the writing (What form will your writing take?)

T—Topic of the writing (What are you writing about?)

In the Centerpiece Lesson Plan I, used RAFT as the culminating activity in a biology lesson on the circulatory system. I chose RAFT for this lesson because study of the physiology of the body is so abstract. We never get to "see" blood circulate, travel through the chambers of the heart, oxygenate cells, or do any of the many wondrous things it does (yes, there are animations and simulations, but they're still not "real"). About all we ever get to see in the flesh is blood clot. So by making it personal, by having students assume the role of a blood cell (or a heart valve, or a ventricle or the aorta) and write an accurate account of blood cell behavior to an audience of their choice, the information becomes less abstract, and thus more memorable. And, in the process of that writing, students learn a great deal about the circulatory system as a whole, thus achieving the content objective.

Brenda Shearer (2000) notes that RAFT serves as an antidote to the "academic dance" we discussed earlier by virtue of its transfer of ownership to students. Shearer comments that when using RAFT, instead of writing as self, the student selects a role; instead of writing for the teacher, the student selects an audience; instead of writing an essay, report, or term paper, the student selects a format; and instead of writing on an assigned topic, the student selects a topic (p. 3). To do a RAFT, students (with teacher guidance) analyze a text or topic of study and decide the role they want to take, the audience they're writing for, the format their writing will take, and the specific topic for the writing. Below are a few of the myriad possibilities (Buehl, 1995):

Role	Audience	Format	Topic
Frontier woman	Self	Diary	Hardships in West
Constituent	U.S. senator	Letter	Gun control
Wheat thin	Other wheat thins	Travel guide	Journey through the digestive system
Plant	Sun	Thank-you note	Sun's role in plant's growth
Repeating decimal	Set of rational numbers	Petition	Prove you belong to this set
Julia Child	TV audience	Script	Wonders of eggs
Huck Finn	Jim	Letter	What I learned on the trip
Trout	Self	Diary	Effects of acid rain on lake

Shearer (2000) found, after using RAFT with many students in various grades, that although students *liked the idea* of RAFT writing, they were frequently frustrated by the ranges of choice they had to make, that is, "going from very little choice to too much choice" (p. 5). She solved this problem by developing ways to "model and map" each step of the decision-making process so that students could succeed. You saw those in our Centerpiece Lesson Plan.

STEP 1: SELECTING THE TOPIC

Students in teams create large maps on chart paper about a topic—for example, endangered species, government, trust, measurement, harmony, volleyball. Teams then select one of the subtopics created by the mapping as the focus of their topic selection and brainstorm and record questions having to do with that subtopic; teams repeat the questioning process with other subtopics to create a bank of possible topics to write about. At the end of this exercise, each team formulates a question that it will answer in its writing.

STEP 2: ASSUMING A ROLE

The teacher guides students through the process of identifying possible roles (repeating decimal, Huck Finn, etc.) by asking each team to brainstorm as many roles as they can for the question they asked. So, for example, if the question is, "How, why, where, and when do earthquakes occur?" possible roles are scientist/seismologist, the San Andreas Fault, a witness to an earthquake, a California resident living on a fault line (Shearer, 2000, p. 216). Then for each role, students ask and answer the following questions:

1. What do I know about this role?
2. In order to assume this role, what will I need to know?
3. What are some sources of information I could explore to do a good job of writing from this perspective?

To answer these questions, students generate modified K-W-L role maps with *Know*, *Need to Know*, *Sources*, and *Learned* at the top. After exploring and answering these questions, students then choose their roles.

STEP 3: SELECTING AN AUDIENCE

Selecting an audience follows the same pattern as selecting a role. Students use the questions they've generated and roles selected to brainstorm (again on chart paper) all the possible audiences for each role. When ideas are no longer forthcoming, students select an audience.

STEP 4: SELECTING A FORMAT

For students to select a format, they must be knowledgeable about the many discourse alternatives available to them. Shearer comments that "formats are more than structures, they represent different ways of looking at the world. . . . The format must not only be appropriate to the role, audience, and topic, it must also reflect the stance and the goals of the writer" (p. 219). So, students need to identify what they know about each format and learn what they need to know to adopt whatever one they pick. They do this by creating the same kind of modified K-W-L chart for formats that they did for audience and roles, and then by researching the one they select. And it is here, in this transformation to a consciously selected discourse form, that students are able to move away from the thinly disguised plagiarism that is so common to written reports.

STEP 5: ORGANIZING INFORMATION AND WRITING

The final step of RAFT is for students to bring together all the information they have gathered about their topic and format and organize it for the final written product. Here again, to be successful, they may need assistance in the form of teacher guidance. Their experience creating maps should be helpful in bringing together all of the resources and decisions they've made to do the RAFT writing.

You can see from the detail in the Centerpiece Lesson Plan and the amount of guidance teachers provide that RAFT is complex and more time intensive that other strategies in this text. One of the reasons it's worth taking the time to do is what I suggested earlier: RAFT makes highly abstract concepts personalized and more easily grasped. Another is that it reveals discourse forms to students that they'd not yet considered. Brenda Shearer states, "One of the problems contributing to plagiarism is that students lack the understanding of discourse forms necessary to transform information" (2000, p. 220). That is, students know of no other forms for writing about subject matter information other than the thinly veiled plagiaristic forms they've used since fourth grade. RAFT gives them new ways to think about writing, new perspectives, and new alternatives for creating text; thus, they are able to arrive at deeper understanding by transforming ideas into their own words and to incorporate new discourse forms into their writing repertoire.

How to do . . . .

RAFT

RAFT provides the opportunity for students to explore many different discourse forms and add them to their writing format alternatives. Like other strategies, RAFT gets less time-intensive as students gain experience and practice with it. RAFT fits quite well as a major activity of an instructional unit. Because it's so appealing to students, it is worth your time to try it. Use the following procedures to introduce RAFT.

1. Determine your unit and/or lesson objectives.
2. Identify topics for RAFT exploration that support your learning objectives.
3. Collect materials you will need for the various maps and charts students will create—chart paper, pens, and so forth.
4. Develop plans for the mapping and research needed to complete each of the steps in RAFT:
   - Selecting the topic.
   - Assuming a role.
   - Selecting an audience.
   - Selecting a format.
   - Organizing information and writing.
5. Establish assessment procedures.

LEARNING LOGS AND DOUBLE ENTRY JOURNALS

LEARNING LOGS

Learning logs—sometimes called *prediction logs*—are special kinds of journals that accompany students through units of study. They are the repository for students' observations, thinking, ideas, plans, accomplishments, procedures, and products during that unit. Teacher-written prompts are used to guide student writing before, during, and after the unit of study and are directed toward the cognitive tasks of focusing, gathering, remembering, organizing, predicting, elaborating, integrating, and evaluating (Thompson, 1990, p. 36). Frequently, the unit-opening prompt is an activity that you and I recognize as the beginning of a TPRC or a K-W-L Plus: "List everything you know about ____." Instead of students recording their list on a TPRC or K-W-L form, however, they record it in their spiral-bound learning log and have access to it throughout the unit of study as was the case in our Centerpiece Web Quest in Chapter 7. Learning logs thus offer the advantage of preserving students' thinking for later consideration.

Occasionally, teachers also use learning logs to deal with procedural issues in the classroom. Nancy Chard (1990) describes a situation in which a group activity was not progressing well: Students were not on task, groups were dysfunctional, and so on. Chard asked students to make two lists in their learning logs under the headings "What Is Working?" and "What Needs More Work?" These lists then served as a springboard for class discussion and decision making regarding continuation of the group project. The project continued.

Learning logs are business; they are filled with all manner of writing, most of which is prewriting or drafting, but all of which has something to do with the progress of the unit under study. Teacher-developed directions, or prompts, help students focus on important aspects of the unit and guide them in planning their participation in it. The key here for teachers is developing generative prompts. Below is an example of how learning log prompts guide students' prewriting and drafting in a social studies class.

LEARNING LOG SAMPLE WRITING PROMPTS *Social Studies*

WRITING PROMPT 1 (BEFORE READING/PREWRITING)
What do you believe the qualifications for voting should be? Why? How are your qualifications like/different from those we currently have? Share your qualifications with your group.

(Students read.)

WRITING PROMPT 2 (AFTER READING/DRAFTING)
Do a survey of the voting habits of your family and friends. Find out how often they vote, why they choose to vote or not, whether they know where their voting place is, and how they arrived at their attitudes, beliefs, and practices. As a "bonus question," ask if they can name their local, state, and national representatives. Write a summary of what you found and be prepared to share it with your group.

(Students share information in small groups.)

WRITING PROMPT 3 (AFTER GROUP DISCUSSION)
Why do you think states have the right to pass their own voter qualification laws? What issues might enter into state laws regulating voting qualifications? What do you think might be the hottest issue today? What are the voting laws in our state?

DOUBLE ENTRY JOURNALS (DEJ)

By now, you're experienced DEJ users, or, at the very least, you've had opportunity to see a number of prereading and postreading DEJ prompts. The DEJ (Berthoff, 1981; Vaughan, 1990) is yet another special kind of journal. In the DEJ, the left-hand page of a spiral notebook is for notes, drawings, observations, ideas, word clusters, and maps (prewriting) that precede a reading or learning event; the right-hand page is for what Vaughan calls "cooking" those ideas and observations after the reading or learning event (drafting a statement of some kind) (p. 69). Writing prompts for the right-hand (postreading) page writing are used with the clear intent of integrating and constructing new knowledge from the linkage between the information contained on the left-hand (prereading) page and the learning event.

Web-based DEJ exercises offer yet another twist. When situated in an e-forum, individual DEJ entries on the Web are public—available to everyone in the forum (limited to class members and the teacher)—and are the basis for class conversation in which ideas and responses are linked and extended through threaded discussions in which the Web page provides a visual record of how each response is linked to one(s) before it. Thus, students write *multiple* responses, in both the pre- and postreading conditions. Thus, also, the teacher may enter the discussion and participate or simply monitor the type and kind of conversation that is occurring.

The same kind of writing prompts illustrated in the section on learning logs are appropriate for use in DEJs (as are the kinds of prompts used throughout this text). DEJs may also be used to develop or reinforce procedural knowledge (that is, how to do a thing—e.g., use library resources), particularly when the class is starting new kinds of research, investigation, or learning. Below are writing prompts for use with DEJs in a music class.

DEJ SAMPLE WRITING PROMPTS
Music

WRITING PROMPT 1: PREREADING; LEFT-HAND PAGE (PREWRITING)

As you listen to the opera *Porgy and Bess*, write down feelings and associations the music and words create for you. Jot them down in any order and any way.

[After listening to the opera and recording feelings/associations, the class shares some of the associations, and then reads the prologue to *The Life and Times of Porgy and Bess* (Alpert, 1990) to learn about how this work was received by music critics and the public, both initially and through the years.]

WRITING PROMPT 2: POSTREADING; RIGHT-HAND PAGE (DRAFTING)

On the basis of what you've heard and felt when we listened to the opera and what you read about how it was received then and now, how would you answer Gershwin's critics?

How to do . . . .

LEARNING LOGS AND DEJS

1. Determine your instructional objectives.
2. Decide how learning logs or DEJ exercises contribute to your learning objectives.
3. Determine when and how you will use learning logs or DEJ writing in your class.
4. Write prompts for learning logs or DEJ entries.

INSTRUCTION THAT GUIDES STUDENTS BEFORE WRITING

BEGINNING RESEARCHERS

Donna Maxim (1990) describes a process she used to guide her students away from the traditional informational report writing mode (in which plagiarism, tracing, and tedium predominated) and teach them how to become real researchers. Maxim used this approach with young children, but it is every bit as useful with students of all ages who have settled into the habit of copying, or downloading, researched information directly from primary and secondary sources and then patching together a "report" that is, essentially, a plagiarized piece of work. Maxim developed her instructional approach in three phases: First, she taught students how to take notes and develop research ideas from listening; second, she developed their ability to read without notetaking and subsequently construct notes; and third, she taught students how to initiate and carry through a research plan by actually doing so. Because this strategy is so clearly directed at teaching students how to gather, synthesize, and record information while doing research, I've categorized it as a prewriting activity that could be one aspect of the writing workshop.

PHASE 1: TAKING NOTES AND DEVELOPING RESEARCH IDEAS FROM LISTENING The program begins by teaching students how to take notes without copying ("reading and writing at the same time," as Maxim calls it) through the simple expedient of teaching notetaking by reading to students rather than having them do the reading themselves. The teacher reads a book or book section to the class. The book may be nonfiction or fiction, but it should have sufficient informational content for notetaking to be relatively easy. After the reading, students are asked to record in their logs (1) facts and information they recall from the reading, followed by (2) questions and speculations these facts and information generate. (A good idea the first time you use this might be to model the process in a whole-class discussion using chart paper to recall facts and write questions so that students can see how the notetaking is done.) After each listening–notetaking experience, students share their individual notes and questions with the class, and the teacher leads discussion in which students speculate as to what research projects might grow out of the information and questions they've collected.

Any number of books, journals, or magazines are appropriate for this exercise. You may find that nonfiction informational pieces are particularly good for initiating notetaking, such as those found in magazines or journals you subscribe to for your classes or such weekly or monthly popular magazines as *Newsweek*, *Time*, or *Sports Illustrated.* Other resources are topical journals such as *Smithsonian*, *Nature Conservancy*, or *National Geographic.* Don't limit the reading to nonfiction, however; any number of fiction books have social and/or scientific import and are highly useful for stimulating research projects. Scott O'Dell's *Island of the Blue Dolphins* (1960), Jean Craighead George's *Julie of the Wolves* (1972) and *My Side of the Mountain* (1959), Harper Lee's *To Kill a Mockingbird* (1960), James Clavell's *Shōgun* (1975), and Anna Quindlen's *One True Thing* (1994) are certainly all reasonable choices. Many, many other books are available. I suggest that you gather lots of books, magazines, journals, primary sources, and other materials related to the area of study you're targeting the research projects for and that you read daily from this pool and have students do the notetaking and question generation at the end of each reading.

PHASE 2: READING AND TAKING NOTES

After students become good at listening and taking notes, they're ready to learn reading and notetaking skills. You begin this phase by distributing informational magazines to the students (back issues of anything you've collected will do). Students are told not to open their magazine but to look at the cover and generate questions they think they'll find answers to on the inside. Questions are recorded in students' logs. Then, students are asked to leave their desks and their lists and pencils and go sit someplace else in the room to read their magazine for 10 minutes. At the end of 10 minutes, they *leave their magazine at the place where they were reading*, return to their desks, and write out any answers they found to their list of questions.

Maxim reports that her students found this exercise very difficult; they wanted to be able to look back at their reading and do the kind of copying–notetaking they'd become so used to. I'm sure you're likely to encounter some resistance to the activity as well, and I further predict that the older your students and the more entrenched their reference-copying habits are, the stronger the resistance will be. Stand firm here. It will take several repetitions of the exercise for students to realize that they can indeed take notes without copying. Keep the source material well within a range of reasonable difficulty (a good reason for using magazines) and repeat the activity frequently.

PHASE 3: INITIATING AND CARRYING OUT RESEARCH

It is useful for the class to be engaged in a unit of study concurrently with the exercises you use to teach and to have students practice notetaking from listening and reading. It is also important that the students see how their newly learned notetaking skills might be applied to a project in that unit of study. As many resources as possible should be made available that are appropriate within the context of the unit—PowerPoint presentations, speakers from educational organizations and governmental offices, the Internet, field trips, movie and television documentaries on videotape or DVD, parents and other individuals from the community, library resources both at school and in the community, and so forth.

In the course of this study, and as students become acquainted with various materials and resources, they should begin recording in their logs ideas and questions that they deem worthy of further investigation. Through large-class discussion and individual conferences, they will frame their research question, consider and list possible resources, and decide on their plan for the research itself. The students then launch their projects and carry them out.

Donna Maxim's approach to teaching students how to become researchers is I think, a particularly sound practice. Essentially, it provides guided, sheltered simulation of a productive research process for students to engage in concurrently with a unit of study for which they will subsequently do research. Implementing this approach is not difficult, but it does require advance planning and thought.

How to do . . . .

BEGINNING RESEARCH

Spending classroom time teaching students how to do research writing is a worthy use of time, it seems to me. Unless we do so, students will find it very difficult to move away from their ingrained habit of copying from resources (which we teachers have, for generations, ignored) and learn the important study skills of summary, synthesis, and transformation of information. However, students who are used to mapping without looking back at what they've read should be better able to make this transition. This instructional strategy fits perfectly with a unit of study that involves a major research project. Use the following procedures to teach beginning researchers:

1. Determine your unit objectives.
2. Collect the following materials:
   - Resources from which you can read passages to students for listening and notetaking.
   - Chart paper and pens for modeling notetaking at various stages.
   - Magazines/articles for reading and notetaking.
3. Read a passage to students and conduct a discussion of the notes that should be taken from that passage; record notes on the chart paper.
4. Read various other passages and have students take notes.
5. Distribute magazines to students and guide them as they
   - Look at the cover and generate questions.
   - Leave desks and their written questions to do the reading.
   - Return to desks without the magazines to write notes and answer questions generated.

6. Conduct discussion of the notes taken during this exercise. Repeat the exercise as needed.
7. Conduct discussion outlining the steps and requirements for the final research project.
8. Design assessment procedures.

WEB SITES AND E-MAIL

Many students routinely seek information at Web sites or through e-mail exchanges. Both of these activities represent important new kinds of prewriting and drafting and involve new standards for both writing and general behavior. Such writing often involves electronic classroom partnerships in which students write e-mail messages to students in other classrooms to find out about the lives of their counterparts across the nation or around the world. Sometimes this exchange includes practice writing and reading in another language (Silva, et al., 1996); sometimes it does not (McCarty, 1998). Web-based writing may be focused on students searching for information from teacher-prepared prompts (Rekrut, 1999), full-blown WebQuest activities, and/or free-form searches. Many students today spend considerable amounts of time gathering information on the Internet. What is important to discuss are the rules and responsibilities for Internet use for class-related tasks.

We all know by now that when using e-mail and Internet sites, such writing and information gathering raises new areas of concern and requires new standards of behavior (Marcus, 1998; Rekrut, 1999). Martha Rekrut notes that it is important for schools and teachers to address these concerns by setting clear standards for Internet use and having clearly stated, explicit prohibitions for student use of the Internet (pp. 551–552). She uses the following set of rules to remind students of the consequences of not abiding by school standards for Internet use:

The following abuses of telecommunications facilities may result in disciplinary action and/or loss of your telecommunicating privileges:

- Using outside private services (BBS or bulletin board systems, commercial services, etc.) that have not been approved by your teacher or principal for in-school use.
- Using school equipment to send messages/files that are mean, threatening, suggestive, obscene, belligerent, or violent.
- Transferring any objectionable material, as defined by current school and community standards.
- Flaming or showing disrespect for any other person.
- Using the equipment to violate any laws, including copyright laws.
- Using the equipment to plagiarize and otherwise use other people's work without their permission.
- Prying into other people's work.
- Keeping others from doing their work.
- Disrupting or downing a system.
- Stealing from others.
- Copying software for which you have not paid.

These statements will undoubtedly change as conditions of the Internet evolve, and you will just as undoubtedly grapple with issues of student use of electronic media and writing in your classroom.

WRITING FROM MAPS

Let us go back to the final exercise from our "Splendid Outcast" story in Chapter 4. After the students had entered the VSS words on their maps, the teacher gave the following directions:

T: Now I want you to go back to your map, and I want you—without talking to anybody and without looking at your story—to find something on your map that really speaks to you, and I want you to write about it in any way you choose. Find something on your map—an idea, a concept, whatever—that really speaks to you, that really capsulizes the story or makes it more meaningful to you or stands out, and simply write in any form you choose about that part of your map. I'm going to give you several minutes to begin your writing. (After several minutes.)

T: I'm going to ask you now to share your writing at your table with your group. Everyone understands that this is the first draft, the first time pencil hits paper. But I want you to read what you've written to the people at your table and then begin making plans for what you could do with this piece of writing—what you *will* do with this piece of writing for developing what it is you've started. Okay? Do that now, please.

(Students read responses to groups.)

(Heard during the group discussions:)

S1: I'll read mine first—it's very short. First of all, I'll tell you where I'm coming from. I see Rigel as [parallel] to many people in society . . . "reverence and hatred rival attention—the reverence we have for the unattainable . . ."

(Various students talking:)

S2: The thing that struck me was that it's not easy to be free.

S3: It's symbolism between Rigel and much of society in the way that a person or a group of people can be viewed in such different ways.

S4: That story gives you so much to think about.

T: [To one group] Begin planning what you will do with this piece.

Notice how this writing event grew naturally and logically from the other lesson activities. Students have already discussed many aspects of the story and its relationship to their own experience and prior knowledge, organized their thinking about the story with maps, and explored various words and concepts connected with the story during vocabulary discussion. Now they are extending all of this with their written response to the text.

EXTENDING SUBJECT KNOWLEDGE WITH WRITING FROM MAPS

This open-ended "ideas that speak to you" assignment is utterly appropriate for curriculum goals and writing in an English class. In your subject area, however, you may wish to focus student attention more directly. In Chapter 4 we asked students to "create a map or visual representation that will help you understand and remember how to do multi-step equations"; writing from those maps could follow from the instruction,

> Go back to your map and think about what you know about solving multi-step equations. Write instructions that will help someone else learn how to do multi-step equations.

In Chapter 5 students created a group map of what they'd learned in a sheltered lesson on forms of energy. Here is a sheltered writing assignment using those maps:

> With your group go back to your map. Decide what you think is most important about issues of renewable and nonrenewable energy. Write a paragraph that explains your group's position on these issues and give scientific information that supports your position. Be prepared to read and discuss your position in class.

ADVANTAGES OF WRITING FROM MAPS

Recall Spivey's (1989) notion that writers transform knowledge from reading (or other learning events) through the processes of organizing, selecting, and connecting ideas. Maps literally *are* each student's prewriting plan; they show what ideas the student selected as most meaningful, how these ideas are connected, and the supporting details for each. Through the process of transmediation (Siegel, 1995), students are able to "reconfigure" content—that is, construct new information, with mapping as the primary vehicle for organizing, selecting, and connecting information. Mapping therefore serves as a productive foundation for student writing to extend knowledge constructed from reading.

Strategic Writers

Mapping, by definition, is an organizational activity; it therefore precedes writing naturally by providing visual representation of students' constructions and organizations of knowledge from a learning event (reading or some other). Mapping thus initiates the prewriting process. Show students on the board how to transform ideas on a map into written text; let the class do this several times as a class activity. Then have them work with partners or individually to do it. Give your students many opportunities to *talk about* how they transform map elements into written text. This will give them much needed practice in the prewriting skills of selecting, organizing, and connecting ideas.

How to do . . . .

WRITING FROM MAPS

When you have students write from maps, keep in mind that the fullness of the mapping activity itself is critical to successful writing. Specifically, writing will be easier and more fluent when students have had sufficient time to develop their maps fully and share and discuss their maps with other students. Because much of the organizing, selecting, and connecting of ideas goes on during the mapping and sharing, student energy can subsequently be directed toward the writing itself. The following steps are useful for implementing writing from maps:

1. Identify instructional objectives.
2. Plan the lesson activity (reading, etc.) and follow-up group mapping activity.
3. Develop writing directions that lead students from important ideas on their maps to decisions, conclusions, or evaluations. Include attention to logic and rationale in the directions.
4. Develop procedures for partnership, small-group, or whole-class sharing of writing; include written responses, if possible.
5. Decide how writing will be used—for example, notes for class discussion, base for revision and further development, or idea for research paper focus.
6. Design appropriate assessments.

JOURNALS

Writing journals are beginning to be seen as standard operating equipment in all secondary classrooms. They've been around a long time in English classes and just recently have begun to find their way into mathematics, physical education (as in Nikki Tran's class), social studies, science, and other subject area classrooms. Journals are particularly useful in classrooms because they lend themselves well to regular, systematized writing times. Spiral-bound, 8 1/2″ by 11″ notebooks are the most commonly used journals, although electronic journals are rapidly gaining favor, and the threaded discussions that are possible on the Web allow journaling to be a class collective event.

EXTENDING SUBJECT KNOWLEDGE WITH JOURNAL WRITING

The purpose of journals in subject area classes is to allow students to keep a running account of their progress and knowledge in a class (Zinsser, 1988) and to explore ideas and issues in relationship to what they know and what they are learning. Usually, journal writing is content specific but open-ended: Students write about their reactions to ideas, grapple with new concepts or skills, ask questions, call for help, or pass judgment on ideas or class events. Other times, teachers focus students' writing with prompts or directions; this may take the form of asking students to describe the meaning of an algebraic sentence, for example (Zinsser, 1988, p. 157), or some other task.

It is important that journals be subject focused so that they perform the function for which they are intended. Everyone must understand that content area journals are not totally free-form; they are not diaries or chronicles of students' personal lives. Rather, they are a forum for students to express honestly their constructions of knowledge and attitudes in a subject area, to ask questions, and to state what they do and do not know. This requires that journal writing become a regular part of classroom routine and, if possible, a daily procedure. If journal writing opportunities are infrequent, students rarely get past their initial tendency to cover their feelings of inadequacy and/or mask honest responses and cannot develop the fluency of expression that allows them to explore areas that baffle or frustrate them. Several authors recommend a "letter to the teacher" format to give focus to student writing about their current progress in class. Whatever the format, journals are universally considered to be "private talk" between teacher and students; any sharing or public revelation of journal content must be done only with the express consent of both.

Journals offer two major advantages to students in learning content. First, they constitute a written record of students' ideas and steps in learning. As such, they allow students to return to their ideas, concerns, insights, and so forth, so that elaboration of barely formed ideas may occur after a time of reflection or as the result of other new learning. Second, because initial ideas and jottings are kept intact in the bound journal (and are not lost in the jumble of notebooks and lockers), they remain available to be mined by the students at a later date when major projects or extended elaborations of class content are to be drafted, revised, edited, and published.

RESPONDING TO JOURNAL WRITING

Generally, teachers collect, read, and respond to journals on a regular basis. Most teachers do not grade the journals per se but rather respond and react to student entries. If grading does occur, it is usually associated with whether the journal writing has been done.

I recall that when I had freshman, sophomore, and junior English class journals to read, I very quickly became overwhelmed by the sheer volume of students' writing and the amount of time it took to read and respond to each entry. I learned I couldn't read and respond to *everything* students wrote. I learned I didn't want 120 journals at the same time (I couldn't even carry them to the car!) because it made the job of responding seem so much more overwhelming. So I set staggered due dates for journals by class (two classes each Friday on alternating weeks) and asked students to designate one entry each week (total of two) for me to read and respond to. I could then spot-check other entries as time permitted but was, at the very least, responsible for reading and responding to the designated entries.

Another very reasonable way to monitor and respond to journal writing is to choose one day each week for the teacher to circulate through the class, stopping at each student's desk to see the pages of journaling the student did that week. The teacher uses a stamp or initial on each page to designate that these pages have been seen, and records a check or some other mark that each student has (or has not) done the requisite journal assignment for the week. This can be done reasonably quickly and while students are actually writing in their journals to a prompt the teacher has prepared. Then once a month or once each grade period, the teacher asks students to use sticky-note paper to identify three (or five or however many) journal entries that the student wants the teacher to read and respond to (teacher's choice as to whether these will be graded). The teacher collects the journals, reads specified entries, and write responses to those entries in each journal. Journals are returned to students the following class period. There are other alternatives and options for responding to journals that are equally useful; decisions about them are usually based on a combination of personal, pedagogical, and curricular variables in combination with a certain amount of trial-and-error adjustment.

JOURNALS IN SUBJECT AREA CLASSROOMS

Because journals are becoming much more common in middle and junior/senior high classes other than English, various alternatives for using journals are appearing in the literature and in classrooms themselves. A common pattern in mathematics seems to be that on arrival in the classroom, students get their journals from the teacher's desk and write for a designated time. Often, students use the journals to think though their experiences (problems and successes) in completing the homework from the night before. Other mathematics teachers use journals at the end of class for students to state in their own words what it was they learned that day, what questions they have, and what they felt they didn't understand. My physical education students report journals being used in a middle school physical education program for the same kind of reflection that Nikki Tran was doing on progress in physical education and health. Social studies and English teachers often use a "Quote of the Day" writing prompt as a way to open class. (One English class I observed called this daily writing period "jotters.") Famous quotes, current-day quotes, quotes from popular television shows, or others are used for students to think about in writing and share their responses for the purpose of connecting the quote both with their own experiences and with the current class topic.

With just a little thought and effort you should find it possible to include journal writing of some type in your classroom, whatever your subject area. Keep in mind that you are not limited to written prompts for student journaling; cartoons, pictures, music, art, and other media are perfectly good resources. Below are journaling prompts for a *Smithsonian* article (Daniloff, 1991) that might be part of a world history, English, or humanities course. The article is about Russian Decembrists forced into exile in Siberia and their wives who followed them.

Writing Prompts (After Reading) Choose one of the prompts below and write your response in your journal:

1. You are Maria Volkonskaya, wife of Decembrist Prince Sergei Volkonsky, ready to join your husband in exile in Siberia. Write a letter explaining why you will leave your infant son to make this 4,000-mile trip.
2. How do you think you would respond to the conditions of life in Siberia? Write a letter describing how the conditions of your exile affect you. What hope do you see?

How to do . . . .

JOURNAL WRITING

Structure is probably the most important element of successful journal writing ventures. I don't think it is an exaggeration to say that most unsuccessful ones have, in all likelihood, been lost for want of structure. It is not enough simply to decide to have your classes do journal writing. Planning must go considerably beyond that and include the following steps:

1. *Decide why you're doing journal writing and how it reflects instructional goals.* Consider carefully your reasons and have them ready to explain to students.

2. *Determine and state explicitly what the daily, weekly, and semester-long policies and procedures are for the journal writing.* Consider and make decisions about all of the following:
   - What effect, if any, will journal writing have on students' grades?
   - When is the best time to write—beginning or end of class?
   - How often shall we write?
   - Shall we simply write, or shall we use a letter-to-the-teacher format, or do I want to develop daily prompts?
   - What is a reasonable timeline and routine for reading and responding to students' journals?

3. *Develop and list expectations for student behavior.* Consider and make decisions about all of the following:
   - Where will I locate journals? Will students bring them, or will I store them? (Many teachers keep journals in their room if they don't have to change rooms. This eliminates many hassles.)
   - How will students get journals kept in the classroom? What is the consequence if students forget to bring their journals from their lockers?
   - What is the signal to start writing? What is the signal to stop?

4. *Develop and list expectations for teacher behavior.* Consider and make decisions about the following:
   - What will I be doing while students are writing?
   - Will I write and share my writing with students?
   - What will be the focus of my response to students' writing?
   - How much of each student's writing will I read and respond to?
   - What is my commitment for returning journals after I've collected them?

QUICK WRITES

Quick writes were described earlier in this text (Chapter 4) as short, open-ended writing opportunities in which students think through their own immediate learning process. They are essentially a tool for reflecting on one's own learning, and they fit into the category of before writing when quick writes are saved and used for the purpose of writing an extended piece about one's learning (not unlike what Nikki Tran is doing). Quick writes are most commonly, but not always, used at the end of the instructional period. Many teachers use quick wr ites in mid-lesson if they suspect that students are struggling. Sometimes, the questions that surface in Quick Writes create breakthrough moments. Certainly, quick writes are appropriate for use in any kind of journal; saving them in a journal also serves to keep them in the context of the lesson for later reference. Quick Writes are wonderfully easy to use and offer illuminating glimpses into students' thinking. Use them liberally.

A FEW FINAL WORDS ABOUT WRITING ACROSS THE CURRICULUM

In Chapter 2, I said that reading and writing are different sides of the same coin. Certainly, there are differences between them, but for the learner, both reading and writing yield constructions of knowledge that support learning. Very few people debate the importance of reading in a subject area as a potent means for learning, yet many people are skeptical about the potency of writing's influence on learning. I hope you no longer are. Your students will benefit enormously from the process writing they do in your class, and the extent to which you make writing a regular, daily part of classroom life is the extent to which you will increase that benefit.

Just as we want our students to be readers who learn more about calculus, world literature, economics, health and fitness, music, chemistry, and much more, from reading, so, too, do we want them to be writers who learn from writing. Joe Bob Briggs (1991), one of my favorite newspaper columnists, gives the quintessential advice for how one becomes a writer. His words resonate just as clearly for writing in subject areas:

> The way you become a writer is you write. Every day. No exceptions.
>
> Nobody believes this. Everybody wants to believe in something called "talent" or "inspiration" or "knack for it." Maybe there is such a thing, but it has nothing to do with becoming a writer. . . .
>
> Nobody can tell you how to write, but there are certain things you can do to get to a place where you can write. There are three of them:
>
> Write every day.
> Write every day.
> Write every day.
> This is all I know.

WHAT THIS CHAPTER MEANS TO YOU

1. Nikki Tran is arriving at some very important insights about her tennis game and herself as a tennis player as she writes in her learning log journal each day. The requirement to keep a journal and construct a formal analysis of her progress in tennis is making her analytical about tennis, able to synthesize the data she collects each day about her tennis playing, and ultimately increases her learning and skill in tennis. Writing and reflecting about one's own learning is equally powerful in all subjects; you want your students to do this.

2. Writing process is not confined to writing in English classes and formal writing. Instead it concerns how we go about articulating knowledge in any subject area. In today's world, composing in hypertext as well as written texts allows students to process knowledge multimodally. To the extent students are required and taught how to the use writing/composing process to construct knowledge in subject areas, they will become deep thinkers and accomplished learners in those subject areas.

3. The writing workshop, RAFT, and other instructional strategies and activities guide students before, during, and after writing. All of these strategies are applicable to your subject area.

DOUBLE ENTRY JOURNAL

Go back and reread your prereading DEJ response. What, if anything, would you do to increase the type and kind of writing adolescents are doing in classes in your subject area? What benefit would you expect to occur as a result of what you would do? How might this benefit extend to students' overall writing proficiency?

FEATURE *WHAT GOES IN MY PORTFOLIO?*

Develop a plan and rationale for incorporating significant writing activities in your classroom. Be sure to explain how your thinking so that parents, or even the principal or school board, will understand why students are doing so much writing in your class. Include in your explanation an answer to the question "How will this writing help my child perform better on achievement tests?"

RECOMMENDED SOURCES

*Alpert, H. (1990). *The life and times of Porgy and Bess.* New York: Alfred A. Knopf.

*Applebee, A. N. (1981). *A study of writing in the secondary school* (Research Report No. 21). Urbana, IL: National Council of Teachers of English.

*Applebee, A. (1983, March). *Writing in the secondary school.* Paper presented at the San Diego State University Conference, "New Directions in Comprehension Research," San Diego.

Atwell, N. (1990). *Coming to know: Writing to learn in the intermediate grades.* Portsmouth, NH: Heinemann.

Atwell, N. (1998). *In the middle: Writing, reading, and learning with adolescents* (2nd ed.). Upper Montclair, NJ: Boynton/Cook.

*Berthoff, A. E. (1981). *The making of meaning: Metaphors, models, and maxims for writing teachers.* Portsmouth, NH: Heinemann.

Blake, M. (1990). Learning logs in the upper elementary grades. In N. Atwell (Ed.), *Coming to know: Writing to learn in the intermediate grades* (pp. 53–60). Portsmouth, NH: Heinemann.

Bolter, J. D. (1998). Hypertext and the question of visual literacy. In D. Reinking, M. McKenna, L. Labbo, & R. Kieffer (Eds.), *Literacy and technology: Transformations I a post-typographic world* (pp. 3–14). Mahwah, NJ: Lawrence Erlbaum.

*Bomer, R. (1999). Writing to think critically: The seeds of social action. *Voices from the Middle, 6*(4), 2–8.

*Briggs, J. B. (1991, June 9). Writers do it daily. *This World*, p. 4.

*Buehl, D. (1995). *Classroom strategies for interactive learning, a monograph of the Wisconsin State Reading Association.* Schofield: Wisconsin State Reading Association.

*Calkins, L. M. (1986). *The art of teaching writing* (2nd ed.). Portsmouth, NH: Heinemann.

*Calkins, L. M. (1994). *The art of teaching writing* (3rd ed.). Portsmouth, NH: Heinemann.

Calkins, L. M., with S. Harwayne (1991). *Living between the lines.* Portsmouth, NH: Heinemann.

*Carr, E., & Ogle, D. (1987). K-W-L Plus: A strategy for comprehension and summarization. *Journal of Reading, 30*, 626–631.

*Chard, N. (1990). How learning logs change teaching. In N. Atwell (Ed.), *Coming to know: Writing to learn in intermediate grades* (pp. 61–68). Portsmouth, NH: Heinemann.

*Clavell, J. (1975). *Shōgun.* New York: Atheneum.

*Daniloff, R. (1991). How Czar Nicholas was outfoxed by the guardian angels. *Smithsonian, 22*(3), 102–113.

*Friedman, T. (July 6, 2006). In the rain forest, lesson of survival and disconnectedness. *The Press Democrat* (reprinted from the *New York Times*), p. B5.

Gee, J. P. (2000). Teenagers in new times: A literacy studies perspective. *Journal of Adolescent and Adult Literacy, 43*(5), 412–420.

Gee, J. P. (2002). Millennials and Bobos, *Blue's Clues* and *Sesame Street:* A story for our times. In D. E. Alvermann (Ed.), *Adolescents and literacies in a digital world* (pp. 51–67). New York: Peter Lang.

*George, J. C. (1959). *My side of the mountain.* New York: E. P. Dutton.

*George, J. C. (1972). *Julie of the Wolves.* New York: Harper & Row.

Graves, D. H. (1983). *Writing: Teachers and children at work.* Portsmouth, NH: Heinemann.

Hagood, M. C., Stevens, L. P., & Reinking, D. (2002). What do *They* have to teach *Us?* Talkin' 'cross generations. In D. E. Alvermann (Ed.), *Adolescents and literacies in a digital world* (pp. 68–83). New York: Peter Lang.

*Jacobs, G. E. (2004). Complicating contexts: Issues of methodology in researching the language and literacies of instant messaging. *Reading Research Quarterly, 39*(4), 394–406.

*Lee, H. (1960). *To kill a mockingbird.* New York: Lippincott.

*Lewis, C., & Fabos, B. (2005). Instant messaging, literacies, and social identities. *Reading Research Quarterly, 40*(4), 470–501.

*Marcus, S. (1998). Avoiding road kill on the information highway. In J. A. Braun, P. Fernlund, & C. S. White (Eds.), *Technology tools in the social studies curriculum* (pp. 362–366). Wilsonville, OR: Franklin, Beedle & Associates.

*Mauney, S. W., Lalik, R. V., & Glasson, G. E. (1995). Looking forward: A science teacher incorporates whole language. In G. Pace (Ed.), *Whole learning in the middle school: Evolution and transition* (pp. 183–203). Norwood, MA: Christopher-Gordon.

*Cited in Text.

*Maxim, D. (1990). Beginning researchers. In N. Atwell (Ed.), *Coming to know: Writing to learn in intermediate grades* (pp. 3–16). Portsmouth, NH: Heinemann.

*McCarty, P. J. (1998). Four days that changed the world and other amazing Internet stories. In J. A. Braun, P. Fernlund, & C. S. White (Eds.), *Technology tools in the social studies curriculum* (pp. 376–380). Wilsonville, OR: Franklin, Beedle & Associates.

*Myers, J., & Beach, R. (2001). Hypermedia authoring as critical literacy. *Journal of Adolescent and Adult Literacy, 44*(6), 538–546.

National Center for Educational Statistics (NCES). (2003). http://nces.ed.gov/

*O'Dell, S. (1974). *Island of the blue dolphins.* Boston: G. K. Hall.

Pace, G. (1995). *Whole learning in the middle school: Evolution and transition.* Norwood, MA: Christopher-Gordon.

*Quindlen, A. (1994). *One true thing.* New York: Random House.

*Rekrut, M. D. (1999). Using the Internet in classroom instruction: A primer for teachers. *Journal of Adolescent & Adult Literacy, 42*(7), 546–557.

*Ruddell, M. R. (2001). *Second year evaluation report: New Orleans consortium for technology innovation and implementation in teacher education (NOC-TIITE).* Unpublished manuscript, Loyola University, New Orleans; University of New Orleans.

*Santa, C. (1988). *Content reading including study systems.* Dubuque, IA: Kendall/Hunt.

*Shearer, B. A. (2000). Student-directed written inquiry: Transferring ownership to our students. In M. McLaughlin & M. E. Vogt (Eds.), *Creativity and Innovation in Content Area Reading* (pp. 209–229). Norwood, MA: Christopher-Gordon.

*Siegel, M. (1995). More than words: The generative power of transmediation in learning. *Canadian Journal of Education, 20*(4), 455–475.

*Silva, P. U., Meagher, M. E., Valenzuela, M., & Crenshaw, S. W. (1996). E-mail: Real-life classroom experiences for foreign languages. *Learning and Leading with Technology, 23*(5), 10–12.

*Spivey, N. N. (1989, November). *Composing from sources: Text and task.* Paper presented at the annual meeting of the National Reading Conference, Austin, TX.

*Thompson, A. (1990). Thinking and writing in learning logs. In N. Atwell (Ed.), *Coming to know: Writing to learn in the intermediate grades* (pp. 35–51). Portsmouth, NH: Heinemann.

*Vaughan, C. L. (1990). Knitting writing: The Double-Entry Journal. In N. Atwell (Ed.), *Coming to know: Writing to learn in the intermediate grades* (pp. 69–75). Portsmouth, NH: Heinemann.

*Zinsser, W. (1988). *Writing to learn.* New York: Harper & Row.

Building Table

CHAPTER 8	RAFT	LEARNING LOGS, DEJ	BEGINNING RESEARCH	WRITING FROM MAPPING	JOURNALS
FOCUS ON	Content information organization and articulation	Content information organization and articulation	Content information research	Content information organization and articulation	Content information organization and articulation
GUIDES STUDENTS	Before, during, and after writing	Before, during, and after reading and writing	Before, during, and after reading and writing	Before, during and after writing	Before, during, and after reading, and writing
USE TO PLAN	Units, semesters	Lessons, units, semesters	Lessons, units	Lessons	Lessons, units, semesters
MAY BE USED	Whole class, collaborative groups	Whole class, collaborative groups	Whole class	Whole class, collaborative groups, partnerships	Whole class
MAY BE COMBINED WITH (known strategies)	DR-TA, DRA, GMA, ReQuest, VSS, TPRC, DIA, REAP, Three-Level Guides, Reading Response Groups, K-W-L Plus, DEJ, journals, Learning Logs	DR-TA, DRA, GMA, ReQuest, VSS, TPRC, DIA, REAP, Three-Level Guides, Reading Response Groups, K-W-L Plus	TPRC, K-W-L Plus, journals, Learning Logs	DR-TA, DRA, VSS, ReQuest, DIA, TPRC, Three-Level Guides, Reading Response Groups, K-W-L Plus, journals, Learning Logs	DR-TA, DRA, GMA, ReQuest, VSS, TPRC, DIA, REAP, Three-Level Guides, Reading Response Groups, K-W-L Plus
MATERIALS PREPARATION	Moderate	Moderate	Light	Light to moderate	Light
OTHER PREPARATION	Moderate	Moderate to extensive	Moderate	Moderate	Light
OUTSIDE RESOURCES	Useful	Useful	Necessary	Useful	Not necessary
HOW TO DO	Page 304	Page 307	Pages 309–310	Page 313	Page 316

CHAPTER 9

ASSESSMENT OF STUDENT PROGRESS IN SUBJECT AREA READING AND WRITING

DOUBLE ENTRY JOURNAL

Draw a line down the center of your page. On the left side of the line list everything you know about assessment. On the right side list what you think you need to know about assessment to be a good teacher. Share your lists with a friend.

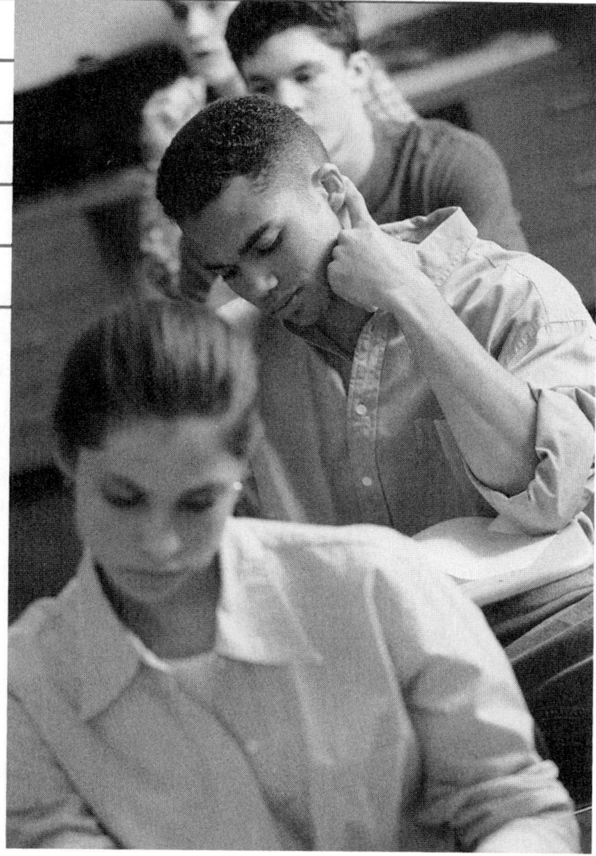

Photodisc Blue/PhotoDisc, Inc./Getty Images

Lonnie Manolili sits in the faculty meeting, his head buzzing with all the new district testing and assessment plans. He looks around the room. Everybody appears to be in about the same shape as he: overwhelmed by all the testing requirements, frustrated by how much time testing and test preparation will take away from teaching and learning in his classroom, and just flat blown away by all the time and energy the district is investing in standardized tests. The bottom line? High test scores.

A few years ago everything was all about aligning the district curriculum with state standards. Working in cross-grade curriculum groups, teachers spent hours doing the alignment and making sure that their district curriculum standards and units of study would prepare kids for the state-standards-based tests. Now everybody's wondering how in the world teachers are going to get kids ready for the newly mandated achievement test that most certainly is *not* aligned with the curriculum. And all three grades—sixth, seventh, and eighth—must take both tests each year.

In the subsequent discussion groups, Lonnie's frustration is palpable, as is other teachers'. Their collective concern is, How can we and our students be expected to produce high test scores when the tests being used are not congruent with the curriculum we teach? He, and the other teachers, have worked very hard this year to implement the new curriculum by getting better at what they do. They entered energetically into professional development workshops this year to fend off their principal's suggestion that they buy the test-preparation materials put out by the state test publisher and use them in English, math, and science classes. *Everyone,* all the teachers in the school, agreed that their preference is to prepare the kids for the test by teaching better, not teaching to the test. So they persuaded the principal to spend the money for professional development instead, which she did. And it's making a difference. Lonnie knows he's a better teacher now; he's learned new teaching strategies (that really work!), his kids are working hard, and he is learning better ways to document students' learning using performance and other assessment strategies. He and the other teachers are just starting to learn how to evaluate students' individual literacy strengths and needs, and he knows that this information will help him work with the kids in his classes who need help. He's really afraid that the new district emphasis on high test scores will convince his principal to go back to her original idea; he's also well aware of the pressure from parents, the school board, and local and state politicians for the school to demonstrate high levels of achievement on the tests. He can see that same concern reflected in the faces of his colleagues as they sit at the table and talk. He feels hollow.

• • •

Evaluation and assessment of student abilities are long-standing issues in public education, especially at the middle school and junior/senior high levels. Few other aspects of secondary education get as much press as student achievement, and it is through evaluation and assessment programs that student achievement levels are measured and reported to the public. High-stakes tests are at the forefront of assessment issues today. John Guthrie (2002) defines high-stakes tests as "A test or testing program [that is] used to make important decisions about individual students, teachers, or schools" (p. 370). He identifies a number of possible important decisions: (1) promotion and retention of students, (2) graduation from high school, (3) improvement of instruction, (4) "takeover" by a state department of education, (5) tracking students into homogeneous classes, and (6) assignment of students into Title I reading or special education classes. Guthrie notes that tracking decisions have lifelong consequences because most students stay in the track to which they are assigned; in fact, however, all of these decision points can have lifelong consequences for students, teachers, and schools.

Part of the high-stakes testing environment today is the public reporting of test scores, school by school; implementation of rating or ranking of each school by the state; and the threat of state takeover if schools do not achieve a certain rating or ranking or make continuous progress. While publishing test scores is not new, rating and ranking systems that carry the consequence of state takeover are; 25 of the 50 states currently attach a takeover consequence to the state testing program (Amrein & Berliner, 2002a). Newspapers and news magazines headline the results, usually with a negative slant ("Standards elude most students") or when positive, followed by a negative tag ("Test scores rise, goals still unmet") (*San Francisco Chronicle*, 2002). Generally, the worse the news, the louder the headlines scream.

Negative stories about test scores and student achievement are not new, they're not confined to one sector of the media, they're not confined to one part of the curriculum—reading seems to get the lion's share, with writing, mathematics, and science running close behind and physical education and foreign language education taking occasional lumps—and they're not likely to go away soon. Those of us who have been in education for a few years have learned to read the stories and to endure. What we know is that these reports—whether negative or positive—and the testing programs behind them tell only part of the story. Although we rejoice when that part is told with reasonable accuracy, we realize that media reports generally leave much of the complexity of student achievement undiscussed. Barbara Fox (1990) summarizes the situation well: "Like a barometer that registers air pressure but does not shed light on the reasons for pressure changes, the NAEP [National Assessment of Educational Progress] reports tell us only how well students are reading; they do not illuminate the reasons for differences in levels of . . . competence" (p. 337).

Those of us in public education and teacher education know that no matter how well teachers teach, and no matter how difficult or complex their teaching circumstances, negative reports will continue. To counter the effects of negative press, *we* must assume responsibility for telling the rest of the story—for illuminating the reasons for differences in students' competence. And we must continue the daily work of teaching school, regardless of how accurately (or inaccurately or incompletely) the story was told in the first place. This means that teachers working in every level of education must be knowledgeable about all types of assessment programs and procedures—classroom, school, district, state, and national—so that we can communicate fully and openly with students, parents, other educators, and the community as a whole about how students (and we) are doing. (For the most current information about national and international assessments, refer to the Web site of the National Center for Educational Statistics, www.nces.ed.gov.) Further, we must also develop and maintain useful, accurate assessment and reporting mechanisms in our own classrooms while monitoring and using appropriately those assessment programs mandated by districts and states.

Our discussion of assessment and assessment programs begins with an overview of key concepts and issues central to various types of achievement evaluation. From there, we will move to discussion of academic standards and formal testing, because of the current prominence of these issues in schools. And finally, we will address ways in which student progress in subject area reading and writing can be incorporated into classroom assessment.

OVERVIEW OF EVALUATION AND ASSESSMENT

Let's start with some operational definitions of assessment language to lend clarity and precision to this discussion. Often, assessment words and terms are used slightly differently from text to text and person to person, even though there is a loosely agreed-on usage standard for each. The definitions that follow represent common usage in the reading/language field and reflect the way terms are used in this text.

ASSESSMENT CONCEPTS AND TERMS

TESTING AND MEASUREMENT

Testing and *measurement* are ways we appraise students' reading and writing abilities using a set of oral or written questions, problems, or exercises. Testing and measurement involve some form of *quantification;* that is, when we give tests, or when we measure reading and writing abilities, we use numbers to express what we find. So we say someone is reading at the "eighth-grade level" or that a student scored "in the 75th percentile" or that "47% of the students in School A scored at or above average" or that a student's SAT verbal score was "563." All of these numbers have accrued rather stable meanings (both denotative and connotative) through years of common usage and reference; these meanings are used to interpret and make decisions about students' abilities and knowledge.

SAMPLING

Sampling is the act of using part of any given entity to find out about the whole. When we give a reading test with 35 questions and use the results of that test to describe someone's reading abilities, we have *sampled,* not evaluated completely, that person's reading behavior. I always think of sampling as "one taste of the gravy," a little sip that allows you to judge, or predict, how the whole batch will taste. Academic test samples, however, are highly vulnerable to error—that is, they often yield inaccurate or misleading results—and the smaller and narrower the sample, the greater the probability of that error. Thus, only broadly based, frequent samples of students' reading and writing behaviors can give us a full understanding of their literacy abilities.

ASSESSMENT AND EVALUATION

Assessment and *evaluation* are words generally used interchangeably to describe ongoing quantitative and qualitative analysis of students' literacy behaviors. However, some educators differentiate *assessment* ("gathering and synthesizing information concerning students' learning") from *evaluation* ("making judgments about students' learning") (McLaughlin & Vogt, 1996, pp. 104, 106). Assessment and evaluation may include testing but are not limited to it; observation, interviews, in-progress analyses, and various other evaluative methods are usually combined with test results to help teachers draw conclusions about students' reading and writing abilities. Assessment and evaluation occur over time, so that sampling yields a profile of reading and writing behaviors across that time.

A great deal of assessment and evaluation go on in teachers' heads as they watch students in their classes, review and grade work, and consider individual and group academic effectiveness, and these analyses are added to the meanings attached to testing numbers to increase the depth of evaluative judgments. So if we know that a student's language score on a test is the 93rd percentile *and* that the student routinely demonstrates well-constructed knowledge comprehension in written and oral work, we know that the student is functioning very well indeed. On the other hand, if the language score is the 93rd percentile and the student's oral and written work are consistently below adequate, then we know we need to find an explanation for the discrepancy between the test score and the student's response to academic tasks.

FORMAL ASSESSMENT

Formal assessment refers to the assessment program or programs usually carried out at the school or district level that typically focus on testing and measurement. It includes district- or state-mandated "off the shelf" achievement test batteries (i.e., tests that are not tailored for specific curricula or populations—the Comprehensive Test of Basic Skills (CTBS) is a popular achievement test, as are the Stanford Achievement Test (the most recent edition is often referred to as Stanford 10), the Iowa Test of Basic Skills (ITBS), and others—as well as state or local formal tests that are standardized on a state or local population—such as the Chicago Academic Standards Examinations (CASE), the Ohio Proficiency Tests, the Texas Assessment of Academic Skills tests (TASS), the Illinois Goals Assessment Program tests, and the Massachusetts Comprehensive Assessment System (MCAS), to name a few. Tests used in formal assessment programs may be norm-referenced or criterion-referenced (see definitions for these testing terms in a later section Testing Instruments), although the majority of formal tests currently administered are comparative (norm-referenced).

Formal assessment programs in high schools generally also include the Pre-Scholastic Aptitude Test (PSAT), the Scholastic Aptitude Test (SAT), and the American College Test (ACT). Almost all schools and school districts participate in statewide testing programs, many of which combine mandatory achievement tests with state or locally designed tests, and may be involved in the NAEP (National Assessment of Educational Progress) test administration as well. NAEP has been administering assessments regularly in a variety of subject areas to nationally representative samples since 1969 (Campbell, Hombo, & Mazzeo, 2000). NAEP is currently reporting long-term trend results, for the years of 1971–2004, and from its most recent reading tests administered in 2005. Formal assessment can involve more than tests, including formal observation (generally done by certified psychometrists or psychologists) and formal consultations, called "staffings," which are led by trained counselors or resource specialists. Counseling, Title I reading, special education, and other programs carry out their own formal assessment programs and procedures in schools and school districts.

Important to understand here is that for most classroom teachers, involvement in the formal assessment program focuses primarily on administering all or part of yearly achievement and other required tests in their classrooms under the guidance of a testing coordinator, counselor, or principal and interpreting test scores to students and parents. (However, involvement may very well also include preparing students to take such tests and worrying about test results when stakes are high—for example, when test scores are used to determine students' progress in school or to evaluate teacher and/or school effectiveness.) Generally, major decisions about formal assessment are made administratively or by faculty with special degrees and credentials (counseling, special education, Title I reading, resource specialists, etc.). In some states, these decisions are made at the state, rather than local, level.

Built into the most recent (2002) reauthorization of the federal Elementary and Secondary Education Act (ESEA), commonly referred to as No Child Left Behind, are high-stakes provisions that will affect teachers, students, and schools for years. All schools are required to submit Academic Yearly Progress (AYP) reports and must test all students in grades 3 through 8 in reading and mathematics each year (Bracey, 2002). In addition, schools have until 2014 for all students to reach the "proficient" level on these tests. According to Gerald Bracey (2002), the law allows each state to define "proficient," but because NAEP already has defined such a level, he expects the NAEP levels will prevail. Bracey and others have previously pointed to the fact that "year-to-year changes in [NAEP] school-level test scores are volatile and often stem from factors that have nothing to do with instruction" (Bracey, 2002, pp. 142–143), and predicted that AYP testing would result in a "sea of bad news" (Doyle, 2002) about test scores and student achievement, even from schools that are currently rated or ranked high. Now, in its fourth year of NCLB implementation, these concerns and others have come to pass.

INFORMAL ASSESSMENT

Informal assessment goes on in classrooms daily and includes all manner of teacher-made tests, structured and unstructured observations, grading procedures and standards, interviews, self-reports, and the myriad things we do to decide how students are progressing. Unit tests are informal assessments, as are teacher observations of students working in collaborative groups or playing a game of softball. Information that teachers gain about students' prior knowledge and experience during a guided discussion and information revealed on students' maps or written responses to text likewise, are also informal assessments, as is the information teachers extract from words and definitions students bring to a VSS discussion.

Central to informal assessment is the notion that we are able to take many more, and more varied, samples of students' abilities and behaviors than formal assessment procedures allow. Thus, we can have a richer, fuller understanding of what students can and cannot do in our classrooms. In some schools where students are grouped in "families" or "schools within a school," informal conferencing among teacher teams regarding student progress occurs regularly, adding further to the pool of knowledge about students' academic performance. Informal assessment and informal conferencing are not to be confused with "incidental" or "chance" or "haphazard" assessment and conferencing; rather, informal assessment and conferencing are planned, systematic, teacher informed and directed, and deliberately comprehensive.

Informal assessment is where classroom teacher responsibility predominates. Classroom teachers carry out the bulk of informal assessment that goes on in schools, although special-class teachers do some informal assessment. It is classroom teachers (not site or district administrators) who are responsible for knowing how to assess, what sampling procedures are most appropriate and useful, how to systematize assessment so that it is not random or arbitrary, and how to communicate results to students, parents, the school, and the community.

AUTHENTIC ASSESSMENT

Authentic assessment refers to systematic sampling of student behavior to see how well and in what ways students are able to do requisite tasks. (The focus in this text is literacy tasks; authentic assessment applies to all other academic areas as well.)

For formal assessment, authentic assessment means movement away from test items that do not resemble real-life literacy tasks (e.g., reading 150-word paragraphs and answering main-idea questions or choosing correct usage responses in sentences and short paragraphs) toward tasks that do simulate real-life experiences (e.g., reading extended complete or excerpted texts and responding to them, or writing extended text)—a movement that poses no small set of problems for test developers and administrators.

For the classroom teacher, authentic assessment is an extension of informal assessment, and includes both content and literacy assessment. It consists of all the assessment practices we discussed in the section on informal assessment, but is made authentic—and therefore more likely to reflect students' true abilities—by adherence to the following standards:

1. *Authentic assessment occurs at short intervals over time.* We get as many samples of students' literacy abilities, or tastes of the gravy, as we can. These intervals are planned and systematic, not left to chance or whim, and include assessment sampling during instruction (evaluation of students as they carry out class activities) as well as sampling of the products of that instruction (evaluation of written work, projects, and the like).

2. *Authentic assessment requires information from a variety of sources.* Tests are considered only one source of information about how well and in what ways students are able to do what we want them to do. Other ways include daily, weekly, and unit work samples; observation during guided and independent class activities; conferences and interviews with students; student self-reports; and conferences with other teachers (e.g., in team teaching arrangements).

3. *Authentic assessment occurs while students are engaged in, or using products from, real reading and writing tasks.* Instead of giving isolated-word spelling/vocabulary tests, teachers note and keep systematic records of students' spelling/vocabulary behaviors both in drafts and in polished written products. Teachers maintain systematic records evaluating and noting students' responses during DR-TA, TPRC, journal writing, and other discussion and writing episodes. Teachers read and maintain records of students' Quick Writes on what the lesson was about and/or what problems were encountered; teachers note what students are able to say in their own words about lesson content or connections students make between the Quote of the Day and class content in journal entries and learning logs. Reading and writing tasks themselves are authentic to the subject area discipline rather than skill-and-drill, isolated, and/or artificial.

4. *Authentic assessment uses teacher observation as a major source of information about how well and in what ways students can articulate content knowledge*, rather than relying on test results or any other single assessment procedure as the sole measure of academic achievement. To become skilled in authentic assessment, teachers learn to observe and analyze student behaviors as these behaviors occur in the course of regular classroom activities; they develop recordkeeping procedures that are efficient, informative, and unobtrusive; and they learn to trust their own judgment on the basis of many samples over time, even when their judgment differs from test results.

ASSESSMENT TODAY AND IN THE FUTURE

The notion of authentic assessment gained rather wide acceptance in the early and mid-1990s; however, informal and authentic assessment approaches are currently overshadowed by policymakers' demand for standardized testing results. Assessment in this country has always focused on testing, with the emphasis waxing and waning with the times. The late 1990s and early-to-mid 2000s seem to be echoing the late 1970s and early 1980s—a time of skill tests, minimum competency tests, and criterion-referenced tests—with the current reemphasis on statewide tests, high school graduation tests, standardized achievement tests, and mandated testing by federal law (No Child Left Behind). The loud and clear message to teachers from every level of administration is, "Test, test, and test some more, and don't bother us with judgments about what you see in front of your eyes on a day-to-day basis." In high schools, all this is *in addition to* Advanced Placement tests, SAT and ACT tests, and, in some states, exams for seniors to compete for scholarships to state colleges and universities. In a meeting I attended just a few years ago, a testing director for a local school district said, "In our high schools, the month of April is given over to testing." In the rather stunned silence that followed her comment, somebody wondered aloud, "Wouldn't that month be a good time for the students to be learning?"

Rather than advocate abolishing tests, educators concerned about authentic assessment recommend *changing the tests* (as we discussed earlier) so that tests more accurately represent what we want students to know and be able to do. In the course of this effort, formal tests will have to undergo some degree of transformation if they are to be aligned with state and local curricula. Unfortunately, a far easier approach, and one that we're beginning to see happen, is to realign state and local curricula to coincide with the tests (Vogler & Kennedy, 2003). Teacher-made tests, as well, must acquire new dimensions. By definition, if we expect tests to yield authentic information about how well and in what ways students are able to do certain things, we must abandon test content and formats directed toward other aims.

STANDARDS AND ASSESSMENT

National, state, and local curriculum standards are the subject of intense interest and effort today. The standards movement is essentially based on the notion that setting high expectations for student performance, stating clearly what the specifics of the expectations, and establishing clear penalties for failure to meet expectations will increase substantially not only the quality of the educational experience but student performance as well. Much of the impetus for national standards grew from the Goals 2000 legislation that was part of the 1994 Elementary and Secondary Education Act (ESEA) reauthorization, which set into motion the adoption of standards by national panels, often sponsored by or connected to national professional organizations, in virtually all curriculum areas. State and local standards followed, developed in much the same manner, and are at the forefront of much that goes on in the name of curriculum and content in all subject areas today. Let me state emphatically: There is absolutely nothing wrong with high standards. Nor is there any reason for teachers, school, and districts *not* to be held accountable for student achievement. My concern, however, is in how the standards and accompanying assessment programs have been implemented. Teachers have been told in no uncertain terms that they are to teach to the standards adopted by their school or community. Indeed, some schools require that teachers' lesson and/or unit plans identify the specific standards being addressed by the lesson or unit (hence the LPs in this text). "Standards-based instruction" is the catch phrase of this philosophy. Opinions differ as to the ultimate success of this approach. Anne Lewis (1995) notes that

> much of the turmoil surrounding standards stems from exaggerated claims by opponents and proponents. Beware of those who say that standards will "save" public education, but be equally skeptical of those who claim that standards will nationalize the curriculum. Neither group is right. (p. 745)

We now have several years of experience with local, state, and national standards and their accompanying tests, and Anne Lewis was right: they have neither saved public education nor nationalized the curriculum. They have, however, created as many problems as they have solved.

Some claim that prior to standards-based reform teachers were free to "do anything they wanted to" in their classrooms. That simply is not true, and the claim itself does a real disservice to the many hardworking teachers who taught before this latest reform. Teachers always have been held to curriculum goals and standards adopted by school districts and have been required to align their curriculum accordingly. Much of the newly adopted state standards grew from the accumulated wisdom from those years.

Well documented now, and contrary to the notion that standards-based instruction and assessment have "reformed" education, are such questionable practices as test tampering (teaching the actual test items, omitting scores, etc.), pushing low achieving students out of school or retaining students in one grade to get better results on the mandated test grade scores, and reclassifying low achieving students as students with special needs to exempt them from taking the test, again for the purpose of achieving better results (Goldberg, 2004). Test preparation programs and consultants have become ubiquitous in middle level and high schools throughout the country, with concern by some (Booher-Jennings, 2006) that resources are being directed away from students who are "below the bubble" to focus on increasing the scores of the potential passers. Equally questionable is implementing an "accommodation" for students with special needs in which the reading test items are read to students, thus changing the test from a reading test to a listening comprehension test (McGill-Franzen & Allington, 2006). Indeed, at least two widely accepted new policies in schools reflect the singular push for high test scores to meet standards, yet neither of these practices has any scientific support.

Curt Dudley-Marling, Janice Jackson, and Lisa Stevens (2006) note the recent "intensification of schooling" typified by greater demand in schools across the country for daily homework assignments for all students—with as much as 30 minutes a day for kindergartners and a regimen of three to four hours per night for high schoolers—leaving little time for leisure activities and pleasure reading or writing. According to Dudley-Marling et al., this practice is "unsupported by research" (p. 751). In fact, it seems to have grown from Newt Gingrich's statement that "every child . . . should be required to do at least two hours of homework a night, or they are being cheated for the rest of their lives." (Spring, 1997, p. 16). Recently, Alfie Kohn (2006), decided to reread the research most cited to support the academic value of homework. In study after study he found little evidence that the amount of homework that teachers assigned or that students did increased middle level and high school students' grades or test scores. What he found instead was that frequently the "researcher's conclusion [was] at variance with his or her results." (p. 17). In other words, even though results showed no evidence that homework increased academic achievement (and on occasion didn't even study homework vs. no homework), researchers arrived at the conclusion that it did anyway. Thus, we must be careful of accepting pronouncements that "research proves" or "there is little doubt" that homework has a positive effect on student learning.

Retaining students—not passing them to the next grade—has reemerged as a highly popular practice in schools, and is often encouraged by rather scornful reference to "social promotion" and validated as an antidote to such practice. Yet, we have nearly 100 years of research on grade retention that does not support it as effective, and experience supports that research. Rarely do retained students catch up to their promoted peers; however, they are considerably more likely to drop out of school. Ann McGill-Franzen and Richard Allington state,

> The repopularization of flunking is odd in an era of evidence-based reform initiatives, if only because a century's worth of research has demonstrated that flunking doesn't work. Flunking does not improve academic achievement over the long run. (2006, p. 764)

The current era of standards-based reform either grew from or has brought with it the hard-line stance of "getting tough on kids" and schools (Dudley-Marling et al., 2006) in which students and schools by the thousands are deemed "underperforming" and not improving. Thus, as Mark Goldberg notes, "a school that moves its English-language learners from, say, the 30th percentile to the 40th percentile can still be labeled as having failed to make AYP if the passing score is set at the 60th or 70th percentile" (2005, p. 390). Even schools that score well above the passing score are labeled "not progressing" if their scores do not go even higher. So it is that the standard(s) for "progress" may be unobtainable, even in very good schools. Goldberg notes,

> Americans will recall that many U.S. schools were actually doing well before the latest national testing movement began. They were graduating young people who went to hundreds of fine colleges, did well, and produced the world's greatest economy and mightiest military force—not to mention high quality of everything from technology and the arts to popular entertainment. (2005, p. 394)

And that, I believe, leads us to the singularly important questions all educators must ask themselves about standards: Why are we doing this? What are we accomplishing? What is it that we have gained and expect to gain further? What should be the relationship between standards and assessment? Answers vary, from fervent belief that standards will raise academic achievement (O'Day & Smith, 1993) to cautious acceptance of standards as part of a larger reform effort (Cohen, 1995) to just as fervent belief that "one size fits few" (Ohanian, 1999a, 1999b). Susan Ohanian notes that in an effort to give weight and scope to standards, framers of state standards have ignored the developmental reality of adolescence—for example, the requirement for adolescents to read *Moby Dick:*

> Now you and I know that anyone who says high-schoolers should read *Moby Dick* (1) doesn't know any fifteen-year-olds; (2) has never read *Moby Dick;* or (3) has read *Moby Dick,* has a fifteen-year-old in the house, and wants to get even. (1999a, p. 5)

James O. Lee (2003) makes the case that for standards to be useful in urban settings, they must be tied to constructivist pedagogy to avoid a "pedagogy of poverty" that is disconnected from students' lives, drill based, and bent on "filling students up" with knowledge (p. 449). He states, "When standards are abstracted out of specific classroom settings by professional organizations and state departments of education and are deemed appropriate for all students, they often fail to connect to the lives of the teachers or their students" (p. 451). His position is echoed by Beverly Falk (2002), who suggests that *good* standards-based reform can happen only when we (1) develop worthy standards, (2) teach the way children learn, and (3) assess to inform and support learning.

You will need to ask and answer questions about standards in your subject area for yourself and arrive at your own conclusions as standards and standards assessment tests play out in your school and teaching experience, and you will undoubtedly participate in standards-based instruction. You will make decisions about teaching to the test, using materials designed by test publishers to coach students in advance of the tests, and what kind of teaching and learning happen in your classroom.

LITERACY ASSESSMENT IN CONTENT AREAS

I think it is safe to say that you will be involved, in one way or another, in grappling with issues related to standards, assessment, evaluation, and testing. The goal of this chapter is to give you a thorough understanding of assessment issues and the means both for understanding school and districtwide assessment practices and for implementing alternative assessment practices in your classroom. Underlying everything in the chapter is the assumption that there is no one, easy answer to the question "How do we best assess student learning?"—with the corresponding assumption that multiple assessment practices are necessary if we are to understand what students know and are able to do. There is also the issue of secondary teachers' need to balance content and literacy assessments. Our emphasis, as you would expect, is literacy assessment, but it is literacy assessment *in the context of subject area learning and teaching*. The rationale here is that knowledge of students' reading and writing abilities in your subject area yields much valuable information to you, including:

- Insight into the substance and extent of students' content knowledge,
- Understanding of what literacy behaviors students need to learn to function effectively in your subject area,
- Indication of what you need to do to assist or guide students' reading and writing in your classroom,
- Identification of students who should be referred for additional evaluation and/or placement in other school programs.

PRINCIPLES OF ASSESSMENT

Assessment in subject area reading and writing, whether formal or informal, must be based on some set of principles, or guidelines, so that we have a means for determining what assessment procedures are and are not appropriate. The following discussion outlines generally agreed-on comprehensive guidelines for assessment at all levels.

1. *Assessment should focus on learning.* The goal here is to encourage, assist, and enhance learning—not to "catch" students unable to do what it is we expect or want them to do. Assessment procedures, therefore, should focus on what students know, rather than on what they don't know, and should occur only after students have been given adequate time to learn. Thus, formal and informal assessment must be aligned with the content and emphasis of the curriculum. Moreover, classroom assessment should, in some manner, reward students for taking risks and for coming close to a targeted goal. One of the most appealing viewpoints in current theory is that we need to value approximation (Cambourne & Turbill, 1987). In other words, we need to understand that "coming close" is a positive, rather than a negative, occurrence—instead of being "wrong," coming close means you are one step closer to being right.

I like the cast that this gives assessment. With it, teachers' attitudes and approaches are "Look how close you came" or "Here's how much my students know," rather than "Look how many you missed" or "Here's how much my students don't know." This positive cast turns us away from a focus on punitive attitudes and behaviors and toward a focus on classroom assessment practices that inform students honestly about what they can do, encourage students to increase the range of things they do well, and allow students to try to do things they have never done before.

2. *Assessment should be equitable.* Equity has to do with fairness, impartiality, and justice. Assessment equity means that evaluation procedures are not simply impartial but fair and just as well—appropriate for all students, regardless of the range of diversity that these students represent. Whatever students' race, gender, abilities, culture, ethnicity, socioeconomic status, or language background, no assessment practices or procedures should systematically bias judgments for or against any individual or group. That's a big order, but it is an important one. Given the diversity of students in today's classrooms, and the probability that your students represent many different cultures, viewpoints, and language and experiential backgrounds, the most reasonable approach is to use a variety of assessment practices that let all students demonstrate their accomplishments as fully as possible. Furthermore, for some students, equity may require that you use special facilities or services for assessment; if this is the case, do so. If appropriate facilities or services are not available, do whatever is necessary to get them or make whatever adjustments are necessary to provide all students equal access to equitable evaluation.

3. *Assessment should be congruent with the aims of the system, the school, and the curriculum.* This sounds self-evident, but it really isn't. For years, we've talked about the importance of "critical thinking," "problem solving," and "higher-order thinking" in education, yet we continue to give teacher-made and published achievement tests that focus on literal-level knowledge. That's not congruent. It is not unusual to find other discrepancies between stated and real values. Districts and schools can and do have statements of education standards that are not fully, or even partially, reflected in the curriculum being taught, available textbooks and equipment, and teaching traditions in the school. When this is the case, serious and extended discussion is required to resolve a basic and crucial inconsistency. Once goals, curriculum, and instruction are in line, assessment strategies must be determined that reflect and support them; these assessment practices must represent what the system and school truly value and what expectations the school holds for students. That's congruent.

4. *Assessment should recognize the limitations of assessment methods.* One of the frustrations associated with evaluation and assessment is that no one assessment procedure is perfect. No matter what means we use to evaluate student progress—giving tests, observing students as they work, grading written work, asking students to self-report, or devising elaborate point systems—error, or bias, intrudes. Of key importance, therefore, is that we understand how each procedure is vulnerable to error, recognize that limitation, and take steps to minimize it. As is so frequently the case, one of the best ways to reduce error is to use a variety of assessment practices, because one procedure's weakness is often another's strength. (For example, multiple-choice tests give us little information about why students responded as they did; learning logs and DR-TA-type discussions yield lots of information on the "why" of students' logic and reasoning.) Using two or more assessment procedures in tandem reveals a truer picture of what students know than any one procedure alone could.

5. *Assessment should reduce competition and increase cooperation in the classroom.* This sounds antithetical to commonly held beliefs about assessment. In fact, much of what occurs in the name of assessment, from elementary school all the way through college and beyond, is based on a competitive model of evaluation in which one "gets ahead" in the world by "beating" everyone else. I've heard all the arguments about competitive grades "toughening the kids up" and how we're doing a disservice to students by not getting them ready for the competition in the "real world." I don't buy those arguments, for several reasons.

First, we have a substantial body of research documenting the negative effects of competition in the classroom (and beneficial effects of cooperation), particularly with regard to academic evaluation (Deutsch, 1949b; Johnson et al., 1981; Slavin, 1980).

Second, the argument in support of competitive assessment flies in the face of what assessment is all about: *The purpose of assessment is to find out how well and in what ways students are able to do what we want them to do.* If that is true, then assessment should increase teacher–student and student–student communication; competition generally shuts communication down. Assessment should build feelings of self-worth and competence; for many students, competition destroys both.

Finally, assessment should take place in an environment of mutual respect, openness, and trust; competition works against all three. I am not denying the presence of competition in middle and secondary schools (or in the "real world"), nor am I saying it should all go away; rather, I am proposing that assessment and grading are not the appropriate arenas in which competition should predominate.

6. *Assessment should include particiption by students.* I suppose it sounds idealistic, and maybe even iconoclastic, to give some of our assessment "power" to students. Yet, this is an area in which a little yielding on our part as teachers can have major benefits for both our students and ourselves. Certainly, many assessment decisions are beyond students' prerogatives, especially with regard to formal assessment, but others are not. Perhaps if we would ask a bit more—ask students what they want to do, ask them to evaluate their own performance, and ask what they think it's "worth"—perhaps if we would listen a little more closely to students' voices and feed what we hear from them into our own agenda and knowledge of what needs to go on in the classroom, students would willingly assume the responsibility. Whatever our goals and beliefs about grading, students need to have some say in how they are assessed.

7. *Assessment should include consistent and meaningful reporting,* which occurs in many ways and on many levels. First, we must give clear, honest appraisal to students frequently and regularly so that they know at all times where they stand with respect to overall achievement and in every class. Second, we need open, consistent communication with parents to give them the same clear, honest appraisal we give students; it is here, however, that communication frequently breaks down.

Many social and economic conditions have led to the widening gap between home and schools—for example, family working and commuting schedules that don't leave time for parents to visit schools; large, impersonal schools that are forbidding and frightening to all but the most secure parents; single-parent families for whom any visit to school requires special child care or work arrangements; immigrant parents who may feel overwhelmed and uncomfortable in schools; teachers and students who commute to schools outside of their living community; homeless students who may not even live with their parents. Nevertheless, we must continue our efforts to maintain contact with parents and reduce the barriers to parental participation in schools. Many schools have launched innovative programs to do just that. In addition to parents, school administrators, district governing boards, and local and state communities must remain informed of the results of assessment programs. It is from the perspective afforded by this widespread reporting of formal and informal assessment results that thoughtful, informed instructional decisions can be made.

FORMAL ASSESSMENT

Formal testing programs are a long-standing tradition in U.S. education. I've already discussed many of the issues currently surrounding formal testing programs; however, it's unlikely that anything will ever override their use. Nonetheless, the issues associated with formal testing need to be understood by policy makers, administrators, teachers, and the public at large. Issues of test validity and reliability, and issues of test pollution and fraudulence, are serious and compelling (Bracey, 2002). They cannot be ignored. Inappropriate use and interpretation of tests, difficulty in reporting the complexities associated with test performance (Fox, 1990), and a changing U.S. school population all contribute to educators' and others' concerns about formal tests. Further, the widespread acceptance of the objectivity of standardized tests is, according to Georgia García and David Pearson (1991), "one of the greatest illusions" of standardized testing. García and Pearson argue that those who "decide what passages to use, what questions to ask, what choices to provide for multiple choice items, and what the 'right' answers are" (p. 15) are subject to the same biases as are classroom teachers. They conclude that "subjectivity can never be avoided, only masked" (p. 15). And finally, the usefulness of standardized test scores for English-language learners, and the effect this testing has on students who are not fully fluent in English, are of continuing concern.

Publishers receive multimillion-dollar returns on yearly test sales and scoring services. Barbara Miner in *Rethinking Schools* (2004/2005) reports that the nonpartisan U.S. Government Accounting Office (GAO) estimates that states will spend between \$1.9 billion and \$5.3 billion between 2002 and 2008 to implement NCLB-mandated tests (let's do the math: 50 × \$1.9 = **\$95 billion**; 50 × \$5.3 = **\$265 billion** over a six-year period). Those estimates are only for the direct costs, and could increase as much as eight to 15 times when indirect costs of implementation, teacher time, administration of "practice" tests, and the like are figured in. When you add to the publisher profits the public's continuing demand for test results (Paris et al., 1991), you begin to see the scope of just the *economic* issues that formal testing raises.

Other issues persist: To give you an example, Figure 9.1 (p. 338) presents the summary of the 2004 trend analysis of the 1971–2004 NAEP results of tests of reading achievement for grades 4, 8, and 12. You can see from this summary that scores have remained relatively stable over the past 35 years, thus refuting the loud cries of "the scores are falling the scores are falling" that have echoed throughout the country periodically during that time. Results from the most recent assessment in 2005 are highly congruent with these trends, with some upward movement in grade 4 (age 9) and somewhat lower scores for grade 8 (age 13). The 2005 mean scores are 262 for grade 8 and 219 for grade 4. The 12th grade (age 17) scores are not yet available for the 2005 NAEP test. The only scores over the years 1971–2004 that are statistically significantly different from the 2004 scores are marked with an asterisk (*); do note that, while statistically significant, these differences represent very small scale score change. For all ages, the 2004 scores

FIGURE 9.1 *National Trends in Reading by Average Scale Scores*

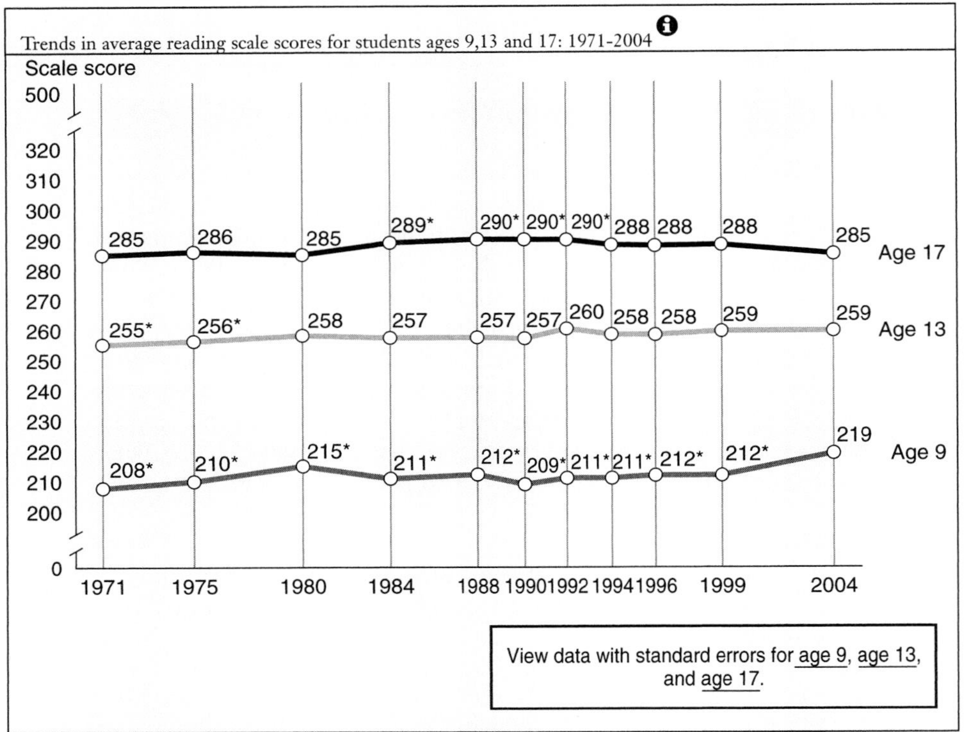

*Significantly different from 2004.
Source: U.S. Department of Education, Institute of Education Sciences, National Center for Education Statistics, National Assessment of Educational Progress (NAEP), selected years, 1971–2004 Long-Term Trend Reading Assessments.

(as well as the 2005 scores) are higher than the 1971 scores (again, evidence that runs counter to the widely believed myth of declining test scores).

These aggregate reading scores look remarkably unremarkable. But let's disaggregate the scores. Here are some of the trends:

- Female students at all three grade levels had higher scores than did their male peers.
- White students and Asian/Pacific Islanders had higher scores than black and hispanic students.
- At all three levels students in private schools outscored students in public school.
- At all three grade levels, students in urban fringe/large town schools outscored students in central city and rural schools.

You can see from just these few trends that there is no short answer to the question "How are U.S. students doing in reading achievement?" And the long answer touches on many, many aspects of life, including such issues as privilege, language, gender, SES, power, culture, home life, and education status of parents. Perry Marker (2003) notes poignantly:

> High-stakes tests have proven to be very reliable predictors of factors related to socioeconomic class and poverty. Standardized testing is a strong indicator of where the wealthiest schools are, and where children of poverty go to school. (p. 5)

Writing assessment and achievement are equally problematic, but with some additional twists: Don Leu and his associates (2002) report that "not a single state permits any student who wishes to use a word processor during state writing assessment." Yet, in a study of the effect of using word processing for the Massachusetts Comprehensive Assessment System (MCAS) testing, Russell and Plati (2000) found that when a randomly assigned subset of eighth- and tenth-graders were allowed to use word processing instead of handwriting the Composition and four Open-Ended items, students performed significantly better when they composed essays on computer. In addition,

- The percentage of students performing at the "Advanced" Level doubled.
- The percentage of students performing at the "Proficient" Level or better increased.
- The percentage of students "Failing" decreased.

They concluded that students should be given the option of word processing their essay section of the test. In addition, given the rapid increase in computer and word processing use and its continued increase for the foreseeable future, writing assessment must be reformed to reflect the fact that more and more students do the bulk of their first draft writing on a computer. Provision for computer use in assessment, however, raises additional issues regarding power, SES, culture, language, home life, and educational status of parents. Michael Russell and Lisa Abrams (2004) surveyed over 4,000 teachers nationwide and found that 30% of the teachers reported that they do not use computers when teaching writing because the statewide test is handwritten. Thus they demonstrate the power of tests to influence classroom practice.

And Edgar Schuster (2004) raises the issue that formal writing tests test only one aspect of the writing process—drafting. The 25–30-minute time limits generally allocated for each writing sample allow precious little time for the other aspects—prewriting/planning, revising, editing, publishing, and evaluating. Schuster notes that by omitting time for revision, writing tests are seriously flawed: "For every serious writer, revision, in the global sense—revision as re-seeing—is *the* vital step in the writing process" (p. 377). Thus, he believes we should call these state *drafting* tests and not confuse the scores obtained with measures of students' writing abilities.

Paris and his associates in 1991 called for serious and concerted effort directed toward formal assessment reform based on important psychometric, political, and psychological issues that traditional testing has raised and on the results of a two-stage survey of test attitudes, beliefs, and practices that they administered to 1,000

Peanuts: © United Feature Syndicate, Inc.

students. What Paris and his associates found is disturbing, particularly with regard to middle school, junior high, and senior high students.

Student responses to the survey indicated that older students are more suspicious of the validity of test scores than are younger ones, have decreased motivation to excel on tests, and believe themselves not to have useful strategies for taking tests. These same attitudes were more recently expressed by students polled about achievement tests (May, 2003) who readily admitted to giving only minimal effort or randomly filling in bubbles on the answer sheet. One student stated, "The state tests make no difference in our lives. It's not like the high school exit exam or the SAT . . . something that matters in our futures" (p. A1).

Paris and associates concluded that yearly testing may have detrimental effects on students and actually depress scores artificially as students progress through school (1991, p. 15). They make the following recommendations:

1. Assessment should be collaborative and authentic to promote learning and motivation.
2. Assessment should be longitudinal.
3. Assessment should be multidimensional. (1991, p. 18)

These recommendations provide useful support for a major reform movement in the field of formal assessment, and they indicate the need for structural change in how we measure students' achievement. Over 15 years later, this change has not yet occurred, even though high-stakes formal tests are now well entrenched in schools across the United States, even in the face of the many questions raised here and elsewhere related to their use (Amrein & Berliner, 2002a, 2002b). What is striking is that we have *no research evidence whatever* that high-stakes testing increases student achievement and learning (Black & William, 1998; Marker, 2003). In a research study that Audrey Amrein and David Berliner conducted using NAEP, AP, ACT, and SAT scores to examine the achievement effects of high-stakes testing in 28 states (2002a), no support could be found for a positive relationship between testing and achievement. They did find some unintended effects (2002b) and concluded the following:

- There is inadequate evidence to support the use of high-stakes tests and high school graduation exams to increase student achievement.
- Higher numbers of low-performing students are being retained in grade before pivotal test years to prepare them for taking high-stakes tests.

- Higher numbers of low-performing students are being suspended before test days, expelled from school before tests, or being reclassified as exempt from tests to prevent low-scoring students from taking tests.
- Higher numbers of teachers are teaching to the tests, limiting instruction to only those things that will be tested, requiring students to memorize facts, and drilling students on test-taking strategies (all of which Meier [2002] suggests the states and test-coaching programs *encourage* teachers to do).
- Higher number of teachers are leaving public school teaching for private schools, which are free of state testing mandates.

It seems clear that formal testing issues will be at the forefront of education conversations for some time. None of the problems has gone away, and the federal legislation assures continued use of standardized tests to hold students, teachers, and schools accountable to specific goals. States, districts, schools, and teachers will have to confront the complexities of formal assessment and make very important decisions about how tests are to be used. Certainly, formal assessment remains popular with the general public, legislators, and policy makers. Whatever the outcome of those decisions, teachers are responsible for knowing how to understand and interpret formal assessment results for their own information and for the purpose of informing students, parents, and the community at large. You need not be a measurement expert to be able to read, understand, and interpret formal test results. You do, however, need a basic understanding of a limited number of measurement concepts. So I present a set of carefully chosen measurement concepts (Mitchell, 1977) here that will afford you a working knowledge of formal testing and the ability to understand the formal assessment instruments used in your school.

TESTING INSTRUMENTS

STANDARDIZED TEST/NORM-REFERENCED TEST

A *standardized test*, or *norm-referenced test*, is a test designed to measure individual performance as it compares to an identified "norm group." The norm group is the set of people, of like age and grade to the students being tested, whose performance set the standard against which the students being tested are measured. Standardized tests are supposed to be administered according to prescribed directions (so that the test group has the same conditions as the original norm group) and are scored by prescribed rules (so that the test group results are scored exactly as the original norm group results). Most of the instruments used in formal testing programs are norm-referenced, standardized achievement tests; all standardized tests I'm aware of are commercially published.

TEST BATTERY

A *test battery* is a group of several tests standardized on the same norm group so that the test scores are comparable. Most of the achievement tests administered by school districts are test batteries that include sections on reading, writing, language, mathematics concepts, mathematics computation, social studies, and science. Some have fewer sections and cover fewer academic areas, whereas others are more comprehensive and include such areas as spelling, listening, and reference skills. The SAT (Stanford 10), the CTBS, ITBS, and the Metropolitan Achievement Test are widely used test batteries. Some people refer to any group of tests administered at generally the same time as a "battery." That's term is technically incorrect because the tests do not fit the condition of having common norm groups; therefore, the results are not truly comparable.

Survey Test/Achievement Test

A *survey test*, or *achievement test*, is a test that measures general achievement in a given area. Survey tests are generally considered to be reasonable estimates of group achievement and not very good precise measures of individual achievement. Unfortunately, survey tests are commonly and routinely used to measure individual reading achievement and progress. Survey tests are found not only in batteries. In fact, there are a number of rather popular secondary survey reading tests: the Gates–McGinitie Reading Test and the Nelson–Denny Reading Test are two examples.

Diagnostic Test

A *diagnostic test* is intended to locate and analyze specific strengths and weaknesses. For the most part, teachers of special classes and counselors are the primary users of diagnostic tests. Generally, these special teachers interpret the results of diagnostic tests to teachers, students, and parents.

Criterion-Referenced Test

A *criterion-referenced test* is a test designed to provide information on a student's specific skills rather than to compare the student to a norm group. Generally, criterion-referenced tests are limited in content and yield scores that have meaning in reference to what the student knows in relationship to a knowledge criterion or standard. Most minimum-competency tests are criterion-referenced; students must score above a certain minimum score, or criterion, to pass. Spelling tests are one kind of criterion-referenced test. Some criterion-referenced tests are commercially published.

TEST SCORES

Raw Score

The *raw score* is generally the number of correct responses obtained by the student. On some tests, the raw score is the number of correct responses minus some fraction of incorrect responses. Virtually all raw scores are computed in relationship to the time allowed to complete the test. Raw scores are used to compute all other scores. You almost never see raw scores when you look at formal test results; rather, you see various converted scores that were obtained from the raw scores.

Mean Score, Median Score, and Mode Score

The *mean score* is the arithmetic average of raw or other scores. The mean is frequently used to compute converted scores. The *median score* is the middle score, the point that divides a set of scores into two equal parts. The median is the 50th percentile. Almost always, the mean and median scores of standardized tests are the same. The *mode score* is the score that occurs most frequently; that is, it is the score obtained by more students than any other score.

GRADE EQUIVALENT (GE) SCORE

A *grade equivalent (GE)* score is a converted score expressed as a grade level for which the raw score is the real or estimated average. GE scores are expressed in terms of grade and month of grade, assuming a 10-month school year. Thus, a GE score of 10.7 means tenth grade seventh month, while 7.2 means seventh grade second month. GE scores are not very useful, even though they are popularly used and often demanded by parents. Because GE scores are converted from raw scores by mathematical interpolation rather than actual comparison with the norm group, they're not very reliable. Just as importantly, they don't have useful meaning. "Tenth grade seventh month" doesn't really tell us where a student stands, either in a real sense or in relation to other students; we have to infer meaning and/or that relationship by our knowledge of whether that student is a sixth-grader, a sophomore, or a senior in high school. And even if we do know that relationship, a 10.7 score obtained by a sixth-grader does not mean that the student should be given reading material appropriate for the end of tenth grade.

PERCENTILE RANK

A *percentile rank*, in contrast, is a converted score that tells the position of the obtained score within a group of 100 scores. Percentile ranks are computed using the norm group scores. For example, a 93rd percentile means that a student scored equal to or above 93% of the norm group and below 6% (99th percentile is the highest percentile rank). Percentile ranks have become a popular way of reporting test scores to the public, frequently with the explanation, "A score of 57th percentile means that the student scored better than 57% of the eighth-graders nationwide." *Percentile ranks have nothing to do with percent of correct responses.* Percentile ranks are reasonably useful scores; I think they're the most useful scores for understanding students' achievement and for talking to students and parents. This is especially true if you place the percentile ranks into some sort of context. I use the context shown in Figure 9.2.

FIGURE 9.2 *Scoring Grid*

90th–99th	percentile:	Superior
80th–89th	percentile:	Above average
70th–79th	percentile:	Above average
60th–69th	percentile:	High average
50th–59th	percentile:	Average
40th–49th	percentile:	Average
30th–39th	percentile:	Low average
20th–29th	percentile:	Below average
10th–19th	percentile:	Below average
0–9th	percentile:	Very below average

STANINE SCORES

Stanine scores are another way to compare a student's obtained score with the norm-group scores. Stanine scores are expressed on a 9-point scale of standard scores (stanine is short for "standard nine"), with the number 5 corresponding to the mean. Because the mean is almost always the median as well, the 5th stanine is approximately the 50th percentile. Although stanines do not correspond exactly with percentile ranks, you can get a very good sense of how students compare with the norm group by looking at stanine scores. Generally, stanine scores are recommended by measurement experts as the most useful score for comparing student progress from one test administration to another.

INTERPRETATION OF TESTS

To understand and interpret formal test results and the various converted scores, you need to know at least three more things.

TEST VALIDITY

Test *validity* refers to how well the test measures what it says it measures. There are all kinds of validity expressions, but probably the most important of these are (1) *content validity*, which is the extent to which the content of the test matches the content of the curriculum, and (2) *face validity*, which is the degree to which the test appears to reflect real-life skills and knowledge. Validity computations are available in every technical manual for every published test. If you have questions about a test's validity, talk to the test coordinator and get a copy of the technical manual to see the validity information.

TEST RELIABILITY

Test *reliability* refers to the extent to which the test is consistent in measuring whatever it does measure. Reliability concerns the accuracy, stability, and dependability of test scores and the amount of confidence we can have that a student's obtained score is real. Reliability information also resides in the technical manual; you should know something about test reliability before you begin interpreting scores and using those interpretations for academic decision making.

STANDARD ERROR OF MEASUREMENT

Standard Error of Measurement (SEM) is a statistic that provides an estimate of the possible magnitude of error present in an obtained score. It is the amount by which the student's obtained score may differ from his or her hypothetical true score because of errors of measurement. SEM is expressed ± x, which is read "plus or minus x." So, if a test has an SEM of ± 4, and a student obtained a score of 32, this would be interpreted to mean that the student's true score is somewhere between 28 and 36. You can see that the higher the SEM, the less reliable the test.

Any movement within the SEM range (e.g., the student's score goes up or down 1 to 4 points) *is considered no movement at all.* Therefore, you cannot say the student's score has "improved" if his or her score is 3 points higher this year over last year; neither can you interpret a score as "falling" if it is 3 points lower. You can see that without knowledge of the SEM, *you cannot interpret test results comparatively.* That is, you cannot compare this year's score to last year's score or one student's score to another's, because you have insufficient information to interpret the distance between scores. If this year's score is 47 and last year's was 44, a SEM of ± 2 makes the difference important; a SEM of ± 4 renders the difference meaningless. As with validity and reliability, the SEM is provided in the technical manual of the test (SEM measures are sometimes called confidence intervals). Request that information from the counselor or test coordinator and be sure to get information about (1) what scores the SEM is in reference to (frequently, raw scores) and (2) printouts or lists of what those scores are for each student.

INFORMAL AND AUTHENTIC ASSESSMENT OF SUBJECT AREA READING AND WRITING

One issue that surfaced earlier in this chapter in our discussions of informal and authentic assessment was the need for teachers to use various sources of information in the evaluation of students' subject area reading and writing abilities. This is because virtually all formal literacy tests and some informal ones, no matter how carefully conceived and developed, engage students in artificial literacy tasks unrelated to school tasks and everyday life reading and writing. Sternberg (1991) points to the short passages, immediate-recall tasks, multiple-choice questions, and single-purpose nature of reading tests; Elbow and Belanoff (1986) note that writing tests lead students to believe that "proficient writing means having a serious topic sprung on you (with no chance for reading, reflection, or discussion) and writing one draft (with no chance for sharing or feedback or revising)" (p. 336). These negative aspects are still present in currently published achievement tests. So if teachers want to know how students really read and write, specifically with regard to subject area materials, then teachers must have information that goes well beyond the results of formal literacy tests.

TRADITIONAL INFORMAL ASSESSMENT

Because our emphasis in this text is on literacy assessment, we are not going to explore all the ways in which subject area teachers have traditionally assessed student learning. For the most part, literacy assessment in subject classes has focused on vocabulary and writing assessment, both of which are legitimate areas of evaluation (adolescents' protestations that "This isn't English class!" notwithstanding). What is most important in both areas is that assessment be a natural extension of effective instruction (see Chapters 4, 5, 6, 7, 8, 10, and 11).

PERFORMANCE ASSESSMENT

Performance assessment and performance exams are viewed as an effective means for authentic evaluation of student progress. Performance assessment requires authenticity, with the intent to make the assessment activity a true simulation of real-life activity.

Dolores Handy (Moje & Handy, 1995) used performance assessment in her Chemistry I class for end-of-semester evaluation of both content knowledge and reading and writing. Well in advance of the exam, Handy asked her students to read two articles, one for and one against the use of DDT; students were to write summaries of the articles and list unfamiliar words and their estimate of the definition of each word. One week before the exam, Handy collected the summaries and word lists and returned them to students with written responses—indications that a student should look again at one of the readings or that their understanding was incomplete or a suggestion to add information to the summary. Students received points toward their semester grade for the notes and vocabulary lists. Then on the day of the exam, students, with summaries in hand, worked in the computer lab to word-process a response to the exam task: that they vote on a ballot for or against banning DDT and write a letter to a government official supporting one of those positions. Students received a grade on their letter for its coherence, appeal to audience, and use of information from the two articles.

One of the ways many teachers grade performance exams and tasks—and other projects as well—is using rubrics: statements describing varying levels of accomplishment on any given task. Below is a rubric I created that could be used to grade the exam in Dolores Handy's class; points could be assigned to each level:

Exceptional:

- Information from the articles is thoughtfully synthesized.
- Information is presented imaginatively and purposefully.
- The letter demonstrates deep understanding both of the chemistry and the environmental impact of DDT use.
- Writing is well organized and cohesive.
- Arguments are explicit, clearly stated, and fully supported.

Thorough:

- Information from the articles is well summarized.
- Information is presented clearly.
- The letter demonstrates clear understanding both of the chemistry and the environmental impact of DDT use.
- Writing is organized and cohesive.
- Arguments are clear, specific, and supported.

Adequate:

- Information from the articles is present but minimal.
- Information is reasonably well presented.
- The letter demonstrates understanding both of the chemistry and the environmental impact of DDT use.
- Writing is somewhat organized and cohesive.
- Arguments are reasonable and at least minimally supported.

Inadequate:

- Information from the articles is msissing, inaccurate, and/or muddled.
- Information is not well presented.
- The letter demonstrates lack of understanding of either the chemistry or the environmental impact of DDT use or both.

- Writing is unorganized.
- Arguments are incomplete or hazy and unsupported.

OBSERVATION AS AN ASSESSMENT TOOL

Observation is probably the single most useful means available for getting information about students' reading and writing abilities (or any other abilities, for that matter). I generally distinguish between "unstructured" and "structured" observation. By "unstructured" observation, I mean those times when you are observing students and are open to any information that may come your way: You are not looking for specific items or particular areas of learning/expertise, but you take note of important information as it is revealed. "Structured" observation, in contrast, occurs when you have clearly identified purposes for observing: Perhaps you want to see what students do when they come to a word they do not know or how students preplan first-draft writing or how well students are able to make and support predictions while reading text. Both types of observation are useful and appropriate in the classroom. Generally, structured observation yields more systematic information, but unstructured observation may be equally productive—we often learn the most important things about students when we least expect to.

NOTETAKING AND RECORDKEEPING WITH OBSERVATION

Critical to the success of any type of observation is that teachers develop and maintain a system of notetaking to record information about and impressions they have of students. This can be as simple and straightforward as having a spiral notebook in which notes are kept in a diary-like fashion by a daily recording of events and insights, or assigning each student a page and entering dated notes as observations occur. Or perhaps a set of 4″ × 6″ or 5″ × 8″ file cards with each student listed on a separate card would be ideal. Some teachers keep Post-it notepads handy for jotting down observations during busy class time; later, they transfer the information to a more permanent record. Another possibility is using a database or word-processing program to establish and maintain observational records. Every teacher needs some system for recording observations; discover what works best for you and use it.

The idea of maintaining notes and records of observations is not new. Teachers used to keep all sorts of anecdotal records of students in the cumulative folders that followed students from grade to grade. Mostly, these notes and comments were focused on students' behavior and represented teacher judgments and impressions based on daily contact with students. Two things happened to change this practice. First, the Buckley Amendment (Family Educational Rights and Privacy Act, FERPA) was passed in 1974. This was a federal statute that decreed that all official school records must be open and available to parents—a condition previously unheard of in U.S. education. In no time, throughout the country, cumulative folders were denuded of all teacher and counselor comments, leaving nothing but test scores and attendance records. The second occurrence was the ascendancy of test scores over teacher judgments as the sine qua non of student evaluation that resulted from the heavy emphasis on testing in the late 1970s and continues today. Fear that teacher comments would be unsubstantiated or biased (and thus vulnerable to legal action) and the availability of "hard data" in the form of test results led to an official stance of evaluation based on test results, with almost no credence given to anecdotal, observational information.

NOTETAKING AND PURPOSES FOR OBSERVATION

It is absolutely imperative that we keep in mind our purpose for observation so that the notes we take and the records we maintain reflect that purpose and not something else. (Otherwise, our notes really will end up being unsubstantiated or biased, which is absolutely unfair to students and just as absolutely vulnerable to lawsuit.) *The purpose for assessment (observation) is to determine how well and in what ways students are able to do what we want them to do in a given subject area—that, and nothing more.* Right now, we are looking at observation of students' literacy abilities as they affect content learning in your classroom—a way to measure the degree to which students are, or are becoming, strategic readers and writers in your subject area. Thus, the notes you take and the records you keep should focus on how well and in what ways students function with your class texts. I recommend that you begin by using some sort of structured observation to assist you in focusing your attention on specific aspects of literacy and to hone your observational skills. Later, as observation becomes second nature to you, you may want to use a more free-form, less structured approach.

THE DEVELOPMENTAL INVENTORY

The Developmental Inventory is an observational instrument I created (Haggard, 1984; Ruddell, 1991) for use during routine classroom activities and/or with written products from these activities. The inventory can be used to evaluate all aspects of language, reading/listening, and writing/speaking. It is designed to guide teacher observation during any of the instructional activities we've discussed in this text—VSS, mapping, writing workshop, DR-TA discussion, TPRC, DIA, learning logs—as well as other kinds of activities that routinely occur in classrooms, including, but not limited to, current-events presentations, chapter discussions, demonstrations, and all manner of media activities. In addition, the inventory is useful for guiding teacher evaluation of written work and other products of classroom instruction. It allows teachers to evaluate students' English-language development in subject areas. And finally, it may also be used for students to reflect on their own literacy development. I call it the Developmental Inventory to focus attention on a basic notion about literacy: that the literacy behavior students exhibit at any given time reflects their current theory of how language works. These theories and behaviors are expected to change over time (i.e., develop), so that language and literacy functioning become more proficient.

The Developmental Inventory is made up of two separate, but generally parallel, lists of language and literacy behaviors focusing on listening/reading (Figure 9.3, p. 349) and speaking/writing (Figure 9.4, p. 350). Within each list are four categories of language and literacy behaviors that contribute to students' ability to use subject area materials and generate text. These categories are:

FIGURE 9.3 *Developmental Inventory: Listening, Reading*

Student Name ______________________________ Grade ________ Date ________
Observation and evaluation of:

LISTENING READING
(circle one)

Instructions: Circle the appropriate letter to describe how each statement fits this student during your most recent period(s) of observation.

U = Usually O = Occasionally R = Rarely

Guides Self Through Text				
1.	Makes predictions	U	O	R
2.	Supports predictions with logical explanations	U	O	R
3.	Uses both prior knowledge and text information to support predictions	U	O	R
4.	Changes and refines predictions as reading/discussion proceeds	U	O	R
Knows How Text Works				
5.	Demonstrates knowledge of common text elements and patterns	U	O	R
6.	Draws inferences from spoken and written text	U	O	R
7.	Understands how to use various source materials and events appropriate to age/grade level	U	O	R
8.	Demonstrates fluency and confidence when engaged with text	U	O	R
Understands Social Aspects of Meaning Construction				
9.	Is aware and tolerant of others' interpretation of spoken language and written text	U	O	R
10.	Supports and maintains own position in face of opposition	U	O	R
11.	Participates in interactions to negotiate meaning construction	U	O	R
Uses Range of Strategies While Listening/Reading				
12.	Raises questions about unknown information	U	O	R
13.	Uses illustrations and/or other graphic information to construct meaning	U	O	R
14.	Relocates and uses specific information to support predictions, inferences, and conclusions	U	O	R
15.	Revises meaning as new information is revealed	U	O	R
16.	Uses a functional system to gain meaning for unknown words (e.g., context-structure-sound-reference)	U	O	R

FIGURE 9.4 *Developmental Inventory: Speaking, Writing*

Student Name ______________________ Grade ________ Date _________
Observation and evaluation of:

SPEAKING WRITING
(circle one)

Instructions: Circle the appropriate letter to describe how each statement fits this student during your most recent period(s) of observation.

U = Usually O = Occasionally R = Rarely

Guides Audience Through Text				
1.	Uses language markers to identify the beginning, middle, and end of spoken or written accounts	U	O	R
2.	Develops and elaborates ideas	U	O	R
3.	Uses descriptive names for objects and events	U	O	R
4.	Provides adequate information for audience understanding of events, ideas, arguments, and accounts	U	O	R
Knows How Text Works				
5.	Demonstrates knowledge of common text elements and patterns	U	O	R
6.	Relates information in a logical sequence	U	O	R
7.	Uses language and sentence structures appropriate to text type and age/grade level	U	O	R
8.	Demonstrates fluency and confidence while speaking and writing	U	O	R
Understands Social Aspects of Meaning Construction				
9.	Understands and appreciates various speech and writing styles	U	O	R
10.	Adjusts language to clarify ideas (spontaneously or over time)	U	O	R
11.	Participates in interactions to negotiate meaning construction and develop elements of text and style	U	O	R
Uses Range of Strategies While Speaking/Writing				
12.	Uses ideas and language effectively to show sequence of events and cause–effect relationships and to support main ideas	U	O	R
13.	Revises extemporaneous speech or first-draft writing to arrive at a more polished product	U	O	R
14.	Develops cohesion through idea organization and language use	U	O	R
15.	Explores topics with some degree of breadth and depth	U	O	R
16.	Develops graphic, spoken, and written text that illuminates meaning	U	O	R

The Developmental Inventories may be reproduced for classroom use.

1. Guides self or audience through text
2. Knows how text works
3. Understands social aspects of meaning construction
4. Uses range of strategies while listening, reading, speaking, or writing

The purpose of the inventory is to guide teacher observation and analysis of students' language and literacy behaviors; it is one way to do structured observation in your classroom and as you grade student work. In addition, it is particularly useful for analyzing how ELL students, or students with special needs, or students who are experiencing problems in your class are able to function with class texts and writing tasks. It is certainly not the only way to assess—there are any number of alternative foci you could have, and just as many different criteria for assessment. Nevertheless, this inventory is a place to start. After you become comfortable with it, you can then adjust, add, or revise according to your own specific needs. Let's now look at the four categories of literacy behaviors that the inventory uses.

1. *Guides self or audience through text.* Whether students are reading with your guidance or independently, whether they are watching a demonstration narrated by you or on a film or videotape or conducting an independent Internet search, or whether they are mapping or writing their response to a classroom event or revising a piece of writing for formal presentation, their ability to generate guideposts for moving themselves through the text of that event is critical to the knowledge that they construct. It is, in fact, a major aspect of strategic reading and learning. So we need to look closely at students' ability to generate these guideposts (guides self or audience through text) to monitor their opportunities for arriving at well-constructed knowledge. While reading, listening to an oral presentation, or watching a demonstration or film, students guide themselves through text by making predictions or asking predictive questions.

A useful way for you to assess how well students do this independently is to observe the extent to which they do it during guided reading and other discussion events. The DR-TA, TPRC, K-W-L, DRA, ReQuest, DIA, and similar instructional strategies are very revealing of students' ability to predict and the extent to which students are able to support and refine predictions as reading progresses. Therefore, they are perfect opportunities for teachers to do structured observations. These strategies, in various ways, allow teachers to evaluate further the degree to which students are integrating prior knowledge with text information throughout the reading event. Remember, our goal here is not to see whether students' predictions are *right.* Rather, we're interested in whether or not students are able to:

- Generate predictions that make sense on the basis of the information students currently have.
- Support their predictions with arguments that are logical and reasonable.
- Connect what they already know with what they are learning.

Guideposts for moving through text are just as important in speaking and writing as they are in listening and reading, but here, the individual must guide the audience, as well as the self, through text. We use any number of speaking and writing conventions to do this. Language markers—words and terms that signal certain text events—are one such convention. When you were young, the words *Once upon a time* signaled the beginning of a story; that's a language marker. In middle grades, students use *The End* liberally to bring their writing to a close; that's a language marker, too.

What you want to observe in students' speaking and writing is their growing sophistication with such markers: opening accounts with statements of time and place ("Yesterday as I was driving to school . . ."); itemizing major points ("First . . . second . . . and finally . . ."); summarizing and recapitulating major ideas ("In summary . . ."); and making use of the many other ways in which speakers and writers guide their audience. Further, you want to look to see how well students decontextualize when writing and speaking—that is, the degree to which they develop and elaborate ideas, use descriptive names for objects and events ("legislative and judicial branches of government" versus "senators and judges"; "sharp liner to right" versus "a hit"), and provide sufficient detail so that the audience didn't have to *be there* to understand the event. Questions you can use to guide your analysis here include:

- Does the description or account make sense on its own?
- Is it understandable without numerous probes for clarification, definitions, and further explanation?

2. *Knows how text works.* One of the most important abilities your students can have is knowing how text and other materials commonly used in your subject area work: how they are organized, what kinds of information reside in them, what information margin notes and footnotes contain, how illustrations and other graphic materials add to or support written text, and so on. Mathematics books, for example, frequently use a format pattern like this:

Explanation and example

Rule, generalization, or formula

Example

Example

(Example)

Exercises

Students who perceive this pattern know where to go when something doesn't make sense; students who don't know the pattern don't know how to get help when they need it. Other texts in other subject areas work differently, and some mathematics books are different from this one. Students seeking information on-line need to know how on-line text works—what a search engine is, how to create good search prompts, what a Boolean search is, how to bookmark Web sites, and such. Critical here is to determine whether your students know how these texts work, how to identify and use patterns useful with specific texts, and how to switch from one text mode to another.

Observing students as they use their texts and when they have questions gives you some understanding of their knowledge of how text works. Similarly, their ability to draw inferences (i.e., see the relationship among the explanation, the rule, the examples, and the exercises), use various source materials (e.g., reference books, online search engines, computer software), and demonstrate fluency and confidence with all kinds of subject-specific text all indicate how well students are able to function in that subject area.

This same fluency and ease need to be established in students' production of spoken and written text in the subject area. In journal entries and Quick Writes, look to see whether students use the text conventions and patterns typical of your subject area and how well they are able to relate information in logical sequence, use the language of the subject area and topic, and develop ideas fluently. Because journal entries and Quick Writes are typically first-draft writing, look also to see how revised and polished efforts contrast with first-draft speaking and writing. Use questions such as the following:

- Do rehearsal and revision increase the student's reading, writing, or speaking fluency?
- Does the student demonstrate knowledge of how the text works?
- Does the student's polished work demonstrate real knowledge of the text conventions of the subject area?

3. *Understands social aspects of meaning construction.* We have already discussed at length the social nature of learning and the influence of substantive discourse on knowledge construction. Students need to understand the value of these interactions as well and to participate actively in many different kinds of small- and large-group events. Sophistication in this area requires students to be able both to "hold their own" (maintain their own position in the face of opposition and present ideas articulately and forcefully) and to understand and appreciate alternative views and perspectives (recognize the validity of other experiences and viewpoints and appreciate the diversity of different voices and writing styles). Helpful questions include:

- Does the student listen to other points of view?
- Is the student's response thoughtful and logical?
- Is the student willing to include other points of view in his or her own thinking?
- Does the student achieve a balance between maintaining his or her own position and accepting others'?
- Does the student understand, appreciate, and use various writing and speaking styles?
- Does the student participate willingly in classroom discussions and other events?

4. *Uses a range of strategies while listening, reading, speaking, or writing.* Students need any number of strategies to be effective language users and strategic readers, writers, and learners. Not everyone agrees on the list of strategies that make students effective, and everyone's list reflects his or her own particular biases. My list is based on what many people believe to be important parts of students' metacognitive strategies for processing language and texts in classrooms. These are things students do that serve to monitor their progress through text and tell them what to do if something goes wrong.

First on the list is raising questions. Next to making predictions, I can think of no more important cognitive act than question asking for monitoring learning and constructing knowledge; I am not alone in this belief (see Manzo & Manzo, 2004; Palincsar

& Brown, 1984). Careful observation during ReQuest episodes reveals a great deal about students' question-asking abilities. Second on the list is students' ability to locate and use helpful information in text: using illustrations and graphics, relocating ideas and information to support predictions and conclusions, and reexamining and changing ideas as new information warrants. Finally, there is the all-important area of how students function *independently* with text when they come to a word they do not know. All of these strategies affect how well students learn the content itself. They are well worth observing while students read text or listen to lectures and demonstrations.

Strategies are just as important in speaking and writing. Here, as with other parts of the inventory, we distinguish between first drafts and polished efforts. However, we begin by looking at how well students are able to marshal thoughts and language to do whatever it is they're trying to do. We also look for progress during the year and observe how students' abilities to articulate subject knowledge develop in correspondence to classroom instruction and activities. Useful questions related to literacy strategies include:

- Does the student raise questions? Are the questions pertinent and useful for arriving at new understandings?
- Is the student able to show sequence of events and cause-effect relationships and support main ideas?
- Does the student understand the importance of drafting and revising in speaking and writing and revise willingly?
- Is the student developing strategies to bring cohesion and organization to his or her work?
- Does the student have a sufficient knowledge base for exploring ideas with breadth and depth?
- Can the student speak, write, and produce maps or other visual representations that illuminate rather than confuse or obscure ideas?

USING THE DEVELOPMENTAL INVENTORY

The Developmental Inventory is usable both during instruction and when you are reading or grading students' work. You can duplicate multiple blank copies and use one each time you observe a student in class or target that student for analysis of written work. You may want to begin by focusing on only one section of the inventory (e.g., guides self and audience through text), or you may want to use selected items from the entire instrument. I recommend that you choose a limited number of students to observe during any given class period, no more than two or three. Then, as class progresses, pay close attention to the responses of those two or three students, keeping notes as you can.

In all likelihood you will want to begin by observing students who do not appear to be strategic readers and writers and/or are having difficulty using texts or completing tasks in your classroom or who do not do well on formal tests. Because of the number of students you see each day, it's not practical to think that you will be doing this kind of structured observation of every student you teach. You might consider, however, spot-checking some of the students with highly developed literacy abilities just to get a sense of what their strengths are. The Developmental Inventory gives you useful information for how you can alter instruction or tasks to provide instructional assistance for students who need it.

Have a copy of the inventory near to consult periodically to remind yourself of what you're looking for in the students' behavior. Focus on what students *can* do, not on what they can't do. Deliberately plan and lead instruction so that behaviors you want to look at are displayed: predicting, elaborating ideas, using graphic information, and so on. Don't forget to continue observing as students work independently or in groups—whether they are reading, writing, or discussing—so that you have a full range of behaviors to record. As unobtrusively and efficiently as possible, take notes and jot down impressions. *As soon as you can after class*, fill out the inventory and make additional notes. Plan time to share with students what you observe so that they will have the same knowledge you have about their language and literacy abilities in relation to your subject area. You may wish to ask all of your students to fill out a Developmental Inventory to reflect on their own literacy; then, with the students you observe, use their reflections and your observations as a basis for discussion.

NOTETAKING AND RECORDKEEPING WITH THE DEVELOPMENTAL INVENTORY
Crucial to the success of observational assessment are the notes you take during your observations and the systematic recording of what you find. The Developmental Inventory is highly useful for recording your observations and making additional notes. By recording information on the inventory and maintaining these records, you will be able to see students' progress over the semester or year they have in your class. If you choose to use the Developmental Inventory with all students, you will be able to see how each individual student progresses, how each class as a whole progresses, and how all of the students you teach in a given year develop as the result of your teaching.

A major value of maintaining systematic records of your observations is that such records legitimize the kind of informal assessment that observation represents. Recall my earlier comments about the demise of anecdotal records in students' cumulative folders and the resulting effect of heavy, and in many districts almost sole, reliance on so-called hard data from tests. Much of this change came about because teachers did not always maintain observational records and notes to support the comments made in cumulative records—the hard data of informal assessment, if you will—and so these records were without substantiation. Also contributing was the fact that, for some students, anecdotal records were wholly focused on negative attributes and what students couldn't or didn't do rather than what they could do. (After the Buckley Amendment was passed, such records were abandoned, in part, because of this negative focus.)

If we are to make observation and informal assessment procedures successful now—as we must do if we really are committed to authentic assessment practices—we must keep careful records to demonstrate that we are not being arbitrary, capricious, or prejudicial in our assessment practices and conclusions. Such well-maintained records will demonstrate that (1) *we are assessing systematically*—in other words, we have specified behaviors that we are observing and goals for the number and kind of observations we make for each student; (2) *we can demonstrate a clear parallel between our instructional goals and the behaviors we are assessing*—in other words, our instructional strategies and classroom activities reinforce the very behaviors we are evaluating, and these behaviors increase and enhance content learning; and (3) *we can demonstrate student progress over time*—in other words, we have numerous samplings of literacy behaviors over semesters and academic years, and we can demonstrate what students can do at the end of the year that they were unable to do at the beginning.

From such careful recordkeeping, we put ourselves in a position to override the hard data of test results *when those samples of student abilities do not accurately reflect what students can and cannot do.* This is how, with informal, authentic assessment practices, teachers come to be able to trust their judgments and to become seen by others (parents, administrators, and the community as a whole) as experts on the issue of student achievement.

I think you can see how truly authentic this kind of observational assessment is and that it meets all of the standards for authentic assessment. Clearly, we are using standard, everyday classroom events and tasks as the basis for the evaluation, as opposed to artificially set up special tasks. Just as importantly, we increase authenticity by *not stopping class to "test" or "observe" how students are doing;* class is going right on. Students are reading, doing experiments, working on problems, using their learning logs, working in small groups, and doing various other activities without interruption. Content learning is progressing. It's only the *teacher* who is stopping periodically to concentrate on students' subject area language and literacy abilities in the context of content learning.

If you choose not to use the Developmental Inventory for this kind of assessment, then it is to your benefit to devise a list of questions or items you will use to guide your observations and record your findings systematically on a checklist or response sheet. This keeps you honest, it reminds you consistently of what you're looking for, and it establishes your hard database.

INTERVIEWS AND STUDENT SELF-REPORTS

Probably one of the most overlooked methods we have for assessing student abilities is simply to ask them what they can and cannot do. Most of the time, especially if they feel reasonably secure with us, they'll tell us. Students have an amazingly accurate view of their own academic abilities; they rarely exaggerate—if anything, they tend to underestimate what they can do.

INTERVIEW ASSESSMENT

Interview assessment has been a recommended education practice for many years, yet teachers rarely do it. Most classroom teachers I know would not consider interviewing to be an important part of their assessment practices. I think that's mainly because "interviewing" sounds so formal and time consuming. Conducting 150 interviews, even distributed over an entire semester, is more than a little daunting. Few teachers have the time, energy, or inclination to do anything like that.

Student interviews do not have to be drawn out, however. We talk to students all the time, both in class and out. If we would use the same mind-set that is appropriate to observational assessment when we're talking to students, we could do interview assessment just as often and just as authentically as we observe. Thus, when a student asks for assistance while reading, we can ask, "What do you do when you come to a word you don't know?" (strategies while reading and writing) and note his or her response. Or we can ask, "When you can't remember how to do the problems in your math homework, what do you do?" (knows how text works); or "How do you find information in an encyclopedia or on the Internet?" (knows how text works); or "When you're getting ready to write, what are the steps of your preplanning?" (guides audience through text; knows how text works). You get the idea. The keys here are to

1. Do this kind of questioning deliberately and systematically.
2. Write down students' responses.

Voilà! Interview assessment.

QUESTIONNAIRE ASSESSMENT

Questionnaire assessment is a form of indirect interview. Many teachers like to have students fill out questionnaires about various aspects of students' knowledge and interest in the subject area. Written questionnaires suffer somewhat from writing-fluency limitations, which may cause students to say less than they would orally, but for the most part, this doesn't seem to constitute a major problem. Because questionnaires so often ask about interests and attitudes, many teachers like to use them as ice breakers; teachers find that students respond readily to them. Figures 9.5 and 9.6 (pp. 358–359) are questionnaire surveys you may wish to use or adapt for your class. You can, of course, use the questionnaire questions in an informal interview.

PORTFOLIO ASSESSMENT

Portfolios have been used for some years as the most useful means of gathering various kinds of evidence to use in the assessment process. Kenneth Wolf and Yvonne Siu-Runyan (1996) define portfolios as follows:

> A portfolio is a selective collection of student work and records of progress gathered across diverse contexts over time, framed by reflection and enriched through collaboration, that has as its aim the advancement of student learning. (p. 31)

In subject area classrooms, portfolio assessment focuses on content learning but may include language and literacy elements as well. Certainly, it seems reasonable to incorporate some aspect of students' reading, writing, listening, and discussing abilities into evaluation of their subject area knowledge.

Portfolio assessment can be used in many variations; consequently, teachers and schools considering a move to portfolio assessment from more traditional assessment procedures are immediately faced with a number of important decisions. Murphy and Smith (1991) suggest the range of decisions to be made:

> In a sense, coming up with a portfolio project is like choosing what to teach. The decision automatically creates possibilities and limitations. In the infinite scheme of what can be taught, teachers choose for their particular classroom communities. In the same way, they can make decisions about portfolios with themselves and their students in mind. (p. 1)

Wolf and Siu-Runyan (1996) identify three different types of portfolios, each with its own primary purpose and emphasis:

1. *Ownership* portfolios, in which students select contents for the purpose of promoting independent learning.

FIGURE 9.5 *Reading Questionnaire*

Student Name ______________________________ Grade ________ Date _________

1. Are you a reader? _______________ (If no, skip questions 2 and 3.)
2. What do you like to read?
   ____
3. What do you like most about reading?
   ____
4. How do you know if someone is a good reader?
   ____
5. How do you think teachers decide who is a good reader?
   ____
6. If you had your choice, what topics or type of books would you like to read for this class?
   ____
7. What books or other things have you read that you'd recommend for use with this class?
   ____
8. What advice would you give someone who wanted to get better at reading (subject area)?
   ____
9. What's the most recent thing you've read?
   ____
10. What did you think of it?
    ____
11. What else would you like to tell me about the reading you do for pleasure or for school?
    ____

2. *Feedback* portfolios, in which students and teachers collaborate to determine contents for the purpose of documenting student learning.
3. *Accountability* portfolios, in which contents are selected by students, teachers, and test directors for the purpose of evaluating achievement.

EARLY DECISIONS FOR PORTFOLIO ASSESSMENT

Several critical questions need to be answered when designing an effective portfolio assessment system:

1. *What are the purposes for this portfolio assessment?* Why am I having students do this—to give them ownership? to document their learning? to evaluate their learning?

FIGURE 9.6 *Writing Questionnaire*

Student Name ____________________ Grade ________ Date ________

1. Are you a writer? ______________ (If no, skip questions 2 and 3.)
2. What do you like to write?
____
3. What do you like most about writing?
____
4. What do you think makes a good writer?
____
5. How do you think teachers decide who is a good writer?
____
6. What kind of writing do you think we will do in this class?
____
7. What kind of writing would you like to do in this class?
____
8. What advice would you give someone who wanted to become a better writer?
____
9. What have you written lately?
____
10. What did you think of it?
____
11. What else would you like to tell me about the writing you do for pleasure or for school?
____

2. *What will be the criteria for assessment?* What evidence am I looking for? What do I want students to demonstrate? How will I make sure students know what needs to go into their portfolios? What kind of mix do I want between daily work, individual work, group work, tests, first draft and polished writing, and outside work?

3. *Whose responsibility is it to do what?* How directive should I be regarding portfolio contents? How much leeway should I give students to determine what they each want in their portfolio? Should I rule certain things out? Should I require certain things?

4. *What will the guidelines be?* How will students know or be able to judge the quality of their own work? By what standards will I judge the quality of their work?

5. *How should materials be collected?* Where will the portfolios be housed? How should materials be presented? What categories of work and what self-evaluations should be included? How many items should be presented for each category of work?

6. *What will the working procedures be?* When and how often will portfolios be evaluated? How will I report evaluation to students? What is my commitment for returning portfolios to students?

POSSIBLE DECISIONS FOR PORTFOLIOS

There are some very reasonable and relatively easy ways to answer all those critical decision questions. Linda Rief (1990) describes a portfolio project in her seventh- and eighth-grade English classes in which she chose to settle the question of who is responsible for what in this manner: She, the teacher, decided the *external* criteria for what goes into the portfolios:

> Each student's two best [written] pieces chosen during a six-week period from his or her working folder, trimester self-evaluations of process and product, and, at year's end, a reading/writing project. (p. 24)

The students decided the *internal* criteria: that is, which pieces they wished to present and the reasons for their choices. I like that plan because it's workable and sufficiently directed by the teacher to guide student development. By no stretch of the imagination is it laissez-faire; nevertheless, it remains open to a significant amount of student choice in the assessment process. (Recall the assessment principle that students should have some say in how they're being assessed. This approach is one way to give students real power in their own evaluation.)

Determining the mix or range of things that can go into the portfolio is another issue. Here is a partial list of possible portfolio contents:

1. *Samples of student writing*, including idea development (brainstorming), first draft, revision and rewrite drafts, and final pieces. Writing samples should show work over time.

2. *Story maps* from in-class and out-of-class reading. Included also should be writing that grew from the mapping experience.

3. *Reading log*, a bibliography or dated list of books the student has read for pleasure and/or in response to class projects, topics, and issues. Writing done in relationship or response to books listed should also be inluded.

4. *Vocabulary journal* or *log* that shows words the student has collected and the definitions she or he has developed for them. Written vocabulary activity work should accompany the journal.

5. *Artwork*, *project papers*, *photographs*, and other products of work completed.

6. *Group work papers, projects, and products.* A written explication of each member's contribution and self-evaluation of how well the group functioned may be included.

7. *Daily journal* of student's personal thoughts, reflections, ideas, and so forth.

8. *Writing ideas,* a list of things the student thinks would be interesting, ongoing writing topics (never a "polished" product).

9. *Observational assessment results,* including, for example, the Developmental Inventory, interviews, questionnaires, and any other checklist or informal measurement used.

10. *Reading response log or writing from assigned reading* during the year (e.g., summaries, notes, feelings, reflections, evaluations, and other responses).

11. *Learning log or double entry journal,* including notes, predictions, essays, social argument, imaginative writing, written responses, analyses and responses, explication, and writing done in a second (or third) language.

12. *Letters or e-mails* exchanged with the teacher, pen pals, classroom visitors, and others in the school and community.

13. *Out-of-school writing and artwork* the student selects to include.

14. *Unit and lesson tests* collected over the grading period and/or academic year.

Students should be given a wide range of acceptable means of demonstrating their ability to meet standards or criteria. You may find it useful to specify various media in determining your external criteria; for example, you may require two pieces of writing, three tests, and five representative homework assignments.

Another possibility is a requirement for self-reflection and self-evaluation. Rief (1992, p. 146) required students to answer the following questions regarding their choice of "two best pieces":

- What makes this your best piece?
- How did you go about writing it?
- What problems did you encounter?
- How did you solve them?
- What makes your most effective piece different from your least effective piece?
- What goals did you set for yourself?
- How well did you accomplish them?
- What are you able to do as a writer that you couldn't do before?
- What has helped you the most with your writing during this trimester?
- What are your goals for the next 12 weeks?

Maureen McLaughlin and MaryEllen Vogt (1996) comment on the importance of self-reflection in portfolio evaluation:

> Self-reflection is the heart of portfolio assessment. It encourages students to ponder what course goals mean and contemplate their ownership of the portfolio process. It tells students that we value their thinking and affords us access to information we've never had in the past. (p. 33)

You may also want to consider other kinds of portfolio materials. For example, you may want to increase the depth of information from tests by allowing students to select some number of tests out of the total given during the grading period, rework/rewrite/redo the chosen test(s), and accompany them with a written self-reflection similar to what students produced on the basis of Rief's evaluation prompts. If nothing else, that would certainly change the role of tests in classrooms. I would also expect that first draft and polished writing, text responses, and other literacy artifacts would be included in just about any portfolio collection. These are authentic representations of students' reading and writing abilities in subject areas and are valuable means for evaluating subject area progress.

MAKING PORTFOLIOS WORK

You must make several other decisions about portfolios. One is how the portfolio will figure in the grade to be assigned for the grade period. Another is how and when you will evaluate the portfolios. I recommend that for each grade period, you do one or more "in-progress" evaluations prior to the final, grade-producing evaluation. The in-progress evaluations allow you to assess the quality of students' work and give them feedback about their work and about the choices they are making while the consequence of risk taking is low. Critical to the evaluation process is that there be a structure for carrying out evaluations systematically and equitably. There are any number of systems for evaluating portfolios; Tierney and associates (1991) recommend various alternative formats. Rubrics are just as useful with portfolios as they are with other projects, both for you and for your students, in defining how portfolios are to be assessed and what differentiates good work from not-so-good work.

The issue of *time* needs to be addressed here. This kind of assessment, where you look at a variety of work students have done and where you respond in writing to each student, takes time. There is simply no glossing that over, and the only way a secondary school teacher with five or six classes a day can possibly find the time is to establish staggered schedules for evaluating different classes. Time commitment is considerable. But even more problematic is figuring out how to get portfolios back and forth from school to home (a wagon, grocery cart, or luggage carrier helps!); unless they're in an electronic format, portfolios can get bulky and heavy. An even better plan would be to use your planning period and some before- and after-school time, and any other at-school time you can find, to eliminate the need to transport portfolios. Many teachers have students present their portfolios individually to the teacher during the last few days of the grading period and set aside class time for the presentations.

Other time-saving and transportation alternatives are possible. One is to have students evaluate their portfolios and submit a written analysis of their evaluation, with selected work samples attached. You, then, would spot-check portfolios in class on an ongoing basis and collect students' self-evaluations at the end of the grade period for determination of final grades. By reducing the bulk of materials you collect (that is, collecting only selected samples of student work), problems associated with transporting portfolios for grading are eliminated and grading time itself is considerably reduced. Another alternative is the growing use of digital portfolios, in which students put their portfolio and explanation on their own web page and the teacher accesses the portfolio from his or her computer. Many commercially produced template programs for digital portfolio development are available now; most are on-line and charge a minimal fee for each student's subscription to the service for a semester.

A FINAL WORD ABOUT ASSESSMENT

I can think of a no more sensitive and politically charged topic in education than assessment. As you can see just from this chapter, assessment issues are complex and thorny, and there are no easy answers. Moreover, shifting social, economic, and political tides influence national, state, and local conversations about assessment, and very few of the conversants have dispassionate views. Daniel Ferri (1999) reminds us that we need to keep assessment and achievement testing in perspective (and reveals a bit of the beauty of children's spirits while he's at it). Here's his story.

In the course of preparing his sixth-grades for their yearly state writing exam, Ferri had his students fill out the Scantron information section—in which they had to fill in circles corresponding to responses to queries about race, ethnicity, age, and so forth—the day before the exam. Because the Scantron readers do not read incomplete or lightly marked boxes and circles on such forms, Ferri and his teaching partner went over the data sheets and put Post-it notes on the worst ones, telling kids to "Print your name more clearly" or "Fill in circles under date of birth" or "Darken circles." The data sheets were returned to the students the next day along with the writing prompt, which was, "Should students be required to wear uniforms in school?" At the end of the testing session, Ferri heard Duane ask Becky, "What did you write about?" (Ferri picks up the story:)

> "Well, I wrote about uniforms," Becky answered. "We all did, it said so on the paper."
>
> "Mine didn't say that," Duane said. "Mine said to write about dancin' circles."
>
> Becky and I both said, "What?" "What did you write about?"
>
> "I wrote about dancin' circles," Duane responded. "Here, I'll show you."
>
> I reached for the pile of prompt pages, but Duane was already rummaging through the stack of test booklets. Becky said, "Those didn't say what to write about!"
>
> "Mine did," Duane answered. He pulled his test booklet out of the stack and pointed to the Post-it stuck to the front page. On that Post-it I had written, "Darken circles."
>
> "See, right here, it says 'Dancin' circles," Duane said. "So that's what I wrote about."

Dancin' circles. Ferri only wishes he could have watched the face of the reader who graded Duane's test. I think I would have loved to have seen that myself.

WHAT THIS CHAPTER MEANS TO YOU

1. Lonnie Manolili's concerns and fears about high-stakes testing are shared by many teachers across this country. You may very well be facing the same difficult decisions he and his colleagues face right now. I encourage you to fight for the choice of better teaching through staff development rather than obtaining materials that will help you teach to the test.

2. There are no easy answers to the many questions raised by high-stakes assessment and standards-based reform. You will sit through many meetings on those topics and engage in many discussions about standards, tests, legislation, and much more. Keep yourself informed about the issues and the way students in your school are performing on mandated tests. Pay attention to NAEP data and show the trend scores when people tell you about declining test scores. Visit http://nces.ed.gov/ at least once a year to look at the most recent data.

3. You must be diligent about informal assessment of your students' achievement to support your evaluation of their progress in your class. Pay attention when they talk and write and do work in your class. Take notes. Keep records. Use the Developmental Inventory to guide and record your observations of those students who might benefit from such.

DOUBLE ENTRY JOURNAL

Look at your prereading DEJ response. How has your understanding of assessment changed? Of the understandings you have now, which do you consider to be most critical to your teaching? Why?

FEATURE *What Goes in My Portfolio?*

Use the Developmental Inventory to observe two students, one of whom is an ELL student, over time in a classroom. Observe all aspects of their literacy: Listening and Reading, as well as Speaking and Writing. Write a summary and analysis of what you observed. Include suggestions for instruction that will assist both students.

RECOMMENDED SOURCES

*Amrein, A. L., & Berliner, D. C. (2002a). *The impact of high-stakes tests on student academic performance: Any analysis of NAEP results in states with high-stakes tests and ACT, SAT, and AP results in states with high school graduation exams.* [On-line]. Available at http://edpolicylab.org

*Amrein, A. L., & Berliner, D. C. (2002b). *An analysis of some unintended and negative consequences of high-stakes testing.* Executive Summary [On-line]. Available at http://edpolicylab.org

Berliner, D. C., & Biddle, B. J. (1997). *The manufactured crisis: Myths, fraud, and the attack on America's public schools.* White Plains, NY: Longman.

Bigelow, B. (1999). Tests from hell. *Rethinking Schools, 13*(3), 3.

*Black, P., & Wiliam, D. (1998). Inside the black box: Raising standards through classroom assessment. *Phi Delta Kappan, 80*(2), 139–148.

*Booher-Jennings, J. (2006). Rationing education in an era of accountability. *Phi Delta Kappan, 87*(10), 756–761.

*Bracey, G. W. (2002). The 12th Bracey report on the condition of public education. *Phi Delta Kappan, 84*(2), 135–150.

Brozo, W. G. (1990). Learning how at-risk readers learn best: A case for interactive assessment. *Journal of Reading, 33*(7), 522–527.

*Cambourne, B., & Turbill, J. (1987). *Coping with chaos.* Portsmouth, NH: Heinemann.

Campbell, J. R., Hombo, C. M., & Mazzeo, J. (2000). *NAEP 1999 trends in academic progress: Three decades of student performance.* [On-line]. http://nces.ed.gov/nationsreportcard//pubs/main 1999/2000469.asp

*Cohen, D. (1995). What standards for national standards? *Phi Delta Kappan, 76*(10), 751–757.

Deutsch, M. (1949a). A theory of cooperation and competition. *Human Relations, 2,* 129–152.

*Deutsch, M. (1949b). An experimental study of the effects of cooperation and competition upon group process. *Human Relations, 2,* 196–231.

*Doyle, D. P. (2002, June). AYP revealed: Now what? *The Doyle Report, 4.* [On-line]. www.thedoylereport.com

*Dudley-Marling, C., Jackson, J., & Stevens, L. P. (2006). Disrespecting childhood. *Phi Delta Kappan, 87*(10), 748–755.

*Elbow, P., & Belanoff, P. (1986). Portfolios as a substitute for proficiency examinations. *College Composition and Communication, 37,* 336–339.

*Falk, B. (2002). Standards-based reforms: Problems and possibilities. *Phi Delta Kappan, 83*(8), 612–620.

*Ferri, D. (1999). Dancin' circles. *Rethinking Schools, 13*(3), 7.

*Fox, B. J. (1990). Teaching reading in the 1990s: The strengthened focus on accountability. *Journal of Reading, 33*(5), 336–339.

*García, G. E., & Pearson, P. D. (1991). *Literacy assessment in a diverse society* (Technical Report No. 525). Champaign, IL: Center for the Study of Reading, University of Illinois, Urbana-Champaign.

*Goldberg, M. (2004). The test mess. *Phi Delta Kappan, 85*(5), 361–366.

Goldberg, M. (2005). The test mess 2: Are we doing better a year later? *Phi Delta Kappan, 86*(5), 389–395.

*Guthrie, J. T. (2002). Preparing students for high-stakes test taking in reading. In A. E. Farstrup & S. J. Samuels (Eds.), *What research has to say about reading instruction* (pp. 370–391). Newark, DE: International Reading Association.

*Haggard, M. R. (1984, November). *Language-based strategies for assessing reading development.* Paper presented at the annual convention of the California Reading Association, Oakland, CA.

*Johnson, D. W., Maruyama, G., Johnson, R., & Nelson, D. (1981). Effects of cooperative, competitive and individualistic goal structures on achievement: A meta-analysis. *Psychological Bulletin, 89,* 47–62.

Kibby, M. W. (1993). What reading teachers should know about reading proficiency in the U.S. *Journal of Reading, 37*(1), 28–40.

*Kohn, A. (2006). Abusing research: The study of homework and other examples. *Phi Delta Kappan, 88*(1), 9–22.

*Lee, J. O. (2003). Implementing high standards in urban schools: Problems and solutions. *Phi Delta Kappan, 84*(6), 449–455.

*Cited in text.

*Leu, D. J., Ataya, R., & Coiro, J. (2002, December). *Assessing assessment strategies among the 50 states: Evaluating literacies of our past or future?* Paper presented at the annual meeting of the National Reading Conference. Miami, FL.

*Lewis, A. C. (1995). An overview of the standards movement. *Phi Delta Kappan, 76*(10), 744–750.

Manzo, A. V. (1969a). *Improving reading comprehension through reciprocal questioning.* Doctoral dissertation, Syracuse University, Syracuse, NY, 1968. *Dissertation Abstracts International, 30*, 5344A.

Manzo, A. V. (1969b). The ReQuest procedure. *Journal of Reading, 13*, 123–126.

Manzo, A. V., & Manzo, U. (2004). *Content area reading: Strategic thinking for strategic learning* (4th ed.). Hoboken, NJ: John Wiley & Sons.

*Marker, P. M. (2003). *One more brick in the wall: High stakes testing in teacher education—The California Teacher Performance Assessment.* Available at http://www.louisville.edu/journal/workplace/issue5p2/marker.html

*May, M. (2003, May 8). State tests get little respect from many students. *The San Francisco Chronicle*, pp. A1, A 19.

*McGill-Franzen, A., & Allington, R. (2006). Contamination of current accountability systems. *Phi Delta Kappan, 87*(10), 762–766.

McKenna, T. (1999). The straitjacket of standardized tests. *Rethinking Schools, 13*(3), 8.

*McLaughlin, M., & Vogt, M. E. (1996). *Portfolios in teacher education: Theory, practice, and promise.* Newark, DE: International Reading Association.

Meier, D. (2002). Standardization versus standards. *Phi Delta Kappan, 84*(3), 190–198.

*Miner, B. (Winter, 2004/2005). Keeping public schools public. *Rethinking Schools.* Retrieved at http://www.rethinkingschools.org/archive/19_02/test192.shtml.

*Mitchell, B. C. (1977). A glossary of measurement terms. *Test Service Notebook, 13.* New York: Harcourt-Brace-Jovanovich.

*Moje, E. G., & Handy, D. (1995). Using literacy to modify traditional assessments: Alternatives for teaching and assessing content understanding. *Journal of Reading, 38*(8), 612–625.

*Murphy, S., & Smith, M. A. (1991). *Writing portfolios: A bridge from teaching to assessment.* Markham, Ontario: Pippen Publishing.

*O'Day, J. A., & Smith, M. S. (1993). Systemic school reform and educational opportunity. In S. Fuhrman (Ed.), *Designing coherent education policy: Improving the system.* San Francisco, CA: Jossey-Bass.

*Ohanian, S. (1999a). One size fits few. *Rethinking Schools, 13*(4), 5.

Ohanian, S. (1999b). *One size fits few.* Portsmouth, NH: Heinemann.

*Palincsar, A. S., & Brown, A. L. (1984). Reciprocal teaching of comprehension-fostering and comprehension-monitoring activities. *Cognition and Instruction, 1*, 117–175.

*Paris, S. G., Lawton, T. A., Turner, J. C., & Roth, J. L. (1991). A developmental perspective on standardized achievement testing. *Educational Researcher, 20*(5), 12–20, 40.

*Rief, L. (1990). Finding the value in evaluation: Self-assessment in a middle school classroom. *Educational Leadership, 47*, 24–29.

*Rief, L. (1992). *Seeking diversity: Language arts with adolescents.* Portsmouth, NH: Heinemann.

*Ruddell, M. R.-H. (1991). Authentic assessment: Focused observation as a means for evaluating language and literacy development. *California Reader, 24*, 2–7.

Ruddell, M. R. (1995). Literacy assessment in middle level grades: Alternatives to traditional practices. *Reading & Writing Quarterly: Overcoming Learning Difficulties, 11*(2), 187–200.

*Russell, M., & Abrams, L. (2004). Instructional uses of computers for writing: The effect of state testing programs. *Teachers College Record, 106*(6), 1332–1357.

*Russell, M., & Plati, T. (2000). *Mode of administration effects on MCAS composition performance for grades four, eight, and ten.* [Online]. Available at http://www.be.edu/research/nbetpp/reports.html

*Schuster, E. H. (2004). National and state writing tests: The writing process betrayed. *Phi Delta Kappan, 85*(5), 375–387.

Sharan, S. (1980). Cooperative learning in small groups: Recent methods and effects on achievement, attitudes and ethnic relations. *Review of Educational Research, 50*, 241–271.

Sherif, M., Harvey, O. J., White, B. J., Hood, W. E., & Sherif, C. W. (1961). *Intergroup conflict and cooperation: The Robber's Cave experiment.* Norman: University of Oklahoma Book Exchange.

Simmons, J. (1990). Portfolios as large-scale assessment. *Language Arts, 67*(3), 262–268.

*Slavin, R. E. (1980). Cooperative learning. *Review of Educational Research, 50*, 315–342.

*Spring, J. H. (1997). *Political agendas for education: From the Christian Coalition to the Green Party*. Mahwah, NJ: Erlbaum.

*Sternberg, R. J. (1991). Are we reading too much into reading comprehension tests? *Journal of Reading, 34*(7), 540–545.

*Tierney, R. J., Carter, M. A., & Desai, L. E. (1991). *Portfolio assessment in the reading-writing classroom.* Norwood, MA: Christopher-Gordon.

Valencia, S. W., McGinley, W., & Pearson, P. D. (1990). Assessing reading and writing. In G. G. Duffy (Ed.), *Reading in the middle school* (pp. 124–153). Newark, DE: International Reading Association.

*Vogler, K. E., & Kennedy, R. J., Jr. (2003). A view from the bottom: What happens when your school system ranks last? *Phi Delta Kappan, 84*(6), 446–448.

Vogt, M. E. 1995, November. *CRA Research Institute: Introduction.* Paper presented at the annual conference of the California Reading Association, San Diego.

*Wolf, K., & Siu-Runyan, Y. (1996). Portfolio purposes and possibilities. *Journal of Adolescent & Adult Literacy, 40*(1), 30–37.

CHAPTER 10

Diversity in the Classroom: Meeting the Needs of All Students

DOUBLE ENTRY JOURNAL

Write the word diversity in the center of your journal page. Around it, write all the ideas and associations you have about diversity. Classify and categorize your associations. Make a semantic map of your ideas.

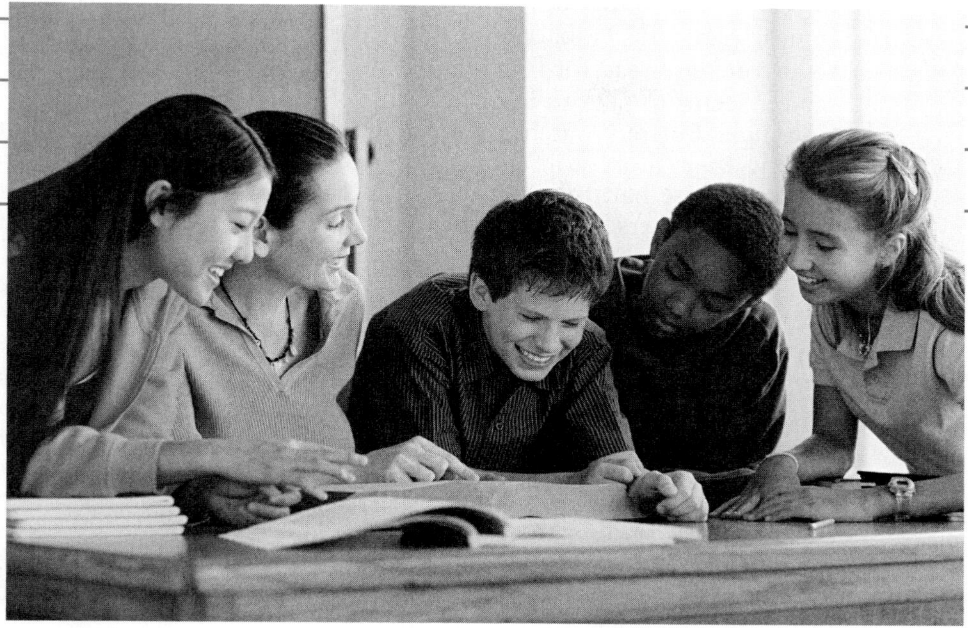

Image Source/Jupiter Images

Derek Stackhouse sits at his desk, eyes not moving from the open book in front of him. "Don't call on me. Please, please don't call on me," he shouts inside his head. He knows better than to make eye contact with Ms. Butrous or anyone else in the room. He can feel the tension in his body—the knot in his stomach almost hurts—but remembers to maintain an outward appearance of insolent cool. He relaxes a bit when Ms. Butrous calls on someone else and the reading begins again. He can't *stand* reading aloud in class with everyone reading along just waiting to catch his mistakes. And he makes plenty. He can't seem to get rid of his nervousness about reading out loud; he can feel his face getting red and his throat tightening up, and he always stumbles through his paragraph in near-panic. It's embarrasing and makes him mad. He can't even listen to anyone else read for fear that he'll be chosen next. And when he does read it seems to take an hour before his heart returns to normal.

Angie Butrous watches with a sinking heart as the kids take turns reading their short story aloud. She made the decision to do this reluctantly because half the class came every day unprepared for discussion, and consoles herself that at least everyone will hear the assignment this way, but she can see with her own eyes that this is not a good use of class time. There's nothing happening in this room and it looks it. There's no energy—just the dead, dull sound of one person reading and no one really listening. And then there's the agonizingly slow turns of the kids who can't read well. She tries to break things up a bit by stopping to discuss the story, but only a few kids (the same few every time) appear to be able or willing to talk during discussion. This is quite a diverse class: lots of kids who are achieving just fine, a few who are really doing well, and another considerable number of kids that she just can't seem to reach. There are ELL students at all of these levels, many kids who've been in classes and school together since kindergarten, and a growing number of kids new to the district. She really wants to meet all their needs and knows deep down inside that there has *got* to be a better way.

• • •

Diversity is becoming the norm in U.S. classrooms. Where once our schools housed populations of relatively similar students, we now find more and more schools with students representing diverse cultures, language backgrounds, family structures, socioeconomic classes, ethnicities, sexual orientations, learning styles, and physical and learning abilities. This new diversity results, in part, from legislation reflecting social changes in the United States, beginning perhaps as early as mandatory attendance laws, but more significantly with *Brown v. Board of Education of Topeka* (1954), which initiated the end of legal segregation of students into racially homogeneous schools. Legislatively mandated changes further increased classroom diversity, with federal law PL 94-142 stipulating the "least restrictive environment" for students with various physical and learning disabilities by mainstreaming them out of special schools and classrooms into regular public schools and classes to the fullest extent possible.

Other social and school conditions add further to the diversity of our classrooms. One such condition is the recent large wave of immigration to this country and, as we noted in Chapter 6, the growing number of children of these immigrants. Qin-Hilliard (2002) notes,

> Today, the United States is again being transformed by large-scale immigration that in sheer numbers has surpassed all previous records. The "new migration," which . . . rapidly intensified in the last decades of the twentieth century, is characterized by a continuous flow of immigrants, especially from Latin America, Asia, and the Caribbean, (p. 393)

The most recent census data reflect this transformation. And adding still further to the mix are special programs directed toward retention of immigrant and indigenous students with traditionally high dropout rates; these populations include teenage mothers, low SES students, gifted minority students, and students with special interests and talents. The net effect is that our schools look different today than they did even a few years ago. It is not unusual today to hear several languages in the halls of middle and secondary schools, and in large urban schools serving immigrant populations, the number of different languages and dialects spoken in one school can be 20, 30, or more. Because of PL 94-142 and the mainstreaming practices it mandated, students who were once sequestered in special classes and schools now are sitting in regular classes—sometimes in wheelchairs or accompanied by guide dogs, note-takers, and American Sign Language (ASL) interpreters, and sometimes physically indistinguishable from their peers. Girls and young women appear in advanced mathematics, science, and government courses in growing numbers, and students of all races, abilities, and talents are given support and encouragement to stay in school and continue on to college or other postsecondary education.

This variation and diversity are further reflected in a perceptible move away from the "melting pot" tradition characteristic of previous immigrant movements into the United States, in which cultural, ethnic, and linguistic groups adopted mainstream values and behavior to assimilate into the majority culture. Now, attitudes lean more toward a "salad bowl" mixture in which groups retain and celebrate their differences and contribute their unique qualities to the larger society (Banks, 2003). Thus, students from diverse cultures, both immigrant and indigenous, are less likely today to seek assimilation by adopting majority traits. Rather, they are maintaining ties with their primary culture by holding on to the behaviors, language, attitudes, and values of the group or groups with which they identify, whether these groups are culturally, linguistically, academically, ethnically, or socially defined. Increasing numbers of students with ties to two or more cultures, languages, or races acquire and maintain cross-cultural values, attitudes, and behaviors and code switch or mix and match at will (Luke, 2002; Moje, 2002).

Diversity, variation, and difference are very much a part of today's schools, and these qualities contribute greatly to providing a rich, multicultural, multiperspective education for all students. The presence of such diversity and difference has caused schools to change from practices that assume homogeneity and from practices that deny or denigrate student characteristics, languages, or qualities. This change is by no means complete; schools and districts are currently increasing their efforts to bring about changes appropriate to the new diversity and will continue to do so in the future. Teachers and administrators in school districts are participating in workshops, in-service programs, and graduate study to increase their understanding of the diverse populations entering schools, whether these populations consist of learning-disabled students, various immigrant groups, gifted students, low-income indigenous and immigrant students, students with physical and health disabilities, students with special talents, bilingual students, or any combination of these.

CENTERPIECE LESSON PLAN

The Centerpiece Lesson Plan for this chapter on diversity begins with the strategy Question-Answer Relationships (QAR) that help students understand how text information combines with their own knowledge base in the construction of meaning. QAR is followed by the Gradual Release Writing strategy that offers a strong scaffolding support for students who may not like to write or who are not very good at articulating information in writing. Both these strategies are highly useful for diverse classrooms and student populations.

QAR, GRADUAL RELEASE WRITING CENTERPIECE LESSON PLAN, *Physical Education*

Lesson: Foul Shot

Course/Grade: Physical Education/7th–10th Grades

Materials:

- Copies of "Foul Shot" poem by E.A. Hoey
- QAR Poster
- Student notebooks
- Pens/pencils

LESSON OBJECTIVES (WITH CONTENT STANDARDS)

Upon completion of this lesson students will be able to

- Analyze the physical, emotional, and social aspects of a critical-moment basketball game foul shot (Standard 2—demonstrates understanding of movement concepts, principles, strategies, and tactics as they apply to the learning and performance of physical activities).
- Connect performance activity with own active living practices (Standard 6—values physical activity for health, enjoyment, challenge, self-expression, and/or social interaction).

LESSON PROCEDURES

Before Reading: Into—QAR

1. Display QAR Poster. *Say:* When you read and answer questions, your answers can come from In the Book—whatever we read *(point to poster)*, answers can come from In My Head—what you already know *(point)*, or answers can come from a combination of the two—the book and what you know. Today we're going to do some reading and I'll ask you questions and where you got the answers—In the Book or In My Head or a combination of the two.

2. Distribute copies of "Foul Shot" to students. *Say:* Poetry is for reading aloud, so I'm going to read this poem to you. You may read along silently or just listen. When I've finished reading, I'll ask you questions.

3. Read "Foul Shot." *Ask:* What made this description of a foul shot so exciting? *After answer, ask:* Where did you get that answer? *(Likely: In the Book and In My Head). Ask:* How do you know the basket is good? *(Answer)* Where did you get that answer? *(Likely: In the Book). Say:* Now I want you to read the poem silently, but this time focus on the physical, emotional, and social events that the poet describes.

During Reading: Through

4. *Ask:* What were the physical events? Where did you get that answer? *Ask:* Why do you think the poet said in line 5, "soothes his hands along his uniform" instead of "<u>smoothes</u> his hands along his uniform"? Where did you get that answer? Everyone stand up. <u>In place</u> you will re-create the physical form of this foul shot as I read the poem. Pay close attention so that your demonstration of form matches the description in the poem. *Read poem, say:* Good. Let's do it one more time. Be sure to pay close attention to how your body feels and is positioned as you re-create the event. *Read.* Great. Now be seated. *Ask:* What were the emotional events the poet described? Where did you get that answer? *As students get familiar with the main categories, begin asking follow-up. Ask:* What were the social events the poet described? Where did you get that answer? *(Likely: In the Book). Ask:* Was that a Right There or Think and Search?

5. *Say:* Now I want you to read the poem for the third time, and this time, try to see the events as if they were a movie playing out the scene as it was described. Ask yourself, have I experienced a similar event?

6. *Ask:* Someone describe for us an experience you've had that was something like this? What was happening with your body? How did you feel? What were you thinking? What did you do right after? *Allow several responses with the same questions following.*

After Reading: Beyond—Gradual Release Writing

7. *Say:* Now let's create an opening sentence or two to begin an account of an experience like the moment in the poem "Foul Shot." How could we begin our account? *Allow students to make many suggestions. Record their sentences or phrases or ideas on the chalkboard or overhead projector. Then say:* All right, we have lots of good ideas. How can we combine these into one or two good opening sentences? *Take suggestions and begin fashioning the first two sentences of the account. Arrive at two generally agreed on opening sentences.*

8. *Say:* Okay, we have our first two sentences. *Read sentences aloud.* Everyone copy these sentences and write at least two more sentences to reflect or describe your own experience <u>and</u> to tell how active living is pleasurable for you.

9. *After students have completed their writing, say:* Turn to a partner or group yourselves in groups of no more than three. Take turns reading your account to each other. After each person reads, the partner or partners should tell that person what they liked most about their account. *Circulate as students read. Listen to full accounts and to partner response.*

10. *Say:* Let's read our poem aloud one more time. This time, you may read aloud with me. Let's be sure to reflect the physical, emotional, and social events in our reading. *Read.*

11. *Say:* Be sure your name is on your account so you can hand it in to me. I understand it's not a polished piece of writing. I want to see what you've written. I will give you a credit for your completed account.

12. *Say:* For the rest of the period, we'll work on foul shots. Squads, to your assigned drill baskets; squad leaders, pick up a basketball. I'll circulate and give you feedback.

LESSON ASSESSMENT(S)

13. Observational Assessment

    - Note how well individual students are able to identify and articulate QARs and how well they were able to analyze the physical, emotional, and social aspects of the poem.
    - Note quality of student contribution of ideas for opening lines for written accounts. Note individuals as they write own sentences. Assist as needed.
    - Watch foul shot practice noting individual student form and success. Give feedback as appropriate.

14. Other Assessment—Read and respond to written accounts; check to see that they include both elements required: description of experience and comment on active living. Grade accounts as completed or not.

THE DIFFERENCE MODEL AS A MEANS FOR VIEWING DIVERSITY

It is helpful to have a framework for understanding diversity in all its forms. Such a framework allows us to gain perspective regarding the broad spectrum of student diversity and guides how we think about and respond to diverse student abilities and needs. The Difference Model framework (Weiner & Cromer, 1967) gives us such a perspective and a positive means for conceptualizing diversity.

Weiner and Cromer identified four models to explain and describe instructional implications for students experiencing reading difficulties. These models grew from research on students with reading problems and were developed to explain characteristics of that population. However, they represent assumptions commonly applied to other types of diversity as well, particularly those involving physical and learning disabilities, cultural and language differences, and socioeconomic status.

The models, each with its own assumptions, diagnostic requirements, and instructional implications, serve as alternate means for understanding diverse student abilities—specifically, language and literacy abilities—in subject area classrooms. In presenting these models as representative ways to view many aspects of diversity, I am extending them beyond Weiner and Cromer's original intent. My thesis here, however, is that one of them, the Difference Model, is useful for responding to all types of diversity and is particularly helpful to subject area teachers in analyzing student needs and developing literacy instruction and support to accompany subject area instruction.

Weiner and Cromer's four models for characterizing problem readers are summarized in Figure 10.1. As you look at these four models, at least two attributes are readily apparent. One is that the first three models have names and assumptions that involve pathology: that is, defect = something *wrong*, deficit = something *missing*, and disruption = something *interfering*. In contrast, the Difference Model implies no pathology: nothing is wrong, missing, or interfering academically, socially, economically, linguistically, or culturally. Rather, something is *different*. The student responds in a way that is simply different from the expected response, and this difference may range from responses that indicate problems or inability to construct meaning to those that go well beyond the expected response.

THE DEFECT AND DISRUPTION MODELS

A second attribute is apparent in the instructional implications of each model. Two of them, *defect* and *disruption*, are well outside the purview of the subject area teacher (see Figure 10.1); the one requires "correction of the defect," whereas the other recommends

FIGURE 10.1 *Four Models for Understanding Literacy Abilities*
From Weiner and Cromer, 1967.

MODEL	ASSUMPTIONS	DIAGNOSIS	INSTRUCTION
DEFECT	Something is *wrong* that causes a problem (e.g., vision or hearing loss).	Find the problem.	Correct the defect.
DEFICIT	Something is *missing* that causes a problem (e.g., word-recognition or comprehension skills).	Find the missing element(s).	Teach student skills that are missing.
DISRUPTION	Some sort of physical or emotional trauma has occurred that *interferes* with reading and causes a problem (e.g., emotional difficulties).	Locate the cause of the trauma.	Remove the source of trauma and/or repair effects.
DIFFERENCE	Some *difference* exists between the student's usual mode of response and the expected mode that causes the problem (e.g., word-by-word reading or noncomprehension).	Identify the area of difference.	Adjust instructional approach or materials, or adjust response mode to minimize difference.

removing the source of trauma and/or repairing its effects. Certainly, teachers are responsible for referring students to specialists when they believe students need vision, hearing, or some other physical screening or emotional or psychological counseling. Nevertheless, there is often a limit to the amount of correction that can be made for any given problem as well as a limit to the range of physical and emotional problems that are correctable.

The fact is, students will be sitting in your classroom with any number of temporary or permanent physical and psychological problems ranging from very mild to major, and you are powerless to change the fact that these problems exist or to make the causal circumstances go away. Sometimes these problems will impinge on language and literacy functioning, and sometimes they will not; regardless, you can't change them. You *are* responsible for the academic and emotional well-being of these students in your classroom; however, you will need to do something other than look for the "defect" and correct it or identify the event that "disrupted" a student's progress. The defect and disruption models simply do not offer productive avenues for subject area teacher action in the face of various kinds of diversity in their classrooms.

THE DEFICIT MODEL

The *deficit model* is equally, if differently, problematic. The deficit model assumes that the best way to handle literacy problems is to look for whatever is missing and then teach it. It is, in fact, the most universally accepted model of instruction in Title I reading programs and many learning disability programs (Johnston & Allington, 1991). I have some serious reservations about the value of this model in any form, as do Johnston and Allington, because of its emphasis on "teaching to the weakness." Essentially, the deficit model suggests that appropriate instruction for students with reading or learning problems involves finding out what students can't do (or don't have), teaching them how to do it, and then having them practice doing it. From just about any perspective, this seems like a questionable practice; it certainly is from the student's vantage point.

Consider for a moment one of the things you do least well (perhaps, for example, batting a softball); now consider having to go to a place and learn about and practice doing that thing for one hour every day, five days a week. That's deficit-model teaching; that's "teaching to the weakness." I don't want to be on the receiving end of it, and I suspect you don't either. Furthermore, I suspect that at one time or another you've been exposed to plenty of instruction in how to do whatever it is you don't do well: *It didn't "take."* No matter how many hours you go to a place and learn about it and practice doing it, instruction probably wouldn't take now. The greatest fallacy, in my mind, about deficit-model teaching is that the model itself fails to account for the fact that whatever it is we're trying to teach now has probably already been taught and was not learned. Continuing to focus on that weakness and not on the individual's strengths is self-defeating.

Aside from these issues surrounding deficit-model teaching in reading classes is the incontrovertible fact that subject area teachers do not have time to teach students "missing" skills unless the skills are directly related to learning in subject areas. This entire book concerns your responsibilities for increasing students' literacy abilities *in your subject area*, and they are considerable. But to expect you as science teachers, social studies teachers, mathematics teachers, and home economics teachers to interrupt subject area instruction to teach the so-called basic literacy skills is unrealistic and unfair.

Much of what goes on in middle and high schools in the name of remedial instruction—in all subject areas—is clearly linked to a deficit model of teaching. More recently, schools have begun to implement remedial and low-track instruction in literacy based on the assumption that the cause of students' literacy problems is "missing" phonics skills. Greenleaf, Jiménez, and Roller raise serious questions about this practice and its assumptions:

> [S]econdary students who struggle to read are increasingly seen as having phonemic awareness or decoding problems that need to be addressed through a systematic reteaching of phonics. The assumption that we have a secondary population of students who missed phonics is a sweeping generalization that is not only false in many of our experiences with struggling readers in middle and high schools, but also dangerous as students are swept out of content area classes into remedial skills-based classes where their self-esteem, motivation, access to knowledge, and academic identities shrink. Why does this misrepresentation of the reading problems students face persist? These are students who can least afford this misguided waste of their time. (2002, p. 488)

David O'Brien (2003) notes the "profound, negative perceptions" adolescents develop of themselves as the result of prolonged placement in programs aimed at fixing deficit skills.

What is usually (but not always) unsaid here is that deficit-model thinking and instruction assume that someone is at fault: either the student is at fault for failing to learn a certain set of skills, or the student's former teachers are at fault for failing to teach them. Neither assumption is useful for helping marginalized readers function in the mainstream.

THE DIFFERENCE MODEL

The *difference model* offers an alternative to the defect, disruption, and deficit models as a way of viewing and responding to diversity, whether this diversity resides in language and literacy abilities or elsewhere. The difference model, as we suggested earlier, assumes no pathology; nothing is "wrong" with the student or missing or interfering with anything. The difference model is neutral in that regard. The teacher does not seek to find problems; rather, she or he identifies the student's response, compares it with the expected response, and evaluates the difference. This is a significant and important change from the other models in the way we look at students. We quit asking, "What's wrong here?" and begin asking, "What is the magnitude and nature of the difference?" We quit blaming students for not being able to do everything, spending hours finding labels and symptoms for so-called problems that seem to grow even larger as we toil, and generally operating from a mind-set of pathology and fault finding.

Of major significance here are the instructional implications the difference model suggests. Recall that in our models chart, the "instruction" section for the difference model reads, "Adjust instructional approach or materials, or adjust response mode to minimize difference." *Here* is where subject area teachers respond positively to diversity in their classrooms, and here is where your responsibility is most important. Notice that the model is still neutral. You are not going to change the instructional approach or materials because something is wrong with the materials or with students; rather, you are doing it because you notice a difference between what your students are doing and what you want them to do. In every sense, this entire book and others like it are about the many ways you can adjust instruction or instructional materials to minimize the difference between what your students are doing and what you want them to do.

AT-RISK STUDENTS, THE DIFFERENCE MODEL, AND DIVERSITY

In her elegant analysis of the parallels between quantum physics and reading theory, Constance Weaver (1994) notes that "when a human observer intervenes to measure some aspect or quality . . . the person *actualizes* one possibility (makes it happen) and collapses all other possibilities (negates the possibility of their happening)" (p. 1188). In other words, the transaction between the observer and the observed creates in a very real way the observer's construction of meaning about the behavior of the observed. I think this is an extraordinarily powerful notion. Applied to the difference model, it suggests that how we view students affects substantially our interpretations of students' behaviors and abilities. If we choose to assume pathology, we will indeed find things "wrong" or "missing" or "defective" in our students; if, on the other hand, we approach students from the point of view of the difference model, we will identify how and in what ways students' responses differ from our expected responses and adjust instruction and materials accordingly.

The difference model also leads us away from the fallacy of associating all diversity (or difference) with the general category of students "at risk." *At risk* is a term that gained great popularity and widespread use over 20 years ago from the widely disseminated and widely quoted study *A Nation at Risk: The Imperative for Educational Reform* (National Commission on Excellence in Education, 1983). My concern, and the concern of others (Pearson, 1990), is that we may label too many students "at risk" by making the definition include students who exhibit any difference from the mainstream—for example, bicultural/bilingual students and students with talents other than traditional academic skills.

There are indeed students in our schools who are truly at risk for failure, and their numbers are greater than any of us wish; but they cannot be defined by diversity or difference alone. I will discuss the specific characteristics of at-risk learners in the next section of this chapter. For now, the difference model is a useful reminder that diversity is not necessarily associated with problems or difficulties; difference is not necessarily the same as "at risk."

It is, of course, impossible to list and discuss every kind of difference or diversity found in today's schools. Nevertheless, there are broad categories of diversity useful for guiding our discussion here; within each of these categories there are variations and individual differences. Let's now look at specific types of diversity and ways that classroom teachers can reduce differences between how students respond and how teachers want them to respond.

MARGINALIZED LEARNERS

Marginalized learners are the kids we've all seen in school who, for a variety of reasons, do not participate in the mainstream activities of the school. It is however, more likely than not that literacy plays a role of some sort in these students' marginalization. Moje, Young, Readence, and Moore offer the following definition:

> Marginalized readers are those who are not connected to literacy in classrooms and schools. Specifically, we identify as marginalized adolescents those who are not engaged in reading and writing done in school; who have language or cultural practices different from those valued in school; or who are outsiders to the dominant group because of their race, class, gender, or sexual orientation. (2000, p. 405)

Marginalized adolescents are the students whom we most frequently consider to be at risk. Rich Vacca and Nancy Padak offer a specific definition of *at risk:*

> In times of war or crisis, men and women serving on the front line are often described as being "in harm's way." They're vulnerable to attack by the enemy and open to physical danger. In times of schooling—our times—some children and youth experience a different type of vulnerability and danger. For a variety of reasons . . . these students are in danger of school failure. They are also in harm's way, but not in the sense of physical danger or attack. Their danger, and society's potential loss, is more social, economic, and psychological in nature. From a school perspective, the students to whom we refer are said to be "at risk." (1990, p. 486)

Central to our discussion in this section are those students truly at risk and, specifically, those at risk of failing to acquire literacy levels necessary for academic success. Origin of birth, ethnicity, and/or language background do not, alone, define the risk. Rather, Vacca and Padak describe such students as fitting into one or more of the following categories (1990, pp. 487–488):

1. *Students who are alienated from a system that has failed them.* These are students who never learned to read effectively and rarely make any attempts to read at all.

2. *Students who learned to read but whose participation in school is marginal.* These students can read but do so only under duress and only to fulfill minimal requirements.

3. *Students who demonstrate characteristics of "learned helplessness."* These students feel that they do not have the resources for overcoming failure, and they are further limited by various other attributes and characteristics. Included in these attributes are (a) narrow understanding of reading processes, (b) lack of metacognitive skills, (c) low self-image, (d) negative attitude toward and interest in reading, and (e) limited set of strategies for approaching reading tasks.

Mike Rose, in *Lives on the Boundary*, depicts poignantly from the students' own perspective the marginal lives of adolescent students at risk:

> You'll see a handful of students far excel you in courses that sound exotic and that are only in the curriculum of the elite: French, physics, trigonometry.

> And all this is happening while you're trying to shape an identity; your body is changing, and your emotions are running wild. If you're a working-class kid in the vocational track, the options you'll have to deal with this will be constrained in certain ways: You're defined by your school as "slow"; you're placed in a curriculum that isn't designed to liberate you but to occupy you, or, if you're lucky, train you, though the training is for work the society does not esteem; other students are picking up the cues from your school and your curriculum and interacting with you in particular ways. . . . You turn your back on all this and let your mind roam where it may. What . . . so many [students] do is protect themselves from such suffocating madness by taking on with a vengeance the identity implied in the vocational track. Reject the confusion and frustration by openly defining yourself as the Common Joe. Champion the average. Rely on your own good sense. F— this b—s—. B—s—, of course, is everything you—and the others—fear is beyond you: books, essays, tests, academic scrambling, complexity, scientific reasoning, philosophical inquiry.
>
> The tragedy is that you have to twist the knife in your own gray matter to make this defense work. You'll have to shut down, have to reject intellectual stimuli or diffuse them with sarcasm, have to cultivate stupidity, have to convert boredom from a malady into a way of confronting the world. Keep your vocabulary simple, act stoned when you're not or act more stoned than you are, flaunt ignorance, materialize your dreams. It is a powerful and effective defense—it neutralizes the insult and the frustration of being a vocational kid and, when perfected, it drives teachers up the wall, a delightful secondary effect. But like all strong magic, it exacts a price. (1989, pp. 28–29)

The picture Rose paints here is all too accurate and all too familiar to those of us who have spent time with marginalized adolescents, and, when accompanied by poverty and racial segregation, the loss, in terms of potential achievement, is extraordinary. Jonathan Kozol, in *Amazing Grace: The Lives of Children and the Conscience of a Nation* (1995), documents the dropout and "discharge" rate of poor, at-risk students in New York City: only 200 graduating seniors in a school of 3,200 students—a statistic describing what he calls "human ruin" (p. 150).

Lance Gentile and Myrna McMillan explain that marginalized students have to deal simultaneously with their lack of academic prowess, which means that they spend days and weeks and years going from the unknown to the unknown, and the stress that accompanies failure to succeed in school. This produces a "fight or flight" reaction in which students either act confrontationally when faced with literacy tasks or retreat altogether (1987, pp. 19–22). Johnston and Allington attribute these behaviors to the "ego-involving situations" so commonly found in classrooms. Ego-involving situations are those in which the public nature of the situation causes one's ego to be exposed (1991, p. 1004); marginalized students have learned to avoid such vulnerability.

INSTRUCTION FOR MARGINALIZED STUDENTS

Certainly, we see marginalized readers and writers in secondary classrooms, and by the time they get there, they have established their own personal responses to school and literacy tasks. Some students may be brash, "difficult," and rejecting of traditional academic values; others may retreat into quiet passivity; and still others camouflage their academic problems with acting-out behavior, clowning, or obsequiousness. Whatever the overt behavior, it is important that these students not be thrust into ego-involving situations; specifically, Gentile and McMillan recommend that teachers not do any of the following with students who have difficulty reading (1987, pp. 3–4):

1. Require students to read aloud in front of other students.
2. Require students to read from books or materials that are long and hard.
3. Ask students to stop reading because they have made too many errors or appear lost or flustered.
4. Require students to do the same kind of reading day after day.
5. Require students to read materials that parallel specific traumatic events in their lives.

This list eliminates three of the most frequent activities associated with textbook reading in subject area classrooms (and, incidentally, at least two of which were operating in Derek Stackhouse's and Angie Butrous's classroom): (1) Round Robin Oral Reading, (2) reading from textbooks that are too difficult for the readers, and (3) unending, unvarying, routine reading assignments and tasks. Earlier, I emphasized in this text that unrehearsed oral reading has no place in the classroom, and I reiterate it here. Unrehearsed oral reading is a source of real fear and embarrassment for many students, and *it does little, if anything, to ensure that they are constructing meaning from text.* In fact, many students are so consumed by the discomfort of anticipating their turn and living through and remembering their embarrassment while reading that very little of their energy can be directed toward cognitive processing of content. Recall Jim Cope's finding (1997) from Chapter 4 that unrehearsed oral reading was the *single* most negative experience reported by adolescents in school, and Harry Singer's point (1970) that "following along" with fluent oral reading is not what marginalized readers and writers do. These students are just as poorly served by inappropriate materials and assignments that do not vary from one day to the next. We've discussed at length in other chapters the importance of friendly, accessible text, as well as the availability of many useful instructional strategies for teaching subject area content and literary skills.

Clearly, we must engage marginalized readers and writers in *task-involving* situations in which students get caught up in the activity and, in so doing, define themselves as successful (Johnston & Allington, 1991). In Chapter 7 we discussed the value of classrooms where students experience this "flow." In addition, we must give these students the support of working with others to achieve academic and literacy success; in this way, they are not overwhelmed by being solely responsible for everything they do in the classroom. We also must provide learning environments for marginalized adolescents that look and feel like the classrooms of accomplished learners.

CLASSROOMS FOR HIGH AND LOW ACHIEVERS

MaryEllen Vogt (2000) describes the results of her research on classrooms for high and low achievers (Vogt, 1989). She notes the differences in students' access to content as well as differences in instructional approach. She found that with the high-achieving students, teachers

- Talk less and encourage more interactions between students themselves.
- Use less structured teaching.
- Frequently include creative and generative approaches to teaching.
- Ask higher-level questions and allow more wait time after questioning.
- Cover more material and spend more time on instruction.
- Provide more opportunities for leadership and independent research.
- Have warmer and more personal relationships with students.
- Hold higher expectations for students' success.
- Praise students for "good thinking" with frequent elaboration of their responses.
- Use a greater variety of instructional materials.
- Spend little time on behavior and classroom management.

However, she found that while teaching low-achieving students, teachers:

- Talk more, with fewer opportunities for students to interact with each other.
- Use more structured teaching with fewer creative and generative methods.
- Ask primarily literal-level questions.
- Allow less wait time after questioning with little elaboration of student responses.
- Cover less material and content.
- Spend more time on behavior and management concerns.
- Provide few or no opportunities for leadership and independent research.
- Have less congenial relationships with students, primarily because of behavior and management issues.
- Hold lower expectations for students' success.
- Praise students for "trying hard" rather than for "good thinking" and successful endeavors.
- Use fewer and lower levels of instructional materials.

It is clear from Vogt's research that classrooms reserved specifically for marginalized readers and writers do not look and feel like the classrooms of accomplished learners, and that the end result is "differentiated expectations for students' success, in the minds of teachers, parents, and even in the students themselves" (p. 5).

And finally, if we are going to change the lives of marginalized readers and writers in any real sense, if we are going to remove the need for them "to protect themselves from such suffocating madness by taking on with a vengeance the identity implied in the vocational track" (Rose, 1989), then we must change the way we view them and the way they view themselves. Paul Crowley (1995) urges us to help marginalized readers revalue the reading process and themselves as readers. He states:

> Middle school is not too late to help readers in trouble. Students come to us with a wealth of language experiences and curiosity that form a solid basis for a meaning-centered reading program. The challenge for us is to strip away the sense of failure, to overcome the defensive attitude, and to involve them as members of a community of readers. This is not an easy task, but helping readers revalue themselves and what they know about reading is the starting point. (p. 11)

We help marginalized students revalue themselves as literate beings by arranging instruction *in every class* so that they are supported and successful, both in becoming increasingly strategic readers and writers and in learning subject matter content. We do this secure in the knowledge that success fosters more success. The extent to which marginalized learners begin to experience the exhilaration of accomplishment and see themselves as competent learners is the extent to which it is probable that they will continue to advance. One does not become an advanced downhill skier without feeling the rhythm of expert skiing. Equally, one does not become an accomplished reader, writer, and learner without experiencing what it feels like to read and write and learn successfully. To make this happen, we must provide "scaffolds"— structures that support students as they grapple with new ideas and new literacy needs (Cambourne & Turbill, 1988). The instructional approaches developed in the next section of the chapter and that you saw in the Centerpiece Lesson Plan for this chapter—as well as those discussed previously in this text—all have built into them various kinds of scaffolds to support all readers and writers, including marginalized learners.

INSTRUCTION IN SUBJECT AREA CLASSES FOR MARGINALIZED READERS AND WRITERS

It is important at this point to state explicitly that instruction in subject area classes for marginalized readers and writers *must be instruction that occurs as a natural part of the classroom and that has content learning as its primary goal.* That means you are not expected to "take students aside" and teach them separately from the rest of the class; nor are you to water down materials, slow down instruction, or otherwise impede the progress of other students in order to teach "remedial" reading and writing.

Rather, judicious choice of well-designed instructional activities that combine literacy and content instruction allows you to teach in such a way that supports the needs of marginalized learners *while providing appropriate, rigorous content instruction for all.* All of the instructional strategies presented in this section are useful for teaching in virtually any classroom, and all of them share characteristics of the kind of instruction that MaryEllen Vogt found to predominate in classrooms of high-achieving students. Only one of them, ReQuest, was specifically designed for teaching readers in trouble, and it has already been discussed as an appropriate content-focused instructional strategy (see Chapter 4). Any of the others could just as reasonably appear in other chapters in this text (e.g., comprehension, reading across the curriculum, or collaborative learning). My choice to include them here is based on the direct and explicit means these activities provide for developing students' metacognitive abilities and knowledge regarding their own literacy and learning. That is, these activities assist students in becoming strategic readers and writers—figuring out how subject area texts work, monitoring their progress through text, and developing effective response strategies for text reading, writing, and other learning events—characteristics associated with good readers and writers and high-achieving students. Our goal here is to adapt instruction and teach students how to adapt their responses so that we minimize the difference between what we want them to do and what they are able to do.

The first four instructional strategies presented here (ReQuest, QAR, ReQAR, VSS) all fit into a category of instruction generally labeled "reciprocal teaching" (Palincsar & Brown, 1984) that has been used successfully to teach marginalized readers and writers. Essentially, reciprocal teaching strategies focus on and strengthen students' proficiencies in four aspects of comprehension: predicting, questioning, clarifying word meanings and ideas, and summarizing. The last two (Gradual Release Writing Instruction, Cone of Experience) provide structure for guiding marginalized learners' writing and group projects. Do note that these aspects of comprehension, writing, and group learning are necessary literacy skills in all subject areas *and* that accomplished learners benefit from attention to them as well.

REQUEST

Although we've already discussed ReQuest as a means of developing comprehension in subject area texts (see Chapter 4), it deserves mention here because it was originally designed specifically for students with reading problems (Manzo, 1969b; Manzo, Manzo, & Thomas, 2004). ReQuest is particularly effective in one-to-one situations with individual students, which is how I used it in my Title I reading classes. As a regular classroom teacher, however, you will rarely have the opportunity to work one-to-one with your students. If you do, ReQuest is a good instructional choice, especially if students have already experienced it in whole-class settings. In that case, when you work with marginalized readers, I recommend that you proceed one sentence at a time, following all the criteria listed in Chapter 4, and that your questions focus both on content information and on useful literacy behaviors for constructing meaning while engaged with text.

You'll probably use ReQuest most often with the whole class and have the combined objectives of increasing content comprehension and providing assistance specifically for marginalized readers. Here again, you may also want to use sentence units for the initial experience (as opposed to paragraphs, which I suggested in our Chapter 4 discussion). In all probability, your targeted students will not be the ones to volunteer a question or a response. Although some people recommend calling on students to get the quieter ones to participate (Helfeldt & Lalik, 1976), I'm hesitant to do this, even when conversation is initially dominated by the better students. As long as everyone is attentive, I'm content to assume that the more vocal students are serving as yet another model of questioning behavior that others can emulate at a later time. If more hesitant students aren't forthcoming relatively soon, then put everyone into multiability groups and let them do ReQuest under the guidance of a peer leader. The smaller groups are less public and therefore less ego involving and threatening to students who are unsure of themselves as readers and learners.

Helfeldt and Henk (1990) recommend combining ReQuest with Question/Answer Relationships (QAR), which you saw in our Centerpiece Lesson Plan. We will look first at QAR, and we will then consider the combination of ReQuest and QAR.

QUESTION-ANSWER RELATIONSHIPS (QAR)

QAR (Raphael, 1982, 1984, 1986) is an activity in which students categorize comprehension questions according to how and from what sources the questions are answered. Raphael (1986, p. 517) uses the schematic shown in Figure 10.2 to describe relationships between questions and answers. This is the QAR porter used in the Centerpiece Lesson Plan.

In the Book relationships are those in which (1) answers are "Right There" (i.e., explicitly stated in one sentence or in two contiguous, pronominally related sentences) or (2) answers require the student to "Think and Search" (i.e., answers are available in one or more forms in text but must be put together from information throughout the reading).

In My Head relationships involve (1) answers that require "Author and Me" (i.e., require readers to combine background knowledge with elements from text in such a way as to integrate prior knowledge and text information) or (2) answers achieved "On My Own" (i.e., come primarily from readers' background knowledge unrelated to text information). The point of QAR is to develop students' understanding that both the text and their own knowledge base are important sources for constructing meaning while reading. Readers are then asked to consider specifically how text and background knowledge interact in the meaning-construction process.

The teacher may initiate instruction in QAR by modeling an introspective process (Helfeldt & Henk, 1990) or by probing students' responses during question-and-answer episodes with such follow-up questions as "How did you know that?" and "Where did you get that answer?" After identifying the QAR taxonomy, the teacher begins making

FIGURE 10.2 *QAR Relationships*

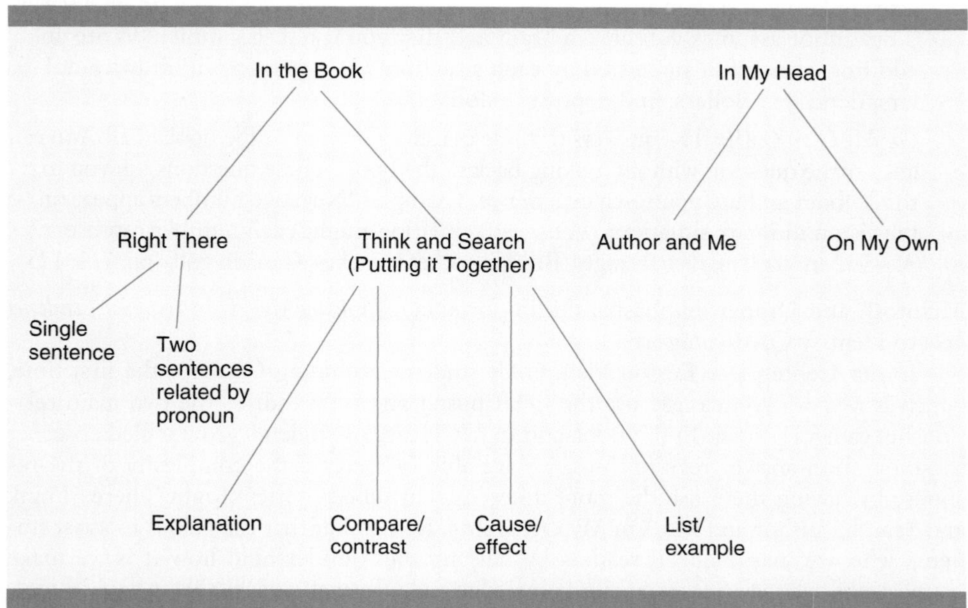

response relationships explicit—for example, "Oh. You had to look in several places *In the Book* to find that answer; that's a *Think and Search*, isn't it?" or "Good. You used information from the book and stuff *In My Head* to arrive at your answer. You were using *Author and Me* there."

Raphael (1986) suggests that teachers may want to begin by distinguishing only between the two main categories—*In the Book* and *In My Head*—and spend some time allowing students to analyze responses on those two dimensions only. After students become comfortable with that analysis, the teacher can begin extending to the subcategories *(Right There, Think and Search, Author and Me, On My Own)*, concentrating first on one main category (e.g., *In the Book*) and then including the other.

Margaret Mclntosh and Roni Draper (1995) taught the QAR strategy to middle-level and high school students in math classes. Here are the definitions they used to explain answer categories:

> *Right There QARs:* The answer is *right there* in the textbook—on the page—in the same sentence. Often the same words that make up the answer are found in the question. Example: "State the slide model for addition."
>
> *Think and Search QARs:* The answer is in the book, but you have to think about it and search for it. The answer is in the text, but not just in one sentence. The words in the question are not the same words that are found in the answer. Example: "Simplify –2 + y + –9."
>
> *Author and Me QARs:* The answers to the questions are not directly in the text; there may not even be an example like it in the text. However, the author has given you information in the text that you have to put together with what you already know and then fit all of this together to let you come up with an answer. The author assumes you have a brain and that you use it. Example: "Write an addition expression suggested by each situation: (1) A person withdraws *d* dollars, deposits *c* dollars, and deposits *b* dollars."
>
> *On My Own QARs:* The answers to these questions are not in the book at all. You can answer the question without looking back in the book. These questions ask you to think about and use your own experience. Example: "Negative numbers appear on television in many situations. What real situation might each number represent? A. –5.32 in stock market averages, B. –9 in rocket launches, C. –3 in golf. (pp. 121, 123)

Mclntosh and Draper emphasize the importance of taking the time to *teach students how* to identify QAR categories.

In our Centerpiece Lesson Plan, QAR students are doing QAR for the first time, which is why we consciously use the QAR poster and only address the two main relationship categories first: In the Book and In My Head. As students grow skilled at seeing these question-answer relationships, we are able to increase the complexity of the response by having them use the more differentiated subcategories (Right There, Think and Search, Author and Me, On My Own, etc.). Remember that the goal is to assist students who are marginalized readers by helping them understand how it is we make connections between our own prior knowledge and information available in text. Notice, there's nothing "remedial" about this lesson; it's absolutely appropriate for the best and least capable readers in the class. The fact that the teacher reads the poem aloud before students read is simply one more kind of scaffolding for marginalized readers.

I deliberately chose to use poetry in a physical education class lesson plan (as opposed to an English class lesson) to highlight Paul Marlette and Christine Gordon's notion that using alternative texts in PE class allows PE to become a "mindful" subject in which students connect with both their physical and cognitive realms (2004, p. 227). This lesson—except for the foul shot practice at the end—could just as easily be used in an English class with a change in emphasis from physical movement to poetic form.

Creating Strategic Readers

Marginalized readers characteristically are nonstrategic. (Recall that earlier in the chapter Vacca and Padak described students truly at-risk to have a "lack of metacognitive skills.") These students have little sense of their own reading abilities, how to connect what they know with new information, or even how to proceed through text efficiently and fluently. The greatest gift we can give them is to help them become metacognitive about reading, thinking, and learning in subject area texts. QAR is an excellent strategy for doing this, as is ReQuest. In each, we ask them to articulate how they're processing text, either by analyzing the relationships between questions and answers, or by learning to ask good questions of text. Use QAR and ReQuest frequently to guide students through your subject texts, especially if you have students who struggle to get through text on their own.

How to do . . . .

QAR

QAR is intended for use in all classes. It is particularly useful for marginalized readers because it highlights the value and importance of connecting prior knowledge and text information. (One way these students' response to text is different from the expected response is that they frequently do *not* make that connection.) It also serves as a basis for developing students' abilities to locate information in text, understand different text structures (e.g., explanation versus comparison–contrast), and recognize whether information is explicitly stated in the text or implied. The following steps will help you incorporate QAR into your question-and-answer discussions:

1. Teach the QAR taxonomy using an illustration such as the one in Figure 10.2.
2. During a question-and-answer discussion, connect students' answers with the QAR taxonomy—for example, "You had to look in several places *In the Book* to find the answer. That's a *Think and Search*."

3. Begin asking students to connect their answers with the QAR taxonomy at the main category level *(In the Book, In My Head).*

4. Continue doing this until students become skilled and confident at it.

5. Have students identify QAR connections using main categories and subcategories *(Right There, Think and Search, Author and Me, On My Own).*

6. Determine assessments.

REQAR

Helfeldt and Henk's (1990) combination of ReQuest and QAR is intended to be used after students are thoroughly familiar with both ReQuest and QAR separately. ReQAR uses the basic ReQuest questioning structure; however, Helfeldt and Henk suggest alternating between student questioning and teacher questioning after each question-and-answer sequence. In its original form (Manzo, 1969a), the ReQuest procedure allows students to ask as many questions as they wish to ask before turning the floor over to the teacher; this is followed by the teacher asking as many questions as she or he wishes to ask. I prefer the original form because it allows the teacher to follow up, as needed, in any areas not covered by students' questions and to provide as extended a model of questioning and answering as he or she deems necessary.

Using the ReQuest structure, ReQAR begins by focusing on the two main QAR categories: *In the Book* and *In My Head.* A student asks a question that the teacher answers in the following sequence:

1. The teacher answers the question.
2. The teacher identifies the QAR category (*In the Book* or *In My Head*).
3. The teacher gives reasons why he or she chose that QAR category.

This same procedure is used when students answer the teacher's questions.

After students demonstrate consistent proficiency in identifying main QAR categories, the second phase of ReQAR is initiated, in which the questioner specifies a QAR category for the answer giver to use, and the answer giver identifies the source, or subcategory *(Right There, Think and Search, Author and Me, On My Own)* used in developing an answer. The sequence looks as follows:

1. The student asks question(s) and specifies QAR category *(In the Book* or *In My Head).*
2. The teacher answers question(s) and identifies QAR source *(Right There, Think and Search, Author and Me, On My Own).*

In the final phase of ReQAR, all identification of QAR categories and sources is done by students. The teacher's role at this point is simply to field answers and questions; students determine which categories and sources describe their own and the teacher's questions and responses.

ReQAR has much to offer marginalized learners. First is the amount of analytical thinking going on in any question–answer episode. My experience with this population of students is that they usually are very good thinkers who haven't had many opportunities or much encouragement to use their intellectual capacities in school. Although they may hesitate at first, when given the opportunity to think and talk and problem-solve, they do so with amazing energy and skill. My experience using ReQuest and creative thinking activities with Title I students taught me that lesson well. ReQuest and QAR each encourage analytical thinking, even when used singly; combined, the effect is enhanced. My recommendation is that you not push quiet or hesitant students into participating during ReQAR; give them time to see how it works, and let them feel comfortable with it. Once the activity is well known, use small groups to make participation easier for them.

Another advantage of ReQAR is that by focusing on answers, the teacher and students will learn just as much about questions. Students who generally lack strategies for getting information and learning school subjects will therefore have access to kinds of questions to ask, kinds of information and combinations of information useful in school learning, and ways to find out what they want to know.

How to do . . . .

REQAR

Helfeldt and Henk recommend using ReQAR over time, and I concur. Like ReQuest, ReQAR will take a little time for its full power to be felt. Make it a short-and-sweet daily routine, gradually progressing from one stage to another. Don't feel pressed to do everything at once. Teach ReQuest first; play with it and let students get comfortable in their new role as question askers. Give them experience in small groups playing the teacher role as well. Then move on to QAR. Spend lots of time thinking out loud analyzing the question–answer relationships, and then draw students' analyses from them with easy, nonthreatening probe questions. After everyone is thoroughly successful with ReQuest and QAR, try the combination ReQAR and use it over time as well. The following steps are useful with ReQAR:

1. After students are familiar with ReQuest and QAR, in a ReQuest discussion, after answering a student's question, identify the QAR category *(In the Book, In My Head)* and give a reason for the category you chose.
2. Continue doing this for a while.
3. After a student answers your question, ask the student to identify the QAR category and give a reason for her or his choice.
4. Continue this until students are skilled and confident doing it.
5. Have a student ask you a question and identify the QAR category.
6. Answer the question and identify the QAR subcategory *(Right There, Think and Search, Author and Me, On My Own)*.
7. Ask students to make all identifications.
8. Determine assessments.

THE VOCABULARY SELF-COLLECTION STRATEGY (VSS)

I mentioned in Chapter 5 the success Brenda Shearer and I had using VSS with a population of at-risk middle school students (Ruddell & Shearer, 2002); in fact, the research we did combined reciprocal teaching with VSS. VSS was wildly popular with these students, and the words these seventh- and eighth-grade "at-risk" students collected were extraordinary. I listed a number of them in Chapter 5; here are a few more: *federation, spelunking, sophisticated, confidential, embezzle, mundane, pinnacle, recapitulate, inhumanity, emissary, reminisce*. We concluded:

> VSS word lists demonstrate that when given the opportunity to select their words, students will consistently choose important, challenging, interesting words to learn. In addition, VSS and comparative test scores reveal that they will learn self-chosen words and their spellings, retain that learning over time, and devote more effort to learning their own words than they will to commercially packaged word lists. (2002, p. 361)

I encourage you to use VSS as one way to meet the needs of marginalized readers and writers. It has a powerful effect.

What we discovered in our study is that using a combination of reciprocal teaching and VSS with marginalized learners caused them to move away from behaviors and attitudes typical of marginalization (learned helplessness, minimal response, alienation) and to replace those with behaviors and attitudes characteristic of high achievers (active involvement, metacognitive awareness of successful strategies, strategic reading and writing). By the end of the year they saw themselves as active, involved learners; very nearly all of them transitioned out of the Title I class into regular classes the following year (Shearer, Ruddell, & Vogt, 2001).

Recently we went back to the high school to see how successful the kids had been in school in the five years since the end of the study (Ruddell, in press). All of them had graduated from high school, the eighth-graders in 2003, and the seventh-graders in 2004. Two of the 17 students had moved away. Of the 15 remaining, two graduated with GPAs between 3.5 and 4.0; 11 graduated with GPAs between 2.5 and 3.49; and two graduated with a GPA of 2.0. On the Wisconsin State Assessment System test administered in 10th-grade, 12 of the 15 students scored in the 5th and 6th stanines, grade level or slightly above; and three scored in the 4th stanine, slightly below grade level. Three students are attending college, two of which were on the dean's list their freshman year. Six of the students went to vocational/technical school, four are working, two are in the military, and one of the students who moved away is known to be in college. This group of students, who scored two or more years below grade level in reading at the beginning of seventh and eighth grades, were very successful in high school, with over half going on to postsecondary education. It appears that they were able to sustain the gains we saw during the year of the study.

GRADUAL RELEASE WRITING INSTRUCTION

Douglas Fisher and Nancy Frey (2003) suggest a way to assist marginalized writers that starts with the teacher doing most of the writing by recording (or "scribing") student' thoughts in class-constructed written paragraphs and accounts. You saw Gradual Release Writing Instruction in our Centerpiece Lesson Plan. Such instruction may be focused on a specific kind of account—for example, a daily summary of what was learned that day—or not, as the teacher wishes. Students contribute ideas, the teacher leads the discussion and assists in shaping the written account, and records the account on the board or computer using an LCD projection screen so that all can see. This is followed by gradual diminution of teacher writing with concurrent increase in student independent and group writing. Fisher and Frey comment on the need for initial teacher participation:

> None of the students were willing to write in front of peers. Years of experience told them that they were not strong writers, and they were unwilling to demonstrate their skill or lack of it in front of the whole class. Thus, the writing done in class was initially teacher controlled. The teacher scribed almost everything, and bits and pieces of language structures and conventions were taught to the students. (p. 399)

The idea here is to begin with teacher-scribed accounts and move students progressively toward independent writing. Here are steps for so doing:

Step 1: After many experiences with group-created and teacher-scribed collective accounts, move to class-created beginning sentences that each student expands by writing one or two additional sentences independently. Fisher and Frey give an example: During a discussion of what constitutes sexual harassment, the class created the following two sentences: "Sexual harassment hurts everyone and makes people feel unsafe. Sexual harassment happens to a lot of people." (p. 399). Each student copied these two sentences and was asked to extend them with one or two sentences written independently. Give the class many opportunities to use expansion of group-created sentences so that students get very good at it.

Step 2: Take one minute each day to do power writing, a writing task designed solely for the purpose to increasing students' writing fluency by having them write as much as they can in a limited amount of time. Marginalized writers benefit from fluency practice because it helps them break out of a long-established pattern of inability to get words on paper. Give students a topic and have them write as fast as they can on that topic for one minute. At the end of the minute, students count their words and record the number on a personal chart. Power writing accounts can be saved and revised or simply saved. Fisher and Frey note that one young man from Somalia who could get fewer than five words on paper in a minute at the beginning of the year had increased to 40 words a minute by January.

Step 3: The final goal is independent writing. Fisher and Frey suggest that continued guidance is necessary to keep marginalized writers from slipping back into old patterns of procrastination and struggle. They recommend that independent writing topics grow from a collective class experience or reading that gives all students lots of background knowledge of the topic on which they will write. For some students, assistance in generating the first sentence or first two sentences may be needed in the beginning.

In describing their adolescent students in this gradual release approach, Fisher and Frey (2003) note:

> The adolescents in this class were interested in discussing their life experiences and the experiences they shared in class. They struggled to write, but they clearly had interesting and profound thoughts to share. As these students became convinced that they would be respected, they were more willing to share their writing with others. (p. 399)

In our Centerpiece Lesson Plan, we did two of the three parts of Gradual Release Writing Instruction. I agree with Fisher and Frey about the power of fluency practice for students who struggle with writing and composition. Students will find it strange at first to be writing as fast as they can for a minute, but they will gradually come to like their increasing prowess at getting words on paper. By all means do have them record their wpm (words per minute) each day. It is in the other two steps—teacher scribing and combining group-created sentences with independent writing—that you help them shape their writing skills so that they become increasingly skilled writers in your subject area. To the extent that you want students to be able to articulate their knowledge in writing, you will need to provide instruction and guidance in doing so. Gradual Release Writing Instruction is an effective way to do so.

How to do . . . .

GRADUAL RELEASE WRITING INSTRUCTION

The goal in this instruction is to provide strong scaffolding for students who have not previously been good writers, to support them as they progress toward fluent writing in subject areas. Thus, the teacher begins by writing for them and gradually lets them become more independent. Use the following steps:

1. Each day have students dictate group accounts, reports, and the like, and write the accounts on the board, on an overhead projector, or on a projected computer screen.
2. As ideas are mentioned, help students shape sentences, ideas, and topics into a coherent account.
3. After students are very experienced at scribed accounts, have students dictate the first two sentences that you write; then ask each student to add two more sentences to the account independently.
4. Add power writing to the daily routine: Have each student write on a topic you give them for one minute. At the end of the minute, have them count their words and record the number on a personal chart. Save these power writing samples and wpm charts and come back to them as desired.
5. Begin independent writing of paragraphs and accounts only on topics the class has discussed at length. For some students you may need to provide the first or the first and second sentences.

6. Give students many opportunities to continue power writing and independent account writing.
7. Determine assessments.

THE CONE OF EXPERIENCE

Project-based learning is yet another way to support marginalized learners (Moje et al., 2000). Richard Sinatra (1991) uses Dale's (1969) "Cone of Experience" as the basis for integrating language and literacy activities into content learning (Figure 10.3). The Cone of Experience approach is a useful way to develop lessons and units that give needed assistance to marginalized readers and writers while teaching content.

The key to the Cone of Experience is designing instruction on a continuum from Activities of Action (including direct, purposeful experiences, simulated experiences, and dramatic participation) to Activities of Observation (including demonstrations,

FIGURE 10.3 *Dale's Cone of Experience*
Adapted from Dale, 1969.

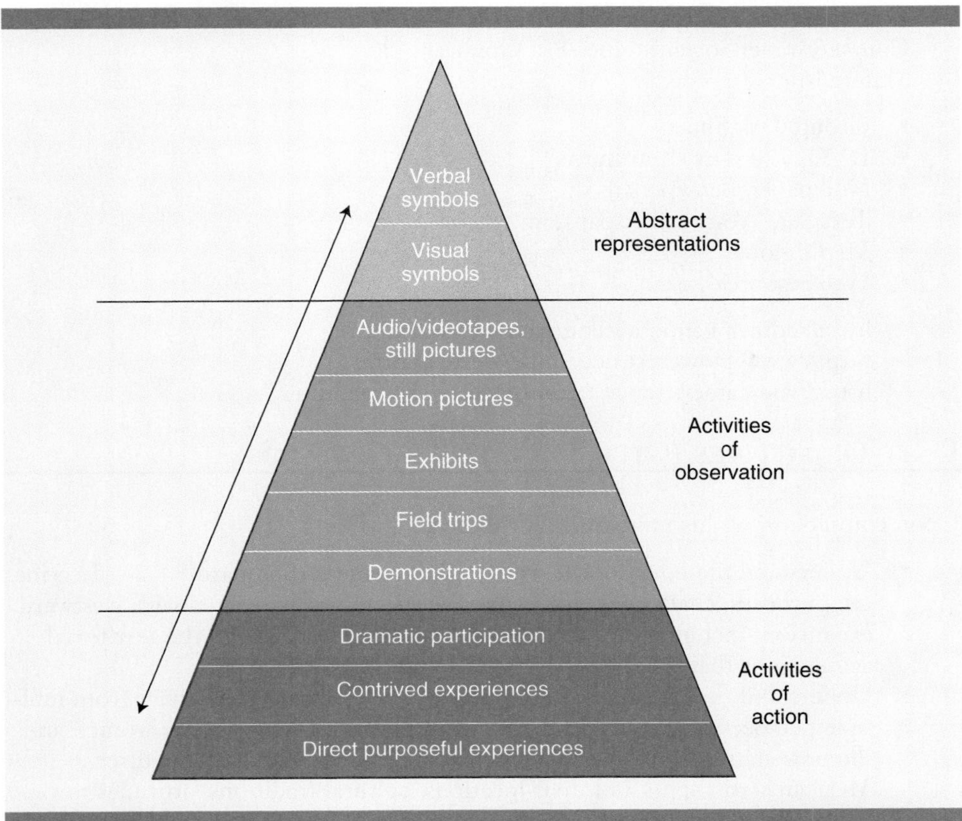

field trips, exhibits, motion pictures, DVDs, audio- and videotapes, and still pictures) to, finally, Abstract Representations (including visual symbols and verbal symbols). Important to the Cone of Experience is that the Action and Observation activities precede and provide the environment and context for Abstract Representation activities, so that by the time students read and write on a topic, they are well prepared and ready to do so.

The lesson or unit should begin with a "hands-on cooperative endeavor," in which students become immersed in the experience and the language of the topic (Sinatra, 1991, p. 427). After the direct experience or simulation activity, the lesson progresses to one or more observational activities that contain elements from the action experience and add to that experience. Finally, students, perhaps back in their groups, launch into full-scale reading and writing about the topic in whatever form and medium best fit the topic itself. Following is a Lesson Plan for a unit using the Cone of Experience.

CONE OF EXPERIENCE UNIT LESSON PLAN, *Social Studies*

Lesson: Westward Expansion
Course/Grade: Social Studies/8th Grade
Materials:

- Group Task Sheets
- DVD, *The West* (Ken Burns)
- Notepaper, pens/pencils
- Text Set, Westward Expansion
- Maps, globes
- Web resources, e.g.:

  http://edtech.kennesaw.edu/web/westward.html
  http://www.snowcrest.net/jmike/westexp.html
  http://www.americanwest.com/pages/wexpansi.htm

UNIT OBJECTIVES (WITH CONTENT STANDARDS)

Upon completion of this unit students will be able to

- Understand the effect of the westward movement (Standard 8.8.2—describe the purposes, challenges, and economic incentives associated with westward expansion, including the concept of Manifest Destiny, and the territorial acquisitions that spanned numerous decades).
- Understand the successes and failures of the westward movement from multiple perspectives (Standard 8.8.3—describe the role of pioneer women and the new status that western women achieved; Standard 8.8.5—discuss Mexican settlements and their locations, cultural traditions, attitudes toward slavery, land-grant system, and economies).

- Understand major challenges faced during the westward movement (Standard 8.8.4—examine the importance of the great rivers and the struggle over water rights).

LESSON PROCEDURES

Before Reading: Into—Activities of Action

1. Students will be divided into five groups. Each group will represent one of the following groups: male farmers/settlers ready to leave Independence, Missouri, on the Santa Fe Trail; wives/daughters and other female family members of the farmers and settlers; Mexican families living in the New Mexico Territory; Native Americans in Kansas, Oklahoma, Texas, and New Mexico territories; and cattle ranchers of various cultures in target areas for settlement.
2. Each group will receive a Task Sheet on which their group identity is noted (e.g., farmer/settler) and the following task is assigned:

   Task: From the perspective of your group, develop a written statement on a separate page of your group's attitude and position regarding westward expansion using the following questions to guide your development of your statement:
   - What is at stake for you in westward expansion?
   - What benefits can/will you get?
   - What are the demands, dangers, and problems for you as a result of the westward movement?
   - What will your responses be? Why?
   - What do you believe is your probability of succeeding? Why?
3. *Say:* Your first task is to work as a group to think about and combine what you already know about westward expansion from the perspective of settlers or women or Mexicans or Native Americans or cattle ranchers. Make a list of what you know and begin writing your statement.
4. After groups have completed their work, *say:* Let's share what we already know. *Allow each group to read its statement. Ask:* What are some of the things we don't know or need to learn more about? *Field responses and make lists.*

During Reading: Through—Activities of Observation

5. *Say:* Here are excerpts from Ken Burns's series *The West* that may shed some light on what we want to know. As you watch make notes of information that will be useful to your group. *Show DVD excerpts.*
6. *Ask*: What new information did you get from the show? *Field responses. After some discussion, say:* In your groups, go back to your task sheets and list possible projects that your group might want to pursue. Remember, you're still representing a specific group in the westward expansion. List resources you wish to use as well. There are lots of books on the cart, and you may look for Web sites as well. You will turn your task sheets in to me at the end of class today. Tomorrow I'll meet with each group to help you define your project.

After Reading: Beyond—Abstract Representations

7. Meet with each group to help them design their project. Each group chooses one or more aspects of its experience in the westward movement to research and presents a written account of its research along with a performance or graphic/visual product. Groups must consult at least one source in each of the following categories:
   - Museum products or visits
   - Realia
   - Web site information
   - Primary documents
   - Historical fiction
   - Biography/autobiography
   - Various kinds of maps

LESSON ASSESSMENT(S)

8. *Observational assessment*—Note students' background knowledge in the initial statement of benefits, problems, demands, dangers, etc. Note how well students are able to work in groups, locate and use information, be productive.

9. *Project assessment*—Grade the written and performance/visual products according to rubrics created. Students receive both an individual and group grade.

How to do . . . .

CONE OF EXPERIENCE

One of the main values of the Cone of Experience progression for lessons and units is that it leads you, the teacher, toward careful consideration of how to establish an environment and context for reading and writing in your subject area. That's a bonus for all students, but it is critical for marginalized readers and writers. The focus on group activities of action is also helpful, giving students an opportunity to contribute a variety of knowledge and skills to the group and then add to their own repertoire of literacy abilities in the abstract representation stage. Use the following steps to develop lessons and units using the Cone of Experience:

1. Identify unit or lesson content and objectives.

2. Determine Activities of Action and the introductory "hands-on" experience.

3. Identify, collect, and/or prepare resources for Activities of Observation.

4. Determine how the Activities of Observation connect to unit/lesson objectives and Activities of Action.

5. Determine alternatives for Abstract Representations and the prompt(s) you will use to guide students in completing Abstract Representations requirements.
6. Establish criteria and guidelines for students to use in meeting the Abstract Representations requirements.
7. Determine how the Abstract Representations requirements connect to the unit objectives and the Activities of Action and Observation.
8. Determine assessments

FINAL WORDS ABOUT MARGINALIZED LEARNERS

Before leaving our discussion about marginalized readers and writers, I think it's important to remember that many of the instructional strategies and activities discussed in other chapters are very helpful for addressing the needs of this group. We needn't discuss them further here, but do review and consider using the following: DR-TA and mapping (Chapter 4); DIA (Chapter 6); TPRC, PReP, and K-W-L (Chapter 7); learning logs and DEJs (Chapter 8). Other project-based approaches will be presented in Chapter 11.

Certainly, all of the instructional strategies and activities recommended for Sheltered Instruction in Chapter 6 are equally beneficial for marginalized readers and writers. Using text sets is especially appropriate for ensuring that marginalized learners have access to many levels and types of texts—fiction, nonfiction, easy books, hard books, journals, picture books, websites, DVDs, and other resources—that allow them to select the texts that give them access to the curriculum.

I remind you also that the most productive approach to minimizing the difference between what you want students to do and what they actually do is to look for students' strengths and build on them. Focus on what students *can* do and look to see how their strengths can be used in your classroom. Elizabeth Moje and her colleagues say it well:

> First, listen to and watch young people in a variety of spaces and contexts, looking for what they *can* do and for ways to bring that proficiency into the classroom. Often, kids who appear to struggle in the classroom are completely different people outside of the classroom. Youth who sit slumped in their desks and scowl when prompted to read or write are often fluent in other languages; can navigate cities with ease; can relate specific scientific information learned from television or from field trips; and can weave colorful cultural tales, classic children's literature, and colorful family stories. (2000, p. 405)

STUDENTS WITH SPECIAL NEEDS

In all likelihood you will have students with special needs in your classroom. Students may be identified variously as having a learning disability, attention deficit disorder (ADD), attention deficit hyperactivity disorder (ADHD), or physical needs with respect to hearing, vision, language, and neurological functioning. For some of these students, your major responsibility will be to make specific accommodations, such as allowing them more time for taking tests, letting them word process rather than hand write a test, or providing seating arrangements in class to accommodate for hearing loss or to make lip reading accessible or to minimize distractions. For others, you will be expected to adjust instruction to meet requirements in the student's Individualized Educational Program (IEP). Both types of accommodation are defined in law, in the Individuals with Disabilities Education Act (IDEA) and PL94-142. You are obliged to understand your responsibilities and to carry them out.

Many of the instructional adjustments recommended for students with special needs are those we've discussed throughout this text—having students make predictions before reading; guiding students before, during, and after reading; using advance organizers and graphic organizers (maps); using multi-modal presentations (as we did when sheltering lessons); presenting information visually; and others (Friend & Bursuck, 1999). A generally important strategy as you consider accommodations for students with special needs is to work with the special education teacher and others to understand the specific accommodations individual students require and to build those into your teaching repertoire.

One approach for giving students with special needs, and in fact all students, the opportunity to work within their area of strength is to arrange assignments and projects with options for alternative means for displaying knowledge. Howard Gardner's notion of "multiple intelligences" provides a framework for doing this (Gardner, 1993). *Verbal-linguistic* intelligence is highly valued in schools and includes all manner of spoken and written reports, essays, and debates; these are the traditional ways of demonstrating knowledge. Gardner suggests other intelligences and other ways of knowing: *Logical-mathematical*—charts, graphs, outlines, maps, diagrams, etc.; *Visual-spatial*—drawings, maps, cartoons, photographs, etc.; *Bodily-kinesthetic*—drama, role-playing, tableaux, demonstrations, buildings, dance, etc.; *Musical-rhythmic*—rap, dance, songs, talkstory, readers theatre, etc.; *Interpersonal*—surveys, interviews, newscasts, newspapers, magazines, biographies, etc.; *Intrapersonal*—journals, narratives, role-playing, autobiographies, letters, etc.; *Naturalistic*—gardening, creek/river restoration, star-gazing, walkabouts, etc. One of the finest social studies teachers I know creates options from each of these intelligences for students to choose how they wish to fulfill requirements for assignments and projects. So they may opt to paint a mural, write a rap song, design a detailed map, or create a PowerPoint presentation instead of writing a traditional report in his classroom. This is one way for you to consider alternatives for students whose strengths are different from verbal-linguistic intelligence, whether the students are identified as having special needs or not. In other words, it is a way for you to accommodate successfully for students with special needs while meeting the needs of all students in your classes.

GIFTEDNESS, GENDER, AND OTHER DIFFERENCES

We've discussed at some length the diverse populations in today's middle and secondary schools. Even if you teach in somewhat homogeneous schools, it's safe to predict that you will have many kinds of students come through your classroom daily.

Over the years, you will undoubtedly see a wide spectrum of human abilities, intelligences, attitudes, behaviors, appearances, and actions. It's impossible to address the needs of each and every one of those students in a text such as this; nevertheless, there are three additional populations I'd like to mention and discuss briefly.

GIFTED STUDENTS

Gifted students may be the most neglected group of students in schools. This is because in so many cases, gifted students are able to achieve, and in fact soar, without very much institutional or classroom attention. Many, many students gifted with extraordinary academic talents delight teachers daily with their wit, insight, and sterling work. For gifted students whose talents lie outside academic areas, challenge or go beyond teachers' understanding and beliefs, or are masked by inability to perform well on standardized academic achievement tests, this is not necessarily the case (Sternberg, 1986). Some gifted students actually have problems in school. Tuttle (1991, p. 373) identifies some of the characteristics of gifted students and some corresponding potential difficulties they may have (Figure 10.4).

FIGURE 10.4 *Characteristics Associated with Giftedness*

Characteristic	Sample Potential Problem
Curiosity	Continually raises questions that sometime interfere with the teacher's lesson; needs access to a variety of materials
Persistence	Focuses on areas of personal interest, sometimes at the expense of work in other areas often required by the teacher; is viewed as stubborn
Critical Thinking	Is reluctant to submit work that is not perfect: may not even begin a project because of feeling that it may not reach own excessively high standards; criticizes peers and teachers, causing negative reactions and feelings
Abstract Thinking	Neglects details once generalizations are mastered; jumps to conclusions about specifics; impatient with teacher's focus on specific steps or details in a procedure; becomes frustrated by others' inability to understand general concepts quickly; designs own procedures that may be in conflict with those taught by the teacher
High Verbal Ability	Dominates class and informal discussions; is sarcastic of others; argues for the sake of argument, detracting from the progress of the lesson; uses humor not always understood or accepted by others

You will find that multiple-ability grouping activities, project-based learning, and many different writing activities lend themselves to individual investigation and enrichment assignments that are appropriate and challenging for gifted students. Such assignments require students to choose areas of personal interest, read and conduct research about the chosen topic, and produce written and other products that reflect their research and learning. Essentially, assignments such as these provide opportunity and encouragement for gifted students to use their individual talents to go well beyond what others in the class are doing on any given topic and allow classroom teachers to make personalized, individual adjustments for students with special talents and above-average intelligence.

Parents of gifted students are often critical of mixed-ability grouping practices because they believe their children will be "slowed down" or held back by other students in the group. *Their concern is misplaced as long as the instruction used with these mixed-ability groups involves complex problem-solving tasks*—and we discuss this kind of instruction at length in Chapter 11. Subotnik (1988) emphasizes the value of interdisciplinary, thematic instruction for gifted students because of their ability to "see relationships and make generalizations" (p. 279). Throughout the literature on giftedness, there is a clear focus on the need for gifted students to be engaged in high-level problem-solving tasks involving intuitive expression, analogies, discrepancies, organized random search, tolerance for ambiguity, creative reading and writing, creative thinking, and visualization (Williams, 1972). Such instruction is very much in line with what should be going on in every classroom and is particularly appropriate for gifted students because it allows full use of their abilities and appeals to their wide range of interests.

GENDER DIFFERENCES

Since the 1980s, pioneering work has been done on the cognitive, moral, academic, and language development of girls and young women by, among others, Carol Gilligan and her associates (1990) at the Harvard Center for the Study of Gender, Education and Human Development; the Education for Women's Development Project (Belenky et al., 1986); Deborah Tannen (1990), in her study of language differences between males and females; Myra and David Sadker (1994), in their longitudinal studies of girls' academic achievement; the American Association of University Women in its national study, *The AAUW Report: How Schools Shortchange Girls* (1992); and Mary Pipher, in her studies of eating disorders and adolescent girls in therapy (1994). This work is significant because so much of our understanding of human development—and preadolescent and adolescent behavior especially—is rooted in theory and research from primarily male populations (Belenky et al., 1986; Gilligan, 1990). It was not until the 1980s that assumptions from male-based theory and research were examined in light of controlled research using female subjects.

What we know from the recent research on female development is that the patterns of cognitive, moral, academic, and language development of girls and young women are different from those of boys and young men. Studies have identified (and continue to identify) specifics regarding these differences. For example, Gilligan (1990) found 11- and 12-year-old girls to be confident, resistant to interlopers or things outside what they know, willing to stand up for their ideas, and willing to disagree—even reluctant to back down. By the age of 15 or 16, however, adolescent girls are likely to have gone "underground" with their resistance and appear much more tractable; they become less confident of their own abilities (or more willing to subordinate them) and focus primarily on making and maintaining connections with others. These connections have been found to be central to women's lives (Miller, 1976), and adolescent girls encountering conflict face the additional dilemma of deciding how (or whether) to protect themselves while simultaneously maintaining connections with others (Lyons, 1990).

The point of this discussion is that the decline in assertiveness and in achievement documented for middle-level and high school young women is deeply rooted in the culture of schools and classrooms as well as in the general social environment. Teachers and researchers report that girls "recede" in classrooms (Barbieri, 1995; Sadker & Sadker, 1994) where boys' voices and participation dominate. Boys' reading problems and their "inability to fit comfortably into the school culture" (Sadker, 2002) are also long-standing issues that have "a lot to do with how we conduct school" (Sadker, 2002, p. 238). Gender stereotypes continue to pervade classrooms and mold teacher and student behavior, even when teachers attempt to be sensitive and responsive to all students' needs. Nancy McCracken (1996) highlights the effects of such gender bias in schools:

> Girls are not the only ones harmed by gender role effects in language arts. While middle school girls have been the focus of much of the recent research on gender bias in the schools, it is important to recognize that all middle school kids, male and female, are harmed by pervasive, unaddressed gender stereotypes in schools, in language arts as well as in science and math. . . . Boys and girls who don't fit the stereotypical gender-role expectations are also profoundly disadvantaged in classrooms and schools where gender stereotypes go unchallenged. (p. 9)

Emerging recently and continuing to be the focus of much academic and popular press attention is the reevaluation of the social, emotional, and psychological development of boys (Hall, 1999). Spurred by Carol Gilligan's revolutionary research on the inner lives of girls, this new body of work looks more closely than we ever have at the seeds of violence in boys and young men (Hall, 1999); the effect that harsh teasing and being at the bottom of the social pyramid has on males' perceptions of their bodies and selves (LeBlanc, 1999); and a pervasive sense of disillusionment and disaffection on the part of young men in a world they believe to have let them down (Faludi, 1999). Current research indicates that boys engage differently in school and that they want and need to start with a real-life problem rather than the abstract issues in a textbook. Jeffrey Wilhelm states, "Shakespeare didn't write *Romeo and Juliet* to torture ninth or tenth graders, he wrote it to explore a human problem. The reason that we still read that play, make movies of it, and perform it, is that problem is still alive" (Harris, 2005, p. 4). Wilhelm's point is that boys need for us to start with the problem and not the play. I couldn't agree more (recall the discussion in Chapter 7 about flow, and discussion throughout this text about starting with what students *know*—their prior knowledge and previous experience—and leading them toward learning what they don't know). David Sadker (2002) admonishes us to address the very real issues that males and females face in school without turning the discussion into a gender war. We must keep sight of the fact that all of these social/emotional effects—for both males and females—have a profound impact on students' achievement in school.

OTHER DIFFERENCES

On occasion, you will have students with special differences who require the services and/or expertise of special teachers and staff. These include severe emotional, psychological, or learning disorders; homelessness and/or migrant family life; severe home and family problems; and physical problems that require in-school treatment, medications, or major accommodations. For students with such differences, you will need to work very closely with special teachers and staff to provide what is best for individuals while simultaneously caring for the needs of the other 30 or 35 students in the class. Your allies in this effort will be counselors, nurses, resource room teachers, vice principals, school psychologists, reading teachers, and various representatives of outside agencies, including social workers, police, psychologists and psychiatrists, physicians and nurses, and university clinical faculty.

Programs for pregnant teens, teen parents, students who have tested positive for human immunodeficiency virus (HIV) or students with acquired immunodeficiency syndrome (AIDS), and teen 12-step drug and alcohol recovery programs may also be operating within the school, or available outside it, and may be a significant part of your students' personal and academic lives. For you to address your students' cognitive needs, to teach them content and develop their ability to read and write in your subject area, you will have to maintain contact with school and community agency representatives who are working to support students psychologically, emotionally, physically, socially, and economically. Working with these professionals also supports you and your efforts in the classroom. As a rule, everyone benefits from close and frequent communication and collaboration.

CREATING LEARNING CLASSROOMS FOR PREADOLESCENT AND ADOLESCENT STUDENTS

Beyond designing and using effective instructional approaches, teachers also need to establish productive classrooms where students feel comfortable and safe, and where learning happens. Teachers don't have to "love" kids to be able to do this, but they do need to like them and understand what lies beneath the surface of the carefully constructed personas that adolescents present to the world. Elizabeth Kean (1991), a high school teacher, writes movingly about what she learned about teaching as she watched her own son progress through adolescence:

> High school students are simply high school students, not underage college kids. Like many inexperienced high school teachers, I'd been teaching literature by trying to reproduce my favorite college classes. Having a child in high school brought me and my embarrassingly unrealistic expectations back to earth. My son also helped me discover a side of my students I would have otherwise missed. Preparing for a 9th grade oral report on Greek mythology, Rob took a Tupperware bowl from the kitchen, covered it with aluminum foil, and wore it as a helmet. I was astonished. He was a jock. He worked at being "cool." Yet he was willing to put a foil-covered bowl on his head in public. (p. 7)

One of the ways we learn about what lies behind students' public faces is in the daily contact and interaction we have with them. Critical to this are the classroom routines, events, and rituals that define the learning environment and that come to define the teacher herself or himself. Much of what I'm talking about here falls under the heading of "classroom management" and has to do with everything from how class is called to order to what the operational classroom rules are and how they are monitored and enforced, to teacher mannerisms and habits, to the consistency of the teacher's demeanor and personality from day to day and week to week. My point is that how the teacher establishes classroom routines, events, and rituals has a major effect on the classroom environment and, therefore, on the human interactions that occur within that environment. This, in turn, affects the substance of what students and teachers say to one another and what they come to know about each other.

Any number of good books are available to guide you in making decisions about how you establish and maintain the environment in your classroom. My favorite, and the one I think all student teachers and new teachers should read (even though it is old), is Jenny Gray's *The Teacher's Survival Guide* (1969); it gives specific, useful, step-by-step advice for establishing an orderly classroom and for developing the classroom management skills that make teaching an art. My own advice for maintaining a classroom environment conducive for getting to know and like students consists of three central rules:

1. Establish clear, explicit expectations and make sure everyone knows them.
2. Be consistent.
3. Have a short memory.

EXPECTATIONS

It matters not how you determine *expectations* for student behavior in the classroom or precisely what those expectations are. You may wish to determine the rules of the road and simply tell them to students; conversely, you may want each class to work cooperatively at setting its own standards. You may find also that your idea of what constitutes appropriate and useful classroom behavior may not match other teachers' expectations. That's okay, too, although I encourage you to check the *Survival Guide* for ideas about appropriateness and inappropriateness. The important thing once these rules or standards have been developed is to make sure they are explicitly communicated to students and, I might add, written and displayed prominently in your substitute-teacher file for the days when you are not in the class. You may even wish to display them in the room. Explicit rules and clear communication are set forth so that everyone in the room knows precisely what these expectations are and therefore has no reason to be unclear or unsure about how to act.

CONSISTENCY

Consistency means that you respond to students and student behaviors pretty much the same way every day. Consistency also means that whatever the classroom rules and regulations are, they are enforced the same way every day and with every student. Whether you choose to run a highly structured classroom or one that allows considerable leeway for student actions is not the central issue; students generally adapt easily to different classroom styles *as long as each style is clearly defined and constant*. What is at issue is consistency. Whatever classroom style choice you make is your choice, but *make it and stay with it*.

Inconsistency is the kiss of death in a middle school, junior high school, or senior high school classroom; students want and need to know what the limits are and how far you are willing to be pushed. If you laugh one day at behavior you censured the day before, or if you allow chaos and out-of-control behavior one day and demand pin-drop silence the next, students will not be able to find the boundary limits or the point at which your flexibility ends. They will keep testing the limits and trying your patience. A true measure of your consistency is the number of times you have to yell or say "Sh!" to quiet the room, the amount of unproductive noise that swells when you turn your back or leave the room, and the degree to which student behavior careens from held-in-check to uncontrolled. If there's a lot, you're not.

Consistency also applies to how you treat students, and the rule here is, don't play favorites. Be thoroughly consistent in your treatment of students. You're bound to like some students better than others: Some students will charm you silly while others will put you off, and you will find it difficult to see any redeeming features about some of the students you teach. These feelings and responses are normal, natural aspects of human interaction. *But when it comes to how you treat students in your classroom, you must set these feelings aside*. Be assiduously fair, objective, and emotionally reasonable in your responses to student behavior, and, I might add, in your grading practices; the consequences for any act and the reward for any work must be absolutely the same for all students.

SHORT MEMORY

Having a *short memory* for what students do wrong is one of the greatest assets you can bring to the classroom. When problems occur, when student behavior is difficult, rebellious, or unacceptable, handle the problem immediately and completely. Get all issues attended to, and apply appropriate sanctions or disciplinary measures objectively and firmly. Then forget it. Be prepared to be stern and unyielding with a student one moment and capable *in the next moment* of addressing that same student in your normal, cheerful voice and accepting manner. That's not a particularly easy attribute to develop, but it's an important one for conveying to students that what is at issue here is their behavior and not themselves. It also demonstrates that you are not keeping a mental scoreboard of student "transgressions" that will accumulate throughout the school year. (Interestingly, the very act of moving rapidly from sternness to normal demeanor in such situations actually does help you avoid starting and maintaining scoreboards.) The ultimate message to students is this: "I may not always accept your behavior, but I always accept you." It's an important message, and it goes a long way in developing liking and trust between students and teachers.

The reason I've taken time to address classroom management issues is my strong belief that chaotic classrooms, or classrooms in which students feel frightened, or angry, or unsure of themselves, yield very little in the way of productive learning. Many different kinds of classrooms, on the other hand, provide positive environments. Characteristic of such classrooms, and notwithstanding a variety of classroom styles, is that students and teachers alike perceive the classroom to be a safe, orderly place where honest mistakes are allowed, risk taking is encouraged, and hard work is rewarded. Further, the class environment must be conducive to such feelings if schooling is going to accomplish its primary goal of educating young people. Students learn very little content, and very little that is positive, in classes where they feel disconnected, angry, or out of control.

THE DIFFERENCE MODEL REVISITED

By this time, it should be clear why I believe the Difference Model is so powerful for explaining student diversity and for developing appropriate instruction to meet various student needs. I like the Difference Model because:

1. It allows us to take a healthy, rather than pathological, look at diversity in all its manifestations.
2. It contains implications for instruction that are reasonable and workable within the context of subject area classrooms.
3. It reinforces the notion that sound, well-developed instructional approaches, with minor adjustments and adaptations, are just as appropriate for "diverse" learners as they are for mainstream learners. That's the whole point of this chapter.

You simply cannot attend to and correct every academic, language, and social-emotional "problem" students exhibit as they file through your classroom at the rate of 150 to 180 per day; such defect- and deficit-model goals are self-defeating, if only because of sheer numbers. You can, however, make needed adjustments in instruction and activities to adapt to differences between student response and your expectations and to capitalize and build on student strengths. Your decision to use instructional activities that support students' language and literacy abilities increases the likelihood that students with diverse abilities, language backgrounds, talents, and skills will succeed in your class.

WHAT THIS CHAPTER MEANS TO YOU

1. You have available many, many alternatives to the Round Robin Oral Reading routine that paralyzes Derek Stackhouse and dismays his teacher Angie Butrous; RROR is *not* a good way to make the curriculum accessible to all students, and it does absolutely nothing to develop students' literacy abilities in content areas. Don't use it.
2. Approaching diversity from the perspective of the Difference Model gives you useful ways to design instructional activities in your class that reduce the difference between what you want students to do and what they are able to do. In addition, it allows you to address the needs of all students in your classroom.
3. Rich, complex instruction using reciprocal teaching and collaborative learning approaches has high potential for meeting the needs of diverse learners, and especially for helping marginalized learners, gifted students, and students with special needs learn content and become better readers and writers.

DOUBLE ENTRY JOURNAL

Go back to your "diversity" semantic map. Rearrange, revise, and add to it in any way you now deem appropriate. Add a place for the category "Teaching I Can Do to Provide for Student Differences." Fill it in with ideas from this chapter (and other chapters) useful for your subject area. Share your map with a partner or a group. Explain how and why you restructured your original map.

FEATURE *What Goes in My Portfolio?*

Develop either a written or symbolic representation of the diversity you see in the school or schools you are in. How does the Difference Model relate to the populations you find there? Include a lesson plan that you would use to create a classroom that looks and feels like a class with high-achieving students.

RECOMMENDED SOURCES

*American Association of University Women (1992). *The AAUW Report: How schools shortchange girls.* Washington, DC: American Association of University Women.

*Banks, J. A. (2003). *Teaching strategies for ethnic studies* (7th ed.). Needham Heights, MA: Allyn & Bacon.

*Barbieri, M. (1995). *Sounds from the heart: Learning to listen to girls.* Portsmouth, NH: Heinemann.

Barbieri, M. (1996). Words under the words: Learning to listen to girls. *Voices from the Middle, 3*(1), 33–40.

*Belenky, M. F., Clency, B. M., Goldberger, N. R., & Tarule, J. M. (1986). *Women's ways of knowing.* New York: Basic Books.

Cambourne, B., & Turbill, J. (1988). *Coping with chaos.* Portsmouth, NH: Heinemann.

*Cope, J. (1997). Beyond Voices of Readers: Students on school's effect on reading. *English Journal, 86*(3), 18–23.

*Crowley, P. (1995). Listening to what readers tell us. *Voices from the Middle*, *2*(2), 3–12.

*Cited in text

*Dale, E. (1969). *Audio-visual methods in teaching* (3rd ed.). New York: Holt, Rinehart & Winston.

Davis, S. J., & Hunter, J. (1990). Historical novels: A context for gifted student research. *Journal of Reading, 33*, 602–606.

*Faludi, S. (1999). *Stifled: The betrayal of the American man*. New York: W. Morrow & Co.

*Fisher, D., & Frey, N. (2003). Writing instruction for struggling adolescent readers: A gradual release model. *Journal of Adolescent and Adult Literacy, 46*(5), 396–405.

*Friend, M., & Bursuck, W. D. (1999). *Including students with special needs: A practical guide for classroom teachers* (2nd ed.). Needham Hgts., MA: Allyn & Bacon.

*Gardner. H. (1993). *Frames of mind: The theory of multiple intelligences*. New York: HarperCollins.

*Gentile, L. M., & McMillan, M. M. (1987). *Stress and reading difficulties: Research, assessment and intervention*. Newark, DE: International Reading Association.

*Gilligan, C. (1990). Teaching Shakespeare's sister: Notes from the underground of female adolescence. In C. Gilligan, N. P. Lyons, & T. J. Hanmer (Eds.), *Making connections: The relational worlds of adolescent girls at Emma Willard School* (pp. 6–27). Cambridge, MA: Harvard University Press.

*Gray, J. (1969). *The teacher's survival guide* (2nd ed.). Belmont, CA: Fearon.

*Greenleaf, C. L., Jiménez, R. T., & Roller, C. (2002). Conversations: Reclaiming secondary reading interventions: From limited to rich conceptions, from narrow to broad conversations. *Reading Research Quarterly, 37*(4), 484–496.

*Hall, S. S. (1999, August 22). The bully in the mirror. *New York Times Magazine*, 31–35, 58.

*Harris, P. (2005). Tackling the challenge of boys' literacy gap. *Council Chronicle, 15*(1), 1, 4.

*Helfeldt, J. P., & Henk, W. A. (1990). Reciprocal question–answer relationships: An instructional technique for at-risk readers. *Journal of Reading, 33*, 509–514.

*Helfeldt, J. P., & Lalik, R. (1976). Reciprocal student-teaching questioning. *Reading Teacher, 30*, 283–287.

*Johnston, P., & Allington, R. (1991). Remediation. In R. Barr, M. L. Kamil, P. B. Mosenthal, & P. D. Pearson (Eds.), *Handbook of reading research: Volume II* (pp. 984–1012). New York: Longman.

*Kean, E. (1991, August). Other people's kids. *Teacher Magazine*, 6–7.

*Kozol, J. (1995). *Amazing grace: The lives of children and the conscience of a nation*. New York: Crown Publishers.

*LeBlanc, A. N. (1999, August 22). The outsiders. *New York Times Magazine*, 36–41.

*Luke, A. (2002, December). *Making literacy policy differently: Globalisation, diversity and semiotic economies*. Plenary address at the National Reading Conference, Miami, FL.

*Lyons, N. P. (1990). Listening to voices we have not heard: Emma Willard girls' ideas about self, relationships and morality. In C. Gilligan, N. P. Lyons, & T. J. Hanmer (Eds.), *Making connections: The relational worlds of adolescent girls at Emma Willard School* (pp. 30–72). Cambridge, MA: Harvard University Press.

Maker, C. J. (1982). *Curriculum development for the gifted*. Rockville, MD: Aspen.

*Manzo, A. V. (1969a). *Improving reading comprehension through reciprocal questioning*. Doctoral dissertation, Syracuse University (University Microfilms No. 70–10, 364), Syracuse, NY.

*Manzo, A. V. (1969b). The ReQuest procedure. *Journal of Reading, 13*, 123–126.

*Manzo, A. V., Manzo, U. C., & Thomas, M. M. (2004). *Content area literacy: Strategic thinking for strategic learning* (4th ed.). New York: John Wiley & Sons.

*Marlette, P. B., & Gordon, C. J. (2004). The use of alternative texts in physical education, *Journal of Adolescent and Adult Literacy, 46*(3), 226–237.

*McCracken, N. M. (1996). Resisting gender-binding in the middle school. *Voices from the Middle, 3*(1), 4–10.

*McIntosh, M. E., & Draper, R. J. (1995). Applying the Question–Answer Relationship strategy in mathematics. *Journal of Adolescent and Adult Literacy, 39*(2), 120–131.

Miller, J. B. (1976). *Toward a new psychology of women*. Boston: Beacon Press.

*Moje, E. B. (2002, December). *Youth's language and literacy practices in enactments of identity*. Presentation at the National Reading Conference, Miami, FL.

*Moje, E. B., Young, E. P., Readence, J. E., & Moore, D. W. (2000). Reinventing adolescent literacy for new times: Perennial and millennial issues. *Journal of Adolescent and Adult Literacy, 43(5)*, 400-410.

*National Commission on Excellence in Education (1983). *A nation at risk: The imperative for educational reform*. Washington, DC: U.S. Government Printing Office.

*O'Brien, D. (2003). Juxtaposing traditional intermedial literacies to redefine the competence of struggling adolescents. *Reading Online*, p. 1. Available at http://www.readingonline.org/newliteracies/obrien2/.

*Palincsar, A. S., & Brown, A. L. (1984). Reciprocal teaching of comprehension-fostering and comprehension-monitoring activities. *Cognition and Instruction, 1*, 117–175.

*Pearson, P. D. (1990, May). *Who's at risk? Our students, our schools, our society? A research and policy perspective*. Paper presented at the annual meeting of the International Reading Association. Atlanta.

*Pipher, M. (1994). *Reviving Ophelia: Saving the selves of adolescent girls*. New York: Putnam.

*Qin-Hilliard, D. B. (2002). Editor's review. *Harvard Educational Review, 72(3)*, 393-398.

*Raphael, T. E. (1982). Teaching children question-answering strategies. *Reading Teacher, 36*, 186–191.

*Raphael, T. E. (1984). Teaching learners about sources of information for answering comprehension questions. *Journal of Reading, 28*, 303–311.

*Raphael, T. E. (1986). Teaching question-answer relationships revisited. *Reading Teacher, 39*, 516–522.

*Rose, M. (1989). *Lives on the boundary*. New York: Penguin Books.

*Ruddell, M. R. (In press). Literacy research, diverse perspectives, and the big tent: An essay review. *Journal of Curriculum Instruction*.

*Ruddell, M. R., & Shearer, B. A. (2002). "Extraordinary," "tremendous," "exhilarating," "magnificent": Middle school at-risk students become avid word learners with the Vocabulary Self-Collection Strategy (VSS). *Journal of Adolescent and Adult Literacy, 45(5)*, 352–363.

*Sadker, D. (2002). An educator's primer on the gender war. *Phi Delta Kappan, 84(3)*, 235-240.

*Sadker, M., & Sadker, D. (1994). *Failing at fairness: How America's schools cheat girls*. New York: Scribner's.

*Shearer, B. A., Ruddell, M. R., & Vogt, M. E. (2001). Successful middle school reading intervention: Negotiated strategies and individual choice. In J. V. Hoffman, D. L. Schallert, C. M. Fairbanks, J. Worthy, & B. Maloch (eds.), *Fiftieth yearbook of the National Reading Conference* (pp. 558-571). Chicago: National Reading Conference.

*Sinatra, R. (1991). Integrating whole language with the learning of text. *Journal of Reading, 34*, 424–433.

*Singer, H. (1970). Research that should have made a difference. *Elementary English, 47*, 27–34.

*Sternberg, R. J. (1986). Identifying the gifted through IQ: Why a little bit of knowledge is a dangerous thing. *Roeper Review, 8*, 143–147.

*Subotnik, R. F. (1988). Teaching gifted students. In J. A. Banks & C. A. McGee Banks (Eds.), *Multicultural education: Issues and perspectives* (pp. 269–285). Boston: Allyn & Bacon.

*Tannen, D. (1990). *You just don't understand: Women and men in conversation*. New York: Ballantine.

*Tuttle, F. B., Jr. (1991). Teaching the gifted. In J. Flood, J. M. Jenson, D. Lapp, & J. R. Squire (Eds.), *Handbook of research on teaching English and the language arts* (pp. 372–379). New York: Macmillan.

*Vacca, R. T., & Padak, N. D. (1990). Who's at risk in reading? *Journal of Reading, 33*, 486–488.

Van Tassel-Baska, J., Feldhusen, J., Seeley, K., Wheatley, G., Silverman, L., & Foster, W. (1988). *Comprehensive curriculum for gifted learners*. Boston: Allyn & Bacon.

*Vogt, M. E. (1989). *The congruence between preservice teachers' and inservice teachers' attitudes and practices toward high and low achievers*. Unpublished doctoral dissertation, University of California, Berkeley.

*Vogt, M. E. (2000). Content learning for students needing modifications: An issue of access. In M. McLaughlin & M. E. Vogt (Eds.), *Creativity and innovation in content area teaching* (pp. 329–351). Norwood, MA: Christopher-Gordon.

*Weaver, C. (1994). Parallels between new paradigms in science and in reading and literacy theories: An essay review. In R. B. Ruddell, M. R. Ruddell, & H. Singer (Eds.), *Theoretical models and processes of reading* (4th ed., pp. 1185–1202). Newark, DE: International Reading Association.

*Weiner, M., & Cromer, W. (1967). Reading and reading difficulty: A conceptual analysis. *Harvard Educational Review, 37*, 620–643.

Wheatley, G. H. (1988). Matching instructional strategies to gifted learners. In J. Van Tassel-Baska, J. Feldhusen, K. Seeley, G. Wheatley, L. Silverman, & W. Foster (Eds.), *Comprehensive curriculum for gifted learners* (pp. 383–394). Boston: Allyn & Bacon.

*Williams, F. (1972). *A total creativity program kit*. Englewood Cliffs, NJ: Educational Technology Publications.

BUILDING TABLE

CHAPTER 10	QAR AND REQAR	GRADUAL RELEASE WRITING INSTRUCTION	CONE OF EXPERIENCE
GUIDES STUDENTS	After reading	Before, during, and after writing	Before, during, and after reading and writing
USE TO PLAN	Lessons	Lessons, semesters	Lessons, units
MAY BE USED	Whole class, small groups	Whole class, small group	Whole class, collaborative groups
MAY BE COMBINED WITH (known strategies)	DRA, GMA, ReQuest, VSS, REAP, learning logs, DEJ	DR-TA, GMA, ReQuest, VSS, TPRC, K-W-L, Three-Level Guides, Anticipation Guides	GMA, VSS, List-Group-Label, semantic mapping, REAP, Journals, learning logs, DEJ
MATERIALS PREPARATION	Light	Light	Moderate
OTHER PREPARATION	Moderate	Light	Moderate to extensive
OUTSIDE RESOURCES	Not needed	Not Needed	Necessary
HOW TO DO	Pages 387–388 and 389	Pages 392–393	Pages 396–397

CHAPTER 11

CONTENT LEARNING, COLLABORATION, AND LITERACY

DOUBLE ENTRY JOURNAL

What experience do you have working cooperatively or collaboratively with others toward a specific goal? How often is such work in your life associated with school—in your role either as teacher or as student? What do you like and not like about working collaboratively? What do you think makes cooperative or collaborative learning successful or not successful? Share your thoughts with a friend.

Spenser Ainsley/The Image Works

Martina Day and Greg Lewis are team teaching their *The Sky's the Limit!* unit, in which her computer science students and his physics students are working collaboratively on projects about space. They have the kids divided in cross-class groups of three to five students each, and right now groups are clustered around every computer in both classrooms to get their projects going. Some kids are accessing Web sites with their cell phones. The unit began yesterday when Martina and Greg introduced the students to the Space Physics and Aeronomy Research Collaboratory (SPARC) and NASA websites where they could explore the instruments, computer models, real-time data, and theories used for space research.

Each group is now continuing its explorations for the express purpose of (1) deciding what question(s) the group wants to pursue for its space-science project and (2) identifying additional websites and other resources for carrying out the project. Animated discussion fills the rooms as kids navigate within and across Web sites and use the class text sets that Martina and Greg had stocked with books, magazines, and journals from the district library. Because the rooms are right across the hall from each other, it's easy for Martina and Greg to move between rooms to answer questions and troubleshoot problems. As they pass each other in the hall they glance warily at the two other rooms in their wing and wonder if the working noise of the groups is bothering anybody.

They are very excited about the unit and the kids' response. There is no playing around going on in either room: The kids are working hard—talking, exploring, debating, planning—and appear to be eagerly engaged and on task. Once the project questions are approved, groups will have to continue working hard to gather the information they need and finally, to create the website and PowerPoint presentation required as the capstone of the project. Martina and Greg are expecting a lot of hard work from their students; they want sophisticated science knowledge and computer skills to result from this unit. Martina taught advanced electronic search strategies at the start of class today, and Greg is getting ready to lead students in summarizing some of the space research information they've found over the past two days. Tomorrow, the groups will look at questions they've generated, add to or refine them, and begin the process of winnowing their questions down to their project focus. All is going well so far.

• • •

Traditional learning models in middle and secondary schools are well entrenched and highly resistant to periodic waves of school reform and restructuring. Consider this description of U.S. classrooms developed by John Goodlad and his research team (1984) and the "frontal teaching" practices they found to dominate classrooms in the early 1980s. Consider also the accuracy of this description with respect to the instruction that goes on in many secondary classrooms today:

> The data from our observations in more than 1,000 classrooms support the popular image of a teacher standing or sitting in front of a class imparting knowledge to a group of students. Explaining and lecturing constituted the most frequent teaching activities, according to teachers, students, and our observations. And the frequency of these activities increased steadily from the primary to the senior high school years. Teachers also spent a substantial amount of time observing students at work or monitoring their seat-work, especially at the junior high level. (p. 105)

Goodlad goes on to emphasize that seat-work activities were rarely focused on constructing or producing knowledge; that "students were not very often called upon to build, draw, perform, role play, or make things" (p. 105); and that most independent work took the form of students working separately on identical tasks rather than individually working on tasks tailored to specific learning styles or circumstances. Thus, the discourse in most secondary classrooms is "fan-shaped" (Martin, 1983), with the teacher at the focal point of the fan. Margaret Cintorino (1993) gives us this picture:

> The teacher stands at the front of the room and addresses the large group. Some of the students listen; some do not. Some of the students accept the validity of the teacher's words and the teacher's right to say them; some do not. Some of the students absorb the teacher's proffered construction of knowledge and alter their own systems of knowledge in response; most do not. It is a difficult and detached way to learn. (p. 23)

Using Paulo Freire's "banking" analogy for schooling, Perry Marker completes the picture of traditional classrooms in U.S. secondary schools:

> [W]e, as teachers, set ourselves up as omniscient and often infallible experts who have a huge cache of facts and information from which students can frequently make withdrawals. And, in most cases, we do not wait for students to make the withdrawal, we conveniently direct deposit the information into students' accounts through lectures, worksheets, and textbooks. Students are at the mercy of the banker, who creates all the rules as to how the bank and the information deposited therein shall be organized, managed and dispensed. (1993, p. 78)

CURRENT APPROACHES TO CONTENT LEARNING

An increasingly popular antidote to the traditional teacher-dominated classroom—in all subject areas—is the notion of constructivist teaching and learning. Mark Windschitl defines the "culture of constructivism" as "a coherent pattern of expectations that underlie new relationships between students, teachers, and the world of ideas" (1999, p. 752). Specifically, constructivist teaching and learning are based on a theoretical stance and teachers' beliefs that

> learners actively create, interpret and reorganize knowledge in individual ways; . . . that their students' background knowledge profoundly affects how they interpret subject matter and that students learn best when they apply their knowledge to solve authentic problems, engage in "sense-making" dialogue with peers, and strive for deep understanding of core ideas rather than recall of a laundry list of facts. (p. 752)

Smerdon, Burkam, and Lee summarize the assumptions on which this theoretical stance and these teacher beliefs rest:

> (1) some of our notion of what constitutes "knowledge" may be culturally constructed, rather than truth or fact; (2) knowledge is distributed among group members and the knowledge of the group is greater than the sum of

> the knowledge of individuals; and (3) learning is an active, rather than passive, process of knowledge construction. (1999, p. 8)

Of particular importance in current constructivist thought are the "new literacies" of today's world and classrooms (New London Group, 1996). These are the multiple and often mixed symbol systems understood and used in highly technical environments, where messages are frequently multimodal and where the technology itself is constantly changing so that new symbol systems and new mixtures within and across systems develop rapidly. In his study of the attributes of new literacy classrooms, Kist (2002) found that students (1) know content; (2) understand different symbol systems and creative forms of expression; (3) understand how to evaluate information from different media; and (4) find the ability to be productive. In addition, Kist found that students and teachers in new literacy classrooms believed themselves to have benefited from:

- Projects.
- Shared responsibility.
- Interdisciplinary curriculum.
- Collaboration.
- Team teaching.

As you can see, these ideas, with the emphasis on students' construction of knowledge and social negotiation of meaning, are highly congruent with the theory and practice we've discussed throughout this book; in this chapter, the focus of discussion is on collaborative learning.

CENTERPIECE LESSON PLAN

The Centerpiece Lesson Plan for this chapter is actually a Unit Plan quite similar to Martina Day and Greg Lewis's *The Sky's the Limit!* unit. It combines a modified K-W-L, Project-Based Learning, and Internet Inquiry.

K-W-L, PROJECT-BASED LEARNING, INTERNET INQUIRY CENTERPIECE UNIT PLAN, *Music*

Unit: Mali to Memphis
Course/Grade: Vocal Music/6th–9th Grades
Materials:

- *Mali to Memphis* CD, Putomayo World Music, 1999
- Handout of musical artists on the CD playlist
- CD and book Text Set, Malian and Memphis-based Blues
- Butcher paper and markers
- Various percussion instruments, drums, blocks, etc.

- 25 copies, *Blues: An Anthology*
- Two laptops with LCD projectors for display of satellite pictures of Mali (http://www.google.com/maphp?hl=en&tab=wl&q=) and Memphis (http://www.google.com/maphp?hl=en&tab=wl&q=)
- 32 Project Work Management Sheets
- Internet access (laptops, desk tops, computer lab, cell phones, etc.)
- Paper, pencils, pens

LESSON OBJECTIVES (WITH CONTENT STANDARDS)

Upon completion of this unit students will be able to

- Recognize and understand Malian (Bambara, Fulani and Songhai) and American blues music traditions (Standard 6.a—identify simple music forms when presented orally; Standard 6.b—demonstrate perceptual skills by moving, by answering questions about, and by describing aural examples of music of various styles representing diverse cultures; Standard 7.a—describe distinguishing characteristics of representative music genres and styles from a variety of cultures).
- Sing American blues standards and accompany singing with percussion instruments (Standard 1.c—sing music representing diverse genres and cultures, with expression appropriate for the work being performed).
- Enjoy traditional and current Malian and American blues music (Standard 6.e—respond through purposeful movement to prominent musical characteristics while listening to music).

LESSON PROCEDURES

Before Reading: Into—K-W-L/Project-Based Learning

1. DAY ONE. As students enter the room and settle into their seats, play the first two songs on the CD, Amadou and Mariam's "Mon Amour, Ma Cherie" and John Lee Hooker's "I'm in the Mood." When ready to open class, *ask*: What kind of music is playing? *Field responses and record them on the board. Guide students to understanding that this is blues. Ask:* What do we know about the blues? *Record student responses on a large piece of butcher paper labeled Know mounted on an easel or taped to the chalkboard.*

2. After a number of responses are recorded and discussed, *say*: The first song you heard was blues from Mali, and the second was Memphis blues. We're going to do a unit called "Mali to Memphis." *Illuminate LCD projectors and show maps of Mali and Memphis. Say:* But first we're going to hear some music from each. *Start the CD album playing enough of each song to fill all but the last five minutes of class. Introduce each selection with the artist's name (writing each on the board) and encourage enjoyment of the music. After listening to the CD, say:* Here is a list of the artists you just heard. Tomorrow we're going to start by adding to our "Know" sheet *(point to sheet)*, so tonight I want

you to ask anyone you know who likes listening to blues music to give you more information. Come tomorrow ready to add to our "Know" list. Feel free to bring in any blues CDs you might have; I'll play them as we work.

3. DAY TWO. Have *Mali to Memphis* playing as students enter. *Say*: Let's add to our "Know" sheet. *Field responses. Read over the entries. Say:* Now you're going to work in groups to create a project your group wants to do about Malian and American blues. *Distribute students into groups of from three to five students. Have them create their own "Want to Know" list and a list of possible projects their group is interested in doing. Circulate and guide/assist groups as needed. Meet with each group to begin process of finalizing project topic. Play blues, both Malian and USA blues, as groups work.*
4. Distribute songbook anthologies and begin teaching a blues song.

During Reading: Through—Project-Based Learning, Internet Inquiry

5. DAY THREE. *Students seated in groups.* Using Internet access introduce students to the Internet Inquiry Web site (http://www.inquiry.uiuc.edu/) where you've registered the class. Demonstrate how groups can use the site to get information and create their project. Remind them of other search resources: Google, etc. Work with each group to finalize project topic. *Say:* Use the rest of class to search for information about your topic. You may check out CDs and books from the CD/book text set cart to use at home tonight. Before you leave class today, fill out the top part of your Project Management Sheets (Group and Members), one for each member of your group and one you'll turn in to me before you leave class. Tomorrow we'll have half the class for your projects and half for singin' the blues.
6. DAY FOUR. *Say*: [Group Name], what are you planning to do today? What do you need? How can I help you? *Record group's response under "Work Planned" on that groups Project Work Management Sheet. Remind students to record on their sheets. Continue similarly with all groups.*
7. *At the end of work, repeat the group poll. Say:* [Group Name] what did you accomplish today? What are your plans for tomorrow? *Record.*
8. Distribute songbook anthologies, sing/learn blues songs.
9. Continue in this pattern until projects are complete.

After Reading: Beyond

10. Students present results of their inquiry project to class.

LESSON ASSESSMENT(S)

11. <u>Observation assessment</u>—Throughout the unit observe students to see that they are understanding musical concepts, inquiry strategies, and organizational/project display requirements. Observe also to see that they enjoy the musical experiences of listening and singing.

12. Project assessment—Using the rubric you designed, grade group projects. Students will receive an individual and group grade.

COOPERATIVE LEARNING AND COLLABORATIVE LEARNING

The literature that supports cooperative learning begins with pioneering work by social psychologists interested in the social effects of cooperative and competitive group environments (Lewin, Lippitt, & White, 1939; Sherif et al., 1961) and specifically in school settings with academic goals (Aaronson et al., 1975). Later, educational psychologists and educators with specialties in various fields adopted cooperative learning as the focal point of study for developing effective instructional practice (Cohen, 1994; Johnson & Johnson, 1979; LittleSoldier, 1989; Sharan & Sharan, 1989/90).

Cooperative learning has for many years enjoyed broad appeal and retains current prominence in educational thought. The literature abounds with various names for cooperative learning, most of which are used synonymously (e.g., "group problem solving," "groupwork," and "group investigation"). An important distinction does exist, however, between *cooperative learning* and *collaborative learning* (even though the terms are often used interchangeably); this distinction centers around who does what planning for whom. That is,

- *Cooperative learning activities* are most often conceived and planned by the teacher and carried out by students in cooperative groups working from teacher direction and assistance.
- *Collaborative learning activities* are projects and ventures that are student directed; i.e., projects planned, developed, and carried out by student groups in consultation with the teacher.

This distinction gets fuzzy in both theory and practice when teacher-planned activities develop a life of their own and new direction as student work progresses, and/or when student-planned activities bog down and require greater amounts of structure and assistance from the teacher. Thus, cooperative activities can become collaborative, and collaborative student planning may require considerable teacher direction. The focus of our discussion is collaborative learning; in those discussions where the literature is specific to one type of learning activity (cooperative or collaborative), I will use that terminology exclusively.

CHARACTERISTICS OF COOPERATIVE/COLLABORATIVE LEARNING

Cohen (1994) uses the term *groupwork* to refer to cooperative learning and suggests that cooperative learning has four key characteristics: (1) delegation of authority, (2) shared responsibility for learning, (3) mixed-ability grouping, and (4) complex academic tasks.

DELEGATION OF AUTHORITY

In cooperative learning classrooms, the teacher, rather than telling students how to solve problems and monitoring the work to prevent error or failures, must *delegate* some of the work of problem solving and self-monitoring to students. That is, she or he allows students to "make mistakes and struggle on their own" toward solution of the problem with which the group is presented (p. 2). This means that cooperative learning activities change a major dynamic of the traditional classroom.

As we discussed earlier, the most common form of instruction in traditional classrooms is lecture and explanation; the teacher's voice predominates, and the students' role is to absorb information, follow directions, and learn the content of the curriculum. In cooperative learning classrooms, on the other hand, *students' voices predominate:* Students do most of the talking, students figure out what to do, and students make missteps and errors along the way. The knowledge that students construct as they negotiate the process of problem solving and working with new ideas, then, becomes the curriculum that is guided and nurtured by teacher construction of complex, productive tasks. I once heard someone say, "The more the teacher talks, the more the teacher learns"; cooperative learning is based on the obverse of that statement: "The more the students talk, the more the students learn."

Shared Responsibility for Learning

The second key characteristic of cooperative learning is that *no one can complete an assigned task without the participation of other members of the group* (Cohen, 1994). Consequently, students teach, assist, and guide one another and give directions, listen, criticize, and complement each other's efforts. Here again, the classroom dynamic changes from one that traditionally has been competitive to one in which individual success depends on group success. This new dynamic does not occur magically, nor can its development be left to chance. Teachers can and must guide students toward cooperative learning behaviors, and we will discuss at length ways to do this later in this chapter. Once students become adept at group participation, however, such creative group problem solving yields important gains for students in the form of opportunities to (1) learn from one another, (2) engage in higher-order thinking, and (3) experience authentic intellectual pride in their accomplishments (Cohen, 1994, pp. 13–19).

Mixed-Ability Grouping

A third characteristic of cooperative learning activities is that *groups are mixed ability and mixed regarding other status characteristics* (gender, race, ethnicity, etc.), so that they represent the classroom and school population as a whole. This is particularly significant for students whose cultural and family backgrounds include core values in which individuals with different strengths and abilities share and help one another as specific abilities are needed (LittleSoldier, 1989). Donna Alvermann cautions, however, that teachers should be cognizant of power relationships between ourselves and our students and among students themselves (1995, p. 285).

Collaborative learning approaches are one way schools can, and do, effect the change from tracked to untracked class placement. In fact, these activities are the most reasonable alternative to the traditional read-lecture-explain-test format that is so difficult to accomplish successfully with mixed-ability classes. In many high schools today, however, there is extraordinary pressure for ability tracking in ever-greater numbers, with the increase of advanced placement (AP) and honors courses, implementation of high-stakes tests, and development of compensatory programs; thus, mixed-ability groups are correspondingly more homogeneous.

COMPLEX ACADEMIC TASKS

Finally, critical to the success of cooperative learning activities are the *tasks* themselves. Cohen recommends that group work tasks have more than one answer or involve more than one way to solve problems; be intrinsically interesting and rewarding; allow different students to make different contributions; use multimedia; involve sight, sound, and touch; require a variety of skills and behaviors; require reading and writing; and challenge students (1994, pp. 57–58).

Clearly, all of these characteristics point to collaborative learning tasks that are complex, rich, and full. Many, but not all, group learning activities require more than one class period to complete; these generally involve rather extended, polished final products. Complex group tasks can be completed in the space of a class period, however; it becomes a matter of adjusting the scope of activities to fit the time and activity constraints of the course.

COLLABORATIVE LEARNING, LANGUAGE, AND LITERACY

Collaborative learning is, by definition, constructivist. What, then, does collaborative learning have to do with developing students' reading and writing abilities? The answer is "a lot." In fact, you already know, or sense, the extent and magnitude of this relationship because of the emphasis placed on it in other chapters of this text and the number of instructional activities developed there that require cooperative group or partnership work to complete.

Ann Shea Bayer (1990) uses Vygotsky's (1978) notions about the social origins of learning to make a case for what she calls "collaborative-apprenticeship learning" (CAL), in which student language and thinking are central to the learning process (Bayer, 1990, p. 18) and are enhanced through social interactions. She, Vygotsky, and others contend that learning is deepened and enhanced through language and social interactions that occur as learning progresses. Bayer makes the following assertions about these interrelationships (the assertions in italics are Bayer's; the explanations in plain text are mine):

1. *Language is the mechanism through which the negotiation of meaning occurs.* Until we can give voice to our thinking, it remains inchoate, confused, and unformed. Language allows us to sort through confusion, name ideas, and mark our own progress toward insight; students cannot effectively learn subject area content without using language to negotiate and construct meaning.

2. *Students need regular opportunities to talk, read, and write as they attempt to construct explanations that make sense to them.* Without these opportunities, students are engaged in what I call "lonely learning," which systematically limits their potential for learning and for increasing their literacy abilities by denying them access to the thinking of those around them. Listening to the teacher's explanation is not nearly as effective in "getting it" as is working through an idea or process with the help of other learners.

3. *Expressive language allows the learner to express freely thoughts, feelings, and opinions about a subject and is the beginning point for coming to terms with new ideas.* Expressive language doesn't sound academic and may, in fact, be mistaken for informal conversation. Nevertheless, it is the language we all use to "noodle" with ideas, explore and experiment, and become accustomed to new concepts and thinking. Expressive language is the language we use before and while we gain mastery over the subject area itself and is often the language we use to rehearse, or "try out," new ideas.

4. *As students work out meanings for new concepts, their talk becomes less expressive and more formal and includes appropriate use of specialized vocabulary.* Students begin to talk, write, and think like scientists, poets, historians, welders, and mathematicians only after they've had many opportunities to try out the language, experiment with new ideas, and explore new ways of thinking. They cannot do this solely within their own heads; they need the audience, the reactions, the other points of view that group interaction provides to extend their own thinking. As Windschitl states, they need "to be witness to and participate in one another's thinking" (1999, p. 753).

If we now add to Bayer's assertions the principles of thinking, reading, and writing set forth by this text, we begin to see the full extent of the interrelationships among collaborative learning, language, and literacy. Essentially, the logic goes like this:

1. Thinking, reading, and writing are cognitive processes that have as their intended outcome the construction of meaning.

2. Language, whether oral or written, is a primary medium through which we explore, extend, and grapple with ideas while thinking, reading, and writing to arrive at new insights and construct new knowledge.

3. Opportunity to use spoken and written language and to share insights, explorations, extensions, and questions with others increases everyone's fund of knowledge, reveals alternative logic systems, influences viewpoints, and enriches the total experience base we can bring to the reading/writing act.

4. This enriched experience, including increased knowledge and alternative logic systems and viewpoints, in turn, increases our ability to construct rich meanings as we transact with text.

Thus, the relationship between cooperative and collaborative learning and students' abilities to read and write in subject areas is a direct and important one, and the relationship between language (including literacy abilities) and subject area learning is just as direct. These extraordinary and singularly important linkages among thinking, language, social interaction, literacy abilities, and subject area learning are sufficiently compelling, I think, for us to conclude that instruction in subject area classrooms must, indeed, account for all these variables and their interactions.

CONCEPT-ORIENTED READING INSTRUCTION (CORI)

Guthrie, Alao, and Rinehart (1997) describe an instructional framework for content learning that combines all aspects of constructivist, integrated, interdisciplinary, and collaborative learning. Figure 11.1 illustrates the seven themes that comprise Concept-Oriented Reading Instruction (CORI): instruction that is Observational, Conceptual, Strategic, Self-directed, Collaborative, Self-expressive, and Coherent. Within the CORI framework, learning begins with *real-world observation*—an opportunity for students to look around them and define what they see, whether this observation is focused on the physics of body movement, the social conditions of a community, animal habitats, or the

FIGURE 11.1 *CORI*

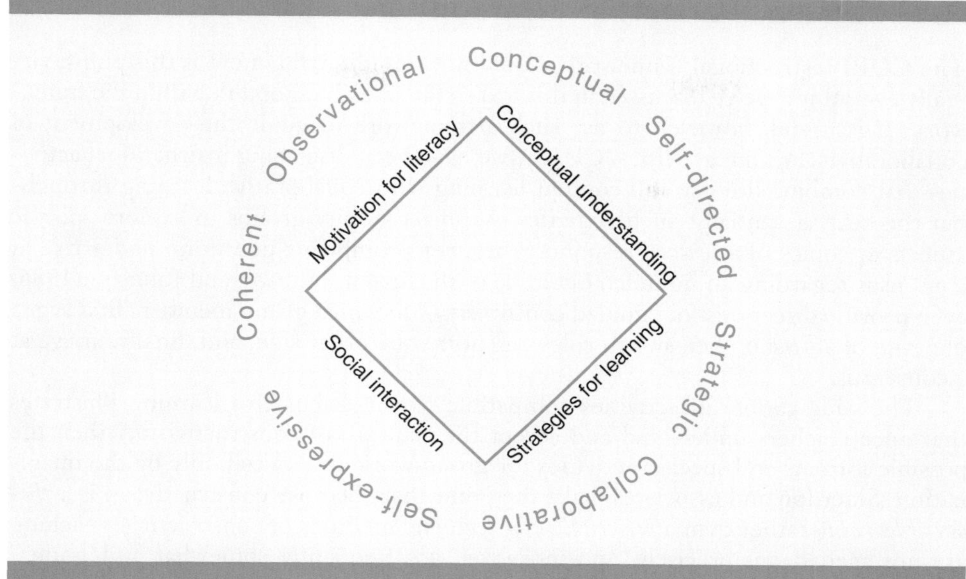

messages about human behavior found in episodes of *Monty Python's Flying Circus*. From these observations and encounters, students develop *conceptual questions* that they want to answer and, with the teacher's guidance, begin shaping these questions into research projects. As students pursue answers to their questions, the teacher provides *strategy instruction*—how to find information online, what resources are available, how to use features of texts to guide the search and make it more efficient, how to redirect a search that hits a dead end, how to differentiate between what we already know and what we want to learn, and so on—to increase students' ability to be strategic as they carry out research. *Self-direction* and *collaboration* are predominant aspects of each group's work in answering questions and communicating findings to the rest of the class. What student groups produce—whether videos, graphs, written reports, illustrations, songs, or plays—are *self-expressions* that are representations of the knowledge that students have constructed. *Coherence* is found in the connections students make between what they know, observe, and learn and in the connections between learning experiences (Guthrie et al., 1997). You can see from this description that Martina and Greg's *The Sky's the Limit!* space unit is based on the CORI framework and further that CORI instruction intends to create the condition of flow we discussed in Chapter 7.

Guthrie emphasizes that when teaching from the CORI perspective, teachers (1) focus on content goals, (2) provide choice for students to make decisions about tasks and texts used for learning, (3) provide hands-on activities related to goals and tasks, (4) use an abundance of interesting texts for learning, and (5) support students' collaboration and discourse around a variety of text types (2004, pp. 11–13).

COLLABORATIVE LEARNING ACTIVITIES TO PROMOTE LITERACY AND CONTENT LEARNING

The CORI instructional framework should not sound terribly new at this point; virtually everything we've discussed in this text so far is easily a good fit within the framework. It is useful, however, to use such a framework to guide the development of collaborative learning activities. Clearly, we have been discussing instructional activities that combine literacy and content learning with collaborative learning throughout this text. Essentially, such activities use mixed-ability groups to explore specific aspects or topics of a lesson, respond to teacher prompts or questions, and arrive at consensus regarding an intended outcome of the lesson. Johnson and Johnson (1986) even provide directions for "guided controversy," in which group members first argue one side of an issue, then switch roles and argue the other side, and, finally, arrive at a consensus.

The wide variety of activities compatible with collaborative learning illustrates that once teachers understand and accept the "culture of constructivism," then the possible formats and specific activities for group work are limited only by the imagination. Smerdon and associates make the point that "because constructivism is a *theory of learning* rather than a *prescription for teaching*, methods of constructivist teaching are not spelled out precisely, and moreover, are frequently somewhat ambiguous" (1999, p. 9). Collaborative learning activities, therefore, can take many different forms; the one constant among them, however, is that they build on students' prior knowledge, emphasize higher-order thinking and problem solving, allow students' voices to predominate, and require group construction of a final learning product (Smerdon et al., 1999).

Collaborative learning activities lend themselves to many different kinds of language and literacy uses. Furthermore, they promote content learning by providing extended opportunity for students to explore and discuss topics, ideas, events, issues, and procedures and to plan and carry out inquiry projects, which address the heart of the content itself. Our Centerpiece Unit Plan and the instructional activities detailed next share these characteristics and are useful collaborative learning activities. Each activity is adaptable in various ways.

PROJECT-BASED LEARNING

Project-based learning, as its title suggests, centers around major projects that students, as a class or in small groups, decide to undertake. Projects may address community needs ("Cleaning Up the Neighborhood"); explore personal, family, and community histories ("The Families, Lives, and Times of Odessa, Missouri"); engage students in exploration of global issues ("Mali to Memphis," "Money Makes the World Go 'Round"); or develop any of a myriad of other big ideas. Effective development of these project topics requires two conditions: (1) topics must grow from students' felt needs and (2) project development involves material from and exploration of multiple resources. Here is a snapshot of a class engaged in project-based learning; notice how this classroom "feels" (notice also how similar it is to Martina Day's and Greg Lewis's classrooms).

> Room 202 at Brooks Middle School has a purposeful hum to it, reflecting the efforts of the community of learners who work there. A quick glance around the room shows clusters of students working together: one group sits on the carpeted floor critiquing questions for a survey on adult and young adolescent television viewing habits; another group huddles around several computers as they complete a simulation on Westward Expansion; still others quietly ponder books or magazine articles; and a group of four stands at a chalkboard in the corner of the room, intently studying a large, schematic diagram of the local hydro-electric plant.
>
> A few moments later the teacher emerges from one of the groups on the floor and moves to a desk in the back where she has a clear view of the room. From this vantage point, she assesses the activities before her. Interestingly, no students approach her until she begins to move from group to group, listening to the discussions, observing and hearing about work in progress—a preliminary copy of the television survey, a summary of James Michener's views on great rivers of the West—and, when asked, offers the name of a professor from the local university, an expert on hydro-electric power. It is obvious the students in this class know what they need and want to do. (Brazee, 1995, p. 445)

Jerry Harste emphasizes the importance of inquiry as the foundation for project-based learning. He is not talking about inquiry as a methodology here, but rather inquiry as a deeply felt, inner need to know. He states, "Viewing curriculum as inquiry means that I envision classrooms as sites of inquiry, or as communities of learners. Inquiry is not a technical skill to be applied at will, but rather a philosophical stance that permeates the kinds of lives we choose to live" (1994, pp. 1230–1231). Inquiry becomes the starting point and sustaining element that propels a classroom project itself and thus emerges as the driving force of project-based learning.

I find the notion of inquiry, as Harste envisions it, to be powerful. Essentially, he is saying that students and teachers should examine what they know, look around their world, and decide what it is they want to know. *Then learning should grow from class exploration of questions generated in determining what the group wants to know.* The idea that deeply felt needs should guide curriculum choices in classrooms, that questions students and teachers ask and then energetically seek to answer are crucial to the implementation of state- or district-mandated curriculum standards, and that intensely focused reading and writing stemming from the inquiry topic may be more powerful than assigned textbook reading and writing of formal lab reports and expository essays is *revolutionary*. And it is worth our attention.

Lucy Calkins (1991) comments on the value of shared experience as the foundation for curriculum planning and asks why we typically plan special events—field trips to concerts, museums, and historical sites; outdoor education overnights or week-long experiences; community service projects—for the *end* of the school year when we could do them at the *beginning* of the year and then use the experience to undergird curriculum for the rest of the school year. I was struck by Calkins's viewpoint several years ago on vacation when my husband and I took a jet-boat trip up the Rogue River in Oregon. It was a full-day trip—we boarded at 7:30 A.M. and arrived back at the dock near dusk, about 8:00 P.M. Parts of the Rogue River are protected by the federal Wild and Scenic Rivers Act, so these boat trips are heavily regulated; the tour guides are experienced and knowledgeable rivermen who narrate and answer questions throughout the day. Trips are run from May 15 through October 15. Figure 11.2 is a map I created of just a few of the things we saw or learned that day. It was such an event-filled day—we saw eagles and ospreys and deer and a bear; we traveled under a beautiful art-deco bridge built in the 1930s as part of the Works Progress Act; we saw people panning for gold and rafting down the river; we ate lunch at a resort that can only be reached by boat—and on the way back I said to my husband, "If I taught school anywhere within a 60-mile radius of Gold Beach, Oregon, I'd be making the arrangements to take my class on this trip next May 16th." Then I remembered Lucy Calkins and turned back to him and said, "No, I wouldn't. I'd do it in September. I'd *start* school with a trip up the Rogue River!" Consider the many projects that could grow from any one or two of the items on my map; consider if *students* had generated such a map and then used questions they developed from their map to guide group projects. Consider also the almost endless possibilities of a semester or year of social studies, science, music, art, English, or humanities class with the theme of *The River*.

FIGURE 11.2 *Concept Map, The River*

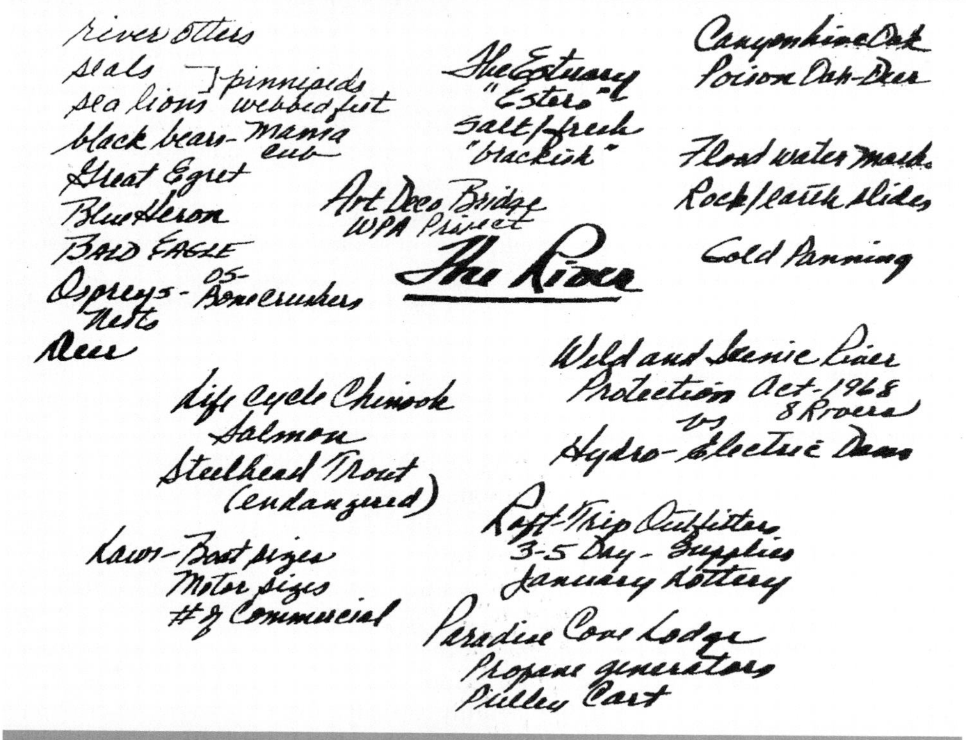

In addition, I like the idea of group projects as a focal point and center for learning. We have all seen preadolescents and adolescents go after an idea or hone a skill with absolute concentration and determination. (Think about their pursuit of athletic, musical, or thespian activities; their amazing ability with electronics—gaming, surfing the Internet, and mixing media; their absorption with coolness and comic books and popular music). *That's* the energy and motivation that projects based on true inquiry capture, and it's the kind of motivation Guthrie and his associates (1997) intend in the CORI instructional framework and what Csikszentmihalyi (1997) had in mind when he talked about "flow." Consider for a moment how, as part of an "Our Bodies, Ourselves" project, student-conducted experiments during a visit to an amusement park (e.g., measurement of wind resistance during roller coaster rides; heart rate and pulse studies on various rides; the speed of the roller coaster in contrast to the speed of the ferris wheel, the carousel, and the bumper cars) lead naturally both to insight and learning and to new questions and additional study. Along the way, students read and write as it serves their project needs.

Our Centerpiece Unit Plan for middle school music class begins with the sound of Amadou and Miriam's haunting "Mon Amour, Ma Cherie" and John Lee Hooker's "I'm in the Mood" ("I'm in the mood, I'm in the mood, mood, mood, Baby, I'm in the mood for love.") and continues with the sound of Malian and American blues for a good portion of the class period. Students are immersed in the music for a significant period of time; they then pool their knowledge about blues to initiate the beginnings of their "Know" list in our modified K-W-L. It is at this point in the unit that student experts may emerge: No matter what the subject area or topic, it is not unusual to find that one or more students have special experience or knowledge about the subject of inquiry, either from family experiences or from their own self-initiated interests. Don't hesitate to capitalize on that expertise. It is at this point also that students are starting to "own" the topic—*their* knowledge is being brought to bear on the subject, *their* experience is coming into play.

Day two opens with another pooling of knowledge, this time from information students got from knowledgeable others. Here again, student choice determined who they asked about blues and the information brought forward. The first half of the period is spent with students in groups deciding what they want to know (W in the K-W-L progression) and beginning to shape their inquiry topic. This is followed by learning a blues song. Note how CORI practices predominate: student choice and hands-on experience. Note also the opportunity for flow experience in this classroom.

As the work progresses, student groups finalize their inquiry topics and prepare for Internet and other exploration to occur.

Do not underestimate how important it is to preadolescents and adolescents for the reading, writing, and work they do in school to be meaningful. In *Reading Don't Fix No Chevys: Literacy in the Lives of Young Men*, Smith and Wilhelm chronicle the richly literate out-of-school lives of adolescent males, along with their very strong antipathy to literacy and learning in school. The students' complaint? School activities and expectations are not meaningful. One student says:

> English is about NOTHING! It doesn't help you DO anything. English is about reading poems and telling about rhythm. It's about commas and crap

For Better or For Worse® **by Lynn Johnston**

> like that for God's sake. What does that have to DO with DOING anything? It's about NOTHING! (2002, p. 119)

Project-based learning is one way for all classes and all subject areas to become meaningful to kids.

To initiate project-based learning in your class, begin as we did in our Centerpiece Unit by leading a class discussion about "Things We Know" about a particular topic (just as you'd do with TPRC or K-W-L). Let students work in pairs or groups to list what they know; give them plenty of time and expect ideas to range considerably. Share these in whole-class discussion. Then let them go back to their partner or group and first list "Things We Don't Know" and later "Things We Want to Know." Perry Marker (1993) suggests the following progression of questions to guide a similar process. He views this as a means for students to develop ideas and issues into thoughtful, transformative projects: (1) What do we know [about this topic]? (2) What don't we know? (3) What do we want to find out about what we don't know? (4) How can we find information? (5) What resources do we have to find the information? (6) How can we present and share our findings? (7) What specific proposals can we make to implement our findings? (pp. 82–83). Either of these approaches for launching inquiry projects may cover several days and may require that you "prime the pump" a bit; students are wholly unused to being asked what they'd like to learn in school and to be given the freedom to develop their own projects. Your role is to assist student groups in shaping project ideas and guiding them as they work in collaborative groups through completion of the projects. Develop procedures and recordkeeping systems *before you begin the projects* so they are ready to go from the start (more about this at the end of the chapter).

INTERNET INQUIRY

New, exciting possibilities exist on-line to enhance project-based learning. Don Leu (2000) recommends Internet Inquiry, a student-directed inquiry activity that has five action phases: (1) question, (2) search, (3) analyze, (4) compose, and (5) publish. As

FIGURE 11.3 *The Cycle of Inquiry*

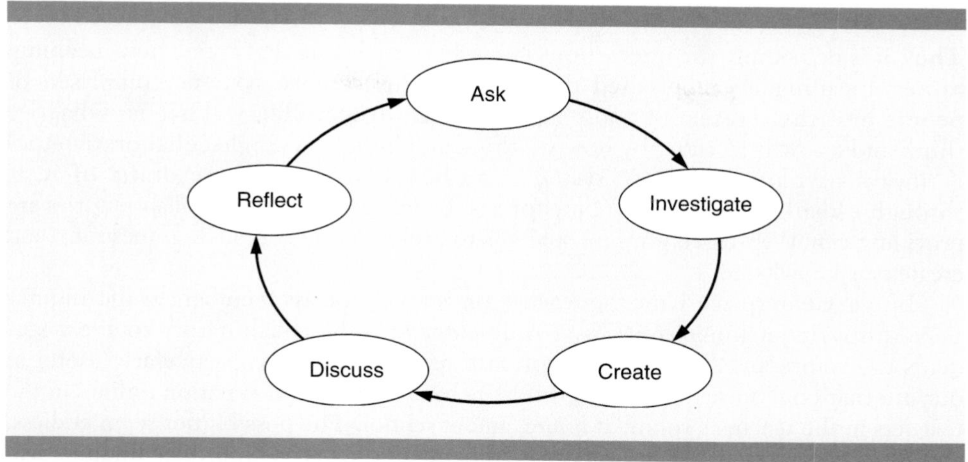

you saw in our Centerpiece Unit, we combined Internet Inquiry with project-based learning; it is also the foundation of Martina and Greg's space unit.

Bruce and Bishop use the Cycle of Inquiry, shown in Figure 11.3, as the foundation of Web-based project learning, which they call the Inquiry Page. They state:

> Students need to learn more than textbook knowledge. Instead they need to be able to examine complex situations and define the solvable problems within them. They need to work with multiple sources and media—not just a textbook. They need to become active learners, to collaborate, and to understand the perspectives of others. In short, they need to learn how to learn, and they must ask (find problems), investigate (multiple sources/media), create (engage actively in learning), discuss (collaborate and debate), and reflect to do that. (2002, p. 707)

Adding to the resources for collective inquiry is the "collaboratory" (a combination of "collaboration" and "laboratory"), which is a virtual workspace or "center without walls" (Wulf, cited in Lunsford & Bruce, 2001), where ideas and technologies are available and shared by a collaborative group with the aim of producing new knowledge. Lunsford and Bruce identify the attributes found in collaboratories:

- Shared inquiry—a common set of problems or issues that participants are working on together
- Intentionality—shared consciousness of the site's status as a mutual project
- Active participation and contribution—members use and add to resources and negotiate with one another over their projects
- Access to shared resources—data, links, research findings, and tools needed by participants
- Technologies—usually Web based

- Boundary-crossings—bridging gaps of geography, time, institutions, and disciplines (2001, p. 55)

Thus, it is not simply the interactions between participants that create new meaning; rather, meaning is constructed through complex activity systems comprised of people and their research tools (Lunsford & Bruce, 2001). That is, what we think and know is affected by how we think and know: "A single collaborative tool is always part of an activity system, as when writers exchange drafts of texts through e-mail for feedback" (Lunsford & Bruce, 2001, p. 53). Collaboratories are providing new Web-based ways for students to explore problems, answer questions, and create new knowledge.

In our Centerpiece Unit the teacher registered all class members at the Inquiry Page (http://inquiry.uiuc.edu/) to provide entry into the collaboratory to allow students to explore and share information internationally. This is particularly useful in our international music unit. Thus, students have available information online, in the text sets in the teacher's room, at home, and at school. The possibilities seem endless, and the technology-based projects that students use for reporting their findings will be made available in the collaboratory for use by others.

Blogs and podcasts can be used as part of Web-based collaborative work and are often found in collaboratories. Blogs are used in project-based learning for student groups to provide links to useful research sites for other groups to use, or as a way for groups to maintain a record of the sites they've used. In addition, blogs are often used to critique other Web materials and/or incorporate "day-in-the-life" narratives and other personal information (Oravec, 2002). Lunsford and Bruce recommend software at www.blogger.com as a resource for creating, managing, and posting blogs to one's own site or to a server. Just recently, Google purchased software for creating blogs as well (*Newswatch*, 2003).

Internet Inquiry and the Cycle of Inquiry both typify Concept Oriented Reading Instruction (CORI), and the message from each (and other inquiry-based approaches) is that the old transmission model of instruction—that is, the teacher standing in the front of the room lecturing or asking questions—is no longer viable in today's world of rapid change and instant information access. Recent published anecdotes of how students use technologies when they are not participating in class events in school reinforce this idea:

> "I use [my handheld Spanish translator] more for Tetris. I won't lie. In Spanish class I'll say I'm looking up words, but I'm playing Tetris" (Eli Macia) . . . "If a student has both hands under the desk, you know they are texting" (Aria Norton) . . . . Newer MP3 players now play video, allowing students to watch recorded shows and movies when they should be listening to a lecture . . . [and] some clothing is now designed for the technology, hiding wires, adding control panels on sleeves and making it harder for teachers to spot. (Halverson, 2006, p. A7)

Active, thoughtful engagement with multiple ideas and resources must be the hallmark of instruction today, and project-based learning and Internet Inquiry are that.

Figure 11.4 lists Web sites that are excellent resources for project-based learning and Internet Inquiry (the "sparc" addresses refer to "Space Research Collaboratory").

FIGURE 11.4 *Project-Based Internet Sites*

Global SchoolNet Foundation: This award-winning website provides examples of past projects and includes information on how to join current projects. Links to additional projects are provided. With over 750 on-line collaborative projects, it bills itself as "the leader in collaborative learning." http://www.globalschoolnet.org/index.html

iEARN: A global network committed to helping young people use the Internet to undertake projects designed to make a meaningful contribution to the health and welfare of the planet. http://www.iearn.org

Global Learning and Observations to Benefit the Environment (GLOBE): A worldwide network of students, teachers, and scientists working together to study and understand the global environment. Students and teachers from over 7,000 schools in more than 80 countries work with research scientists to learn more about our planet. http://www.globe.gov/globe_flash.html

The Genesis Mission: Website created and maintained by educators at Mid-continent Research for Education and Learning (McREL). It offers quality, standards-based instructional materials related to the Genesis mission of the National Aeronautics and Space Administration (NASA). There are many opportunities for teachers, students, and community members to participate in the mission. http://genesismission.jpl.nasa.gov/

The Inquiry Page: The site created by B. C. Bruce and his colleagues to implement the Inquiry Cycle and is simultaneously a website, a community of learners, and a research project. It is designed to support teachers and learners of all ages in development and implementation of inquiry projects. http://inquiry.uiuc.edu/

The Space Physics and Aeronomy Research Collaboratory (SPARC): Site that brings together an international community of space, computer, and behavioral scientists to create the infrastructure needed for Internet space study. http://intel.si.umich.edu/sparc/

Windows to the Universe: Site funded by NASA, which invites teachers, students, and the public to explore using actual instruments, computer models, real-time data, and theories scientists use to study space. In addition, it offers outlines of classroom activities and opportunities to "ask a scientist" questions. http://www.windows.ucar.edu/sparc/

How to do . . . .

PROJECT-BASED LEARNING AND INTERNET INQUIRY

Launching a project-based learning and/or Internet Inquiry unit is an act of faith—faith in students' ability and desire to explore questions deeply, faith in the power of student-directed learning, and faith in one's own ability to manage the whole thing. In the last section of this chapter, I give some suggestions for the managing part; here are the things you need to do to get projects started:

1. Decide what stimulus you will use to get students thinking about what they know and don't know about a big topic. Will it be a walk around the community? ads you've collected from magazines and other media? a movie or videotape? quotations you've gleaned from newspapers or from conversations you've heard in your classroom?
2. Present the stimulus and guide students' discussion of what they know, don't know, and want to know. You may do a K-W-L for this part.
3. Guide students in grouping "want to know" ideas and questions into categories of interest.
4. Allow students to form groups according to the broad categories and continue exploring their topic. Guide groups in generating the question(s) they wish to explore.
5. Lead a discussion of possible resources and their location.
6. Identify specific expectations for the outcome of the project—what students are expected to produce, how productions will be graded, group responsibilities, and so forth.
7. Oversee group work.
8. Guide final presentations.
9. Determine assessments.

THE GROUP READING ACTIVITY (GRA)

The Group Reading Activity (GRA) (Manzo, 1974) divides responsibility for initial learning and presentation of topic information among five or six collaborative learning groups within the classroom. The teacher determines topic divisions and assigns a topic and corresponding textbook (or other) reading to each group. For example, for a unit on the Middle Ages, the following topics and assignments might be made:

Topic	*Assignment*
Byzantium	pp. 115–119
Peoples, Cultures, and Leaders	pp. 119–126
Feudalism	pp. 126–131
Crusades, Religions, and Religious Leaders	pp. 135–142

Town, Guilds, and Merchants pp. 142–147
Education, Science, and Art pp. 147–151

Additional resources are available in the room and in other areas in the school.

Each group must determine (1) what is the most important information in the assigned textbook reading; (2) what, if any, other information and resources are needed to understand the topic; and (3) how the group can best present the topic information to the rest of the class. Presentation options include written summaries and outlines, annotations, oral reports, electronic presentations, panel discussions, dramatizations, audiovisual presentations, and any other type of product useful for informing the class and preparing everyone for unit evaluation.

After group deliberations, the teacher appoints a student critic from each group to move to another group and listen to the proposed ideas for class presentation. The student critic is expected to provide constructive criticism. Groups use this information to revise and rearrange their proposals, which they then present to the teacher. The teacher consults with the group and assists further in adapting the presentation plans, if needed. Groups complete all preparations and do the presentations.

The class then works as a whole to determine what areas of the unit need further research and study as well as how that study could be carried out; students are encouraged to "rapid read" those sections presented by other groups. Final arrangements for follow-up activities are made. At the end of the unit, student knowledge is evaluated using assessment strategies that are appropriate to the students, the unit, and the type of information learned.

How to do . . . .

GRA

I like the GRA because it requires precisely the kind of social and verbal interaction Bayer described as being so critical to learning and because it meets the standards for CORI as well. The focus is evenly divided among collaboration, reading, language interaction, learning, teaching, and production of a teaching aid. Writing is used spontaneously and naturally throughout and is often the chosen medium (or a major aspect of the chosen medium) for transmitting information to the rest of the class. The GRA is readily adaptable to units of various sizes and lengths and fits reasonably into most subject areas. The following steps should assist you in using the GRA:

1. Determine the material to be studied and the lesson or unit objectives.
2. Divide the reading material into four, five, or six topic sections.
3. Establish four, five, or six cross-ability and cross-status groups. The number of groups should correspond to the number of topic sections established.
4. Assign one topic of the reading material to each group. Each group is to determine (a) what is the most important information in the section,

(b) what other information is needed to understand the topic, and (c) how the group can best present the topic to the rest of the class.

5. Appoint one student critic from each group to listen to another group's plan for presenting its material to the class.
6. Allow time for the student critic to make constructive recommendations.
7. Consult with each group regarding its plans for presentation.
8. Allow time for presentations to be finalized.
9. Have groups present.
10. Conduct full-class discussion for further clarification and research of project ideas.
11. Determine assessments.

GROUP INVESTIGATION

Sharan and Sharan (1980) developed the Group Investigation approach, which uses interest-centered cooperative groups as the means for students to plan and carry out extended project investigations and productions. They propose a six-stage progression of cooperative events:

Stage 1. Identify the topic and organize research groups

Stage 2. Plan the investigation

Stage 3. Investigate

Stage 4. Prepare a report

Stage 5. Make final presentations

Stage 6. Test and evaluate

Huhtala and Coughlin (1991) decided to use Group Investigation for a Middle East unit in an interdisciplinary, team-taught, sophomore English and government class beginning in the fall of 1990. This was a timely decision and a daring one, given the subsequent need for them to teach world events as these events were happening during the buildup to the 1991 Persian Gulf War. Huhtala and Coughlin describe the successes and the problems they encountered in using Group Investigation for the first time. Of real import is that, problems and all, in comparison with other, non-teamed classes, in the Group Investigation class, "Absenteeism was reduced by a third. Grades of D and F were reduced from twenty to thirteen percent" (p. 50).

OTHER COOPERATIVE/COLLABORATIVE LEARNING ACTIVITIES

JIGSAW GROUPING

Jigsaw Grouping is well known and frequently used in one form or another. Jigsaw Grouping was introduced by Elliott Aaronson for the purpose of encouraging active participation in group settings by students from different ethnic, cultural, and racial backgrounds (Aaronson et al., 1975). Jigsaw Grouping is based on the characteristics of a jigsaw puzzle: Students are given interlocking parts of a whole picture; each student learns and communicates her or his part, but no one can see the whole picture until all of the parts are in place.

To do Jigsaw Grouping, the teacher establishes mixed-ability groups of four to five students and assigns one-fourth or one-fifth of the unit of study to each student. Students read their own part and meet with members from other groups who were assigned the same part; this new group meets to discuss and clarify their understanding of the material read and, in the course of that discussion, becomes the expert group on that section of the unit. Members then return to their original groups to teach the group the important information from their part. The group then works to incorporate these interlocking parts into a construction of the whole unit. Following this initial shared teaching, the group may go back to any or all parts of the material to gather additional information or clarify areas of confusion.

The following lesson plan written by an experienced and excellent Spanish teacher, Dianne Metzger, shows how jigsaw grouping can be combined with TPRC and prereading vocabulary instruction in a Spanish 3 class that is reading and interpreting a Pablo Neruda poem. This combination is equally useful in other classes as well.

TPRC, PREREADING VOCABULARY INSTRUCTION, JIGSAW LESSON PLAN, *Foreign Language (Spanish)*

Lesson: "La Tortuga"
Course/Grade: Spanish 3/11th–12th Grade
Materials:

- "La Tortuga" by Pablo Neruda, *¡Ven Conmigo*!, Holt, 2000
- CD Soundtrack from "Il Postino," Miramax Hollywood Records, 1995
- "Turtle" graphic organizers in green or brown on white poster paper
- Colored permanent markers
- Small sticky-notes
- Overhead projector
- Overhead transparency with vocabulary words
- 11″ × 17″ cardstock
- Dice

LESSON OBJECTIVES (WITH CONTENT STANDARDS)

Upon completion of this lesson students will be able to

- Read and analyze a poem in Spanish (Standard 1.2—students understand and interpret written and spoken language on a variety of topics; Standard 2.2—students demonstrate an understanding of the relationship between the products and perspectives of the cultures studied).

LESSON PROCEDURES

Before Reading: Into—TPRC, Prereading Vocabulary Instruction

1. Divide the class into groups of five. Give each group one of the turtle graphic organizers on poster paper and a marker in a contrasting color. *Say:* In the next seven minutes think about everything you know about turtles. Write the words or phrases of what you know in the turtle graphic. *(You may wish to display your own turtle graphic with a few common-knowledge words/phrases.)*

2. After students have finished brainstorming, ask each group to hang or prop its turtle graphic in different parts of the room. Give each group a supply of sticky-notes. *Say:* With your group, walk around the room to read each of the other groups' graphic. Put a sticky-note beside any entry on a graphic that your group doesn't understand or agree with. When you've finished, go back to your own graphic and revise or add any information you wish.

3. When all groups have completed revisions, *say:* What are some things that all groups had on their graphics? What are some things only one or two groups had? *Allow time for questions and clarifications. Have information on hand to support this discussion.*

4. Read or tell a short biographical sketch of Neruda. Have students jot down information under columns titles, "Lugares donde vivió" (Places where he lived), "Sus publications" (His publications), and "Cuantos años tenia en puntos" (His age at important points in his life). *Say:* Okay, now I'm going to draw a timeline of Neruda's life. You tell me where to enter places he lived, his publications, and important points in his life.

5. Play a short selection from the soundtrack of the film "Il Postino," e.g., Ralph Fiennes's reading of "Ode to the Sea." *Ask:* What do you think "no, no, yes" represents in this poem? Why do you say that? Why do you think Neruda mentions seven of everything? What makes a poem a poem? From what we've talked about so far, what do you think you might find in a Neruda poem titled, "La Tortuga," The Turtle?

6. Read "La Tortuga" to the students in Spanish, allowing them to read silently on their own copies.

7. Write vocabulary words on the overhead ("olas"—waves, "plateada"—silver-colored, "ambarinos"—amber-colored, "rapiña"—bird of prey, "desfiar"—to defy) and accompany with visuals, pictures, and/or clarifying explanations in Spanish.

During Reading: Through—Jigsaw

8. Leave the turtle graphics and vocabulary words, visuals, and explanations up to assist with comprehension.

9. Have students remain in their groups. *Say:* Each group will write in Spanish a two to three sentence interpretation of "La Tortuga." In your group now number-off, 1–5. *After students have finished, say:* Number 1s, you are responsible for the opening section of the poem, "La tortuga" through "profundo

mar." *Write assignment on the board.* Number 2s, next section, "la tortuga" through "y las olas." Number 3s, section "la tortuga" through "y no lo sabe." Number 4s, "De tan vieja" through "planchar." And number 5s, "Cerró" through "piedras." You will all become experts on your section, so to do that I want all number 1s to meet here *(gesture to location)*, number 2s here *(and so on)*. In your expert groups, read your section in Spanish and as a group translate into English. You know where the dictionaries are if you need them. Then discuss *in Spanish* the meanings you perceive in your section. *Circulate and assist as needed.*

10. *After expert groups have finished, say:* Okay experts, return to your home group. Starting with number 1, give your English translation. Then discuss *in Spanish* the meanings the expert groups found and develop your two to three sentence interpretation. You will share your interpretation with the class, then you will turn it in for me to review. *Allow groups plenty of time to share translations and discuss interpretations. Assist them as needed. When groups are ready, say:* Who wants to share first? *Conduct discussion using the following questions as appropriate:* What is the English translation of "De tan vieja se fue poniendo dura"? What simile does Neruda use? Why do you think he chose that particular comparison? Do you think it is apt? Why or why not? What animal would you choose to represent life? Why?

After Reading: Beyond

11. Distribute one 11″ × 17″ cardstock page to each student. *Say:* Fold your paper in half so that you have two 8-1/2″ × 11″ sheets *(demonstrate)*. Go back to the poem and choose two quotes that you think are interesting. Write one quote around the perimeter of each sheet on facing halves of the paper *(demonstrate)*. After you've done that, illustrate your quotes using marking pens.
12. *After students have finished, say:* In your home groups, share your quotes and illustrations. I'll bring a die for you to roll to determine who will present their work to the class.
13. *After groups have finished, say:* Who will share with us first? *Continue around groups.*
14. Hang the papers around the room for other classes to enjoy.

LESSON ASSESSMENT(S)

15. Observation Assessment—As students discuss and work in small groups note conversational skills and check for understanding of vocabulary, idioms, and abstract concepts.
16. Product Assessment—Read and respond to the group written interpretations of "La Tortuga"; review and grade quotes/illustration papers that choose to submit in their grading period portfolios.

Slavin (1986) expresses concern over the use of Jigsaw Grouping with typical classroom texts. His point is that most texts are not written so that unit sections can be easily separated out; the only way teachers can make the sections independently comprehensible is to rewrite and/or add considerable amounts of text (p. 339). I agree, in part, with Slavin; I've used Jigsaw Grouping with adults and have encountered this problem. On the other hand, many texts are readily subdivided into sections that stand alone.

Even when a text does not lend itself to subdivision, however, the following are ways around the problem that do not involve extensive rewriting:

1. Use library and other resource materials to supplement the classroom text so that comprehensible, free-standing text units are put together from various sources.

2. Combine Jigsaw with an adapted TPRC or K-W-L, as our "La Tortuga" lesson plan did, in which groups list and record everything they know about the lesson topic before reading, share these with the class, and then read their assigned sections of the unit and do their expert grouping. The TPRC/K-W-L brainstorming thus provides a common core of background knowledge that assists students in constructing meaning as they read separate sections of the unit.

3. Help students become accustomed to a situation in which *some of the information they need is missing*. In this case, part of the purpose of the expert group discussion would be to identify information gaps, propose alternative ideas for filling those gaps, and predict how some of the pieces of the Jigsaw will ultimately fit together. This approach also encourages students to work cooperatively to elicit important (perhaps missing) information from one another during discussions, a central point of the exercise itself.

Note the scaffolding provided by Jigsaw grouping, and the way it also follows CORI practices.

How to do . . . .

JIGSAW

Jigsaw grouping can be such a valuable addition to your teaching repertoire that you would do well to consider using it in your classroom. It is easily combined with other instructional strategies, including TPRC, mapping and VSS. Below are steps for implementing Jigsaw.

Jigsaw

1. Determine the material to be studied and the lesson or unit objectives.
2. Divide the reading material into four or five roughly equal sections.
3. Establish cross-ability and cross-status groups of four or five students each; the number of students in each group should correspond to the number of sections of reading material.
4. Assign one section of the chapter (or other reading material) to a student in each group so that the total reading assignment is covered within each group.
5. Allow reading time.

6. Ask all students assigned to each section (e.g., section 1, section 2) to meet in expert groups to (a) consider, discuss, and clarify the information in their assigned reading and (b) prepare for returning to their original groups and teaching the material to that group.
7. Convene original groups for students to teach their part of the reading to other group members.
8. Conduct full-class discussion of the chapter or other reading material for further clarification and/or research.
9. Determine assessments.

CREATIVE THINKING–READING ACTIVITIES (CT-RAS)

Creative Thinking–Reading Activities (CT-RAs) (Haggard, 1978) are short, warm-up activities for developing students' creative problem-solving abilities. CT-RAs require cooperative learning groups to generate (1) as many possible solutions as they can think of for a problem or incongruity and then (2) combine possible solutions or generate from them a final solution that the group determines to be the "best" according to a given criterion.

CT-RAs use standard creativity tasks such as *Unusual Uses* ("Think of all the unusual ways you can to use a brick"), *Circumstances and Consequences* ("What would happen if we all had eyes in the backs of our heads?"), *Product Improvement* ("Think of all the ways you can to improve school desks"), and *Inventions* ("With your group, think of as many ideas as you can for a new toy. Invent a toy, name it, and write out directions or explanations for it."). These may be used in their "pure" form (e.g., "Think of as many uses as you can" for any common object) or adapted to a specific content area (e.g., "Think of as many unusual games as you can using a volleyball" or "Invent a tool to be used around the house in the year 2020"). Consider that only a relatively short time ago, a subject-specific CT-RA could have been "What would happen if the Berlin Wall fell?"

In completing the CT-RA, groups are required to follow the original ground rules Alex Osborn developed (1963) for brainstorming:

1. Don't criticize anyone's ideas, not even your own.
2. List as many ideas as possible.
3. Engage in freewheeling at will—the wilder the idea, the better.
4. Form new ideas by combining and adding to ideas already listed.

After the brainstorming, the groups use their list of possible solutions to arrive at a final answer; they may be asked to decide their final most useful answer, their funniest answer or combination of answers, or the solution they think is most likely to occur in the future. These final answers are then shared with the whole class.

USING CT-RAS

CT-RAs are easy. They can be done in 10 to 15 minutes at the beginning or end of the class period (5 minutes of brainstorming; 5 minutes of polishing final solution; and 5 minutes of sharing with whole class) and can then be recalled for application to subject content. They're also good for days when interruptions or an altered school schedule destroys the continuity of the class routine (i.e., days with assemblies, early dismissal, pep rallies, field trips, etc.).

I used CT-RAs for one full semester in a high school remedial reading class and discovered at least four things. First, my "low academic" kids were marvelously creative. Anyone who didn't know this was a remedial reading class and who observed the students' CT-RA discussions would have labeled my students "bright." (My students *were* bright, by the way.) The students certainly looked and acted bright doing CT-RA; this is the group that wanted to improve school desks by putting hydraulic lifts on the legs so the students in the back of the room could see as well as the ones in the front!

Second, my students *loved* doing CT-RAs. For many of them, it was the first time they'd ever *felt* bright, in control, and powerful in the classroom. They were certainly NOT the lethargic, disengaged students so often associated with remedial reading classes. If I tried to cancel CT-RAs, the students let me know about it in no uncertain terms. Never have I had such a population of students complain so much if I canceled a school task.

Third, I learned that the interest inherent in the task overrode all problems associated with cooperative group work. I had no difficulty with students staying on task or with students participating cooperatively. Keep in mind that these were the students whom most people would predict would be the *least* likely to work well together; many of them were considered by other teachers and students to be the most difficult in the school.

Finally, I learned to capitalize on the thinking students did during CT-RA and transfer it to academic tasks. So when a freshman student asked me how to write the paragraph on skiing he needed to take to his English class, I could begin by saying, "Remember the thinking we did this morning in our CT-RA [unusual uses]? Sit down, and *using that same kind of thinking*, list everything you know about skiing." He did this without hesitation and without needing clarification. After that, we clustered his ideas and narrowed them down, and he wrote his paragraph.

The importance and value of the small- and large-group discussions in CT-RA cannot be overemphasized. Although high achievers and/or highly verbal students may initially dominate the small cooperative group discussions, this lasts only until the hesitantly offered suggestion of a quieter member knocks everyone's socks off for its wit, its wackiness, or its sheer beauty. As groups share their efforts in full-class discussion, "oohs" and "ahs" echo spontaneously around the room when particularly ingenious responses are read. Students quickly learn that these comments are frequently contributed by class members who rarely contribute anything to class.

A CT-RA ACTIVITY: BIOLOGY

Bob Tierney (1985) describes a CT-RA-like activity he uses in his tenth-grade biology class in which each student draws an animal, real or imaginary, with a felt-tipped pen. Students then cut their animals out, cut off the head, and pass the head to the student sitting next to them. Students paste the new head on the animal body they've retained. Tierney then provides the class with a list of Latin and Greek word roots and asks each student to give his or her animal a scientific name and write a description of the animal's habitat and behavior. Students read their descriptions to one another and group the animals according to similarities. After this, Tierney launches his lesson on binomial nomenclature and classification.

This lesson needs only the addition of cooperative groups to make it a cooperative CT-RA. After the new animals are pasted together, groups or partners (rather than individuals) brainstorm possible names, habitats, and behaviors for each person's animal. Using these ideas, students then work individually to write descriptions of their animal's habitat and behavior. Small groups reconvene to share names and descriptions and determine tentative criteria for classification of the animals in that group. Oral summaries of the small-group discussions are then shared with the whole class.

How to do . . . .

CT-RA

Creative problem solving is fun and becomes increasingly so as it is shared with others. Creativity is based on incongruity and freewheeling mental play; it therefore invites spontaneity and risk taking, wild speculation, and humorous response. (Be prepared for noise and laughter.) CT-RAs lead to wonderfully generative thinking that produces innovative, unpredictable solutions to problems. That does *not* mean the solutions or answers are frivolous. They are the models and prototypes of solutions that come from brainstorming and creative problem solving *in subject areas.* The fact that they are fun does not make them less academic. The fact that they are done in small-group cooperative settings means that they stimulate precisely the kind of social and language interaction that content learning requires. The following steps should be useful in developing CT-RAs for your classroom:

1. Decide how CT-RAs fit into the curriculum, unit, and/or lesson plans (daily, periodic; general, specific).
2. Write CT-RA prompts and final answer criteria—for example, "What would happen if everybody all over the world recycled paper, plastic, and glass?" The final answer criterion is to choose the answer you think most likely to happen.
3. Divide students into cross-ability and cross-status groups.
4. Allow 5 minutes for brainstorming, 5 minutes for considering a final answer, and 5 minutes for group sharing of answers with the whole class.
5. Conduct full-class discussion to determine possible follow-up of ideas generated.

ASK SOMETHING

Paul Crowley's Ask Something approach (1988) is based on the notion that students can improve writing drafts by learning from peer reactions. Students bring to class a piece of their writing; it may be from learning log entries, a piece of writing done after reading, or the result of a direct teacher assignment. Students work in small groups where each student passes his or her paper to the person on the left (or right). Students read the new papers and write at least one question in the margin or at the bottom of the paper that they believe needs to be addressed. The papers are then passed to the next person for the same purpose. When all members of the group have asked one or more questions, papers are returned to the author. Authors then choose which questions they wish to address and make revisions. After the initial activity, groups may reconvene to share their revised work, discuss particularly useful questions, make plans for final revision, or do any combination of the three.

The value of Ask Something is its demonstration of how writing can be a collaborative process in which, once again, students assume most of the responsibility for the learning event. Clearly, any content can be addressed in the writing itself, whether it is analysis of a mathematical procedure, elaboration of a current event, literary response, or recordings taken during a science project. The teacher's role here is to monitor individual and group progress.

AMBIGUITY, RISK, AND COLLABORATIVE LEARNING

By now, I've become so convinced of the value of collaborative learning that the advantages seem self-evident to me. Certainly, I incorporated more and more group work into my own classes over the years. Early in my university teaching career, I taught almost totally from a lecture–demonstration model that was more lecture than demonstration. I was a good lecturer; I knew my stuff, I had an upbeat and dynamic speaking presence, and I threw in stories and dramatic humor to keep things interesting. My students left the room each class period shaking their aching hands and telling me how *much* they'd learned. They not only performed admirably on my rather rigorous tests but also gave me very high teaching evaluations and wrote personal notes to me about how they liked the class. There was no reason to change—until I began to think about the incongruity of my standing in front of a class lecturing about the importance of language interaction for content learning (I was the only one "interacting!") and until I perceived that having students work through new ideas in small-group discussion and written products might be more important than giving tests to see how much course content they could remember. And so I changed. Beginning in my second or third year of university teaching, I began adding more and more small-group discussion and participation so that, even in so-called lecture classes, not a class period went by without one or more extended periods of small-group collaborative learning.

My decisions about collaborative learning grew from a combination of classroom experience, what I know and am still learning about language interaction and content learning, and my own research and study. I've spent some time examining issues related to ambiguity and risk in the classroom, specifically with regard to how students construct meaning when faced with ambiguous classroom tasks (Ruddell, 1991a), and have hypothesized about a certain type of advantage collaborative learning activities provide.

Ambiguity refers to the extent to which a precise and predictable formula for student action in generating a task product is defined (Doyle & Carter, 1984); that is, a task is considered ambiguous when students are not told everything they need to know or do to fulfill task requirements. Research suggests that students disambiguate classroom tasks in one of two ways: (1) reducing the task to a low-level, formulaic assignment (Doyle & Carter, 1984) or (2) redefining or reconstructing the task itself (Murphy, 1988). Interacting with ambiguity in classrooms is the element of *risk*—or the degree to which students face negative consequences for failure to meet task demands. When both ambiguity and risk are high, students are persistent in their efforts to reduce one or both (Doyle & Carter, 1984).

Collaborative learning activities reduce individual student risk in the face of complex, ambiguous classroom tasks (Ruddell, 1991b); this is important because complex, ambiguous classroom tasks very often are precisely the kinds of tasks that require higher-order thinking and lead to real learning in content areas. Reduction of risk comes in collaborative groups not only from the psychology of "strength in numbers" but from many other sources as well. By reducing risks, collaborative learning activities offer the following advantages (elements of the CORI model are boldfaced in the discussion below):

- *Collaborative learning activities focus on student construction of knowledge through* ***observation*** and active search for meaning rather than reproduction of answers from text. Students do indeed engage in higher-order (i.e., constructivist and collaborative) learning tasks that are nonformulaic and for which there are no pat, easy answers. Learning is active, assertive, and student-directed.

  Furthermore, with rapidly expanding online resources, such as collaboratories, blogs and the like, web-based projects may involve students working collaboratively in classrooms across the nation and across the world, thus "knocking down the classroom walls" (Roerden, 1997) in ways we never had dreamed possible.
- *Collaborative learning activities allow student thinking to determine much of the content of lesson discussion and the lesson itself.* Recall my earlier statement that students' **conceptual questions** and constructions of knowledge become the curriculum; this occurs when complex, ambiguous tasks allow exploration of many resources and multiple viewpoints in the process of problem solving. This is not "out-of-control," directionless curriculum; rather, it is true connectedness between what students know and what they are learning.
- *Collaborative learning activities place the teacher in the role of facilitator of learning and friendly monitor of classroom events.* The teacher serves as an important resource person as students work through collaborative tasks. The term *friendly monitor* is intended here to convey the idea of a mentoring teacher role. The teacher as facilitator is always aware of curricular and student needs but steps back sufficiently to allow student **self-direction**.
- *Collaborative learning activities contain guidelines, guideposts, and directions for focusing responses.* Students are not expected simply to sink or swim; rather, students are taught to be **strategic** learners. Scaffolding activities and resources, including teacher modeling, guidance, and strategy instruction, are available as students need them to support learning.
- *Collaborative learning activities encourage independent thought and action.* Collaborative learning activities leave plenty of room for students to be **self-expressive**

and independent thinkers. Because of the high ambiguity and low risk, students are free to make choices and pursue uncharted waters without fear of being "wrong"; teacher guidance and support encourage this process.

- *Collaborative learning activities provide "practice time" for rehearsing new ideas, thoughts, and theories.* Progression from expressive to formal language occurs during the self-expression of practice time. As students manipulate ideas in language, they begin to see nuances and make important connections between prior knowledge and new learning. Their efforts are informed by insights and ideas expressed by others and lead to construction of **coherent** theories and knowledge.
- *Collaborative learning activities require much oral and written interaction between classroom participants.* This includes all participants, students and teachers, who **collaboratively** sort through the ambiguities and make sense of the task and the new learning. Further exploration of ideas occurs in the course of students engaging in language interactions.
- *Collaborative learning activities promote interdependence with peers and other resources.* Although this may seem to contradict the idea of developing independent thought and action, it does not. Independence and interdependence are both very important cohabiting qualities for student collaboration and are quite capable of coexisting. It is through this combination that students come to trust their own voice and viewpoints while listening to and understanding many voices and other viewpoints. This is particularly important in classrooms and schools in which students with homogeneous experiential backgrounds and values are being joined by students with diverse cultures, attitudes, values, and ideas (LittleSoldier, 1989).

PROCEDURES FOR IMPLEMENTING, GUIDING, AND EVALUATING COLLABORATIVE GROUP WORK

If I had to identify the single greatest barrier to group learning in classrooms, it would undoubtedly be the concern teachers have about "turning the class loose" or "losing control" in the classroom. This is a well-founded concern: We've all seen or experienced classrooms that were out of control. Consider your experience for a moment, however, and you'll probably conclude that most of the time, students working in groups did not cause the problem. Other things did, and those other things would have been present whether or not the class was in small groups.

It would be foolish to claim that there are no potential problems associated with collaborative group instruction. Of course, there are; but careful planning can do much to reduce the probability that such problems will occur.

PREREQUISITES TO GROUPING FOR COLLABORATIVE LEARNING

Preparation for collaborative learning is essential to success. In schools or districts in which students are experienced group workers and learners, preparation and prior planning for cooperative or collaborative work need only be minimal. If students are not used to working with one another, then preliminary planning must be detailed and carefully thought out. At the very least, you should arrange the following conditions before using collaborative learning groups in your classroom:

1. *Before you even consider moving students into learning groups, you must establish an orderly learning environment.* This does not necessarily mean pin-drop quiet or even quiet most of the time. It does mean that whatever the class rules and expectations are, everyone knows them and generally abides by them.

2. *Your classroom should demonstrate to all who enter a clear focus on learning.* There can be no mistaking that this is a classroom in which everyone works and everyone gets things done. Expectations are high, and teacher behavior consistently reflects this.

3. *Whatever your class is, it is consistently that.* Students can trust that teacher behavior, expectations, and responses will be much the same day in and day out. Decide, and let students know, what you will tolerate and what you will not. Maintain a generally even disposition and don't play favorites. Expect adolescents to test the boundaries, and respond to each test the same way you responded to the one before and the same way you will to the one after.

INTRODUCING COLLABORATIVE LEARNING GROUPS

One attitude that will serve you well in introducing collaborative learning activities is that it is worthwhile to spend a little time introducing and clarifying collaborative learning concepts before attempting to have students work in learning groups. Time spent here is small in comparison to time spent reducing chaos or confusion and removing problems. Consider doing the following:

1. *Physically arrange the room to be as conducive as possible to accommodate interactions and resource needs of collaborative learning groups and your sightlines in the room.* Try to plan the room arrangement to reduce noise, movement, and confusion and to maximize your ability to observe working groups. Recall the teacher in Room 202 whose desk is in the back of the room "where she has a clear view of the room." That's what you want. You will also need to consider specific needs and equipment for your subject area. If you do not have your own room, plan ways to rearrange and arrange back quickly and quietly each class period.

2. *Establish working rules for the operation of learning groups.* These may be developed collaboratively with your class, or you may announce and explain them. Rules need to account for

a. Procedures for getting into and out of groups each day.
b. Amount of movement permissible in the room during group work (e.g., you may want to specify that only two people may be up and moving around the room at a time).
c. Movement to other resource areas in the school (the library, film room, storage area, computer lab, etc.).
d. Signals for starting and stopping work each day.

e. Instructions/procedures for using computers and other classroom resources (especially cell phones if you allow them for Internet research).
f. The signal you will use to get students' attention when the room is noisy with working conversations.

MaryEllen Vogt (1996) suggests that a useful beginning activity for introducing collaborative group work is to engage students in a conversation about what constitutes an effective working group. This may be initiated by asking, "What do participants do when a group is working well?" As students brainstorm ideas ("listen to one another," "do the work you say you're going to do," "be prepared," "don't fool around," "encourage others' participation," etc.), the teacher records ideas on the board. After the brainstorming, students select one social skill (e.g., "listen to one another") and as a group develop a Looks Like/Sounds Like/Feels Like chart that summarizes what a learning group will look and sound like when it is operating well. Figure 11.5 shows what a chart might look like for the social skill of "listen to one another." It is worth the time it takes to explore a variety of social skills in this same manner before beginning the group work and then posting the charts in prominent places in the room. On occasion, you may refer to the charts to help students remember the characteristics of effective group membership.

ESTABLISHING ROLES FOR INDIVIDUALS IN COLLABORATIVE LEARNING GROUPS

Most teachers using groups for the first time like the idea of role assignment because it adds structure that helps students understand specifically what it is they are to be doing. Just as importantly, role assignment gives a clear message to students that this is business; it has certain *goals*, certain *expectations* for student performance, and certain *structures* to guide student behaviors. Such messages go a long way in developing students' abilities to work independently. Over time, specific roles are rotated among

FIGURE 11.5 *Looks Like/Sounds Like/Feels Like Chart*

Social Skill: **Listening**

Looks Like	**Sounds Like**	**Feels Like**
Heads nodding	One person speaking	I am important
People are interested	A "busy buzz"	What I have to say is important
People are leaning forward	Questions and answers	What I think matters
There is eye contact	Appropriate disagreement	I can help others figure things out
People are taking turns	People are reading and learning	Good

group members so that everyone has an opportunity to assume each role. The following roles are useful for learning groups (each role may not be necessary every time groups function, depending on the group task):

- The *facilitator* is responsible for moving the group process along, making sure everyone has a chance to participate, encouraging reticent members, helping talkative members curb their input, and making sure the task is completed.
- The *recorder* is responsible for keeping notes and informal minutes of the discussion, ideas generated by the group, alternative solutions, explanations, and any other important information; the recorder does the final write-up, as needed.
- The *timer* allocates and monitors time so that all parts of the task are completed as required; the timer notifies the group throughout of time considerations.
- The *worrier* is responsible for worrying about content and procedural issues—for example, whether the group is "bird walking" (off the subject), whether the ideas being generated are on track with the task goal, whether the operational "grand plan" of action can be accomplished in the time available, and so forth. The worrier begins most sentences with "I'm worried that . . ."
- The *reporter* is responsible for reporting progress and/or final solutions to the class during wrap-up time; the reporter may also be responsible for taking periodic reports of the group's progress to the teacher.

For some collaborative learning activities, you may want to add the following roles:

- The *messenger* serves as liaison between the group and other groups, the resource center(s), and/or the teacher; the messenger may be the only group member designated to be out of the group working area without special permission.
- *Set-up/clean-up* people are responsible for collecting and returning materials and equipment, checking to see that personal belongings and trash are removed from the working area, and requesting any additional materials and equipment the group needs.
- The *author* is responsible for final write-up of a written report or project using material and drafts developed by the entire group. There may be two or more authors per working group.
- The *editor* is responsible for reviewing and revising drafts developed by the authors and/or other members of the group. The editor works closely with the authors in production of the final product. There may be two or more editors per working group.
- The *checker* makes sure that individuals have completed their work and submitted it to become part of the group product and helps authors and editors meet deadlines.

There are clearly overlaps across roles, places where two roles could be combined, and perhaps a gap or two from the perspective of your subject area, and that's fine. These roles are not etched in stone; many can be adapted to a given subject area or class, and roles can be added as needed. Similarly, the responsibilities I've attached to each role have been refined over time based on group learning activities in my classes and on what others have described. They, too, are recommendations only and should be adapted to fit the needs of a given task, class, and teacher.

One cautionary note about group roles is warranted: Bonnie Raines, in a master's thesis study of collaborative literature group discussions in the middle grades, found that assigning roles and requiring students to facilitate or lead discussions did not always produce positive results (Raines, 1991). Because of inexperience, facilitators sometimes asked questions that interrupted the flow of discussion and limited student thinking or speculation. Raines found that groups in which students were given clear discussion tasks and worked as a group toward that task, rather than in specific roles, produced higher-level discussions than did structured, role-assigned groups.

In your subject area and for the cooperative and collaborative group tasks you develop, group roles may not be an issue; it may be that the choice of whether or not to assign them is clear and compelling. You may find it helpful, however, to monitor the effectiveness of assigning group roles, to try various arrangements, and then to make adjustments as needed.

GUIDING COLLABORATIVE LEARNING GROUPS

The teacher's role as students work in groups is a critical one. Whatever you do, don't be misled into thinking that once the groups are operational, your work is over—far from it. You have many important functions to perform, even though they differ significantly from traditional teacher roles. As groups work, you should do several things.

STAY WITH THE ACTION

One of the most valuable "teacher rules" for effective collaborative group learning is that the teacher's time when groups are working should *not* be used to grade papers, plan other instruction, leave the room, or do any of the paperwork or various other tasks that you have to do. Recall Martina and Greg and the teacher in Room 202 moving among groups and observing from the back of the room. Plan on doing that. You need to be alert, "with it," and on top of things at all times.

STAY AWAY WHEN YOU SHOULD

Probably the hardest thing for you to do is to stay back and let students work. If you don't already know how to do it, learn to tune in and out of group discussions from a distance; you'll be surprised how easy it is. You'll see groups having problems and be tempted to settle the issues. Resist the urge. Give them some time to make mistakes or work through solutions themselves.

GET CLOSE WHEN YOU SHOULD

When you see a group that appears to be off task, go stand near it; you may or may not want to have any verbal interaction whatever with the group. Simply stand there and see whether your presence gets the group back on task. You may see a group caught in a problem too large or too complex for students to work out; ask if there is any way you can help. Periodically stop by each group and ask how students are doing, if they need anything, and what you might do to facilitate their progress. Be particularly watchful, alert, and close when group work has implications for student safety.

TEACH STUDENTS INQUIRY AND PROJECT STRATEGIES AS THEY ARE NEEDED Recall the "mini lessons" we discussed in Chapter 7 for teaching students how to do the kind of writing you want in your classroom. The same kind of instruction is highly useful for teaching kids how to go about doing research for their projects. In Martina's and Greg's unit, Martina began the day's work with a mini lesson on using search engines effectively. Her next lesson may be on how to create and post blogs. You may want to teach your students how to use probes that measure motion, or how to record observations, or how to find books and other resources in the university research library. Whatever. Spend five minutes or so teaching just that one thing that they can apply immediately in their project searches.

HELP GROUPS SUMMARIZE LEARNING AT THE END OF EACH WORK PERIOD Getting into the habit of summarizing progress and learning each day is one of the hallmarks of accomplished learners because the very next thought that comes to mind is the one that begins planning for the next day. Greg Lewis is getting ready to lead just such a discussion so that students take the time to stop and think about what they've learned and how that fits with what they already know. From that thinking will grow a focus on what still needs to be learned.

PROJECT MANAGEMENT

When students are working in collaborative groups, and especially when the work they are doing is project based, one of the most important things you can do to make the experience successful is to maintain an organizing system that assists students in focusing their attention and energy each day on the work at hand. A very simple way to do this is to provide time at the beginning of class each day for stating the work to be done today and at the end of class for reflecting on the day's accomplishments and planning for the next day's work. I recommend a "status of the group" roll call (adapted from Atwell 1998) at the beginning of class that asks each group in turn, "What are you doing today?" and "What do you plan to accomplish?" At the end of class, guide students similarly in reflecting on the work done; this gives groups and individuals opportunity to monitor their own progress ("What did we accomplish today?" and "What will we be doing tomorrow?") and share with other students and the teacher what they've found in their research and/or problems they're encountering. Analytical discussion of this kind increases students' ability to self-monitor their working progress and develops their planning and strategic inquiry skills. It also keeps you informed of the progress they're making and provides information for your recordkeeping and evaluation procedures.

Figure 11.6 on page 448 illustrates one way to maintain records of group planning and progress. Make a copy of the Project Work Management Sheet for each working group. Put the group's name or project topic at the top and list all group members in the space allotted. Each day at status-of-the-group roll call, record (in abbreviated form) each group's outline of its plan for the day. Later, during reflection time ("What did you accomplish today? What do you need for continued progress?"), record group accomplishments. Make note of any other pertinent information. I recommend strongly that you distribute this form to students and require that they keep track of their own work planned and accomplished each day.

FIGURE 11.6 *Project Work Management Sheet*

Group (Topic name): ______________________

Members: ______________________

____

____

____

____

Date	Work Planned	Work Accomplished

Creating Strategic Learners

One of the ways to teach students how to guide themselves in the inquiry process is to show them the value of taking stock at the beginning and end of each work period. Thus, they become strategic—purposeful and planned—self-directed learners. And thus, they become increasingly able to direct their own learning independently.

EVALUATING AND GRADING COOPERATIVE/COLLABORATIVE GROUP WORK

Evaluation and grading are critical components of successful collaborative group functioning and are made all the more so by the fact that we don't have a group work evaluation/grading tradition to guide what we do. Ultimately, you'll have to decide how and what you want to evaluate from the group work, and each decision will be based on the complexity and extent of the group task and the product from the group interaction. It's difficult to give hard-and-fast rules here; however, I recommend that you seriously consider using some form of rubric for evaluating final products. Following is a sample of a rubric for grading projects:

EXCELLENT

- The topic is very well conceived and thoughtfully considered.
- The information demonstrates thorough research from a wide variety of resources.
- The information is presented clearly, imaginatively, and purposefully.
- The product demonstrates deep understanding of the topic.
- The product is notable for its organization and cohesion.
- The product is extremely well presented and polished.

VERY GOOD

- The topic is well conceived and thoughtfully considered.
- The information demonstrates substantive research from a variety of resources.
- The information is presented clearly.
- The product demonstrates clear understanding of the topic.
- The product is well organized and cohesive.
- The product is well presented and polished.

GOOD

- The topic is generally well conceived and considered.
- The information demonstrates solid research in some variety of resources.
- The information is generally well presented.
- The product demonstrates understanding of the topic.
- The product is adequately organized and cohesive.
- The product is adequately presented and polished.

UNACCEPTABLE

- The topic is poorly conceived and considered.
- The information demonstrates little or no research from few resources.
- The information is poorly presented.
- The product demonstrates little or incorrect understanding of the topic.
- The product is poorly organized and incoherent.
- The product is poorly presented and unpolished.

If you wish to involve students in creating rubrics for grading projects—and I strongly encourage that you do—one way to teach them how to determine rubric levels is to lead them in an exercise in which the class collectively develops a rubric for assessing pizza. Announce that they're going to describe the characteristics associated with good and bad pizza on a scale of one to five, one being the worst pizza, and five being the best. Lead the discussion in which you write on the board under numbers 1–5 the words and phrases students suggest. Help them shape the final rubric. After they've done that, then have them think about how they'd describe the best and the worst projects and guide the creation of the assessment rubric.

In addition, Perry Marker (personal communication, 2006) recommends the following guidelines for class presentations:

- The purpose of a group presentation is for students to *learn from one another* in a collaborative manner.
- Each presentation should focus on *different* information; groups do not need to be working on the same topic.
- Provide a *specific set of guidelines* for the presentation—e.g., use two or more intelligences; no reading of the presentation; it must involve all members of the group, incorporate visuals, etc.—these guidelines may be built into the class rubric for grading projects and presentations.
- Have each group *add its own individual requirement* to the guidelines.
- Have groups *present to small groups* rather than the whole class and present several times.
- *Do not have presentations for every project*—use other forms, such as posters, learning stations, reflective "what I learned" writing, etc.
- *Make sure the audience has something to do as a result of the presentations*; e.g., write questions for an exam, write an evaluation of the presentation that serves as a portion of the final grade, etc.
- *You, the teacher creates the groups*—until students are very experienced and trusted group workers do not let them group themselves; consider students' strengths and social characteristics and weigh status issues as well in forming groups.

Generally, product grades in project-based learning are group grades. You will also need to evaluate individual students' contributions to the project as groups did research, planned final products, and developed them. I recommend incorporating individual and group self-evaluations into the determination of individual grades. Specific recommendations for grading follow.

GRADING CRITERIA

Before launching collaborative learning groups, decide on your grading criteria and procedures and do not deviate from them. Unless what you devised is patently unfair, capricious, or prejudicial, continuing with flawed procedures generally causes fewer problems than does changing grading criteria and procedures in midstream. If you do see a need to change, find a way to remove or reduce the effect of the flaws. Be sure your grading criteria and procedures are clearly outlined for students.

GROUP AND INDIVIDUAL GRADES

Consider awarding a group grade for the final product with provision for some type of individual evaluation. This may require that students keep individual journals chronicling their own participation and contributions to the group effort. You may want to include some sort of individual assessment—an individually written or developed product (test, essay, etc.) based on the group work.

STUDENT PERCEPTIONS OF GROUP PROGRESS

Consider also administering a questionnaire periodically to see how students perceive the progress of the group project. Cohen's questionnaire (1994) is based on students' perceptions of how interesting and difficult the work was, how actively the individual participated, and how effective the group was in allowing equal participation by all students. You can write a short, five-minute questionnaire for use to maintain periodic connection with student perceptions.

SOME FINAL WORDS ON CONTENT LEARNING, COLLABORATION, AND LITERACY

In most of the other chapters, I've developed my own "final words." In this one, I want to use the words of one of my students. Below is an excerpt from an end-of-semester report written by David Hathorne (1991) about his field experience in secondary reading. This excerpt just about says it all in summarizing our discussion of cooperative/collaborative learning, literacy instruction, and subject area learning. (I might add that it does so with delightful humor and eloquence.)

> One of the more significant events which occurred while I was observing the class, and certainly the event most relevant to the teaching of reading and writing in a math class, was a cooperative unit on geometrical measurements. The lesson to be learned was ostensibly how to use geometry to make indirect measurements—that is, measurements that would be otherwise difficult or even impossible to make. And, in fact, methods for making such measurements were learned, but so were other things, such as how to interpret, how to think, and how to write clearly.
>
> The easy and most obvious way to teach such a lesson would be to give the kids a set of instructions and then let them make the measurements. That would have worked, and something of value would have been learned, but Janie (not her real name) was more clever than that. What she did was to divide the class into teams of four students and give each group a very sketchy set of instructions. The tasks to be performed were described, and the instruments to be used for each task were enumerated. Some hints as to how to go about making the measurements were given, but students had to use preexisting knowledge and a bit of intelligence in order to come up with complete schemes to make accurate measurements. Each group was required to pool their geometrical resources and write out a complete description as to how the measurements were to be made. This report was handed in and graded before the actual field work was performed.
>
> Now this in itself constitutes, in my opinion, one excellent lesson. It has math, it has groups, it has thinking, it has writing. What more could one ask for? Well, this is where Janie put the most interesting spin on the project. When the groups got the reports handed back, they each got a report written up by another group. So to do the actual measurements, the groups had to pretend that they didn't know how to proceed, and follow explicitly the set of instructions written by another group. Keep in mind that the groups knew

that this was going to happen, so, in addition to the grade they received on the initial report, there was an element of competition between groups to produce the best report . . . .

Even though I took no part in writing the initial report, I did get to join one of the groups in the actual performance of the measurements. Our tasks were to measure the height of the school library clock tower, the height of the flag pole, the distance across the street in front of the school, and the height of a tree on campus. Each of these measurements was done using a different method. The first one required the use of a large sighting protractor, which the students were required to construct. The day before the measurements were to occur, I took it upon myself to construct the protractor for our group. It turned out to be a super-deluxe whizbang unit with custom sighting arm, tripod mount, and bubble leveling device for precision accuracy. This did not hurt getting me in good with my group, and besides it was fun to make. So we gathered our data, did our calculations, and got our answers. Pretty damn good ones too!

But the real capper to the whole exercise occurred when we all gathered back in the classroom. Each group, it seemed, was absolutely convinced that the set of instructions they wrote up was a masterwork of mathematical prose—elegant in its conciseness and sheer genius in its clarity. The piece of trash that they had to work with, however, they were convinced had been dashed off by a group of crazed opium-eaters coming down from eight days on bad stuff. There's a lesson there somewhere. The most difficult part for me was letting the students do most of the work. It was, after all, their exercise and not mine.

WHAT THIS CHAPTER MEANS TO YOU

1. Martina Day and Greg Lewis have created an optimal opportunity for their students to engage in collaborative projects and to learn a whole lot of physics and computer science along the way. This kind of content learning is truly powerful and stands in strong contrast to read-the-book-answer-the-question-listen-to-the-lecture instruction. Students are definitely DOING things. Think of ways to you can convert a unit of instruction in your class from the traditional mode of lecture/discussion to project-based. Consider how you can use technology in your unit.

2. The CORI framework suggests that learning should be Observational, Conceptual, Self-Directed, Strategic, Collaborative, Self-Expressive, and Coherent. Project-based learning and other group learning activities are all or most of those. Pay attention to how your instructional approach meets these criteria and strive to meet them all.

3. Directing project-based learning effectively requires thoughtful planning, preparation, and management. Use the suggestions in this book and your own experience to establish structures and routines that will support students' work in project groups.

DOUBLE ENTRY JOURNAL

Go back and look at your prereading DEJ notes about your own experiences with collaborative learning. Given those experiences and what you've learned reading this chapter, how do you think you might effectively use collaborative learning groups in your classroom? What steps will you take to make such learning a positive experience for students? What do you see as the pros and cons of using collaborative learning activities in your subject area? How willing would you be to try your hand at integrated studies? Share your ideas with a friend.

FEATURE *What Goes in My Portfolio?*

Work with a friend or colleague in a different subject area to create the broad outline for an integrated unit of study in your two subject areas featuring collaborative group work. Include in your outline the stimulus for initiating the unit, the steps you'll use to guide students in conceiving and developing their group projects, possible final products, timeline, management strategies, and grading procedures. Use as many on-line resources as make sense in developing your outline.

or

Write a letter to parents explaining your reasons and procedures for collaborative group learning in your classroom. Be sure to include information about how your instructional practice will benefit their children.

RECOMMENDED SOURCES

*Aaronson, E., Blaney, N., Sikes, J., Stephan, C., & Snapp, N. (1975, February). The Jigsaw route to learning and liking. *Psychology Today*, 43–50.

Aaronson, E., Stephan, C., Sikes, J., Blaney, N., & Snapp, M. (1978). *The Jigsaw classroom*. Beverly Hills, CA: Sage.

*Alvermann, D. E. (1995). Peer-led discussions: Whose interests are served? *Journal of Adolescent & Adult Literacy, 39*(4), 282–289.

*Atwell, N. (1998). *In the middle: Writing, reading, and learning with adolescents* (2nd ed.). Upper Montclair, NJ: Boynton/Cook.

*Bayer, A. S. (1990). *Collaborative-apprenticeship learning: Language and thinking across the curriculum, K-12*. Mountain View, CA: Mayfield.

*Brazee, E. (1995). Tracking the middle grades: National patterns for instruction. *Phi Delta Kappan, 71*, 445–449.

*Bruce, B. C., & Bishop, A. P. (2002). Using the Web to support inquiry-based literacy development. *Journal of Adolescent and Adult Literacy, 45*(8), 706–714.

*Calkins, L. M. (1991). *Living between the lines*. Portsmouth, NH: Heinemann.

*Cintorino, M. A. (1993). Getting together, getting along, getting to the business of teaching and learning. *English Journal, 82*(1), 23–32.

*Cohen, E. G. (1994). *Designing groupwork* (2nd ed.). New York: Teachers College Press.

*Crowley, P. (1988). Ask something. In C. Gilles, M. Bixby, P. Crowley, S. R. Crenshaw, M. Henrichs, F. E. Reynolds, & D. Pyle (Eds.), *Whole language strategies for secondary students* (p. 47). New York: Richard C. Owen.

*Doyle, W., & Carter, K. (1984). Academic tasks in classrooms. *Curriculum Inquiry, 14*, 129–149.

Eeds, M., & Wells, D. (1989). Grand conversations: An exploration of meaning construction in literature study groups. *Research in the Teaching of English, 23*, 4–29.

*Goodlad, J. I. (1984). *A place called school*. New York: McGraw-Hill.

*Guthrie, J. T. (2004). Teaching for literacy engagement. *Journal of Literacy Research, 36*(1), 1–30.

*Guthrie, J. T., Alao, S., & Rinehart, J. M. (1997). Engagement in reading for young adolescents. *Journal of Adolescent & Adult Literacy, 40*(6), 438–446.

*Haggard, M. R. (1978). The effect of creative thinking-reading activities (CT-RA) on reading comprehension. In P. D. Pearson & J. Hansen (Eds.), *Reading: Disciplined inquiry in process and practice, 27th Yearbook of the National Reading Conference* (pp. 233–236). Clemson, SC: National Reading Conference.

Haggard, M. R. (1979). Creative thinking-reading activities (CT-RA): Catalysts for creative reading. *Illinois Reading Council Journal, 7*, 5–8.

Haggard, M. R. (1980). Creative thinking-reading activities (CT-RA): Bridging the gap between creative thinking and creative reading. *Reading Newsletter, No. 10*. Boston: Allyn & Bacon.

Haggard, M. R. (1986). Instructional strategies for developing student interest in content area subjects. In D. Lapp, J. Flood, & N. Farnan (Eds.), *Content area reading and learning: Instructional strategies* (pp. 70–80). Englewood Cliffs, NJ: Prentice-Hall.

Haggard, M. R. (1989). Reducing ambiguity: How students and teachers make sense of school. In S. McCormick & J. Zutell (Eds.), *Cognitive and social perspectives for literacy research and instruction, 38th yearbook of the National Reading Conference* (pp. 445–451). Chicago: National Reading Conference.

*Halverson, N. (August 14, 2006). A lesson in tech. *Press Democrat*, pp. A1, A7.

*Harste, J. C. (1994). Literacy as curricular conversations about knowledge, inquiry, and morality. In R. B. Ruddell, M. R. Ruddell, & H. Singer (Eds.), *Theoretical models and processes of reading* (4th ed., pp. 1220–1242). Newark, DE: International Reading Association.

*Hathorne, D. (1991). *Reading curriculum field experience*. Unpublished manuscript.

*Huhtala, J., & Coughlin, E. B. (1991). Group Investigation, democracy, and the Middle East. *English Journal, 80*, 47–52.

*Johnson, D. W., & Johnson, R. T. (1979). Conflict in the classroom: Controversy and learning. *Review of Educational Research, 49*, 51–70.

*Cited in text.

Johnson, D. W., & Johnson, R. T. (1986). *Learning together and alone* (2nd ed.), Englewood Cliffs, NJ: Prentice-Hall.

*Kist, W. (2002). Finding "new literacy" in action. *Journal of Adolescent and Adult Literacy, 45*(5), 368–377.

*Leu, D. J. (2000). Developing new literacies: Using the internet in content area instruction. In M. McLaughlin & M. E. Vogt (Eds.), *Creativity and innovation in content area teaching* (pp. 183–205). Norwood, MA: Christopher-Gordon.

Leu, D. J., & Kinzer, C. K. (1999). *Effective literacy instruction, K-8* (4th ed.). Upper Saddle River, NJ: Prentice Hall.

Leu, D. J., & Leu, D. D. (1999). *Teaching with the Internet: Lessons from the classroom* (2nd ed.). Norwood, MA: Christopher-Gordon.

*Lewin, K., Lippett, R., & White, R. (1939). Patterns of aggressive behavior in experimentally created "social climates." *Journal of Social Psychology, 10*, 271–299.

*LittleSoldier, L. (1989). Cooperative learning and the Native American student. *Phi Delta Kappan, 71*, 161–163.

Luke, A., & Elkins, J. (1998). Reinventing literacy in "new times." *Journal of Adolescent and Adult Literacy, 42*, 4–7.

*Lunsford, K. J., & Bruce, B. C. (2001). Collaboratories: Working together on the Web. *Journal of Adolescent and Adult Literacy, 45*(1), 52–58.

*Manzo, A. V. (1974). The group reading activity. *The Forum*. College Reading Special Interest Group. Newark, DE: International Reading Association.

*Marker, P. M. (1993). Not only by our words: Connecting the pedagogy of Paulo Freire with the social studies classroom. *Social Science Record, 30*(1), 77–90.

*Martin, N. (1983). So all talk is significant. *Mostly about writing*. Upper Montclair, NJ: Boynton.

*Murphy, S. B. (1988, February). *The problem with reading tasks: Watching children learn*. Paper presented at the annual meeting of the Eastern Educational Research Association, Miami Beach, FL.

*The New London Group. (1996). A pedagogy of multiliteracies: Designing social futures. *Harvard Educational Review, 66*(1), 60–92.

*Oravec, J. A. (2002). Bookmarking the world: Weblog applications in education. *Journal of Adolescent and Adult Literacy, 45*(7), 616–621.

*Osborn, A. F. (1963). *Applied imagination* (3rd ed.). New York: Scribner's.

Paratore, J. R., & McCormack, R. L. (Eds.) (1997). *Peer talk in the classroom: Learning from research*. Newark, DE: International Reading Association.

*Raines, B. (1991). *Response and collaboration in literature discussion groups: A two-year study of an intermediate grade classroom*. Master's thesis, Sonoma State University, Rohnert Park, CA.

*Roerden, L. P. (1997). *Net lessons: Web-based projects for your classroom*. Sebastopol, CA: Songline Studios, Inc.

Ruddell, M. R. (2000). Dancing as fast as we can: Developing literacy, content, and curriculum. In M. McLaughlin & M. E. Vogt (Eds.), *Creativity and innovation in content teaching* (pp. 281–298). Norwood, MA: Christopher-Gordon.

*Ruddell, M. R.-H. (1991a). Student's metacognitive response to ambiguous literacy tasks. *Reading Research and Instruction, 31*, 1–11.

*Ruddell, M. R.-H. (1991b, May). *Use of ambiguous literacy tasks: Guiding students toward complex comprehension*. Paper presented at the annual meeting of the International Reading Association, Las Vegas.

Sharan, S. (1980). Cooperative learning in small groups: Recent methods and effects on achievement, attitude and ethnic relations. *Review of Educational Research, 50*, 241–271.

Sharan, S., & Sharan, Y. (1986). *Small-group teaching*. Englewood Cliffs, NJ: Prentice-Hall.

*Sharan, Y., & Sharan, S. (1989/90). Group investigation expands cooperative learning. *Educational Leadership, 47*, 17–21.

*Sherif, M., Harvey, O. J., White, B. J., Hood, W. E., & Sherif, C. W. (1961). *Intergroup conflict and cooperation: The Robber's Cave experiment*. Norman, OK: University of Oklahoma Book Exchange.

Slavin, R. E. (1980). Cooperative learning. *Review of Educational Research, 50*, 315–342.

*Slavin, R. E. (1986). A cooperative learning approach to content areas: Jigsaw teaching. In D. Lapp, J. Flood, & N. Farnan (Eds.), *Content area reading and learning: Instructional strategies* (pp. 330–345). Englewood Cliffs, NJ: Prentice-Hall.

*Smerdon, B. A., Burkam, D. T., & Lee, V. E. (1999). Access to constructivist and didactic teaching: Who gets it? Where is it practiced. *Teachers College Record, 101*(1), 5–34.

*Smith, M. W., & Willhelm, J. D. (2002). *Reading don't fix no Chevys: Literacy In the lives of young men*. Portsmouth, NH: Heinemann.

*Tierney, B. (1985). In the fifth grade, they all raise their hands. *Learning*, *85*, 34.

*Vogt, M. E. (1996). Creating a response-centered curriculum with discussion groups. In L. B. Gambrell & J. F. Almasi (Eds.), *Lively discussions: Creating elementary classrooms that foster engaged reading* (pp. 181–193). Newark, DE: International Reading Association.

*Vygotsky, L. (1978). *Mind in society: The development of higher psychological processes*. Cambridge, MA: MIT Press.

Wenger, E. (1998). *Communities of practice: Learning, meaning, and identity*. Cambridge, England: Cambridge University Press.

*Windschitl, M. (1999). The challenges of sustaining a constructivist classroom culture. *Phi Delta Kappan*, *80*(10), 751–755.

Building Table

Chapter 11	Project-Based Learning	GRA	Group Investigation	Jigsaw	CT-RA
Focus On	Integrated content learning	Content reading and discussion; information organization and artic-ulation	Content reading and discussion; information or-ganization and articulation	Content reading and discussion; information or-ganization and articulation	Content problem solving; reading and writing articu-lation
Guides Students	Before, dur ing, and after reading and writing	Before during, and after reading and writing	Before during, and after reading and writing	Before, during, and after reading and writing	During read-ing and writing
Use to Plan	Units, semesters	Lessons, units	Units, semesters	Lessons, units	Lessons, units, semesters
May Be Used	Collaborative groups	Collaborative groups	Collaborative groups	Collaborative groups	Collaborative groups
May Be Combined with (known strategies)	VSS, writing workshop, journals, learning logs	VSS, GMA, writing workshop	DR-TA, DRA, writing workshop, journals, learning logs	VSS, GMA, REAP, writing workshop, journals, learning logs	TPRC, GMA, semantic map-ping,writing workshop, journals, learn-ing logs,DEJ, Group Investigation
Materials Preparation	Light	Moderate	Light	Moderate to extensive	Light
Other Preparation	Moderate	Moderate	Moderate	Moderate	Moderate
Outside Resources	Necessary	Necessary	Necessary	Necessary	Not needed
How to Do	Page 430	Pages 431–432	———	Pages 436–437	Page 439

CHAPTER 12

DEVELOPING LIFELONG READERS AND WRITERS

DOUBLE ENTRY JOURNAL

List as many books, articles, and other materials as you can that you read more for pleasure than for study. What makes such reading pleasurable? On what occasions do you write "just for the fun of it"? What, if anything, does the reading and writing you do "for fun" have to do with you as a learner and as a subject matter specialist?

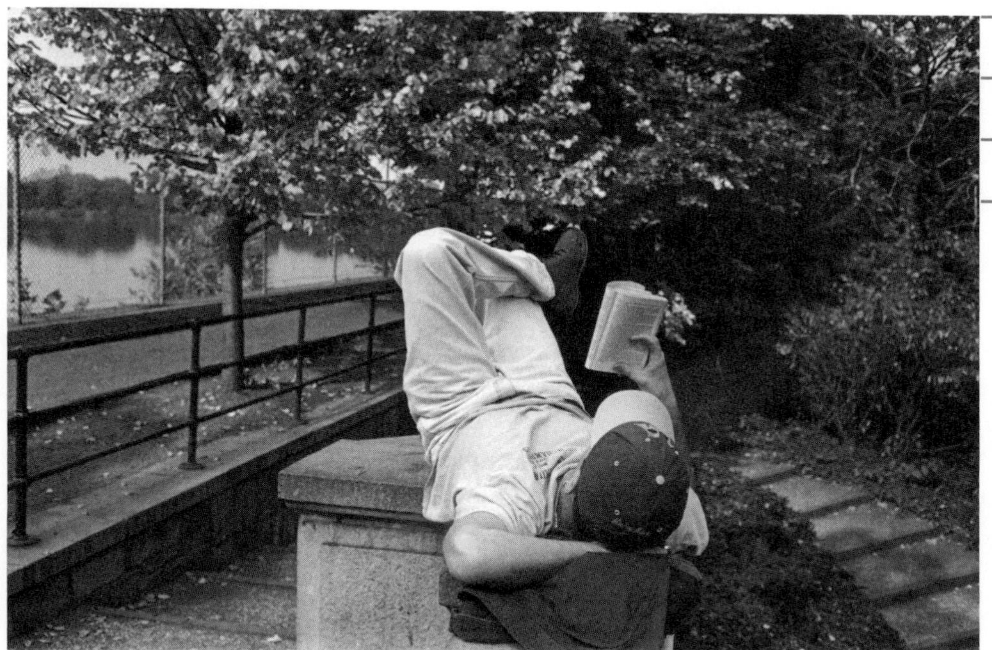

James Carroll/Stock, Boston

C.J. Robinson is just about to jump out of her skin. She cannot *wait* to get to school today. And is she ready! She remembers the feelings she had two weeks ago as if it were today. Mr. Carter, her humanities teacher, is making the announcement—everyone has to read "a pleasure reading book" as part of the unit on Transitions—and she feels the familiar dread, the anger, that raw feeling in her stomach. She doesn't read for pleasure. She just can't read books. She hates to read and barely manages to get through most of her class assignments. She's had lots of help from the resource room teacher, but she still can't get over that feeling of being overwhelmed by page after page covered with letters and words. Mr. Carter must have seen her distress. He came over to her desk and asked if she could meet with him for a couple of minutes during tutorial. When she came in, Mr. Carter handed her the book, *Chinese Handcuffs*, and said, "C. J., this is a great book. I've read it, so I know. It's about kids making all sorts of transitions, and I think you'll like it. Plus, I've had lots of kids tell me it's one of their favorites. I know this is a big reach for you, but I want you to try. Try reading some of *Chinese Handcuffs* each day. If you find that you can't do it, all you have to do is let me know. I think you're going to be successful."

And guess what! She *did it!* She read the whole book and is ready to contribute her ideas about transitions from the viewpoint of this book in class today. The book is awesome. It's written so well that you can sort of see everything in the book taking place. She actually enjoyed reading and found that she was reading well beyond the time she had planned to read each night. She actually finished the book early!

The unit is so cool. They're doing lots in their groups—reading history and newspapers, listening to music, watching videos, finding information on the Web, and now today each member of the group will tell how their book connects with everything else. And she, C. J., will be able to join right in. It feels good. It makes her proud that she read the whole book. Since Cris Crutcher has written so many other books, she's thinking about trying another one.

• • •

INVITATION

If you are a dreamer, come in,
If you are a dreamer, a wisher, a liar,
A hope-er, a pray-er, a magic bean buyer . . .
If you're a pretender, come sit by my fire
For we have some flax-golden tales to spin.
Come in!
Come in!

I begin this chapter with Shel Silverstein's "Invitation" (1974) to turn your attention to the teacher's role as an opener of doors. Everyone who has read and loved (and reread and loved some more) Silverstein's *Where the Sidewalk Ends* knows that on the pages behind the poem, "Invitation," lies a world that is forever interesting, joyful, and touching for readers anywhere between the ages of four and 104. Silverstein's poems open doors by saying things we've never said before, finding unerringly the points of universal experience, and leading us to self-discovery through humor and Silverstein's own healthy irreverence tinged with a sweetly sane view of the world and the humans in it. If all we had to do was read Shel Silverstein poetry to students all day, discipline problems would go away, kids would rush to get to our classes, and life at school would be fine indeed!

Of course, we can't read wacky and wonderfully insightful Silverstein to students all day, but just the thought of it gives us a yen to do something more than preside over days and months of the unending passive routines in school.

OPENING DOORS

"Opening doors" is about capturing students' natural curiosity, interest, and energy and showing them the possibility of new ideas and new ways to view the world of a particular subject area. It occurs when teachers slip quietly from the role of teacher into the role of mentor, spending much less time telling and much more time suggesting, encouraging, pointing the way, identifying resources, and monitoring students' independent progress.

When I think of mentoring and opening doors, I always think of Auntie Mame (Dennis, 1955), that exuberant, irrepressible, bohemian aunt who, in 1929, took her orphaned nephew to rear in the midst of freethinkers, cocktail parties, an ever-changing apartment decor to match her own changing personal interests (Siamese to Southern Belle to ultramodern), and an incipient stock market crash. Auntie Mame opened doors of delight, wonder, and new ideas to Patrick:

> "My dear, a rich vocabulary is the true hallmark of every intellectual person. Here now"—she burrowed into the mess on her beside table and brought forth another pad and pencil—"every time I say a word, or you hear a word, that you don't understand, you write it down and I'll tell you what it means. Then you memorize it and soon you'll have a decent vocabulary. Oh, the adventure," she cried ecstatically, "of molding a little new life!" She made another sweeping gesture that somehow went wrong because she knocked over the coffee pot and I immediately wrote down six new words which Auntie Mame said to scratch out and forget about. (p. 22)
>
> I still have some of the vocabulary sheets of odd information picked up at Auntie Mame's soirees. One, dated July 14, 1929, features such random terms as: Bastille Day, Lesbian, Hotsy-Totsy Club, gang war, Id, daiquiri—although I didn't spell it properly—relativity, free love, Oedipus complex—another one I misspelled—mobile, stinko—and from here on my spelling went wild—narcissistic, Biarritz, psychoneurotic, Shönberg, and nymphomaniac. (p. 24)

I know full well who opened the door to reading for pleasure for me. It was my parents. My mother read to us from the time we were very young, and I cannot have been more than three or four years old when she first took my sister and me to the local school library and let us check out books (while she checked out her own). My favorites then were the "*Watchbird*" books that taught comportment and manners to young children. My memories of going to the library are rich—the smell of books in the library; the feel of the hard, cold floor as I sat and looked through the big picture books; the librarian's special pencil with a purple stamp protruding from the sharpened end for stamping the due-date card that went in the pocket in the front of the book (a memory definitely not available to the millennials). Later, I can remember *waiting* for the day when I was old enough to check out eight books at a time! (I don't remember how old I had to be to gain this prerogative, but I do remember chafing at the four-book limitation.) And then, when I was 13, my father introduced me to the mystery books written by Mary Stewart and let me in on his preference for keeping two books going at one time: an upstairs book for bedtime and a downstairs book for when you ran out of things to do.

TEACHERS WHO OPEN DOORS

Teachers, of course, have for generations opened doors for students, and often they do so by capturing students' avid interest in a subject and thereby transforming them from students who "study math" (or any other subject) to students who "*do math*" (or any other subject), and doing math or science or literature or football means one reads and writes in that area for the rest of one's life, regardless of whether that lifelong involvement is part of a career choice. That is what this chapter is about: turning students into avid learners and lifelong readers and writers in your (and other) subject areas and engaging their interest and energy for independent learning that goes well beyond the confines of classroom and school walls. And it does not seem too great a stretch to suggest that when students connect with teachers who open doors, they begin forming the habits of mind that lifelong literacy requires—avid reading and writing, energetic inquiry, and active pleasure in reading, writing, and thinking.

OPENING DOORS TO LIFELONG LITERACY

> Reading for pleasure is an extraordinary activity. The black squiggles on the white page are still as the grave, colorless as the moonlit desert, but they give the skilled reader a pleasure as acute as the touch of a loved body, as rousing, colorful, and transfiguring as anything out there in the real world. And yet, the more stirring the book the quieter the reader, pleasure reading breeds a concentration so effortless that the absorbed reader of fiction (transported by the book to some other place and shielded by it from distractions), who is so often reviled as an escapist and denounced as the victim of a vice as pernicious as tippling in the morning, should instead be the envy of every student and every teacher. (Nell, 1994, p. 41)

In virtually every discussion of literacy in the media today, there is the unremitting message that adolescents and adults don't read very much for their own pleasure. Recent research about adolescent pleasure reading is mixed. Linda Strommen and Barbara Mates (2004) conducted a written questionnaire survey of 151 sixth- and ninth-grade students to identify those who were *Readers*, for whom reading is a "significant, pleasurable, recreational activity," and *Not-readers* who "seldom or never choose to read for pleasure" (p. 189). They found only 12 Readers (a meager 8%). The other 92% of the students were Not-readers. Interestingly, both categories of students were distributed across reading achievement levels, "Several Not-readers were honors students, while a few Readers claimed to struggle with reading and reading assignments" (p. 191).

These results are somewhat different from those obtained by the 2003 Young Adult Library Services Association Teen Read Week survey of adolescent pleasure reading interests and practices. International in scope, but heavily weighted by U.S. teen respondents—76% of a total of 3,677 preteens and teens who responded to the survey—the survey is conducted online and is voluntary. Results of this survey yield a rather positive view of adolescents as active and avid pleasure readers. Following are some of the findings of this survey, and while these results may not be a representative sample of all adolescents, they are strikingly similar to previous survey results and do tell us something about the teens who did respond:

- 54% agreed or strongly agreed that they read constantly for their own pleasure and love it.
- 50% agreed or strongly agreed that they didn't have much time to read for pleasure but like to when they get a chance.
- 36% said they read outside of class for pleasure on a daily basis, and another 16% said they read for pleasure at least twice a week.
- 26% agreed or strongly agreed that they only read what they are supposed to for school.
- 21% agreed or strongly agreed that they basically don't read books much at all.

And additional mixed results come from a very recent poll conducted by the Yankelvich, a consumer trend tracker (2006) of kids' (ages 5–17) reading habits. The results indicate that

- 80% of 9–11-year-olds, 69% of 12–14-year-olds, and 54% of 15–17-year-olds described themselves as medium- to high-frequency readers (reads from four to six times a week to every day).
- Nearly two-thirds of kids surveyed agree that they need to be a strong reader to get into college.
- Four in ten of kids use technology for recreational reading, usually a computer, and many of these are high-frequency readers.
- 46% of the 15–17-year-olds identified themselves as low-frequency readers (reads two to three times a month).
- 40% of teens think reading for fun is important.
- Three times as many boys than girls think reading for fun is "not at all" important.

Contrasting also to the large number of Not-readers in the Strommen and Mates study is the incredible popularity of books and book clubs. Never in this country have bookstores been so large—look at your nearest Borders or Barnes & Noble—nor has competition to sell books been so fierce: Right after Borders and Barnes & Noble started putting small bookstores out of business, Amazon.com, Zooba.com, and other online bookstores came along and began underpricing them! The greatest loss in all of this is that small local bookstores frequently can't survive the competition; the big plus is that clearly, somebody out there is reading and enjoying books.

Two recent events in the book world support this conclusion. One is the incredible popularity—on at least two continents—of the *Harry Potter* book series, with each new book availability date breathlessly announced by the media and the books being read by children and adults alike. Tickets for Rowling's 1999 national book tour sold out everywhere she went, and well before the first *Harry Potter* movie, middle-level students in one of my local schools did the very serious work required to translate and actually play the game of Quidditch sans the magic aspect of the game played in the book itself (Smith, 1999). The world holds its collective breath waiting for each new release of *Harry Potter* books (complete with all-night parties at bookstores across this country and presumably around the world).

The second newsworthy event was the equally incredible popularity of books selected by Oprah Winfrey for Oprah's Book Club (discontinued in April 2002 and reconstituted in 2003 as the "Traveling with the Classics" book club), which created a nationally shared experience of reading and discussing books. Certainly, book clubs have been around for many years, but they have generally been attended by a very small fragment of the general public and often have been associated with special-interest groups—study groups, support groups of one kind or another, social groups or clubs, academic affiliations, and so forth. Not so today. Oprah Winfrey opened a door that led to (or caused to be noticed) book clubs everywhere—large- and small-city newspaper book clubs, "One Book, One City" book clubs, Mother-daughter book clubs, online book clubs, and others. According to a 2000 survey, 5 million Americans are active in book clubs (Mnookin, 2003). The most recent U.S. census report (December, 2006) projects that in 2007 Americans will spend $55.5 billion to buy 3.17 billion books. Everyone's getting into the act, and what a wonderful thing that is.

FINDING OUT ABOUT READERS AND WRITERS

One of the most important things you can do is find out about your students as readers and writers. I'm talking here not just about knowledge of students' basic reading and writing abilities but about students' literacy attitudes, interests, and proclivities as well. And I'm suggesting that every teacher needs to get this information.

"Why," you ask, "do I, the physical education [music, art, science, math, vocational education] teacher, need to know about my students' reading and writing interests, attitudes, and habits?" The answer is, because you cannot really understand your students, individually or as a group, until you have a sense of how they view themselves; so much of school is tied to literacy that students' self-esteem at school is often rooted in their literacy behaviors and interests. Gaining access to students' literacy attitudes, interests, and habits gives you real insight into their attitude toward your subject area, other subject areas, school in general, and themselves as learners. This understanding is critical to our goal of developing lifelong readers and writers; we need to know what kind of readers and writers students are now; how they view themselves as readers, writers, and learners; and what interests they have. Such knowledge, in turn, allows us to connect students with the right book or right idea and encourage their continued interest, involvement, and participation in learning.

QUESTIONNAIRES

Questionnaires are useful instruments for finding out about students; they are generally nonthreatening and may be used at various times throughout the year. Recall (or go back and look at) the reading and writing questionnaires that were introduced in Chapter 9. These questionnaires reveal students' literacy attitudes, interests, and behaviors and are open-ended enough to allow widely diverse responses. Whether you decide to use them early in the year or semester (as ice breakers, as mentioned in Chapter 9) or later, be sure you emphasize to students that the questionnaires have no bearing on grades. You may want to consider letting students choose whether to sign the questionnaires or respond anonymously; signed responses will give you individualized information, and anonymous ones will give you a sense of group attitudes, interests, and habits.

Questionnaires are intended to give you an overview of how students view their own literacy abilities, how they see school literacy, and the kind of reading and writing and other literate activities they do independently and of their own choice. It may be just as revealing to do this without knowing specifically who thinks what as it is to have identities divulged. On the other hand, you may want detailed information about each student. Use your judgment in deciding which you wish to do. Understand that you may find out also how students use literacy in new times—e-mailing, instant messaging, reading or writing graphic novels, Web surfing, reading or writing zines, and so on. This is important information in understanding the multiple literacies of today's youth.

Feel free also to adapt the questionnaires to your own subject area and the area of student interests and attitudes that are important to you. I may not have included questions that you'd like to ask, or I may have asked questions that you do not consider useful. Note particularly items six and seven on each questionnaire. These are intended to tap resources and ideas students have that may be incorporated into class content and materials options. Avid readers and writers may contribute especially good suggestions here.

These certainly are not the only questionnaires available for surveying students' reading and writing habits, although I like them because they're short and sweet and they get at important attitudes, interests, and habits. Nancie Atwell (1998) includes similar, but slightly longer, open-ended reading and writing surveys in her text. The "BJP Middle/Secondary Reading Attitude Survey" (Baldwin, Johnson, & Peer, 1980) is intended for anonymous student response in order to provide information about how students as a group view reading (Figure 12.1 on page 466). Readence and his associates assert that reluctant and/or less proficient readers may react negatively to questionnaires that reveal each individual's identity; such students may respond by writing down what they believe the teacher wants rather to hear than what they really feel (p. 190). That can happen, but here again, you may want to give students the choice of putting their name on a questionnaire or not, as they wish.

FIGURE 12.1 *The BJP Middle/Secondary Reading Attitude Survey*

Directions: This survey tells you how you feel about reading and books. The survey is not a test, and it is anonymous. It will not affect your grades or progress in school, but it will help your school to create better programs. Answer as honestly as you can by circling the letters which tell how you feel about each statement.

SA = Strongly agree A = Agree D = Disagree SD = Strongly disagree

1.	Library books are dull.	SA	A	D	SD
2.	Reading is a waste of time.	SA	A	D	SD
3.	Reading is one of my hobbies.	SA	A	D	SD
4.	I believe that I am a better reader than most other students in my grade.	SA	A	D	SD
5.	Reading is almost always boring.	SA	A	D	SD
6.	Sometimes I think kids younger than I am read better than I do.	SA	A	D	SD
7.	I enjoy going to the library for books.	SA	A	D	SD
8.	I can read as well as most students who are a year older than I am.	SA	A	D	SD
9.	I don't have enough time to read books.	SA	A	D	SD
10.	I believe that I am a poor reader.	SA	A	D	SD
11.	I would like to belong to a book club.	SA	A	D	SD
12.	I like to take library books home.	SA	A	D	SD
13.	Teachers want me to read too much.	SA	A	D	SD
14.	You can't learn much from reading.	SA	A	D	SD
15.	Books can help us understand other people.	SA	A	D	SD
16.	I almost always get As and Bs in reading and English.	SA	A	D	SD
17.	I like to have time to read in class.	SA	A	D	SD
18.	Reading gets boring after about ten minutes.	SA	A	D	SD
19.	Sometimes I get bad grades in reading and English.	SA	A	D	SD
20.	I like to read before I go to bed.	SA	A	D	SD

60–80 = Good
40–59 = Fair
20–39 = Poor

Scoring: The positive items are 3, 4, 7, 8, 11, 12, 15, 16, 17, 20. Give four points for an SA, three points for an A, two points for a D, and one point for an SD. For the negative items, 1, 2, 5, 6, 9, 10, 13, 14, 18, 19, score four points for an SD, three for a D, two for an A, and one for an SA. Scores can range from 20 to 80.

TALKING TO AND OBSERVING STUDENTS

It's amazing how much information you can get by simply noticing the books and other things students bring to your class each day. Some of this cargo is regulated by where students' lockers are in the building in relationship to your classroom location, but for the most part students carry with them the things that are personally meaningful to them. Pay attention, and you'll see all manner of things (some of which, perhaps, you'd just as soon not see).

See what books students read when they have free time in your class. A standing, and cardinal, rule of my classroom always was: "Bring some sort of pleasure reading material to my class every day." Possibilities were broad—comic books, magazines, library books, books from home, paperbacks, fiction, nonfiction; limitations were narrow—no nudity and no smut. Students were told that they needed free-reading material available in the event that they finished all their work and had class time to fill; a penalty was assessed if students were observed with time on their hands and no book or magazine to read.

The refrain I used was: "You never have nothin' to do as long as you've got your free-reading book in my class." Students who did find themselves without a free-reading book were allowed to choose something to read from materials available in the room (after the penalty); they were not allowed to go back to their lockers to get their own. Quiet reading time was frequently enjoyed by the entire class for the 5 or 10 minutes before dismissal; on days in which schedule disruption was so intrusive as to destroy any semblance of normalcy—when the whole school's collective attention was on picture day, prom, or the championship game, and sometimes in that week before winter holidays or the last day of school—I used quiet reading time for part or all of a period as a means of calming the crowd, restoring everyone's jangled nerves, and/or providing relief from a day of unabated excitement and anticipation.

Granted, I was an English teacher, but it should not be just in English classes that students read something interesting to fill time or as a reward for getting work done. Nor is it only English teachers who occasionally want to calm students a bit in times of high excitement. I think it would be a good idea for a "bring a free-reading book to class every day" standard to be adopted by an entire school to promote independent and pleasure reading.

John Shefelbine (1991) makes the point that good readers are students who read a lot outside of school and outside school assignments. This *practice reading*—just like practice playing the piano or playing basketball—is the key to high-level accomplishment (p. 6). Anderson, Wilson, and Fielding (1988) found that as little as 10 minutes a day of reading outside of school contributed positively to students' reading proficiency and growth and that teachers' attention to and provision for reading that goes beyond class assignments contributed significantly to students' overall reading abilities as measured by achievement tests. It seems very reasonable that the findings of Anderson and associates (1988) hold true for writing. If I were teaching now, I'd give students an option; to fill free time in my class, students could (1) read their free-reading book or (2) write in their journal housed in my class. Given the emphasis today on achievement test scores, especially reading and writing scores, it would seem doubly important that students be encouraged in every class to do what we know helps increase those scores: read and write independently.

You may be uncomfortable with the idea of letting students read just any free-reading book in your class or write on topics outside your subject area. If you are, fine. Stock up on books and magazines that you *do* approve of, or prepare a list of books and other reading material that students can read when they have extra time in your class. Prepare a file box of general writing prompts that are appropriate to events and content in your classroom—for example: "What I found hardest about today's class." Use content-based free-reading and writing activities to demonstrate to students that reading and writing are pleasurable and esteemed free-time activities. If you can also impress on them that reading and writing *in your subject area* are pleasurable, so much the better.

When students routinely engage in independent reading and writing in your classroom, your role is to pay attention to what they read and write. See what books and magazines are on their desks; chat with them about their reading and writing. Share books you are reading or have read and make suggestions and recommendations. You will learn an enormous amount about students as you talk about reading and writing with them and observe them as they read and write independently. You will learn what interests them and what doesn't and see them from a new perspective. In the meantime, your attention, willingness to share your own pleasure reading and writing with them, and knowledge of books, magazines, articles, and ideas that coincide with their interests will validate their reading and writing behaviors. As students see that you value literacy and that you promote and engage in avid reading and writing, they, too, will begin to adopt such attitudes and behaviors.

BECOMING FAMILIAR WITH GOOD BOOKS FOR PREADOLESCENT AND ADOLESCENT READERS

As I mentioned earlier, I've been an avid consumer of books since before I learned to read, so this part has always been easy for me. When I began teaching, I decided that a standing, and cardinal, rule for myself would be "Always read from the library your students read from" (not good grammar, but good advice). And my first year of teaching (sixth grade) offered me the opportunity to go back and read some of the books I'd read as a youngster. My very first book that very first year was *Caddie Woodlawn* (Brink, 1935); I went on to read *My Side of the Mountain* (George, 1959), *Big Red* (Kjelgaard, 1945), *Up a Road Slowly* (Hunt, 1966), and many, many others. When I began teaching high school. I rediscovered *A Tree Grows in Brooklyn* (Smith, 1943) and Mazo de la Roche's *Jalna* series (1944); I discovered *The Outsiders* (Hinton, 1967), *Mrs. Mike* (Freedman & Freedman, 1965), Le Carré's *The Spy Who Came in from the Cold* (1963), and, of course, Paul Zindel's *The Pigman.* Over the years I read a lot of books in those libraries, and my students soon learned that I was a reliable source for recommending good books. They knew I never told them I liked a book unless I did, and they knew that if I hadn't read the book I would tell them. Actually, they began recommending books to me.

Sadly, our most recent research indicates that teachers—even English teachers—are often unfamiliar with the books that preadolescents and adolescents like to read (Applebee, 1992; Krickeberg, 1996; Samuels, 1982). In a national survey of English teachers, Sandra Krickeberg found that "teachers have personally read very few notable young adult novels" (1996, p. 2). She also found that teachers believe such novels are appropriate only for ninth- and tenth-grade average and below-average students. Krickeberg concludes, "Young adult literature presents realistic portrayals of adolescents and topics relevant to their lives. Teachers' lack of knowledge about young adult literature appears to limit its inclusion in literature classes" (p. 2). I would add that this lack of knowledge about what kids are reading not only limits the possibilities for literature study, but also severely limits teachers' knowledge about the kids themselves and makes it impossible to achieve the goal of developing lifelong readers and writers. I recommend that you consider rediscovering some old favorites or discovering other books from the library your students use. It's easy, interesting, and great fun.

CLASSROOM CLIMATES FOR LITERACY

One very useful exercise is to look around classrooms (your own included) and begin thinking about how classroom environments encourage or discourage literacy. It doesn't take much to create a literate environment. You need books; to get them, you can join paperback book clubs, subscribe to magazines relevant to your subject area, use as much as you can from your yearly budget to buy books, accept offers of giveaways from the librarian, or bring books and magazines from home. You need bookshelves, bookstands, writing folders, journal storage space, and shelves; for these, you may need to beg, borrow, and build whatever you can, scavenge from storage rooms, or consider shopping at a cut-rate office supply outlet. You need time; all this requires is that you allocate reading and writing time each day, use a variation of mandated free-reading and -writing options in your class ("You never have nothin' to do"), and talk about books and literacy between classes when students cluster around and want to talk.

Consider also how you can make pleasurable reading and writing central to your classroom curriculum. As you read and become acquainted with interesting trade books, find ways to incorporate parts or whole books, fiction and nonfiction alike, into the major materials and resources you use with a given unit. Look for opportunities for students to write about how their lives and experiences intersect with classroom content. Interesting, vital materials and ideas for teaching content in all subject areas abound. Use them. Learning does not have to be drudgery; find and use the materials that make learning exciting.

READING WITH STUDENTS SUSTAINED SILENT READING (SSR)

Sustained Silent Reading (SSR) (McCracken, 1971) is probably the most widely used approach for encouraging reading in classrooms. SSR is a time when everyone in the classroom reads (teacher included), and everyone reads a book or magazine of his or her own choice (a *Newsweek* "Buzzwords" column once reported that students have dubbed SSR "Sit down, Shut up and Read"! [Zeman, 1991]). SSR periods can be anywhere from 5 to 15 minutes long, although most people use 10 or 15 minutes. Central to SSR is that the time is spent reading for pleasure; textbook reading, doing homework, and working on book reports are all not allowed.

Getting started with SSR requires some planning and thinking. You will need first to explain the activity to students (many of them will be experienced SSR-ers from elementary school) and define policies and procedures. Decide how many minutes make sense for your students; to begin, it's usually a good idea to underestimate, rather than overestimate, time. (You can always add minutes gradually to work up to an ideal time.) Decide what will signal start and stop time and other "rules of the road"—what reading matter is permissible and what is not, what bonus will be given for good performance and what penalty for poor performance (pluses and minuses, points, etc.), and other details.

In my classroom, I required students to use only free-reading material for SSR (applying the same possibilities and limitations mentioned earlier on page 464) and banned textbooks from my or any other class. I used the tardy bell as the signal for reading to begin the 15-minute SSR period, and I gave the signal when to stop. I awarded grades for SSR: *A* if you did it, *F* if you didn't. It only took about three days for kids who'd rarely seen an A on anything to begin collecting them routinely. My directions were: "During SSR, you must read; if you are not reading, you must at least be turning pages and passing your eyes over print. Neither talking nor sleeping counts as SSR." I spent a minute or two observing as students settled into reading and then began reading my book. I was able to monitor student participation quite nicely by looking up occasionally and sweeping the room with my eyes. (Pin-drop quiet rooms, however, require very little monitoring.)

In some districts, whole schools take time out for SSR every school day; during schoolwide SSR, everyone reads (students, teachers, the principal, the janitor, the secretaries, etc.), and special accommodations are made for visitors arriving at the school during that time. One of the high schools where I supervise student teachers uses schoolwide SSR every day for the 15 minutes following lunch period. Everyone carries a book or something to read to class and reads until the bell sounds. Douglas Fisher (2004) writes about the resuscitation of an all-school SSR program in an urban high school in which 75% of the over-2,000-student population are English Language Learners and 99% of the qualify for free lunch. Essentially, teachers felt that the kids weren't participating in SSR and that they needed either to fix the program or end it. Through their efforts at gaining schoolwide support, reallocation of resources for SSR books for every classroom, systematic data collection, and ongoing support from the administration, they "learned that SSR is effective if done well, and we created a way to make sure that it was being done well" (p. 149). Jim Trelease (1995) describes the turnaround brought about in a middle school of 400 students in Boston by a principal who instituted SSR, among other new activities, as part of a campaign to improve students' academic performance. In this school, SSR was done the last 10 minutes of every school day, and every teacher in the building was assigned to participate with a group of students. Initially viewed with skepticism and some resentment by some teachers, whole-school SSR became quite successful. Trelease describes the effect:

> Within a year, [the principal's] critics had become supporters and the school was relishing the quiet time that ended the day. The books that had been started during SSR were often still being read by students filing out to buses—in stark contrast to former dismissal scenes that bordered on chaos. (p. 20)

I *really* like the idea of teachers reading with classes. In your classroom, you may not want to do it every day as I did. Try two or three times a week, always on the same schedule; or alternate SSR with journal writing or some other activity. You may wish to encourage schoolwide adoption of SSR. The main thing is to do it—to read. You'll be surprised at how interested students are in what you're reading; you may also be surprised to find that students begin listening to your recommendations for books more attentively or even begin asking you to suggest good books to read. If you have an avocation or hobby, bring something to read that reflects it; let kids see a side of you they don't know about. All of this has real impact on students. Through such activities, you become a model of literate behavior and you develop bonds with students that otherwise could not be.

READING TO STUDENTS

Reading to students is just as important as reading with them. Jim Trelease, in his *Read-Aloud Handbook* (1995), makes a strong case for both. According to Trelease, reading aloud to students does "what the great art schools have always done: [provide] 'life' models from which to draw" (p. 20). I read to my university students every class period, and you should have seen the faces of my "Reading and Writing Across the Curriculum" class students the very first time I did. They were shocked, and a little embarrassed, by a grown woman standing there in front of other grown men and women reading Dave Barry's hilarious "How to Make a Board" (1982). I read everything to them—excerpts from favorite books, columns from newspapers and magazines, Shel Silverstein, children's books, adolescent literature, cookbooks, new discoveries and golden oldies, and on and on.

I wanted to prove the point that no one ever gets too old to enjoy being read to and make the point that my students should read to their middle school, junior high, and high school students, too. The first point always got proven (and I hope the other point got made). By the third or fourth week, students saw me reach for my reading material, and they began to put things away and *arrange* themselves for the reading. I was always surprised by the number of full-grown adults who close their eyes to listen to me read.

Read to your students. Read what *you* like, and they'll like it, too. I once charmed a very difficult freshman English class (right after lunch, 24 boys and two girls, low-achieving/difficult student group) into cooperative, productive behavior by reading *They Call Me Mr. 500*, by Andy Granatelli (1969) to them for five minutes after 10 minutes of SSR every day. The class came to me straight from after-lunch playground activity and exuberance and could not seem to make the transition to academic tasks successfully; we needed something to calm the exuberance and turn their attention to schoolwork. The book did it. Thus, it was not "wasted time." I found we accomplished more in the remaining 40 minutes after the reading than we could in the 55 minutes without the transition activity.

A few days after I began reading to the students, an interesting thing happened. I had the only copy of the book owned by our library, but I looked up one day to see Larry Baldwin (one of the most difficult students in this very difficult class) reading along with me in what was clearly a library-owned copy of the book (it had the protective transparent library cover). Because I was reading out of the copy from the school library, I knew that Larry had made the effort to go to the neighborhood public library to find the book. He probably had to *get* a library card to get that book. As far as I'm concerned, that's success.

I am always astonished at what reading to students accomplishes. With my adult students over the years, I've seen some amazing things on the last night of class when they read to one another: Once a man *sang*, a cappella, a song that was part of the novel of Appalachia he was sharing with us; another young man read one of John F. Kennedy's speeches (about 10 minutes long) completely with a JFK accent; and yet another student fought back tears repeatedly, *but kept on going*, as she read to us from a novel paralleling the life of her immigrant grandmother.

In a survey of middle school content area, reading, and special education teachers Lettie Albright and Mary Ariail (2005) found that 86% of the 141 middle school teachers they surveyed read to their students. Most teachers read aloud one to two times a week. Their four top reasons for reading aloud were (in order) to (1) model good reading practices (e.g., fluency, intonation, rhythm), (2) make texts more accessible to students who struggle, (3) ensure or increase comprehension/understanding of text, and (4) reinforce content knowledge. Other reasons included increasing student enjoyment, improving listening skills, creating community, stimulating critical thinking, and enriching students' lives. These and other reasons support the practice of reading aloud to students. If they're read to in every class, if the physical education teacher and the mathematics teacher and the social studies teacher and music teacher all periodically and consistently read newspaper stories and articles or book excerpts and poems to them, how much more powerful that would be. How much more likely it would be that we could create a nation in which "90 percent of the children can read and willingly choose to do so" (Trelease, 1995, p. 18), and, I might add, a nation where 90 percent of the adults can read and willingly choose to do so.

WRITING WITH STUDENTS

Just as we can implement SSR, so can we have periods of sustained writing. I've known teachers and schools to refer to it as Sustained Silent Writing (SSW); as I mentioned in another chapter, one school I know calls it "jotters." With the growth of the process writing movement, the frequent presence of journals and learning logs in middle and junior/senior high classrooms, writing workshop, and the ideals of writing across the curriculum, students much more commonly write in many subject area classes today than they did even a few years ago.

WRITING TO STUDENTS

One of the most effective vehicles for writing to students is their journals. Many teachers and students like the letter format for corresponding back and forth, for commenting on ideas in each other's previous letters, and as a way of conveying important information to one another (Atwell, 1998). Graves (1990) recommends this as a way to share responses to books and other reading that students and teachers do. He comments on how dramatically the writing changes when students quit writing neutral accounts and summaries of their books and begin writing about their responses to the books. He marvels further over how dialogue is often sustained for several weeks about a single subject (p. 56).

This kind of writing is substantially different from the notes in the margin and other notes we frequently write to students to alert them to things that are missing or wrong or need fixing in their work. Journal letters are exchanges between individuals writing as equals. They become another powerful tool for making literacy natural, easy, and self-sustaining.

USING LITERATURE IN CONTENT CLASSES

I've already mentioned a number of ways to use literature in content classes: reading to students, reading with them in SSR, reading books from their library and talking about those books, and encouraging students to read for pleasure in your class. Mr. Carter connected students' pleasure reading to his Transitions unit in a very creative way: having students decide and share with other students how the book they were reading illustrated some form of transition. All of these are perfectly reasonable and easy ways to bring literature into content classes. What must be emphasized here is that, always, the goal of using literature in content classes is *not* for the purpose of "literature study"; that is, we are not going to deconstruct the novel or the poem. Rather, the goal is to bring to the study and learning of specific content the perspectives and ideas that various literary forms provide, including nonfiction. So, for example, in the study of the history of the Gold Rush, you might include excerpts from J. S. Holliday's extraordinary book, *The World Rushed In*, chronicling the experience of those who traveled to the gold fields and those who stayed home through diaries and letters from travelers themselves and their loved ones at home. Biography is easily incorporated into the study of virtually every subject area. One student teacher I know chose to introduce his geometry unit by reading excerpts from the novel *Flatland*. A colleague just told me of an M.A. student who, for his thesis study, is using literature circles in an AP history class.

Recall in Chapter 11 the suggestion I made about a thematic unit titled *The River* that could be created for science, social studies, music, art, English, or an integrated humanities curriculum. All manner of literature is appropriate for use with a river theme. Text sets are a perfect way to use literature related to a theme. Gather (purchase or borrow from the library) four or five copies of each title so each student can read one of the books. As I described in Chapter 6, the text set includes fiction and nonfiction, possibly poetry and biography, picture books, CDs, DVDs, visuals, websites, and magazines of the *Smithsonian* or *National Geographic* type. Students read the different texts and with teacher guidance relate their text to the theme as a whole and to the information shared by other groups (refer back to Chapter 7 for suggestions of prompts to use to guide student group discussion of their reading). Recall also from Chapter 6 the value of text sets for sheltering instruction, and from Chapter 10 the discussion about using text sets to meet the needs of diverse populations in your classroom. Each student may read just one of the texts in the set or may read two or three on a rotation basis. *Life on the Mississippi*, *River Running*, *Love in the Time of Cholera*, Stephen Ambrose's *Undaunted Courage*, *Island of the Blue Dolphins*, Ken Burns's PBS *Lewis and Clark: The Journey of the Corps of Discovery*, http://www.americanrivers.org, http://nps.gov/rivers (website of the Wild and Scenic Rivers), and *Wind in the Willows* are texts that could be part of a Text Set for a unit with a river theme.

RESOURCES FOR DEVELOPING LIFELONG READERS AND WRITERS

One of the first issues to be addressed as you decide how independent reading and writing will be used in your class is what and where are the resources available to support your decision to do so. Specifically, you will want to know where you can go to locate the kinds of books kids really like to read and where you can get ideas for encouraging students' writing. There are many, many resources available to you.

RESOURCES FOR INDEPENDENT READING—FINDING GOOD BOOKS

SCHOOL LIBRARIANS

The very first resource I can think of for finding books is your school librarian. School librarians know and love books; all too often, however, they are viewed as catalogers and library monitors rather than what they really are—veritable storehouses of knowledge about books and what kids like, what's new, what's old and still usable, what books would be perfect to use with your unit on "transitions," and a host of other important areas. Working with the librarian, you can put together text sets on a topic or theme to be kept in your room during a unit of study, make arrangements for bringing or sending your students to the library during class periods, gain access to on-line resources and book lists and other resources, and accomplish any number of useful goals.

I always made a point of getting to know my school librarian very early in the academic year and found my success rate over the years to be 100%. To a person, they were cooperative, delighted to offer services and have the opportunity to be a resource to students, willing to try various joint ventures and plans for accommodating my and the students' needs, and utterly generous with their time and knowledge.

STUDENTS

Another major resource for books is the students themselves. Students know what books they like and don't like, and they will tell you. Furthermore, they are quite willing to hold on to their own beliefs and opinions, even when those do not coincide with adults' beliefs and opinions. In the early 1970s, when *The Exorcist* (Blatty, 1971) hit the bestseller lists and details from the movie production became common fodder for gossip columns, this lengthy book (about two inches thick in paperback) became the reading rage in high schools. Never mind that teachers didn't consider the book appropriate, never mind that it was anything but "young adult" fare, and never mind that it was not particularly easy readings—kids read it (many of them the very students everyone believed to be "low," "slow," or "below" readers).

Adolescent readers are not at all averse to reading the complete works of any given author. Steven Krashen (2000, personal communication) calls this "narrow reading" and makes the point that some students—students who find reading difficult and/or ELL students who need assistance with English—benefit from confining their reading to one author (or one genre) because of the considerable redundancy that occurs when reading one author's writing or one genre repeatedly. This redundancy makes the reading progressively easier; students then read more, and their reading improves because of this continued reading practice. This is a rather nice way of scaffolding students' progress toward increased reading ability. Stephen King's books are so popular that kids want to read all of them, as they do Paul Zindel's, S. E. Hinton's, Judy Blume's, and others'. Adolescents also like book series; many of you may be graduates of the *Dune* series (Herbert, 1965), the *Narnia Chronicles*, or even the old perennials *Nancy Drew* (now enjoying renewed popularity) and the *Hardy Boys*. As I mentioned earlier, the *Harry Potter* series continues to be the hottest reading game in town right now among young adolescents.

PUBLISHED BOOK LISTS AND ONLINE RESOURCES

Any number of excellent book recommendation lists are available for assisting you in selecting titles for your own reading, gathering books for in-class use, or making suggestions to students. Most of these lists are annotated or provide discussion of some type about the content and quality of the books appearing on the list. They are in addition to standard review sources such as the American Library Association *Booklist* and the *Hornbook* magazine and major newspaper review sections (e.g., the *New York Times*, the *Christian Science Monitor*, and others). Every edition of the middle school journal produced by the National Council of Teachers of English, *Voices from the Middle*, contains book reviews by middle school students themselves. Each volume of the *Journal of Adolescent* and *Adult Literacy*, published by the International Reading Association, includes a section of reviews of books for adolescents.

Here are two listing of teens' top book choices that were part of the Teen Read Week 2003 Summary:

The Best Book You've EVER Read (for pleasure or school) Ties are ranked together.

1. The *Harry Potter* series
2. *Holes*
3. *The Outsiders*
4. *Lord of the Rings*
5. The Bible
6. *The Giver*
7. *Hatchet*
8. *Men in Black*, *Tuck Everlasting*
9. *To Kill a Mockingbird*, *Where the Redfern Grows*
10. *The Little House on the Prairie* Series, *The Princess Diaries*, *Ella Enchanted*

The Best Book You've Read in the PAST YEAR for FUN

1. The *Harry Potter* series
2. *Holes*
3. *Lord of the Rings*
4. *The Princess Diaries*, *A Child Called "It"*

5. *Sisterhood of the Traveling Pants*
6. *Alice* series
7. *Cat in the Hat*
8. *Hatchet*
9. *All American Girl*
10. *Chicken Soup for the Teenage Soul*

There are also many online resources about books for youth and adolescents, the lists of which change rapidly. Here are a few I found: http://www.ala.org/ala/yalsa/teenreading/teenreading.htm, http://www.lazyreaders.com, and http://www.grouchy.com/angst/mixedupfam.html. There are many other lists out there. Just type "teen books" into Google and you can pick and choose. I encourage you to find sites where students and teachers recommend good books.

RESOURCES FOR INDEPENDENT WRITING—GETTING GOOD IDEAS

Good ideas for writing generally are ideas that grow out of our own experiences. Stimulating students' writing is simply a matter of triggering remembrances or exploring current experiences or events that are interesting and important in our daily lives. So a major source you can use is your own ideas about linkages between community, national, and world events and the lives of your students and/or yourself. Look around you, read the newspaper, watch CNN and MTV, and choose one event; then develop a question that allows students to link that event with their own lives, a memory, or something they know. Their writing may explore that issue, draw and explain the parallel, or discuss insights revealed by the analogy.

Students' lives, and your own, are marvelous resources for writing. Donald Graves (1990) emphasizes the value of daily events and observations as sources for writing. These may be "little" events—savoring morning solitude or experiencing the buoyancy and exertion of a good swim—or they may be larger—feelings about community or world events, enumerations of lifetime goals, or speculation about how one's knowledge in an academic discipline fits into "the grand scheme of things." The stuff of daily living is very much an appropriate topic for writing.

Memory in particular can be the source for much writing. David Fisher and Patty Brown (1990) provide the title annotation "Use your recollections of the past to bring pleasure to the present" in *The Book of Memories*. In this book, Fisher and Brown and their colleagues ask questions and recommend the following:

> Read the question or suggestion, then just close your eyes and think about it. The idea is not just to remember something, but to savor that memory, and enjoy the feeling that it provokes—the way something looked, or smelled, or sounded, the way something felt in your hand. (p. 8)

From these vivid recollections, interesting and exciting writing can occur. The questions in *The Book of Memories* make perfect writing prompts; here are a few:

- What was your favorite picture of yourself as a child?
- What was the hardest you ever laughed?

- What was the biggest or ugliest bug you ever tried to kill?
- What was your most memorable birthday party?
- Who taught you to read?
- To whose house did you and your friends usually go to play?
- What was the best time you had being late?
- What was the most embarrassed you've ever been on a date?
- What were some of the cafeteria classics in grade school?

You get the idea. There are many more in the book, and reading them makes you think of others. There's no reason why questions such as these, those that tap areas of common experience and nostalgia, cannot be slanted toward subject area experiences. Below are some topics I created for activating students' memories surrounding content learning and subject area classes:

- What was your moment of greatest exhilaration in a physical education class?
- What was the biggest breakthrough you ever made in math?
- What was your greatest project flop in home economics class [or wood/metal shop]?
- What piece of art or music took your breath away?
- Describe the sights, sounds, and smells of the science lab.
- How does clay feel in your hands?
- How do you know when you've hit the tennis ball just right?
- What unit in social studies touched your life the most?
- What literary character would you most like to have as a friend?
- What science discovery had (or has) the greatest impact on your life?

Finally, you may find video or Web-based material and information to be a useful resource for writing ideas. With the availability of many high-quality full-length movies and television programs today and the written and visual information on the Web, video and other media resources can and should be used to stimulate writing or serve to mediate reading and writing. Many of the books students read independently, and many fiction and nonfiction books highly useful with thematic and other units of study, are also available in movie or documentary form on videotape or DVD. By all means, use these liberally. Students who might not be able to read the original text gain access to ideas and experiences from video showings; students who wouldn't be caught dead reading a book often spend hours surfing the net and respond eagerly to new ideas in writing.

Some of your students may be zine readers and/or writers. Zines are, by definition, from the fringe and are often outlawed in schools, but nevertheless they can serve as an important source of adolescent reading and writing. Zines are alternative press, and often present ideas, written expression, and ways of thinking that are counter to accepted "right" ideas, writing, and thought. Prominent in the writing in zines is the theme of "kids who got kicked out of school for publishing a zine." From their study of two young women zinesters, Barbara Guzzetti and Margaret Gamboa (2002) recommend that zines should not be brought into the classroom curriculum:

> [T]o do so would put restrictions on writing a zine, and thereby defeat the purpose and fun of creating a zine—the freedom to write with no rules. Rather, these zinesters suggested that teachers adopt a stance that promotes the ethic of zines—do-it-yourself. (p. 39)

If you're not familiar with zines, type "zines" into Google and you can find lots of information, reviews, and examples of zine writing. Many zines are published online.

SOME CONCLUDING THOUGHTS ABOUT DEVELOPING LIFELONG READERS AND WRITERS

I am absolutely convinced of the importance of working to create lifelong readers and writers. It does us no good to teach students how to read and write if they choose not to, and it does us no good to promote learning in subject disciplines if students are unable to further that learning independently. We *know* how to make students good readers and writers: Give them lots and lots and *lots* of practice reading and writing. We also know that English teachers cannot be expected to assume sole responsibility for providing this practice. A powerful message is sent only when *all* middle school and junior/senior high teachers own part of that responsibility and when all teachers willingly become openers of doors.

Once, in the course of counting ballots for middle school students who had voted for their favorite book, I came across this response: "I haven't read any book for the past 12 years. So, I can't list any." Coming from a student who is 12 or 13 or 14 years old, this is, I think, an eloquent and poignant reminder of the result when students *don't* choose to become lifelong readers and writers. We as teachers have, at the very least, the important responsibility of providing encouragement, time, and opportunity—of opening the door—for students to choose otherwise. Wayne Otto (1990) states, "Giving students time to be with books sets up a context where it's not just the books that are valued, it's the personal and social interactions with books that count" (p. 214). When students come to value their "time with books" and writing time, then we can rest assured that they will continue to read, write, and learn well after they leave our classrooms and schools. That's the point, after all.

WHAT THIS CHAPTER MEANS TO YOU

1. C. J. Robinson had the very good luck to have the right book put into her hands at just the right time, and it transformed her. Mr. Carter had the knowledge, perception, and experience to be able to give her that book. We don't succeed like this every time, but when teachers know their students and know the books that teens like to read, it can happen more often than not. You can get to know kids and books well, too.

2. No matter what your subject area, you can find little and big ways to encourage students' independent reading and writing and connect it to your subject area. When you choose to do that, you not only enrich kids' lives, but you increase their content knowledge and contribute to their reading and writing achievement as well.

3. There are many, many resources for learning about and using independent reading and writing in classrooms, some of which are right in front of your eyes each day in class and many of which are easily found online. Spend some time exploring those resources and considering how you can use them to increase your students' learning in your classroom.

DOUBLE ENTRY JOURNAL

Go back to the prereading list of reading and writing that you considered enjoyable. List ways you could include that type of reading and writing in your curriculum. How and when could free reading and writing (SSR/SSW) occur in your classroom? Share your thinking with the group.

FEATURE *What Goes in My Portfolio?*

Create an annotated bibliography of good books for preadolescent and adolescent readers to read—books they'll read for pleasure or for their own information. Get ideas for book from kids, librarians, your own favorites when you were a teen, booklists, and on-line. Or develop annotated lists of text sets of literature you can use in your class.

RECOMMENDED SOURCES

*Albright, L. K., & Ariail, M. (2005). Tapping the potential of teacher read-alouds in middle schools. *Journal of Adolescent and Adult Literacy, 48*(7), 582–591.

*Anderson, R. C., Wilson, P. T., & Fielding, L. G. (1988). Growth in reading and how children spend their time out of school. *Reading Research Quality, 23*, 285–303.

*Applebee, A. N. (1992). Stability and change in the high school cannon. *English Journal, 81*(5), 27–32.

Applebee, A. N., Langer, J. A., & Mullis, I. V. S. (1988). *Who reads best? Factors related to reading achievement in grades 3, 7, and 11*. Princeton, NJ: Educational Testing Service.

*Atwell, N. (1998). *In the middle: New understandings about writing, reading, and learning* (2nd ed.). Portsmouth, NH: Heinemann.

*Baldwin, R. S., Johnson, D. D., & Peer, G. G. (1980). *BJP middle/secondary reading attitude survey*. Bookmatch. Tulsa, OK: Educational Development Corporation.

Benson, H. (2003, June 20). Harry Potter mania raises security issues. *San Francisco Chronicle, D1*, D 20.

*Fisher, D. (2004). Setting the "opportunity to read" standard: Resuscitating the SSR program in an urban high school. *Journal of Adolescent and Adult Literacy, 48*(2), 138–149.

*Fisher, D., & Brown, P. (1990). *The book of memories.* New York: Putnam.

*Cited in text.

*Graves, D. H. (1990). *Discover your own literacy.* Portsmouth, NH: Heinemann.

*Guzzetti, B. J., & Gamboa, M. (2002, December). *Exploring teen zines: Adolescent girls writing differently on their own.* Paper presented at the annual meeting of the National Reading Conference, Miami, FL.

Hatty, M. (1999, November 12–14). Harry Potter author reveals the secret . . . *USA Weekend.*

Hochman, D. (1999, November 19). Mugglemania. *Entertainment Weekly.*

*Krickeberg, S. K. (1996, April). *A national teacher survey on young adult literature.* Paper presented at the meeting of the International Reading Association, New Orleans.

*McCracken, R. A. (1971). Initiating sustained silent reading. *Journal of Reading, 14,* 521–524, 582–583.

*Mnookin, S. (2003, March 3). Not your mom's book club. *Newsweek,* p. 43.

*Nell, V. (1994). The insatiable appetite. In E. H. Cramer & M. Castle (Eds.), *Fostering the love of reading: The affective domain in reading education* (pp. 41–52). Newark, DE: International Reading Association.

*Otto, W. (1990). Bernie and me. *Journal of Reading, 34,* 212–215.

*Samuels, B. G. (1982). *A national survey to determine the status of the young adult novel in the secondary school English classroom, grades 7–12.* Dissertation Abstracts International, *43,* 2224A (University Microfilms No. 82–29347).

*Shefelbine, J. (1991). *Encouraging your junior high student to read.* Newark, DE: International Reading Association.

*Smith, C. (1999, October 27). SR kids make fiction reality. *Press Democrat,* B1, B3.

*Strommen, L. T., & Mates, B. F. (2004). Learning to love reading: Interviews with older children and teens. *Journal of Adolescent and Adult Literacy, 48*(3), 188–200.

*Trelease, J. (1995). *The read-aloud handbook* (3rd ed.). New York: Penguin.

*Yankelvich (2006). *Kids and family reading report.* www.scholastic.com/readingreport.

*Zeman, N. Bureau Reports. (1991, September 9). Buzzwords. *Newsweek,* p. 6.

LITERATURE CITED

Abbot, E. A. (1884). *Flatland.* London.

Ambrose, S. E. (1996). *Undaunted Courage.* New York: Touchstone.

Barry, D. (1982). How to make a board. *New Shelter Magazine.*

Blatty, W. P. (1971, 1984). *The exorcist.* New York: Bantam.

Brink, C. R. (1935, 1990). *Caddie Woodlawn.* New York: Macmillan.

Crutcher, C. (1990). *Chinese handcuffs.*

de la Roche, M. (1944). *The building of Jalna.* Boston: Little, Brown.

Dennis, P. (1955). *Auntie Mame.* New York: Book-of-the-Month Club.

Dixon, F. W. (1985). *The Hardy boys.* New York: Simon & Schuster.

Freedman, B., & Freedman, N. (1965, 1984). *Mrs. Mike.* New York: Berkeley Books.

George, J. C. (1959). *My side of the mountain.* New York: Dutton.

Granatelli, A. (1969). *They call Mr. 500.* Chicago: H. Regnery.

Grahame, R. (1995). *Wind in the Willows.*

Herbert, F. (1965). *Dune.* New York: Berkeley Books.

Hinton, S. E. (1967). *The outsiders.* New York: Viking.

Holliday, J. S. (1982). *The world rushed in.* New York: Simon & Schuster.

Hunt, I. (1966). *Up a road slowly.* Chicago: Follett.

Huser, V. (2001). *River running.* Mountaineers Books.

Kjelgaard, J. A. (1945). *Big red.* New York: Holiday House.

Le Carré, J. (1963, 1984). *The spy who came in from the cold.* New York: Bantam.

O'Dell, S. (1960, 1987). *Island of the blue dolphins.* New York: Dell.

Paterson, K. (1980). *Jacob have I loved.* New York: Harper & Row.

Silverstein, S. (1974). *Where the sidewalk ends.* New York: Harper & Row.

Smith, B. (1943, 1968). *A tree grows in Brooklyn.* New York: Harper & Row.

U.S. Census Bureau (December, 2006). *Statistical abstract of the United States: 2007.* Washington, DC: U.S. Census Bureau.

Zindel, P. (1968, 1983). *The pigman.* New York: Bantam.

INDEX

A

B

C

D

E

F

G

H

I

J

K

L

M

N

O

P

Q

R

S

T

U

V

W

Y

Z